1990

THE MENTALLY RETARDED CHILD

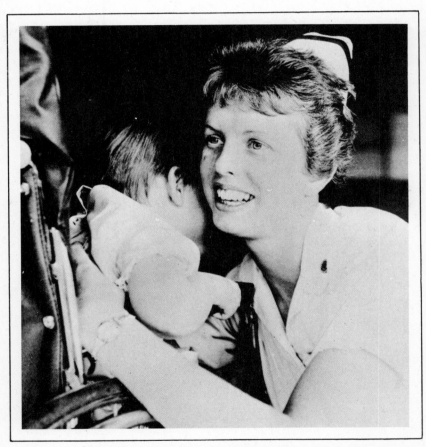

(Courtesy of Plymouth Center for Human Development, Northville, Mich.)

THE MENTALLY RETARDED CHILD

Development, Training, and Education

Fourth Edition

MAX L. HUTT
Consulting Psychologist
formerly, Professor of Psychology
The University of Detroit

ROBERT GWYN GIBBY
Director, Drs. Gibby & Gibby Jr., Ltd.
formerly, Chief, Psychology Service
McGuire V. A. Hospital, and
Professor of Psychology
Virginia Commonwealth University

ALLYN and BACON, Inc.

Boston   **London**   **Sydney**   **Toronto**

To my wife, Anne
Who has taught me the meaning of love
MLH

To my wife, Cathry
Whose love, understanding, and help
are still constant
RGG

Copyright © 1979 by Allyn and Bacon, Inc.
Copyright © 1976, 1965, 1958 by Allyn and Bacon, Inc.
470 Atlantic Avenue, Boston, Massachusetts 02210

Library of Congress Cataloging in Publication Data

Hutt, Max L
  The mentally retarded child.

  Bibliography: p.
  Includes index.
    1. Mentally handicapped children.   I. Gibby, Robert
Gwyn, 1916-   joint author.   II. Title.
[DNLM: 1. Mental retardation. WS107.3 H982m]
HV891.H8 1979   616.8'588   78-26311
ISBN 0-205-06520-1

Printed in the United States of America.

Contents

137, 143

V   EDUCATION: OBJECTIVES, METHODS, AND
THERAPY

Preface

The phenomenon of mental retardation has many faces. Mental retardation embraces affective, motivational, attitudinal, and social characteristics of the individual. It includes, also, physical, physiological, and neurophysiological features. Moreover, genetic, constitutional, social-cultural, and emotional factors may contribute in varying degree to mental retardation. Some of the characteristics of mental retardation can be prevented and many can be modified by early programs of intervention. Effective educational and training programs can do much to improve the functioning and adjustment of retarded individuals.

As a result of continuing research and experimentation, a virtual revolution has occurred in methods of assessment and treatment. In this volume, we have attempted to explain and document these changes. However, in the legitimate fervor to correct abuses and inadequacies in past methods, there has been an alarming tendency in some quarters "to throw out the baby with the bath water." Much that has been painfully learned has been temporarily abandoned; much that is "new" has been accepted too uncritically. Our aim, in this book, has been to provide a balanced and critical review of both old and new. We must always be alert to the empirical question: "How adequate is the evidence for the effectiveness of this method of assessment or treatment?"

A critical, but often neglected, issue concerning mental retardation is the significance of the personality, both as a possible cause and as a consequence of retardation. The problem of personality adjustment must be carefully considered in any assessment and treatment program. We have therefore attempted to build a bridge between our knowledge of personality characteristics and cognitive impairment.

In general, the present revision attempts to provide a balance between "the old" and "the new." It reviews both old and new evidence concerning etiology, assessment, prevention, intervention, education, and treatment, being constantly alert to the dignity and worth of the retarded individual. It is mindful of the "inalienable rights" of all handicapped persons to have a significant role

ix

in their own destiny and in participating more effectively in the community. Hence, the present edition has been reorganized in some major respects.

Parts I and II provide basic foundations for understanding mental retardation. Part I discusses the history of mental retardation, basic concepts and definitions, definitions and theories of intelligence and its measurement, classification and the issue of labeling, characteristics of many types of mental retardation, and finally etiology of the condition. Part II then presents some basic conceptions of developmental and adjustment processes and begins the task of relating these concepts to problems of assessment, education, training, and therapy of the retarded. We have selected aspects of the "old" and the "new" for Parts I and II that seem to be most relevant to our purposes. Undoubtedly we have neglected some material and overemphasized other material that other people might find less relevant. However, we have exercised our best judgment and have felt obliged to neglect some areas or findings in order to prevent this volume, already quite comprehensive, from becoming too cumbersome.

Part III is concerned exclusively with problems and methods of measurement and assessment. A broad sampling of assessment has been incorporated here, including some of the most promising newer methods. An understanding of assessment methods is needed to insure the maximal use, both by teachers and specialists, of findings about the individual, which can help in providing better education and treatment. The current disputes about the measurement of intelligence are particularly relevant for teacher and administrative personnel. The *process* aspects of measurement have been emphasized, as well as some of the most serious misconceptions about the nature of supposedly valid tests. At the same time, emphasis is given to the predictive and planning characteristics that assessment provides, so that we do not disregard the values of assessment simply because all methods of measurement, no matter how sophisticated, have their limitations and ultimately require an integrative interpretation using data from sources other than the measuring instrument itself. The field of measurement is burgeoning, especially in the area of measures of early developmental characteristics, and relatively new approaches have developed to measure social adaptation and cognitive functions.

Part IV is a new addition to the text. It introduces the reader to current conceptions and methods of early intervention, placement, and training for retarded infants and children. This area has shown highly promising results and is relevant even to the worker who deals exclusively with school-age children. Part V focuses on the school years, emphasizing principles of learning, education, and counseling. The emphasis on the unique child with a special constellation of traits and abilities is examined so that individualized programs may be more effectively developed by teacher, parent, and specialized personnel when relevant.

Finally, Part VI presents an overview of the present field of mental retardation, considers where we have been, where we are, and where we may be going. Problems involving public policy are considered and related to current difficulties in providing adequately for all retarded individuals.

It is our hope that this work will assist all people who work with the mentally retarded. It will be abundantly clear that there are many unresolved issues and much that we do not know. Rather than attempting to provide "answers" by fiat, we have frankly acknowledged our areas of ignorance and dispute, making clear our own prejudices when we were aware of them, and openly defining the nature of the unresolved issues. Recent programs in the field have demonstrated that it is possible, on the one hand, to reduce sharply the incidence of mental retardation, and on the other hand to improve significantly the skills and adjustment of many retarded persons. However, the problem of mental retardation will always be with us; the best plans cannot eliminate it. The problem is particularly poignant and salient for the parents of retarded children, but it also is a problem that all of society must share.

Mental retardation is, most of all, a deeply human problem and, in one way or another, affects the lives of us all. To the extent that we understand those problems more fully, we will also more fully understand the problems of all of humanity. To phrase this another way: much of what we learn about mental retardation is applicable to all people; much of what we learn about all people is applicable to those who are mentally retarded.

ACKNOWLEDGMENTS

This edition of *The Mentally Retarded Child* could not have been written without many sources of support. First of all, I wish to acknowledge my indebtedness to the many retarded children and adults with whom I was privileged to consult and whom I tried to assist through a variety of clinical methods and educational programs. The rich lode of material one gains from working closely with individual retarded persons cannot be gained simply from the analysis of research studies, no matter how significant such studies may be. The amazing flexibility and adaptiveness of such individuals, as well as the frustrating problems they present, can only be fully appreciated from intensive, individual experiences. As the reader will realize, I have tried to cull the field of research and theoretical publications in an effort to provide a broader perspective and enrich our understanding of mental retardation. I have used fairly extensively the work of Dr. Robert G. Gibby from the previous editions. Findings from new areas of study have been added and integrated into the context, where relevant.

I also am indebted to the many teachers and parents of retarded children who have shared with me their hopes, their frustrations, their ideas, and their experiences in training. Quite often, the person who is most intimately involved with a particular retarded child, whether teacher or parent, knows more about the child and understands him or her better than the "professional expert."

I wish to acknowledge gratefully the many suggestions and criticisms offered by people who read and reviewed the manuscript in its entirety. The book has benefited immeasurably from their ideas. On some points some reviewers and I have remained in disagreement, and I have had to exercise my own judgment; some disagreements may reflect the diversity of opinion about theories and methods that are so prevalent in the rapidly changing field of mental retardation. For whatever shortcomings there may remain in this volume, I must assume full responsibility. Both the readers of this work and I must remain indebted, however, to Nicholas J. Anastasiow, Barbara Edmonson, James J. McCarthy, Jack B. Share, Beth Stephens, and Glen E. Thomas for their comments on the manuscript of this edition of The Mentally Retarded Child.

I also wish to acknowledge the gracious assistance of Ms. Kirsten Lietz, librarian for the Institute for the Study of Mental Retardation and Related Diseases of the University of Michigan. Her immense familiarity with the literature of the field was of great help.

Max L. Hutt
Ann Arbor, Michigan

We missed the aid and guidance of Mrs. Catherine E. Gibby, who took great responsibility for the preparation of the manuscripts of all of the preceding editions.

R. G. Gibby
Richmond, Virginia

THE MENTALLY RETARDED CHILD

PART
I

NATURE OF RETARDATION:
HISTORY, CHARACTERISTICS,
AND ETIOLOGY

– 1 –

Introductory Comments
on Mental Retardation

As the term implies, *mental retardation* is a condition in which the cognitive development of the individual is inferior to that of average individuals of a similar age. Such a definition is imprecise; it also fails utterly to convey the enormous complexities involved in the conception of mental retardation. For instance, the initial statement tells us nothing about the *degree* of retardation that is required before one can properly apply the term. Nor does it indicate whether all mental or cognitive abilities are necessarily retarded. Nor does it suggest that other abilities *not* commonly referred to as *mental* are also affected. Beyond such considerations are such issues as: What caused the phenomenon of mental retardation in a particular case? Was it present from birth? Is it remediable? What are its consequences? and, Which criteria or which measures are used in determining that there is some degree of mental retardation?

This chapter will introduce the reader to some of these issues. We will present a preliminary conceptualization of mental retardation, an historical orientation concerning the problem so that we may see where we have been on this issue and where we are currently, an overview of the size of the problem of mental retardation, and an elucidation of the major issues that we will confront in later chapters.

It may be helpful, first, to examine a few cases of presumptive mental retardation in order to provide concrete illustrations of the behaviors that occur. We say "presumptive" because the behaviors seem to fall within the category frequently labeled "retarded," but as we shall see, not all of such cases meet modern criteria of mental retardation. We also should caution the reader that some terms we will use in describing these cases have a technical meaning with highly specific connotations. These technical terms will be defined in later sections of this volume as we discuss the relevant issues.

THE CASE OF JOHNNY JONES

The case of Johnny illustrates some of the problems of a mildly retarded child. In many respects, Johnny is typical of other mentally retarded children, but like all other human beings, Johnny also is a unique individual, with his own special characteristics.

Johnny appears to have lived a life full of varied frustrations. When one first meets him, in his fourth-grade class, one is struck by his attitude of despair and hopelessness. He is about a year older than his classmates (he has just turned ten years of age), sits alone in his seat near the window, and fumbles with the pages of the book on his desk. The teacher is reading some material from the fourth-grade reader, but Johnny seems to be uninterested. The rest of the children are following the teacher in their own texts, but Johnny's attention appears to be wandering. Soon, the teacher, after a few reproving looks in his direction, walks over to him to see whether she can be of help. She finds Johnny is looking at the wrong page, questions him about what he has been doing, finally finds the right page for him, and walks back to her desk to continue with her reading. The class is annoyed by this interruption in the exciting material the teacher was reading and has waited impatiently for her to resume. But Johnny has lost interest, and soon his head drops on his book as he gives up his hopeless task of attempting to follow the print.

Johnny has not learned to read! He can understand many spoken words and even some simple phrases, but he is unable to gain a comprehensive understanding of the material even when it is read to him. He seems to get tired easily when the reading lesson arrives, and he frequently gives up and goes to sleep. His inability to cope with the reading lesson has been a problem since he started school, and it has been a serious obstacle since the second grade (which he was forced to repeat).

When he entered school at the age of six years, his mother had a conference with his teacher. She told the teacher that Johnny had always "seemed a little slow," but that he was a good boy, and she asked that he be given special help and encouragement. He had seemed to be a perfectly normal baby, she told the teacher. He was the first child in a family of three children, with a brother two years younger and a sister three years younger. He was slow in beginning to talk, but he was able to say a few words at two years of age. His speech had "always" been infantile, and he seemed to prefer "baby talk" even when he was six years old. He had also been slow in learning to walk, although his parents had made special efforts to encourage him. Shortly after he had begun to walk (at two years of age), his brother was born, and Johnny, receiving less attention and love, reverted to creeping and crawling. He also was late in learning bladder and bowel control, his mother explained, and after he had established fairly good control, he went back (regressed) to soiling and wetting at five years of age. With help he overcame this difficulty, however, and was fully trained once again at the age of six.

His mother stated that he had never been a "problem" at home although he had had severe temper tantrums from two and a half to four years of age. She thought that his tantrums were "brought on" by measles and scarlet fever, because he had seemed temporarily more irritable after these illnesses. When his teacher asked about his relations with his brother and sister (siblings), his mother commented that there had been some jealousy and rivalry, but that the parents would not tolerate such attitudes. Johnny soon learned to get along with his siblings and preferred the company of his brother to other children of his own age. This preference became something of a problem because the brother tired of Johnny's constant companionship, and Johnny was often left to play by himself. He had never seemed to be interested in, or able to get along with, boys of his own age. Frequently, they would take advantage of him and lead him into mischievous behavior. At other times, they would not include him in their games. Gradually, Johnny had begun to stay by himself and play with his dog or work with his Erector set. He learned to use a few simple tools and would spend hours making things.

Johnny never liked school. In the first grade he managed to get along, but frequently he had to be prodded into going to school. His teacher reported that he was the slowest child in the group. He was not particularly troublesome, but he had difficulty learning any of the things the other children seemed to learn easily. He usually stayed by himself and had to be urged to participate in group activities. He seemed listless and fatigued. When he did show some interest in something, it soon waned. At times he would doze off in the classroom. It was suspected that there was something wrong physically, but a medical examination was entirely negative, and it was finally concluded that he was "lazy." However, he did show considerable drive and continued interest when he was engaged in "making things" in school.

He was promoted to the second grade because it was the school policy not to "fail" children at the end of the first year. His second year at school was much more difficult for him. He had difficulty in all school subjects except handwriting and spelling, in both of which he did fairly well. His greatest trouble was in reading, and he had almost as much difficulty with simple arithmetical computation. He was given some special help at school, and a tutor was employed at home, but to no avail. Finally, he was referred to the school counselor, who reported that Johnny was retarded in intelligence. He had obtained an IQ score of 63 on a group test of intelligence given to him by the counselor. It was suggested that he should be given continued special help in school and that he should be made to repeat the second grade.

During his second experience in the second grade, Johnny's school work continued to be very inferior. The principal, during a conference with Johnny's mother, suggested that Johnny needed placement in a class for retarded children, but since such a class was not available in the school, Johnny's teacher was asked to provide a simplified program of studies for him. But his school conduct became more unsatisfactory despite this special program. Occasionally he would "play hookey." He would have to be brought to school by his mother to ensure his attendance. He seemed to resent his younger brother, who was attending the first grade in the same school and who was doing good school work.

Near the end of the year, Johnny was referred to a child guidance clinic in a nearby city. There it was determined that his IQ score on an individual intelligence test was 67 but that his school achievement was below the level expected of his mental age. According to the clinic's report, he was unable to read phrases or sentences, he had poor memory abilities, and he could not concentrate for any extended period of time. The clinical psychologist reported that Johnny felt hostile toward both of his siblings and was highly ambivalent toward his mother. The psychologist said that Johnny had a moderate emotional maladjustment due to frustrations in school work and excessive parental pressure to do well in school. It was suggested that the pressure be reduced and that Johnny be transferred to a school with a class for retarded children of his own age group. The parents resented these suggestions and were unwilling to move the family from the small town where they lived to a larger city whose school system provided "special classes." Further tutoring was attempted at home to get Johnny "up to grade." The parents could not "understand" why Johnny was so dull. After all, the mother explained to the teacher, both of the parents had graduated from high school and both of the other children seemed to be above average.

Despite unsatisfactory work, Johnny was promoted to the third grade. In this grade he seemed to like his teacher, who took a special interest in him. He was permitted to spend most of his time drawing and making things, and his interest in school increased. He no longer had to be "urged" to go to school. The teacher was a very warm person who tried to deal with each child on an individual basis. Even Johnny's reading of words began to improve, although no special tutoring was provided at this time. Johnny reported at home that he liked the class because it was smaller than his previous classes and because he could spend so much time on his "projects." His reading vocabulary reached the beginning second-grade level, although his reading comprehension was still well below that level.

Since Johnny's school work continued to be very poor in the fourth grade and his withdrawal behavior became more pronounced, he was referred again to the psychological clinic in a nearby city. This time a more extensive evaluation was made. Once again he attained an IQ rating of retarded, his score this time being 71. Interviews with both Johnny and his mother revealed that Johnny was often despondent, that he flared up occasionally at home, that both of his parents were severely disappointed in him, and that they made frequent unfavorable comparisons with the younger brother. It was also learned that Johnny was unwanted when he was born. The parents had felt that they did not want a child at that time because of their precarious financial situation. His father had been particularly upset by the financial burden that a child presented. The parents attempted to accept their new child, but they admitted that their resentment often showed in their early attitudes toward him. Johnny's slow progress added to their irritations, and subsequently, when their second child was born, at a time when their financial position had become more favorable, the parents tended to show more interest and pleasure in the new arrival. It became more clear that Johnny's problems were complicated by the unfortunate attitudes his parents showed toward him and by the unfavorable comparisons that they frequently made with his siblings. The clinic staff concluded that his difficulties due to inferior intellectual capacities were greatly increased by this home situation, by the explicit and implicit pressures exerted on him by the home and the school, and by his growing sense of rejection and inadequacy. They proposed a "total program" of mental hygiene in *the home, a carefully specified special program of school activities, and psychological guidance for both Johnny and his mother.*

A great deal can be learned from Johnny's case. At this time we will note some of the crucial factors; we will discuss the other issues in later chapters. Johnny is a boy with limited general intelligence (a mildly retarded child). His three reported IQ scores of 63, 67, and 71, which were reasonably close in agreement, indicated that he had retarded intelligence. (A child with exactly average intelligence would hypothetically score 100 on an intelligence test.) Thus, a major factor in Johnny's poor school work was his relatively limited intelligence. Children like Johnny usually progress much more slowly than average children in many aspects of their general development and learn much more slowly in school, particularly in the traditional academic subjects. Under optimal conditions, when home and school expectancies are geared to the children's actual abilities and potentialities, special provision can be made to adapt their environment to their actual level of ability. But in Johnny's case, conditions were not optimal.

Johnny was not doing as well in school as his actual mental ability would warrant. At the time of his last clinical examination, when he obtained an IQ score of 71 at the age of ten years and four months, his obtained mental age was seven years and three months. This meant that his mental level of development was equal to that of average children who were seven years and three months old. Therefore, he had the potential to do school work at the level of children near the beginning of the second grade. Yet the clinic found that in academic subjects (principally reading and arithmetic), he was even below that level. This was true despite the facts that he had repeated the second grade and that he had obtained special tutoring at school and at home. His emotional maladjustment and his frustrations with his school environment probably had contributed significantly to his relatively inferior achievement for his mental level.

From a review of the history of this case, it becomes clear that many factors in the home may have contributed, in the first place, to Johnny's poor emotional adjustment. The initial attitudes of his parents, their inappropriate expectations of him, and their unfavorable comparisons with his more fortunate siblings (who apparently were not retarded) played their part. His illnesses, shortly after his brother was born, probably added to his difficulties, both in their direct effect of temporarily reducing his physical ability and in their indirect effects of gaining him additional special attention and fostering regressive behavior. Thus were developed the initial stages of his maladjusted behavior, which in turn contributed to his later difficulties in adjusting to the school program.

Johnny's withdrawal behavior (his aloneness, his depression, his "dozing," his "laziness," and his infantile mannerisms) may be interpreted as defensive attempts to cope with his problems. His truancy may be similarly understood. The attempts by parents, teachers, and tutors to get him to learn more rapidly and adequately were probably perceived by him as further evidence of rejection and as further evidence of his inadequacy. It is interesting to note that he had the greatest success with his "warm" teacher in the third grade who made no attempt to pressure him, who respected his integrity as an individual, and who provided him with a program in which he could both be and feel successful.

This case raises many questions concerning methods of guidance that might have been effective for Johnny and his parents, and many questions concerning school policies that might be developed for children like Johnny. Many issues need to be raised concerning areas of accomplishment that one may reasonably expect from such children. These matters will be deferred, however, until later sections of this book in which their discussion will be more appropriate.

The next two sets of presentations provide quite differing stories. In the first, two preschool children are considered and the effects of special stimulation programs on their total development are noted. The last case illustrates how severe cultural deprivation (along with poverty) can contribute to severe social maladjustment together with poor academic accomplishment and lowered self-esteem and lowered aspiration level.

THE CASES OF KEVIN AND BART*

When the two boys came as three year olds to the Happy Learners Center, no one dreamed they would eventually be admitted to a regular public school kindergarten class. Now, at five and one-half years old, they are ready. Arrangements for enrollment have been made.

The Happy Learners Center is one of a series of preschools within a five-county region that integrates a few handicapped children into each of their regular programs. The rationale for doing this is based on the idea that children learn a great deal from other children.

Kevin came to Happy Learners by way of a Headstart Program and a local children's rehabilitation institute. His condition was described broadly as a "general failure to thrive." He was thin, withdrawn, and unable to walk or talk, and he failed to respond to all family efforts to toilet train him. The parents were frustrated and impatient with his lack of development.

Bart, a child with Down's syndrome, was referred by the local association for retarded citizens shortly after his family moved into the community. He was an only child who seemed happy and secure enough, but he showed signs of developmental delay characteristic of the syndrome.

Each boy had a daily one-half hour period working on individualized objectives with a resource teacher. The rest of the time was spent in regular programs. Simultaneously, the resource teacher worked with the parents, aiding the families to continue working on simple special objectives at home.

At first, Kevin responded mainly to the daily individualized program with his resource teacher. According to her, his earliest response was in learning to

*Quoted from: President's Committee on Mental Retardation. Report to the President: Mental Retardation: Century of Decision. Washington, D.C., March 1976.

move. "Kevin was helped to crawl up and down steps. This discovery seemed to please him, and he began to show an eagerness to try other things. Next he stood up, holding a chair and pushing it. Then he used a plastic ball bat to steady himself. After that, he took off! Walking became fun for him, and it opened the way for the next thing we worked on, which was a game of touching other children and letting himself be touched."

Bart's early learning experiences were quite different from Kevin's. "Although Bart benefited from our individualized period, he liked being with the rest of the children. In group singing, finger plays and games, he began to mimic the other children. This kind of 'modeling' was encouraged."

Now at age five and one-half, the boys have mastered toilet training and self-help skills. Both can print their first and last names. They can count to 20. They know their addresses and telephone numbers. They can recite the alphabet. Kevin has become a more sociable person. Bart has achieved a remarkable increase in his attention span and can speak longer sentences, even though the muscular impediment to his speech is still apparent.

This vignette is remarkable in some respects. Above all, it illustrates how much can be accomplished with early and persistent training experiences coordinated between school and home. Kevin's case might have soon become "hopeless" unless early intervention had occurred. Bart's case might have shown far less progress without such early intervention. The importance of continuous training in basic motor and perceptual skills is clearly documented in Kevin's instance and seems to have led to changes in self-concept and social behavior. The importance of 'modeling' in Bart's experience indicates the probable usefulness of such types of learning for some children. Although the two boys had very different characteristics, both profited enormously from individualized and appropriately tailored instruction. Later in this volume, we will discuss in detail the two types of mental retardation from which these children suffered. Kevin's condition at age three was one of apparent, overall retardation in development: physical, motoric, perceptual, linguistic, and social. In the past, children with Bart's condition, Down's syndrome, frequently were placed in state institutions for the retarded in which they often failed to thrive and then died at a relatively early age. As it is, the future is brighter for both children than could have been anticipated from their conditions in earlier years.

THE CASE OF HENRY DISTAL

Our next case will be presented here very briefly. The complex problems involved deserve detailed and careful consideration, but many of their technical aspects can only be understood fully after the reader has acquired a more sophisticated understanding of the diagnostic and pathological issues that will be presented later in this volume. At those points in the book, we shall refer to some of the problems involved in this case.

Henry was first seen by a psychologist after he had been referred by a court because of juvenile offenses. At that time he was almost 14 years old and had reached the seventh grade in elementary school. The court was interested in understanding the causes and nature of his delinquency. Although that was the problem presented, we shall focus our discussion on other factors that came to light.

Henry was diffident, seemed hardly interested in the consultation, responded for the most part laconically, and did what he was asked to do with little involvement and with minimal effort. The school reported that Henry was very retarded in all academic areas. In fact, on standardized tests, he achieved a reading comprehension level of about mid-third grade, and his achievement in arithmetical reasoning was even lower. Although the examining psychologist attempted to motivate Henry for both the interviews and the psychological tests, he reported that Henry showed little interest.

On a formal, verbal test of intelligence, he obtained an IQ score of 74; on a nonverbal test his IQ score was even lower (67). Clearly, one might think that Henry was retarded. However, qualitative features of Henry's performance on these tests indicated that he might have higher capacity than his IQ scores indicated. In exploring this possibility, the psychologist administered a test of perceptual-motor ability, the Hutt Adaptation of the Bender-Gestalt Test (see chapter 11). This test is essentially nonverbal and provides an assessment of specific aspects of perceptual and motor development. The results on this test were extremely uneven; in some respects Henry's perceptual-motor abilities were as low as the seven-year level, but in others they were at the fourteen-year level!

Aspects of Henry's performance suggested that he suffered from some form of organic brain disturbance. This possibility was checked out in two ways. First, he was referred to a neurologist for intensive examination. The results were entirely negative. Second, some portions of the Hutt Adaptation of the Bender-Gestalt Test were administered under special experimental conditions. These conditions were designed to evaluate the extent to which poor motivation and poor work habits adversely affected his performance. It was discovered that Henry could perform at his own chronological level on most perceptual-motor tasks when he was intensely motivated and when he applied himself with great effort. On some of the tasks, however, he showed somewhat immature perceptual-motor behavior, but the previous suggestion of organic impairment was no longer present.

Now, for the first time, the psychologist began to explore factors in Henry's background that might explain these phenomena. The school had very little information about his background. School personnel stated that Henry had lived in his present community for only seven months, and they did not have a record of his previous school background. The family were then contacted, and they, together with Henry, supplied details of his background.

Henry had been raised in a very poor section of Appalachia. His father had completed only three grades of elementary school; his mother had left school in the fourth grade. The father had been a coal miner but was unemployed more often than not. There were seven other children in the family, and four children had died in early childhood. The family usually lived under conditions of extreme poverty. The children attended school infrequently; at times they found temporary employment doing odd jobs. Not only was the home impoverished finan-

cially, but the family provided extremely little intellectual or cultural stimulation of any kind. There was little involvement between the parents and the children. Illness and malnutrition had become a way of life.

When Henry was about thirteen years old, the family managed to move north to the large city where they now lived. There, school attendance was required, but Henry found himself utterly unable to cope with either the academic material or the style of life, which was utterly foreign to him. Truancy and delinquency soon followed.

In this case, we see the grave consequences of extreme *cultural deprivation*. But the case exemplified more than just inadequate stimulation from the culture; Henry also was deprived economically and emotionally. Under these circumstances, it is not surprising that he was not stimulated to develop in many areas of his life. Getting by with as little effort and involvement as possible became his style of life. Emotional and intellectual privation led to lack of total development.

In such cases as this, how meaningful are the results of formal, standardized intelligence tests that assume a "normal" background of intellectual, educational, and cultural experience? How is one to judge what might have been if conditions had been more favorable? And, given the circumstances as we found them at the time of examination, what now could be done to ameliorate the situation? These issues require assiduous consideration.

Was Henry mentally retarded? Although such cases have often been so diagnosed, the evidence indicates otherwise.

Was Henry impaired in his functioning? Clearly—although we have hardly begun to delineate the many areas of his impairment.

How often are cases that simulate mental retardation the result of early deprivation of mental and emotional stimulation? Later, we will examine the evidence on this score. It is far too easy to assume there is retardation when, in fact, there has been, not a lack of original endowment, but an absence of effective conditions for growth and development. And how do more subtle conditions of emotional and cultural deprivation affect the intellectual and personality development of the child?

Society has, by and large, failed to deal with these issues, and scientific research is still limited in its answers. But the problems are far-reaching, as we shall see, and require intensive analysis. Our major point here, however, is that many instances of apparent mental retardation are, in fact, examples of impairment in development due to factors other than inferior endowment.

PRELIMINARY CONSIDERATIONS
OF THE CONCEPT OF MENTAL RETARDATION

Throughout this volume, we will attempt to develop inductively a comprehensive conception of mental retardation. First, however, we will explore some common definitions of the term and examine some historical views of mental retardation.

In earlier times, the term *feebleminded* was applied to people with mental retardation. This term was based in part on the preoccupation with the most severely retarded individuals, and often with individuals residing in state and other institutions for such persons. In part it rested on the assumption that the problem was one of defective, usually inherited and defective, intelligence. Indeed, in the latter part of the nineteenth century, feeblemindedness was thought to be caused by a disease and to lead frequently to delinquent or criminal behavior. Only in the early part of the twentieth century were systematic attempts made to differentiate, segregate, and treat individuals thought to be mentally defective. The work of Alfred Binet, with the collaboration of Théodore Simon, culminated in the development of a standardized intelligence test, which, it was thought, could accurately measure "intelligence."

The earliest definitions of mental retardation, after the advent of the intelligence test, were based almost exclusively on the degree of deficiency in general intelligence, as measured or estimated. Thus, it was thought that anyone achieving an intelligence quotient (IQ) below 70 was in the mentally retarded range. Based on the work of Lewis M. Terman (and later, of others) who developed the original Stanford-Binet Intelligence Test (a modification and refinement of the Binet-Simon test, adapted for the United States), individuals were classified into three broad ranges of mental retardation; Morons (with IQs from 50 to 70); Imbeciles (with IQs from 30 to 50); and Idiots (with IQs from 0 to 30). Intelligence was then regarded as a unitary phenomenon, properly evaluated by a standardized intelligence test, hereditary in origin, and varying in the population from a very low level (that of idiots) to a very superior (or genius) level. The cut-off point of an IQ of 70 was arbitrary; below this IQ it was assumed (with some empirical evidence in support of the assumption) that there were approximately 3 percent of the population (see chapter 2 for a more detailed discussion of this issue).

Although many people contended that other criteria were needed, the usual practice in diagnosing mental retardation was almost exclusively the IQ measure, with the exception of cases based on mental retardation due to some specific organic reason. As we shall see, the early definitions of mental retardation that were proposed by authorities in the field usually included criteria other than intelligence. Nevertheless, children were routinely diagnosed solely on the basis of IQ. We stress this point because this practice led to widespread misdiagnosis, and only in recent years have corrective efforts been made to abandon this highly hazardous procedure.

In chapter 2, we will consider in detail some aspects of the nature of intelligence. Here, it is necessary to examine some critical questions. First, What is intelligence? There is no clear consensus on this issue; indeed, some people would have it that "Intelligence is what intelligence tests test." Hence, we are left with the proposition that the nature of intelligence is what is revealed by our commonly used tests of intelligence. Yet, these tests were developed, in the first instance, to deal with a pragmatic question: How can we segregate the nonlearners in school from the learners? This is what Binet set out to do at the turn of the century. His test was designed to measure "scholastic aptitude." Although it did this reasonably well (test scores correlated fairly well with progress in academic learning), it was designed neither to measure some specific set of cognitive abilities, which were clearly defined as "intelligence," nor to allow for the effects of wide variations in cultural influences that might seriously affect test results. (We have considerable evidence on this score, as we shall see in succeeding chapters.)

As it happens, therefore, when individuals are evaluated by means of a standard intelligence test, it usually is assumed that that individual has had a personal-experience background that is comparable to others on whom the test was standardized. Most minority groups, which are deviant in personal experience from the majority group, those close to the poverty level, and those with extreme cultural deprivation do not meet this assumption. Hence, most tests of intelligence that are administered to them *are inapplicable*.

Even if one had a culture-free test of intelligence (and there are no such instruments nor are there likely to be any), one would still be left with the question of what constitutes intelligence. Is it a unitary ability, or is it composed of many separate abilities? For example, does intelligence consist of such abilities as: reasoning, abstraction, memory, mathematical ability, perceptual maturity, mechanical ability, social sensitivity, and others? If so, how are these abilities related to each other? And how do they relate to subsequent success in academic subjects, in social management, in occupational skills, and in family adjustment? All of these, and many other aspects of effectiveness in living, may be differently related (and, in fact are differently related) to the usual measures of intelligence.

A related question is the degree of possible modifiability of the intelligence test score. As we shall see, research has clearly indicated that many (perhaps all) aspects of intellectual functioning can be modified—some of it drastically—especially if there is considerable modification in early learning experiences (before five years of age). Some people still maintain that intelligence is almost entirely dependent on hereditary factors. They tend to argue that modifiability in both intelligence and in intelligence scores is due to faults of the tests—their imperfect reliability. We clearly disagree with this position and shall cite evidence to support our position. In any case, if intelligence is modifiable, even within limits, how can we rely alone on the intelligence test score?

For some time now, however, authorities have suggested that more than a deficit in intelligence is involved in mental retardation. Tredgold and Soddy (1970) have arrived at a conception of mental retardation as follows (after having earlier relied almost exclusively on a conception based on intellectual deficit alone):

> . . . a state of incomplete mental development of such a kind and degree that the individual is *incapable of adapting himself to the normal environment* [italics ours] of his fellows in such a way as to maintain existence independently of supervision, control, or external support.

It will be noted that this definition stresses poor mental development, even though it considers that only when this (presumably) results in inferior adaptation is the term *mental retardation* applicable. It assumes that low intelligence leads to such maladaptation, and not the reverse. Nevertheless,this conception includes social adaptation as a central criterion.

Doll (1941a) is both more explicit and more restrictive in his conceptualization:

Mental deficiency is a state of social incompetence obtained at maturity, resulting from developmental arrest of intelligence because of constitutional (hereditary or acquired) origin: the condition is essentially incurable through treatment and unremediable through training except as treatment and training instill habits which superficially compensate for the limitations of the person so afflicted while under favorable circumstances and for more or less limited periods of time.

Doll also states (1941b):

. . . we observe that six criteria by statement or implication have been generally considered essential to an adequate definition and concept. These are (1) social incompetence, (2) due to mental subnormality, (3) which has been developmentally arrested, (4) which obtains at maturity, (5) is of constitutional origin and (6) is essentially incurable.

Again we find *social incompetence* stressed as the ultimate criterion. Doll distinguishes between *feeblemindedness* and *intellectual retardation. Feeblemindedness,* to Doll, is an incurable condition characterized *always* by social incompetence, whereas *intellectual retardation* implies the possibility of attaining social competence. Doll insists that a diagnosis of feeblemindedness cannot be made until all six criteria listed above are met.

Benoit (1959) has expressed dissatisfaction with many definitions of mental retardation because they usually state the existence of a functional defect without reference to the total sociocultural background (the *social milieu*) of the individual, or they define the behavioral problem or retardation in dead-end terms. He offers as a substitute a formulation based on Hebb's (1949) theory of the organization of behavior. Benoit views mental retardation:

as a deficit of intellectual function resulting from varied intrapersonal and/or extrapersonal determinants, but having as a common proximate cause a diminished efficiency of the nervous system thus entailing a lessened general capacity for growth in perceptual and conceptual interpretation and consequently in environmental adjustment.

According to Benoit, this Hebbian type of definition is more fruitful than others in the literature since it directs attention to how a basic lack in the individual originates, suggesting that retardation is due to impaired efficiency of the nervous system. Benoit deplores the dichotomy of an *organic vs. familial* etiology and feels that his definition avoids that pitfall by placing all retarded persons in the same group, since the Hebbian formulation "neither assumes nor denies a structural defect in the central nervous system at the root of the diminished capacity for perceptual and conceptual integration."

The American Association on Mental Deficiency has redefined mental retardation as follows (Grossman, 1973):

[Mental retardation is characterized by] significantly subaverage intellectual functioning existing concurrently with deficits in adaptive behavior and manifested during the developmental period.

The term *subaverage* is further defined as a level of performance that is at least one standard deviation below the population mean for the age group involved.* The upper age limit of the "developmental period," although not rigidly specified, is regarded as being approximately sixteen years. Even though this definition of mental retardation has precipitated some controversy (see chapter 3), it may be helpful in that it clearly delineates a highly specific group of individuals according to sharply defined criteria. This definition of mental retardation will be employed in the present text.

The position of the AAMD was considerably influenced by such workers in the field as Zigler (1965), who suggested that adaptive and motivational factors were highly important in the development of the *cultural-familial* category of mental retardation. Zigler's position was that these retarded persons differed from normals in the hierarchy of reinforcers for which they expended effort. Such individuals, because of adverse social and educational experiences, tended to be outer-directed; that is, they looked for, and needed, external cues and motivations rather than performing on the basis of self-contained, but learned, reinforcers. Zigler contrasted these retarded persons with retarded persons from the biomedical category in which cognitive inferiority was based on organic factors.

As we shall see, many workers in the field of mental retardation now believe that the so-called cultural-familial mental retardation is reversible. As Begab (1974) put it in his presidential address to the AAMD: "The dynamic nature of mental retardation denies the long cherished bromide of 'once retarded always retarded.'" Begab believes we now are in a position, with our present knowledge, "to reduce significantly the prevalence of mental retardation."

At this point, it will be helpful to differentiate between *retarded* mental development and *arrested* mental development. *Retarded* mental development refers to a slow or inferior developmental rate present in the child from the *time of birth*. *Arrested* mental development refers to a cessation or diminution in the rate of mental growth due to injury or disease that occurs *after birth*. (These points will be elaborated on in following chapters.)

Mental retardation also can vary in *degree* or *level*. The American Psychiatric Association attempts to deal with this problem by distinguishing three major levels, as follows:

1. Mild deficiency. Children at this level can profit from a simplified school curriculum and *can* make an adequate, though modest, social adjustment.
2. Moderate deficiency. Such children need special academic and vocational training and guidance but do not require institutional care.
3. Severe deficiency. These children need institutional or some type of custodial care.

A detailed discussion of systems of classification of mental retardation appears in chapter 3.

*The standard deviation is a statistical measure that indicates how a group of scores cluster around the average, or mean, score in a normal distribution of scores. It is represented by the Greek letter *sigma* (σ) and is also abbreviated as SD. For a full discussion of the meaning and derivation of sigma, the reader is referred to an elementary text on statistics.

The World Health Organization has proposed that children whose intellectual deficit is severe enough to result in academic disability be regarded as *mentally retarded* children, bearing in mind, however, that academic achievement is not the sole criterion on which such a diagnosis is based. If one accepts this point of view, then the total range of intellectual deficit encompassed by the group is considerable.

The condition of mental retardation, in fact, is found in other groups of children in addition to the so-called trainable and educable mentally retarded children who first come to mind and on whom attention has been primarily focussed in the recent past. It also includes children who, because of limited intellectual capacities, find it impossible to keep up with their chronological age group in the elementary school or to complete an academic high school course successfully.

The behavioral reactions of the mentally retarded child are the product of *many interacting forces*. The attitudes and actions of the child's family, neighbors and schoolmates, and society generally, as well as the child's inferior intellectual capacities, codetermine the child's reactions. We are concerned primarily with the reasons *underlying* behavioral reactions. Such an approach is termed a *dynamic approach*. It is different from the traditional manner in which mental retardation has been regarded.

The dynamic viewpoint asserts that each individual is unique; that intellectual functioning, rather than being solely dependent on constitutional factors, is the complex resultant of many interacting factors, among which motivation and cultural experience are very important; and that improvement in mental functioning may result from significant intervention that stimulates development and adaptation. If, like the AAMD, we employ both intellectual and adaptive factors in our conception of mental subnormality, then many individuals who were formerly labeled mentally retarded would be excluded from this classification, and the widely accepted notion that the mentally retarded group comprises 3 percent of the population would be rejected in favor of a much lower percentage (Mercer, 1973b).

Thus, our brief introductory excursion into the meaning of the term "mental retardation" has shown that there have been highly significant shifts in our conception of the nature of this phenomenon. From the earliest conceptions, in which the condition was entirely attributed to biological and hereditary factors, the condition is now attributable to social-cultural factors, as well. From a viewpoint that stressed the intellectual deficit, almost to exclusion, we have shifted to one that embraces social-cultural and adaptive features. From a position in which we lumped all retarded individuals into a category without significant intraindividual variations, we have come to see that retarded persons vary tremendously from each other with highly important intraindividual differences in their makeups. And, from a position in which mental retardation was regarded as irreversible, we have come to recognize that prognosis is limited, in large part, by the specific conditions of development and training that nurture and foster growth and encourage individualization.

One might say, with some exaggeration, that there are as many different kinds of mental retardation as there are retarded persons. Each retarded individual has a unique makeup. Each needs to be treated in an individualized fashion, tailoring the training and education to the unique pattern of assets and liabilities. In short, each retarded person is nonreplicable, despite some common attributes, and each deserves the maximum opportunity of achieving full potential and the most creative utilization of his personality. The person whom we call "mentally retarded" is not irretrievably bound by the particular limitations he/she* may have in the cognitive domain; like all other persons he is, in fact, a highly complex organism with both assets and liabilities, with unique needs, motivations, and a spirit that needs to be cherished.

A BRIEF HISTORICAL SURVEY

In order to gain some perspective on the problem of mental retardation, on its effects on the individual and on society, and on our present methods of dealing with all of these issues, a brief historical summary may be helpful. As we shall see, in one sense we have come full-circle from believing as Itard and Séguin did that retarded individuals could be trained and educated so that they could function "normally" in society, to the position that most retarded persons and especially the severely and profoundly retarded persons always needed institutionalization and could never be expected to join the mainstream of society, to a popular current position that all (or almost all) retarded persons should be "normalized" (Wolfensberger, 1972). Some people now believe that public, residential institutions for retarded persons should be completely eliminated and even that special education classes are unnecessary and produce harmful segregation. How much of such an ideal approach is possible or even practical? Our historical survey will help us gain a better perspective.

Before the twentieth century, interest in mentally retarded children had waxed and waned for several hundred years. In the eighteenth century, the nature of mental retardation was brought to spectacular public attention by Jean Itard. He undertook the task of educating "up to a civilized state" a young boy who had been living in a wild and savagelike condition in the woods of France. This boy, called the Wild Boy of Aveyron, was about eleven years of age at that time. Although Itard did not meet with much success in his educative attempts, the publicity the case attracted served to stir up considerable interest in the problems of mental retardation. Several schools for the mentally retarded were established in Europe. The prevalent theory at that time was that mental defect was amenable to education. It soon became apparent, however, that even though the children placed in special schools did show remarkable growth and progress, particularly in areas of habit development, there were limits beyond which they could not reach. The work of Itard was followed in Europe by Edouard Séguin, who later migrated to the United States, where he became a leader in educating state legislatures and the public to the problems of the mental defective.

*Throughout this volume, the pronouns *he* and *she* will be used interchangeably to refer to all people in general.

Dugdale's report *The Jukes* (1877) is based on studies over a number of years. He studied the social adaptations of five generations of a single family, whose members had extensive antisocial records. Although Dugdale concluded that "crimes against society" were transmitted along family lines, he did *not* believe that this transmission was necessarily on a hereditary basis. Society, however (probably because of its tendency to project its inner fears), jumped to the conclusion that hereditary transmission of mental retardation was proved by Dugdale's study, despite the fact that only *one* out of the 709 subjects studied by Dugdale had a certified record of feeblemindedness.

Many misconceptions were held both by the general public and by professional workers during this period. Some of these were that mental deficiency is a disease; that delinquent and criminal behaviors are a direct consequence of mental deficiency; that education is of no value in the treatment of mental deficiency; and that mentally retarded individuals should be kept in prisons or in homes for paupers. Thus, whereas some attempt at segregating the mentally retarded was attempted, very little provision was made for their special education or training.

In the early part of the twentieth century, some attempts at differentiation in the segregation and treatment of the mentally retarded began to appear. Institutions and special schools were established for their care and training. Probably much of this more desirable attitude was made possible by the development of intelligence tests. (It is interesting to note that this movement originated in France.) In 1904, Alfred Binet and Théodore Simon developed the now famous Binet-Simon test to identify mentally retarded children in the public schools. It has been translated and revised for use in many countries throughout the world. In this country the best known revisions were made by Goddard, Yerkes, Kuhlmann, and Terman. Intelligence tests made the measurement and detection of mental retardation more accurate, and their use stimulated important movements in planning more effectively for children in the public schools.

During World War I, intelligence tests—particularly those designed to be administered to a number of persons at the same time (group intelligence tests)—were widely used in the armed forces. The country was shocked to hear that almost half of all the army recruits had a mental age of twelve years or less. Later, surveys of school populations yielded similar results. This raised a storm of controversy regarding the nature of intelligence and the meaning of the term *feebleminded*. It was first decided that something was wrong with the tests and the interpretations made of their results. Soon, however, it became apparent that test results were invalidated by many conditions (such as educational and cultural experiences), that the intelligence quotient alone was not an adequate criterion of mental retardation, and that there were many other problems concerning the proper use and interpretation of intelligence test scores.

Research was stimulated, and many studies were done on such problems as the inheritance of mental capacity, racial differences in intelligence, and relation of IQ to occupational level. Many previously held conceptions were found to be invalid and had to be discarded. The oversimplified concept that intelligence was a unitary trait transmitted on a Mendelian hereditary basis had to

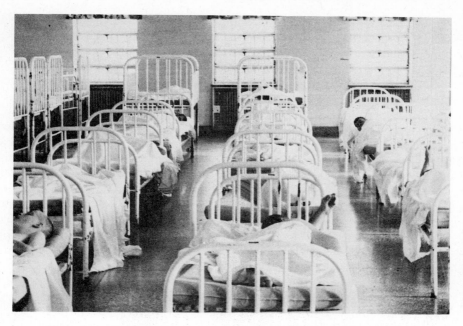

Old-style institution. (From Blatt, *Souls in Extremis*, Boston, Allyn and Bacon, 1973, p. 44. Reprinted by permission of the photographer, Mark Blazey)

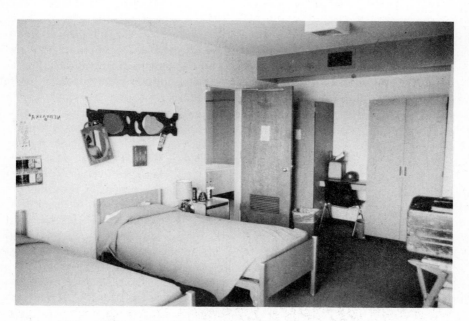

Modern Residential Facility. (Courtesy of Richard S. Mitchell, Southgate Regional Center, Southgate, Mich.)

be thrown overboard. It was seen that the apparent race differences in intelligence often were the result of the bias of the test in favor of one racial group over another. It also was evident that many factors other than intelligence were significant in predicting ultimate vocational and educational levels.

The research and the resulting controversies during the early part of the twentieth century proved to be quite valuable. Gradually, revised conceptions of the nature of intellectual functioning and the nature of mental retardation developed. Increased and improved provisions for educating mentally retarded in the public schools were made. Moreover, the changing attitudes toward mental retardation prompted innovations in methods of training and education, not only in the public schools, but in some of the residential institutions as well.

By 1955, it was possible to see some of these changes in perspective. In an editorial written for a journal on mental retardation, Hungerford (1955) was able to delineate three major shifts during the previous 100 years or so. During the first period, dating from about 1850 to about 1900, there was an emphasis on the development of institutions for the retarded. The next phase, lasting until about 1950, emphasized the development of special classes for the trainable retarded in the public schools. The third phase, which then began, saw a gradually increasing emphasis on research and experimentation with new methods of training and teaching.

Hungerford believed that "institutions were built to last, and unfortunately they did." The last part of this quotation refers to the developing attitude that many of the children who were institutionalized did not belong in institutions and could have fared better in other settings, possibly in community homes. He also stated that special classes had failed but that they did produce a significant amount of movement among the *parents* of retarded children. We shall comment on both of these observations shortly. But in Hungerford's view the movement of the parents resulted in a number of important gains. Parents felt less stigmatized if they had a retarded child and they began to believe that heredity was not the major cause of this condition. They also became aware of the rights of retarded children to adequate treatment and education as well as for a chance at happiness. And finally, by refusing to accept the prevalent notion that seriously retarded children were doomed to lives of perpetual custody, they were able to conduct the most "practical research" in the 1950s.

Since the 1950s, we can discern four major new developments that have greatly accelerated the concern and provision for the mentally retarded. The first major development came as a consequence of President Franklin D. Roosevelt's concern with the problems of poverty and economic depression. In seeking to reduce poverty, he initiated many programs and sought the allocation of funds to implement such programs and to stimulate research on the causes and consequences of poverty. One research study thus motivated was done by Ginsberg and Bray (1953). They found that during World War II more than 700,000 persons had been rejected for military service because of mental retardation. Moreover, they found that there was a clear association between rejection rates and the incidence of classification for mental deficiency!

In the 1960s, a more focused attack on the social origins of mental retardation (as well as on other causes) began with the report of President John F. Kennedy's Panel on Mental Retardation (1962). In part, this report concluded that there is "accumulating evidence that a host of social, economic, and environmental factors—often categorized as *cultural deprivation* [emphasis ours] —are correlated, or associated to a high degree, with the incidence of mental retardation, especially in its milder manifestations. . . ." Public interest in these findings led to allocation of funds by Congress and grants from foundations that made possible extensive research, as well as many innovative and experimental approaches to treatment.

The panel's report was followed by several others,* which maintained professional interest in the field by bringing together the latest findings and by pointing out needs and developing trends. The reports encouraged interdisciplinary study and research and stimulated the use of methods and data from the several disciplines in relation to the problems of mental retardation. One striking sociological concept to come out of the 1969 committee was that of "the six-hour retarded child." This was based on the finding that many children who were termed retarded, especially those from impoverished areas or from ethnic minorities, seemed to function within normal limits in their homes or in their neighborhoods, but because they were viewed as mentally retarded when they went to school, they tended to function as mentally retarded individuals in that setting.

The third, and perhaps the most important, development was the activity of the National Association for Retarded Children in promoting training programs, legislation, and research. This association was formed in Minneapolis, in 1950, by forty-two parents who were frustrated by the gross deficiencies in provisions made for the training and education of their own, as well as other, retarded children. By 1965, the organization had a membership of more than 100,000, with scores of local chapters and state organizations. Using their own resources, but seeking the assistance of professionals, the members promoted countless programs, local clinics, legislation, and workshops. They were not to be denied, and their voices have been heard.

The fourth set of developments, set in motion by the preceding activities and findings, and reinforced by both professional and lay concerns, can be called the period of "humanization of the mentally retarded." Many factors were involved in this drama. Concerns about the negative and even brutal effects of institutionalization; research and concerns about the effects of special education classes on the personality and achievement of mildly and moderately retarded children; research on the effects of classification and "labeling"; a series of court cases (which we will review later in this volume) in which the legal

---

*See the following reports by The President's Committees on Mental Retardation: *A First Report to the President on the Nation's Progress and Remaining Great Needs in the Campaign to Combat Mental Retardation* (Washington, D.C.: U.S. Government Printing Office, 1967); *The Six-Hour Retarded Child: A Report on a Conference on Children in the Inner City* (Washington, D.C.: U.S. Government Printing Office, 1969); *MR 70: The Decisive Decade* (Washington, D.C.: U.S. Government Printing Office, 1970); *Entering the Era of Human Ecology* (Washington, D.C.: U.S. Government Printing Office, 1971).

rights of the retarded and the culturally deprived were defined and established (called "advocacy" for the retarded); mainstreaming into regular classes or regular nonacademic programs for the retarded; newer methods of assessment and newer approaches to assessment of the handicapped; research on new teaching approaches (such as "diagnostic-prescriptive teaching" and programmed instruction); and, behavioral and other therapeutic programs with research indicating their values for the retarded—all of these and many other factors culminated in the passage of P. L. 94–142 by the U.S. Congress and signed into law by President Gerald R. Ford on November 28, 1975. This law, which is the result of a series of refinements of the Education of the Handicapped Act, begins by stating: "There are more than eight million handicapped children in the United States today." It provides that there shall be free public education for *all handicapped children* between the ages of three and eighteen years by 1978 and for all between three and twenty-one years of age by 1980. We will discuss the provisions and implications of P. L. 94–142 in other chapters of this book, but we cannot overemphasize the vast effect of both the expenditure of rapidly expanding federal funds for states meeting these provisions, as well as of the highly specific criteria and goals established as part of this Act. Truly a revolution has occurred in attitudes toward the retarded (as well as toward all other handicapped persons) and in attempts at relatively "normal" types of placement for them with special programs to provide maximal growth and attainment. The question arises: Will the public, parents, educators, and other professionals be able to meet the challenge that has been posed? We shall have much to say about that query at various points in this volume.

Although we will later discuss all of these features of developments during the late 1960s and in the 1970s, we should like to add a footnote on two of them at this point—reactions to residential institutions and reactions to education for the retarded in special education classes.

Public residential institutions for the retarded were developed, as we have indicated, to provide some appropriate treatment for these individuals, but over the years following their establishment, many problems and even abuses developed. Economic and ethnic considerations often were more influential in determining institutional placement rather than educational, psychological, or medical considerations. In the 1950s the National Association for Retarded Citizens became active in seeking to correct these wrongs and to foster the development of adequate alternative community programs. Between 1964 and 1969 the American Association of Mental Deficiency evaluated 134 of the public institutions, utilizing its Standards for Residential Institutions, and found that 60 percent were overcrowded, 50 percent were rated as below standard, 80 percent did not meet standards for attendant/resident ratios, and 60 percent did not have adequate space for programming the activities that were supposed to be provided (Helsel, 1971). Although by this time most states provided for some type of public education for the more severely retarded, few states provided adequate funds or implementation of programs.

Evaluations of the effects, especially the detrimental effects, of institutionalization through numerous research studies revealed that institutionalization decreased the achievement and adjustment of individuals placed in such programs as compared with other individuals who were placed in homes or in community-based settings (Lyle, 1959; Sternlicht and Siegel, 1968; Centerwall and Centerwall, 1960). Of 190,000 residents in such institutions in the late 1960s, the proportions of moderately, severely, and profoundly retarded were about equal, yet most of the moderately retarded could have, presumably, made an adequate or better adjustment at home or in community programs (Baumeister, 1970; Conley, 1973). The photographic evidence produced by Blatt and Kaplan (1966) shocked the public and educators. They revealed that many residents were poorly fed and poorly clothed and that some were found walking around in the nude.

These and other factors produced great shifts in public attitudes and in the development of alternate programs, especially for the moderately retarded who had previously been improperly placed in institutions. Scheerenberger (1976) has indicated that there has been a consistent trend in restricting placement in institutions between 1968 and 1974, so that in the former year institutions had a population of 60 percent of its residents in the severely and profoundly retarded categories, whereas by 1974 the proportion in these categories was 71 percent. Deinstitutionalization, by itself, is insufficient, however, as we shall see later; improved programming for those who must (possibly) be institutionalized and adequate alternatives for those who are placed in alternative settings must be provided.

The problems in the area of special education classes and programs are even more complicated. Special education classes were provided in this country at about the turn of the century, although their extensive use began in about the mid-1960s, in order to insure more effective education for the retarded, especially the trainable and educable retarded (mildly and moderately retarded). A series of studies evaluating the efficacy of such placement brought conflicting results, but the negative findings of some studies caused many educators to become greatly concerned. In 1968, Dunn wrote an article forcefully decrying the negative effects of special education classes (Dunn, 1968). Many educators took up the issue and called for the total abolishment of special education classes (Hammons, 1972). There developed an intense emphasis on "mainstreaming." Some of these attempts were ill-conceived and poorly planned; many were unrealistic. Finally, even Dunn was forced to conclude (Dunn, 1973):

> Accompanying the trend to integrate retardates into general education has come the realization that most children from standard English speaking homes with IQ's in the 50's cannot function in an academically oriented class. Thus more and more of these students are likely to be classified as moderately retarded and placed in self-contained special educational facilities.

Later chapters will consider the issues more fully, examine the evidence on the values and limitations of special education for both mildly and moderately retarded individuals, and consider possible solutions and programs.

THE MAGNITUDE AND SIGNIFICANCE
OF THE PROBLEM

It is very important for planning purposes to know the size of the problem we are dealing with. We also need to know the size and geographic distribution of various aspects of the problem. For instance, it would be helpful to know what proportion of retardated individuals is found in the cities and in the rural areas, and similarly it would be helpful to know whether there are greater numbers of retardated persons in the North, South, East, or West. It is even more important to know how many retardated persons are in each of the several general categories: from mild to profound. Beyond such types of data we should know how many retardated persons are being served and how many are not, as well as what kinds of services are needed. These are a few of the types of statistics we need to know if we are to attempt to provide meaningful and appropriate programs of training and education. Hence, we shall provide some relevant data on these and other aspects of the general problem of prevalence of mental retardation.

We should add at once that the significance of the problem of mental retardation extends far beyond the retardated individuals themselves. Not only are these individuals involved in our planning and its consequences, but so are the immediate families of the retardated, for they bear the direct effects of proper or improper provision for them. Beyond the immediate families also is a significant effect on the society at large, as we shall see. In addressing itself to some of these expanding effects, the President's Committee (1976) noted: "Depending on where and how we draw the line, retarded people in the United States number between four and six million. But a *vastly greater number* [emphasis ours] themselves are affected. Their immediate families embrace at least 20 million . . ."

Some Preliminary Definitions

The following discussion uses a number of terms to describe segments of the population of retardated persons, and we should be clear about their meanings. In speaking of the size of the problem of mental retardation, we usually refer to *prevalence* and occasionally also speak of *incidence*. *Prevalence* refers to the number (sometimes proportion) of mentally retardated persons actually found in a given population at a given time. Incidence refers to the degree or frequency of occurrence; it is sometimes spoken of as the *rate of occurrence*.

We also will refer to the various grades of mental retardation, ranging from the borderline (which the AAMD no longer considers as mental retardation) through the levels of *mild, moderate, severe,* and *profound*. Table 1.1, based on IQ scores alone, indicates the respective ranges in IQ for the Stanford-Binet and the Wechsler intelligence tests for these various levels of retardation.

Some of the data concerning prevalence and also concerning adequacy of treatment programs deal with two relatively separate categories of retardation: the organic-retarded (also referred to as biologically retarded), and the cultural-familial retarded (sometimes referred to as the familials). When mental

TABLE 1.1.   Levels of Mental Retardation and
Corresponding IQ Scores

Level	Stanford-Binet IQ	Wechsler IQ
Borderline	69–84	70–84
Mild	52–68	55–69
Moderate	36–51	40–54
Severe	20–35	25–39
Profound	19 and below	24 and below

retardation has been caused by some overriding, biological interfering factor, it is called *organic*. Most of these individuals are found among the severely and profoundly retarded groups. When, however, mental retardation is due to other conditions, it usually is referred to as cultural-familial.

Problems in Estimating Prevalence

It might seem, at first, that there should be little difficulty in calculating the number of retardated persons in a given population (or in estimating them), but, in fact, such calculations are far from easy. One problem is the criteria we employ in designating an individual as retarded. Experts have not yet arrived at a consensus with respect to suitable criteria. Even though there now is widespread conviction that, in agreement with the AAMD, both intellectual and adaptive levels should be considered, most diagnosticians do not actually employ adaptive criteria in their diagnoses. If we employ only IQ and adopt the usual cut-off score of IQ 70, we should expect that 3 percent of the population would be considered retarded. This figure would have to be modified, however, since many retardated individuals die earlier than the nonretardated, and the percentage would differ, therefore at different age levels. On the other hand, if we employ both intellectual and adaptive criteria the percentage would be lower; Dunn (1973) estimates that the percentage would be about 1 percent of the total population.

If we do agree on the criteria, how are we to measure them validly? IQ tests, as we shall see, are affected by the cultural-educational conditions in which individuals are reared. If we use them, we must still *interpret* their meaning not only in terms of the cultural-educational factors that may affect the results of the test, but also in terms of other factors that may influence test results, such as the motivation of the subject while taking the test, the adequacy of the examiner, and the type of test (or tests) used. Tests of social adaptation are even more difficult to interpret and to construct. Problems of interpreting the results of both types of tests will affect our estimates of prevalence of mental retardation.

If we use other criteria, such as those proposed by Mercer (1973a), which define mental retardation from a "social systems perspective" in terms of achieved status and the role played in a social system, we can readily see that the problems of measurement and, therefore, of estimating prevalence of mental retardation, become more complicated.

Criteria aside, other difficulties exist. Where do we find people who are presumably retarded so that we can assess and count them accurately? Most retarded children are so recognized at about the time they enter school or shortly thereafter because they exhibit difficulties in mastering the academic subjects. But before this period, unless a child shows gross developmental retardation or unless a sensitive parent or pediatrician notes signs of such retardation, there is far less likelihood that the child will be properly evaluated. Hence, estimating prevalence in the preschool years presents special problems. In recent years, special projects have been developed to insure early identification of retardated children since this would make corrective and habilitative efforts more effective. But how about the older retardated persons? Some of them may have dropped out of school or left school for various reasons. How can we count such people accurately in our census?

The problem of obtaining a complete sample of retarded individuals has been attacked in various ways. One way is to take intensive surveys of a restricted sample. Selected samples have involved retardated persons in public institutions, in child and maternity clinics and hospitals, and in a restricted geographic area. Some of these samplings are cited in our study of prevalence.

Findings Concerning Prevalence and Incidence

Because of the problems of variable criteria and sampling, estimates of prevalence used to vary greatly. For instance, Wallin (1958) reviewed 60 studies of prevalence during the period from 1894 to 1958 and found that estimates varied from .05 percent to 13 percent of the population. Currently estimates are less variable. Dingman and Tarjan (1960) attempted to estimate the total number of retarded individuals in the United States, and suggested that, conservatively, some 5,714,255 such individuals were in this category. This figure is close to that of the President's Committee of 1976 we noted earlier. The estimated prevalence offered by Dingman and Tarjan for the various levels of intelligence were: between IQs 0 and 20, 87,500; between IQs 20 and 50, 350,000; and between IQs 50 and 70, 5,276,555.

As far back as 1953, Tizard prepared an article for the World Health Organization. In it he commented on the prevalence problem in relation to school-age individuals.

At the present time the proportion of children considered educationally subnormal in different countries varies from about 1 percent to 4 percent; a further 6 percent to 9 percent are so dull as to require special assistance within the normal school system. . . . the needs of infants and preschool children have been overlooked, and it is evident that much uncared for subnormality must exist within children of preschool age.

More recently, the U.S. Office of Education (1976) estimated that for the period of 1971–1972, in the 5–19 year age range, 2.3 percent were classified as mentally retarded; 1.5 percent were mildly retarded, and 0.8 percent were moderately or severely retarded.

We probably can rely on the figures supplied to the President's Committee (1976a) by the National Association for Retarded Persons, which estimates the numbers of retarded persons in the United States, by degree of retardation, as follows:

Mild	5 million, plus
Moderate	360,000
Severe	280,000
Profound	143,000.

The proportions of retarded persons in the various categories, when evaluated solely by intelligence level and solely by adaptive level of behavior, among children, appear in Table 1.2. Again note that as judged by intelligence, slightly more than half of the people in this selected sample seen in health clinics are borderline or lower. Roughly the same proportion are judged to be without retardation in terms of adaptive criteria. However, there is a striking difference between the percentages based on intellectual and adaptive criteria when we examine the most serious categories of retardation: the severe and the profound. The proportion judged to be so seriously retarded by adaptive criteria (about 21 percent) is more than twice that of those judged so retarded by intellectual criteria (about 10 percent).

Now let us examine the problem in terms of additional factors other than intelligence and adaptation. What does the prevalence situation look like when we consider the numbers of retarded persons in various socioeconomic strata, in various ethnic groupings, in terms of geographic distribution, and other such categories?

We have seen that poverty and social-cultural deprivation make their significant contribution to behaviors we have evaluated as retarded. It is quite clear that the effects of "social deprivation" are differentially related to degree of severity of retardation. Kirk (1962) estimates that there are about 50 cases of educable mentally retarded children (also called educable retarded) per 1,000 school children in poverty areas, whereas there are only 10 such cases per 1,000

TABLE 1.2.   New Patients in Maternal and Child Health Mental Retardation Clinics by Intelligence and Adaptive Behavior Levels, Fiscal Year 1972*

Intelligence Level (N = 22,728)		Adaptive Behavior Level (N = 18,484)	
No retardation	39.7%	No retardation	38.4%
Borderline	21.5%	Mild (level–1)	22.6%
Mild retardation	17.4%	Moderate (level–2)	17.7%
Moderate retardation	11.5%	Severe (level–3)	12.7%
Severe retardation	6.6%	Profound (level–4)	8.7%
Profound retardation	3.2%		

*From: President's Committee on Mental Retardation. *Mental Retardation: the Known and the Unknown.* Washington, D.C.: DHEW Publication No. (OHD) 76-21008. (Adapted from: U.S. Department of Health, Education, and Welfare. *Children Served in Mental Retardation Clinics–Fiscal Years 1970–1972.* Rockville, Maryland: Maternal and Child Health Services, 1972.

in high economic areas. Similarly, Tarjan et al. (1973) show that most cases of mental retardation in the IQ range from 50 to 70 come from low socioeconomic areas, whereas there is no significant difference in incidence of cases below IQ 50 between different socioeconomic groups. Presumably, the most seriously retarded suffer from organic defects that are largely unrelated to socioeconomic conditions; they result from birth defects, prenatal disease, and serious postnatal disease.

In an intensive survey in one area of California, Mercer (1973b) showed that there was the expected prevalence of 3 percent of individuals with IQs below 70; but when clinical judgments of retardation were made for individuals with IQs below 50 there was *more than six times the expected percentage of .04 percent* in this category. This group also had significantly more physiological defects than the group with IQs above 50. Hence, Mercer suggested that mental retardation may consist of two nonhomogeneous groups, the organic-retarded and familial-retarded. Thus we see that social-cultural factors affect the incidence of milder degrees of retardation far more than they do the more serious degrees, and we also note that organic cases of retardation, usually found in the most severe cases, are not so affected and probably should be thought of as belonging to a different category of retardation.

The relation of mental retardation to ethnic origin also is very interesting. We should state at once that there is little evidence of significant differences in intelligence among different ethnic groups, but that *presumed differences in intelligence* often are alleged to exist when inadequate allowance is made for differences in social factors and their effects on most intelligence tests (see chapter 2 for further discussion of this problem). Ethnic groups that have suffered from poverty and deprivation, frequently display greater difficulty in adapting to conventional school learning situations; their retardation in conventional learning is reflected in their lower intelligence test scores and they have frequently been mislabeled as mentally retarded.

Conley (1973) made an extensive analysis based on twenty epidemiological studies of whites versus nonwhites, and of poor versus higher socioeconomic groups. In general, the prevalence rate for retardation was found to be the expected 3 percent, but mental retardation was found to occur about 6 to 7 times more frequently among the nonwhites than among the whites, and about 13 times more frequently among the poor than among the middle- and upper-economic groups. Mercer (1973a) found that in a group of Mexican-American children, 14.9 percent were labeled mentally retarded on the basis of conventional intelligence tests, but that only 6.0 percent were so labeled when judged on the basis of adaptive behavior criteria. Even more striking was the finding that when judged on the basis of *culturally adjusted tests* only 1.5 percent were judged to be retarded!

The literature is replete with studies on racial intelligence and on ethnic differences in intelligence. We shall discuss some of these studies in later chapters of this book. However, we must make two points now. (1) Alleged differences in intelligence among different ethnic groupings usually have been based on grossly inadequate studies with improper allowance for the effects of cultural differences on test scores. (2) Much harmful practice has occurred in improperly labeling children from some ethnic groups (especially ethnic minorities) as mentally retarded and improperly providing for their educational needs.

It has been known for some time that retardated individuals are unevenly distributed in different geographic areas of the country. In the past, some of this variability was attributable to differences in economic status of these regions and differences in funds allocated for detection, training, and education. Sloan (1955) reported, for example, the incidence rate for retardated persons in public and private institutions varied from 39.91 per 100,000 of the population to 126.77 per 100,000 over the four geographic areas of the country, as Table 1.3 indicates. Sloan also reported variability in incidence rates for the separate states; these incidence rates per 100,000 varied from 4.50 to 164.77. Such data demonstrated the highly unequal assistance offered to persons in need of institutional treatment at the time.

The figures for the retardated who are served by public education also are of interest. The greatest number of these were served through placement in special education classes, although since the early 1970s other arrangements have been developed. If we examine the figures for enrollment in special education for the entire country, we note that for 1948, shortly after special education began to be popular, 86,980 pupils were enrolled in such classes (Mackie, 1969). By 1958, the number had jumped to 223,477 (Martin, W. E., 1970) and by 1968 the figure was 872,113 (Martin, 1971). In the years after 1968, since other arrangements began to be made to meet the needs of many retarded pupils, we can gain a better picture of how these pupils were served by examining the percentages who were served and not served by public education—through any of the rapidly diversifying programs. The President's Committee (1976a) estimates that in 1972 only about 50 percent of the population of retarded children was "served" in public education and 50 percent was "not served." By 1975, the respective percentages were 83 percent and 17 percent. The U.S. Office of Education estimates that in 1976 the respective percentages were 90 percent and 10 percent. Thus, the majority of those individuals enrolled in public education (mainly the borderline, mild, and moderate retardates) were being "served" after 1975. However, insufficient funds often were allocated by state and federal agencies to meet the real educational needs of these individuals.

TABLE 1.3.   Persons in Homes and Schools for the Mentally Retarded

Area	Total Population	Public and Private	Rate per 100,000	Public	Rate per 100,000
U.S.	150,697,361	134,189	89.00	125,650	83.37
N. East	39,477,986	50,048	126.77	45,273	114.67
N. Central	44,460,762	50,997	114.70	48,696	109.53
South	47,197,088	18,838	39.91	18,038	38.22
West	19,561,525	14,306	73.13	13,643	60.74

Reproduced from W. Sloan, "Some statistics in institutional provisions for the mentally handicapped," *Amer. J. ment. Defic.,* 1955, 59, 380–387.

TABLE 1.4.   Prevalence of Handicaps Associated with Retardation*

Handicap	Total %	%, Partial Handicap	%, Severe Handicap
Speech	54.5	33.4	21.5
Upper limbs, fine control	43.9	34.9	9.0
Upper limbs, gross control	42.4	34.2	8.2
Ambulation	42.3	32.4	9.9
Emotional disorders	42.0	35.7	6.3
Vision	26.8	20.9	5.9
Toilet training	22.5	10.2	12.3
Seizures	17.3	15.1	2.2
Hearing	14.9	11.5	3.4

*(Adapted from Conroy and Derr, 1971)

We already have commented on the problems of the institutions for the mentally retarded. In 1975, approximately 190,000 residents were housed in such institutions (Vitello, 1976). Most of these individuals were in the severely and profoundly retarded categories, and about half of them were under 20 years of age. With the passage of new federal legislation, we can expect that an increasingly larger percentage of these individuals will be relocated in community settings and in the developing public educational facilities being provided for them.

We also should note in this discussion of prevalence that many retarded persons have one or more associated handicaps. Hence, they need special provision both for habilitation purposes and for appropriate educational treatment. In a nationwide survey of community and residential facilities, Conroy and Derr (1971) have ascertained the percentages of individuals who have handicaps in several areas other than that of retardation. Table 1.4 presents these data.

From these figures, we can readily see how widespread the problem of associated handicaps is among the retarded. Of particular interest to us, as clinical psychologists and proponents of the psychodynamic approach to mental retardation, is the high percentage of behavioral and emotional disorders. Although only 6.3 percent of cases are characterized as "serious," the fact that the total percentage is 42.0 suggests that the emotional needs of the retardated must be given adequate consideration in any program designed for their improvement.

All in all, the problem of mental retardation is seen to be a massive one; it is a problem that·affects the lives not only of the immediate families concerned, but also the lives of all of us. We need to understand the problem in all of its complexity so that we can develop rational and effective methods of prevention, alleviation, education, and training. As we have seen, great strides have been taken along these paths in recent years, but so much remains to be learned and to be done that we cannot afford to become complacent about the problem.

– 2 –

Intelligence: Theories, Measurement, and Relation to Mental Retardation

In this chapter, we will consider what intelligence is purported to be, how it has been measured, how it is distributed in the population, and what its relationship is to mental retardation. All present conceptions of mental retardation, and all as far back as we know, have held that this condition involves a significant deficit in intellectual functioning. Even if we were in full agreement on what intelligence is, and even if we were certain that our measures of intelligence were entirely valid, many unanswered questions would still remain. Some of these questions are: What causes inferior intellectual functioning? Is the deficit irreversible? Is it a uniform deficit covering all mental functions? and, Is intellectual deficit the only or primary criterion of mental retardation? But, as we shall see, there is considerable disagreement about all of these issues.

There also is considerable and sometimes acrimonious argument about the value of intelligence testing and about its uses and misuses. We believe that the *proper testing* of an individual's general intelligence can serve very useful functions, but that: (1) the evaluation of intelligence is not a mechanical or routine task; and (2) the significance of the nature of the individual's intellectual functioning cannot be determined on the basis of the intelligence test alone. Some people would dispense entirely with intelligence tests, citing their many difficulties, their uncertain degree of validity, and their lack of relationship to other important aspects of the personality and social adjustment. We agree, on the other hand, with those who find that the proper evaluation of intelligence can contribute greatly to the appropriate guidance and training of retarded individuals.

THEORIES OF INTELLIGENCE

As we consider the history of the conceptualization of intelligence and its measurement, we shall note that we have come almost full circle from the

31

position held in the late nineteenth century to the position advocated by some people today.

Pre-Binet Conceptions of Intelligence

Psychologists working in laboratories in Germany explored many psychological problems by means of scientific laboratory studies. Their approach to measuring intelligence involved the measuring of simple quasiphysiological indicators of physiological reactivity. Thus, they measured reaction time, rote memory, skin sensitivity, and similar psychophysiological functions. These functions were believed to be measures of the quality of efficiency of the entire nervous system and therefore could represent an index of mental efficiency. It was believed that measures of restricted, simple samples of such behavior were the most reliable and even the most valid. This approach strongly influenced psychology in other countries, especially in the United States, until well into the twentieth century. Unfortunately, it was found that these physiological measures did not correlate highly with academic success or, later, with other criteria of intellectual ability.

Binet's Conception of Intelligence

Alfred Binet was asked by the school authorities to develop a means by which slow learners in school could be distinguished from other school children. The aim was to select slow learners and provide them with special training. Binet's thinking was influenced by French and British psychologists and philosophers. He could not read German so the work of the German psychologists did not influence him. Moreover, Binet, whose training was in law and medicine and who had worked in psychiatric clinics and hospitals, wanted to discover in a practical way how slow learners differed from other learners. He spent many hours interviewing children and trying to devise procedures for evaluating general traits that would relate to academic performance. His approach was both *global* and *pragmatic*. Theoretical considerations were minimal. He tried to include in the test he was developing items that tapped broad aspects of mental functioning and that would differentiate bright from dull children. He also wished his test to differentiate older from younger children.

Thus, the Binet-Simon test of intelligence, which was finally developed in 1904, was a composite of many kinds of test items and seemed to measure broad aspects of mental functioning. Binet developed the concept of *mental age*. Mental age was the average age of test items that each had been assigned to on the basis of experimental findings. That is, the child was assigned a mental age that corresponded to the chronological age category in which he could pass about 50 percent of the items. Thus, Binet's measure of mental age indicated the age level at which a child could be expected to function in mental and academic work. Binet viewed intelligence therefore as a composite of complex and varied mental functions, the average performance on which indicate the person's level of mental maturity. Above all, Binet's test was designed to predict scholastic performance.

Spearman's Conception of Intelligence

By the 1920s, many American English psychologists were publishing accounts of their research on the nature of intelligence. Spearman, an Englishman, was an experimental psychologist who was influenced by the traditions of other English scientists. Based on an extensive series of research studies, he concluded that one fundamental *general factor* underlies all manifestations of intelligence. He called this factor *g* (Spearman 1927). According to Spearman, individuals are born with different amounts of *g*, although *g* also is influenced by experiences in life. The *g* factor is involved to some extent in all behavior of the individual, and some behavior is heavily dependent on this factor. Some types of activity depend on specific abilities, called *s*. Each *s* factor is specific to a given activity. Spearman thus proposed that two types of major factors are involved in an intelligent behavior: a common factor (*g*) and a specific factor (*s*). Individual differences in intelligence are due primarily to individual differences in *g*. According to this theory, the mentally retarded child is deficient in the amount of *g* he possesses.

Thorndike's Theory of Intelligence

In direct opposition to Spearman's unitary concept is the concept proposed by Thorndike (1926). He concluded that intelligent behavior is the function of highly specific abilities, and that general intelligence is merely the aggregate of those specifics. Unlike Spearman, Thorndike did not believe there is such a trait as *general intelligence;* rather, he believed there are many specific intelligences. According to Thorndike, there may be as many specific intelligences as there are different kinds of intelligent behaviors. However, he also believed that all of these specific intelligences may be grouped into three major categories. Thorndike called these categories *abstract, mechanical,* and *social* intelligence. Of the three, abstract intelligence correlates the highest with achievement in academic subjects.

Thorndike's view of the nature of intelligence is clearly expressed in his statement concerning individual differences: "... the person whose intellect is greater or higher than that of another person differs from him in the last analysis in having, not a new sort of physiological process, but simply a *larger number* of connections of the ordinary sort" (emphasis ours) (Thorndike, 1926).

Factor Analytic Theories of Intelligence

With the development of *factorial analysis of traits,* research was stimulated into the structure of the behaviors involved in intellectual functioning. Factor analysis is a statistical procedure in which many presumably well-constructed tests are given to a large population and the minimum number of relatively separate or unique parameters (or types of abilities) necessary to accommodate the results is extracted. Some of these factorial studies attempting to describe the *structure* of intelligence were directed at testing L. L. Thurstone's findings (1938) of twelve primary traits. Most of the studies were done with normal subjects, primarily with older children and adults.

Perhaps the work of Guilford and his associates (1971) best represents the current findings concerning the structure of intelligence. Guilford believes that intelligence consists of five *operations*. He defines them as "*cognition* (knowing or grasping items of information); *memory* (putting information into storage); *divergent production* (searching for and retrieving alternative items of information from storage to meet a certain need); *convergent production* (searching for and retrieving an item of information fully satisfying a particular need); and *evaluation* (judging whether an item of information satisfies given specifications)." In addition to these operations, according to Guilford, mental functioning is characterized by two other dimensions: *content* and *product*. Each dimension has a specific number of characteristics. Putting the separate characteristics of all three dimensions into all possible combinations yields a total of 120 unique intellectual abilities.

Guilford thus has found that there is no general factor of intelligence; rather, there are many, relatively uncorrelated, unique intellectual abilities. Moreover, he has found that these abilities do not develop at the same rate as they would if they proliferated from a single source; they "emerge more or less on their own at different times."

Turning to the problem of the structure of intelligence in the retarded, as contrasted with the normal, and using his own data as well as that of other researchers [notably Dingman and Meyers (1966)], Guilford found that the structure of intelligence in the retarded is basically similar to the structure of intelligence in normal subjects. However, there are also differential abilities within these two populations, some of which may be particularly important for planning educational programs and for individualized training.

Cattell (1971) has found what he calls *fluid* and *crystallized* factors in intelligence, based on his factorial studies. He believes that fluid intelligence represents the person's *potential* intelligence, largely independent of educational and social learning but dependent on incidental learning experiences and basic aspects of the environment. Crystallized intelligence depends on formal education and includes skills normally taught in school. It is of interest to note that Cattell (1964) attempted to construct a "culture-fair" test of intelligence, but his efforts in this direction, like those of others, have been disappointing.

Information Processing

With the advent of sophisticated theories about communication processing and with developments in computerizing knowledge, there has followed, almost inevitably, a conceptualization of intelligence based on models of information processing. A fusion of the work of experimental psychologists and learning theorists has led to the study of such processes as the receival, storage, and retrieval of information in the human organism. In turn, this has brought interest in the nature of sensory processes, coding strategies, and memory functions. Again, as in the late nineteenth century, it has been found that there are large individual differences in the efficiency of such processes. These considerations concerning processes in cognition have suggested a theory of intelligence based on the organism's efficiency in processing information. Hunt et al. (1973) have constructed measures of such functions and propose them as measures of intellectual behavior. Scores on such measures are related to scores on standard intelligence tests, particularly on verbal tests, but the relationship is far from being either high or perfect. Workers in this field of information processing believe that this is as it should be. They argue that information processing taps more basic, and therefore, somewhat independent functions.

As noted earlier, we appear to have come almost full circle from the early days of experimental psychology, when basic psychophysiological processes were given priority in learning about individual differences. Although newer terms and somewhat broader functions are being conceptualized and measured in information processing, the approach is still essentially molecular rather than molar. And we have seen how in earlier days such measures were limited in their prognostic usefulness. It remains to be seen whether the developments of information-processing methods of measuring "intelligent behavior" will lead to more fruitful results.

Cognitive Styles

Closely related to the development of factor analysis of intelligence is the research on cognitive styles. Workers in this area recognize that individuals with similar levels of mental maturity (as measured by a conventional intelligence test) and individuals with disparate levels of intellectual maturity differ in the specific intellectual strategies they characteristically use in dealing with their life situations. Thus, some individuals may reveal a high level of verbal reasoning or verbal abstraction, others may show high ability in various memory tasks, and others may demonstrate high ability on spatial or mathematical concepts. More accurately, we should speak of profiles or patterns of cognitive style. Our immediate concern is whether there are distinctive cognitive profiles that distinguish retarded individuals from the nonretarded. To answer this question, we must review some of the issues and evidence on factors related to cognitive style.

One early focus in studies of cognitive style dealt with the possible relationship of cognitive style to ethnic and social class differences. A study by Lesser, Fifer, and Clark (1965), often criticized on methodological grounds, but whose findings were nevertheless replicated later, evaluated the performance on various tasks of 320 first-grade children from Chinese, black, Puerto Rican, and Jewish ethnic backgrounds. There were 160 children from each group, equally divided by sex. Using the Hunter Aptitude Scales, measures were obtained on verbal skills, numerical skills, reasoning skills, and spatial perception skills. Differential patterns of functioning were demonstrated for each ethnic group, with the following specific rankings (from highest to lowest):

Verbal: Jews, blacks, Chinese, Puerto Ricans
Numerical: Jews, Chinese, Puerto Ricans, blacks
Reasoning: Chinese, Jews, blacks, Puerto Ricans
Spatial: Chinese, Jews, Puerto Ricans, blacks.

This study, like others that followed, demonstrated that there were characteristic differences in specific cognitive abilities and in the profiles of these abilities associated with both ethnic origin and social class.

Hertzig et al. (1968) attempted to answer the more difficult question of whether different cultures actually "teach" differing cognitive skills by virtue of their differing cultural experiences. In a longitudinal study, they compared children from working class Puerto Rican families with children from middle-class, white American families. They gathered data based on the Stanford-Binet (given when appropriate in Spanish to the Puerto Rican children) and extensive observations of behavior during testing and other experiences. Verbatim transcripts were made of both behavior and verbalizations. They found significant differences, which they attributed to the cultural patterns in the homes. The Puerto Rican children used language as freely as did the American children, but they used it quite differently, using actions rather than language to express many of their responses. They responded with gestures, distractions, social interactions and, sometimes, with "passive unresponsiveness." On the other hand, the American children were clearly work-oriented, used verbal abstractions with facility, and persisted at the tasks with considerable effort. It is interesting to note that most children in both groups came from stable families so that disruptive family circumstances did not contribute to the class and ethnic differences that were found.

Based on their own studies and the research done by others, Golden and Birns (1976) conclude that social class differences in cognitive style clearly emerge by three years of age. In one study, (Golden and Birns, 1968), they used a variety of tests including both verbal and nonverbal ones. A critical variable in this study of white boys was the differing educational levels of their mothers. The education of the mothers was dichotomized as high education (college graduate) and low education (not beyond high school). No differences were found in the two respective groups of children on learning tasks under nonverbal conditions. However, differences were found favoring the high education children on performance involving verbal conditions and on tasks involving delay. No differences were found on tests of spatial perception involving embedded figures. It seems reasonable to conclude from all of the studies that the specific culture of the home, and particularly the nature of the child-mother interactions in language and social behavior, influence the learning strategies and cognitive strategies of the children in decisive ways.

As we shall learn, many retarded children come from homes with poor social stimulation experiences, and particularly from homes in which linguistic experiences of the kind middle-class Americans employ are limited or lacking. Although it does not follow that poverty, by itself, leads to poor early stimulation of infants and children, it often accompanies such lack of stimulation. Perhaps more important are the differences in styles of child rearing that ill equip many children from low socioeconomic levels or from minority cultures with the kinds of cognitive skills required in middle-class schools. Thus, as we shall later learn in abundant detail, such children "behave" in a retarded manner in the conventional academic school situation. They are retarded in learning, but whether they are truly retarded intellectually or are simply different is another matter.

Some Comments about Theories of Intelligence

We have seen that intelligence has been variously defined and conceptualized. Not only is there a lack of full consensual agreement concerning the nature of intelligence, but it also is obvious that social-cultural developments and philosophical considerations play an important role in how we conceive of intelligence.

Wechsler (1958) deplores the fact that many people feel that intelligence is not adequately defined. He states that the difficulty is not so much that psychologists cannot agree on a definition of intelligence, but that intelligence itself is not a tangible entity. Rather, it is a limiting construct—an abstract rather than a material fact—and for this reason, it is known only through its properties and effects. According to Wechsler, any definition must be concerned ultimately with what intelligence involves and what it distinguishes, rather than with what it is. As he succinctly states: "We know intelligence by what it enables us to do." Wechsler defines intelligence operationally as the aggregate or global capacity of the individual to act purposefully, to think rationally, and to deal effectively with the environment. Further, he stresses that many determinants other than intellectual ability per se are involved in intelligent behavior. These include the goal-directed nature of the behavior, drive, incentive, and personality variables.

Although the definition of intelligence is somewhat arbitrary, depending in large part on one's philosophical view of the world and the nature of human beings, our position—based on clinical experience with a great variety of cases, as well as on the accumulated experimental and research evidence over the past decades—is a *dynamic* one. It is well known that infants are born with certain different characteristics that predispose them to interact with their environments in different ways. This interaction between organism and environment is not mechanical, but dynamic. The organism *reacts selectively* to the environment, seeking out stimulation that it craves, blotting out other aspects of the environment, and integrating these behaviors in accordance with its own goals and (later) values. Thus, the growth and development of the individual is not merely dependent on what he is born with. It also is influenced by external factors impinging upon him. Growth may be retarded, accelerated, or otherwise modified by these dynamic interactions.

As we shall see later in this chapter and throughout this book, the behavior that we call "intelligent" is not solely determined by genetic endowment, nor is it a simple, unitary phenomenon. There are many kinds of intelligence, and they are viewed and valued differently by different people and their societies. Some aspects of intelligent behavior are rather easily modifiable; other aspects can be modified only with great difficulty. We have been accustomed to think of such things as *abstract reasoning ability* and *general learning capacity* as being the core of intelligent behavior. In some societies, prudent behavior, social adaptability, or sensitivity to environment is highly valued as indicative of intelligent behavior.

Our society has taken for granted, to a large extent, that intelligence is what our conventional intelligence tests measure; but these tests were mainly designed to measure and predict academic performance. Traditional intelligence tests do not correlate perfectly with each other. In fact, tests designed to measure intelligence in infancy and early childhood have a relatively small relationship with tests designed to measure intelligence in later years. The commonality among these tests may vary as much as 40 to 80 percent. Even the same test given to the same person within relatively short intervals may give varying results, depending on the person's motivation at the time of testing, the circumstances of the testing, and the examiner administering the test. Intelligence tests that are commonly administered during the school years are typically "loaded" with measures of verbal abilities. They primarily measure one's abilities to *learn, remember,* and *synthesize* verbal materials. Such abilities may be markedly influenced by early experiences with verbal stimulation in the home, parental attitudes toward verbal communication, and incentives to acquire such abilities provided by home and community. If these factors were constant across the population, and predictions of academic success were then based on measures of these factors, we could expect a much greater degree of constancy in the later growth of tested individuals and a higher degree of predictability of later attainment. But these conditions do not hold across the board. Evaluation of the person's training experiences therefore needs to be scrutinized very carefully so that predictions of later development may take them into account.

These arguments should not be taken as a blanket repudiation of the value of standardized intelligence tests. Such tests have great value in determining *current, general, academic aptitude* and in placing students in school. However, they do not predict specific learning potentials and should be evaluated in terms of many relevant factors that could bias results—both in the short run and in the long run.

It might be well to emphasize two points concerning currently used intelligence tests, especially the Stanford-Binet and the Wechsler tests. 1. These tests were designed to measure scholastic aptitude, especially the kind of aptitude that plays an important role in verbal and general academic functions. As such, they have value *providing* the assumptions required for their validity (adequate previous stimulation and verbal learning, adequate motivation, and appropriate conditions of testing) are met and *providing* that any deviations from meeting these assumptions are properly taken into account in interpreting the results. 2. Factor analytic studies depend for their findings, in the last analysis, on the nature of the specific tests and the functions they involve that are used for the analysis. Such analyses cannot tell us what intelligence is! They can only tell us how most economically and most efficiently to describe (or name) the functions measured by the selected tests (or test items). The concept of intelligence is, in fact, an arbitrary formulation. If we keep in mind that for the most part the *usual* tests of intelligence measure a general kind of scholastic potential and also that a "potential" is only a "given" for the moment and may change under differing conditions, we can find important values for their use.

Some of the newer conceptualizations of intelligence have led to differing methods of measuring intelligence and "intellectual potential." We shall present samples of such methods in chapter 11.

FURTHER ASPECTS OF THE CHANGING CONCEPTION OF INTELLIGENCE

A much-needed reorientation thus is taking place in our view of intelligence. However, a basic issue concerning intelligence remains to be resolved. On the one hand, we can regard a person's intellectual *capacities* as being relatively fixed and static. That is, a person is born with a *fixed* intellectual capacity that is manifested from birth onward—it is a constant. On the other hand, we do *not* need to regard intellectual *functioning* as being such a constant, but as a *variable* depending on the interaction of many complex forces, both internal and external to the individual. It is thus a resultant—a product. If we assume that intelligence is constant, then programs for mentally retarded children will need to stress custodial care and the vocational training that is possible for persons of limited basic capacities. If we accept the interactional concept, then programs will have to try to improve the intelligence-operating level of mentally retarded children, especially mildly and moderately retarded children.

We are faced on the one hand with accepting the status quo of the child, and on the other with rejecting the fact that the condition is fixed. Further, important action implications stem from these two concepts of intelligence. If we accept the interactional concept, then we may do much more from the preventive standpoint. Influences or factors involved may be manipulated, which may prevent defective intelligence. If we accept the constancy concept, then intervention and prevention programs become more limited.

The older theories of intelligence tended to view it as a sort of separate entity within the child, relatively independent of outer influences such as environmental and social institutions and values. Gradually, this viewpoint began to change, and the effects of outer influences were recognized. However, even then intelligence continued to be regarded as a separate entity. Newer approaches view intelligence as but one part of the total dynamics of the child, one that is related to the child's total personality and its functioning. The human being functions as a total integrated organism, and therefore those aspects we call intelligence cannot be separated from the total functioning of the child—it is a manifestation of the total personality picture.

Fromm and Hartman (1955) have dealt extensively with this point of view. They discuss the many factors that interfere with the manifestations of the child's "true" intellectual potentials. These include: (1) neurotic inhibitions (such as inhibition of curiosity and aggression), physical handicaps, and emotional deprivation; (2) learning disabilities (such as inhibited curiosity and specific fears); and (3) temporary intellectual dysfunctioning based on emotional conflict (such as examination fear, fear of exhibitionism, and need to exceed potentials).

Some workers in the field go much farther than this. They believe it is inappropriate, or even misleading, to think in terms of *general intelligence* as measured by standardized tests. Bijou (1966) for example, prefers to think in terms of a *functional analysis* of behavior. He stresses that behavior should be assessed in *field situations,* that is, in the natural settings in which it occurs. Such careful observations of behavior over succeeding sessions lead, he believes, to effective assessment of behavior, its antecedents, and the kinds of activities that are needed to reinforce it. The observations lead to unique programs for each individual, designed to maximize growth. As a consequence, the child is not erroneously labeled according to a general and abstract concept such as *intelligence,* and he is not stereotyped and limited. Bijou rejects such general terms as *learning disability* for the same reasons.

There are many advantages to this viewpoint, and there is suggestive evidence that it offers considerable promise. But whether the concept and measurement of intelligence should be abandoned or neglected is another matter. What is especially valuable in Bijou's approach, aside from the specific merits of specially designed learning programs for each child, is that it eliminates the erroneous assumption that limited *general intelligence* necessarily means limits on all kinds of cognitive learning or all kinds of effective adaptation.

Cromwell (1967) also rejects the conventional definition of intelligence that emphasized only its cognitive aspect. Instead, he views intelligence as "the generalized adequacy an individual is able to maintain in achieving the goals and meeting the demands of his environment." Thus, he defines intelligence operationally, making no distinction between cognitive process and product. Cromwell also suggests that intelligent behavior must be defined in terms of a sequence of observable behaviors. In that way specific behaviors can be identified, and they often can be trained, improved, or made more efficient. Intelligence is not viewed as a constant, but rather as a composite of many factors, some of which may improve over time whereas others may not improve or may even show decrements. Cromwell points to Butterfield's summary (1967), which does, indeed, indicate how environmental factors may cause change in such specific abilities.

Piaget's Theory

In sharp contrast to other conceptions of intelligence as consisting of factors (whether general or specific), Piaget's formulations deal with the *development of cognitive processes* in the individual. Piaget's views have begun to have a significant impact on methods of education and are particularly relevant for the education of the retarded. At this point, we wish to present a preliminary summary of some of his views, leaving for later chapters discussions of details of his theory and applications to the problems of training and educating retarded pupils.

Piaget's theory of the development of cognitive processes (intelligence) formulates his understanding of how the environment is perceived and becomes "known" to the individual (1952). Four general conditions influence the rate of development of such cognitive processes. (Cognitive processes include the development of motoric skills, perceptual skills, language and thought.) The four conditions are: heredity and internal maturation; the nature of the child's physical experience in the early years; social transmission (educational stimulation in the broadest sense); and equilibration (which we shall define presently).

The infant's earliest behavior is determined in large measure by the specific reflexes of which the infant is capable, largely by reason of inherited structures. In the process of behaving, two features may be noted: *assimilation* and *accommodation*. Assimilation involves a "grasping" of occurring events and their incorporation into one's experience. As a child sucks, not only is the sucking repeated, but also a variety of elements in the recurring experience prolong the experience and produce an adaptation in the response itself. Thus, putting out one's tongue, placing one's fingers into the mouth, some degree of "looking and searching," and other corollary behaviors occur and are incorporated into the sucking response. In this manner the infant learns to *accommodate* its behavior to the newer elements in its ongoing experience. These primitive and simple accommodations are highly important in their portent for further behavior development.

The processes of assimilation and accommodation interact and produce a new *equilibrium* in behavior. Equilibration requires energy, which is provided as the child is increasingly challenged by its changing environment. A challenging environment—one that is not overwhelming to the child but that provides stimulation and experiences for which the child is maturationally ready— enables the child to develop new *schemata* (or behavioral structures) that either replace older schemata or in which older schemata are incorporated. *Means-ends* behavior emerges (the gradual development of intent), and the increasing complexity in the organization of behavior produces new needs for the individual.

The next stages in the development of intelligence involve: *secondary circular responses* (using external objects in the environment to satisfy needs) and other ever more complicated phases in equilibration so that the individual uses more and more complicated behavioral processes in satisfying needs and in mastering the environment. Perception becomes more adequate, memory processes more effective, and thinking procedures more mature.

Piaget attempted to demonstrate that all children pass through the same stages of development but that they differ in the ages at which they enter these stages and the rates at which they progress. Aside from hereditary influences, the rate of development depends in large part on the kinds of experiences and stimulation provided for the child. Also critical for the later development of intelligence are the basic experience in *behavioral actions* in which the child engages and the *energy* expended by the child in mastering the environment. Lawrence and Festinger (1970) confirmed that effort is required for optimal learning. Bosiclair and Dubreuil (1974) and Pinard and Lavoie (1974) studied children in various parts of the world (Canada, Switzerland, Martinique, and Rwanda) and contrasted children receiving traditional school programs with those receiving action-oriented programs including many motoric and play situations, especially group play. The latter groups were accelerated in their development of perceptual, linguistic, and symbolic skills. These and other studies seem to indicate that: (1) when children are provided stimulating experiences appropriate to their stage of development; (2) when they are given the opportunity to expend energy in motoric and other play activities; and (3) when they have to find their own solutions through experimenting, arguing, and discussing—they develop at a faster rate and achieve higher maturation in mental operations.

Piaget's theory is a dynamic one that provides a clear developmental emphasis in the development of intelligence. His conception of intelligence is not testable by means of the conventional tests of intelligence, but it can be evaluated by appropriate, alternative methods (Duckworth, 1964). The implications of Piaget's formulations are manifold. Intelligence is not a static quantity. Although there are inborn limits to the full development of intelligence, these limits are modifiable and the range for differential development is extensive, providing active, challenging, and appropriate experiences are offered through which the child *learns to learn*. Poverty of experience, according to this view, can be devastating and its effect has been extensively studied and verified through many studies, which we shall refer to in later chapters.

DISTRIBUTION OF INTELLIGENCE

We all know that there is a vast range of intellectual ability among children. Some children are markedly inferior, and others, by contrast, are markedly superior in intelligence as measured by intelligence tests. Most children, however, cluster around a central point in the distribution of intelligence that is called the *mean,* or *average.* A particular child may rank at any point on this continuum from very inferior to very superior, according to the amount (*quantity* or degree) of intelligence possessed. In addition, the child may differ from others in the kind (*quality*) of intelligence that is characteristic of him.

It is important that we consider how intelligence, from a quantitative point of view, is *distributed* (that is, spread out) in the general population. Most

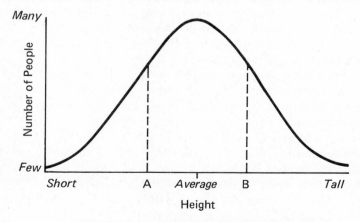

FIGURE 2.1.   Normal Distribution Curve

human traits are distributed among the total population in a characteristic pattern. For example, if we took all the people in the world and arranged them in order according to their height from tallest to shortest, we would find that a very small percentage would be exceedingly tall, the greatest percentage would be average in height, and a very small percentage would be exceedingly short. If we graphed the number of people of each height, we would construct a curve similar to that shown in Figure 2.1. Any given individual would rank, according to height, at a specific point in this distribution.

The distribution depicted by this curve is representative of most human traits, such as height, weight, mechanical aptitude, physical strength, dependency on others, and aggressiveness. This curve also results when the distribution of intelligence in the general population is plotted. Such a curve is known as the *normal distribution* curve, or the curve of *normal probability*. When a human characteristic is distributed in this way, there is a clustering around the average, central point of the curve, and decreasing frequencies as we move toward either *tail* (end).

One representative curve of the distribution of intelligence in white American-born children was constructed by Terman and Merrill (1937). They plotted it for the IQ of 2,904 children between two and eighteen years of age, who were tested with the L-M form of the *Terman-Merrill* test (see chapter 4). This curve is reproduced in Figure 2.2.

According to the data accumulated by Terman and Merrill, the statistical average in IQ is calculated to be 100 (on the 1937 revision of the *Binet* intelligence test), but children whose IQs fall between 95 and 104 are considered to be *average,* or *normal,* in intelligence. Approximately 3 percent of the total group fall below an IQ of 65 and are considered to be *feebleminded.*

It also is important that we pay particular attention to the distribution of IQs around the *mean.* The standard deviation (SD) of the curve plotted by Terman and Merrill is 16.4 IQ points. Statisticians have determined that the following statistical relationships *always* hold for any normal distribution of measurements: 68.26 percent of the population fall between points one SD above and one SD below the mean; 95 percent fall between 2 SDs above and below the mean, and 99.7 percent fall between points three SDs above and below the mean.

Since the mean of the distribution of IQs on the *Terman-Merrill* test is 100, and the SD is 16.4 points in IQ, approximately 68 percent of all children have IQs (on this particular test) between 84 and 116 (between one SD above and one SD below the mean); 95 percent have IQs between 67 and 133 (between two SDs above and two SDs below the mean); and approximately 99 percent (almost all) have IQs between 51 and 149 (between three SDs above and three SDs below the mean). Although the numerical value of the mean IQ and the size of the SD vary according to the specific intelligence test used (since any specific test has some errors of measurement), it is believed that intelligence is distributed over the total population according to this pattern regardless of the test used for its measurement.

However, some authorities believe that although intelligence is nor-

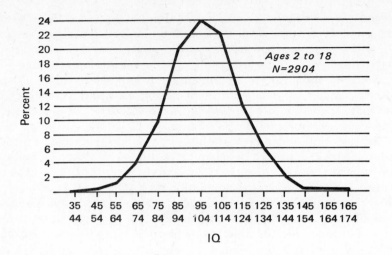

FIGURE 2.2.   Distribution of Composite L-M IQs of Standardization Group (From L. M. Terman and M. A. Merrill, *Measuring Intelligence.* Boston: Houghton Mifflin, 1937, p. 37.)

mally distributed over an unselected population, the lower range of the total distribution is not normally distributed. In support of such a contention, some surveys have indicated that there actually are many more very severely retarded persons than would be predicted from the normal curve.

Dingman and Tarjan (1960) analyzed expected and actually occurring frequencies of mental retardation. They estimated that there were actually 334,421 more persons below IQ of 70 than would be predicted from the normal distribution curve and then constructed a new curve based on their data. This curve is shown in Figure 2.3.

The distribution of intelligence depicted is in fact a *combined* curve, made up of two components: (a) a normal curve based on the theoretical *general population;* and (b) a truncated normal curve based on the excess frequencies. According to Dingman and Tarjan, the mentally retarded segment of the curve is composed of two subgroups. One represents the lower end of the normal distribution curve of intelligence; the other, the "excess" instances with a separate frequency distribution. The curve of the latter group is cut sharply at IQ zero, since this degree of retardation is "incompatible with life." We have noted that Mercer's study (1973b) confirms this finding.

From inspecting the curve in Figure 2.3, it is apparent that mental retardation is *not* a point on the curve; it is, rather, an area under the curve that describes a *range* in intelligence. Thus, mentally retarded children range over a significant portion of the total scale. So do "normal" or "bright" children. In other words, any particular grouping of children designated by any descriptive term varies in degree of intelligence, and often will show as much (or even more) inter-group as intra-group variability.

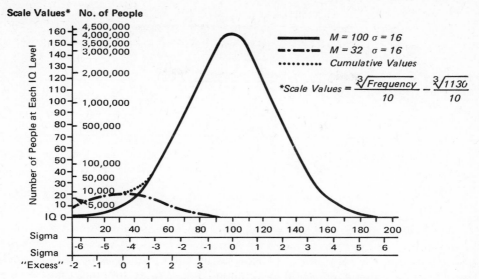

Scale Values*   **No. of People**

Number of People at Each IQ Level

$M = 100 \ \sigma = 16$
$M = 32 \ \sigma = 16$
Cumulative Values

$$\text{*Scale Values} = \frac{\sqrt[3]{Frequency}}{10} - \frac{\sqrt[3]{1130}}{10}$$

FIGURE 2.3.   Frequency Distribution of IQs, Assuming a Total Population of 179,000,000. (From *Amer. J. ment. Defic.*, 1960, 64, 991–994.

PATTERNS OF MENTAL GROWTH

Many studies have dealt with the relationship of growth in mental abilities to increase in chronological age (see, for example, Wechsler, 1950; Bayley, 1955). There are some points of divergence in these studies, largely because different investigators have used different measures of mental ability or have applied them to different groups of children. But if these differences are considered, the major findings of such studies tend to agree quite closely.

The typical curve representing the growth of intelligence, when smoothed out, assumes the form of a modified semi-parabola. Inspecting this curve indicates that mental abilities grow rapidly in the periods of infancy and early childhood. These periods of rapid growth are followed by a period of slower growth until the *apogee* (maximum) is reached during early adulthood. Thorndike (1926) stated that there is a cessation in growth of mental ability at about age 21, and many authorities tend to agree that measured intelligence generally shows no increment beyond that age. After that point is reached, no apparent change occurs for a number of years (there is a *plateau* in the curve). But in the middle years of life there is a slight decrement in intellectual functioning, and this decrement increases with increasing chronological age. In *senescence* (old age) there is a gradually increasing decrement in mental abilities as measured by present intelligence tests. (This does not mean that people cannot learn anything more after young adulthood or even in old age, but only that mental *capacity*, or the general *rate* of learning, reaches a peak in young adulthood and decreases in later life.)

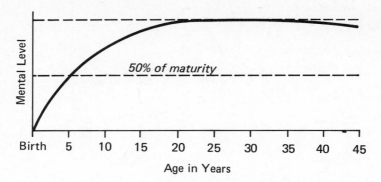

FIGURE 2.4.   Growth in Intellectual Ability, from Birth to 45 Years

Several exceptions to the general findings noted above must, however, be noted. First, it has been found that when some method of *absolute scaling* has been applied to the test data, the shape of the curve is different. Absolute scaling refers to a statistical method of obtaining units of measurement that are consistent in value throughout the range of scores and development levels. This refinement in scoring attempts to correct for obviously unequal units of, say, mental age scales in which differences of a year in mental growth at younger ages are not comparable to differences of a year at older ages. Thurstone and Ackerman (1929), for example, applied the method of absolute scaling to the data from 4,208 children and adolescents on the *Stanford-Binet* test. Figure 2.5 represents the type of curve that resulted.

Thurstone's data also demonstrated a second exception to the general principles of mental growth we have discussed: different intellectual functions

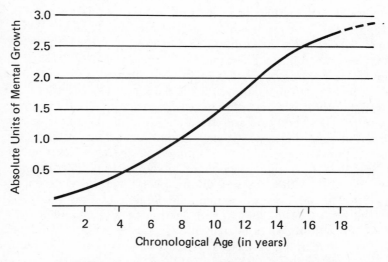

FIGURE 2.5.   An S-shaped Curve of Mental Growth

mature at different rates. At the extremes, *verbal comprehension* reaches 80 percent of maturity at eighteen years of age, whereas *perceptual speed* reaches 80 percent of maturity at twelve years of age. Other aspects of intellectual functioning, such as *reasoning, memory,* and *numerical facility,* reach equivalent degrees of maturity at intervening age levels. It must be noted that these findings are based on the then-current conditions of child rearing and education. It would be interesting to evaluate the development of these different intellectual processes under differing conditions of training and development. We suspect that training exerts some influence on rates of maturation, as Piaget suggested and as some of the research we quoted indicates.

A third exception to the general growth curve originally proposed is that different intellectual functions decline in efficiency after the apogee (high point) has been attained. It had been assumed, before adequate research on this subject, that: (a) all intellectual functions declined after a certain age, and (b) all intellectual functions declined at about the same rate. Both assumptions have been found to be false. In a study by Bayley (1955) referred to earlier, it was found that when a group of adults who were previously identified as highly intelligent were retested, they showed significant gains in intelligence until age 50 and beyond. One wonders whether such findings are due to continued interest of such people in intellectual endeavors and the consequent restimulation that their efforts involve. With regard to differential decline of differing abilities, evidence (Hallenbach, 1963) indicates that this is, indeed, the case. Many factors may contribute to such differential decline, such as the extent to which intellectual functions depend on sensori-motor processes (which may decline due to aging), and the extent to which new learning is required in the living process or is otherwise motivated. Of course, a serious brain dysfunction may cause intellectual impairment, especially in certain areas of behavior dependent on specific cortical effectiveness; but brain damage in general has not been found to produce a decline in intelligence in old age (Aring, 1957).

Finally, it should be emphasized, as we shall attempt to do throughout this book, that there are considerable individual variations in the growth curves of different people. Garrison has pointed out that even though the mental growth curves of superior, average, and dull children differ in some respects, they all conform to the same general pattern. This point is illustrated in Figure 2.6. The three curves represent the mental development of (1) superior, (2) average, and (3) dull children. Although the pattern of growth is essentially the same for each group, the differences between the curves become greater with increased chronological age. As Garrison points out, the backward child tends to become more inferior when compared with the average as he gets older, and the superior child becomes even more superior.

The uniqueness of the pattern of mental growth of each individual is shown in Figure 2.7. Note that the mental ages of the five subjects (all boys) were the same at the chronological age of seven years, but differences in mental ages were pronounced at the chronological age of seventeen. The *rates* of growth also are markedly different from one child to another, with each child having his own unique pattern of mental development. Garrison points out that one should not

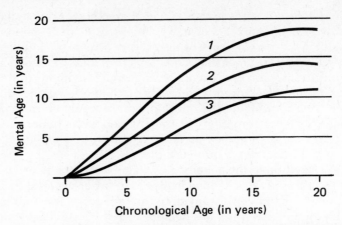

FIGURE 2.6. The Mental Development of (1) Superior, (2) Average, and (3) Dull Children (Karl C. Garrison, *Psychology of Adolescence*, 5th Ed., © 1956, Prentice-Hall, Inc., Englewood Cliffs, N.J., p. 79.)

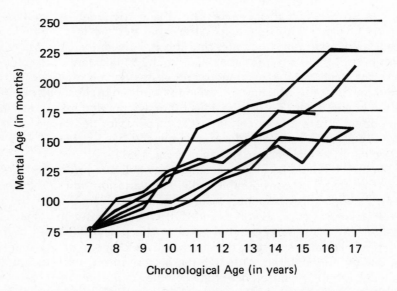

FIGURE 2.7. Diverging Individual Mental Growth Curves (From Karl C. Garrison, *Psychology of Adolescence*, 5th ed., © 1956, Prentice-Hall, Inc., Englewood Cliffs, N.J., p. 83.)

conclude that a child is mentally inferior merely because he develops slowly. A superior child may be slow in getting started, and a dull child may make an impressive beginning.

INTELLIGENCE TEST SCORES AND BEHAVIOR

The score on a standardized test of intelligence has important values. Among these is the significant correlation of such scores with *academic performance*. As we have seen, however, such scores also have serious limitations. For one thing, they do not correlate perfectly with scholastic achievement; if they did, they would not be needed! For another, they do not predict equally well the different aspects even of academic learning; they are better in predicting reading achievement and arithmetic reasoning than spelling, or achievement in history. McCulloch and his coworkers (1955) found that intelligence tests did not predict the capacity of mentally retarded individuals to learn words through repetitive training. Recent studies have shown the great variability in learning different skills under different conditions of training of retarded individuals with similar intelligence scores. (See chapters 11, 12, and 13.) And, of course, the score on a test is the result of many factors other than intelligence, such as the personality of the individual, motivation for doing well, and prior training and education. But when properly employed, intelligence tests can play a significant role in various educational procedures, as we shall see, and in helping to make appropriate administrative decisions concerning placement and readiness for certain learning situations.

Historically, two types of intelligence test scores have been used; the *mental age* score and the *IQ* score. They have differing meanings and differing functions. The mental age (MA) concept was introduced by Binet as a mathematical measure of the mental age level that the individual possessed at a particular time. It simply indicated that on a certain test, presumably measuring general intellectual development, the individual had attained a level comparable to the average of individuals of that age. Thus, an eleven-year-old child who has a mental age of nine is comparable in "general intelligence" (assuming the test results are valid) to average nine-year-olds (as represented in the sample of children on whom the test was standardized). The MA is an important measure since it gives a precise standard for making one kind of important judgment. In general, it would not be expected that such an eleven year old would be able to compete successfully with average children of his own age in academic tasks, but it would be expected that he had the intellectual capacity for doing such work in competition with average nine year olds or with other individuals at the nine-year mental age level.

As we have seen, the MA, as measured by an appropriate intelligence test, is a measure of mental maturity. The IQ, on the other hand, is a measure of brightness, or relative intelligence. The IQ measure was introduced by Terman in connection with his standardization of the *Stanford-Binet Intelligence Test* and was obtained by dividing the obtained mental age by the individual's chronological age, and multiplying the result by 100 (to remove decimal figures). Thus, if a child of eight years obtains an MA of ten years on an intelligence test, his IQ would be 125, whereas a child with the same chronological age who obtains an MA of six years, would have an IQ of 75. The first child would be considered "bright" and the second child would be considered "dull." Such IQ measures tell us what the expected rate of development of intelligence is rather than what the level of mental maturation is.

There are several problems with IQ measures. We will first focus on the units of measurement. Does a 10-point difference in IQ above the average (an IQ of 110) indicate the same degree of difference in brightness as an IQ difference of 10 points below the average (an IQ of 90)? Similarly, does an IQ of 130 represent as much deviation from 100 (in a positive direction) as an IQ of 70 (in a negative direction)? To insure that such differences are quantitatively equal, we must be sure that the units on which the quotient is based also are equal. But, as we have seen, mental growth does not proceed at the same rate throughout life, nor does it proceed in a straight line. Another way of looking at this problem is to compare the distribution of test scores at differing ages. On the 1937 edition of the *Stanford-Binet,* for example, the standard deviation (the SD is a measure of variability) was 12.5 at age six and 20.0 at age twelve. Thus, a child who retained the same relative position, one standard deviation above the average, at ages six and twelve, would obtain respective IQ scores at these two ages of 125 and 140—a considerable difference. To correct for this difficulty, Wechsler, in developing his tests, used the relative position of the test score for a particular age (or SD units) as the basis for calculating the IQ score. (Terman and his collaborators have developed similar procedures for the 1960 edition of the *Stanford-Binet.* See chapter 11.) When calculated by comparing an individual with individuals of comparable age, this problem with the meaning of IQ scores is solved.

There are other problems, however. Does an individual's IQ score remain constant over an extended period of time, even assuming that the same types of test items and appropriate methods for calculating the IQ are utilized? As we shall see, IQ scores can vary over time—sometimes considerably—depending on such factors as the reliability of the test, conditions of the testing, and intervening educational and intellectual experiences. The critical questions here are: how much error of measurement is involved in the IQ measure; and, how much variation in IQ can be expected under changing conditions?

Both the MA and IQ scores have value and in our judgment should not be disregarded. A major difficulty, however, is that we tend to rely excessively on scores of any kind. Once we have a mathematical score, we tend to assume that the score is an absolute measure and an adequate and accurate characterization of the individual. An IQ of 60 does not necessarily mean, for example, that the individual is mentally retarded, nor do two individuals each of whom scores an IQ of 60 have *the same profile* of mental abilities. Intelligence test scores simply are samples of behavior obtained under certain conditions. Like any sample, their values and limitations must be carefully taken into account.

To emphasize the points we have been making, we cite two examples of errors that could be made, and in one case were made, if test scores are not properly interpreted. These cases are, admittedly, exceptions but they point up the need for clinical judgment in interpreting intelligence test results.

The Case of Carole

Carole, a seven-year-old girl, achieved an IQ score of 68. Despite the low level of Carole's test performance, the psychologist concluded that she was a child of good average intelligence and that the test score was depressed because of Carole's severe fear of the testing situation. She had formerly attended a one-room school and was now attending a large city elementary school. He recommended reevaluation at a later date after she had become accustomed to her changed situation.

The Case of Howard

Howard presented a much more complicated problem. He was first seen by the senior author when Howard was slightly less than six years of age. He had been evaluated previously by a psychiatric service and found to show severe disturbances in speech (echolalia, or repetitive sounds or words in speech), interpersonal behavior (schizoid and autistic), and mental development (mentally retarded by at least one year). The examining psychologist had given him an inappropriate form of the Wechsler (the WISC, which is intended for much older children), along with personality tests that were inappropriate for his age level and his capacity for responding. Moreover, this psychologist reported that "he will have adjustment problems all of his life." (Such an unwarranted long-term prognosis is a dangerous procedure.) He was later evaluated in a psychiatric hospital for children, since the parents were obviously distraught by the findings and sought additional professional guidance. Here, much more careful and sensitive evaluations were made. This hospital suggested that "longitudinal study is definitely indicated," but found Howard to be "low normal in intellectual level," based on the WPPSI (a form of the Wechsler intelligence test appropriate for Howard's age).

Howard was seen by the present writer about eight months later when Howard was nearly six years of age. Careful histories were taken from both parents before he was seen. It was learned that he had had severe and restrictive training during his infancy by a governess who was left in charge while the parents were away on extended trips. The parents did not learn until later that Howard had been so severely restricted! As soon as they did, they took corrective measures, but a great deal of harm had already occurred. Howard was a very anxious child and was seriously delayed in many perceptual and motoric areas of development. He engaged in a great deal of fantasy, seemed little interested in other children or able to relate to them, and had developed a highly repetitious speech pattern (which was incorrectly labeled "echolalia"). The examiner noted a slight degree of dysplasia (abnormal development) of Howard's head and learned that there were some difficulties in the birth process. These and other factors had contributed to his slow development in some areas and to his erratic behavior.

He was examined by a variety of perceptual-motor and intelligence tests, suitable for his age, only after ample time had been taken to develop thorough rapport and a friendly relationship had been established. It was clear that he was retarded in some aspects of both gross and fine coordination as well as in social *skills. On the other hand, he had a vocabulary level that was about two years above his age level, his fantasy (while sometimes unrelated to the reality situation) was creative and original. Many aspects of thinking and judgment were clearly above average. However, attention span and memory span were inadequate for his age.*

It seemed clear that Howard was not only not a retarded child and not an autistic child, but also that he was emotionally disturbed and was retarded in some basic areas of development. On the other hand, he was definitely superior in many areas of intellectual functioning, despite his handicaps. Howard had been misdiagnosed.

A corrective program was begun with the full and spirited cooperation of the parents. Play and social situations were developed for the home to stimulate growth in interpersonal areas. Some individual therapy was provided for Howard to release his anxieties and to help him use his fantasy in a constructive fashion. Later, he was enrolled in a preschool program and given special training in sensory and motoric areas as well as in social interaction. The parents also needed reassurance and guidance.

One year later Howard was seen again. He had made remarkable progress. His IQ score was now estimated to be at least 130! His vocabulary and reasoning were at least two years above his age level. Motor development had become almost normal, and sensory processes as well as perceptual skills were at least average. He still had some difficulty in interpersonal relations and occasionally his ability to attend was inadequate. However, all of the new findings suggested that with continued special care and training he would make a superior adjustment and progress at a superior rate in school subjects.

Cases such as Howard's indicate how tests can be used effectively to judge current abilities and misused to overgeneralize inaccurately and to prognosticate improperly. In each case, the intelligence test score told us how the individual was then functioning; in each case, individual factors in terms of background had to be considered.

Constancy of Intelligence Test Scores

This brings us to a consideration of the much-debated question of the constancy of the intelligence test score—that is, How stable is such a score over a period of time? The research literature is replete with apparently conflicting studies; some maintain that the score remains fairly constant, others stress that it is variable and shows considerable fluctuation. Much of the difficulty in dealing with this problem may stem from attempts to overgeneralize about the matter of constancy as well as from a tendency to identify test scores with behavioral aspects of intellectual functioning. In part, when talking about IQ constancy, we need to consider the characteristics of various groups of children rather than to generalize for all children. The IQ has different meanings, depending on the group to which it is applied. Thus, an IQ derived for a mentally retarded group has a *different* reliability than one for an average group. Similarly, IQs obtained for infants are less reliable than those for adolescents.

Let us consider measures of intelligence for young children. How constant are their intelligence test scores from year to year? Goodenough (1951) critically evaluated the results of intelligence tests given to infants and children between two and three years of age. She pointed out that (1) they did not necessarily have the same predictive value for later mental development as those given after school age; and (2) they were not necessarily reliable. Goodenough felt that tests given in early life had little value for prognosis; further, scores on such tests often were inaccurate even at the time of administration.

The constancy of the measured intellectual functions fluctuates with the intellectual level of the group examined. In general, as pointed out earlier, those children with IQs around the average tend to have more constant IQs when tested a second time than either the very bright or the very dull children. We are here concerned only with the constancy of measured intellectual capacities in the below-average groups. The true scores of children with low intelligence test scores contain a larger probable error of measurement than those scoring around the average.

We know that marked fluctuations in the IQs of children testing below average do occur, apart from the statistical variation cited above, when they are retested. Repeated studies have been made of children who were reared in undesirable environments and later placed in more favorable surroundings. In such instances there have been, at times, considerable increases in intelligence test scores. The following are examples of such studies.

Long ago, Skeels and Dye (1939) studied the effects of differential stimulations on mentally retarded children. Originally, they were interested in two illegitimate children whose mothers were feebleminded. The children were in an orphanage. At the age of 1½ years, they were examined on the *Kuhlmann-Binet Test* and achieved IQs of 46 and 35 respectively. Behaviorally their actions also were typical of mentally retarded children. They were accordingly transferred to an institution for feebleminded children. Six months later they were reexamined and found to have IQs (again on the *Kuhlmann-Binet*) of 77 and 87. A year later their IQs were found to be 100 and 88. At about 3½ years of age, they were 95 and 93. It was found that the two children had been greatly liked by the ward attendants, who played with them, took them for rides, and in general provided them with a positive *therapeutic* climate.

Following this initial experience, thirteen children were transferred from the orphanage to the institution for feebleminded. The mean IQ of the group was about 64, with a range of 35 to 89. The children also showed the behavioral characteristics of retarded children. As a control, they were compared with twelve children of similar intellectual level and behavior who were retained in the orphanage. In the institution for the feebleminded the children were placed in wards with older and brighter children. According to Skeels and Dye, the environment of the transferred group was positive and stimulating, whereas that of the control group tended to be the opposite. They were then reexamined psychologically. The experimental group showed a mean increase in IQ of 27.5 points, but the children in the control group all decreased in IQ.

There are, of course, many factors to be taken into consideration in evaluating the Skeels and Dye study. The positive emotional environment provided for the experimental group may be important, as well as the fact that deprivation at an early age generally is believed to hinder the psychological growth of the child. On the other hand, one might argue that the reason for the change in IQ was that the tests given were unreliable, or that they were administered improperly. We are not, however, concerned at this point with the reason for the change per se. The important fact is that the original measure of intellectual functioning did not remain constant, but *changed* over a relatively short period.

Marchand (1956) studied a group of 123 retarded individuals before and after they were placed in employment outside an institution. He concluded that:

1. Eighty percent of these individuals had higher IQs after having had such employment experiences. Of the group, 50 percent increased from 1 to 9 IQ points, and 38 percent increased from 10 to 31 points in IQ.
2. There are consistent differences in the drive, attitudes, and facades of the individuals who developed significantly as well as those who did not show such change.
3. The average rise of the experimental group was 9.2 points of IQ, whereas the group with which they were compared (the control group) showed a mean drop of 1.4 IQ points.

Cultural factors also may affect the intelligence test score. This conclusion has been demonstrated repeatedly. A study of this phenomenon was reported by Fahmy (1954). He tested a group of children from an extremely restricted environmental section of Egypt. Four tests were given to the group. On the *Porteus* the mean score was 76, on the *Goddard* 74, and on the *Goodenough* 50, but on the *Alexander* it was 97. The children had no adequate conceptions of straight lines and had no drawing experience. These abilities were heavily weighted in the first three tests. However, the *Alexander* test involves the manipulation of colored blocks; colors were highly important in the children's culture. Fahmy feels that this study furnishes ample evidence of the effect of culture on the intelligence test score. If a child is moved to a different culture and is tested with an instrument based on the new culture, then changes in his test score may be expected.

In order to highlight the effects of short- versus long-term intervals between retestings, we will cite two representative studies that are fairly typical of the findings of many other studies.

Collmann and Newlyn (1958) studied changes in the *Terman-Merrill* IQs of 182 retarded children who were retested within a period of one year following the original test. The correlation between the two obtained IQs was .93, and of the 182 cases, only two of the IQs rose by nine points and only five cases fell six points. These were the extreme shifts that occurred in IQ from test to retest. This study suggests that the IQs of retarded children tend to be stable within a period of one year.

Alper and Horne (1959) studied IQ changes in a group of fifty children institutionalized over a long period of time. They had been tested originally with the 1916 *Binet,* and were all retested with the *Wechsler Adult Intelligence Scale.* The minimum retest interval was 17 years and 9 months, the maximum was 35 years and 3 months, and the mean time between tests was 25 years and 9 months. It was found that in some cases there was considerable shifting of IQ within a narrow range, but there were few extreme shifts. The differences between the mean *Binet* and mean *Wechsler* total IQ scores was not significant. It was concluded that there is a tendency for the IQ of institutionalized children to remain relatively consistent.

When we review the available evidence, we are forced to conclude that intelligence test scores need not remain constant from time to time. This conclusion is particularly true when we consider the performances of a specific individual as opposed to those of a group. Social and cultural forces, personality factors within the child, the circumstances surrounding the test administration, as well as statistical artifacts of test construction (i.e., peculiarities of scaling methods), are all factors that influence the production of an intelligence test score. These factors will be discussed in detail in chapter 11. At this point, we simply wish to underscore the limitations of any score derived from an intelligence test. We agree with Hunt (1961), who, after an exhaustive review of the evidence concerning factors that may influence such scores, said: ". . . deprivations of experience have been found to make a difference in the rate at which infant organisms develop behaviorally," and these deprivations "call the assumption of predetermined development into serious question. . . ."

In evaluating the performance of an *individual child,* we must recognize that many factors other than genetic endowment may have influenced the outcome. Intelligence, even as measured by valid tests, is *a product of many interacting factors* and, in any case, does not adequately represent the child's capacity for learning and adapting. Above all, we must avoid the assumption that a particular IQ score will necessarily remain constant.

The interaction of environmental factors and cognitive functioning has been highlighted by several studies. Such interaction is especially noticeable in situations in which children have been deprived of social and intellectual stimulation in their early years of development—for example, in slum areas and in ethnically deprived groups.

Heber and his coworkers (1970, 1972) investigated the effects of early intervention in preventing retarded intellectual functioning in a socioculturally deprived area of Milwaukee. In a sample population of blacks with an average IQ of 86.3, 22 percent had IQs below 75. From this sample, Heber and his coworkers selected forty mothers, all of whom tested at an IQ score below 70. The investigation assigned this subpopulation randomly to either an experimental or a control group. They also employed what they called a *contrast group:* the other siblings of the children in the study. The investigators applied intensive stimulation to the infants of the mothers in the experimental group, beginning at about birth and continuing through the preschool years. At four months of age the infants were enrolled in an infant education center. Throughout the program, the mothers in the experimental group were given training to improve their methods of child care and homemaking techniques. At about the fourth year, all of the infants were retested, as were the children in the contrast group. It was found that the experimental children now had an average IQ score of 128, the control group had an average IQ score of 94, and the contrast group had an average IQ score of 85.

This study has been criticized on methodological grounds, and it has been pointed out that the experimental group had training on items sampled by the intelligence tests. Nevertheless, the very high IQs obtained by the experimental group and the difference of 34 IQ points between the experimental group and the control group are not to be gainsaid. It also is interesting that the children in the contrast group, who might have been expected to show about the same average IQ as their mothers, instead were at least 15 IQ points higher. It is probable that the training the mothers received had some effect on their interactions with these older children. In general, then, even allowing for some effects of uncontrolled factors, the experimental procedures appear to have produced significant increments.

Another study correlated ethnic background, adaptive behavior, and measured IQ. Adams et al. (1973) compared four groups of children: twenty-six black males, twenty-four black females, thirty white males, and twenty-nine white females. The children ranged in age from four to seventeen. As measured by the *Vineland Social Maturity Test* (see chapter 11), blacks and whites did not differ on social quotient. As measured on an IQ test, however, more blacks than whites were classified as "very impaired." Thus, if IQ score alone had been used to rate the maturity designation, the black group would have been adversely classified.

Studies like this again emphasize the importance of considering more than the IQ measure in the total evaluation process. They point up the wisdom of including some evaluation of adaptive behavior to arrive at a more accurate estimate of the individual's capacity. Intelligence tests have their important place in this evaluation process, but social conditions, educational opportunities, and other specific aspects of behavior also must be given very careful consideration.

A related issue is the effect of attendance in nursery schools in stimulating cognitive and adaptive development. There is ample evidence, which some workers in the field are still unwilling to accept, that attending nursery school can have both short-term and long-term effects on such development. Much of the evidence that is currently available on this issue has been summed up by Spicker (1971); Lichtenberg and Norton (1970); and LaCrosse et al. (1970). There also is considerable and expanding evidence that the intervention and remedial training in infancy can markedly affect intellectual and adaptive development (see chapter 12.)

FACTORS CONTRIBUTING TO MENTAL IMPAIRMENT

We have seen that intelligence test scores and also intellectual functioning in general can be improved or be impaired by certain classes of factors. Since mental impairment often wears the mask of mental retardation, it is important to understand the nature of the conditions that can produce such an effect.

Some children function somewhat, or considerably, below their *native potential* for intellectual functioning. Just how many cases of this kind there are is not known, although widespread clinical experience suggests that the number may be very great. In fact, Tarjan (1960), who differentiates two groups of mental retardates as *physiological* (those who rarely show stigmata and whose retardation is attributable to psychogenic or functional causes) and *pathological* (those who have some demonstrable organic basis for their retardation and show concomitant somatic involvements), estimates that the former group outnumbers the latter by a ratio of 16 to 1. Many children tend to function as mentally retarded because of types of personality disturbances that produce *inhibition in intellectual functioning*. If these personality disturbances are resolved, the children tend to function at considerably higher mental levels.

Mental impairment may be said to exist whenever an individual is functioning below the intellectual level of which he would be capable were it not for some interfering and remediable factor. It is *not* to be confused with a test rating of mental retardation that is due to invalid or faulty administration of the test. In mental impairment, the individual not only tests lower than his potential but also behaves at an inferior level in his total adaptation to the world.

Three main categories of factors may produce or contribute to mental impairment. One is *cultural deprivation*. Cultural deprivation is frequently, but not necessarily, associated with very low socioeconomic status. It may be due to cultural poverty in the home, to very inadequate and inferior schooling, or to serious inconsistencies in cultural experiences. In any case, the environment is seriously deficient in providing stimulation for intellectual growth and, after a time, the individual may behave as though he were retarded in native intellectual endowment. (See chapters 6 and 11 for further discussion of this problem.)

A second major category of causes of mental impairment is *physical injury or disease*. Sometimes a disease may so debilitate a person that his intellectual functioning is impaired until that condition has been corrected or compensated for. Severe anemia is one example of such a condition; tuberculosis is another. Other diseases may affect a person's functioning for shorter periods but may nevertheless cause impairment in mental ability during such periods. Injuries, especially those causing sensory impairment, may adversely affect mental functioning. Other conditions, such as severely enlarged adenoids, may interfere with effective sensory functioning or with general physical well-being and therefore indirectly affect mental functioning. In general, the kinds of conditions we are discussing produce a *temporary arrest* in mental development and, as a consequence, an *impairment* in mental functioning. Such conditions should be distinguished from those that affect the central nervous system (particularly the cortex), sometimes causing permanent arrest and retardation.

Finally, there is the category of *psychological factors* that may cause impairment in mental functioning. This is a highly complex category. All of us have heard of cases of severe psychological disturbances, notably cases of *psychosis* (insanity), in which impairment in mental functioning may occur. But even much milder cases of personality disturbance may produce some degree of mental impairment. Common examples of such cases include the under-achiever in school who functions below mental potential, but who does not necessarily show mental impairment of the degree that would cause the child to be confused with a case of mental retardation.

Because of a great variety of etiological factors, impairment in mental functioning may be associated with various types of personality difficulties. Fear of failure, low aspiration level in achievement, fear of rejection, fear of group situations, and fear of teachers may be associated with mental impairment. When any of these or other conditions cause the child to function on intelligence tests and in other behavior as if he were a case of true mental retardation, he may be categorized as showing mental impairment.

We should like to highlight one type of psychological disturbance that can contribute to this end result and that frequently goes undetected. That is the type of case in which severe anxiety, especially when present from infancy, may cause the child to *withdraw* from full interaction with, and participation in, the environment. As a result of the anxiety, the personality may become *autistic* or *schizoid* (see chapter 9); that is, it may *avoid* responding to stimulation. Such children may not show any bizarre behavior manifestations; they may be quiet and even compliant; they may not look outwardly disturbed. But their *resulting inhibition in mental functioning* may closely resemble the condition of true mental retardation. The mental inhibition and impairment may, in such cases, actually be the major clinical symptom of the personality disturbance. In these cases, and in all other types of personality disturbances in which impaired mental functioning occurs, improvement in the personality adjustment, together with whatever other corrective measures might be indicated, can be followed by improved total behavioral functioning, including intellectual behavior.

– 3 –

Classification and Labeling:
Issues and Solutions

Science generally has proceeded by attempting to classify the phenomena under study, thus providing some degree of order, and then analyzing under natural or experimental conditions the various classifications of phenomena. In this process, it often is learned that the classification scheme that has been utilized is based on faulty assumptions, and the scheme is then altered or abandoned. The history of the study and treatment of mental retardation has followed this pattern. Many conditions that were formerly called mental retardation or mental deficiency are no longer so characterized. Moreover, it has been learned that there are differing kinds of retardation—differing both in degree of deficit and in significant qualitative aspects of the human organism. Some people even have gone so far as to abandon the adjectival modifier "mental" and have focused, instead, on the repertoire of "retarded" behaviors that are "shaped by events that constitute [its] history" (Bijou, 1966).

The problem of "labeling" has similarly undergone extensive scrutiny. The term "mentally retarded" as well as other terms that have been used to describe different classifications of the retarded often have been found to be inaccurate, derogatory, and creating adverse conditions for education, training, and social adjustment. Some people have advocated the total elimination of labels.

Yet classification and labels are necessary not only to study and treat the phenomena under consideration, but also to provide the support for appropriate programs toward such ends.

This chapter will consider these issues and some of the solutions that have been proposed.

HISTORICAL SYSTEMS OF CLASSIFICATION

Before the advent of intelligence tests and the great contributions of Alfred Binet, classes of mental retardation were not clearly discriminated and persons with obvious limitations in mental capacity were called *idiots.* This term is defined in the Oxford Universal Dictionary (1955) as: "A person so deficient mentally as to be incapable of ordinary reasoning or rational conduct." Quite obviously such a definition leaves much to be desired. It links irrational behavior with mental deficit, and it fails to define the degree of deficiency with any degree of accuracy. Moreover, the term came to be synonymous with high social disapproval and disparagement. For instance, a corollary definition given in the same work was: "A term of reprobation: A blockhead, an utter fool. . . ." Later the term *imbecile* was applied to the whole range of mental retardation. Still later the term *feebleminded* was utilized, and the designation of idiot was reserved for the lowest levels of retardation and the term imbecile was applied to higher levels of retardation. The general term *ament* was later applied to the whole range of mental retardation.

These early approaches to the classification of mental retardation were not only crude but also reflected the popular notions concerning the retarded; namely, that they were indigent, irresponsible, subject to alcoholism and sexual debauchery, and criminally predisposed. Little effort was made to distinguish the effects of mental retardation per se from the effects of frequently miserable conditions that contributed to the social maladaptation and inefficiency of some retarded individuals.

Classification Based on Intelligence Tests

With the introduction of the *Binet Intelligence Scale,* and later with the development of other versions of this and other tests and the concepts of MA and IQ, classification of mental retardation was based on the *measured intelligence test findings.* Utilizing the MA concept proposed by Binet, the American Association for the Study of the Feebleminded distinguished three classes of mental retardation: idiots, imbeciles, and morons. The idiot level consisted of individuals with MAs up to and including two years; the imbecile level was from three to seven years, inclusive; and the moron level was from seven to twelve years, inclusive. These MA limits applied to the expected MA at maturity.

When IQs were employed some years later, the traditional classification was based on this measure. We shall note the approximate IQ limits that were employed since the limits differed with different tests, especially the Terman revision of the Binet (the *Stanford-Binet*) and the *Wechsler Intelligence Tests.*

The lowest category is idiot, applied to individuals obtaining an IQ in the range from 0 to 29. It must be said that both Terman and Wechsler were well aware of the limitations of an IQ score in defining mental retardation and noted that factors other than intelligence might influence the obtained IQ score. Nevertheless, the practice to utilize the IQ score alone in arriving at a diagnosis became widespread, often with disastrous results. We note this point in discussing the category of idiocy because, as we shall see, individuals in this category often have serious biological handicaps that make the validity of the usual intelligence tests questionable.

Children within the idiot category usually are unable to learn to care for themselves in even the most elementary fashion unless they are given special and prolonged training. Even then, some cannot attain competence in such skills. They have to be protected from physical dangers, and they may need close supervision in most activities. Speech functions tend to be grossly retarded and remain at a primitive level. Some never develop speech functions at all. Soiling is quite frequent and becomes a health and custodial problem. At an adult age, most individuals in this category still need close supervision and guidance. If they are able to attain any degree of social usefulness they need not only prolonged and intensive training but also a simplified and protected milieu within which to function.

The next higher category is imbecile. The IQ range is approximately 30 to 49. Such individuals generally are able to learn to dress and engage in many useful personal functions provided they are given appropriate training when they are ready for it. Bladder and bowel functions can be controlled with training in most instances. They learn to speak reasonably well and to communicate fairly effectively. Vocabulary tends to remain rudimentary, however. Higher-grade imbeciles can learn to read simple reading matter, can learn to write some words, and can learn to engage in many useful and productive tasks with appropriate training. In a complex social setting, most will require continued guidance and protection, but can become useful members of society, as recent research has shown, if provided with training and careful guidance.

Ranking above the imbecile is the category of moron. The IQ range is approximately 50 to 69. Individuals in this category are generally able to profit considerably from carefully tailored training and education. They learn to take care of their basic physiological needs, communicate effectively, and are able to learn to read and write—if only at simple levels. Special training can be highly effective with such individuals. Many become quite competent in manual activities and many are able to gain useful employment. Some learn to support themselves. Many marry and live in a community effectively if they are given continued guidance and counseling.

The highest category based on IQ scores is that of the borderline retarded. The IQ range is approximately 70 to 79. Most of these children are not recognized as having retarded mental capacities until they reach school age, and they may make an effective adjustment to their peers prior to this age. When they reach school age they frequently are seen as "slow learners." They especially show difficulty in learning reading and arithmetic. Improved methods of school training often are of considerable value to them, and they may make surprisingly good progress under such conditions. They usually are able to learn social and vocational skills and can make good adjustments.

Within the educational community, two terms have been widely employed in recent years to describe the upper ranges of the mentally retarded— since until very recently the lower ranges were customarily placed in institutions or in private facilities. Individuals with IQs in the range from about 50 to 70 or 75 have been categorized as *educable mentally retarded,* and those in the IQ range of 25 to 50 have been designated as *trainable mentally retarded.* In the 1970s, as a result of legal decisions, children with IQs below 25 sometimes were referred to as "the right to education children." Differing educational programs and differing placements within the school system were provided for "educables" and "trainables" as well as, most recently, for some of the "right to education children."

Classification based on intelligence test results alone contains many hazards and inadequacies, apart from the limitations of any intelligence test in adequately describing the broad range of cognitive functions. As we have noted, individuals with similar IQs and MAs vary considerably not only in their cognitive abilities but also in their physical and social characteristics. Moreover, rates of development for individuals with similar intelligence scores differ considerably. For these and other reasons, improved methods for classification have been attempted and are still being developed.

Lewis's Classification

This is one of the older classificatory systems. Like many others, it suggests a twofold classification based in part on the presence or absence of organic brain damage. Lewis (1933) called one category the *pathological* group. In this category are placed children whose intellectual deficiencies are attributable to some organic brain damage or pathology. Such conditions are considered *abnormal variations* from the normal. He termed the second category the *subcultural* group. Children in that group have no demonstrable brain injuries, and no other physical pathology can be found. Lewis felt that these children are the *extremes* of the normal variations in intelligence that can be expected, assuming that abilities are distributed in the population from very low to very high. He does not consider these children *abnormal* variants like those in the pathological group, but *normal* variants.

Strauss's Classification

An approach to classification based, at least in part, on *etiological* (causative) factors was made by Strauss and Lehtinen (1947). They postulated two major groups of disorders: (1) *exogenous* conditions and (2) *endogenous* conditions. The children in the exogenous group are essentially brain-injured children. Damage to the brain can have occurred before, during, or following birth. However, Strauss and Lehtinen did not include in this category those children who show signs of gross neurological involvement; they limited it to children who have no motor disabilities but whose test performance indicates some brain damage. Sometimes the damage to the brain is such that neurological examination does not elicit any signs of the damage. It is manifested by subtle alterations in the functioning of the child as revealed by psychological tests. The endogenous classification refers to children who have no brain damage but are nonetheless mentally retarded.

Kanner's Classification

Kanner (1949) introduced a classification of mental retardation that may be termed, in effect, a pragmatic grouping. Basing his categories on the behavioral reactions of the child, he proposed three major groups:

1. *Absolute feeblemindedness.* Children in this category would stand out as "different" in any situation. Their deficiency is so great that they *cannot be helped* significantly at home and so need institutionalization.
2. *Relative feeblemindedness.* In this category are placed children whose limitations are related to the society in which they live. They cannot comply with its intellectual demands.
3. *Apparent or pseudofeeblemindedness.* For various reasons, children in this category act *as if* they were feebleminded, but they actually are not feebleminded. They have the potential for adequate performance.

Benda's Classification

Benda (1952) was concerned with classification of children who were regarded as being *intellectually inadequate* (those with IQs ranging from 50 to 70). According to Benda's proposed classification, there are five major categories of such children:

1. *Emotionally disturbed normal children.* These children score low on intelligence tests because of factors outside the intellectual field. Because of their low scores, they are thought to be mentally retarded.
2. *Mentally ill children with low intelligence.* These children are unable to cope with the test situation in a successful manner and score low in spite of their adequate intellectual potentials. Their inability to function adequately is due to a serious emotional disorder, such as childhood schizophrenia or infantile dementia. (See chapter 9.)
3. *Biologically normal children with low intelligence.* These children have no demonstrable biological involvements, but have a low degree of intelligence. They are a normal part of our population.
4. *Children with oligoencephaly.* Children in this classification are considered pathological because of their overall constitutional inadequacy.
5. *Brain-injured children.* These children are considered by Benda to be more or less accidental cases of mental retardation. Brain injury may result from such causes as birth trauma, infectious diseases, and metabolic disorders.

Although Benda constantly refers to the psychological test performance in his classification scheme, he expresses the opinion that an adequate diagnosis also rests on many additional factors.

CLASSIFICATION OF THE AMERICAN ASSOCIATION ON MENTAL DEFICIENCY

In 1959, on the basis of a coalescence of opinion about criteria for classifying mental retardation, the AAMD proposed a classificatory system that has been widely accepted (Heber, 1959). This system actually includes two subsystems: a medical basis of classification and a psychological and adjustmental basis. Over the years, a number of refinements and redefinitions have been made. The most recent form of the system, published in 1973, is the one that we shall present (Grossman, 1973).

The medical classification is mainly of concern to medical specialists, and we shall refer to it only briefly. It involves eight categories* of physical, etiological factors, the last of which overlaps considerably with the psychological and adjustmental set of criteria. The categories follow:

1. Retardation caused by infection
2. Retardation associated with disease or intoxication
3. Retardation associated with trauma or a physical agent
4. Retardation associated with disorders of metabolism
5. Retardation associated with new growth (such as *tuberous sclerosis*)
6. Retardation associated with unknown prenatal conditions
7. Retardation associated with unknown disease but with structural reaction manifest
8. Retardation associated with only functional reaction manifest

Although the system presumes that the physician can directly establish the specific causal agents for mental retardation in categories 1 through 7 at least, in actual practice determining cause is often difficult. Frequently, the physician will have to obtain significant data by reviewing the child's developmental history or by observing his behavior and symptoms. In such instances he will have to make a careful clinical judgment.

The psychological and adjustmental classification involves measurement or evaluation of *intelligence level* and *adaptive behavior*. Mental retardation is considered to be present when there is "significantly subaverage general intellectual functioning existing *concurrently* [our emphasis] with defects in adaptive behavior . . . manifested during the developmental period." In other words, the designation of mental retardation involves the presence of *both* subnormal intelligence and subnormal adaptive behavior. Since these phenomena involve different assessment problems, we shall discuss them separately.

Assessment of intelligence usually involves the administration of one or more intelligence tests (see chapter 11). A psychologist usually administers and interprets the test, and she may use whichever test she believes is most appropriate for the individual being evaluated. When the findings from a test or tests are of uncertain validity, the clinician must assign appropriate weights to the data or make a clinical judgment about them. This proviso acknowledges the difficulty that may arise in obtaining valid test results. The tests that are recommended for most cases are. the *Cattell Infant Intelligence Scale,* the *Stanford-Binet Intelligence Scale,* and the *Wechsler Intelligence Scale for Children.*

When the measure or estimate of IQ score has been obtained, the individual is assigned, *in terms of intellectual functioning,* to one of the levels of retardation indicated in Table 3.1. Each level is defined by the amount to which the IQ score is *below* the average of a given test in terms of standard deviation units. Note that there are only four levels of retardation, ranging from *mild* to *profound.* In the earlier manuals developed by the AAMD there were five levels, but the borderline level now has been eliminated, and the present manual recommends the use of the term *borderline intelligence* instead of the earlier

*The classification scheme of the AAMD is under constant review by one of its committees, and currently is in another stage of revision as this book goes to press.

TABLE 3.1.   AAMD (1973) Levels of Measured Intelligence in Terms of SD Units

Retardation Level	Range in SD Values	Range in IQ Scores Stanford-Binet	Range in IQ Scores Wechsler Test
Mild	−2.01 to −3.00	68 to 52	69 to 55
Moderate	−3.01 to −4.00	51 to 36	54 to 40
Severe	−4.01 to −5.00	35 to 20	39 to 25
Profound	Below −5.00	19 and below	24 and below

term *borderline retardation* for persons whose IQ scores are above the classification of *mild retardation* (between 1 and 2 SD units below the average).

The assessment of adaptive behavior is much more difficult and subjective. According to the Manual, adaptive behavior involves a "composite of many aspects of behavior and a function of a wide range of specific abilities and disabilities." Two instruments that are suggested for assessing adaptive behavior are the *AAMD Adaptive Behavior Scale* and the *Vineland Social Maturity Scale*. The validity of these and other tests of adaptive behavior is far less widely accepted than the validity of intelligence tests, so the clinician also must use other sources of data, including observation of the child's daily behavior, to arrive at an evaluation. The major areas of adaptive behavior specified by the AAMD include the following: independent functioning, physical development, economic activity, communication, number and time use, and social activity. The following examples demonstrate how different combinations of specific behaviors are associated with different levels of retardation.

At three years of age a person would be moderately retarded; at six years, severely retarded; and at nine years, profoundly retarded if the following actions indicated *highest level* of adaptive behavior.

Independence: Tries to feed self with a spoon
Physical: Walks alone steadily
Communication: Uses four to six words; communicates many needs with gestures
Social: Plays with others for short periods

On the other hand, the following behaviors would indicate mild retardation at six years, moderate retardation at nine years, severe retardation at twelve years, and profound retardation at fifteen years, if they were the highest level displayed by the subject:

Independence: Feeds self with a spoon or fork; may spill some
Physical: May climb steps using alternate feet
Communication: Vocabulary of more than 300 words
Social: Engages in group activities and simple group games

Not all workers in the field of mental retardation accept the classification proposal offered by the AAMD. A fundamental type of criticism is offered by Bijou (1963), who objects to the reification of the concept of intelligence. His position is that intelligence is a hypothetical construct and the term *general intelligence* should not be employed at all. He argues that *intelligence* can never be observed directly; it can only be inferred from behavior to which we append the adjective *intelligent*. He would prefer that we seek out observed and functional relationships between a subject's behavior and the events in his life that immediately preceded it. This technique requires study of the continuous interaction of the individual with the environment. Bijou defines the retarded individual as one who "has a limited repertory of behavior evolving from interaction of the individual with his environmental contacts." He believes that such a definition will lead to more accurate prognosis and reduce or eliminate false conceptions of *incurability*. (We shall discuss Bijou's position more fully in later chapters.)

Another type of criticism concerns the inclusion of *adaptation* as part of the concept of mental retardation. Clausen (1971), for example, offers these objections: (1) The concept of adaptive behavior is ill-defined, and there is no adequate scale to measure it; (2) if adaptation is defined in relation to the settings in which it is manifested, measuring it will require a large, unwieldy number of instruments; (3) the classification blurs the distinction between mental retardation and emotional disturbance; and (4) adaptive behavior may be more affected by interaction with sociocultural factors than measured intelligence is. These are important criticisms, but in our opinion they are beside the point. What is crucial is our conception of mental retardation, and that is, in large part, a matter of one's orientation. If we are concerned about the predictive power of a classification scheme, or even about its meaningful relationship to some aspects of behavior, there is enough empirical evidence (much of which is reviewed in this volume) to justify the approach of the AAMD. Moreover, as Leland (1972) explains, the AAMD proposal requires some degree of evaluation of the subject in naturalistic observations; therefore, fewer persons are likely to be inappropriately labeled mentally retarded.

Justifiable as the AAMD classification criteria are, in our opinion, many professionals still tend to base their diagnosis on intelligence test results alone, even when measures of social adaptation or social maturity are available. As an illustration of this tendency, the findings of Adams (1973) may be of interest. For Adams's study, one hundred mentally retarded children between the ages of five and sixteen were chosen randomly from all of the referrals for psychological evaluation to the Illinois State Pediatric Institute. All the children had been given a standardized intelligence test (usually the *Stanford-Binet*) and the *Vineland Social Maturity Scale*. Thus, the workers in this agency had evidence relating to both dimensions of the AAMD classification proposal. The evaluation of mental retardation (or nonmental retardation) that would have been obtained for these cases using the IQ score alone correlated .94 with the IQ measure (almost perfect correlation), but only .71 with the social quotient measure. Put another way, when the IQ measure was partialled out, the category assigned correlated only .18 with social quotient. Thus, these psychologists relied almost exclusively on the IQ measure for their classification of mental retardation.

Apparently, we still have a long way to go before we can be sure that all of the pertinent facts in a case are properly considered.

As we have noted, there are serious problems in estimating and evaluating *both* intelligence and social adaptation. With regard to the former, we agree with Tarjan (1972) who, despite reservations about the adequacy of intelligence tests, states: "... given care and attention to detail, an IQ test remains the best way of making comparative judgments of intellectual ability within a given culture." With regard to social adaptation, continuing efforts to devise improved methods of measuring the phenomena are producing more effective instruments, especially in the younger age ranges (see chapter 11).

Although there are other proposals for classifying mental retardation, we have reviewed sufficient representatives and utilized schemes to offer the reader some perspective on the problem. We shall employ the AAMD classification throughout the remainder of this volume since it has been widely adopted and its values far outweigh its limitations.

PROBLEMS IN CLASSIFICATION

Classification of retarded children is important for several reasons. It is convenient, enabling us to compile data under appropriate headings for future analysis and study. Classification helps us understand how a particular child may be expected to respond, since we know some things about other children in this group or *class*. Classification also may help us clarify problems of etiology (or causation). Further, adequate classification would simplify the process of surveying the extent of the problems of mental retardation in society and would help us make comparative studies of different groups.

There are, however, many problems inherent in devising an adequate system of classification. If, for example, we attempt a classification based on the behavioral reactions of retarded children (like some of the cited systems of classification), we need to take into account the fact that children with the same kinds of behavior or symptoms often have very different underlying problems. In the first place, a symptom may be the result of very different causes or processes. Let us consider, as an example, the behavioral reaction of bed-wetting (enuresis). This may be the result of some neurological disturbance; it may be caused by a severe emotional maladjustment; it may be a reflection of training practices in toilet control; it may be due to a disturbance in gastrointestinal functions; *or it may* be due to conditions associated with mental retardation. In the second place, a given form of behavior may have different implications, depending on the way it is used and the personality of the particular child using it; and the same behavior may have a different significance at different times in the life of the same person. For example, thumb-sucking is viewed quite differently in a three-year-old than in a ten-year-old child. Therefore, to base a system of classification of mental retardation on behavioral reactions alone presents many difficulties.

If, on the other hand, we attempt to base a system of classification on underlying causes or dynamics, our problems are complicated. The same cause may produce different reactions in different people. There is no single cause for an abnormal form of behavior; causation is complex. Several component causes may jointly contribute to the result. Let us look, for example, at birth injuries to children as a possible etiological factor in some forms of mental retardation. All classification schemes based on causation (and also some others by implication) have the *birth-injured* child (or some other designation meaning essentially the same thing) as one category. Although they may appear to be rather easily described, birth injuries are very difficult to classify. Several attempts have been made to relate the type and extent of a brain injury to the type and degree of mental retardation. One way of doing this is to examine the brain of a mentally retarded person following death and then to attempt to relate the injury (if any is found) to the retardation. An example of such a study is that of Malamud (1954). He reviewed autopsy findings and noted, "It is concluded that an etiological classification of mental deficiencies is not warranted in the present state of our knowledge."

It also is unsatisfactory to base a system of classification entirely on the results of intelligence test performance. To do so would be to assume that the results of such a test are entirely valid manifestations of intellectual capacity and that other factors need not be considered. Such an assumption is not warranted. One example of the problems posed by invalid IQ measurement is noted by Matheny (1967). He points out that an obvious penalty for incorrect or unstable IQ classification is the use of suboptimal therapeutic procedures. It also is obvious that too low or too high expectations of a child's abilities will deleteriously bias the reinforcing behavior of parents and teachers alike. It is less obvious, but true, that incorrect IQ classification tends to result in the inadequate evaluation of the effects of therapeutic procedures, because appraisal of a therapeutic program is based on the direction and amount of IQ change. If the IQ classification is not valid, then IQ changes related to therapeutic programs tell us nothing valid about the success of these programs. It is likely that some of the children considered for therapeutic programs vary demonstrably in their range of abilities.

A comprehensive and extensive review of the issues and evidence concerning classification was part of the focus of The Project on Classification of Children. This project was held under the auspices of the National Advisory Committee (and included both professionals and laymen) and an Inter-Agency Force (and included nine federal agencies) (Hobbs, 1975). Seven major conclusions were offered, of which we wish to highlight three now (leaving the others for discussion at later points in this book). One conclusion was that despite its difficulties, "Classification of exceptional children is essential to get services to them." Another was that categories and labels are powerful instruments for social regulation—often used to obscure covert or hurtful purposes. The third conclusion was that "Categories and labels may open up opportunities for children, facilitate passage of legislation, . . . and provide a rational structure for administration of governmental programs." This project also strongly advised and encouraged the use of *profiles,* in which specific assets and liabilities are charted, as a more effective way than general categories of insuring individualized instruction for all exceptional children. Some states have, indeed, adopted sophisticated profile procedures for estimating specific services needed for individual children. It should be noted that many states require classification and labels to establish eligibility of retarded children for services for retarded pupils.

A CONTEMPORARY VIEW OF MENTAL RETARDATION

We now are ready to attempt a conceptualization of the many kinds of phenomena that are included within the general classification of *mental retardation.* We shall continue to use this general classification to embrace the wide variety of behaviors that are subsumed under this caption, recognizing that the classification applies to people with varying characteristics.

1. *The term mental retardation should be applied only to those individuals whose intellectual functioning has been significantly depressed from birth.* Several terms in this criterion require explicit definition. By *intellectual functioning* is meant the general level of cognitive functions that are properly evaluated by a well-standardized general intelligence test. It is recognized that it is difficult to assess accurately the general intellectual level in infancy or even in early childhood. It also is recognized that intelligence tests for the very young attempt to assess somewhat different functions than such tests for older individuals, in part because different functions mature at different stages. Moreover, the test (or tests) must be evaluated in terms of: appropriateness for the individual; reliability of findings; and internal consistency of the results. This evaluation requires clinical skills and allowance for contaminating factors such as: the social-cultural experience of the individual; the motivation and cooperation of the subject in taking the test; and current, and possibly transient and interfering factors, such as state of health, sensory handicaps, and the like.

By *significantly depressed* is meant a deviation from the average that is accurately and statistically significant. The criterion that we will use is a deviation below the average for the age that is two or more standard deviations.

By *from birth* is meant that the individual has never manifested observable, functional behavior in the intellectual realm that can be assigned to a higher category than that of mental retardation. Thus, we are excluding cases in which intellectual functioning was better but in which a transient factor, such as postbirth injury or disease, produced an arrest in mental development.

2. *The term mental retardation should be applied only to individuals whose social adaptation has been significantly inferior from birth.* Again, several terms in this criterion require explicit definition. *Social adaptation* is, at present, difficult to define precisely or to measure accurately. Nevertheless, using the best available instruments for assessment (both naturalistic and standardized), the level of social adaptation refers to behaviors (intra- and interpersonal) that indicate the adequacy of the individual in making appropriate adaptations in social skills for that stage of development. We accept the AAMD's parameters of

social adaptation: independence, physical skills, communication, and social skills.

The criterion for *significantly inferior* is that of two standard deviations below the mean for the individual's age.

3. *We conceive of mental retardation as being the end-product of the dynamic interactions within systems of functioning in the individual and between the individual and the environment.* Thus, we do not posit the primacy of hereditary factors in the determination of mental retardation. Rather, we conceive of mental retardation as that of a *primary developmental defect* in which both genetic and environmental factors, in interaction, play a role. Genetic factors may set upper limits for these developments, but the behavior is determined by the interactions within the subsystems of the individual and the interactions of the total organism with its external environment.

4. *We conceive of mental retardation as a condition of the whole individual.* It is not simply defective intelligence or defective social adaptation, but rather the total adaptation of the individual who is retarded. At the same time, we recognize that some aspects of functioning may be above average or only moderately below average while others may be much more depressed. In other words, there may be considerable intraindividual variability in behavioral functions, although the individual may still be mentally retarded.

5. *Classification of an individual as mentally retarded should not imply that the individual will be unable to make an effective contribution to society or is an inferior citizen.* The ultimate kind of adaptation that a mentally retarded person makes is a function of many factors: our views and evaluation of the person as a person and as a member of the community; the types of training and education that are given; the degree of complexity and stress of the community in which he lives; the kind and quality of support and guidance given.

There is no doubt that the classification of mental retardation has, in the past, been opprobrious. This is not the fault of the label but rather of society's attitude towards that label. Even if we attempted to avoid all verbal labels and identified mentally retarded individuals as "Type A" or "Type B," and so on, the opprobrium would be there unless our attitudes toward handicapped individuals were changed radically. We shall have more to say about these attitudes later in this work.

Let us therefore turn out attention to the issue of labels.

ISSUES INVOLVED IN LABELING

An adequate evaluation of the issue of labeling requires an understanding of the complex social and legal aspects of the problem as well as that of social-cultural factors culminating in certain attitudes toward those who are "labeled." For these reasons, our present discussion should be regarded as introductory. Later (in chapter 17), after we have reviewed some of these issues, we shall consider the issue of labeling in greater depth.

The term *label* was originally used to denote a strip of paper or cloth attached to an object so as to identify it quickly. Through wide use, the term came to identify classes of objects, events, or persons usually for purposes of quick or easy identification. In educational usage, labels were used to designate types or classes of pupils so that they might be placed in special classes or special programs and offered the types of educational experiences that were deemed most suitable for them. However, the general characteristics that were meant to apply to persons with that label often served to obscure the individual differences among them. When this happened, especially with "massed educational programs," the unique characteristics of individuals with a given label often were lost sight of.

Labels can be thought of as a crude attempt at classification. They can serve useful purposes if they are used to identify quickly those in need of special attention or consideration. They can produce ill effects not only if all persons with a label are treated in the same manner—even if that approach might be useful generally—and significant differences are obscured or disregarded, but especially if the label carries some derogatory meaning. Thus, one would not think of such labels as "superior" or "bright" or "gifted" as being derogatory. But such labels as "mentally retarded" and "slow learner" tend to have derogatory implications. Hence, many educators and other types of professionals sought to discard all labels, or to discard at least those that were thought to be negatively loaded in meaning. Others sought to substitute less opprobrious labels so as to diminish or eliminate the supposed ill-effects of those labels.

The issue of labeling became quite heated in the 1960s, when educators were trying to improve the educational training of the mentally retarded and to provide more individualized teaching. As we have noted, some advocated the total abandonment of all labels applying to this group of individuals. Others, like Dunn (1963), suggested other terms as a replacement; Dunn proposed using the term *general learning disability*. Some preferred the general term *handicapped*. Such efforts introduced more confusion than clarity. The term *general learning disability* was confused with the shorter term *learning disability*, which has quite different meanings. The latter term was generally applied to individuals who had special problems in learning despite average or superior intelligence. The term *handicapped* has been applied especially to those with physical disabilities, and was not necessarily applicable to those with mental retardation.

Some labels that have historical interest but that are no longer employed may be noted at this point. We have mentioned the terms *moron, imbecile,* and *idiot* that were previously used to designate the different degrees of severity of mental retardation. By common consent they have been abandoned as carrying highly negative connotations. We have substituted the terms *mild, moderate, severe,* and *profound,* which currently imply severity of retardation on a statistical basis and do not necessarily suggest any implied derogation of the person. We shall see, in later sections of this book, that other terms that have been found repugnant have been abandoned. One striking example is the term *mongolism,* used originally because individuals with this condition showed physical characteristics of some Mongols; the term now employed for individuals with this disease is *Down's Syndrome.*

If we do employ a label such as mental retardation, are we likely to do the individual a disservice? The opponents of any form of labeling have contended that it has two main unfortunate consequences: it tends to create inferior self-percepts; and to reduce efforts to improve the functioning of the retarded. Mac-Millan et al. (1974) reviewed the literature on the subject and concluded that there were six major, presumed negative effects of labeling: (1) rejection by peers; (2) poor level of aspiration; (3) lowered expectations by teachers for achievement of pupils; (4) poor self-concept; (5) poor chance for success in marriage or employment; and, (6) dislike of the label. They also concluded that the research evidence for such conclusions was ambiguous and insufficient except for that of retarded individuals disliking the label. There is confirmatory evidence for number 6 (Guskin et al., 1975).

Nevertheless, Mercer (1975) found that 65 percent of children with "stigmatizing" labels were viewed as normal by social systems other than the school system. In other words, it was primarily within the school system that retarded individuals were seen as retarded—and perhaps the children therefore tended to react as if they were retarded. It seems reasonable to assert that within the school system in which mental retardation is reflected in slow academic learning, such children would be seen as inferior by both themselves and their teachers no matter what the label was. The problem here is that we tend to value people for achievement alone rather than for other qualities. Such a problem reflects the attitude of our society rather than any inherent difficulty due to the label alone. The corrective also seems clear, if not easy to achieve: to change the attitudes of our society about mentally retarded persons, especially the attitudes of school personnel. Fortunately, based on anecdotal evidence in the literature on mental retardation, this seems to be happening, even if frustratingly slowly.

The findings and recommendations of The Project on Classification of Children (Hobbs, 1975) may have lent considerable impetus for changing our practices as well as our attitudes. They recommend that government funds be allocated not on the basis of categories of deviant behavior and development, but rather on the basis of services needed. As we noted previously, while noting some of the values of categories, they have proposed that profile systems be developed and utilized to specify the particular needs of each individual child. They note that the available, simple classificatory systems "obscure both the uniqueness of individual children and the similarities of children assigned to various categories."

We believe that some of the new and innovative methods of improving training, which focus on specific disabilities in behavior and remedial techniques for modifying them, have significant value. But we must caution that, too often, the remedy is applied without respect for etiology or causation. It has become fashionable, in some circles, to disregard problems of etiology entirely when planning the child's educational program or environment. In our view, that is a serious mistake. It is true, as critics of etiological factors have stated, that what really matters is current performance, and that particular attention must be given to specific assets and disabilities. That is an important correction in orientation. But disregard of etiology can have grave consequences, and even when it doesn't, it can limit the educational program's effectiveness.

Rather than talk in generalities, let us look at some specific types of problems. Let us examine the case of a child who seems poorly motivated for school work, is easily distracted, tires easily, and does very poorly in his first-grade subjects. His performance shows a general learning disability in most areas. Diagnostic-prescriptive teaching is attempted by the resource room teacher and creative behavioral conditioning is attempted. But the child's behavior becomes worse: he withdraws from social intercourse more frequently or even goes to sleep. Moreover, his interest in school work decreases, and he fails repeatedly even on carefully designed tasks. Should his prescriptive program be modified? This might appear to be the answer to many who favor looking only at current behavior and performance. However, physical examination might reveal that the child suffers from a mild diabetic condition, that his blood level is poor, and that he needs specific medical attention, far more rest for the time being, and less pressure to learn more rapidly.

Another type of example is furnished by the case of Johnny Distal, cited in chapter 1. Analysis of his cultural-educational history and his marked irregularities in amount and types of schooling was very important and suggested new approaches to his problems.

Let us consider a third example. A 6½-year-old child showed considerable difficulty in the early stages of perceptual discrimination and in reading. He often reversed letters or confused them. He often failed to distinguish between figure and ground. He showed difficulty in recognizing or in reproducing simple spatial forms such as a square and a rectangle. In this case it was learned, through thorough psychoneurological and neurological examination, that he was suffering from a lesion in the anterior frontal and parietal regions of the brain. Neurological treatment plus psychoeducational retraining were necessary.

Finally, let us examine the case of a nine-year-old boy who frequently kicked other boys and who was doing very inferior work in his special class. Target training was attempted, and behavioral modification also was used to get him to learn to stop kicking and to improve his academic performance. In this case, too, the consequences were unsatisfactory. He did, in fact, stop kicking other boys, but he became more sullen and belligerent, in general, using vulgar terms to deprecate other boys and often getting into fist fights. His school work became worse, and he began to engage in truancy. Referral for social and psychological evaluation revealed that he rated at about average on intelligence tests but that he was extremely unhappy and frightened by home conditions. The father was an alcoholic and frequently beat up his wife and children. Divorce was a constant theme in the home. Arguments were intense and frequent. The mother was desperate but thought she had no place to turn for help. In this case, the boy's lack of involvement in school and his fear-resentment of other boys (and of teachers) were directly related to events in his home. Only when these were dealt with—when his problems were understood by the school, when he learned to develop a trusting and understanding relationship with a teacher, and when he was motivated to work toward goals that seemed meaningful and important to him—did his behavior and his achievement improve.

These are not hypothetical cases but are drawn from our experiences. They serve to illustrate the importance of knowing the *etiology of the problem* as well as its *current manifestations.* They point up the usefulness of knowing as much as possible about the developmental nature of the condition under study and as much as possible about general and specific methods of treatment and training.

They also serve to point up an important issue concerning the label we tend to attach to children. Any general label, whether it be *mental retardation, general learning disability, perceptual handicap,* or *behavior maladjustment,* has its limitations. The label applies only to a *general class of persons* and rarely, if ever, fits the individual case completely. Moreover, the label is insufficient by itself! It is insufficient because it does not enable us to give an accurate prognosis in a given case and it does not specify what remedial steps need to be taken. Finally, the label may suggest that little can be done to improve things.

There does not appear to be an easy answer to this problem. Labels (or classifications) have their purpose, even if they often have been misused. Perhaps a more complete, descriptive label that includes known etiological factors and descriptive samples of relevant behavior would be more useful and less misleading. But more than just labeling, no matter how accurate and individualized, is needed. There also is a need to get to know the particular child thoroughly, at all levels of functioning; to understand the meaning of specific limitations or handicaps; to realize the value of specific assets; to know the variety of means and methods for improving or counterbalancing the condition; and, above all, to think critically and deeply about the problem and to judiciously try out (in the light of all the data) tried or innovative methods for retraining. Sometimes, even intuitive understanding of a child can lead to more complete evaluation and effective methods of experimental treatment or reeducation! Above all, it is the attitude of society toward the mentally retarded (the attitudes of the community, the school, and the school personnel) that must be modified. As long as we consider those with inferior abilities as second-class citizens and view them in some derogatory manner, we shall tend to stigmatize them, no matter what label we choose to employ or to abandon.

— 4 —

Some Common Characteristics
of Mentally Retarded Children

We have emphasized that each individual is unique and never entirely replicable in another individual. The classification of retarded individuals of the AAMD into general categories of retardation from the mild to the profound is not meant to indicate that each category is homogeneous with respect to any behavioral variable, whether it be intelligence or social adaptation. Each retarded child who is placed for purposes of designation into one of the categories of mental retardation is different from every other child in that category, sometimes astonishingly so. Such variations occur in every domain; even within the domain of general intelligence, and within the limits of the guidelines for a particular category of intelligence, children with the same IQ score differ remarkably in various aspects of intellectual behavior. Sontag et al. (1977) argue that within the categories of severely and profoundly retarded, in which one might expect some degree of homogeneity, such individuals "vary spectacularly" in individual potential. They reject the "label" of severely/profoundly handicapped since, they state, that "children so labeled [do not] have a homogeneous pattern of neurological impairment." Although the position of Sontag et al. may not be held universally among all experts in the field, it is clear that the degree of heterogeneity within the categories of the mildly and moderately retarded is quite extensive.

Nevertheless, mildly and moderately retarded individuals differ as groups in many important respects from those with superior intellectual assets, and they also differ as groups from those with inferior intellectual assets. Were this not the case, there would be no point in considering general categories of degree of retardation. Therefore, although it is important to recognize the uniqueness of each individual, it also is important to recognize and consider characteristics that tend to differentiate the several categories of retardation. We emphasize this point because the pendulum that has swung so far in the direction of asserting that each retarded person must be described in terms of his or her specific traits and abilities has caused us to lose sight of these general characteristics. We have begun to consider not the child who is retarded, and who therefore presents special problems and needs because of this fact, but a disembodied set of highly specific abilities. The danger is, therefore, that the very critical objective of providing the optimal conditions for education and training will be lost sight of in the exhortation to improve "target behaviors" or specific symptoms. What will have been gained if in the attempt to improve effectiveness of the educational milieu we have neglected the human being whom we are trying to assist: self-regard? motivational requirements? capacity for coping with complex situations? effectiveness with family and with peers? A balanced perspective is required so that we can value each individual for what he is and yet recognize the general characteristics of his limitations and so provide the appropriate climate, environment for learning and growing, and the specific experiences that may be helpful. Admittedly, this is no simple task; but refusal to deal with the realities does not make it any simpler.

In this chapter, we will attempt to summarize the findings concerning common characteristics of the retarded. Because of significant differences between the mildly/moderately and the severely/profoundly retarded, we shall divide our presentation into two general sections. We shall postpone to the next chapter a full discussion of etiology and its implications citing etiology in this chapter only when it is particularly relevant.

CHARACTERISTICS OF MILDLY/ MODERATELY RETARDED

As we have noted, we shall follow the AAMD (1973) classification for designating the levels of intelligence of retarded individuals. Thus, those who are classified, on the basis of IQ score, as mildly retarded have IQs in the range of 55 to 69, and those who are classified as moderately retarded have IQs in the range of 40 to 54 (based on *Wechsler Intelligence Test* results). The lowest level of the moderately retarded therefore is 60 IQ points below the theoretical (and statistical) average. Since progress in learning most cognitive tasks depends heavily on the level of intelligence, we can see that there is a general and severe disparity between those with retarded intelligence and those with average intelligence.

Differences in Intellectual Functioning

Although the intelligence test does not measure all possible cognitive and associated abilities, the IQ score does, if valid, offer us a general view of the individual's potential for learning many academic skills. In order to conceptualize the significance of differences in this regard of the mildly and moderately retarded individuals from those with average general intelligence, let us consider the data presented in Table 4.1.

We have chosen to illustrate the differences in mental maturity at ages

TABLE 4.1.   Comparison of Mental Ages of Average with Mildly and Moderately Retarded Children

Chronological Age (in years)	Average	Mildly Retarded		Moderately Retarded	
		Upper Limit	Lower Limit	Upper Limit	Lower Limit
2	2.0	1.4	1.1	1.1	0.8
6	6.0	4.1	3.3	3.2	2.4
10	10.0	6.9	5.5	5.4	4.0
14	14.0	9.7	7.7	7.6	5.6

2, 6, 10, and 14 years to emphasize the widening differences between these groups of individuals over the years. At age two years, before much cognitive development has occurred in formal areas, the maximum difference in mental age of the mildly and moderately retarded individuals from average individuals is only 1.2 years, and it is only 0.6 years at the least. At this age, many retarded children within these categories will not seem, to the casual observer, to be very different; they may seem, only to be somewhat slower in such aspects of development as age of walking, development of speech, and social communicativeness. By the age of six years, when formal schooling is usually begun (although with newer programs, this may occur much earlier), the differences are quite pronounced. At the lower limit of the moderately retarded classification, the mental age difference is 3.6 years from that of the average child, and it is already 1.9 years for the child at the upper limit of the mildly retarded group. Such differences are strikingly evident in the children's success with academic learning and are frequently responsible for referral to a learning specialist or to a psychologist to determine what the difficulty may be.

The differences in mental maturity between retarded and average children become progressively greater with age, so that by 14 years of age the maximum difference is 8.4 years in mental age. In other words, the child at the lower limit of the moderately retarded group has not yet caught up with the mental age level of the average child of six years. Unless special provisions have been supplied during prior school years, this child has not only failed to learn what the average child has learned but also has experienced continuing and severe frustration, possible humiliation, and almost irreparable damage to self-regard. These figures are intended only to illustrate the enormous differences in general learning capacity between some of the retarded and the nonretarded; they do not tell us how to manage such differences educationally or socially, nor do they tell us of the many similarities in other respects between retarded and nonretarded children.

What these figures suggest is that the learning problems in many areas of academic achievement, particularly in language, reading, and arithmetic are quite different for the retarded; the greater the degree of retardation, the greater are such problems. On the other hand, there are many areas of learning in which the retarded are not so handicapped, and in some, depending on circumstances of their experience, some retarded children are equal to or even superior to nonretarded children. We shall examine and evaluate such differences and similarities in later sections of this book.

Variability in Behavioral Performance

Retarded children are not equally deficient in all areas of behavioral functioning or in physical development. On the contrary, not only is there considerable variability in level within the categories of both mildly and moderately retarded children, but there also is considerable variability within each child. To emphasize this point two relevant studies will be cited. In one by Klausmeier and Check (1959), the performance of inferior, average, and superior children, approximately nine-and-one-half years of age, was evaluated by means of sixteen measures of physical, intellectual, academic, and personality characteristics. The specific functions investigated were height, weight, strength of grip, number of permanent teeth, bone development of hand and wrist, IQ, reading achievement, arithmetic achievement, language achievement, emotional adjustment, achievement in relation to capacity, self-concept, expression of emotion, behavior pattern, and child's estimate of own learning abilities. On nine of these measures (weight, number of permanent teeth, carpal age, emotional adjustment, achievement in relation to capacity, integration of self concept, expression of emotion, behavior pattern, and estimate of own abilities), these retarded children with IQs in the range from 55 to 80, did *not* differ significantly from either average children (IQ from 90 to 110) or superior children (IQs above 120). The low IQ group was lower, however, from both other groups in strength of grip, reading achievement, arithmetic achievement, and language achievement. This study also indicated that *intraindividual variability* in three academic functions (reading, language, and arithmetic) was greater within the average group than in either of the other two groups. In general, there was considerable intraindividual variability for many individuals in all of the groups. Although the level of retardation used in this study extends above the currently used upper limit for mildly retarded individuals, it illustrates the heterogeneity of individuals irrespective of their intellectual classification.

The other study we will cite illustrates the variability of intellectual and social-adaptative behaviors of retarded individuals. Adams et al. (1973) compared fifty blacks with fifty-nine whites of both sexes on an intelligence test and on the *Vineland Test of Social Maturity*. The subjects of the study ranged in age from four to seventeen years. They found that on the basis of IQ alone more blacks than whites were classifiable as mentally retarded. However, there was no significant difference between the two ethnic groups in SQ (Social Quotient). This investigation suggests that: (1) no single measure can serve to characterize an individual adequately; and, (2) even "valid" measures of intelligence can discriminate against certain ethnic groups. We shall have much more to say about the latter point in connection with our review of ethnic factors and intellectual functioning.

Characteristics of Physical Development and Performance

We have indicated that most mildly retarded children and many moderately retarded children are indistinguishable from average children in physical appearance and in physical development and performance. Now we shall examine this proposition in greater detail. Physical appearance of the mildly retarded, especially in the upper ranges, is truly indistinguishable from the physical appearance of children with average intelligence. As we proceed down the intellectual scale, differences in physical appearance become more evident; and when we reach the lower ranges of the moderately retarded group, such differences become more frequent and more obvious. This is particularly true for moderately retarded children whose mental handicap is caused, at least in part, by certain specific clinical conditions (to which we shall refer in the section on the severely and profoundly retarded). Such aspects of physical appearance and gross physical development as height, weight, facial expression, absence of physical stigmata, and gross coordination are essentially indistinguishable between the higher mildly retarded and average children. As the level of intelligence becomes more deviant, so too does physical development, in that such development tends to be a bit slower and less adequate. As a group, the mildly retarded and, to some extent more so for the moderately retarded, such individuals are somewhat inferior in gross aspects of physical development including age of walking, ability in running, ability to climb, and some aspects of fine coordination (Thurstone, 1959b).

We would like to make a special point of the frequent observation that the lower ranges of the mildly retarded and the whole range of the moderately retarded frequently offer evidence of "dull facial expression." Although the observation may be accurate, such "dull expression" may be the result not of mental retardation per se, but of such other factors as: lack of an appropriately stimulating environment, especially among the lower social classes; undernourishment or malnutrition; and inadequate opportunity for social interaction. Each of these factors is quite complex. For the moment it may suffice to indicate that children from lower classes are frequently deprived of both educationally and intellectually stimulating experiences during infancy and early childhood, and at the same time, are offered inadequate diets (Das and Pivato, 1976). There appears to be an interactive and augmenting effect of poor nutrition and inadequate stimulation. In turn, alertness, active attention, and social interaction are diminished. The "dull look" may well be an end result of such circumstances. On the other hand, "aggressive" improvement in nutritional patterns, with accompanying social stimulation, can significantly improve "appearance" and social activity in physical domains (Riccuitto, 1973).

Sensory-Motor Skills and Perception

We have grouped perception with sensory-motor skills because these behaviors in infancy and early childhood are intricately interwoven. Perception refers to *an organized pattern of behaviors in which the individual interprets or of-*

fers meaning to sensations that are present. This may be contrasted with input to the senses in which the individual "feels" light, or warmth, or coldness, or a localized pain (Gibson, 1963). Sensations are primary elements of experience and depend on the development of certain biological structures within the body. People collect information about their body (internal environment) and world (external environment) through the sensations that they are able to experience. The senses usually work in unison, rarely in isolation, and enable individuals to have these primary experiences involving self and the immediate world. The sensations that a mildly or moderately retarded child experiences are equivalent, so far as we know, to those of the nonretarded child, although by virtue of limited experiences, the retarded child may have less or less varied experiences. But sensations lead to perceptions. In turn, sensations depend, in part, on motoric behavior, which, in turn, depends on biological maturation. Thus, to see something requires an active motoric response, not only in moving the head so that the eyes can sight something, but also in "scanning" the object with many small eye movements in order to sense it more completely. The same is true of other sensations, although some of the nonvisual sensations may require less significant motoric behavior. Thus, in some measure, to obtain a sensation requires some activity on the part of the individual, and to make a perception requires the coordination of such sensations and their interpretation into some meaningful pattern.

We have made these preliminary observations so that it can be understood that these behavioral responses are not simply passive responses to stimuli but are an active process in which the maturity of the biological organism and active interaction of the organism with its environment determine the response. It follows that either when the biological organism is deficient or retarded in the development of appropriate structures or when there is limited stimulation (in intensity, variety, and frequency), perceptual development may be retarded.

Except when there is gross impairment of the central nervous system (CNS), (as is the case with many severely and profoundly retarded individuals), sensory and sensory-motoric development may be expected to develop adequately, unless there is severe limitation of sensory experience (Spitz, 1949; Yarrow, 1963). However, retarded individuals tend to be slower in the development of sensory motoric behaviors than are nonretarded individuals. Studies in this area, and particularly studies by followers of Piaget's theory of cognitive development, have shown that sensory motoric development in retarded children is slower in rate, but not different in quality, from that of nonretarded children (Braga and Braga, 1974; Lerch et al., 1974). Thus, from this viewpoint, unless there has been deprivation of stimulation and nurturance, such children may be expected to attain further developmental steps in sensory motoric behaviors. With appropriate experience and training, they usually can achieve adequate sensory motoric abilities, except in the case of those at the lower levels of the moderately retarded (or at lower levels). Nevertheless, intensive training in early developmental skills can improve the rate of development and the integration of various skills. Guides for such training are available (Wabash

Center for the Mentally Retarded, 1977), and special methods for infants and young children with CNS deficiencies can be helpful (Kephart, 1971).

The development of motor abilities, depending in part on sensory development, generally is slower in mentally retarded children than in nonretarded children (Rarick, 1973). The term *motor skills* refers to the child's abilities to use muscular controls in handling or manipulating objects as well as in coordinating physical movements of the body. Fleishman (1964) has proposed that the term *motor abilities* be used to refer to the general trait inferred from consistent patterns of behavior on performance tasks. Despite extensive research efforts, much of it stimulated by the Joseph P. Kennedy, Jr., Foundation, there is no consensus on the major components involved in motoric abilities, nor is there evidence for any *general factors* of motor ability. On the contrary, motor proficiency seems to consist of both group factors and specific skills involving control, speed, power, and timing and coordination. A comprehensive study by Rarick and Dobbins (1972), which included 261 mildly retarded children and 145 nonretarded children of both sexes, found that from about 8 to 11 factors accounted for the motoric behaviors that were assessed, depending in part on the age of the individuals in the subgroups that were studied. Of these factors, four accounted for most of the variance: strength-power-body size, body fat, fine visual-motor coordination, and gross coordination of limb and body movement. Rarick and Dobbins also found that the factor structure of motoric abilities was less well defined in the retarded population than in the nonretarded population. It is interesting in this regard that the retarded group had significantly more body fat than the nonretarded, indicating perhaps that they engaged in fewer physical activities. However, it must be cautioned that this finding may not be indicative of the indigenous nature of retardation per se; here, as in many other areas, studies of the retarded may confound the effects of retardation with socioeconomic status, cultural factors and resulting experiences, nutritional patterns, and the like.

A comprehensive review of pertinent studies in the area of physical development and motor development of retarded persons (Bruininks, 1974) has offered several major conclusions that we feel are indicative of our present state of knowledge in this area. (1) Generally, intelligence level and measures of motor proficiency are more highly correlated among the retarded than among the nonretarded. Although the structure of motor abilities in the retarded is similar to that of the nonretarded, it appears to be less well differentiated, especially among the mildly retarded. (2) As the severity of intellectual deficiency increases, motoric performance becomes increasingly inferior. In general, both gross and fine motoric behavior are poorer among retarded individuals than among nonretarded individuals. (3) The mentally retarded are generally most deficient in the areas of equilibrium, locomotion, complex coordination, and manipulative dexterity. (4) Many factors, other than mental retardation per se, may contribute to the discrepancy in motoric performance between retarded persons and nonretarded persons, such as nutrition, amount of experience, motivation, and the like. (5) Generally, the mentally retarded are closer to their chronological age peers in motor development than in intellectual development.

(6) Programs of training, and especially "diagnostically based programs of training," can produce significant improvements in motor development.

The problems of evaluating the perceptual behavior of mentally retarded children are many and varied. In the first place, perception does not occur in a vacuum; it involves motoric behavior, motivation, attention, and goal-directed behavior. In the second place, perception becomes integrated with many higher-order functions, such as language, conceptualization, and fantasy. Authorities frequently speak of perceptual-motoric behavior in attempting, at least, to differentiate these relatively less complex behaviors involving perception from more complex behaviors involving higher order processes. Many have thought that the development of normal behavior "depends on a normal perceptual environment" (Hebb, 1958). It has been held that the mentally retarded, especially those with severe or profound degrees of retardation, lack the most basic perceptual-motoric skills and that they need persistent and intensive training to remedy these defects (Kephart, 1967, 1971). We shall subsequently review the effects of such training. It also has been held that the retarded are inferior in habits and skills of attention and that defects of attention contribute to poor perceptual and perceptual-motoric skills. It has been found that in young normal children, central and incidental learning are positively correlated, whereas the correlation between the two types of learning is negative among older children. Thus, with young retarded children whose perceptual behaviors may be retarded in some respects, since selective perception and mental age are related (Hallahan et al., 1973), much usual incidental learning that one takes for granted with the nonretarded does not occur. These are some of the issues that must be considered in evaluating the findings of research studies on perception.

The literature dealing with problems of perception is vast. It is beyond the scope of the present volume to organize and summarize all of that material, but we shall present the findings most relevant to the mentally retarded child. The retarded child differs from the normal child in several important perceptual attributes, although he does not differ in others. Some studies indicate that there are no real differences between retarded children and normal children in perceptual reactivity. This was the conclusion, for example, in a study by Belmont, Belmont, and Birch (1969). They studied perceptual organization in various groups of educable mentally retarded children on responses to the Rorschach card stimuli. (See chapter 11 for a discussion of the *Rorschach Test*.) The subjects, ranging from eight to ten years old, were compared with average children of the same age.

It was concluded that the mentally retarded children were, in general, as perceptually reactive as the children of average intelligence. However, retarded children were less able to analyze their percepts adequately, and they tended to force on their percepts inappropriate organizations that did not conform to the reality features of the Rorschach stimulus blots. Further, it was concluded that retarded children were less able to use verbal clues as an aid in organizing their perceptual responses, and those responses were less influenced by factors related to social interactions. The study suggested that the mentally retarded children with organic brain damage differed from those without demonstrable brain damage in their perceptual behavior. Children without brain damage tended to show a significantly greater restriction in the range of content in their responses. This finding suggests that those children might conceivably have had a higher initial level of intelligence.

The retarded child *does,* however, manifest difficulties in *forming* adequate perceptions. This does not mean that there is a deficit in the particular sensory organ (e.g., the eye or the ear) but that the perceptual integration and interpretation of the incoming stimuli are faulty. Deich (1968) explored the reproduction and recognition functions of mentally retarded persons as indices of perceptual impairment. The subjects of her study were twenty-two institutionalized mentally retarded individuals with an average intelligence quotient of 45 and twenty kindergarten children with an average IQ of 111, who were equated with the mentally retarded on the basis of mental age. After they were screened for recognition of color, the subjects were asked to reproduce thirteen red and white designs selected from the *WISC* and *WAIS* block design tests. (See chapter 11 for discussion of these tests.) Immediately afterwards they were given a recognition test composed of a series of thirteen colored photographs, each consisting of one of the original designs and seven alternatives, one of which matched the original. All of the retarded individuals who did not understand the task were eliminated from the sample. Both groups did significantly better on recognition than on reproduction. However, the retarded group scored significantly lower than the kindergarten children on both tasks. The interaction effects for the groups and methods were not significant; therefore, it was concluded that the main effects were independent.

Deich then studied a second group of subjects, seventeen of whom were institutionalized retarded individuals with a mean IQ of 55 and eighteen of whom were third graders of average intelligence. The groups were comparable in mental age. The same procedures were repeated. Again, similar results were found.

Deich then designed an experiment to determine whether chronological age or mental age was responsible for the lower recognition score of the kindergartners. The subjects of this experiment were thirty-one bright kindergartners who were compared with a number of children from the first experiment. Their average mental age was higher than that of the total original group. The procedures were repeated again. The comparison of the bright and average kindergartners showed the same level of performance in both groups on both reproduction and recognition tasks, suggesting that chronological age was a primary factor in the increasing ability of normal subjects to respond correctly. Deich concluded that the retarded individuals were perceptually impaired and that they did much more poorly than normal people on tasks requiring reproduction or recognition.

Guyette et al. (1964) investigated aspects of spatial perception in mentally retarded individuals. They studied thirty mentally retarded males between the ages of thirteen and twenty-one years, testing them on their perception of the verticality of a luminous rod in a dark room under variation of body position. They concluded that the developmental change in the effect of body tilt on perception of verticality that occurs during the course of normal growth is retarded in mentally retarded subjects. Their results shed light on some aspects of cognitive organization in mental retardation—that is, the relationships between the processes underlying space perception and other cognitive operations. They raised the question whether there is retardation in the emergence of developmental changes that occur in more normal subjects. They also suggested the possibility that some behaviors become manifest that are unique or are different from those that are observable in the ontogenesis of normal people. Significant changes were observed in the effect of body tilt with increase in age. Guyette et al. concluded that their findings were consistent with the orthogenetic principle that states that development proceeds from a state of lack of differentiation (which in this case was seen as a lack of differentiation between self and the object) to a state of increased differentiation. The principle implies that in the early stages of development a lack of differentiation of self and object manifests itself in two ways. One such manifestation is *egocentricity,* in which proximal stimuli are interpreted in terms of one's own body position. A second is *stimulus boundness,* in which the organism changes readily in keeping with the changes in the stimulus.

These problems in perception create many problems for retarded children as well as for their parents. Difficulties in perceptual behavior may be intimately related to many aspects of everyday behavior and may, consequently, produce significant problems in adjustment and independence. For example, retarded children, like all others, frequently ask, "When will you let me drive the car?" For parents of children with moderate degrees of retardation, this question, like many others that involve the adequacy of their children's perceptual-motoric behavior, requires a definite answer. Fortunately, there has been some research on this type of issue that can be helpful.

Egan (1967) has made a study of the competency of educable mentally retarded children in activities involved in driving a car. His subjects included a group of eighteen educable mentally retarded students and a randomly selected group of eighteen regular-class students. Each group had six girls and twelve boys, ranging in age from sixteen to nineteen years. The IQ ranges of the groups varied considerably. The IQs of the educable mentally retarded group ranged from 47 to 75, and none of the children in the control group had an IQ significantly below average.

Some highly significant differences were found between the groups. There was a marked deficiency in the mentally retarded child's ability to gauge the distance between automobiles. Egan felt that this was a serious problem, citing one case in which death was directly attributable to this lack of judgment of distance. There were no differences on visual acuity and on other visual tests. However, on complex reaction and steadiness tests, the educable mentally retarded child scored considerably below the regular students. In a comparison of the actual driving records of both groups of subjects, it was found that the retarded children were unable to make quick and accurate appraisals of approaching obstacles. They also showed marked difficulties in making correct adjustments in driving. Egan believed that the educable mentally retarded child tended to concentrate on the road ahead, and this resulted in failure to assess the speed of the car by checking the speedometer. This failure, in turn, resulted in difficulty in controlling speed.

Egan found that the educable mentally retarded children had, on the average, two accidents compared to one accident in the randomly selected group. He thus demonstrated that in their actual driving records, the mentally retarded children showed a relative inability to react quickly in tight situations, and that on performance on both physical tests and written examinations, they operated at a marginal level.

As we noted earlier, a number of studies have attempted to evaluate the effects of various training procedures in improving perceptual-motoric performance and increasing learning. Studies conducted with mildly retarded children on the effects of training procedures recommended by Kephart and his coworkers have yielded conflicting results. Thus, Fisher (1971) studied the effects of training procedures with three groups: a perceptual-motor training group over a period of four months; a control group; and another control group (to control for the so-called "Hawthorne effects"—effect of other nonexperimental factors, such as increased attention). These nine-and-one-half-year-old children were judged to be deficient on the basis of findings on the *Purdue Perceptual-Motor Survey*. Although some increases in perceptual-motoric skills were found in favor of the experimental group, no significant differences were found in intelligence (as measured), achievement, or on the *Purdue Perceptual-Motor Survey*. In an earlier study with mildly retarded children (about 10–11 years of age), Haring and Stables (1966) did find that perceptual-motor training with the experimental group produced significant gains in perceptual-motoric skills in comparison with a control group. The group receiving training maintained their superiority over the control group when reexamined about four months later. We might say, in passing, that studies with severely retarded children generally indicate that, at least insofar as perceptual-motor behavior is concerned, specific training tends to produce significant improvement in such skills. Maloney et al. (1970) and Morrison and Pothier (1972) did find such effects of training procedures with severely retarded institutionalized males. However, little is known concerning the long-term effects of such training or of the consequences in terms of intellectual functioning or achievement. There is suggestive evidence, however, that with both moderately and more severely retarded children, at least, improvement in deficiencies in the perceptual-motoric area may have important effects in adaptive and intellectual functioning (Hutt, 1977a; Gallager, 1960).

Attention Span and Memory

A great deal of retarded children's difficulty with school work, and perhaps even in adjustment, may be due to poor habits and skills in attending and to poor memory, especially short-term memory. As an example of the importance of these processes Ellis (1963) has proposed that much of the poor performance and behavioral limitations of the retarded can be traced to poor short-term memory. Hence, it will prove useful to examine these processes.

Studies of attention have had a long history. It shall not be our purpose to examine this history in detail, but some landmarks may be of value in understanding our present conceptions. Until the advent of experimental studies of attention following World War II, two views of the nature of attention predominated. Titchener and his followers held that attention was synonymous with conscious clarity and was thus a characteristic of sensory experience. This was the *structuralist* viewpoint. In contrast was the position of William James (1890), which defined attention as a *selective act;* i.e., the individual never experienced most of the multitude of stimuli that impinged on the senses. This *functional* viewpoint stressed that only what the individual is interested in and selectively attends to registers. We have only recently begun to appreciate the significance of James' theory as it relates to attention in the behavior of retarded children.

As new advances were made in the field of neurology and psycho-neurology, some clarifications of the process of attending were made. It became clear that since the brain (in particular the cerebrum) was always active, attention to a new stimulus required *active intervention* by the subject in order to become aware of the new stimulus. Thus, for example, a highly distractible child (and many retarded children, especially those with brain damage, are highly distractible) might not be aware of the introduction of a new stimulus and thus could not learn much about it. Also, the discovery of the reticular activating system (Lindsey, 1951) and Hebb's theory of the organization of behavior (Hebb, 1949, 1958), which held that through the activating properties of the reticular system that relayed information back and forth in the cortical, subcortical, and midbrain areas, and through the gradual establishment of learned "cell assemblies" and "neurological phase sequences," growth in behavioral characteristics (learning) took place. Hebb held that the learning of phase sequences through repeated excitation of patterns of "cell assemblies" depended on appropriate stimulation; stimulation must be novel but not too dissimilar from previous experience. Excessive familiarity leads to loss of interest and thus to nonsustained phase sequences—too little arousal of interest and attention. On the other hand, when the situation is too unfamiliar, the development of phase sequences is not maintained and interest wanes. (We shall see later how the concepts of anxiety and of Piaget's sensori-motor phases offer different or additional explanations of the same phenomena.) The most recent work in the field of attention has come from the applied research of psychologists interested in human engineering. This work has demonstrated that the person is quite limited in the capacity to process information, and that the most effective learning occurs when selective attention is properly guided and supported.

Turning now to the findings on attention, it is generally accepted that the mildly and moderately retarded child has a relatively inferior attention span than the nonretarded child. In general, capacity for both selective attention and attention span are a function of mental maturity. Thus, for example, Hallahan et al. (1973) were able to show that there were no significant differences, even with brain-injured children, between impaired and normal children of the same mental age. Martin and Powers (1967) also showed that the attention span of the retarded child was inferior, although they believed that it could be improved by training.

Short-term memory is closely related to ability to attend. Hermelin and O'Connor (1964) investigated the short-term memory of normal and subnormal children. Twelve normal children and twelve subnormal children were matched for mental age and then compared on a measure of immediate memory. A faster *decay rate* was found in the subnormal than in the normal group. It was found that the input of material in addition to the material to be remembered produced interference and immediate memory decay. Interpolated unfamiliar words proved more effective as interference than familiar ones for normal children, but the reverse was found to be true for the subnormal subjects. Immediate memory in normal children was better than that of subnormals of similar mental age, and the older children did better than the younger ones. It was concluded that a stimulus trace has less duration in subnormal children than in normal children. The minimum delay that was obtained from the subnormal children was about 1 second, whereas normal children responded after about .5 second. Hermelin and O'Connor felt that this finding indicated that fading of the stimulus trace in subnormal children may have begun before the first repetition of the material could take place. They concluded that short-term memory functions differ significantly from long-term memory functions in retarded children.

Hermelin and O'Connor also studied longer-term memory in the retarded. They concluded that the degree of complexity and structure in the stimulus displayed determines the *rate* of learning, but not the *amount* of retention. Further, they pointed out that long-term memory of well-learned material is relatively good even in children ranking at the lower levels of the moderately retarded.

Berkson et al. (1961) reported on short-term memory in retarded children. They studied stimulus trace effects, using electrophysiological measures, and found that the effects of a brief stimulus lasted for a longer period in normals than in subnormals. They concluded that this finding may be related to retention deficits of subnormal children. Baumeister and Ellis (1963), in a related study, postulated that because of impaired neurophysiological reverberation circuits, a stimulus has less intensity and duration in subnormals than in normals.

In these and other studies, the differences between retarded and nonretarded persons are compounded by differences in mental age. In an attempt to control for this factor, Ray and Shottick (1976) compared educable mentally retarded (EMR), trainable mentally retarded (TMR), and normal children of the same mental age. They tested memory span, short-term memory, and long-term memory (after 48 hours). They found that: (1) there were no significant differences among the groups in memory span; (2) the educable mentally retarded were superior to both of the other groups in short-term memory; and, (3) the normals were superior to the EMRs and the EMRs were superior to the TMRs in long-term memory. The last finding might be explained, they believe, in terms of age differences and differential familiarity with the "objects" of the study. One wonders why EMR children were superior to both of the other groups in short-term memory, and here again experiential factors may be responsible.

Although most studies have indicated that attention span and both short-term and long-term memory are inferior in the retarded as compared with nonretarded of comparable chronological age — and this is true for a wide variety of objects and situations — these differences may be due in large part to differences in mental maturity. However, other factors that may contribute to the differences are: interest and motivation, amount of experience with the material, relevance of the material in the daily lives of the subjects of the studies, and attitudes and values toward these functions by school and by home. Perhaps one of the most important implications from all of the studies is that both the content of what is taught and the appropriate "pacing" of what is taught (appropriate to the mental maturity and experiential development) are critical.

Speech and Communication

Speech and communication are so intricately related that we shall treat these topics together. Van Riper (1972) has defined speech disorders as speech that "deviates so far from the speech of other people that it calls attention to itself, interferes with communication, or causes its possessor to be maladjusted." Many other authorities would not include the last phrase as an essential criterion of speech defects, but it is true, nevertheless, that many persons with speech disorders also are disturbed in other aspects of their behavior. This may be particularly more likely in cases with stuttering defects, but maladjustment sometimes accompanies other types of speech problems, such as those involving articulation, voice disorders, delayed speech, cleft lip and palate, and speech disorders associated with impaired hearing. Moreover, speech and language development are related to mental age (Carroll, 1964) and so it is not surprising that mentally retarded individuals show a greater incidence of speech problems than normal individuals of comparable chronological age. Of course, factors other than mental retardation per se contribute to speech and communication difficulties among the retarded. Since many cultural-familial retarded come from homes with poor socioeconomic status and with poor language background (especially with bilingual background), their speech problems are compounded. An additional factor is that many severely and profoundly retarded persons suffer from brain damage, which often interferes with effective speech patterns.

It should not be thought that mental retardation, except when complicated by disorders of the central nervous system, is the cause of speech defects. Travis (1931) long ago stated that both may result from a common defect in the development of the central nervous system. Bereiter and Englemann (1966) have shown that factors other than maldevelopment of the central nervous system account for delayed speech and language. They found that children from homes with deprived culture were retarded by about one year in vocabulary, grammar, and length of sentence when they reached the preschool level. Yet it is clear that for most retarded children specific remedial training in speech and communication can be about as effective as it is with normal children (Rigrodsky and Steer, 1961; Smith, 1962). Hence it is highly unfortunate that insufficient personnel and speech programs are available to such individuals. The improvements in adjustment and in overall functioning that such training can offer can be highly significant including improved self-percept and improved acceptance by peers. Schiefelbusch (1963), in a report to the President's Panel on Mental Retardation in 1962 and in an analysis of the development of communication skills of the retarded, proposed that considerable increases in training programs were warranted. Since most children attain good communication skills by about six years of age, one would expect that if the retarded were given speech and language training during their preschool years and later, most of them could acquire adequate skills in these areas.

The incidence of speech disorders in the retarded has been subject to extensive studies. Schlanger (1953) found that among mildly and moderately retarded children, voice defects (in 62 percent of the cases) and articulatory defects (in 57 percent of the cases) were the most common. Stuttering was present in 20 percent of the cases. Tarjan et al. (1961) found that among institutionalized individuals, from 80 to 100 percent, regardless of IQ, had speech problems. Voice disorders are particularly common among the severely and profoundly retarded, and are common (described as husky and monotonous) among children with Down's syndrome (West et al., 1957). Stuttering has been found to occur much more frequently among retarded than among normal persons (Schlanger, 1953; Goertzen, 1957).

Language development (sentence length, vocabulary, and appropriate syntax) is delayed in the retarded. However, it is noteworthy that one study (Wood, 1960) with a sample of 1,200 children who showed such delay found only 20 percent of the retarded with delayed language development. Wood pointed out that some children may erroneously be diagnosed as mentally retarded because of this language handicap. In general, there is a positive relationship between the developmental rate of language development and of intellectual development; but this is not the case with institutionalized children. Blanchard (1964), for example, found that retarded persons in institutions seldom progress beyond about four years of age in speech and communication. Some of this may be due to neurological defects among such cases, but we suspect that much may result from very inadequate stimulation and social interaction among such individuals in such settings.

Social Behavior and Social Adaptation

An individual's social behavior and methods of social adaptation are very important not only for personal adjustment but for success in many types of interpersonal and vocational situations. Although considerable research has been conducted on the social characteristics of the mildly and moderately retarded child, little is known that can be entirely attributable to the level of intelligence per se. As we shall see, mentally retarded children in this range are purported to display many unfavorable social attributes, as a class, but the findings are confounded by many factors other than the degree of retardation. The socioeconomic background, the opportunities for socialization, the nature of the school placement and school experience, and the attitudes of others toward the retarded (peers, teachers, and other adults), as well as other factors contribute their share to the retarded child's social behavior and to self-percept. At the lower levels of retardation (severe and profound), severe limitations in intellectual capacity as well as incapacitating physiological defects significantly limit social acuity and judgment. At all levels, institutionalization may have profound, negative effects on social behavior.

Only in recent years has systematic research been done on the question of the meaning of social adaptation. Nihira and coworkers (1969, 1970) attempted to determine the number of factors or components that comprise social adaptation. Based on a checklist of observable behaviors, Nihira found that, in children and adults, three components could be described: (1) personal independence; (2) social maladaptation; and, (3) personal maladaptation. The findings from the two studies clearly revealed how different were the patterns of adaptation of the retarded from the nonretarded; retarded individuals were clearly inferior in social adaptation, as a group. The findings also indicate that within the retarded group there are wide differences in social adaptation.

To illustrate another side of the complexity of factors contributing to degree of social maladaptation, quite apart from the nature of prior social experiences, let us look at the findings of a study by Jacobs and Pierce (1968). They were interested in determining the degree to which characteristics associated with brain damage were responsible for rejection by peers. Their subjects were 155 moderately and mildly retarded children ranging in age from six years eleven months to nineteen years nine months. They dichotomized the subjects into two groups based on the number of medical and behavioral observations. Group A, consisting of sixty-six Ss (thirty-eight males and twenty-eight females), had four or more characteristics commonly associated with brain damage; Group B, consisting of eighty-nine Ss (forty-two males and forty-seven females), had three or less of these characteristics. The characteristics were specific learning disability, hyperkinesis, impulsivity, emotional lability, short attention span, perseveration, "soft" neurological signs, WISC indicators, abnormal EEGs, and seizures. The groups were equivalent in IQ and chronological age.

Each subject was asked two questions: (1) Which of the boys and girls in the class would you most like to work with on some special project? and (2) Which of the boys and girls in the class would you most like to play with outside of school? It was found that the children who displayed four or more of the characteristics commonly associated with brain damage were rejected significantly more often, and accepted significantly less often, than those with three or less of these characteristics. Jacobs and Pierce thus concluded that characteristics commonly associated with brain damage, and not mental retardation per se, were associated with rejection and nonacceptance by peers. They also found that the greater the number of brain damage characteristics that were present, the more frequent was the rejection rate. The specific characteristics that were most likely to lead to rejection were: short attention span, hyperkinesis, emotional lability, and impulsivity.

In considering the social adaptation of mildly retarded children, we must rely largely on studies conducted with children who were segregated into special education classes for the retarded. Later, we shall review in detail studies attempting to assess the relative effects, across many dimensions, of special class placement versus regular class placement, or mainstreaming. At this point, we wish to cite some findings based on our current knowledge.

Epstein et al. (1975) analyzed the implications of special-class placement in terms of impulsivity in the behavior of such children. It has generally been found that such children show a considerably higher incidence of impulsivity in cognitive behavior than other children. A proposed remedy is to utilize special methods of teaching, such as highly explicit instructions and modeling, in order to help reduce such impulsivity. Many studies comparing the social behavior of retarded children in special classes with the behavior of such children *after* they have been integrated into regular classes or *with* children of comparable intelligence in regular classes have found that integration facilitates many aspects of social adaptation. Thus, Gampel et al. (1974) found that mildly retarded children, *after* integration into regular classes, behaved more like the nonretarded children with whom they were now associating than the retarded children they had associated with previously. Bruininks et al. (1974) also found that retarded pupils are rated higher on sociometric measures after they have been integrated into regular classes.

Studies such as these. support the value of mainstreaming retarded children in terms of social adaptation and better peer acceptance. But, as we have indicated, many factors other than regular class versus special class placement affect social behavior and social acceptance which we will try to elicit in our later discussion of the values and limitations of mainstreaming. As an example of how other factors may influence the results, we can cite an interesting study by Gottlieb (1974) in which Norwegian retarded children, who have much more opportunity to interact socially than American children placed in special classes, were found to have less favorable attitudes toward retarded children than do American children. The study was based on an analysis of 285 Norwegian children and 231 American children, in the age range of ten to fourteen years. The reasons for such cultural differences are difficult to define, but attitudes of the culture toward the retarded probably play an important role.

The attitudes of the culture toward the retarded and the roles the culture assigns to the retarded, as we have indicated, probably are significant in the social adaptation of the retarded. For example, Willey et al. (1973), in analyzing the stereotypes for normal, educable mentally retarded, and orthopedically handicapped children, offered two sets of findings. One was that mentally retarded children were played with less often than were nonretarded children by children from other groups. The other was that in experimentally arranged situations to test for sociometric choices, mentally retarded children were chosen less often in games in these situations. In general, normal children preferred social interaction with orthopedically handicapped children than with retarded children. This appears to be clear evidence that, insofar as these findings are generalizable, culturally derived attitudes contribute to our stereotypes. Consider, for example, what the findings might have been a decade or so ago, when the attitudes toward the orthopedically handicapped were less favorable than they currently are. Gottlieb and Davis (1971) also found that mentally retarded children were rejected more often in experimentally devised situations. In some special class situations, in which perhaps the social milieu encourages social interaction with normals, such children may be given more sensitive understanding and consideration than retarded children who are not enrolled in special classes (Peterson, 1974).

When surveys are conducted to evaluate the nature of the social adaptation of the retarded, it is generally found that they show less adequate skills in coping with social situations (Lawrence and Winschel, 1973), are therefore more easily frustrated, show more evidence of internal conflict (Lawrence and Winschel, 1973), and have relatively low self-concepts (Tymchuk, 1973). On the other hand, there is at least reasonable doubt that such findings can be attributed to an intrinsic relation to mental retardation. In fact, Affleck (1976) has shown that some role-taking skills are *not* correlated with either MA or IQ, at least within certain ranges of intelligence. The role played by the members of the family also is critical with respect to the social adaptation of the retarded (Wolfensberger, 1967). It also is very important that adequate social stimulation be provided (neither too much protection nor too little stimulation) from infancy on. Not only may social behavior thus be properly encouraged, but cognitive skills also may be developed that would otherwise be delayed or absent. Montenegro, Lira, and Rodriguez (1977) are conducting a long-term study in Chile in which the effects of stimulation programs, beginning as soon after birth as feasible, are being evaluated. In this program, guidelines are provided with respect to what may normally be expected at each month of development, and stimulation is provided by a psychiatrist, psychologists, nurses, nurse's aides, and the mothers in order to encourage development in coordination, other aspects of motor development, language behavior, and social behavior. The program is based, in part, on methods derived from Piaget's conception of intellectual development. Many children are involved in this program: 124 in three experimental groups, and 343 in two control groups. No children in the experimental group were excluded because of conditions of prematurity, disease during pregnancy, or disease during delivery, and some children in the experimental group were from the low socioeconomic group. Results with the experimental groups, based on developmental findings up to 21 months of age, seem to indicate that this intensive and carefully monitored stimulation program produces significant gains for these children in comparison with children receiving no special stimulation. Further, it has been found that with such experimental stimulation, these children do not develop significantly differently from middle high socioeconomic children. Good stimulation programs can, in fact, considerably increase the social development of retarded children, in many instances. It is not clear, as yet, how persistent these improvements are and how they may affect other areas of behavioral development. What is clear is that many retarded children can be greatly helped in their social behavior. It also is clear that therapeutic programs can be used successfully, in the classroom as well as in the home, to reduce or eliminate many kinds of undesirable social behaviors. We shall examine such therapeutic procedures in later chapters of this book.

Academic Performance

Most of the traditional academic skills depend on the level of mental maturation, some much more than others. In general, it has been learned that such academic areas as reading and arithmetical reasoning are highly dependent on the level of intelligence. On the other hand, some academic skills are far less dependent on level of intelligence. In all academic subjects, however, many other factors can contribute to the level of performance, and in chapter 15 we shall indicate in some detail what these factors are and how significant they may be. At this point it will be well to emphasize that the prior experience of the pupil, interests and motivations, and especially methods of teaching, can significantly influence both the rate of learning and the level of accomplishment.

We shall attempt to summarize some of the most important findings concerning the learning of academic subjects in a few propositions.

1. *As many educators have demonstrated, and as Piaget has emphasized repeatedly, the child's readiness for specific kinds of learning will markedly influence the rate and level of accomplishment.* Many retarded pupils come from backgrounds in which there has been highly limited experience in certain areas such as language, varied sensory-motor activities, intellectual and cognitive stimulation, and the like. Moreover, they often have lagged behind in progressing through the stages of intellectual experience—in part because of these other deprivations—so that when they enter preschool or elementary school they are both unprepared and unmotivated for the "standard" academic experiences. This may help to explain why Woodcock and Dunn's comprehensive study (1967) found no significant differences in effectiveness of six different approaches to teaching reading to educable mentally retarded children. On the other hand, when appropriate and relevant experiences were provided first or as part of the learning experience, significant gains could be achieved, as other, more recent studies have shown. For example, a study by Anderson and Coleman (1977) with children showing a retardation in language development of at least two years (some children were retarded in all developmental areas) attempted to improve expressive language by first providing experiences with language comprehension. Using a receptive/cognitive approach and providing various strategies involving motor responses, bodily means of expressing recognition of language concepts, visual problems presented through drawings and pictures, and the like, and *not requiring* any verbal expressions (although these were reinforced when they occurred spontaneously), they found that these children could be taught language concepts in short periods of time. Moreover, the gains seemed to be maintained over a period of time during which follow-up occurred. The investigators report that motor activities and cognitive readiness appeared to be highly important in teaching language expressiveness for these children. As another example, Brown and coworkers (1971, 1974) have demonstrated that by

using behavioral task-analysis (see chapter 11), trainable retarded pupils could be taught skills in functional reading and in arithmetic with considerable success. In task-analysis, the specific skills that are lacking and the specific kinds of readiness are assessed so that individually tailored learning experiences may be provided.

2. *Generally, formal academic work should be introduced at a later chronological age for retarded pupils than is usual for nonretarded pupils.* The time before the introduction of formal academic instruction need not be wasted. On the contrary, there can be a rich harvest from varied and interesting activities dealing with the child's immediate needs (perceptual, motoric, emotional, and cultural) while cognitive development is stimulated and reaches the level needed for more formal academic learning.

3. *The content of academic learning should be closely geared to the child's immediate needs as well as prior experiences.* The immediate needs of the retarded child often have been in conflict with the needs of the teacher/ educator. Not only has learning many academic skills been seen as the first priority by the school system (often reinforced by the wishes of the parents), but all else also has been considered as wasteful or irrelevant. In recent years this orientation has been considerably altered. Nevertheless, the child's immediate needs often have been disregarded in order to "maintain standards" or to prove "accountability." Immediate needs may require learning to understand and communicate about daily experiences the child encounters both at home and in the community, as well as in school. They may involve learning to cope successfully with the physical environment. They may involve the enjoyment and enrichment of sensory experiences. And, we believe, they should, above all, be designed to enhance the child's sense of worth and understanding. Too often, we find, the child's skills or deficiencies, and only these, are assessed, and these other dimensions of assessment are neglected. But, as we shall see, good assessment requires acknowledgment and evaluation of the child's interests, needs, and fears as well as of areas of competence and deficiency.

CHARACTERISTICS OF THE SEVERELY/ PROFOUNDLY RETARDED

The children in these categories are retarded in the intellectual and social adaptive domains, and they also typically have some physiological/ physical limitations due to a variety of prenatal and genetic conditions. Some of the most severely handicapped show gross physical abnormalities; many presumably or clearly have some brain pathology. We shall discuss the most common clinical types of severely/profoundly retarded, indicating what we have learned about etiology and the effects of early intervention/rehabilitative programs. Our discussion of the latter two topics in this chapter will be limited to immediately relevant findings; we shall discuss problems of etiology more systematically in the next chapter and programs for intervention and training in later chapters.

Down's Syndrome

Down's syndrome was discovered in 1844, but it was not until 1959 that Lejeune demonstrated that it was due to the presence of an extra chromosome. Nearly a century earlier, in 1866, Langdon Down described the condition as a clinical entity. It was previously called mongolism due to the almond-shaped, slanting eyes that are a prominent feature of many children with the condition. That name has been abandoned because it often carried with it derogatory implications. At one time, the condition was thought to be caused by a genetic predisposition (inherited), but attempts to confirm that theory have been unsuccessful and have been discredited.

The physical symptoms of Down's syndrome are clearly recognizable. In addition to the characteristic features of the eyes, the most common physical symptoms are a fold in the skin of the eyes (*epicanthic* fold); a deep transverse fissure of the tongue; an absence of definite patterns in the lines of the palms of the hands; close-set, deep eyes that often are strabismic (cross-eyed); flattening of the bridge of the nose; a flaccidity (*hypotonicity*) of the muscles (they appear to have little tonicity or tone); thick, stubby hands; very small fingers, often with only one crease; short stature; subnormal weight; lax bone joints (many Down's children are double-jointed); and, occasionally, peculiarly shaped deformities of the ears. Occasionally there are other physical symptoms.

Down's syndrome child. (Courtesy of Birth Defects Clinic, University of Michigan.)

The intellectual development of the individual with Down's syndrome is quite variable, although at one time it was thought that all such children were severely retarded (in the "imbecile" range). Not only do such children vary in general intelligence from severely/profoundly retarded through the normal range, but the course of their intellectual development can be significantly influenced by the nature of the early training and affectional experience they are offered, and by the persistence with which such training is carried out over time. For example, Hayden and Haring (1977) have shown that between birth and twelve months of age, Down's children perform 62 percent of tasks performed by normal peers, but that after two years of age show "a pattern of continuously decreasing levels of relative performance." However, Down's children who attended the Model Preschool Center for Handicapped Children "appear to be leveling off at approximately 95 percent of normal development." Moreover, there was evidence that the earlier the special program was initiated, the greater was its value. This study involved 94 children over a two-year span and employed a variety of tests (*Peabody Picture Vocabulary Test* or the *Stanford-Binet Scale;* criterion-referenced testing; and information from parents that was coded and calibrated); hence, its results offer strong evidence of the value of special training. A control group of children who did not attend the Model Program leveled off, during the same period, at 61 percent of normal development. Previous studies have shown that Down's children living at home have IQs in the range of 50 to 70, whereas those in institutions have IQs in the range of 20 to 30 (Wunsch, 1957).

There is a great deal of anecdotal evidence that under special conditions or in special circumstances such children can display remarkable intellectual abilities. In one reported case, Nigel, a Down's child, wrote his own autobiography, which was published by his father (Hunt, 1967). Nigel wrote beautifully and sensitively, and he had an intense love of music. Of course, he was also limited in other respects. He was unable to master certain arithmetic concepts and his thinking was in concrete terms.

The senior author has had occasion to follow the progress of a Down's syndrome individual over a thirty-year period. At five years of age, when he was first seen in consultation, his mother was concerned primarily about plans for his schooling or possible institutionalization. She had been advised by her pediatrician that the child might never learn to talk and would need intensive institutional care (this occurred when the child was a little over one year of age.) The mother had insisted that the child remain at home, and she, the father, and an older brother had begun an intensive program of training for the child, commencing at about two years of age. When I saw the child, he tested at an IQ of 89 (with some variability on subtests of the *Stanford-Binet*), could communicate very effectively, and had an estimated perceptual-motoric development of slightly less than five years. We advised delaying formal schooling (there was no appropriate program available) for at least another year or two, meanwhile offering to provide supervision of training at home by the parents. This child entered regular classes at seven years of age (in the first grade) and progressed through elementary and secondary schools at a normal rate. At the last formal testing (with the *Wechsler Intelligence Scale*) at seventeen years of age, the obtained IQ was 111. At thirty-nine years of age, this adult was conducting his own business (a retail grocery), was married, and was financially in the lower middle socioeconomic class! This case is admittedly quite exceptional, but points up the variability in functional ability of individuals with Down's syndrome.

Much has been published concerning the personality characteristics of Down's children. They often have been described as placid, good-natured, cheerful, even-tempered, and amenable to social control. Experience has shown, however, that not all Down's children fit this stereotype. Menolascino (1965) studied a group of eighty-six Down's syndrome children over a five-year period. These children, eight years of age or less, showed a 13 percent incidence of severe psychiatric problems. This figure compared with that of 15 percent found by other workers. By comparison, a group of 616 additional retarded children also studied by Menolascino was found to have a 30 percent incidence of severe psychiatric disorders. In general, Down's children were found to have an incidence rate for severe psychiatric disorders comparable to that of nonretarded children, but about half that of a heterogeneous population of retarded children.

A more recent and intense study of Down's infants, from six to eighteen months of age, yields similar findings (Baron, 1972). These 18 infants were living at home and were extensively evaluated with a specially constructed *Temperament Profile* used in a longitudinal study of both normal and handicapped children. Baron found no significant difference in temperament of Down's children compared with "other children," but stated, "Some [Down's children] may be easy to raise and others may be difficult." In contrast, Thomas and Chess (1977), in a report of other children evaluated in the longitudinal project, indicate that mentally retarded children, in general, show slightly more of the "signs" of the Difficult Sign Syndrome (a scale of problem behavior) than the normal sample.

Schlottmann and Anderson (1975) compared twelve children with Down's syndrome with twelve other retarded children living in an institution. Based on observational study of these children in dyadic interaction in free-play situations, they found that these two groups of approximately twelve-year-old children were most noticeably different in several social behavior categories. The "mongoloid children" were more sociable and more gregarious, and the male "mongoloids" showed the greatest social superiority.

In short, we may conclude that children with Down's syndrome are about as likely as normal children to have personality disorders, but they are *less likely* to have such disorders than other retarded children.

Now let us turn our attention to the etiology of this condition. The President's Committee on Mental Retardation (1976b) estimates that one child in every 600 to 700 births is born with Down's syndrome. The condition is not rare, therefore, but what causes it? Years ago, Goddard (1926) proposed that ". . . the sole and adequate cause is to be sought in the condition of the mother during pregnancy." This conclusion is an example of oversimplification. We have learned that there are three main forms of Down's syndrome. The most common is trisomy #21, in which there has been a *nondisjunction* of the pair of chromosomes designated #21.

A chromosome is a rod-shaped body in the nucleus of the cell; it is composed of genes that are the biological units of heredity. (See chapter 5 for a discussion of genetic mechanisms.) Normally, during the process of cell division (*mitosis*) in pregnancy, twenty-three pairs of chromosomes are formed. Of these, twenty-two pairs, called *autosomes,* govern the broad range of developmental features in people, and the twenty-third set (labeled XX in the female and XY in the male) governs sex characteristics. The chromosomes are arranged in a particular order and have discernible structures. In trisomy #21, the two chromosomes designated #21 fail to separate (nondisjunction), and when the ovum unites with a normal sperm an extra chromosome may be attached to chromosome #21 (hence, *trisomy*).

The photograph illustrates the trisomy #21 found in a male with Down's syndrome. Advanced technology is required to construct this kind of photograph (called a Karyotype), first using an electron microscope to photograph chromosomes in a single cell, then matching each of the chromosomes with its mate.

The developments that made possible the techniques for analyzing tissue cultures grew out of intense research on cancer during which it was learned how to grow cells *in vitro.* Thus it was that in 1959 Lejeune and coworkers (Lejeune et al., 1959) were able to ascertain that children with Down's

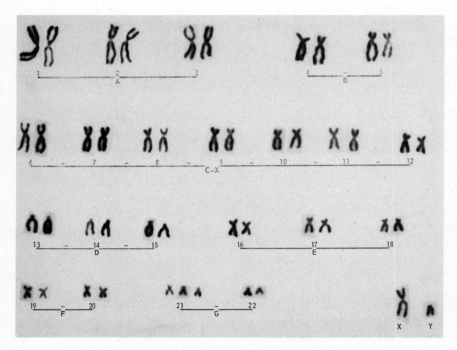

Karyotype showing trisomy #21 in a male with Down's syndrome. (Prepared by Anna W. Carr, Cytogenetic Laboratory, Medical College of Virginia, Richmond, Virginia.)

syndrome had forty-seven instead of forty-six chromosomes in their tissue culture.

The "abnormal condition" within the mother, which Goddard had previously proposed to account for Down's syndrome, led to an *exhaustion theory* (Baroff, 1958) because it had been found that such children were more frequently born to mothers who were advanced in age (over forty years). The theory was buttressed by other possible explanations of exhaustion of the mother—for example, disturbed metabolism. However, there was conflicting evidence showing that the condition of the father might be a contributory cause, and some mothers who were not "exhausted" gave birth to such children. More recent research has indicated that, indeed, with increasing age of the mother there is increased susceptibility to damage in the mother's egg cells (Koch and Dobson, 1971). This has been shown to be an *associated factor* and not necessarily a *causative* factor. The same study indicates that other factors are associated with Down's syndrome, such as exposure to radiation during preovulation, repeated abortions, and poor spacing of pregnancies. Down's syndrome may, in fact, occur at variable ages of the mother. Koch and Dobson offer the following incidences for various age groupings: .33 for ages 29 years and below; 1.67 for ages 30–34; 3.57 for ages 35–39; 14.29 for ages 40–44; and, 25 for ages 45–49. Thus, increasing age of the mother is clearly an associated factor in the condition, with ages above 39 showing a much higher incidence of this condition.

We have had to revise some of our previous beliefs about the cause of Down's syndrome. We have learned that the father, as well as the mother, may be a causative agent. The condition may occur in families of any socioeconomic status. More than a single occurrence may take place in a given family, but this is rare. And, finally, the age of the parents is a variable factor and varies in interaction with other factors. Moreover, it has been established that trisomy #21 is rarely inherited, although the genetic mechanisms are not fully understood.

There are techniques for detecting the probability of Down's syndrome during pregnancy and, therefore, of aborting the pregnancy. These are highly complicated medical and moralistic issues that we shall not discuss.

As we noted, there are other forms of Down's syndrome. One form is *familial* (previously termed familial mongolism). This is attributed not to nondisjunction but to *translocation* (or attachment of one chromosome to another). Such translocations may have occurred in the grandparents, and the Down's child carries both the translocation and an extra, unattached chromosome of the same type. This is an inherited condition. It is different from trisomy #21, and parental ages are *not* correlated with its incidence.

A third form of the condition is called *mosaicism* and is a consequence of chromosomal anomaly. During the development of the embryo, a cell divides unevenly, resulting in one cell with forty-five chromosomes and one with forty-seven chromosomes. The cell with forty-five chromosomes dies, but the cell with forty-seven chromosomes develops independently of the cells with the normal number of chromosomes. Persons with this condition may vary widely, some showing typically Down's features and others developing quite normally.

Work is continuing with chromosomal anomalies. Trisomal disturbances involving chromosomes 13 and 18 as well as deletions of chromosome 5 tend to result in severe mental retardation. Other physical anomalies also may result such as prominent nose and narrow pelvic angle that are antithetical to the usual Down's syndrome features. Recent studies summarizing ongoing research also indicate that there are complex interactive effects of hereditary and environmental factors, making the precise contribution of each quite difficult to determine (Stern, 1973; Ehrman et al., 1972).

Cretinism

In sharp contrast to Down's syndrome is the condition of cretinism. The specific cause of this condition has been well established. It is attributable to an insufficient secretion of the thyroid glands. The cretin may be born with a rudimentary thyroid gland (*hypothyroidism*), and in some instances the gland may be entirely missing. Two types of cretinism have been identified: the *sporadic* (or scattered, isolated) and the *endemic* (or regional). Endemic cretinism is most common in specific areas of the world; in the United States it seems to be found most frequently in the Great Lakes region and in some of the far western states. These regions are the so-called goitrous regions, regions in which an adequate amount of iodine does not occur naturally in the water and soil.

Cretinism is easily recognized within the first four months of the infant's life, unless the condition is very mild. Physical symptoms include small stature (*dwarfism*); short, thick legs; a disproportionately large head; short, broad hands with fingers that have square ends; dry, coarse, and scaly skin; a large and protruding tongue; peg-shaped, chalky teeth, which usually are delayed in eruption; everted lower lip; swollen eyelids and eyes that are half-shut; lowered basal metabolic rate with little perspiration; a short, thick neck; delayed sexual development; and a hoarse, thick, and strident voice.

In temperament, cretins are, as a group, rather resistive and stubborn in their relationships with other children and adults. They tend to lack spontaneity in their behavioral reactions. Their behavior is not usually troublesome; it tends to be placid and taciturn rather than quarrelsome and aggressive.

In intelligence, cretins show a wide range of capacities. They may range anywhere from the profound through the mild retarded level of retardation, and some attain a borderline classification.

If cretinism is untreated, it tends to become progressively worse. Then the special physical characteristics become more and more pronounced, until the cretin begins to look, in early adolescence, somewhat like a very aged and wrinkled old man. However, if medical treatment is instituted at an early age, much, if not all, of the unfavorable symptomatology may be avoided. In such instances, the mental capacity may reach an average level.

There are infrequent cases of cretinism that develop after birth. In such cases, deficiencies in thyroid functioning may result from breakdown or disease of the thyroid gland or from disease of the endocrine system, particularly of the pituitary gland. In all such cases, thyroid production has been blocked and atrophy of the thyroid gland may result. In rare instances, there may be destruction of the thyroid gland during embryonic development even when the mother has not suffered from iodine insufficiency; Wilkins (1960) has suggested that some pathologic agent may be responsible for such destruction.

The later the time at which treatment is started, the more unfavorable is the prognosis. Medical treatment must be continued throughout life. There may be some cases in which there are complicating defects in cerebral development that thyroid treatment cannot correct even if it is initiated at a very early age. When the condition of cretinism is particularly severe, the child may die at an early age. In such cases, however, death is due to complicating factors other than the hypothyroidism itself.

Since it is important that the treatment of cretinism be initiated as early as possible, the need for immediate diagnosis of the condition is evident. Lowrey et al., (1958) studied a group of forty-nine cretins to determine the earliest age at which a reliable diagnosis of cretinism could be made. They concluded that such a diagnosis could be made in most cases by as early an age as three months, and certainly by the age of six months.

It should be emphasized that cretins need much more than medical treatment, even though that is vital to their condition. Because of delayed development, they experience, even at best, special problems in adjustment and adaptation. Experience has shown that they can profit from educational, social, and vocational guidance. The parents, too, need help in understanding the problems of these children and in learning how best to help them.

About 5 percent or less of institutionalized mental defectives are cretins.

Microcephaly

There are two forms of Microcephaly: *primary* (also called genetic or familial); and, *secondary* (also called exogenous). The major physical symptom is a small skull (the criterion is 13 inches or less in a six-month infant, and 16 inches or less in an adult) that is conical in shape. Measurement is made of the maximal fronto-occipital circumference. The head is not only small in size but also long in shape (dolicocephalic). The forehead recedes. The face, however, is not as small as the head, in contrast to the proportions of head and face of the midget, in whom both face and head are proportionately small. Microcephalics show a flattening of the back of the head, which has caused some individuals to apply the term *pinhead* to them. Although muscular ability is adequate, their small stature, curved spine, and disproportionately long legs (and arms) cause them to walk in a peculiar fashion, somewhat resembling the gait of a monkey. They have a miniature brain and simplified cerebral structure. The primary type of microcephaly is almost always severely retarded mentally.

About one percent of institutionalized retarded persons are microcephalics. Most require custodial care since they do not develop normal speech patterns and require personal care in feeding and toilet activities. Although institutionalized microcephalics may live as long as other non-stigmatic types of mentally retarded persons, they sometimes die at an early age due to complications or illnesses.

The primary form of microcephaly is attributed to a single recessive gene (Böök et al., 1953). Fortunately, it is quite uncommon. It also is less common than the secondary type of microcephaly (Brandon et al., 1959).

Secondary microcephaly may be caused by a number of exogenous agents. Among these the most common have been: excessive irradiation (during the first trimester of pregnancy); inadequate supply of oxygen to the developing brain of the fetus; and, infections of the mother during pregnancy. Some cases of microcephaly due to X-ray treatment of the mother during pregnancy have been reported (Jervis, 1959), but this cause of microcephaly has become extremely rare since pregnancy tests are routinely done before irradiation treatment during childbearing age.

Unfortunately, excessive irradiation was present during the atomic blast at Hiroshima, and one of the many terrible consequences was the irradiation of pregnant women. Wood, Johnson, and Omori (1967) studied 183 children who had been subject *in utero* to radiation. During a twenty-year follow-up period they found 31 percent who were microcephalic. Forty-one percent of these microcephalic individuals were judged to be mentally retarded. They found also that fourteen of the seventeen subjects whose head size was two to three standard deviations below the mean for the general population had normal intelligence, however. There were fourteen children whose head size was three or more standard deviations below the mean, but only four of these were mentally retarded. Findings such as these indicate that not all secondary types of microcephaly are invariably accompanied by mental retardation.

Secondary microcephaly embraces all levels of the intellectual range, except, perhaps, the very superior. Martin (1970) conducted an exhaustive study of 500 patients at the John F. Kennedy Child Development Center from 1963 to 1968. Of these, 202 cases were found who were microcephalic. Each of these children met the criterion of a head circumference of more than two standard deviations below the mean for the general population. The mean age of the children was 6.1 years. All socioeconomic classes were represented in the sample. On the basis of test results with the *Stanford-Binet*, the *WISC*, or the *Yale Schedules*, it was determined that 27 of these children had IQs of 80 or higher. Four children were found to have evidence of organic brain damage, including seizures, deafness, perceptual dysfunction, and congenital rubella. Eleven of the 27 children were diagnosed as having minimal brain dysfunction. Thus, current evidence indicates that microcephalic children of the secondary type may be found in all the ranges of intelligence. Their physical symptoms also are quite variable. Some may have all of the usual symptoms of the primary type of microcephaly, but most show fewer physical symptoms.

Most microcephalic children are temperamentally fairly alert and even vivacious. They often display a sense of well-being (*euphoria*), but their interests shift rapidly from one object to another. If they are in the range of the severely retarded, they tend to imitate the behavior of other people (*echopraxia*) and they tend to use repetitive speech sounds (*echolalia*). Children with secondary microcephaly, however, often attain normal speech and communication.

Hydrocephaly

Hydrocephaly is a condition in which there is a disturbance in the flow of cerebrospinal fluid. In the most common form of congenital hydrocephaly, in which an obstruction prevents this flow, the skull may become greatly enlarged due to the accumulation of the fluid. If this blockage occurs soon after birth, before the sutures of the skull are closed, the increasing pressure on the brain may cause considerable damage. The blockage may involve excessive formation of cerebrospinal fluid, or inadequate circulation, or inadequate absorption. The causes of this condition are unknown; suggested causes are: advancing maternal age (Collmann and Stoller, 1962), encephalitis, tumors of the brain, meningitis, other types of infections, and other conditions. In addition to the enlargement of the cranial vault and the skull, other physical sequelae may include a thinning of the cerebral cortex, an enlargement of the upper part of the face, and visual impairment. In severe cases, the bodies of the children are very slight and their necks cannot support the excessive weight of their heads. The level of intelligence varies with the timing and amount of cerebral damage although, unless corrected early, the mental level usually is in the range of the severely retarded; in some instances, the child may attain average intelligence. Convulsive seizures often accompany the clinical picture, and optic atrophy (due to degeneration of the optic nerve) may result.

Treatment has involved the use of drugs in some cases (Elvidge, Branch, and Thompson, 1957) and surgical measures in other cases (Ransohoff, Shulman, and Fishman, 1960; Jervis, 1959). One of the most successful operative procedures involves implanting a shunt in order to maintain effective flow of cerebrospinal fluid from the brain into a vein in the neck. Special diets to reduce the accumulation of fluid also have been attempted.

In the secondary type of hydrocephalus, maldevelopment of brain tissue causes an accumulation of cerebrospinal fluid in the spaces within the skull. In such cases, there is no enlargement of the skull, or only slight enlargement, and there is no increased intracranial pressure. Brain damage is typically far less than in the primary form.

Medical diagnosis is difficult in borderline cases. Fortunately, hydrocephaly is uncommon, occurring in about one percent of institutionalized cases.

Familial Amaurosis

There appear to be four varieties of this very serious disease. The form that strikes during early infancy, usually toward the end of the first six months of the infant, is called *Infantile Amaurotic Idiocy* (also *Tay-Sachs' Disease*, after the two persons who studied it at the end of the nineteenth century), and is thought to be due to a single autosomal recessive gene inherited in accordance with Mendelian ratios (see chapter 5). It is found most frequently in Jewish infants of eastern European extraction. The neuropathological findings involve a lipid (mostly ganglioside) and obvious swelling of all of the neurons of the body. It is a degenerative disease ending in early death by or before four years of age. Despite its presumed genetic basis, evidence indicates that other factors are operative. For instance, it is known that one of a pair of the same-sexed twins may develop the disease while the other does not. After early, apparently, normal development, the infant begins to regress neurologically. The child begins to show developmental retardation, visual failure, and hypersensitivity to sound and light. Later, blindness, severe intellectual retardation, seizures, and many neurological manifestations occur. Prostration and severe vasomotor disturbances may occur before death.

Late Infantile Amaurotic Idiocy (Bielschowsky-Jansky Disease) occurs somewhat later than Tay-Sachs' Disease, usually after three years of age, and has a much slower course. Deterioration is not so marked. It occurs more frequently in non-Jewish families than the earlier form. Instead of the typical "cherry red spot" found in the retinas of infants with Tay-Sachs' Disease, there is pigmentary degeneration of the retina, but blindness, incoordination, and psychotic-like features occur.

Juvenile Amaurotic Idiocy (Vogt-Spielmeyer's Disease) occurs between five and six years of age. The nature of the penetrating lipid in this condition is unknown; the clinical picture involves mental deterioration, blindness, convulsive seizures, and spastic paralysis. Death occurs by or before eighteen years of age.

Kuf's Disease has its onset in adolescence, has a slow development, and has a pattern similar to that of the Juvenile form.

There are other quite rare clinical forms of severe mental retardation that need not be presented. However, reference will be made to some of them in the following chapter.

Hydrocephalic child responds to affectionate puppy. The retarded child needs to give and receive love. (Courtesy of University of Michigan Information Series.)

– 5 –

Etiology and Intervention

It is highly unusual to discuss etiology and intervention in the same chapter. By etiology we mean causation, and by intervention we mean methods or experiences that may influence the course and outcome of a condition. Conventionally, these two topics are considered separate and independent issues. But in the case of the condition (or more accurately the many conditions) we have chosen to call mental retardation, causation and outcome are complexly and intimately interrelated. We have learned that many forms of mental retardation are, at least, socioculturally influenced, if not determined. As we have learned to apply effective early intervention procedures, some "potentially" retarded conditions are avoided or are significantly ameliorated. In such circumstances the questions arise as to whether mental growth was inhibited, delayed, or distorted by insufficient and inappropriate stimulation during a critical period of development, whether some individuals "require" more stimulation for growth than others, and whether the distorted growth was due to an indigenous characteristic or to an exogenous inhibitor. In many cases, the interactions of etiological and intervention factors are complex and obscure. (Parenthetically, this is one of the reasons for such highly emotionally loaded arguments by adversaries in the heredity-environment controversies; ambiguity leads to anxiety and projection.)

But, one may ask, what could be the possible rationale for discussing conjointly etiology and intervention in other cases presumably involving genetic or congenital causative factors? Here again, we have learned that it is seldom, if ever, possible to assign the "cause" of retardation exclusively to "inborn" characteristics. In discussing the causation of mental retardation, Stern (1973), a eugenicist, points out that in about half of the cases, no etiological diagnosis can be applied even though about 37 percent of cases of mental retardation are attributable to genetic conditions. Others (Ehrman, Omenn, and Caspar, 1972) have asserted that the interactions between heredity and environment are highly complex, and that many behavioral functions show differing variances (attributable, causative factors) for genetic versus experiential factors (Vandenberg,

Stafford, and Brown, 1968). Language development, the development of perceptual speed, reasoning, and motor ability are differentially dependent on genetic and environmental conditions. In addition, there is hope that many biochemical contributors to or determiners of mental deficiency can be controlled or modified with increasing knowledge of metabolic pathways and the development of new infusion methods (Begab, 1974). Congenital conditions, including malnutrition, the effects of prematurity, and infectious agents are clearly modifiable and even preventable. Hence, the adverse effects of most genetic and congenital contributors to mental retardation can be controlled or modified or compensated for with increasing technology for intervention.

It is no longer appropriate, therefore, to discuss etiology in isolation from prevention and intervention. To do so, augments the mistaken belief that the situation is "fixed" or "static" rather than interactive and dynamic. The more we learn about etiology, the more we learn about possible intervention methods; the more we learn about intervention, the more we learn about etiology. This is not to say that all mental retardation is preventable, but its incidence is surely reducible if we apply what we already know and improve our intervention procedures.

PROBLEMS OF CLASSIFICATION OF
ETIOLOGICAL FACTORS

From what has already been said, it is clear that any attempt at classification in terms of etiology runs into difficulties. Classification usually is based on the presumed cause of the mental retardation. When the definition of retardation is limited to a sociolegal condition, which is more restrictive than the 1973 AAMD concept, as many as 85 percent of retarded individuals fall into the category of "etiology unknown" (Dunn, 1973)—a much higher percentage than that offered by Stern. When the AAMD definition is used, as many as 94 percent would be classified as of unknown etiology (Grossman, 1973). However, whichever definition is accepted, whether these or those offered by other authorities and other professional organizations, most workers would agree that a relatively small percentage has a "known etiology" or that a given etiological factor is the only relevant factor in the development of the retardation.

We have chosen to adopt the Grossman scheme of classification, which proposes nine main etiological groupings. This scheme is not without its difficulties, since even in clear pathological conditions more than one factor may be involved. For example, the categories of *gestational* disorders and of *metabolic and nutritional* disorders, which are considered as separate categories, clearly overlap. Deviations occuring during gestation that produced prematurity and low birth weight often are associated with malnutrition or inappropriate nutrition, and cause and effect are difficult to disentangle. Moreover, although prematurity and very low birth weight often are associated with retardation, the relationship is neither inevitable nor entirely uncorrectable.

Keeping these limitations of any system of classification in mind, we shall begin our discussion of etiology by discussing chromosomal problems. First, it might be helpful to divide the broad range of classificatory categories, as Jervis (1959) has done, into *physiological* mental deficiency and *pathological* mental deficiency. The physiological category includes conditions that are not due to either specific endogenous (primary) factors or specific exogenous (secondary) factors. This category is also called *aclinical,* and more recently *cultural-familial.* The pathological category includes *both* exogenous factors (inherent in the genetic constitution) and specific endogenous factors (such as infections, trauma, toxin, and the like).

CHROMOSOMAL ABNORMALITIES

In order to understand these abnormalities, which depend, at least in part on genetic mechanisms, we will first present a brief discussion of the major genetic mechanisms.

Chromosome, Genes, and Dna

The unit that carries the genetic information on which traits are based is called a *gene.* Each gene occupies a particular location on the chromosome. Chromosomes are so named because to study and identify them a staining process is used. After staining, they acquire a "colored appearance." All human cells contain twenty-three pairs of chromosomes, or forty-six chromosomes in all. In normal cell division (*mitosis*) these 46 chromosomes are duplicated. However, at the particular stage that occurs in preparation for the union of the sperm cell with the egg cell, this process is altered. During that period, the number of chromosomes is reduced by half (*meiosis*). Thus, the sperm and the egg cells each contains twenty-three chromosomes. The embryo receives twenty-three chromosomes from each parent, thus having twenty-three pairs of chromosomes in all. Chromosomes vary in both size and shape. Forty-four of them are called autosomes and the others (an X from the mother and an X or Y from the father) are called sex chromosomes. If there is any variation in the process of cell division or in the arrangement of the chromosomes, serious abnormality may result.

Although each gene carries a particular trait, the genes may act singly or in combination. Moreover, genes can be either *dominant* or *recessive.* Gregor Mendel reported on the rules of inheritance in 1866. He studied peas since he could manipulate the breeding process and study the effects over successive generations. He observed that when he crossed purebred red peas (with red flowers) with purebred white peas (with white flowers), all of the first-generation peas bore red flowers. However, when he crossed some of the second-generation peas with each other, some bore red flowers and others bore white flowers. He thus determined that red was a dominant gene and white was a recessive gene.

The probable effects of crossing dominant and recessive genes in human beings is illustrated in Figure 5.1.

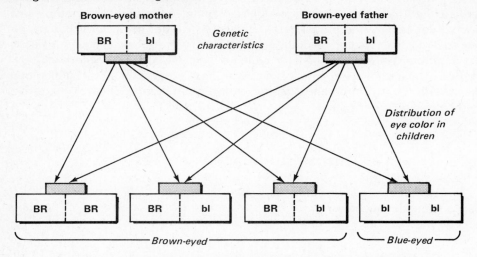

FIGURE 5.1.   Probable effects of crossing dominant and recessive genes, illustrated for eye color. (BR for brown is dominant and bl for blue is recessive.)

Note that in this illustration both "parents" are *heterozygous* (each has a dominant and a recessive gene) although both manifest brown eye color. If they have four children, the probability is that one will be homozygous (with brown eyes), two will be heterozygous (with brown eyes), and one will be homozygous (with blue eyes). Of course this probability would be more likely with a much larger number of children than four.

In addition, since there are twenty-three pairs of chromosomes, the number of possible permutations of these pairs is 2^{23}, or two to the twenty-third power, thus leading to a probability that two children from the same parents would have one chance in 70 trillion that the two will have identical chromosomal combinations. Taking these facts into consideration, we can see that depending on the combination of chromosomes, the dominant or recessive character of the genes, and the possible combinative action of the genes, the possibilities for variation are tremendous. It also has been learned that the majority of mental abnormalities result from the action of recessive genes, thus making the incidence of mental abnormality on this basis infrequent.

As we have noted, genes are the carriers of inherited traits. But the situation is even more complicated than this statement suggests. Not only do genes tend to act in combination (polyogenesis), but some genetic information also is transmitted through the cytoplasm (a fluid) from within the cell membranes. Unlike the contents of chromosomes, in which similar amounts are transmitted in cell division, cytoplasm may be *differentially distributed*. This is one reason that identical twins fertilized from the same egg (*monozygotic twins*) may have *different* characteristics.

Moreover, environmental factors and mutations also can produce radical changes in the offspring. For example, deprivation of oxygen (*anoxia*) in the young fetus can alter the expected characteristics and produce brain damage or death. Anoxia can be caused by various birth difficulties arising from such factors as breech delivery, excessively prolonged (and excessively short) period of labor, and a knotted umbilical cord. Such damage is greatest, in general, during the first trimester of gestation. Infections of the mother, such as rubella (German measles) also can produce serious disturbances. Thus, prenatal and environmental factors may interact with genetic development to alter grossly the development of the beginning organism. Hebb (1958) listed six types of factors that may influence the developing organism: genetic, chemical, traumatic, chemical (postnatal), constant sensory change (both pre- and postnatal), and variable sensory experiences (both pre- and postnatal). Of these factors, only one (genetic) is entirely heritable. Methods that minimize prenatal environmental damage, or eliminate such damage, can prevent the occurrence of subsequent abnormalities.

The genetic code of the DNA also can be affected by mutations. "Natural" mutations develop over a long period of time. In addition, there are rapid mutations produced by extreme conditions, such as those that accompanied the atomic blast at Hiroshima. Such mutations affect the immediate progeny and also can be passed on, through alteration of base code of genetics, to later generations.

We have spoken of the "genetic code." Knowledge of this code became available through the discoveries, mainly, of three Nobel prize winners who were awarded this distinction in 1962: Maurice H. F. Wilkins, Francis H. C. Crick, and James D. Watson. This code, which is the chemical structure of the material of heredity, consists of four base compounds in the DNA (deoxyribonucleic acid). The order of appearance of these compounds in the two strands of the *helix* (a curved form similar to a spiral) governs the transmission of genetic information. The cells also contain RNA (ribonucleic acid), which serves as a messenger in transmitting genetic information from the DNA to protein and enzyme manufacturing sites in the cell. All of the cells in a human being contain the same inheritance.

Despite all that has been learned about transmitting genetic information, many questions remain unanswered. It is not understood, for example, why some cells become muscles and others become neurons, although some theoretical explanations have been offered. The nature of cell development is not clearly understood, although current research is attempting to find some answers. It is believed that there are critical periods in cell development that can be influenced by experimental means. If current research develops means of altering and controlling cell development, many diseases could be controlled or eliminated. There also is the fear that such experimentation could lead to disastrous results with unknown consequences. Consequently there is considerable misgiving about permitting such experiments, especially if there are not highly strict safeguards. The prospects for genetic and human engineering are both stupendous and frightening!

Types of Chromosomal Abnormalities

We will discuss the two types of chromosomal disorders and illustrate some examples of each. The two types are: chromosomal disorders due to a dominant gene and chromosomal disorders due to a recessive gene.

We already have discussed one type of disorder due to a dominant gene (Down's syndrome, in chapter 4). Other diseases falling in this category are: tuberous sclerosis, neurofibromatosis, and acrocephaly. These are rare conditions and only one, tuberous sclerosis, will be presented as an example. Among the recessive gene disturbances, the most important are: Turner's disease, Klinefelter's syndrome, phenylketonuria, and glactosemia, along with microcephaly, and the various forms of amaurotic idiocy (which were presented in chapter 4).

Tuberous sclerosis. This disorder is an example of the relatively rare occurrence of mental retardation associated with a dominant gene. The assumption of genetic transmission is largely based on studies of family pedigrees (Borberg, 1951). However so-called incomplete forms of this disease also occur, which makes diagnosis difficult and the study of genetic transmission more difficult. This condition is found in about 0.5 percent of institutionalized cases. When the condition is due to a dominant gene, transmission occurs even when half of the parental genes are normal; i.e., it is a heterozygot condition.

The usual clinical picture (syndrome) involves mental deficiency, skin manifestations (*adenoma sebaceum*), and epileptic convulsions. Retardation is usually severe or profound and sometimes increases with age. The skin condition may not be present in infancy, but develops in later childhood or adolescence. Convulsions usually are severe and are of the grand mal type. Intracranial calcifications may be seen in skull X-rays. There is no known specific treatment for this condition. There often are benign tumors in the kidneys, brain, heart, and lungs. When malignant tumors occur, life expectancy is shortened.

We cite this condition to illustrate the transmission of a disease by a dominant gene. Evidence shows (Chao, 1959) that 50 percent of children from a parent with this condition are affected, as would be expected.

Turner's disease. This disease is one of the two sex-linked diseases that we shall discuss. It is associated with the absence of one of the X chromosomes (XO instead of XY). Patients with this disease usually are chromatin negative; i.e., they have one X chromosome and no Y chromosome. The presence of the disease is usually discovered when menstruation begins, or later, because secondary sex characteristics fail to develop in such cases. Examination reveals that the gonads are rudimentary. Not all cases develop mental retardation (Haddad and Wilkins, 1959), but they often show learning disabilities.

Klinefelter's disease. This is another disease associated with gene recessive characteristics that affects only males. Also known as *testicular fibrosis,* it is a metabolic-endocrine condition (hence it might also be classified among the metabolic disturbances), and like Turner's disease, it usually is discovered at puberty or later when such female characteristics as feminine breasts and sparse pubic hair are noted. Other characteristics may include high-pitched voice, scanty hair on the chest, and difficulty in achieving erections. The individual has an extra X chromosome (XXY instead of XY); this can be determined by a buccal smear. Testosterone injections may be administered because of the testicular deficiency.

According to Mosier and Dingman (1960) about 1 percent of institutionalized male retardates have this condition, although it may be more common in the general population. The usual degree of mental retardation associated with this condition is mild or moderate, although the mental level may vary somewhat.

Many psychological problems are associated with this condition, both in its "true" form and in other forms (such as XXXYO). Because of the metabolic disturbance and the associated physical feminine characteristics, secondary adjustment problems are likely to arise. "Intervention" for medical and also for guidance and psychotherapeutic purposes can prove very helpful for both the patient and his family.

Phenylpyruvic Oligophrenia (Phenylketonuria). Phenylpyruvic acid is found in the urine when certain physiological processes within the body are disturbed. Presumably, it is found in the urine of normal persons. It has been found in certain groups of mentally retarded people, particularly those with severe retardation. About 1 percent of institutionalized persons show this condition, known as phenylketonuria. It is attributable to faulty metabolism, which also produces lowered intellectual functioning. There is some evidence to indicate that phenylketonuria is inherited. No known neurological abnormalities accompany the condition.

The history of the discovery of phenylketonuria is interesting. (Centerwall and Centerwall, 1961). The recognition of this disease resulted from the fortuitous observation of a Norwegian mother of two mentally retarded children. In actively seeking a specific cause for the retardation, she noticed that her children's urine smelled different from that of other children. Her observation eventually came to the attention of Dr. A. Fölling, a physician in Oslo, who finally uncovered and described the condition known as phenylketonuria. The illness also is known as Fölling's disease, in honor of its discoverer.

The disease process is complicated, but it is one of the few *known* and *preventable* forms of mental retardation. Blattner (1961) estimated that the condition may occur once in every 25,000 to 40,000 births, and that sixth-tenths of one percent of institutionalized mental defectives suffer from phenylketonuria.

Williamson and his coworkers (1968) studied the incidence of phenylketonuria in school-age retarded children. They were primarily interested in developing procedures for mass screening of the children. In a sample of 32,818 children, which included 88.3 percent of the total of available children in the state, they located 68 children suffering from phenylketonuria. Of these, 26 were newly identified and 42 were known cases. The prevalence ratios of phenylketonuria by type of handicap were 1:750 for the educable retarded; 1:175 for the trainable retarded; and 1:105 for the retarded in a state institution.

Kugel and his associates (1966) compared two laboratory techniques for the early detection of phenylketonuria. As we have previously pointed out, early detection is important so that treatment can be instituted early. The study of Kugel et al. was based on 2,600 newborn infants upon whom simultaneous determinations for serum phenylalanine were made using both the LaDu (1963) and the Guthrie (Guthrie and Susi, 1963) techniques. The study showed that the LaDu test was a more sensitive index for determining serum phenylalanine. However, the Guthrie test, while only roughly quantitative, was found to compare favorably in all instances with the LaDu test. This work is particularly significant in that it provides additional confidence in the use of the Guthrie test for mass screening purposes. That test offers a practical procedure for the early detection of phenylketonuria in newborn children who are still in the hospital.

A genetic defect produces abnormalities in enzyme formation. The liver enzyme phenylalanine hydroxylase is either entirely absent or is reduced in its activity to 7 to 10 percent of the norm. Because of this enzymatic defect, phenylalanine, an essential amino acid present in all food proteins, is not oxidized to tyrosine. It accumulates in blood and spinal fluid, and possibly in the brain, and is excreted in the urine as phenylpyruvic acid. Additional metabolic products (such as *phenylacetic acid*) also are formed and are found in the body tissues. Further, other enzyme systems that are necessary for normal brain functions also are adversely affected.

The disease may be diagnosed as early as the third day of life by a very simple urine test, which is very fortunate, since the studies show that the earlier the disease is treated the greater is the probability that the mental defect can be arrested. It has been held that unless treatment is initiated before the age of three years, the cerebral changes resulting from the faulty metabolism tend to be irreversible, and the condition of mental retardation cannot then be alleviated. Treatment consists, for the most part, of dietary manipulations to compensate for the enzyme deficiencies. A high blood concentration of phenylalanine is found in rats that have been fed on diets high in tyrosine. This high level has been found to be accompanied by a decrease in learning ability.

Mentally retarded children suffering from phenylketonuria *may* show severe maladaptive behavior. Bjornson (1964) has reported on the behavioral reactions of such children. He noted that schizophrenic-like symptoms may be expected in *some cases,* but no general pattern of behavioral reactions differentiates the child with phenylketonuria from other retarded children. Bjornson did observe, however, that the condition should be suspected in children who show dull expressionless faces, negativistic behavior, unreal emotional outbursts, and speech disturbances, even though the IQ is not below the dull normal level. Bjornson concluded, after reviewing the available literature, that no consistent behavior pattern was described for the phenylketonuric child, and that no "specific categorizable psychological defect exists."

A long-term research project on phenylketonuria was begun at the Faribault State School and Hospital in Minnesota (Bruhl et al., 1964). It had been assumed that mental retardation could be prevented in children suffering from phenylketonuria by placing the children on a phenylalanine-restricted diet in early infancy. This study observed the effect of a phenylalanine-restricted diet over a longer period of time than had previously been used. It was concluded that the symptoms associated with untreated phenylketonuria arise from two separate factors. One of these is a toxic syndrome that is reversible in a comparatively short time when the excessive concentrations of phenylalanine and their abnormal consequences in metabolism are reduced in blood and tissues. The second is an irreversible structural change associated with organic brain damage and resulting in arrested mental development at an early age. Bruhl et al. believe that it is possible to relieve the toxic syndrome, but it is apparently impossible to undo whatever brain damage has occurred through the *prolonged action* of metabolic changes. Hence, they stress the critical importance of diagnosing phenylketonuria in early infancy and starting the phenylalanine-free diet within the first few months of life before irreversible brain damage has occurred.

Although the primary disturbance in phenylketonuria appears to be biochemical, in many instances organic brain damage or cerebral dysfunction, as diagnosed from EEG tracings, tremors, and problems in coordination, accompany the disorder. However, very little attention has been given to the disturbances in personality that often occur. Steisel and his coworkers (1967) turned their attention to these disturbances, studying the interaction patterns among children with phenylketonuria. They pointed out that the personality of PKU children generally is described as spanning the range from reactions that are mildly or moderately neurotic to reactions that are characteristic of psychotic-like states. Some authors dichotomize the behavior reactions of PKU children as being either hyperactive-destructive or passive-pathetic.

Steisel and his coworkers studied four groups of subjects: normal, retarded and/or brain-damaged, psychotic, and PKU. There were thirty-eight subjects in the PKU group, twenty-three in the retarded group, twenty-six in the psychotic group, and ten in the normal group. The mean age for the PKU group was 8.4. It was 7.7 for the retarded group; 8.6 for the psychotic group; and 5.8 for the normal group. The behavior of these children in a playroom was observed through a one-way screen. The room contained only the experimental materials. The furniture consisted mainly of two chairs and a desk. On a shelf, in full view of the children, were various toys that they could use.

Several judges evaluated the interactions. On the total interaction scores, the PKU group was found to perform significantly poorer than normal, but significantly better than psychotic children. Differences between the PKU group and the retarded or brain-damaged group approached statistical significance, but on separate comparisons for three social-stimulus conditions, the differences between the two groups were found to be *not significant.* The PKU group was found to be the most heterogeneous in interactive behavior, and the clustering of scores suggested that phenylketonuria is behaviorally not a unitary disorder. Correlations of intelligence criteria and interaction scores for the PKU group further indicated that the interaction measure may tap functions not assessed by standardized IQ tests. However, the basic conclusion appears to be that behaviorally, PKU children are certainly not a homogeneous group. They are markedly heterogeneous as far as the research personality variables are concerned.

The research and treatment on phenylketonuria, once a major cause of mental retardation but now very infrequent, illustrate several considerations. One, of course, is that early intervention, in this case, medical and physiological intervention, is critical for some conditions. Another is that biological insult, or organic brain damage, can have a variety of consequences, depending on the history of the individual, the ways in which the individual is treated (biologically and psychologically), and the nature of other aspects of the individual's make-up. Finally, the psychological aspects of the individual's reactions and their impact on others cannot be neglected either in terms of diagnostic evaluation or in terms of guidance and/or psychological treatment.

Galactosemia. Donnell and his coworkers (1961) have described a disorder known as galactosemia, which is related to mental retardation. They state that galactosemia is a hereditary disease caused by an inborn error of metabolism that occurs in approximately 1 in 40,000 to 60,000 births. It is thought to be transmitted by an autosomal recessive gene. The faulty metabolism is due to a defect in the enzyme galactose-1-phosphate-uridyl-transferase, which fails to convert galactose-1-phosphate to utilizable glucose. This failure is responsible for damage to the developing brain, liver, lens of the eye, and kidneys, and possibly to other organ systems as well. If the condition is untreated, cataracts, cirrhosis of the liver, and mental retardation may result. The genetic, chemical, developmental, and nutritional aspects of galactosemia have been reported by many other workers.

If the diagnosis of this condition is made early in life and if treatment to remove the major source of ingested galactose is instituted, the damaging effects of the disease can be circumvented. Treatment involves the use of a galactose-free diet.

An interesting hypothesis about this condition has been suggested by Fishler et al. (1966). They hypothesized that varying degrees of dietary management will affect brain function and will be reflected in psychological tests. They hypothesized that children with effective dietary controls would demonstrate normal physical development and intellectual achievement, and in contrast, mentally retarded children whose dietary management was poor would reveal a decrement in mental functions.

They studied a total of thirty-four galactosemic patients, eighteen boys and sixteen girls, over a period of eight years. The oldest child was seventeen years of age, and the youngest was two months of age. Assessment of mental status was performed by using the *Cattell Infant Intelligence Scale* for children under the age of three years. The *Stanford-Binet* or *Wechsler Scale,* the *Draw-a-Person Test,* the *Bender-Gestalt Test,* the *Sentence Completion Test,* the *Thematic*

Apperception Test (TAT), and the *Rorschach Test* were used with older children. (See chapter 11.)

Their findings supported the hypothesis that galactosemia responds well to dietary treatment. When treatment was instituted early, physical development and intellectual progress were usually excellent. However, older children in this study often exhibited visual-perceptual problems that were severe enough to cause them marked difficulty in academic work. The investigators found a general personality profile (based on data from the projective psychological tests) involving excessive shyness, signs of anxiety, and other personality deviations in early adolescence. They believe that their findings firmly indicate that the damaging effects of the disease, which ultimately lead to physical and mental retardation, can be prevented by dietary treatment.

This hypothesis has been explored in several later studies. Kalckar, Kinoshita, and Donnell (1973) tested the relative effect of immediate treatment versus the effect of treatment that was initiated later. They compared pairs of siblings (ten in all) whose treatment was initiated at different ages. Those siblings for whom treatment was begun at a later age had a mean IQ of 91, whereas their younger siblings whose condition was diagnosed promptly (since the older siblings had already been diagnosed), had a mean IQ of 102. In another study (Nadler, Inouye, and Hsia, 1969), the mean IQ of children with galactosemia was 91 whereas the mean IQ of siblings who did not have this condition was 110. Kalckar et al. (1973), in summarizing the results of studies in three different centers that have attempted follow-up of children with galactosemia, state that treated children generally manifest good physical health although they tend to develop more slowly (have smaller height and weigh less than the norms), and tend, as a group, to have lower IQs than their unaffected siblings; but they also point out that the effectiveness of treatment seems to be clearly correlated with the age at which such treatment is initiated: the earlier treatment is begun, the better the outcomes in the aspects of development that were assessed. The final statement of the long-term effects of treatment has not yet been written, but Fishler's hypothesis seems quite reasonable.

ABNORMALITIES ASSOCIATED WITH METABOLIC OR NUTRITIONAL CONDITIONS

As we have learned, many diseases related to a recessive gene produce disturbances in metabolism. We have discussed some examples of such conditions including Tay-Sachs' disease, galactosemia, and phenylketonuria, in which specific types of metabolic disturbances are present. We also have learned that environmental and genetic factors interact and, especially in pregnancy and early infancy, the tendency toward the development of symptoms caused by the genetic *susceptibility* to the condition can be counteracted or even eliminated, in some instances.

Sometimes the same condition can be produced by *either* genetic or nongenetic factors, as is the case with microcephaly. Some workers have chosen to call the apparently nonhereditary form of a disease that usually is produced by genetic factors the *phenocopy*. On the other hand, it has become clear that mental retardation can be caused by severe malnutrition, and that some aspects of cognitive functioning, such as attention, curiosity, and alertness are particularly so affected. We will discuss the category of metabolic and nutritional abnormalities after chromosomal abnormalities in order to highlight both the contrasts and the similarities. We again will see that it is extremely difficult to disentangle the specific contributions to mental retardation of the hereditary and nonhereditary factors.

Metabolic Disturbances

Metabolic disturbances may involve disorders of carbohydrate formation (such as galactosemia), disorders of protein and amino acid metabolism (such as phenylketonuria), disorders of lipid (fat) storage (such as Tay-Sachs' disease), disorders in the synthesis of thyroid hormone (such as hypothyroidism), and disorders of mucopolysaccharide storage (such as Hunter's syndrome and Hurler's syndrome). Although most such metabolic conditions are associated with recessive gene characteristics, and therefore are presumed to have a hereditary basis resulting in the faulty metabolism, only in the past few years have sophisticated biochemical methods and studies begun to elucidate the specific mechanisms involved and the possibilities for effective treatment or prevention. These highly technical developments should yield better understanding of many of the conditions we have already discussed, and the knowledge from such studies will be more widely disseminated. We will discuss briefly two additional syndromes (Hunter and Hurler) as illustrative of such developments.

Hunter's Syndrome. This is an X-linked disease involving a disturbance in lipid metabolism. As a result of degradation of complex carbohydrate substances, there is an increase in mucopolysaccharides. As in most instances in which high caloric but low protein and vitamin balances are found, mental deterioration can occur, especially if the imbalance affects the fetus during the last six months of the pregnancy or during the first six months postnatally. In the case of Hunter's syndrome, there is a gradual mental deterioration. For reasons not yet fully understood, these children seem to become hyperactive and irritable. The detection of this condition cannot be made by gross inspection at birth since, at this time, most children with this disease appear to be about normal However, laboratory studies of enzymes, prepared from blood plasma and urine, can be utilized for diagnosis, and therapy can be begun. Such therapy, termed *replacement therapy,* involves a culture prepared from patients with a different type of enzymal disorder that can be introduced into the blood stream of the affected individual.

Hurler's Syndrome. This is a much more severe disturbance than Hunter's syndrome. It involves the accumulation of mucopolysaccharide (containing sugars and uronic acid) in the meningeal membrane (the covering of the brain and spinal cord). As the disease develops, many physical symptoms become evident: dwarfed size, large head (hydrocephalus due to the accumulation of excessive liquid in the brain cavity), enlarged spleen, enlarged liver, and noisy respiration. These are manifestations of the faulty metabolism. Mental and physical deterioration are rapid and severe after the first year of life. Again, as with Hunter's syndrome, new developments in biochemistry may make possible treatment during infancy that was formerly unknown. There are many questions concerning the possible effectiveness of such treatment that only further research and experimental treatment programs can answer.

Nutritional Disturbances

In this section we will discuss disturbances due to faulty nutrition of the mother during pregnancy, and of the infant and child after gestation. *Faulty nutrition* is not simply a matter of inadequate food available, but may involve inadequate balance in food intake required for a healthy pregnancy and for healthy development of the infant. On the other hand, *malnutrition* usually refers to inadequate food intake, which, of course, also may be accompanied by faulty nutrition. As we will see, the problems of faulty nutrition and malnutrition are complexly interwoven with ecological and genetic factors, and the specific effects of each factor are difficult to disentangle and evaluate. It might be thought that nutritional disturbances occur only in impoverished societies, or in countries ravaged by war or pestilence. Even in our own "affluent society," however, malnutrition of children is more widespread than is commonly recognized. We shall turn to this issue first.

Malnutrition in the United States. In 1968, the CBS television network presented a dramatic account of malnutrition in this country (CBS-TV, 1968). It reported that not only is a large segment of our population insufficiently nourished, but also many citizens actually suffered from chronic hunger. It is likely that this program was stimulated in part by the publication of a special report prepared for the President of the United States by a committee of the National Health Institutes (National Association of Health, 1967) and a prior publication "Infant Mortality" prepared by the Children's Bureau of the Department of Health, Education, and Welfare (1966). These reports and programs revealed shocking conditions and were, in some measure, responsible for the initiation of Head Start programs and extensive food programs in the public schools and nursery centers. (We will discuss the Head Start Program later in this chapter.) It was found that many pregnant mothers and thousands of preschool children had insufficient nourishment to meet basic biological requirements. The 1966 report found that the neonatal mortality for nonwhite infants "was 64 percent above that for white infants . . . ", and reported that this gap "between the death rates for white and nonwhite infants became wider in recent years." The 1967 report stated: "The international ranking of the United States in infant mortality has dropped steadily in the past decade. In 1955, the United States ranked eighth with a rate of 26.4 per 1,000 live births. The present rate of

24.8 now places the United States in fifteenth position among the developed countries of the world."

Not only has there been much needless death among infants in this country (due to malnutrition plus unavailable medical care), but also many infants of malnourished mothers who have survived suffer from disabilities and abnormal development, including mental retardation (Kawi and Pasamanick, 1959). Such disabilities tend to strike the lower socioeconomic strata with far greater frequency than other economic strata, and the burden has fallen most heavily on the infants of black mothers, as a study in Baltimore revealed (Pasamanick et al., 1956). Despite some programs initiated by federal and state agencies, the deplorable condition of malnutrition still exists today in a substantial percentage of newborn infants.

Effects of Malnutrition and Faulty Nutrition. The peak of brain development in the fetus is during the third trimester of pregnancy. Malnourished pregnant mothers and their malnourished fetuses often suffer from insufficient nutrients to maintain cortical development of the fetus. There is usually a deficiency of protein and DNA content to maintain such development (Beargie et al., 1970). Moreover, prematurity, which can be caused by inadequate maternal nutrition, results in underweight and undersized newborn children. Although it is not prematurity per se that inevitably results in brain damage and poor cortical development, this is often the case. Moreover, if the infant, whether premature or normal term, continues to receive inadequate nutrition after birth, especially during the first six postnatal months when the brain is still developing rapidly, both intellectual and general development can be seriously affected (Manocha, 1972). In general, the infant with low protein intake is likely to suffer most severely. And if the mother suffers from low protein-caloric malnutrition (termed P–C–M), the mother's lactation may be insufficient for the infant's basic biological needs.

We have indicated that it is difficult to assess the effects of malnutrition alone because of the interaction of many factors that affect the amount of food eaten, the particular diet that is utilized, the health status of the mother, and complications of disease and infections that may be present, quite apart from the nutritional inadequacies. Moreover, the kind of stimulation and the amount of stimulation provided to the developing infant, including emotional and intellectual interactions, differ in varying cultures and in varying socioeconomic strata within a given culture. Such variations in the amount and kinds of stimulation provided involve not only what the baby is fed, but also how the baby is fed, what kinds of physical stimulation are offered during the feeding, the amount of visual and auditory stimulation that is present, and the "tension pattern" between mother and child.

Among the presumed effects of malnutrition, Riccuitti (1973) found that there was poor arousal (inadequate response to stimulation), poor attention, and reduced motivation. In an attempt to elicit the relative contributions of nutrition and type of stimulation, Das and Pivato (1976) have been doing studies of high- and low-caste children (from Brahmins and Harijans, respectively) in India. The research population consisted of nine- to twelve-year-old boys from urban and rural areas. The two groups of high- and low-caste children were selected to be comparable in physical size; each group contained children in the upper fourth in height and the lower fourth in height. All subjects were given a variety of psychological tests, including subtests from the *WISC; Raven's Colored Progressive Matrices; Figure Copying; Memory for Designs; Word Reading;* etc. The researchers concluded that there were significant deleterious effects produced by poor nutrition and associated ecological factors on cognitive performance. The urban group was found to be superior to the rural group on some cognitive tests. The differences between castes were significant and greatest in the rural group. Although they were unable to discover the relative contribution of malnutrition and poor stimulation, they concluded that these conditions, *acting together,* significantly inhibit cognitive functioning and intellectual development.

Another interesting study was reported by Lloyd-Still et al. (1974). In their attempt to disentangle the effects of nutritional and stimulation factors, they studied children with *cystic fibrosis.* These children tend to be malnourished due to their pancreatic insufficiency. The group studied came from the middle class for the most part; it was therefore assumed that they did not suffer from the usual negative effects of socioeconomic deprivation. The study presented findings for these children at various stages of their development. It was found that before age five years, these children performed less adequately on an intelligence scale (*Merrill-Palmer Test*) than their siblings who did not have the disease, but later there were no significant differences between the children with cystic fibrosis and their siblings in intelligence (*WISC*), motor development, and social maturity. This study does point up the capacity of children who have nutritional deficiencies to overcome some of the cognitive (and other) possible deleterious effects when considerable attention is provided and adequate compensatory training and stimulation are offered. It does not suggest, however, as some seem to have concluded, that serious nutritional deficiencies can be entirely compensated for.

As we have suggested, all of the evidence to date indicates that faulty nutrition can have seriously deleterious effects on the fetus during the critical periods occurring during the last six months of pregnancy and during the first six months postnatally (Manocha, 1972; Winick and Rosso, 1967). The findings of Wigglesworth (1969) that fewer brain cells and retarded brain development accompany malnutrition, and that uterine malnutrition in the mother causes malnutrition in the fetus and accompanying placental disorders (Gruenwald, 1963) have never been disputed. On the other hand, massive and persistent intervention programs, supplying appropriate nutritional supplements including a high caloric diet and appropriate medical care can dramatically reduce the incidence of prematurity, infant mortality, and many of the deleterious physical and mental effects that might otherwise have been expected (Klein et al., 1977). We cannot agree with the conclusion of Robinson and Robinson (1976) that "Within the range of nutritional deprivation likely to be encountered in the developed nations, ... diet apparently plays a minor role in producing irreversible CNS changes [changes in the central nervous system] and consequent mental retardation." Our conviction to the contrary, despite our knowledge that malnutrition and/or faulty nutrition and social-cultural effects tend to be interactive, is buttressed by clinical and experimental evidence from studies on rats (Chase, et al., 1971; Winick and Rosso, 1973) which clearly reveal such effects as gross reduction in number of brain cells, defects in myelin growth of the brain, and imbalanced growth of the cerebellum.

POSTNATAL BRAIN DAMAGE AND DISEASE

We have deviated somewhat in this classificatory category from the proposal by Grossman. Grossman calls this category "Gross Postnatal Brain Disease." Damage to the brain, however, may occur before birth, as we have seen, and in addition some of the effects of such damage may not be evident until later in the life of the infant or child. Moreover, the damage may be the result of some gross impact on the brain (such as that produced by anoxia) or it may be the result of a disease process. Similarly, damage or disease affecting the brain may occur postnatally, but the conditions that make this damage possible may already have been "set" before birth. It is admittedly difficult to separate these various conditions in an entirely satisfactory manner. For these and didactic reasons we prefer to discuss under one caption all types of damage to the brain in which the major effects occur after birth.

Types of Brain Damage

There are two major types of brain damage: *histogenic* and *chemogenic*. *Histogenic* refers to lesions of the brain; *chemogenic* refers to the deleterious effects of some toxic agent. Toxic effects, in turn, may be the result of a disease process (as in the case of encephalitis, commonly called "sleeping sickness") or the result of the introduction into the system of some poison from an external source. On the other hand, lesions to the brain may result from physical injury, or from disease, or from degenerative cellular changes within the brain. In both histogenic and chemogenic damage, the brain damage may be either grossly visible or microscopic.

We have previously discussed tuberous sclerosis, a condition in which, in the classical form when the results are quite grave, tumors develop in the brain (as well as elsewhere). Such tumors are clearly histogenic, yet the causative factor is a dominant gene. There are other conditions in which lesions of the brain may produce mental retardation. One of these is chorea. In the classical form, *Huntington's chorea,* the evidence suggests that inheritance of a congenital predisposition due to a dominant gene is responsible. This disease is symptomatically characterized by choreic movements (involuntary, jerky movements), usually becomes manifest in the third decade of life or later, and in its classical form leads to severe mental deterioration, including severe mental retardation and psychosis (of the schizophrenic type).

Now let us examine some more common examples of histogenic and chemogenic involvements.

Histogenic Involvements. Perhaps the most common histogenic disorders of children resulting in mental retardation are those involving direct brain damage. Research studies have shown that despite popular belief, blows to the head seldom cause this kind of brain damage. Slight injuries to the brain from accidental blows on the head are not rare. Many persons—probably all of us—have at one time or another suffered a severe blow. But usually, there are no significant aftereffects. Yet if parents note that their child is functioning at a retarded level following such an accident, they all too frequently attribute the condition to a "brain injury" caused by the accident. It is easier and more comfortable to do this than to look for less obvious reasons.

Siegal (1953) has classified the various forms of injury that may occur to the brain. These are: (1) concussions, caused by a blow to the head, the effects of which are disseminated throughout the brain rather than localized; (2) contusions in which there is a definite lesion; (3) lacerations; and (4) hemorrhages, which may be mild or extensive enough to involve the entire brain.

Brain damage that occurs before the age of three years may lead to a condition in which the child is unable to control his muscular movements. Both large and fine muscular controls may be impaired. There may be spasmodic jerkings of the hands, head, or feet, and voluntary movements such as reaching for an object are very difficult to perform. This condition is known as *cerebral palsy.* The extent of the motor involvement may vary from slight impairment to the most severe, where no voluntary controls can be maintained. Sometimes the child may drool, and there may be very severe speech difficulties.

Although children suffering from cerebral palsy may be of average or even superior intelligence, the incidence of mental retardation is very high. Approximately half of such children tested have been reported as mentally retarded (Goodenough, 1956). This is, of course, a far higher percentage than is found in the general population.

Probably the most common cause of histogenic brain involvement in children is birth trauma—the so-called *birth injuries.* Sometimes physical damage that occurs during the birth process is very important in causing mental retardation. The birth process often is violent and may produce, in addition to its psychological effects, physical trauma with far-reaching consequences. Despite the plasticity of the child's brain at birth, prolonged labor, severe physical stress or pressure, or the use of instruments may cause serious injury to the brain. Hemorrhage may result, for example. Many studies have demonstrated that birth injury may produce mental retardation as one of the consequences (see Sechzer, Faro, and Windle, 1973).

As Whitney (1955) states, birth is one of the most acute emergencies encountered by a person during life. He summarized the types of common birth injuries that may lead to mental retardation as follows: (1) asphyxia (lack of oxygen); (2) injuries to the cerebrum; (3) peripheral nerve injuries; (4) fractures and resulting complicating factors; (5) soft tissue damage; and (6) injuries to the viscera.

Although medical care now is greatly improved generally and there are safeguards against injuries and oxygen disturbances during the birth process, the lower socioeconomic strata often do not have adequate medical care, and significant birth damage may occur. Even under the best of medical care, there may be birth damage. The most common forms of such damage are *hypoxia* (a condition in which there is a physiologically inadequate supply of oxygen to the tissues) and *oxygenation* (saturation with oxygen). As we have learned from our previous discussion, an insufficient supply of oxygen may be available to brain tissue due to external causes (*anoxia*). But there also may be an inadequate use of oxygen due to deficiencies of the organism. Graham et al. (1963) studied 116 preschool children born at full term but hypoxic and compared them with 239 preschool children on the basis of a variety of tests and clinical observations. Thirty-six of the hypoxic children had suffered no other complications at birth; the remainder did have some other complications. It was found that the hypoxic children revealed more frequent neurological disturbances and showed poorer perceptual and cognitive functioning than did the other children. They also were rated lower on several personality measures. As a group, however, they did not show such other signs of brain damage as hyperactivity and impulsivity; some of them did. The results clearly indicated the adverse effects of the hypoxia, but it was not clear why more hypoxic children did not reveal other signs of brain damage. It is possible that some suffered only minimal brain damage and that some were able to compensate for such damage.

Excessive administration of oxygen is, fortunately, now quite rare during the birth process. During the birth process, excessive administration of oxygen can cause damage to the new organism, especially if the baby is premature. One study investigated the effects of prolonged use of oxygen during the birth process (Bender and Andermann, 1965). Infants who had been exposed to such conditions frequently showed such after-effects as blindness and mental retardation.

The developing human organism at birth is vulnerable to many kinds of "insult," although it is remarkably plastic and capable of resistance if it is otherwise healthy. Thus, once again we can see that, even in instances of trauma to the organism, the interaction of the organism and its environment is responsible for possible adverse effects.

In a comprehensive study of the effects of anoxia on the subsequent development of the child, some interesting and challenging results were obtained. Thirty cases of anoxia were selected for study from over 40,000 babies born at the Chicago Maternity Center (Benaron et al., 1960). Of these 30 babies, 24 had *severe apnea* and 6 had *moderate apnea*. (Severe apnea is indicated when the baby does not breathe within thirty seconds of birth, is either livid or pallid, and appears dead.) The duration of apnea was from ten to thirty minutes for nineteen of these babies, and longer for the rest. The "experimental" children, who were examined at ages three to nineteen years, were compared with two groups of control children, matched for sex and age. One group consisted of siblings; the other, of nonsiblings. All of the mothers of the control groups had experienced natural labor. A variety of tests (including three different tests that could yield measures of intelligence) were administered. The finding of greatest pertinence to us was that 20 percent of the experimental group measured mentally retarded on the intelligence tests, as compared with 2.5 percent of the control groups.

This and related results caused the authors to conclude that "severe anoxia *may have deleterious results* in later life [italics ours]." The fact that not all severely anoxic children later became retarded reinforces the conclusion that it is not the organic deficit alone that may produce deficiency in intellectual functioning, but the way the whole organism reacts to the damage. This conclusion also is reinforced by another surprising finding, namely, that there were four anoxic children with *superior* IQs (over 110) in the experimental group, but none in the control groups.

Although this latter finding is not statistically significant, it and related findings point up the complicated and interactive way in which *various factors* contribute to the end result. If, indeed, it turns out that proportionately more children who had anoxia than those who experienced normal birth have superior IQs, one would have to consider how this came about: whether the organism, in defending itself against the severe trauma, compensated by developing more rapid maturational growth tendencies; whether the complicated biochemical adaptation to anoxia produced both favorable and unfavorable results in all or in only some cases; whether the special, intensive care given to anoxic babies contributed significantly to their pattern of development; and so on.

Chemogenic Involvements. As noted earlier, chemogenic involvements result from the effects of various toxic agents on the brain tissue. They include reactions to poisons taken into the body (such as alcohol and carbon monoxide); poisons resulting from internal physiological malfunctionings (such as endocrine disturbances); toxic effects of various disease processes (such as encephalitis); and lack of an adequate oxygen supply to the brain tissues. It might well be argued that there is destruction of tissue in chemogenic instances as well as in those that we have described as histogenic. There is, in fact, much overlap between the two classifications, but we may distinguish between the two on the basis of *primacy* of cause. If there is no chemical change preceding the damage, then it may be regarded as histogenic. Such a distinction, of course, is somewhat arbitrary.

Lippman et al. (1958) have reviewed some of the more important aspects of the biochemical bases of mental deficiency. According to these researchers, differentiation should be made between conditions resulting from hereditary biochemical defects and those resulting from a biochemical trauma to the fetus. In either event, however, the behavioral anomalies that result tend to be quite similar.

When such conditions affect the neurological mechanisms, they have far-reaching consequences. One of the diseases affecting children is *encephalitis lethargica*. The first serious study of this condition was made by von Economo in 1917, during the time of the great epidemic in Europe. The disease reached epidemic proportions in the United States in 1918. At that time it often was confused with influenza. Mild attacks of the disease may go unnoticed, but the behavioral residuals, such as increased irritability, aggression, and dependency, may be very serious. The mental retardation that often results also may be profound. The specific bacterial agent responsible for the disease has not yet been definitely isolated, but it is thought to be a filtrable virus. The disease may take many forms and may be either acute or subacute. It may be ushered in slowly and may be accompanied by prolonged sleep or lethargy, delirium, or various eye complaints. There may be muscular contractions ranging from tics to convulsions, or there may be postacute symptoms of overtalkativeness and hyperactivity. The extent of the resultant intellectual impairment is proportional to the involvement, and careful psychological handling, either under the supervision of a psychiatrist or a clinical psychologist, is usually desirable to deal most adequately with the aftereffects.

A number of infections and viruses are important developmentally. One of these is *syphilis*. If there is spirochetal (a type of spiral microorganism) invasion of the nervous system of the fetus, mental retardation, along with other symptoms, may result. At one time, syphilis was an important causative factor in mental retardation, but with the advent of premarital tests for syphilis and other public health measures, it declined drastically in importance. Unfortunately, a recent increase in venereal disease has made syphilis a more serious causative factor again.

A type of viral infection that was at one time thought to result in a very high percentage of death and congenital anomalies of babies is *rubella* (German measles). Some investigators reported such sequelae in 50 to 75 percent of rubella cases if the fetus contracted the disease within the first trimester. However, more recent studies have shown that other factors were not adequately considered, and the percentage is now given as about 10 percent (Skinner, 1961). The symptoms of rubella in the infant may occur in various organs or systems, but for our purposes it is worth noting that rubella associated with the first trimester accounts for mental retardation in about 50 percent of such cases. Rubella was first shown to be a congenitally significant condition when an Australian ophthalmologist found that many babies with cataracts had mothers who had contracted rubella during their pregnancy. There are a number of methods of treatment, including vaccination and passive immunization (which requires giving the pregnant mother a serum taken from babies who have rubella).

One type of flu, *cytomegalic virus,* may cause mental retardation (Weller and Hanshaw, 1962). The consequences of other types of flu are, fortunately, less serious, so far as we know.

Rh Factors. Rh factors are complicated substances that occur in the red blood cells of the majority of people. These substances consist of protein molecules that enable the body to "recognize" what is normal for the body and what is an "invader." The body forms antibodies to combat the "invaders." People with Rh factor have Rh-positive blood. People lacking the Rh factor have Rh-negative blood. When a mother with Rh-negative blood has a baby with Rh-positive blood, the mother begins to develop anti-Rh antibodies. With later pregnancies, the number of antibodies increases. Thus, after the mother's quantity of antibodies has increased sufficiently (usually after the first pregnancy), the mother's body begins to attack the Rh-positive blood of the infant she is carrying. Such a baby has a jaundiced appearance at birth. An analysis of the blood of the baby and the mother will reveal the incompatibility of their blood types, and the baby's condition can be corrected by blood transfusions of Rh-negative blood. If this is not done, the baby's development may suffer severely.

In recent years, other methods of treatment for this condition, other than through blood transfusions, have been developed. The first modification involved the administration of antibodies (anti-Rh antibodies) from the blood of mothers who had previously been sensitized by Rh-positive blood transfusions. As immunization programs decreased the number of such sensitized mothers, it became necessary to find other means of immunization for remaining mothers. This has been accomplished by the immunization agent (called *Rhogam*), which is produced with the use of volunteer males with Rh-negative blood who are injected with Rh-positive cells.

The incidence of the Rh factor as a cause of physical and mental abnormalities (known as *kernicterus*) used to be as high as .5 percent (Clarke, 1973) for all pregnancies. Fortunately, its incidence has been sharply reduced in this country and can be entirely eliminated by appropriate intervention. Thus, it now is possible to control one possible cause of mental retardation.

INFECTIONS AND INTOXICANTS

As we have indicated, the brain of the fetus is most susceptible to damage from infectious or intoxicant agents carried by the mother during the first three months of pregnancy. Although the placental barrier usually is able to protect the fetus, acute conditions may produce irreversible damage. We have discussed some examples of disease processes that affect the fetus, such as rubella and syphilis. When damage to the fetus occurs during the first trimester of development, when it is most vulnerable to infection and toxic conditions in the mother, damage can be very severe. Not too long ago, we witnessed the horrendous effects of the administration (especially in Germany) of thalidomide to pregnant mothers. Thalidomide is characterized as a mild drug, yet mothers who took this drug during early pregnancy bore babies with severe physical deformities. Every once in a while we hear of other toxic agents (teratogenes) that carelessly or inadvertently get into the blood stream of pregnant mothers, with horrible effects on their newborn children or on their pregnancies. In Michigan, such an agent, polybrominated biphenyl (PBB), was inadvertently mixed in the grain of farm animals. The infected cattle transmitted this poison to mothers, who ate meat that was infected with as yet not fully known results in the offspring but with sufficient evidence to indicate that much harm has resulted.

Hence, although the placental barrier helps prevent damage to the fetus, it is not an impermeable barrier. About twenty drugs are known to cause fetal abnormalities (Shepard, 1974). In general, antibiotic drugs, cortisone, quinine, sedatives taken in large amounts, methadone, morphine, and heroin can severely and adversely affect the fetus, especially during the first three months of pregnancy (Blatman, 1974). Tranquilizers, too, taken during pregnancy can increase the incidence of mental retardation and physical abnormalities of the newborn (Milkovich and Van den Berg, 1974).

The baby and young child also can be seriously affected by the ingestion of poisons, even if these are quickly removed from the system. One of the most serious conditions that produced irreparable damage to the central nervous system of young children was lead poisoning. Babies would lick or chew materials coated with paint containing lead and develop lead poisoning. Fortunately paints no longer are made with a lead base, but lead paint is still present in old furniture and the walls of old buildings.

We also should mention that anesthetics administered during labor can produce damage to the fetus. In recent years, the use of anesthetics during the birth process has been discouraged and, when necessary, their use is much more carefully monitored.

TRAUMA AND PHYSICAL AGENTS

Grossman includes within this category any of the physical factors that can cause damage to the developing fetus as well as during perinatal and postnatal periods. We have presented evidence concerning the effects of injury to the brain resulting from such conditions as physical injury to the brain, inadequate or excessive oxygen, and chemical agents.

Another factor that can produce damage to the developing fetus is X-ray irradiation of the mother. There is some evidence to indicate that excessive exposure of the pregnant female to X-ray irradiation is associated with certain forms of mental retardation. Murphy and his co-workers (Murphy, et al., 1942) investigated this relationship and reported that 51 percent of the children of 53 mothers who received X-ray therapy during pregnancy were in some way abnormal. Of the total group of children, 26 (or 49 percent) were classified as microcephalic. On the other hand, only 4 percent of the children of 256 mothers receiving such treatment before a pregnancy were abnormal. Only one child in this latter group was diagnosed as being microcephalic. Courville and Edmondson (1958) state that mental deficiency resulting from exposure of the fetus to X-ray radiation is not rare, but they cite 60 such cases that have been reported in the literature. They believe that the clinical picture tends to be constant for such cases, being that of microcephaly. These findings have been substantiated by other workers.

Care is now taken to prevent undue or unnecessary X-ray irradiation of pregnant mothers, especially during critical stages of pregnancy. However, when X-ray or other forms of intense radiation are experienced by mothers during such periods, as when Hiroshima and Nagasaki, Japan, experienced massive atomic bombings, there was a high frequency of infants with mental retardation (accompanied by microcephaly in some cases) in comparison with expected frequencies (Wood et al., 1967).

GESTATIONAL DISORDERS

Disturbances during the gestation period can result in prematurity or postmaturity. We have discussed the causes and consequences of prematurity. We should add that one negative consequence of prematurity, apart from the hazardous condition of the newborn due to inadequate physical development, is that such babies frequently were placed in incubators and were not given any form of sensory stimulation. During normal parturition, the baby is provided with normal stimulation within the womb, due to metabolic activity of both mother and fetus and due to the mother's activities. Since many premature babies seem to develop in slower or even in a retarded manner, it has been thought that some of this slower growth might be counteracted by providing the prematurely born infant with special stimulation as soon after birth as is feasible. Studies completed thus far have yielded equivocal results concerning gains that stimulation provided by the nursing staff or by mothers (e.g., Powell, 1974). Such stimulation has involved sensory activities for the babies or closer emotional interactions between mother and child. The evidence does indicate that there is greater-than-expected development of the infant after birth, but the relative gains are not maintained. The reasons for this are not at all clear at this time, and better and longer-term follow-up studies are needed.

RETARDATION FOLLOWING PSYCHIATRIC DISORDER

This category includes cases of mental retardation that are associated with psychiatric disorder in the parents, especially in the mother. Psychiatric disorder usually is taken to mean that the condition is one of a severe neurosis or a psychosis (such as schizophrenia). There is little definitive evidence concerning the possible effects of such conditions on the child during early periods of development. Beier (1964) did conclude that there were more cases of mental disorders among the retarded than in the general population, and he found schizophrenia, especially, to be more common. However, he did not attribute a causal role to mental disorders in the production of mental retardation.

Our view is that much more than severe psychiatric disorder is involved in the possible connection between emotional health and mental retardation. The emotional health and adjustment of the mother (or parental surrogate) and its effect on the development of the child have been studied extensively in developmental studies of both normal and abnormal children; we shall refer to such studies and their implications in chapter 6. It is possible that it is not the emotional disturbance of the parent per se that may contribute to the infant's retarded development, but rather the interactive effect of such disturbances with other factors in the environment and other factors within the child that contribute to possible impairment in cognitive and adaptive development. Put in simplistic form at this point for didactic purpose, the more vulnerable the child, and the less adequate the sensory and emotional stimulation provided, the more likely is it that some or all aspects of personality development will be retarded. Retardation may be experienced in motoric development, in sensory development, in cognitive development, and in social-adaptive development, or in all of these spheres.

ENVIRONMENTAL INFLUENCES

We have seen that mental retardation may be accounted for in about 80 to 90 percent of all cases by "environmental factors." These cases have been termed *cultural-familial,* but now are usually called *psychosocially disadvantaged.* Such factors as the following may be included within the complex of environmental influences: deprivation of cultural stimulation, especially in the early, formative years; low socioeconomic status with its accompanying inadequate nutritional conditions; emotional stress within the family, and especially from the parents; inadequate sensory-motor experience; low level of aspiration within the family; inadequate verbal stimulation; inadequate interpersonal experiences; inadequate social stimulation and social acceptance; and, inadequate intervention measures (medical, social, intellectual) to compensate for or to correct faulty or inappropriate patterns of behavior or intellectual development. These factors are considered so important that we shall devote an entire chapter (chapter 6) to presenting developmental patterns of growth and adjustment.

PSYCHOLOGICAL EFFECTS OF BRAIN DAMAGE

We have discussed various forms of brain damage to children, ranging from direct injury to brain tissue to damage resulting from the interaction of very complex internal processes. When the large body of literature on brain damage to children is reviewed, we find that there is a marked overlap in the effects of different types and degrees of such damage. For example, the damage to intellectual functions is not significantly different in chemogenic and in histogenic disorders. There are, however, certain basic considerations that may be summarized from such studies.

First, the specific impairment in intellectual functions is related to the area of the brain damage, regardless of the cause of the damage. Even though very little is known, comparatively speaking, concerning the characteristics of various areas of the brain, certain areas have been related to specific functions. The visual, hearing, touch, pressure, speech, and motor areas have been fairly well defined and localized, although the major portion of the brain is still an unexplored region. However, experimental work is difficult. As Cobb (1944) pointed out, for example, lesions destroying exactly the same areas in two different brains might not result in exactly the same symptom. The effects depend on the personality and general physical characteristics of the particular child, as well as on the area of the brain involved. The residual damage may vary from very severe intellectual impairment, in which the child functions at the lowest mental level and requires complete and constant care, to very mild impairment, in which there are only slight aftereffects involving intellectual functioning. For example, a child may function very well in most other respects, but develop a reading disability because of a birth injury that produced a mild and diffuse hemorrhage.

It is clear, however, that brain-damaged children tend to perform lower on measured intelligence than comparable children without such damage (Bortner and Birch, 1969, 1970; Reitan and Boll, 1973). Once such damage has occurred, the general level of intelligence tends to be as constant as is that of other children, except in instances in which specific effects of damage of a more limited kind (such as motoric functioning and perceptual speed) can be overcome or compensated for by intensive remedial training. It also has been shown that damage to the dominant hemisphere of the brain (usually the left hemisphere) tends to have much more adverse consequences for those aspects of cognitive functioning dependent on linguistic skills and abstract reasoning (Reitan and Boll, 1973; Hutt, 1977a). Note that we have stressed the qualifier "tend" to all of our general conclusions. We have done so because although we have tried to summarize the generalizations from a variety of studies, there are many exceptions depending on the kinds of factors we have noted.

The brain damage, even when it produces no deficit in intellectual functioning, may cause extensive changes in emotional reactions, which then produce impaired intellectual functioning. The child then may function at a somewhat lowered intellectual level and appear to be mentally retarded even though he may still possess average or even superior intellectual capacities. Organic brain-damaged children generally tend to have lowered memory and attention spans. They tend to respond impulsively, and they cannot tolerate tensions. They are restless and engage in excessive motor activities to discharge their tensions. Depending, of course, on the age at which the injury occurred, the child's psychological reactions to the injury may be profound.

Third, as we have repeatedly stressed, the child reacts to his organic brain damage as a unitary organism. It is not only intellectual factors, but *all* aspects of the child that are involved. This conclusion has been particularly stressed by Goldstein (1942) in studying brain-damaged adults. Goldstein points out that an injury to the brain produces deep changes in some of a person's performances; the individual no longer can do things in the same way or as well as formerly. The individual becomes a different person in many respects, both behaviorally and in basic personality characteristics.

It is possible that brain damage producing significant decrements in behavioral functioning may be insufficient in extent to be detected by the usual neurological examination. Further, the behavioral reactions resulting from slight damage may be different from those resulting from extensive damage to the brain.

Knobloch and Pasamanick initiated research into this area (1959). They hypothesize what they term a *continuum of reproductive casualties,* which postulates a fatal component of cerebral damage and a sublethal component that results in a series of syndromes, depending on the degree and location of the cerebral injury. Three specific prenatal and paranatal factors are associated with this continuum: (1) premature birth, (2) toxemia, and (3) bleeding during pregnancy. To investigate the effects of more minimal brain damage, Knobloch and Pasamanick compared 500 premature babies with 492 normal infants up to forty weeks of age.

They found that the premature babies manifested evidence of cerebral damage by the presence of clear but minimal deviations from the normal neurological patterns. Of considerable significance was the finding that these deviations were more or less compensated for neurologically by the age of fifteen to eighteen months. Behaviorally, the premature children showed an increased incidence in sucking, hypertonicity, hypotonicity, twitches, convulsions, feeding problems, and crankiness over the normal infants.

One additional finding also is of considerable importance. Knobloch and Pasamanick concluded that the degree of tension manifested by the mothers of the premature children was positively related to the degree of neurological damage present; that is, the greater the extent of the damage to the brain tissue, the more tension was manifested by the mother. It may well be that the adjustment of the brain-damaged child to the damage is made more difficult by the tension state of the mother.

We have seen that the effects of organic damage to the same brain area vary in different children so greatly that we cannot adequately predict what psychological defects will result from damage to a specific area — or, conversely, we cannot predict precisely the area of damage from a knowledge of the symptoms alone. It thus is a mistake to talk about the "brain-damaged child," as many people do. It is a *specific child* who shows such a condition. That child's reactions to the organic brain damage, how the child deals with changed conditions, the behavioral reactions engaged in, and the altered emotional reactions shown are all functions of the total personality. *What must always be considered are the total reactions of the child to the damage.*

THE ROLE OF HEREDITY AND CULTURE

Society always has been prone to attribute most maladaptive forms of behavior to the presence of an inherited trait. Criminal behavior of the adult and delinquency of the child often have been wrongly ascribed to heredity. Mental retardation is no exception to this tendency. Such common remarks as "It's in the blood" and "It's inherited" reflect the attitude and ignorance of the public. As we pointed out in chapter 1, Dugdale's work on the Jukes family was immediately interpreted by the public as proof of the inheritance of complex behavioral maladaptations, even though his findings provided no evidence for such a conclusion.

Actually, we know very little about the inheritance of intellectual characteristics, although there has been a great deal written on the subject.

There are many obstacles to adequate research on this topic. Difficulties arise because of the complex nature of intelligence and of mental retardation itself and because of the technical problems in exploring any area of human genetics.

Several factors make investigation of mental retardation very complex. One concerns the criteria by which retardation is determined. We have seen that a single test of intelligence is insufficient to establish the diagnosis. And in many investigations, the researcher does not have direct access to the subjects under study and so does not have even one test that can be interpreted directly. Instead the researcher must *estimate* the degree of deficiency by studying judgments made by someone who does know the subjects. Such judgments are influenced by the criteria employed by the judge, as well as by that person's adequacy as a judge. Moreover, the ratings made by a judge in past years, whether based on a single test score or on a number of test scores, may have little validity for the current period, since criteria of mental retardation vary with time.

Another factor that complicates investigation is the heterogeneity of the phenomena of mental retardation. Retarded persons do not, in fact, constitute a homogeneous group; a variety of biological and sociological conditions contribute to retardation. If a single type of mental retardation is selected for study, or if a single trait of the mentally retarded person is selected, the results obtained are not generalizable for other types or traits. Similarly, if a particular level of retardation is studied, the conclusions may be at variance with those obtained from other levels.

Still another problem concerns the methodology that can be employed in such studies. In research on animals this problem is readily solvable, but experimental manipulation of human beings for breeding purposes cannot be attempted. Other types of controls in research also are difficult to apply. For example, since human beings do not mate at random, the methods of statistical analysis that depend on random sampling are not appropriate. It also is difficult to measure precisely the relative effects of environmental factors on behavior, just as it is difficult to control for variation in environmental influences by statistical means.

These and other difficulties in research on the role of heredity encourage a spurious interpretation of the results according to the bias of the investigator.

We shall review and summarize representative and significant studies on the *relative effects* of heredity and environment on the development of intellectual functioning; but before doing so, it might be well to present several critical propositions concerning the subject matter under review.

Some Basic Propositions

1. *Intelligence is not a unitary phenomenon.* We have seen (chapter 2) that intellectual functioning can be subsumed under a number of different factors. Moreover, the number and nature of these factors differ depending on the investigator, the measuring instruments that are employed, and the type of population studied, among other things. Hence, to speak of the "inheritance of

intelligence" is misleading. More properly, we might speak of "the relative effect of hereditary influences on a designated 'intellectual trait.' "

2. *The factors that are included within the rubric "intelligence" are largely a matter of definition.* In the contemporary scene, we are likely to assume that such "cognitive" functions as judgment, abstraction, and linguistic skills (functions that are clearly related to academic learning) are to be included in the realm of "intellectual functioning." Although factor analytic studies have helped determine which traits "belong together" (and, we might add, under certain specified conditions), they have not and cannot determine which traits we wish to specify as "intellectual" or "nonintellectual." Consider, for example, what might have been included in the intellectual domain in the Stone Age. Might not motor strength and motor coordination have been considered evidence, then, of superiority, even of intellectual superiority? In recent years, we have begun to judge that some basic sensori-motor processes (or schema, if we follow Piaget's thinking) are important components of intellectual development in the formative years.

3. *Environment is not a unitary phenomenon.* We are accustomed to speak of "inferior environment" and "superior environment" as if these environments differed in a single, quantitative characteristic. Children from "deprived environments" may be deprived in some, or even in most, significant aspects of their environmental experience, but they may be exposed to other features in their environment that can only be described as "enriched" or "superior." If this thought seems strange, it may simply be that we tend to lump certain features of the environment together as "significant" and dismiss others as "trivial." For example, children from lower socioeconomic strata may be deprived of adequate linguistic experience (although not necessarily so), but they may have enriched physical and motoric experiences (they play rougher and may fight more often). There are relative strengths and weaknesses in every environment.

4. *We should properly think in terms of hereditary tendencies rather than in terms of hereditary traits.* What is inherited is a tendency or a potential toward certain kinds of development (with rare exceptions), but the development of that tendency (whether it is augmented or retarded) depends, in varying degrees, on intrauterine and postnatal environmental circumstances.

5. *Physical, mental, and social development of the organism depends, in varying degrees, on the nature and timing of intervening factors.* Some developmental patterns can be altered, for better or worse, by early and even prenatal interventions; others can be altered, for better or worse, by postnatal interventions. In general, the earlier the intervention and the more appropriate it is, the greater the degree of acceleration or improvement that may be expected.

In examining the research literature that follows, it might be well to keep these five basic propositions in mind.

Research Evidence and Findings
on the Nature-Nurture Controversy

Several studies have used twins as the subjects of their investigations. Sometimes the development of identical twins reared together or reared separately have been investigated. Sometimes findings on identical twins have been compared with findings on fraternal twins and with siblings. In considering the findings of such studies, one should be alert to several problems that plague the interpretation of the results. One is that identical twins do not have exactly the same heredity even though both have developed out of a single egg. Another is that when twins are reared in the same family, they do not necessarily have the same environmental conditions. There may be differentiated patterns of physical care as well as differential patterns of social and emotional interactions. Such differences should tend to decrease the similarities of results obtained in testing them. Still another problem is that when twins are reared separately, the age of separation of treatment, and the degrees and qualities of the differences can exert a significant impact on the findings. And when the results on twins are compared with the results on siblings, then differences in hereditary factors as well as differences in environmental factors need to be taken into account.

Perhaps the classic study in the field was reported years ago by Newman, Freeman, and Holzinger (1937). They analyzed the results on intelligence tests, personality questionnaires, and achievement tests administered to identical and to fraternal twins. They compared the identical twins who were reared together with those who were reared apart. The twins who were reared apart had been placed in different homes at varying ages, and the *differences in the home environments* to which they were exposed were not maximal. Assuming that the twins presumed identical were in fact identical (establishment of this fact is not as simple as it was formerly thought to be) and that they therefore came from the same heredity, an analysis of differences between them associated with differences in their environmental experiences is crucial in determining the limits heredity imposes on intellectual functioning.

The researchers found that, in general, the correlation coefficient in measured intelligence for all of their identical twins was .88, a relationship that is quite high. For fraternal twins the correlation coefficient was .63, suggesting, on the one hand, that heredity plays an important role, yet indicating, on the other hand, that environmental factors are not insignificant.

When the data were analyzed fully, the relative effect of environment became more significant! The researchers found, for instance, that the correlation coefficient on intelligence of identical twins *who were reared apart* dropped from .88 to .77. The differences in intelligence tended to be closely related to the degree of difference in environment. Intrapair differences in IQ ranged from 1 point to 24 points. Thus, taken together, these data indicate the considerable effect of environmental factors.

Burt is another investigator who has studied the intelligence test results with numbers of twins.* He has summed up his findings in two major reports (1957, 1966). In the 1957 study, very high correlations were reported for thirty pairs of twins reared in separate homes from the time of birth. On an adjusted assessment of intelligence, the correlation for the twins was .88. It was .68 on measures of educational achievement. He concluded that although there were both unifactor and multifactors in the inheritance of intelligence, mental retarda-

---

*Recent reports by investigators (see 1977 issues of APA *Monitor*) have cast grave doubt on the validity of his reported findings. It has been suggested that some of his data were "faked."

tion is an inherited characteristic. According to Burt, large deviations in intelligence may be attributed to major genes and smaller variations may be a function of multiple gene effects. He concluded that three-fourths of the total variance in mental ability is due to genetic factors. In the 1966 report, Burt offered findings on fifty-three pairs of identical twins who were separated within the first six months of life and who were reared in relatively different environments. For all twins, the correlation coefficient was .86. For a subgroup of twenty-seven pairs who were separated within the first month, the correlation was .84. He also reported on ninety-five pairs of identical twins who were reared together. For them, the correlation coefficient was .92. Although Burt noted that there was a correlation of .26 between cultural differences and IQ differences, he still maintained that genetic factors were largely responsible for measured intelligence.

Not only did such studies purport to demonstrate that intelligence is primarily a function of genetic factors, but other studies also were offered to show that behavior disorders were correlated with mental retardation and hence that *both* mental retardation and behavior disorders were determined by some pathological physical structure (Neuer, 1947). In commenting on such implications, Anasti and Foley (1948) pointed out that if such relationships were the resultants of a genetic predisposition, the specific limit-setting genetic factors needed to be demonstrated, and such evidence was not available.

Erelenmeyer-Kimling and Jarvik (1963) reviewed the literature on this problem and concluded that hereditary factors could be assumed to account for 50 percent of the variance in intellectual development. However, Jensen (1969) defended the nature side of the nature-nurture controversy and claimed that 80 percent of the variance in intelligence was attributable to heredity. Jensen did acknowledge that extremes in environmental deprivation could *significantly impair* intellectual functioning. Jensen went further and stated that there are innate differences in intelligence between the races, and that, in particular, blacks are inferior to whites. There is the clear implication in the article that Jensen accepts these conclusions as valid, since he makes little allowance for the cultural bias and fallibility of tests and gives no real consideration to contamination of the findings by failure to control for social class. Some workers in the fields of mental retardation, social psychology, and clinical psychology strongly and bitterly attacked Jensen. Resolving the heredity-versus-environment issue is highly important, because certain races and ethnic groups are stigmatized and discriminated against in school and society, which contributes to their cultural deprivation.

The relative effects of both heredity and environment on the development and functioning of intelligence is an especially important, if unsolved, problem. As we shall see, it is clear that inferior cultural and educational experiences can produce a significant decrement in the functioning of intelligence, and if this is so, then we must consider what the limits are within which the forces of hereditary and cultural origin can effectively operate. Because of considerations like this, we have tried to distinguish between *mental retardation* and *mental impairment*. A number of investigators have taken a similar position. For example, Sarason and Gladwin (1958) and Masland (1958) attempt to distinguish between *mental deficiency* (intellectual defects attributable to heredity, disease, or injury), and *mental retardation* (intellectually defective functioning present when an individual fails to use native potentials).

As we have said, there is ample evidence that inferior cultural-educational experience can depress the IQ. Studies of Canal Boat children (who lived in very inferior and socioeconomically deprived circumstances), gypsy children (who had little opportunity for formal schooling) (Gordon, 1924), Kentucky mountain children (who lived in extreme isolation and at low cultural and economic levels) (Asher, 1935), and black children (who moved from inadequate to fairly adequate schooling opportunities) (Klineberg, 1935), have shown how serious this effect can be. In chapter 2, we examined a number of other studies bearing on this problem and indicating, generally, the same kind of findings: namely, that prolonged exposure to inferior cultural experiences serves to depress the IQ as measured on standardized tests.

Other studies indicate that the reverse trend is possible when children are exposed to superior educational or cultural opportunities, especially if this is done at an early age. We shall refer to two classic studies that pointed up this possibility. (See chapters 2 and 12.)

Burks (1928) studied more than 200 foster children who were adopted *before twelve months of age*. On the basis of their known sociological backgrounds, she assumed that these children, who were tested when they were from five to fourteen years of age, would measure, on the average, about 100 in IQ. However, she found that they actually tested, on the average, at 107.4 in IQ, a gain she attributed to their relatively superior foster environments. The change from a very poor home environment to a very superior environment resulted in a shift of about 40 points in IQ. Burks also found that the correlation coefficient between the social status of the true parents and the IQ of the children who had been living with foster parents was only .07; if inheritance plays a major role in determining IQ, the correlation would have been substantial.

Even more revealing is the study by Wellman (1940) on two groups of nursery school children. One group came from homes of low incomes and the other from homes of middle-class incomes. Over one year, both groups gained 6.6 IQ points. That this gain was not an artifact of the effect of practice on the tests, nor was it a temporary effect of an enriched school experience, was indicated by the fact that in follow-up studies, these children tended to retain their improved position on IQ scores.

Other studies, including recent studies on the effects of early intervention programs during the preschool years and before, have highlighted the kinds of changes in intellectual functioning that are possible.

We should like to cite the evidence from a study by Skodak and Skeels (1949). In this study, the intelligence of one hundred adopted children was correlated with the intelligence of their biological mothers. The correlation was found to be .44, a still considerable relationship. However, in a later study by Skodak (1950), it was found that when *unrelated children* were adopted into the same home, their intelligence correlated to the extent of .65, a figure comparable to the correlation of siblings reared together, and close to that of *fraternal twins!*

In a previous study, Skeels (1938) had found that in some cases, when foster children were placed in homes that were superior in socioeconomic status to that of their true parents, the children's IQs rose, and the correlation of their IQs with those of their true parents dropped to about .00.

Ferment was added to the controversy by Skeel's follow-up to his study on mentally retarded children (Skeels, 1966). His findings indicated that children who were placed in adoptive homes of good cultural levels and who were given special attention became normal children, whereas those who had been retained in institutions were significantly less self-sufficient and held menial jobs. Such findings suggest that cultural and emotional factors influence not only measured intelligence but also effective levels of human performance.

Jensen (1969) criticized Skeels's study (which did have methodological problems), stating that Skeels's evidence does not contradict the theory of the inheritance of intelligence and suggesting that the adopted children had been born with normal intelligence but their intellectual functioning had been depressed by extreme cultural deficits.

Nevertheless, recent and more sophisticated studies, in which very early intervention through special educational experiences for the infant and very young child and through involving the mother in such educationally enriching experiences for the child, have clearly demonstrated the positive effects of such programs for disadvantaged children. (See chapter 12.) Thus, Karnes, Hodgins, and Teska (1968) indicated that such programs can have great value in improving the functional level of intelligence. In a program emphasizing special training in linguistic and cognitive skills, an experimental group in contrast with a control group receiving traditional preschool training showed clear superiority in this disadvantaged population. After seven months of such training, the experimental group was superior in intelligence, visual perception, and reading readiness. Other early intervention programs have yielded similar results. Payne and Mercer (1974) summarized some of these gains in evaluating Head Start programs. A long-term program, known as the Milwaukee Project (Garber and Heber, 1973), and a special training program for infants (Lambie and Weikart, 1970) have demonstrated that early and intensive educational experiences can improve intellectual and social skills to a significant degree in "high risk" children (i.e., children who might otherwise be expected to show retarded intellectual development).

It is still too early to write a definitive evaluation of the effects of such efforts, especially over longer-term periods, but it is quite evident that intellectual functioning can be either improved considerably, or can be affected adversely under varying conditions of rearing and training. Differences in the types of experiences provided for infants and young children between low and higher socioeconomic strata have still to be documented adequately and their effects explored fully. A very important contribution to such possible research evaluations has been provided by Kagan (1970). He has isolated a number of significant dimensions in which such strata tend to differ: use of language, mental set, degree and type of attachment (between child and parent), capacity for inhibition, personal sense of effectiveness, expectancy of failure, and types and degree of motivation.

THE NATURE AND EFFECTS OF INTERVENTION

We have seen that many types of intervention can affect the course of development, and even the course of life. Etiology is not fixed and immutable in many, if not most, instances. Genetic counseling may reduce the conception of some children who might otherwise be doomed to irreparable damage and severe abnormality. Counseling and appropriate medical treatment during pregnancy can alter the course of development (more specifically, of maldevelopment) during pregnancy. Nutrition can affect development during the gestation period. The process of birth, with its attendant hazards, physical and emotional, can be affected by a great variety of conditions, some of which we have noted. And following birth, especially during infancy and early childhood, intervention programs involving guidance and training of the mother (and family), intensive training in appropriate sensory, motoric, and emotional experiences, and linguistic and cognitive training—all of these plus effective medical supervision and nutrition, can affect in a positive manner not only physical and mental development, but also can influence the development of attitudes, expectancies, self-evaluation, aspiration, and effectiveness in adaptation to, as still, unknown degrees.

The remaining chapters of this book will examine in detail many aspects of such programs of intervention, trace their outcomes, and attempt to provide a meaningful evaluation.

PART
II

DEVELOPMENT
AND ADJUSTMENT

— 6 —

Development of the Individual

Thus far, we have discussed some aspects of the nature of mental retardation, the nature of intelligence and its manifestations, the prevalence of mental retardation, issues in classifying the retarded, common characteristics of the retarded, and the etiology of mental retardation. We have become aware of the many ways in which retardation may be manifested, the many and interacting factors that may lead to retardation, and some of the factors that may help to prevent or to ameliorate the condition. Implicit in much that has been presented is the conclusion that the personality and social adaptation of the individual are essential parts of the "syndrome" we choose to call mental retardation. However, we have still to delineate what characteristics of the personality and what features of social adaptation are part of or contribute to the condition of mental retardation. Nor have we discussed what is cause and what is consequence.

It is our position that far too little attention has been given to the influence of developmental experiences, in general, and to personality factors, in particular, as they are related to retardation. As we shall see, many studies have demonstrated that mentally retarded individuals, in general, have more behavior problems than the population as a whole. Other studies have shown that degree of psychopathology may be causatively related to mental retardation in some instances. Yet little is known concerning the possible relationships of disturbances in developmental experiences and of emotional disturbances to disability in mental and social functioning of retarded persons. Too little also is known concerning the reverse relationships; that is, how emotional disorders may follow from the condition of mental retardation.

To illustrate the significance of these propositions, consider a sampling of some critical issues. How much and in what way does malnutrition contribute to cognitive impairment or to reduced drive for achievement? Does low socioeconomic status per se contribute to cultural deprivation? Does cultural deprivation contribute to retarded sensory and perceptual development? How does it contribute to inadequate interpersonal skills and to inadequate learning

141

experiences in preparation for later school learning? How do inadequate or traumatic experiences in the first years of life influence self-percept, aspiration level, expectancy of success, communication skills, and capacity to reason? These are some issues that knowledge of normal and pathological development can help us understand more adequately and assist us in constructing appropriate rehabilitative and training programs.

The issues that relate to the possible effects of social and emotional maladjustment are equally relevant. Are some types of mental retardation the result of either social maladaptation or of emotional difficulties? Do emotional difficulties reinforce the syndrome of mental retardation? Do some types of emotional maladjustment masquerade as mental retardation? Can improvement in emotional and social adjustment by appropriate programs of education and treatment reduce the prevalence of mental retardation or decrease the degree of such retardation?

Chapters 6 through 10 address these and related issues. Whenever possible, we will attempt to relate findings and theory concerning these areas to a better understanding of the problems of mental retardation and to specific methods of teaching and training. Some of the implications will be delayed until we discuss educational programs in the chapters that follow Part II.

This chapter will discuss findings and theories concerning individual patterns of development.

EARLY DEVELOPMENT

Prenatal Conditions

We already have referred to some prenatal conditions that may affect the gestation of the embryo and the subsequent development of the organism. At this point, we shall discuss a few of the relatively more common phenomena that may occur during this period.

During pregnancy, the fetus is well protected in its very special environment. The placental membrane surrounding the fetus serves as a barrier against most forms of possible infection. Nevertheless, the fetus can be damaged, and occasionally infections may be transmitted to the developing organism. The most important period during which damage may occur is the first trimester, or the first three months. Generally, the later the damage or infection, the less likely it is to have significant effects. However, each organ or system has its own *critical period* of development. For example, the critical period for the development of the lens of the eye is the second four weeks. For the heart it is the entire first trimester. The brain, on the other hand, has a more prolonged critical period, encompassing the entire nine months of prenatal development, although the first trimester is most likely to be critical.

Infections and Viruses. We have discussed (chapter 5) some of the viruses and infections that can influence the course of the infant's development. Although most of these conditions are now relatively easy to diagnose and to treat, they sometimes occur undetected, especially in families with inadequate access to preventative medical care or with inadequate awareness of their importance. Some of these conditions may have very serious consequences for the child. Others may affect not only the well being of the infant but also the attitudes of the family toward the infant. In turn, even when the physical effects are not, in themselves, serious, the psychological effects may be important.

Other Physical Complications. In chapter 5 we alluded to some physical conditions that affect the fetus. Here, we wish to highlight a few additional complications. One is *ingestion* of drugs by the mother during pregnancy. We noted previously that a startling incidence of this factor occurred some years ago when mothers who had taken the drug *thalidomide* (most of them in Germany, where the drug was frequently prescribed) gave birth to babies who were severely deformed. The effects were most pronounced when the drug had been taken during the first trimester. Many other drugs taken during the same period of pregnancy (e.g., antibiotic drugs, cortisone, and quinine) may affect the physical and neurological development of the fetus, in some cases contributing to mental retardation.

Anything producing *anoxia* (loss of oxygen supply to the brain) in the mother also may adversely affect, sometimes seriously, the development of the fetus.

Prematurity is another condition that sometimes contributes to mental retardation. It is thought to be responsible for about 25 percent of all neonatal deaths and for about 15 to 20 percent of all cases of mental retardation (Gold, 1962). One cause of prematurity is improper or inadequate medical care during pregnancy. Another general factor is *malnutrition*, which we discussed previously. We have seen that the socioeconomic level of the family may contribute to both prematurity and malnutrition, and also that the diverse patterns of living within a socioeconomic status, depending on social customs and patterns of child rearing, may contribute to the maldevelopment of the fetus. In New York City, a study conducted by the Institute of Medicine (1973), showed for example that the mortality rates per 1,000 live births differed dramatically among different ethnic groups and differing educational levels of the mothers. For instance, the mortality rate for black mothers with only elementary education was 50.7, whereas that for white mothers with similar education was 32.8. On the other hand, the mortality rate for black mothers with a high school education was only 31.9, whereas for white mothers it was 14.7. It was suggested that the total care of the fetus is linked to many interlocking factors, but poor care contributes to poor prenatal development and even death of the child at birth.

Excessive Emotional Levels. Folklore contains many unsubstantiated stories of associations between the mother's extreme emotional excitement during pregnancy and the newborn's abnormal birth or development. It has been difficult to obtain rigorous evidence of the effect of maternal emotions on the development of the fetus, but enough is known about the physiological consequences of intense emotion on other biological functioning to make the association a probable one. Experimental work in this area is quite convincing, at least insofar as it applies to animals. For example, Thompson (1957) was able to demonstrate that anxiety states in rat mothers during pregnancy can have significant effects on the birth weight, motor development, and activity level of their babies. In human beings, it has been shown that hypertension in the mother may lead to fetal loss and serious birth anomalies (Montagu, 1950). It also has been shown that mothers who scored high on anxiety questionnaires administered during pregnancy had more frequent complications at the birth of their babies and gave birth to abnormal babies more frequently (Davids, Spencer, and Talmadge, 1961). In such studies, it must be emphasized, the observed associations between the intense emotional state of the mother and the abnormality of the baby also may have been caused by factors the studies did not control for.

Stott (1966) has produced a challenging review of the effects of various forms of stress during the prenatal period. Physical or emotional stress, especially during the later stages of pregnancy, can have a variety of adverse effects on the psychological development of the infant. According to Stott, the stress triggers genetically determined mechanisms, which then bring about subtle impairment of the fetus, particularly in the brain. He pointed out that medical advances have increased the chances of survival of such fetuses and infants more than they have decreased congenital impairment. Unfortunately, this conclusion is still true today.

The Birth Process. We have noted that many factors may influence the course of fetal development. A baby has a genetic inheritance, and that potential is influenced by his intrauterine environment. As his capacities begin to mature and unfold, they may be further affected by the birth process itself. The process of being born is not merely a matter of biological sequences. It is influenced in many ways by the conditions of birth: the physical nature of the birth process, the mother's attitudes (particularly her anxieties), and the medical-physical assistance given during the birth process. Many other factors influence the birth process, such as the effects of cultural attitudes toward birth, the contemporary medical philosophy that may "bend" medical practice in one direction rather than another, and the food intake of the mother. Margaret Mead (1949) noted that the Tchambuli people were aware that external factors could influence the birth process: "The birth is hard, said the Tchambuli, because the mother has not gathered enough firewood."

Our special interest is on the effects of the birth process on the infant. There is little doubt that extreme conditions of birth, such as prolonged labor, excessive or insufficient supply of oxygen to the infant during birth, prematurity or postmaturity, and abnormal birth position may have deleterious effects on the infant's subsequent development. We have noted that *anoxia* may produce retardation in mental development and prolonged infantile behavior (Benaron et al., 1960). But normal birth conditions also may be significant!

Otto Rank (1929), an early psychoanalyst, postulated the position that the shock of birth, even normal birth, was so great for the infant that it created a reservoir of anxiety. He believed that the sudden impact of new stimuli (such as changes in light, temperature, and pressure), plus the separation of the child from its mother, suffused the infant with anxiety, producing relatively persistent anxiety reactions that differed significantly among children. Later, Greenacre (1943) summarized the clinical and research evidence on the relationship between the birth process and anxiety and cautiously concluded: "Variations in the birth process may . . . increase the [organic] anxiety response and heighten the anxiety potential, causing a more severe reaction to later [psychological] dangers in life."

There now is little doubt that both psychological trauma and physical trauma can cause irreparable damage to the neonate and can even cause death if the trauma is severe enough. Years ago, Wile and Davis (1951) demonstrated that increased trauma at birth can produce increased irritability, hyperactivity, and other unfavorable effects in the infant. More recently, Davids, Spencer, and Talmadge (1961) demonstrated that mothers with emotional problems, in comparison with mothers who are better adjusted, have more frequent complications during the birth process, such as unduly prolonged labor and delivery problems. On the physical side, although medical procedures are far more adequate than formerly—especially for more affluent families—complications and serious infections still occur and can produce significant damage to the infant. For example, Shuman, Leech, and Alvord (1974) did a study of 248 autopsies of babies. They found that there was frequent brain damage related to the *use of a soap* that had been used in bathing neonates to prevent infection! The soap (hexachlorophene soap) has since been banned by the Food and Drug Administration. Such toxic agents are especially likely to cause severe harm in babies that are underweight or otherwise malnourished and who therefore are less able to resist infection. When babies suffer less severe damage due to physical and especially psychological trauma, the effects may appear to be less dramatic, but the decreased ability of the infant to cope with subsequent stress (or their greater *vulnerability*) may increase the problems for both them and their mothers in the early phases of development. The baby's limited capacity to respond and develop may frustrate the mother who, in turn, may be less effective in coping with the baby's needs. Thus an inadequate interactional pattern of reciprocal behaviors may be established which further handicaps the baby's development.

The First Postnatal Years

At birth and shortly thereafter, the baby has a repertoire of behaviors—some quite specific and some quite diffuse. The former class of behaviors consists largely of reflexes, such as the eye blinking reflex and the swallowing reflex. These are essentially involuntary behaviors that are automatically evoked by the appropriate stimulus. The latter class consists of dispositional tendencies, such as tendencies to be active, tendencies to be curious about the environment, and tendencies to react passively. These diffuse patterns of behavior are aroused by both internal states and by general classes of external events and are modifiable in terms of the infant's "learning experiences."

Kagan (1969), on the basis of extensive research of his own as well as on the basis of the integration of previous research data, concluded that babies differ in at least four fundamental attributes: vigor of activity; degree of irritability; stimulus satiability (or the rate at which the baby gets habituated with a particular pattern of activity); and threshold of attention change. These congenital characteristics are the consequence of genetic and prenatal experiences and tend to "condition" those who deal with the baby to respond in differential ways. Thus, babies *actively influence* the behavior of those around them, and in turn are affected by the responses that they help to evoke. We stress this point because it seems to us to have far-reaching implications. In short, the baby does not simply mature and unfold its inborn characteristics, but develops in a context, which, in some measure, it helps to create.

But the baby's development is still contingent—in as yet unknown degree—on the external factors that impinge on it. Behavior can be modified by many phenomena. Some of these are: normal growth processes; nutritional schedules and the manner in which such schedules are applied; shock or excessive stress; inconsistencies in life circumstances; disease processes; types and amounts of specific learning experiences; observational or modeling experiences; mediational cognitive processes (especially language and other forms of communication); chemical or biochemical agents; injury or disabling neurological conditions; injury to or loss of sensory organs or mechanisms; externally inhibiting agencies; and types of motivation that are furnished. The baby is not, thus, a preformed miniature of the later adult that will contain all of its "given" characteristics, but is an organism with certain potentials that are modifiable depending on later circumstances. In the case of cultural-familial retarded individuals, in which impoverishment in suitable physical and social characteristics is likely, much of the retardation may be a consequence of such limiting or nonstimulating features of the environment. (See the discussion of early intervention programs in chapter 12.)

We now will review Freud's and Piaget's formulations concerning these early experiences in order to gain some conceptual basis for our later discussion. These are two systematic theories that can assist us in planning more effective training and educational programs.

Freud's position. Freud (1943) proposed that babies have sexual needs that are important to their normal development. This proposition was shocking to Freud's contemporaries, and it is still unacceptable to many clinical workers today, although evidence to substantiate this theory is quite extensive (Hutt and Gibby, 1959). In brief, Freud's position was that the sexual drives are with us from birth to death; that they include the drives for affectional gratification and affiliation; that they take different forms during the several stages of life, acquiring their adult form only after puberty; and—most important of all—that their appropriate satisfaction produces more pleasure and more favorable effects on development than any of the other biological drives.

Freud stated that the first phase of sexual (or more accurately, psychosexual) development, which he termed the oral period, normally lasts for about one and a half years. During this time the infant is chiefly concerned with taking in nourishment and other forms of gratification. This process is centered around the mouth—around the *oral* region. The oral region includes the mouth itself, the immediately surrounding areas, and the upper portion of the gastrointestinal tract.

At first the child takes in nourishment through a process of rather passive sucking. The child's very life depends on such an activity, for the intake of food is vital to existence, but more than nourishment itself is involved. Along with the taking in of the food, the child also "takes in" some of the characteristics of the mother, or mother substitute. Studies have shown that if the mother is, for example, a compulsive person, the child will tend to become somewhat compulsive. A study made by Fries (1946) is interesting. It revealed that when infants are taken care of by compulsive nurses, some of the nurses' tension is somehow transmitted to them and they show more *startle* reactions (reactions to noise or any other sudden stimuli) than those taken care of by quiet, or more composed, nurses.

Much more than the mouth and surrounding areas is involved in the oral development of the child. As the baby sucks on the mother's breast or on the nipple of the bottle, she begins to look at the person who is feeding her. She begins to grasp at the bottle or breast, and so begins to learn to feel. The gratification of the oral needs of the child thus means much more than the intake of sufficient and proper nourishment.

There is ample experimental evidence to substantiate this point of view. When a baby gets insufficient opportunity to suck at the breast of the mother or at the nipple of the bottle, perhaps because of an insufficient feeding period or an inappropriate condition of the nipple (the nipple of the breast may be inverted or the hole in the nipple of the bottle may be too large, for example), the baby will seek to gratify his need to suck by sucking fingers or toes or some other object.

Children also vary in their inborn needs. Some require a greater amount of oral gratification than others (Sterba, 1942). Some persons believe that prenatal conditions may set up particular predispositions. Whether or not the differences are due in large measure to the innate constitution of the child, all authorities agree that variation in oral needs exists. Nevertheless, how a child develops depends greatly on the conditions of training and weaning.

If, when the child is ready to give up the mouth as the primary zone of pleasure and move on to another, he is not encouraged to do so but, rather, is reinforced in oral activities by excessive gratification, he will tend to remain *fixated* at that level. (*Fixation* is the tendency to retain a mode of behavior or to "overlearn" it because of receiving too little or too much gratification from it *when it is the primary mode of satisfaction* in one's maturational development.)

Although we have attempted to present a fair summary of both theory and research evidence concerning a baby's needs, the conclusions we have offered are by no means unchallenged. The major reason for this, apart from the methodological difficulties of providing rigorous controls for the factors involved, is that methods of providing oral gratification interact with the infant's temperament (and strength of drives). Thus, in a well-designed study of the effects of feeding experience, using forty-seven boys and forty-seven girls from the longitudinal Berkeley Guidance Study, Heinstein (1963) concluded that the significance of *single variables* describing the feeding experience was not established. For example, he found that it made little difference whether the baby had been reared with the breast or the bottle as the major source of nourishment.

In contrast, Murphy et al. (1962) studied more complex, general patterns of infant-mother interaction. She found that there were many positive relationships between infant and oral gratification and such behavioral consequences as sense of self-esteem, ability to regulate the impact of the environment, and adequacy of perception. Yarrow (1954) attempted to reconcile these two, apparently opposing, positions. He suggested that frustration of the oral needs during infancy may lead to fixation. On the other hand, excessive prolongation of such feeding experiences also may lead to fixation. His findings imply a *phase-specific* characteristic of these drives. His findings and those of later workers indicate that such phase-specific features differ in different individuals, at least in developmental span. Hence, a flexible schedule in which the mother is sensitively and appropriately responsive to her infant generally leads to the most competent and integrated behavior in the later development of the child. We do not yet know whether retarded children, as a group, differ from other children in this aspect of developmental timing, although we strongly suspect that they do. If so, such children may be slower in gratifying their oral needs. They may need more, but not excessive, gratification until they are able to move on to a higher developmental level.

It appears that a child who has become fixated at a particular developmental level will tend to retain the psychological characteristics of the modes of behavior relevant to that period to an excessive degree. The child will then continue to employ these modes even when they are no longer appropriate. During the oral level of development, the outstanding mode is passivity, and the primary method of gratification of needs by the child is through passive sucking. Fixation at this level leads to overemphasis of passivity in the personality of the child.

Only in recent years have the possible effects of the earliest physical and psychological experiences of the baby (and of the mother and the father) received the systematic and intensive study that is warranted. It now appears that such experiences can profoundly and persistently influence the patterns of subsequent development of the child. For example, a series of studies were carried out by Klaus and Kennell (1976). These investigators studied the effects of keeping the mother with her newborn infant together versus separating them immediately after birth and for the next few days. In some modern cultures, ostensibly for aseptic reasons, babies are separated from their mothers after birth (except for a short "identification" period) and taken care of in hospital nurseries. In a few other modern cultures (such as in Denmark) such practices are not followed. In one of their studies, Klaus and Kennell randomly assigned one group of fourteen mothers and their normal, full-term babies to conditions of prolonged and continuing intimate interactions. Another group of fourteen mothers, also randomly selected, and their babies were assigned to the conventional "routine conditions" of separation. The first group (experimental) arranged to have the mothers given their babies for one hour during the first two hours after birth, and for five extra hours each day for the next three days. The other group of mothers (controls) got a glimpse of their babies at about six to eight hours after birth for "identification," and then had visits with their babies lasting about 20 to 30 minutes for feeding purposes, every four hours. The mothers were matched for age, and marital and socioeconomic status. The babies were equated in sex and birth weight. Both mothers and children were studied during the period immediately following birth and for a subsequent five-year period. During the period immediately following birth, the experimental mothers *fondled* their babies more and had significantly more "en face" (direct visual focusing of mother's eyes with baby's eyes) relationships. At the five-year follow-up, the children from the experimental group had significantly higher IQs and more advanced scores on language tests. The authors concluded: "These findings suggest that just sixteen extra hours of contact within the first three days of life affect maternal behavior for one year and possibly longer, and they offer support for the hypothesis of a maternal sensitive period soon after birth." In other words, the pattern of intimate interactions that is begun directly after birth, with the increased stimulation and communication provided, seems to persist over time and to influence favorably development of the child in a highly significant fashion.

We will have more to say concerning the phenomenon of "bonding" or "attachment" that occurs during early infancy and later infancy, but we wish to emphasize at this point the salience of these early experiences. Condon and Sanders (1974) have shown that the infant "sees, hears, and moves in rhythm to his mother's voice in the first few hours of life, resulting in a beautiful linking of the reactions of the two in a synchronized 'dance' between mother and infant."

This process of linking or bonding or attachment, which is to a large extent species-specific (i.e., there is a preference for linkage to one's own species) has been more clearly delineated in studies by Harlow and by Sackett in studies of monkeys. In general, these studies seem to show that a primary drive, call it love or sex, that is more basic than other drives, such as hunger, needs to be satisfied *if normal development is to occur.* Put in popular terms, love makes it possible for the developing organism to develop curiosity, adapt socially, and thrive in the context of stimulating and satisfying interpersonal experiences that include play, sensori-motoric experiences, and communication. For instance, Harlow (1971) summarized his findings with monkeys raised under differing conditions. In one series of studies, Harlow studied monkeys that were raised with surrogate mothers (monkeys constructed of wire and cloth) compared with monkeys raised with real mothers. Although food and warmth were equally available to both sets of monkeys, those raised with surrogate mothers, with soft cloth covering, clung to them, explored more and seemed "secure," in contrast to those raised with no mothers or wire mothers (without cloth to cling to). Later, Harlow studied the effects of deprivation (i.e., monkeys raised in isolation). Comparisons of monkeys raised under deprived conditions with those raised with cloth mothers or real mothers indicated that deprivation of normal social, maternal contact produced disastrous effects; the more deprivation, the greater the adverse effects. The signs of retardation were many: failure to relate, failure to learn grooming, less curiosity, greater isolation, greater amount of "rocking" activities. Harlow concluded that there was a critical period for rhesus monkeys to establish attachment—the first six months of life—and that failure to establish such attachment with its compendium of physical and social experiences leads to severe damage and retardation. Sackett (1970) showed that rhesus monkeys raised in isolation or only with peers during this critical period later showed a preference for adult rhesus females. Sackett also demonstrated the potency of certain kinds of visual stimuli (pictures of other monkeys in "threat positions") in evoking primary fear responses after 80 days of age. In general, Sackett concluded ". . . partial isolates are deficient sexually, and show low levels of play, environmental exploration, and positive affiliative behaviors. . . ."

These and other studies can be regarded as confirmations of Freud's formulations concerning the significance of: critical periods of development; the importance of satisfying the primary drives involved in love; the importance of significant and stable early interpersonal experiences in providing the base for a wide variety of sensori-motoric experiences to assist the maturational process in normal development. We have referred to the "irreversible effects" of early deprivation. This is the phrase many workers use. However, we shall wish later to examine how and under what conditions such effects are reversible or can, at least, be offset.

During the first few months, the infant continues to use the oral zones to satisfy needs for passively "taking in." Then, gradually, he begins to use them for new purposes. The child begins to put objects into his mouth, and to bite and chew them. During this period, teeth and jaw muscles develop. The child now has a more active means of coping with the environment—a weapon with which he can, for instance, inflict pain or irritation on the mother. He also can expel food that he has taken in—"spit it out." This new phase in the oral period, the so-called biting period, is important in that it marks the beginning of more active interaction between the child and the mother.

The child is now capable of playing a more active part—is less passive and can show both *positive* and *negative* feelings toward objects. (The term *object* includes both inanimate objects [things] and animate objects [animals and people].) Just as the first stage of the oral level, that of sucking, may be regarded as one of *passive* taking in, the second may be regarded as one of *active* taking in. The child often experiences conflict over the use of these two methods, which adds to ambivalent feelings. The way in which the mother responds to the child's need for biting, to the pain inflicted upon her while feeding, and to the ambivalence toward her may have much to do with whether or not the child is fixated at this level.

Fixation at the *oral biting* level has been posited to affect the personality traits later shown by the child. For example, *sarcasm* is associated with fixation at this point. We commonly speak of a person with a "biting tongue," or a "sharp tongue," or we say that the person uses "biting sarcasm."

It is believed that the retarded child, like all other children, goes through these phases of emotional growth. Clinical evidence, however, suggests that the retarded child experiences greater difficulty than the average child in giving up one mode for another. The maturational process is slower, and there is a tendency for such a child to retain immature modes of gratification longer. Such behavior is further reinforced by the attitudes of society in general and the mother in particular.

Weaning presents problems and is a source of irritation to the mother. She feels, perhaps, that the neighbor's child has already given up his bottle, so "why shouldn't my child?" Her irritation thus serves to induce further anxieties in the child. Premature weaning attempts may create severe frustrations and conflicts in the child. These serve to reinforce the fixations of the retarded child at the oral levels. Such fixation tends to perpetuate oral (or immature) traits. It also means that the child is less able to proceed to the next developmental level and to renounce needs for oral satisfaction.

We shall cite three examples of evidence bearing on this general theoretical position of Freud's. One comes from research studies on the effects of early experiences on children's personality development. A study done by Brody (1970) at the Menninger Foundation in Topeka, Kansas, showed that the nature of the infant's feeding experience (that is, how the infant was handled, responded to, and the like) was clearly related to the pattern of behavioral development. An accepting and warm relationship seemed to produce the most favorable outcomes. Another study, by Escalona (1945) indicated that when mothers were high-strung, their babies also tended to be high-strung and were disturbed in the total food-intake process. These studies indicate the kinds of relationships that have generally been established in relatively recent research. In general, such evidence may be taken to indicate that the nature of oral experiences is relevant and important, at least in its immediate effects on the infant's personality development. A third study by Brody and Axelrad (1970) made an intensive analysis of 118 infants and their mothers, measuring aspects of maternal behavior and their effects on the development and the personality of the infants at six weeks, six months, and one year. They conclude: "We have found an empirical relationship between types of mothering and aspects of infant development...." They found that "better" mothering was closely associated with "better" development of the infants, and that "poorer" mothering was associated with "poorer" development.

There is other evidence that deals with the effects of unfavorable, or traumatic, experiences during the first year or early period of life. Again, workers are not entirely agreed on the implications of these findings, but it now seems reasonably clear that separation from the mother, or placement in an institution in which the infant receives inadequate affectional and physical stimulation and gratificaton, may result in adverse personality development. Spitz (1948) was able to show, for instance, that separation from the mother and insufficient fondling and affection could not only retard development but could also actually lead to the infant's death, or at least to severe depression. In fact, a review of the literature on maternal deprivation led one author to conclude that this condition is deleterious and should be avoided if at all possible. Recent studies (see chapter 12) indicate that such deleterious effects are not necessarily irreversible.

Enlightened policy today indicates that when infants have to be separated from their mothers, a good foster mother should be obtained, and if institutionalization is required for some period of time, careful attention should be given to providing the infant with a suitable *mother substitute* and substantial physical stimulation and psychological interaction.

The importance of this problem for mental retardation was, perhaps, best stated in the report of the President's Panel on Mental Retardation (1962):

> The effects on infants of institutional placement in early life has been studied more intensively than any other similar environmental experience. As a result of these findings, more infants are placed in foster homes in preference to institutions. . . . The separation of infants from their mothers or substitute mothers may affect the former adversely. Infants who react negatively to separation live a depressed existence with low physical and intellectual achievement.

All of the evidence suggests that it is quite possible that a considerable percentage of cases of mental retardation result, at least in part, from unsatisfactory emotional experiences during the first year or two of life. This hypothesis has been given far too little emphasis in discussions of mental retardation, in our opinion, with the result that study of the specific mechanisms by which many cases of retardation may be induced has been delayed and ameliorative methods have not been instituted.

Piaget's position. Now let us examine, by way of contrast, Piaget's position to which we have referred previously. Piaget sought to distinguish his views concerning the development of the individual from those of Freud's, stating that there was an antithesis between the two. We do not believe that these theories are in any sense antithetical but rather that they are supplementary. Although Freud emphasized the centrality of instinctual life and the maturational view of development as a consequence of gratification versus frustration of these instinctual needs, he, like Piaget, emphasized the egocentrism of the infantile state (its narcissism) and the gradual development of the personality as it progressed through the several critical stages. Piaget, too, saw the infant as egocentric and the ego state as that of an undifferentiated condition, but he emphasized the sequential nature of the development of *cognitive structures* through which the child got to know both self and the world. Piaget emphasized the successive *schema* that invariably developed and that depended, in large part, on the nature of the specific experiences to which the infant was exposed.

When Piaget speaks of intellectual development, he includes more than is customarily conceived under that rubric; he includes the child's growing self-concept, a sense of competency, and motivation to deal with the external world—although he constantly emphasizes the cognitive features of this development. He suggests that four classes of factors influence the rate of this development: heredity and internal maturation; physical experience; social transmission (education in its widest sense); and equilibration (which we shall presently define). The infant is dominated by diffuse patterns of behavior and its experience is dominated by momentary sensations and motoric responses. This is the period of sensorimotor schema. It is the period of nonsymbolic sense impressions. During this stage, everything is *assimilated* through reflex behavior and sensorimotor experience. Assimilation involves the incorporation of reality into already existing mental structures. As long as assimilation remains the only process, the infant's mind remains unchanged. However, since reality does not continue to "fit" the internal schema, the infant eventually has to learn to *accommodate;* i.e., to learn to "grasp" that there are discrepancies that must be adapted to. This process of accommodation produces changes in the internal structures until *equilibration* is achieved. Equilibrium is achieved by a balancing of assimilation and accommodation and requires energy and *active learning and remembering.* It is emphasized that optimal learning requires *active* learning experiences by the child, as Festigner and Lawrence (1962) demonstrated experimentally. Piaget's view of these early learning experiences is, in one sense, broader than Freud's (Piaget and Inhelder, 1969). Such learning involves experience in all sensory modalities (grasping, sucking, looking, listening, feeling, and the like). Prerequisites for accommodation and assimilation involve presenting the infant (and later, the child) with new experiences with which it is *challenged* and for which it has developed the necessary structures (schemata). Thus, the provision for progressively more challenging sensorimotor experiences and activity by the child in coping physically with these experiences is essential if effective learning is to take place.

Piaget believed that all children go through the same invariable stages of development (Piaget, 1970), but that retarded children demonstrate a slower pace of development and may not reach the highest stages of cognitive development of cognitive schemas. This finding has been confirmed in cross-cultural studies (Bosiclair and Dubreuil, 1974; Pinard and Lavoie, 1974) and in research studies of the retarded and visually handicapped (Stephens, 1977). His emphasis on the critical nature of early sensorimotor experiences as a base for learning and for self-confidence, leading to further skills and motivation in higher order learning, is only now beginning to be fully appreciated by educators (Furth, 1977; Piaget, 1975).

In a peculiar sense, Piaget seems to have neglected the role of emotions and conflict in the development of normal children as well as of retarded children. Affect gets lost, somehow, as focus is placed on cognitive structures and schemata. On the other hand, Freud seems to have neglected the critical role of diverse sensorimotor experiences, and of the psychosocial context of development, as he focused on instinctual development and frustration. In our later discussion, we will attempt to synthesize these theories as we suggest modifications in our remedial and educational programs for the retarded.

First, let us turn our attention to the issue of the development of basic trust and identity in children, and note how this influences subsequent development and adaptation.

THE DEVELOPMENT OF BASIC TRUST AND IDENTITY

The previous section dealing with the possible effects of deprivation on personality development highlighted a problem of great importance. As the President's Panel on Mental Retardation reported (1962):

> The majority of the mentally retarded are children of the more disadvantaged classes of our society. This *extraordinarily heavy* [italics ours] prevalence in certain deprived population groups suggests a major causative role, in some way not fully delineated, for adverse social, economic, and cultural factors. . . . Deprivation in childhood of opportunities for learning intellectual skills, *childhood emotional disorders* which interfere with learning, or *obscure motivational factors* [italics ours] appear somehow to stunt young people intellectually during their developmental period.

It is quite possible that unsatisfactory early experiences, including unsatisfactory emotional experiences, can generate a tendency to avoid coping with the world and its problems; to withdraw from active participation in dealing with one's problems; and to develop far less adequately than would otherwise be the case. *Parents from the more disadvantaged sectors of our society may contribute a disproportionate share of the problems of mental retardation in children, not simply because they are inferior socially and intellectually, but because their severe problems make it more difficult to provide the consistent emotional warmth and security that stimulate children to become curious about their world and to learn about it.*

Some years ago, Erikson (1964) formulated a theoretical explanation of what he termed "basic trust," based on his extensive clinical observations as well as the work of others. He was concerned with the problem of how the infant learns to trust herself, and thereafter the world, so that she is able to express her potentiality rather than to curb it. In recent years workers (Bayley and Schaefer, 1960) have explored the conditions fostering security in the self, calling the personality variable that of *security-insecurity*. This variable refers to the degree of *self-confidence* the individual develops.

Erikson hypothesized that basic trust develops out of the complex of conditions during infancy and early childhood that afford maximal opportunity for action, thought, and expression of feeling *without excessive threat or interference*. Establishing such conditions requires that the infant's needs be met or anticipated with some degree of regularity. It involves not only the satisfaction of biological needs but also an appropriate general pattern of satisfaction of early psychological needs for protection and warmth. As the infant is taken care of in this way, she learns to trust the world and gradually develops appropriate self-confidence. The development of this basic trust in oneself makes possible the use of inner potentials and prevents the blocking of emotional and intellectual development.

A study by Sears and his colleagues (1957), based on intensive interviews with mothers, throws some light on this process. This study showed that one of the two patterns that were most important in determining child-parent relationships and the development of the child's personality was the *warmth* of the mother-child relationship. In homes where the relationship was warm, the child tended to be secure; in homes where the relationship was *cold*, the child tended to be aggressive, had feeding problems, and was generally insecure.

Basic trust seems to be markedly conditioned by the experiences that lead to "bonding" (in the first few weeks) and "attachment" (during the period from four months to about one year). As Bowlby (1969) has suggested, five specific kinds of behavioral activities are at the core of attachment: sucking, crying, smiling, clinging, and following. These are reciprocal activities in which the child and mother interact as each learns the other's pattern of behaviors and accommodates to them. *Eye-contact* has been noted as a highly important ingredient in this process (Wolff, 1963). During these multiple activities between mother and child, the child begins to develop an initial schema that defines the self. When conditions are adverse, as when the infant is separated from the mother after attachment has become established or when there are significant inconsistencies in the pattern of relationships, and the pattern of attachment is disrupted, typical patterns of maladjustment result. As Averill (1968) has shown, this maladjustment is characterized first by *distress and protest* and is then followed by *despair or depression*. Finally, if separation is continuous, the infant will show *detachment* and the condition may lead to very profound disturbance in the personality, including *autism* and *psychosis*.

The foregoing discussion of attachment and separation should not be taken to indicate that only a dyadic relationship between mother and child, consistent over time, is necessary for attachment and healthy growth by the infant. Other patterns also may be satisfactory. In some cultures, the father may assume the caretaker role. In still others, the relationship between mother and child may be supplemented by cooperative, group patterns of living. For instance, in Israel, when children are reared in a Kibbutz, the mother tends to her child's biological and social needs (along with the father), for several hours each day, but during working hours, the child is taken care of in a group by well-trained nurses and given ample experience in socialization (Rabkin and Rabkin, 1969). This pattern seems to be consistent with the needs of the culture and provides, as well, for dyadic and intense relationships between mother and child.

However, as study of cultural differences also demonstrates, when children do not receive intense, intimate, and consistent mothering of some kind, including sensorimotor experiences, retardation in development is likely to result. Ainsworth (1967) compared the development of two groups of Ganda, East Africa, infants raised with differing experiences. In one group, children raised in the bush received much physical contact with their mothers. They slept with their mothers and experienced considerable holding, rocking, and social stimulation. The other group of Ganda children were raised by Western methods in a nearby city. They slept alone in their cribs, were often alone, and had much less sensorimotor experience with their mothers than the bush group. Ainsworth found that the bush group of children was superior to the city group in age of attachment, crawled some seven weeks earlier, and showed accelerated motor development—even superior to that of American infants.

Favorable experiences during these formative months lead not only to healthy attachment and superior sensorimotor abilities, but also to a sense of basic trust and a healthy sense of identity. In turn, this leads to more curiosity about the world, better habits of attention, and greater mastery of bodily functions and aspects of reality. On the other hand, unfavorable experiences can lead to a lack of basic trust, a poor sense of identity, detachment from reality, and slow or poor mastery of bodily functions. If children are endowed with somewhat inferior cognitive potential, one may infer that general retardation of development will be that much more likely and severe if unfavorable conditions during the period of infancy prevail.

PERCEPTUAL ADIENCE–ABIENCE
AND PERSONALITY DEVELOPMENT

Considerations we have discussed thus far are related to a theoretical formulation developed and tested over the past decade or so. Hutt (Hutt and Briskin, 1960) originally proposed the concept of perceptual adience-abience to account for some clinical observations he had made. It was noted that individuals differed in their characteristic mode of relating perceptually to their world: some seemed to be perceptually "open" whereas others seemed to be perceptually "closed." These observations were based on the test behavior of persons who had more or less psychopathology and were correlated with their perceptual-motoric style on the *Hutt Adaptation of the Bender-Gestalt Test* (see chapter 11). It was noted that: (1) the more severe the degree of psychopathology, the more perceptually abient (avoidant) was the test behavior, whereas the less severe the degree of psychopathology the more adient (approach oriented) was the test behavior; and (2) within a particular category of psychopathology (except at the levels of severest psychopathology), individuals varied considerably in their perceptual adient-abient style. Additionally, clinical and therapeutic observation seemed to indicate that those who were perceptually adient were much more likely to benefit from learning of many kinds, including therapy, whereas those who were perceptually abient were much more highly resistant to change and much less likely to profit from new learning experiences.

Let us attempt to elucidate the concept of perceptual adience-abience. (For a detailed discussion of this concept, see Hutt, in press.) It was assumed that individuals varied on a continuum from adience to abience. Those who were adient in perceptual style were more likely to be "open" to new experiences, to see and experience more, and to be more adaptable to changing circumstances than those toward the abient end of the continuum. The latter were more likely to be "closed" to perceptual and other experiences and were more likely to resist change. It was thought that the style of perceptual adience-abience was established relatively early in life (during the formative, infantile period), and once established would tend to become more and more stable, thus suggesting a basic feature of the personality. It was hypothesized that this aspect of perceptual style was largely the result of formative experiences during infancy, especially, and possibly during early childhood years, although genetic predisposition also might be a factor. Individuals who were deprived of adequate visual stimulation or who experienced traumatic or highly inconsistent experiences would tend to become perceptually abient (perceptually avoidant), whereas those who experienced appropriate and fairly consistent experiences would tend to become perceptually abient. Perceptual adience-abience was viewed, therefore, as a primary aspect of perceptual style and as a defense interpolated between the organism and the world. Not only lack of adequate visual stimulation was important to the type of perceptual defense, but so too were the total interactions, emotional and cognitive, between infant and the world. This perceptual style, in the visual domain, was regarded as highly sensitive to such interactions since, as experimental evidence has amply documented, the visual mode is one of the primary modes of interaction by the infant with the world. When faced with traumatic experience, the infant can learn self-defense by turning his head so as not to see the "threat," he can shut his eyes, and he can finally learn to deactivate, to a large extent, the whole process of seeing. Since the infant learns to accommodate to his world in terms of what he sees or fails to see, the visual-perceptual mode is highly significant.

Perceptual abience thus is a primary means of defending against the viewing or experiencing of a "hostile" or "threatening world," or a world that is impoverished in providing consistent pleasurable visual experiences. As a primary defense, it underlies other primitive defenses, such as repression, denial, regression, and projection (see chapter 7). Once developed as a defensive style, perceptual abience operates to exclude visual sensations; one simply does not "see" them. Hence, it is more primitive than later defenses, which require cortical operations that distort or isolate the sensation once it has been "received."

On the basis of 12 test factors scorable in terms of test behavior from the HABGT,* a score on perceptual adience-abience can be derived. The Adience-Abience Scale was derived from preliminary clinical experience and try-out with a wide variety of clinical subjects and then tested experimentally. In the first study, the Scale was applied to a population of 200 institutionalized, deaf retarded patients (Hutt and Feuerfile, 1963). A random sampling of 30 cases from this population was used to refine the scoring method as well as to obtain preliminary data. The 30 cases were dichotomized into high adience and high abience subpopulations and six criteria were utilized to test the general hypothesis that the more adient deaf retarded, in comparison with the more abient deaf retarded, would have better intellectual and interpersonal skills. All but one of these one-tailed tests proved to be significant at the .01 level or better, indicating the probable construct validity of this scale. In a cross-validation study, using the remainder of the population, four of the original criteria were re-

*Hutt Adaptation of the Bender-Gestalt Test.

tained and three new criteria were added. The findings were strongly supportive of the construct validity of the *Scale*. Sample findings indicated: age of admission to an institution for the retarded was highly significant in its relationship to adience-abience (the younger the age, the greater the degree of abience); degree of psychopathology was significantly related to scores on adience-abience; level of intelligence, in this highly restricted sample, was significantly related to adience-abience (on two measures, one nonverbal and the other verbal).

Other studies have explored various issues concerning the *Scale* and its reliability and validity. A series of studies with both children and adults has shown that the *Scale* has both high interscorer reliability and test-retest reliability (Hutt and Miller, 1975; Hutt and Dates, 1977). Validity studies have encompassed a variety of criteria, and some of these studies are still in process. Credidio (1975) has confirmed the construct validity of the *Scale*. Hutt (1977a) has shown that the scale differentiates between those hospitalized schizophrenics who improve and those who do not, and he also has shown that schizophrenics with higher adience scores have greater "inner resources" than those who rate lower on the *Scale* (Hutt, 1969). He has also shown that individuals who are higher on adience manifest greater improvement with therapy (Hutt, 1969). And Hutt, Dates, and Reid (1977) have found that adience is helpful in predicting frequency of recidivism in a male, delinquent population.

Our findings suggest that the phenomenon of adience-abience may be highly significant in predicting the effects of intervention or new learning experiences, and that, perhaps differing methods of intervention are required for those who are adient than for those who are abient. In general, although relative degree of adience-abience does not shift much or at all over time or with intervening learning-therapeutic experience (Hutt and Dates, 1977), improvement in behavior can be differentially effective for those differing in their relative position on the adience-abience continuum. For young children, and especially for young retarded children, appropriate and differential treatment intervention seems to be necessary depending on the relative degree of adience or abience (Hutt, 1976). As we shall see when we discuss intervention programs for the retarded, we can, perhaps, improve our successes and reduce our failures if we provide early and, especially, appropriate experiences that take into account the specific personality attributes of the individuals involved as well as their specific abilities and disabilities.

THE MATURATIONAL PROCESS

All of us have *grown up*. If we observe children around us we can readily see that growth has occurred in a large number of physical, social, and mental characteristics. Physical growth is the type most easily observed. A very good example of such a growth process is the development of the infant's ability to walk. Another example is the development of teeth at various age levels. A more accurate name for this particular type of growth, or unfolding, process is *maturation*.

Through the mechanism of heredity, each infant develops the potentialities for many personal characteristics. Examples of bodily characteristics are color of hair and color of eyes. Besides such specific physical phenomena, the organism has inherent potentialities that are not immediately evident at birth. For example, the newborn child cannot talk, walk, or exercise sexual functions, yet potentialities for these activities are already present. They are *latent,* and later, at the appropriate time, they will gradually come to fruition and become manifest. This process of development is implied when we speak of the *maturation* of a particular function. Both physical and psychological characteristics are subject to maturational processes.

Perhaps one of the most striking examples of the maturational process is the development of physical sexual characteristics. In females, menstrual activities and mammary glands develop at puberty. Corresponding changes in anatomical and physiological sexual characteristics occur in males. Nothing in the appearance of the young child suggests that these vast biological changes will occur at a later time, but the *potentialities* for these developments are present at birth and, of course, in the fetus prior to birth.

The maturational process can be greatly influenced by either internal or external environmental conditions. The maturational process is the result of interactions of biologically inherent characteristics and postnatal internal and external environmental conditions.

A child cannot be taught any activity or function until the particular processes involved have reached an adequate maturational level. We cannot teach a newborn child, for example, to walk, to speak, to read, to climb, or to engage in any other intricate or coordinated muscular activity until that child is physically mature enough to do so.

There have been many experiments concerned with the maturational process. Poulsen (1951) conducted an interesting experiment with newborn chicks. They were kept in darkness for four days. When they were placed in the light, they pecked at all sorts of objects. However, after only four hours of such random pecking activity, they then pecked only at food. Many other experiments indicate that restricting the activity of a child does not necessarily inhibit the maturational process and the future exercise of that activity. An example of such a study is the experiment of Dennis (1940) on Hopi children. Immediately following birth, the Hopi child was bound to a board, hindering the movement of arms and legs. Dennis compared the average age of walking of sixty-three children treated in this manner with forty-two Hopi children who were not bound. He found no significant difference in the age at which each group started to walk.

However, in a later study, Dennis (1960) compared three groups totaling 174 children reared under markedly different conditions and found evidence suggesting that the effects of deprivation in some kinds of experience may be very profound. Children in two of the groups had been placed in institutions in Teheran before they were one month old. These children were placed on their backs in individual cribs and were given minimal interpersonal stimulation—practices that were typical of many such institutions. Children in the other group were placed in a demonstration institution that incorporated modern ideas of child rearing. These children were comparable in genetic background to those in the other institutions. There were enough adults available to see to it that the children received considerable personal attention; the children were held frequently and were often placed in a sitting position. These children showed little or no retardation in motor development, whereas those in the first two groups showed serious retardation. In the second year, 60 percent of the children in those groups were unable to sit up alone, and at four years of age 85 percent were still unable to walk alone. Moreover, these children showed disturbances in the usual pattern of maturation of locomotor development.

In this chapter we shall discuss the maturation of psychological functions. These include language functions, emotional functions like smiling and crying, and many aspects of interpersonal behavior. Generally speaking, such behaviors tend to follow a *maturational pattern;* that is, they evolve in a particular sequence. Sometimes these patterns emerge even under adverse environmental conditions and emerge at the usual periods. On the other hand, there is evidence that development of these and other behaviors may be retarded, sometimes extremely, when appropriate interpersonal experiences are lacking or minimal (Davis, 1947).

A child's intellectual capacities also are influenced by the maturational process. At first, the child's growth in measured mental abilities is rapid; as the child grows older, the rate of increase starts to decline, until a leveling-off point is reached. The rate of maturation of intellectual functions varies for different persons.

Figure 6.1 portrays the rates of development for three groups of children: group A, composed of normal children; group B, children who are mentally retarded; and group C, children who originally were normal in intelligence but, because of some brain pathology, suffered impairment in their intellectual functions.

The vertical dimension represents intellectual capacity, and the horizontal dimension represents chronological age. The curve for group A shows a rapid increase during the early years and a gradual leveling-off between the ages of fourteen and eighteen. The curve for group B shows a similar rapid increase during the early years, but the rate of increase is *slower* than for group A, and the curve reaches its maximum at a point *below* that of group A. The curve for group C, on the other hand, increases at the same rate as for group A but shows a sudden stop due to some pathological factor.

Each individual follows the general curve of maturation but has a unique maturational rate. Some children mature intellectually at a slower rate than others, and some mature at a much faster rate.

THE INFLUENCE OF THE FAMILY
DURING THE FORMATIVE YEARS

The major influence acting on the child during preschool years usually is the family. In our culture the mother is most important in the beginning. Later, the father becomes more significant, and the other children in the family also

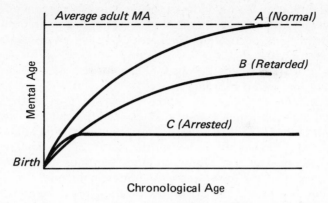

FIGURE 6.1.   Normal, Retarded, and Arrested Mental Development

contribute to the developing child's personality. It should be remembered that the ways in which the members of a family deal with the young child is not only a function of their particular personalities; it is also a function of the culture in which the family lives. Child-rearing practices differ markedly in different cultures. It seems self-evident to state that a good family climate may affect the child's development favorably and that a bad family climate may affect it adversely. But what is a good family climate? And what specifically are its effects? These are some of the questions to which we shall now turn our attention.

The Freudian Position—Anal Period

The most explicit theoretical treatment of the influences of the home on the child's development during early life has been that of the psychoanalytic school. Its formulations were derived, in the main, from clinical observations of neurotic adults and were constructed from the data they furnished in the course of their own treatment. Later, psychoanalysis of children furnished additional data. Still later, research studies investigated these formulations. We shall examine this theoretical position because of its historical importance as well as because of the salience of the hypotheses it offers. We should keep in mind that the direct application of the theory to retarded children has certain dangers. Later, we shall examine some of the research evidence seeking to test, amplify, or revise the theoretical formulations.

Of course, psychological factors in mental retardation do not always account for the impaired mental condition, as we amply documented. However, when such factors are relevant they are profoundly significant. Many careful case studies have demonstrated how dramatic the improvement may be when unfavorable psychological factors are eliminated.

For example, Goodnick (1959) presents a well-documented case study in which the patient's retardation could be ascribed, not to organic injury or inferior original intellectual equipment, but to specific, unfavorable psychological conditions in prior years. We agree with the position of Eisenberg (1958), who states, "We should no longer wonder at the evidence of dysfunction in either [intelligence or emotion], in the presence of disorder in the other, but rather ask: By what mechanism has it occurred in the particular case, and by what means may it be remedied. . . ."

Now let us look at the psychoanalytic position as it describes development following the period of infancy.

As the child continues to mature, it begins to give up the mouth as the primary source through which many satisfactions are achieved and moves on to using another bodily area for such purposes. Usually, starting at about the eighth month of life and ending at about the fourth year of life, the *anal* region assumes primary importance. The anal region includes the anus, the buttocks, and the surrounding regions of the lower end of the intestinal canal. It is capable of offering highly intense emotional satisfaction to the child as soon as his biological development has made it possible.

In general, during the second year of life, the *anal expulsive period,* expulsion of feces is pleasurable to the child. This pleasure is reinforced in many ways. Perhaps most important are the reactions of the mother, who conveys her own pleasure in observing her child's development of bowel control. When excessive reaction is expressed by the mother over this act, it becomes even more important to the child. However, the act of expulsion of the stool may be painful at times, so the child develops some ambivalence toward it. This ambivalence may be greatly increased by the mother's insistence that the baby have a bowel movement on demand, especially if voluntary control over the act is not adequately developed. For a mentally retarded child this is an even more serious problem, since control may develop at a slower rate.

Cultural factors affect anal training. In cultures insisting on rapid, rigid, and harsh toilet training practices, the psychological damage to the child and the consequent fixations that develop around this anal phase are likely to be marked.

During the first stage of the anal level of development, then, the child secures gratification through the passage of stools. This gratification is not only physical; it also is psychologically reinforced or diminished by the feelings expressed by the mother. During the second stage of anal development, the child attains more gratification by retaining or withholding the stool than by passing it. Unless their parents stop them, many children will play with their stools. If strong prohibitions against such exploratory activities have been invoked, the child (and later the adult) may develop excessively negative reactions to fecal matter.

Fixation at the anal level will tend to occur if there has been either *over-* or *under*gratification of the child's anal modes of behavior. Such fixation has an effect on the future personality structure and characteristics of the child. According to the theory, it tends to produce three major personality characteristics: (1) miserliness, or excessive thrift—*parsimony;* (2) obstinacy, or excessive stubbornness—*petulance;* and (3) meticulousness or excessive orderliness—*pedantry.* Although these traits may arise from other sources, the primary source is said to be fixation at the anal level of development.

Toilet training is thus just as important in the psychological development of the child at this level as weaning at the oral level. No matter how careful the mother is in initiating toilet training at the appropriate time, it still involves some degree of frustration to the child. The child must learn to "socialize" toilet habits so that they are congruent with cultural patterns.

In summary, these are the dynamics of this conflict: (1) The child feels hostile toward the adult (the mother) who is forcing her to give up her freedom. (2) The child is afraid to express this hostility since she may be deprived of the love she needs and wants from her mother. (3) The child projects hostile wishes on the mother—that is, tends to see her, rather than self, as hostile. (4) Since she wants to be loved, the child *identifies* with her—that is, *interiorizes* the mother's wishes about toilet training (makes them her own wishes)—and develops some control over bowel movements.

The anal phase often has been called the period of *socialization*. It is the time when the child, now more able to communicate with the world, is expected to learn the prohibitions of the culture, to develop some moral habits, and to develop some personal habits of cleanliness.

The mentally retarded child experiences great difficulties in coping with the problems of the anal period. In the first place, this child tends to be strongly fixated at oral levels, so has less psychic energy to proceed to the next level. In addition, frustrations during the anal period tend to be greater than those of other children, and adjustment is more difficult. Slowness in developing verbal skills retards socialization further. General slowness in maturation often means that the retarded child is subjected to toilet training activities long before being ready for such a program. Many times the child is not even physiologically ready to establish controls over bowel and bladder functions when such training is initiated.

A fairly common problem in the relationship of the retarded child to the mother during this period is *overprotection* by the mother. Too often she is overly solicitous about the child's welfare. (This frequently has been called *Momism* in popular literature.) One reason for this reaction is the guilt she feels over her child's retardation. She wrongly feels responsible for his condition. When overprotected, the retarded child has too little stimulation to mature to the level capable of being reached or to give up more infantile behavior, and in many instances becomes very passive, dependent, demanding, hostile, and aggressive.

Walker (1950) points out that with the mentally retarded child, toilet training is a delayed process, and sometimes it is never accomplished. He states:

> Can we be certain that the defective does not find some degree of emotional fixation in his untidiness? If we take a defective who has accomplished toilet training and attempt to engage him in play demanding his becoming dirty we often meet with resistance. Parental concern over the prolonged toilet training may have developed a compulsive attitude for both parent and child. Perhaps the child finds activity so closely allied to what has been a difficult developmental problem, an emotionally undesirable form of endeavor.

A special problem during the anal period is the development of language, which brings with it enriched possibilities for interpersonal communication. It is in this area that children from disadvantaged homes may suffer the greatest impairment. It has been shown that a nonstimulating home can produce impoverishment in vocal interaction (Keller, 1963). That, in turn, can result in poor auditory vocal discrimination (Clark and Richards, 1966). Therefore, profound retardation in language development and social maturity may ensue, resulting in retarded cognitive development (Hess and Shipman, 1965). Various programs have been initiated to compensate for these lacks in disadvantaged children. Head Start, for example, attempted to supply some of the missing experiences. In a longitudinal study, some children, at age four, were placed in a compensatory preschool program for one or two years. An important part of this program involved greatly enriched language experience. Karnes and coworkers (Karnes et al., 1969) found that one group gained an average of 14 IQ points, and another group gained 24 points. In recent years, intensive intervention programs have been initiated in many parts of the country.

As we have noted earlier, such compensatory experiences may do much more than simply improve specific skills. They may stimulate curiosity and motivate learning and outgoing behaviors that, in turn, enable the child to enrich the world he lives in.

In addition to the evidence we have already cited demonstrating the possible positive effects of more favorable environments, there are other pertinent studies. Goshen (1963) found that failure to provide adequate linguistic stimulation can unfavorably affect cognitive development. Richards and Sands (1963) investigated the relative effects of home, foster home, and institution on retarded children. They found that the home environment was superior, producing not only higher measured intelligence, but also more favorable personality and social characteristics. Of the factors in the home that contribute to such favorable development, linguistic stimulation and interaction are crucial (Freeberg and Payne, 1967). This is not at all surprising, since stimulation in language development is fundamental to cognitive and social adaptation.

Another aspect of personality development during the anal period is the development of the self-concept. According to Cobb (1961) there are five stages in the early development of a positive self-concept: primitive differentiation and integration; naming, identifying, and generalizing; development of attributes of the self; the definition of levels of aspiration; and, adolescent revision of the self-concept. The mentally retarded individual tends to experience delay and confusion in the positive development of the self-concept because, on the one hand, motoric development tends to be delayed especially if the child is not provided with environmental experiences that promote such development, and on the other hand, linguistic development proceeds even more slowly than physical development, thus tending to produce confusion in self-concepts. Chasey et al. (1974) were able to demonstrate that training in physical development on a programmed basis, as compared with only nonprogrammed recreational activity, resulted in more positive self-image among institutionalized children. Confirmatory evidence of the importance of such experiences was supplied by Zisfein and Rosen (1974), who found that both verbal and nonverbal self-estimates of the self were independent, to a large extent, of the level of IQ. Years ago, Guthrie et al. (1961, 1964) were able to demonstrate that positive self-attitudes were derived from engaging in cooperative and socially approved behaviors.

The Psychoanalytic Position—Phallic Period

The *phallic* period extends from three to seven years. The primary zone through which gratifications are received and drives are discharged during this period is the genital organs. Since the maturation of the personality characteristics of the boy is different from that of the girl during this period, we shall discuss the process in each separately. For more detailed analysis of the psychoanalytic theory of the phallic period see Brenner (1973) and Breger (1974).

Maturation in Boys. The primary zone in the boy during this period is the penis and the area surrounding it. It is now well established that boys engage in an increased amount of masturbatory behavior during this phase. When disappointments, frustrations, or failures are strong, such activities increase even more. If masturbation is severely prohibited by the parent, it is likely to be engaged in on the sly. If there are strong guilt feelings about masturbatory activities, as is frequently the case, regression to either oral (like thumb-sucking) or anal (like becoming constipated) modes of behavior may result. Sometimes, children who are very severely disturbed masturbate almost constantly, and they handle and fondle the penis continually even though no orgasm is experienced.

There are important psychological changes during the phallic period. Under normal circumstances, before entering this level, the boy already has developed a very strong emotional attachment to his mother. He has become dependent on her, since almost all of his physical, social, and emotional needs have been met by her. During this period the boy also has learned to love his father, but his relationships with his father are much less intense than his relationships with his mother. There are many reasons for this: the father played a significantly less important role than the mother; the father caressed and fondled the boy less than the mother; and the father did not meet all the needs of the boy in the same manner as the mother.

The boy's relationships with both parents during this period are ambivalent. Although the boy loves his mother, he also is often irritated and frustrated by her. At times he feels very hostile and has other negative feelings toward her. His relationship with his father also contains hostile elements.

On the whole, life would be fairly satisfactory in the home, despite the boy's frustrations and ambivalences, if it were not for the development of a triangle—a three-way relationship between the boy, his mother, and his father. This triangular relationship, termed the *oedipal situation,* is the primary conflict faced by the child during this period, and it usually causes difficulty. Prior to this, the boy encountered three major crises: the trauma of birth, the trauma of weaning, and the trauma of toilet training. This fourth—the oedipal trauma—is probably the most crucial of all.

The little boy is quite content to be with his mother during the day—to play with her, to receive her attention and affection, and, in short, to be in the very center of things. But in the evening, when the father comes home, things become quite different. Usually the mother devotes much of her attention to her husband, she may hug and kiss him, and in general she spends a lot of her time with him. To a large extent she temporarily rejects her little boy, and he is told eventually to go to bed and "go to sleep." The father thus becomes an object of special hostility, since he appears, to the boy, to be depriving him of the intense emotional satisfactions he expects from his mother. Also, and this is of great importance, the father is feared for many reasons: he is the boy's rival for the mother; he is much bigger and can harm the boy; and he becomes the outward representation of the little boy's own guilt and fears concerning the situation.

This is the central core of the oedipal conflict in the boy. It is complicated by many other factors. In the first place, the boy has many female as well as male characteristics, partly because of his identification with his mother. In the second place, all children are bisexual to some extent (the proportion of male and female hormones is never 100 percent of one to 0 percent of the other in any person, and the physical characteristics are never entirely male or female). In addition, the mother herself may have many masculine qualities, and the father may have many feminine qualities.

The normal boy, after a period of considerable stress and conflict, finally learns to identify with the father and give up much of his identification with the mother. In other words, he manages to repress his oedipal wishes for his mother and assumes a more masculine role. His behavior toward the mother changes markedly at this time; he often becomes negativistic toward her or appears to be distant or removed from her. In taking on his masculine role he usually places a great deal of importance upon the physical signs of his masculinity.

In this way, the normal boy learns to give up his infantile ways of behaving and progresses toward puberty. This period is marked by intensive growth in many directions, for both the boy and the girl. It is characterized by an increasing amount of exploration and curiosity. Physical abilities of many kinds have become well established, and the child can locomote, thus establishing better contact with a larger world. The eyes, the ears, and the other sense organs have assumed more mature functions and have become more important for discovering the widening world of reality. Intellectual development also has gone on apace, and enables the child to integrate his new knowledge and to use it effectively.

Maturation in Girls. Progress through the phallic level and resolution of the oedipal conflict is more complicated for girls than for boys. Like the boy, the girl identifies first with the mother and obtains similar attention and emotional gratifications from her. Also like the boy, she receives primary satisfaction from the genital region. During this period the girl, like the boy, learns to identify with her father, but here we find important complexities in the process of feminine maturation. The girl now has one additional phase through which she must pass—she must give up her identification with her father and reestablish her identity with her mother. Only in this way can she assume and accept the role of a female. This brief précis of the oedipal situation for girls is an oversimplified statement of a very complex process.

Difficulties of the Retarded Child. The mentally retarded child, boy or girl, has an unusual amount of difficulty in dealing with the problems of the phallic period. He has less energy to apply to its resolution, since he has not adequately resolved the problems of the oral and the anal levels. His fixations during those periods make it easier for him to regress to those levels when he is faced with oedipal conflicts. He basically is unready to cope with the traumatic experiences of this level; therefore, he develops many behavioral disturbances.

The attitudes of the mother to her retarded child, furthermore, are not conducive to an easy solution of oedipal conflicts. Her relationship to such a child is likely to be emotionally complex and oversolicitous because of the child's difficulties; hence, effective changes by the child are more difficult to achieve.

The process is further hampered by the specific disabilities of the retarded child. His intellectual development is such that he cannot integrate new knowledge or use it effectively. He still does not comprehend the growing world of reality and has problems in perceiving external events.

The retarded child often does not adequately resolve oedipal conflicts. The boy continues to be dependent on his mother, and he may not be able to assume an adequate masculine role. The girl, too, retains her primary identification with the mother. This has significant implications for her later emotional behavior. For both, the oedipal period is fraught with difficulties in mastering interpersonal skills.

The solution of oedipal conflicts can be greatly influenced by the emotional adjustment and psychological sophistication of the parents.

Some Experimental Evidence

The general theory of personality development cannot be tested *in toto*. Rather, specific subdivisions of the theory have to be evaluated separately after being formulated in some testable form. Then the interrelationships of the various elements affecting development have to be considered.

Many studies have dealt with the effects of the climate of the home, and we have already referred to some of these. In a series of well-designed studies at the Fels Research Institute, in Yellow Springs, Ohio, it was demonstrated that the experiences of children during the formative years greatly affect their personality development. For instance, it was shown that "accepted children" tend to be more alert mentally, as well as more friendly and more responsive (Baldwin, 1949). In contrast, rejected children are less alert mentally, do more poorly in school work, are more unstable emotionally, and tend to be apathetic or rebellious more frequently.

Kagan and Moss (1958) were able to show that emotional disturbance has a significantly depressive effect on intellectual functioning. Another group of research workers has demonstrated that the patterns of relationships between mother and child are generally consistent with the predictions derived from psychoanalytic theory. Blum (1959) has shown that there is a large and significant relationship between the combined rigidities of the mother and father and that of their four- and five-year-old children, the correlation being .50. And in an intensive longitudinal study that extended into the adolescence of the children who were evaluated, Peck (1958) found that ego strength (see chapter 10) and friendliness, absence of unnecessary guilt and hostility, and spontaneity in behavior were related to home climate that was lenient, democratic, and relatively consistent.

The effects of severe toilet training and of correlated suppressive training procedures in the home have been well documented by Symonds (1938). His own research evidence indicates that such types of experience lead to personality maladjustment, various forms of inhibition in mental and emotional expressiveness, and withdrawal or compensatory aggressive behavior.

In what we regard as a classic study, Watson (1957) evaluated the effects of strict versus permissive home discipline on children coming from "good" homes. Among other things that make this study impressive is the fact that it deals with home situations that are not abnormal in the usual sense; i.e., economically abnormal or emotionally abnormal. The evidence from this research is quite clear in indicating that even though permissive homes do not have a monopoly on producing all of the favorable effects on personality development, they clearly excel in the production of the following kinds of behaviors: friendliness, low hostility, independence, spontaneity, creativity, and originality. Watson adds, ". . . no clear personality advantages were associated in general with strict discipline in a good home."

We have cited the previous studies to illustrate the kinds of findings that have accumulated from empirical research. Not all studies report similar confirmations of the general psychoanalytic position, and certainly not all workers interpret their findings in terms of this theoretical framework. Nevertheless, the preponderance of evidence certainly is not in disagreement with the basic propositions offered by Freud, although many extensions and modifications of his theory are evidently needed.

Some evidence is particularly intriguing. Hall and Domhoff (1963) made an extensive study of 3,874 dreams reported in eleven separate investigations. The study of dreams tells us something of what is going on within the recesses of personality and throws light on its unconscious components. (See chapter 7 for further discussion of such phenomena.) Hall and Domhoff found ubiquitous sex differences in the dreams of males and females. Moreover, these differences were consistent with the Freudian position. The content of the dreams and the types of conflict that were represented confirmed the nature of both the oedipal conflict, in general, and the delayed resolution of this conflict in girls, in particular.

Considerable research has been done on the effects of separation of a child from parents (Yarrow, 1964). In general, it has been found that separation experiences can have deleterious effects on personality development, unless provision is made to counter such experiences with good relationships, favorable emotional experiences, and necessary therapy. When children have been deprived of relationships with parents and are placed in institutions, they tend to be duller than those who continue to have contact with their parents (Pringle and Bossio, 1968).

The other side of this problem — effective interaction between mother and child on a continuing basis — has been documented by Clarke-Stewart (1973). She studied the interactions of mothers and their first-born children and found the major maternal variables were: social stimulation, affection, contingent responsiveness to and acceptance of the child's behavior, stimulation of the child in play activities, and appropriate maternal behavior in relation to the child's age and ability. There was a highly significant correlation between the overall quality of the mother's (consistent) adequacy of care and the child's degree of general competence.

Piaget's Position: Preschool and Later Years

As we noted, Piaget made highly significant contributions to the theory of intellectual development and tied his thinking about intelligence closely to the development of the personality. We should note that intelligence, for Piaget, is the "coordination of operations." Such "operations" have two essential characteristics: (1) they are reversible; and, (2) they are internalized. In a reversible operation, nothing that the child has internalized is lost; it can be used even when the objective situation has been reversed. Thus, when the child can deal with numbers or quantities so that they can be added as well as subtracted from each other because the quantities (or their conceptual aspects) are "conserved," reversibility is demonstrated. One of Piaget's classical experiments demonstrated that 5-year-old children were incapable of reversibility (and thus of conservation). The child would be shown two glasses of equal shape, each filled with colored water, and would be asked whether they contained the same amount of water. Typically the child would reply in the affirmative. One glass of water would then be poured into a taller and thinner glass. The child would then be asked whether this glass contained the same amount of water as the other, less-tall glass, and would typically respond that the taller glass contained more water. However, a 7-year old would typically respond that both glasses still contained the same amount of water. This experiment also demonstrates the other "operation"; — internalization. An internalized characteristic reveals a mental representation that can be manipulated.

Piaget believes that each individual invariably manifests the development of intelligence as the individual progresses through four major stages, in the order noted. Retarded individuals pass through the same sequence in their development but may never achieve, as do normals, the flexibility of thought, the ability to classify and reclassify, the ability to group and regroup, and reversibility of thought with the ease or thoroughness of those who are intellectually more advanced (Stephens, 1977). The four stages are:

I. Sensorimotor stages (from birth to about 1½–2 years);
II. Preoperational stage (from 1½–2 years to 7 years);

III.   Concrete operations stage (from 7 years to 12 years); and,

IV.   Formal operations stage (from age 12 years up).

We have previously discussed some of the major characteristics of the first stage. This is the stage before the acquisition of language and one in which reflex behavior and accommodations of means to new ends are acquired, the beginnings of primitive deductive thinking appear, and perceptual and motoric behaviors are coordinated.

In the second or preoperational stage, the child begins to learn the use of symbolism or intuitive thought. The child at first engages only in imitative acts, but as she begins to experience some frustration, because the reality world cannot be assimilated without accommodation through equilibration, she learns to manipulate in her own mind thoughts without sensations or actions. According to Piaget, this stage is critical if the child is to progress effectively to the later stages of concrete operations and true representational thought. If the child does not have available "an area of activity whose motivation is not *adaptation* [our emphasis] to reality but, on the contrary, *assimilation* [our emphasis] of reality to the self, without coercion or sanctions" (Piaget and Inhelder, 1969), she cannot succeed in the needs of her personality and of moving forward intellectually. Thus, Piaget favors challenging the child by providing her with ample opportunities for play and exploration with materials and situations that are appropriate to her developmental level but that are, at the same time, novel and somewhat difficult. In this way, intelligence is fostered through the equilibration of assimilation and accommodation. Symbolic play, with idiosyncratic meanings for the child, plus the use of language in social accommodation are seen as essential for the stimulation of intellectual growth. It is through the use of symbolic play that the child learns to master the environment through "the resolution of conflicts" that reality provides.

In the third stage, the child's words and images become articulated into concepts and rules. Sensorimotor thought gradually is replaced with true mental representations: the ordering of events, conservation, and the ability to reverse these and apply them to new situations. Systematic thinking becomes evident and the "fallibility" of parental figures becomes more evident to the child. The child learns to use logic and to adapt to his world through his use of logic. He begins to consider alternative explanations of a given phenomenon or problem. He has become far less egocentric in his thinking and adaptive processes. These latter phenomena in thinking and adaptation become clearly evident and "structured" in the final stage of cognitive development—the stage of formal operations, beginning at about 12 years of age.

Piaget's emphasis on the centrality for intellectual development of sensorimotor activities is sometimes disputed. Nevertheless, most studies that have been undertaken to test aspects of his theory seem to offer confirmation. In the study by Stephens (Stephens, 1977) cited previously, when seventy-five retarded pupils (IQs between 50 and 75) were compared with seventy-five nonretarded pupils (IQs between 90 and 110) in three age groups (6–14 years; 10–16 years; and, 14–24 years), significant differences in Piagetian tasks (conservation, logical operations, operational and symbolic activity, and formal operations) were found between the retarded and the normals at all age levels, and the differences were not accountable for in terms of CA or MA alone. It also was found that retarded pupils showed an arrest in the development of reasoning, but they continued to develop in reasoning—at a decelerated rate—to age twenty years and beyond. Piaget has shown not only that appropriate sensorimotor experiences and symbolic play are important for cognitive and affective development, but also that intellectual development is highly dependent on interest and motivation (Piaget, 1970; Stephens, 1977).

FURTHER PSYCHOSEXUAL DEVELOPMENT

The life period most marked by visible signs of the inner turmoil of emotional conflict is adolescence. This is the period so frequently attacked bitterly in popular journals and newspapers because it is attended by delinquent behavior and by other forms of aggression and defiance of cultural conventions. During adolescence, most children are required to begin making some prevocational decisions and to take appropriate steps to assure themselves of relevant education, training, and experience. For the retarded child, the difficulties of this period are inordinate and may be crucial in determining the kind of adjustment made in later years. In this section, we shall briefly discuss the general features of personality development during adolescence. In later chapters, we shall deal specifically with problems of adjustment, problems of education and training, and problems that society needs to resolve.

In the normal child, puberty ushers in the beginnings of adult sexuality, although there may be a long delay before society permits a person full gratification of such sexuality. The period is marked by intense upsets in all spheres, both physiological and psychological, and these "storms and stresses" are particularly pronounced in the mentally retarded child. With the biological development of the child there is a resulting intensification of the sexual drives; there are rapid physiological changes such as secretion of sex hormones, increase in the size and sensitivity of sexual organs, and development of secondary sex characteristics. In the psychological development there is the reemergence of intense sexual feelings and the presence of many contradictory impulses within the child, such as the need for independence and the need for dependence, or the need for sensuality and the need for asceticism.

There also are other complications. During this period there is a reactivation of older conflicts that may have been adequately controlled by the child's defense mechanisms up to this point. Further, our society does not permit gratifications of the child's increased sexual drives.

The child strives toward two major goals during this period. First, the child tries to achieve sexual gratification, either directly or symbolically. Second, the adolescent strives for a sense of independence and self-esteem. The number of avenues open, however, is limited by the customs and practices of society. Intense needs continue to exert pressure, and guilt feelings and anxieties are pronounced. These problems may often overwhelm the ego, and the child may react to them by either excessive withdrawal or excessive aggression or other forms of rebellion against the parents and society in general. It often is difficult for the parents to understand and tolerate all the upheavals going on within the child. Sensitive handling of the adolescent is necessary so that the child's older problems will not be reactivated and new ones will not be created.

The adolescent boy wants a job; he wants to be self-sufficient; he wants a hot rod so that he can feel a sense of power and masculinity. He likes to dance, to have heterosexual relations, and to relieve his sexual tensions to some extent. He is in a constant state of turmoil. Superego* forces alternate between being excessively harsh and punitive on the one hand and excessively permissive on the other. Finally, some degree of harmony is achieved, and the superego demands are not so excessive in either direction.

Puberty is an excessively difficult period for the mentally retarded child. He has the accumulations of fixations at oral, anal, and phallic levels and the constant pressure of conflicts that have remained unsolved throughout his life. The added problems of adolescence impose a further burden and additional conflicts upon him (and his parents).

The mentally retarded child is not adequately equipped to assume the independent role that society sometimes demands. He tends to continue to be dependent, although at the same time he is aware of a growing need for independence. The pressures of society, as well as those within the family situation, make it exceedingly difficult to adjust successfully to the demands of puberty and adolescence.

FACTORS INFLUENCING THE PERSONALITY DEVELOPMENT OF THE RETARDED CHILD

We now will summarize factors that, according to present evidence, significantly influence the course of personality development of retarded children. Most of these factors are also relevant for so-called normal children, but their salience for retarded ones may be somewhat different.

The biological equipment with which a child is born determines the *initial* tendencies manifest in the child's behavior. Whether the child is inferior or superior, excitable or lethargic, and whether the child is prone to stress reactions or can tolerate stress quite well are "givens" in the organism at birth. Some children develop and "unfold" more slowly than others. Hence they need more time and more specific and detailed instruction to enable them to master what may be simple adaptive problems for others. The retarded person tends to become more frustrated more easily than do more superior contemporaries. Retarded individuals may need more prolonged care, protection, and warmth. They may be adversely affected by the expectancies of parents and older siblings who are frustrated by relatively slow development. Consistency in training procedures and great tolerance for slowness in developing and mastering adaptive behaviors are especially important for them.

*The superego refers to moral values and conscience that have been internalized and serve as motivators of behavior.

It has been demonstrated by both clinical studies and research investigations that some persons with potentially normal or even superior intellectual capacities are thwarted severely in the early experiences they have in meeting their biosocial needs. Parental rejection, separation from parents, rigid training schedules, and a repressive home climate may, separately or in combination, produce avoidance reactions and (in the extreme) severe psychological withdrawal, low drive for accomplishment, and other forms of emotional disturbance. These forms of behavior may then form part of the pattern involving intellectual retardation. The child may learn, as Gardner (1961) has put it, to have a "low expectation level that his efforts will lead to success in problem solving."

Moreover, the child's early lack of success in coping with the problems of adaptation to the expectancies of the environment may produce further abasement of self-regard, which in turn may lead to further loss of drive in successful adaptation. This early lack of success may be attributable to constitutional inferiority in some, to slow developmental rates in others, and to frustrating experiences in still others.

Since society is geared to the normal child, retarded children may experience a disproportionate share of failures and frustrations in early life at home and later in school. They may experience such failures in the psychosexual sphere as well as in the other emotional and intellectual spheres of interaction. Retarded children need ample time for growth and detailed, supervised learning experiences that will encourage a self-regard that is trustful and optimistic. They need special encouragement and positive reinforcement in their attempts to cope with new learning situations, and unwitting rejection must be avoided by not expecting of them more than they can reasonably accomplish.

Most retarded children come from culturally deprived homes and suffer further deprivation of favorable emotional, cultural, and intellectual experiences as a consequence. For such children, massive preventative programs need to be instituted to compensate for their deficiencies—at the community level and in special educational agencies. As we shall see in later chapters, special guidance is needed in both home and school. (See chapters 10 and 13.) The community needs to learn how to deal with retarded individuals, whether they have a constitutional deficiency or some severe emotional impairment. Research has pointed up the difficulties retarded individuals experience in attending to relevant stimuli, as well as the improvement they demonstrate when tasks are properly graded or when special learning procedures are applied (Ware et al., 1962; Zigler and Unell, 1962).

It also is worth noting that our review of the evidence, both in the present and previous chapters, seems to indicate that retarded individuals may, as a group, be more vulnerable to stress than normals. *Vulnerability* can be conceived of as a tendency to develop psychopathological behaviors rather than coping behaviors when the organism experiences either psychological or physical stress. In view of deficits in neurological development and organization that severely and profoundly retarded persons frequently have, their vulnerability may be relatively high. Hutt (1977b) has indicated that high vulnerability predisposes the individual to many forms of psychopathological defense, rather than, necessarily, to a specific form of psychopathology. Falconer (1967), who calls this factor "thresholds of liability," similarly argues that this factor is general in nature rather than disease-specific. Recent biogenetic studies have indicated that such vulnerability is due to a polygenetic basis rather than to a simple or single genetic basis (Blan, 1977). We know too little, as yet, about the antecedents and consequences of such vulnerability, but from what we already know it is reasonable to infer that such vulnerability, coupled with the unusual stresses and deprivations that many retarded persons experience, can markedly reinforce retarded behavior as well as other pathological effects.

And, finally, there seem to be critical periods in the adjustment of the retarded. Although it is impossible to divide the life span into artificially separate periods, it is helpful to think of the first year of life as being especially important, both in assessing the individual and in providing appropriate, and therefore emotionally satisfying, experiences. This is followed in importance by the preschool years, when early patterns of interpersonal relationships are learned; and then by the early adolescent period, when there is a resurgence of old problems as well as new ones for the retarded individual. All are critical periods when the several factors—biological, psychological, and cultural—may have their greatest impact.

THE SALIENCE OF FREUD'S AND PIAGET'S THEORIES FOR RETARDATION

We have presented only selected and central features of Freud's and Piaget's theories. Both have made epochal contributions to theories of human development and to factors that may enrich or impede developmental behavior. Neither theory explains, or attempts to explain, all of human development, but no other theories have offered such incisive views of this process nor such systematic presentations. Other theories and research findings will be summarized in later relevant sections of this book in order to enlarge and "fill in" our understanding.

Both Freud and Piaget emphasize the egocentric and narcissistic character of infant behavior and the high degree of dependence infants have on the nature of their early experiences. Freud posits the centrality of sexual drives (needs for affection) and the effects of frustration of these drives on subsequent. development and maldevelopment. "Bonding," attachment, exploratory activities involving sensual gratification, parental acceptance, and gradual socialization involving appropriate gratification as well as adaptation to reality demands at critical periods highlight Freud's theory. As we shall see in later chapters, psychopathological development produced by inadequate satisfaction of these "needs" is accompanied by defensive operations of the ego, particularly, and may severely distort or delay intellectual development as well as personality development in general. Looking at the retarded from the Freudian position can help us to understand the retarded more completely and to provide the preventative or ameliorative conditions that are needed. The *process* of becoming retarded as well as the *dynamics* of the retarded person can be better understood and dealt with. The retarded child needs not only corrective intellectual experiences, important as these may be, but also help in improving social adaptation, by resolving conflicts and blocks, so that total growth in adaptation may be accelerated.

Piaget has made particularly significant contributions to our understanding of intellectual behavior. Like Freud, he stresses the inevitable sequence of phases in development and the need for *appropriate experience* at each stage. The value of his observations and theoretical formulations concerning early sensorimotor experience and the central value of a stimulating early environment that encourages the infant, and later the child, actively to explore the world and to meet success in learning to accommodate and equilibrate, have only recently been given the prominence they deserve. He has offered precise statements concerning the nature of cognitive operations that can enable us to evaluate more adequately shortcomings in a child's behavioral development and to provide means for correcting them.

It is in ways such as these that both Freud and Piaget have enriched our conceptualization of human development and, as we have attempted to demonstrate, have supplemented each other. In later sections of this volume we also will see that both men have contributed immeasurably to our understanding of moral development and to the significance of this development for effective human development and adaptation. And, as we shall see, an appreciation of the theories of both men will enable us to put to better use some of the recent advances in behavior modification and, even more specifically, in perceptual-motor training—as well as other aspects of specific "target behavior" training—so that we can better tailor educational programs for the maximum benefit of the retarded individual.

— 7 —

Conflict and Anxiety

In the previous chapter, we learned that the development of the personality depends on the interaction of the organism with experience. We can no longer naïvely hold the view that all of a person's characteristics simply emerge from within in the course of maturation. Development of intellectual capacities, in particular, is crucially dependent on the *kind, amount,* and *timing* of experiences. For convenience, we may distinguish two major types of general experience that have an impact on personality development: (1) *deprivation* of relevant stimulation needed to foster development and (2) *conflict* in satisfying needs that motivate behavior.

J. McV. Hunt (1961) marshals evidence dramatically supporting the proposition that intellectual development may be grossly retarded (as well as facilitated) by variation in relevant sensorimotor stimulation. Deprivation of such stimulation, particularly in the early periods of development, may retard intellectual development by as much as 50 percent. We shall refer to such evidence from time to time to point up the fact that retarded functioning is not a matter of inferior genetic inheritance only, as is so commonly believed. The majority of the mentally retarded come from inadequate social-cultural environments in which some deprivation is likely to occur (see Mittler, 1977).

The effect of conflict on personality development and intellectual functioning has been given relatively little research attention in discussions of the retarded. Not only has it been assumed that such people are born retarded and "stay that way," but it also has been assumed that conflict plays only a minor role in the development of retarded functioning. Only in recent years, and usually only in connection with exceptional cases, has attention been pointed toward the severely debilitating effect of severe or prolonged conflict on intellectual development and functioning.

Our major purpose in this chapter is to examine the concepts of conflict and its major consequence—anxiety—and to consider the probable relevance of such phenomena to the development of retarded children. Although evidence specifically relevant to retardation has been rapidly accumulating within the past few years, most of what we know at present applies to relatively normal populations, and we shall have to extrapolate these findings to the population of the retarded to a considerable degree. Our conclusions must therefore be regarded as only tentative, although we believe they are important. We rely on the reader to evaluate our implications cautiously.

PSYCHOLOGICAL CONFLICT

Conflict is the simultaneous arousal of two or more sets of motives that are antagonistic to each other. As an example, we may cite the case of a person who simultaneously wishes to attend a party and go to the theater. If both motives are strong and the satisfaction of one means that the other cannot be satisfied, then conflict may become quite intense. In this example, we assume that the person is fully aware of both sets of motives and can make a deliberate choice between them. The person also may decide to satisfy one set of motives now and try to satisfy the other set at another time. In any case, the stronger set of motives will usually prevail, and some degree of reduction in tension will then result.

However, even in this relatively simple type of conflict situation, inability to make some choice will result in continuing tension until some other behavior reduces it. And continuing tension, if severe, may reduce intellectual judgment temporarily, divert attention from relevant "facts of the situation," and have other disabling effects. On the other hand, *moderate* degrees of conflict and ensuing *moderate* tension may sharpen intellectual judgment and increase attention to relevant stimuli, and the reduction of the tension state by choice and gratification of one set of motives may be experienced as pleasurable. Such kinds of conflict situations are common in life generally, and research evidence indicates that moderate tension, accompanied by relatively accurate awareness of its source, usually improves performance, especially on simple tasks (Spence, 1958; Spielberger, 1966).

Conflict may, however, involve unconscious motives. The concept of the *unconscious* will be discussed fully in the next chapter, but at this point we can conceptualize it as a state of lack of awareness of the motivation that is operating. There are many commonplace examples of unconsciously motivated behavior (Hilgard, 1977). "Forgetting" to make an unpleasant telephone call or to do something else one dislikes is the kind of unconsciously motivated behavior with which all of us are familiar. Getting a headache before a party one thinks one would like to attend, but of which one is unconsciously fearful, is another example. Becoming afraid in a situation that, from a rational viewpoint, should not lead to fear is still another example of the operation of unconscious motives.

In conflicts, either or both of the sets of motives may be unconscious. A person may have tendencies to behave in a certain way of which he is totally unaware, and when these tendencies are unopposed by external barriers to their gratification or by other unconscious internal tendencies, they may be acted on impulsively. Many cases of antisocial, impulse-driven behavior (e.g. fire-setting) may be explained on the basis of unconsciously motivated behavior that is unopposed by other internalized motives. On the other hand, many guilt-ridden people are unable to function effectively because they are experiencing conflict between two sets of antagonistic and unconscious motives.

Unconscious conflicts, it is believed, are extremely important in the development of disturbed states of behavior (Hutt, 1977b). Since the source (or sources) of the conflict is unknown to the person, she is unable to resolve it. At the same time, she unconsciously prevents herself from discovering the motives in conflict, because the very fact that they are hidden indicates that, for some reason, they are intolerable and therefore have to be guarded against. Since all motives seek expression, she expends much psychological energy repressing them (see chapter 8 for further discussion of this point).

One of the major motives of all human beings is to seek affection and acceptance (to gain love). In retarded individuals, this psychosexual set of motives often is in conflict with other motives involving fear of criticism, fear of rejection, and fear of ridicule. In the school situation, in particular, when the mentally retarded child has learned that he cannot live up to the standards expected of him, and has learned to anticipate not only failure but also rejection, there may be a sharp and intense conflict between striving to perform to gain acceptance and being afraid to perform because further rejection is expected. The whole school situation may become unconsciously threatening, and the conflict experienced may become so severe that withdrawal (at a psychological level) may be the only apparent solution. Inattention, lack of interest, and constant lethargy and fatigue may be the observable symptoms of this kind of intense conflict. Or, in a distorted manner, the retarded pupil may unconsciously pit individual strength against the school (teacher), using refusal to learn as the main means of defiance and self-assertion. The child's behavior says, then, in effect, "See how strong I am. No matter how hard you may try, you cannot make me learn." In clinical practice, one finds that this kind of disturbed reaction occurs fairly frequently as the pupil's *passive oppositional* "solution" to the conflict between a wish to be loved and a fear of being deprecated.

The Case of Helena

This eleven-year-old girl came to the attention of the senior author when the parents and the school sought consultation concerning more effective methods for teaching her. At this age, she still had not learned to read even at the primary grade level, her other academic achievements were below her presumed mental age, and she utilized only nouns in her attempts at communication. She had been evaluated previously by a number of psychologists and learning specialists and had been assumed to be at the lower levels of the mildly mentally retarded. She had been given speech therapy, beginning at about four years of age, and she had attended special education classes ever since starting school at the age of six years. No one had thought of her as having any personality problem although she appeared to be shy and withdrawn; on the other hand, she was likeable and never caused any serious difficulties in her relations with peers and teachers.

The parents reported that Helena had suffered anoxia at birth (inadequate supply of oxygen) and that this was apparently responsible for her mental retardation. They also reported, however, that during infancy she appeared to be normal and developed fairly well in physical and personality characteristics until about two years of age. At that time, they noted that she showed retardation in her subsequent development (and even some regression) in almost all aspects of her physical, social, and intellectual development.

In school, Helena was moderately cooperative although she made little effort to learn, giving up quite easily. When the slightest "pressure" was applied to get her to exert more effort, she would immediately begin to cry and offered a "helpless" attitude to those attempting to stimulate her.

The results of previous psychological evaluations were reviewed before Helena was seen in consultation. At 4 years and 4 months, she was given the Cattell form of the Binet Intelligence Test at a pediatric unit of the local hospital and obtained an IQ score of 58. At CA (Chronological age) 5-4, she was reexamined at the same hospital and obtained an IQ score of 62 ôn the Stanford-Binet. At CA 7-4, this test was readministered by the school psychologist and an IQ score of only 46 was obtained. At 11 years and 0 months, shortly before she was seen in consultation, she was reexamined by another school psychologist, who gave her a number of psychological tests. On the Leiter International Performance Scale, her IQ was 57; on the Peabody Picture Vocabulary Test her "mental age" was 5-5, slightly below that obtained on the Leiter Scale; on the vocabulary subtest of the WISC-Revised, her vocabulary was approximately five years. Surely, Helena was a mentally retarded child!

The reported pattern of normal development followed by subsequent arrest in development (and possible regression) suggested that some factor or factors might have been responsible for the change in developmental patterns, although both parents (both of whom were intelligent as well as professional persons) offered no clue that this might be so. Further and more detailed inquiries about the circumstances during the period of reported developmental change revealed that a sibling had been born when Helena was 11 months of age. The excitement of the new arrival, and the shift of attention to this new child seemed to upset Helena very markedly. Shortly after this, Helena developed a febrile condition with a high fever but she seemed to suffer no ill consequences. However, once again attention reverted to the newborn and once again Helena "felt rejected." The parents were able, after this further review of the history, to "remember" that Helena's shift in behavior began at about one year of age (and not at two years, as had previously been reported). The present writer also obtained all of the medical records including the birth records and subsequent developmental records after birth until nine months of age (at a Well-Baby Clinic). There was no report of anoxia (!), and all medical data indicated that Helena was a well baby who showed normal physical, neurological, and mental development. The parents now "remembered" that they had never been told that Helena was "anoxic" but only began to think of this as a possibility after she began to demonstrate some signs of retardation.

A careful psychological evaluation then was conducted to assess Helena's present abilities and potential for growth and development. Part of this procedure included "experimental-clinical" evaluation (see chapter 11). There were indications that Helena had far more potential than she had demonstrated, that she was passively oppositional and did not attempt many tasks of which she was indeed capable, and that she had constructed a simplistic world for herself in which few demands were made on her because she was "retarded" and in which she could receive an inordinate amount of special attention. Although there were difficulties in habits of attention, in the integration of data from multiple sources of stimulation, and in the sequential processing of data, there also was evidence that, when "required" to perform better, she could use language much more effectively than she had ever demonstrated, had superior visual memory, had at least average perceptual-motoric abilities for her age, and could engage in some thinking processes at a level considerably above her presumed mental age.

These and other findings (not reported because of their technical nature) led to the hypothesis that Helena was not mentally retarded, was highly conflicted and anxious, and had developed an oppositional but passive mode of relating to the world. Conferences with parents and school personnel led to the formulation of a remedial program at both home and school that would help to supply needed skills but, above all, that would constantly challenge Helena to function more effectively. Within two months' time, she had begun to respond far above her previous level of accomplishment in communication and linguistic skills, in social adaptation, and in many cognitive tasks. As of this writing, despite some periods of mild regression, she has continued to make increasingly better progress in her academic work in school and a much better social adaptation at home.

It now seems clear, in retrospect, that Helena was highly conflicted and anxious during and shortly after the period when her younger sister was born and withdrew into her passive-oppositional pattern of behavior as a defensive means of attempting to cope with her problems and of seeking and obtaining "special attention" for her needs. This pattern was reinforced over the years. It also is possible that her high fever interfered with neurological patterns of integration at a critical period in infancy and for a time contributed to her difficulties and her "solutions." In passing, it should be noted that there was no current evidence of neurological disability or impairment.

This admittedly exceptional case is cited to illustrate the severe ravages which a high degree of conflict and anxiety can cause.

Unresolved, unconscious conflicts produce persistent tension or anxiety (see next section). The effects of this anxiety may not only produce the immediate effect of diminished effectiveness, but may also have crippling effects on the development of the person's ego. (See chapter 8 for a discussion of this concept.) There also may be the cyclical effect of persistent, unconscious anxiety leading to reduced energy and effectiveness, leading to decreased intellectual functioning, leading to increased conflict, leading to still additional anxiety, and so on. For the retarded pupil who is already handicapped in an ability to deal with the complex social and intellectual demands of the school situation, this cycle may be devastating indeed. When a pupil has been culturally deprived, and when the capacity to cope with conflict has already been impaired (as is the case with many retarded children), the effects of anxiety are more likely as well as more significant.

Other theories of conflict have been developed by various workers in the fields of personality development. By way of contrast with the psychoanalytic viewpoint we have presented, it may be fruitful to consider one of these. Shaffer and Shoben (1956) give a very clear exposition of conflict theory, following Lewin's formulation (1935) of personality theory in many respects.

First, they distinguish between *frustration* and *conflict*. *Frustration* is defined as a condition in which external factors (a person, a person's behavior, or a situation) prevent the reduction of an aroused drive. Blocking of the drive leads to variations in behavior, increased intensity of the drive (frequently), aggression (sometimes), or regression "from better organized to more primitive behavior." *Conflict* is defined as the simultaneous arousal of two or more "antagonistic patterns of motivation" that cannot be satisfied at the same time. Shaffer and Shoben maintain that frustration may lead to conflict in the following way: When the frustrating object is feared, but love from that object is needed (note that this already implies conflict), the frustration leads to aggression, but this learned fear acts as a thwarting motive to the aggressive drives.

Shaffer and Shoben propose (following Lewin) that all conflict may be understood as "an interaction between an individual and the events of his environment." Every object or person in an individual's psychological environment either attracts (has *positive valence*) or repels (has *negative valence*). The degree of attraction or repulsion (or strength of the valences) may vary. Shaffer and Shoben suggest that there are three types of conflict: (1) *approach-approach* conflict (two positive valences that cannot be satisfied simultaneously), (2) *avoidance-avoidance* conflict, and (3) *approach-avoidance* conflict. They believe that the most severe, or most disturbing, type of conflict is the approach-avoidance type when the avoidance motive is based on fear.

A theory such as this serves to clarify many of the phenomena of emotional disturbance. It is not incompatible with the psychoanalytic theory discussed previously. However, one may question how well it accounts for the genesis of many kinds of conflicts.

ANXIETY

Anxiety is a common experience that we have all shared. We have undoubtedly felt anxious from time to time and have been aware of fluctuations in the intensity of our anxiety. If we analyze our experiences when we are anxious, we probably will note that we feel somewhat "disorganized." We may feel that something "bad" is going to happen to us. We dread something, and yet we are not quite sure what it is we dread.

Anxiety is not the same thing as fear. For example, we fear crossing a railroad crossing when a train is approaching, or walking in front of an oncoming car, or remaining in a building that is on fire. *We fear something specific that is consciously known to us.* In an anxiety reaction, we have somewhat similar feelings, but *we do not know exactly what it is that arouses these feelings within us.* The specific object or situation that induces the anxiety reaction is not known at a conscious level.

All human beings experience numerous anxieties. An example of a common anxiety situation is the birth process, which presumably induces severe anxieties in the newborn child. Freud (1936) emphasized the importance of the fact that the infant emerges into an environment that is very different from that of prenatal existence. He stated that the child is suddenly exposed to a flood of stimulation that it is totally unable to handle. According to Freud, this is the first significant danger situation to which we all are exposed, and it serves as the model for all our future anxieties.

Other authorities have differed with this viewpoint. Rank (1929) feels that birth strongly shocks the child, both physiologically and psychologically, thus creating a reservoir of anxiety that is released throughout life. Freud views the birth process as the physiological model of later anxiety; Rank views it as the source of the anxiety itself. Greenacre (1945) takes a position somewhat between Freud and Rank. She feels that constitutional factors, prenatal experiences, the birth process, and the situation immediately after birth all play a part in creating within the child a predisposition to anxiety. Greenacre states that this basic anxiety differs from later anxiety in that it operates on a reflex level and has no psychological content. Fodor (1972) feels that birth is almost always traumatic. We shall discuss the relation of the birth process to the development of the personality in chapter 8. At this time, we focus on the birth process as an example of an anxiety-producing situation to which all human beings are exposed (see Cattell, 1950).

The very young child has basic needs that he is totally unable to gratify or satisfy by his own efforts. An example is the infant's need for food. He cannot satisfy hunger until he is fed by another person, usually his mother. No action of his can satisfy his need for food; it must be satisfied by outside sources. A tension automatically results in the child whenever this need is present. If hunger is not satisfied immediately, he experiences pain and discomfort. The chief point with which we need to be concerned here is that the child experiences impulses and needs that are not gratified immediately. This may create very strong anxieties, which may be overwhelming. The research by Brody and Axelrad (1970) clearly demonstrates this finding.

Since the ego structure of the very young child is weak, he experiences anxieties in a very passive manner and is unable to control them (see Brenner, 1973). As the ego matures, however, the child learns to anticipate dangers. Then the child experiences a reaction similar to the earlier, more primitive, states of anxiety, but at a much less intensive level. This reaction is similar in *quality,* but not in *quantity,* to the earlier and more primary anxiety centered around the need for nourishment. The new type of anxiety, brought about by the ego's anticipation of a future danger, may be regarded as a warning signal, for it initiates a defensive reaction to guard against the anticipated threats. We experience this type of anxiety when we automatically and unconsciously perceive something as threatening. Then we try to do something about it to allay the anxiety aroused by this anticipation.

We may regard all anxieties, in the last analysis, as unconscious fears of experiencing a threatening and damaging state. Anxiety may be regarded as a fear that one's ego will be overwhelmed by a situation it cannot master. Basically, anxiety stems from the apprehension that impulses (id impulses according to the psychoanalysts) cannot be controlled. If, however, there have been no serious disturbances in ego development and the ego has matured sufficiently, impulses usually are not perceived as threatening, so no overpowering anxieties are aroused.

At times, the child is totally unable to handle anxieties. If a child has many repressions that have resulted from previously threatening situations, the slight anxiety that is added by an additional threat of danger is enough to "blow the whole situation apart," and overwhelming anxiety results. The ego's signal of a possible approaching danger in this instance not only fails to avoid a threatening situation but actually precipitates an exceedingly serious situation.

The newborn child's anxiety when needs are not satisfied immediately is automatic and is specific to certain situations. That is a usual reaction. As the ego develops, anxiety serves ego functions. Normally the anxiety reaction is controlled by the ego and is used by the child as a warning signal to avoid further disorganization. When ego control fails and anxiety becomes overwhelming the child reverts to the original primary anxiety stage. That is an abnormal reaction.

A special type of anxiety is known as *guilt*. We all have had the experience of feeling very guilty about some things without knowing why we feel that way. Feelings of guilt are centered around such thoughts as "I have done wrong" or "It was not right." The core of the special anxiety we know as guilt is the ego's warning, "Do not do that or something terrible will happen to you." The guilt feelings that a child experiences arise primarily from fear of abandonment by parents because of something bad that the child did or wished to do. These feelings are quite specific. What is really feared in a guilt reaction is that there will be a loss of those pleasant feelings of well-being, security, and protection that all children desire. (See Lewis, 1971, for a sophisticated discussion of the nature of guilt.) We may summarize all of these feelings under the general term *self-esteem*. In guilt, the child fears the loss of self-esteem. Anxiety, in general, warns the child not to undertake a particular course of action, but guilt feeling develops when the child has behaved in such a way that the loss of approval by the loved one seems warranted.

Anxiety, then, may be regarded as a danger signal that is felt and perceived consciously by the child, although the origin of the anxiety, or its underlying cause, is always unconscious. Anxiety always originates from a threat from within the personality. This internal threat, however, may be initiated or modified by the child's external situations. The physiological symptoms of the child's internal conflicts are expressions of the defensive forces through which the child attempts to control anxieties.

As a result of anxiety, the functions of the ego are inhibited, since ego functions are preoccupied in the defensive struggle. Since the retarded child has an impoverished or inadequate ego, ego functions tend to be disturbed even more than those of the normal child.

Thus far we have presented the traditional psychoanalytic viewpoint on anxiety. That theory helps us understand many aspects of the phenomenon, especially the relationship of anxiety to behavioral disturbances in the retarded child. However (as Freud and many later psychoanalysts have acknowledged), this theory still leaves many critical questions unanswered. In the following pages, we shall present some of the experimental and clinical data on this subject and propose some extensions and modifications of the psychoanalytic theory of anxiety.

A review of much of the experimental evidence is presented in a number of books. May (1950) develops a general theory of anxiety. In a book by Hoch and Zubin (1964) several authorities present summaries of their positions. There already are considerably more data than these volumes present, since the experimental work in this area is in a state of active ferment. Cattell (1957) for example, has summarized some of his speculations. A more recent and comprehensive review of theories and effects of anxiety is available in an excellent volume edited by Spielberger. (1966). Of special interest to those who work with infants and very young children is the book by Brody and Axelrad (1970), noted previously. They trace the interactions between anxiety and ego formation under different conditions of the mother-child relationship.

At least two basic questions remain to be answered about the conceptualization of anxiety. The first asks whether or not anxiety is a unitary phenomenon. In other words, is there simply one kind of anxiety that may vary in intensity but not in its quality or characteristics? The second question is whether or not the amount of anxiety and the stage of the child's life at which it is manifested have differential effects on behavior. That question includes such subsidiary questions as these: Under what conditions does anxiety result in psychopathological behavior? Can anxiety serve to facilitate learning and affect adjustment favorably? Is there a relative degree of anxiety, which may vary for the individual during different stages of life, that is optimal for adjustment? This whole intriguing problem area is vitally significant to an understanding of personality in general, as well as to the psychopathology of the mentally retarded child.

Various investigators (such as Hoch and Zubin, 1964) have taken the position that there is an infinite variety of anxieties. Evidence for this position rests on the demonstration that various kinds of stress may separately induce anxiety reactions. Nevertheless, reaction to stress may not be quite the same thing as basic anxiety. In both there may be increased activity of the autonomic nervous system, disorganized responses and *hyperactivity* (more than normal activity) at the motor level, and feelings of tenseness or panic. However, there may be a significant difference between reactions to specific stress (or *trauma*) and reactions to anxiety as we are using the term. In the latter, we have postulated an unconsious element (the child is unaware of the real danger factor), whereas in the former the danger is known and may be perceived or dealt with more or less directly. Again, in anxiety, the whole ego appears to the child to be threatened, whereas in stress the ego may be only partially involved or not involved at all (see Sarason and Mandler, 1952a; 1952b).

Several recent studies support the theoretical formulation that basic anxiety (usually called *anxiety trait*) is distinguishable from stress anxiety reactions (usually called *anxiety state*) (Spielberger et al., 1970). This distinction is useful in that it leads to better prediction of performance. For example, Hodges and Felling (1970) showed that anxiety trait led to fear of failure and to loss of self-esteem when there was psychological stress. In other words, there appears to be a built-in susceptibility to new stressful situations that may adversely affect certain kinds of performance. Later, we shall see how important this is for retarded individuals.

Some workers have defined what is called *test anxiety* (a reaction to the specific stress of the test situation). Wine (1971) has reviewed the literature on this concept and believes that children who have high test anxiety (or are high in anxiety state) learn to become more alert to evaluative cues but become less alert to task cues. In other words, such children are more concerned about self-worth and therefore function less effectively in the stressful task. Children who are low on test anxiety are able to focus more effectively on the task at hand. However, Sarason (1972) found no difference between three experimental conditions designed to test the effects of reducing test anxiety. In the first, reassurance was given; in the second, *task orientation* was provided; and in the third, *motivating task orientation* was given. Contrary to expectations, Ss (subjects) with high test anxiety were superior to Ss with low test anxiety under all conditions. However, although this was a sophisticated study, many possibly significant factors were not controlled. It would be important to learn how retarded children—having high or low anxiety state and differing in test anxiety—do under varying conditions.

There is another, and perhaps even more basic, difference between anxiety and disturbed reactions to stress. In basic anxiety, the child behaves as if there is a built-in anxiety "structure"; that is, the child is unable to deal with the situation realistically, is unable to modify ways of coping with the difficulty, and continues to respond with relatively *stereotyped* behavior and with anxiety when the stress situation (objectively) is no longer present. Thus, the child has a reservoir of anxiety that discharges whether the objective reality calls for it or not. This discharge may be direct, in which case the anxiety is directly expressed, or it may be indirect, in which case inner equivalents or symptomatic derivatives may be substituted for the emotional part of the reaction.

Stress reactions may gradually give way to anxiety if a child meets repeated stress situations that she cannot master, if the intensity of the stress becomes sufficiently great, or if the child is too immature to cope with the stress. In such a case, perception of the real danger becomes more and more distorted, more repression occurs, the ego becomes less adequate and more rigid, and fear is finally replaced by anxiety; there is then an "unknown factor." A child who already has much anxiety is likely to be disproportionately affected by stressful situations to the degree that the stress involves the security of ego. Hence, stress is more stressful when the subject is younger and less competent and less experienced in dealing with it, and when the ego is more likely to be overwhelmed, as in the mentally retarded child.

It can be readily understood that stress or shock to a child may result in increased anxiety. It may be more difficult to conceptualize the effects of actual or anticipated separation from, or rejection by, an important loved object (such as the mother) although common knowledge tells us that such experiences may result in at least severe depression. The psychological meaning of separation as a vital threat to the ego, particularly as it affects young children, is highlighted by a number of studies. Anna Freud and Burlingham (1973), who studied the effects of such separation in England during World War II, point out that with young children, particularly between the ages of two and four years, separation from the parents may produce severe and persisting anxiety reactions and neurotic behavior. Separation, rather than the fear of being hurt physically, was more often than not the decisive factor in the development of such reactions.

Studies by others not only have confirmed this conclusion but also have shown that severe depression (sometimes called *anaclitic depression)* and other clinical conditions tend to result from such separation during the first year of life. The reaction tends to be more severe when a good or fairly good relationship had already existed between mother and child. Similar, but usually milder, reactions have been reported in soldiers who became anxious, depressed, and disorganized when they were simply removed from their homes or home towns and their families, long before they were subjected to actual threat of physical injury or to more threatening battle conditions (Grinker and Spiegel, 1945).

In such studies, separation easily may be seen as a threat to the ego, in conflict with drives for security, affection, and the preservation of the status quo. When such stress is introduced early in the life of the child, when the ego is still weak and cannot institute appropriate defensive measures, the effects on the ego tend to be proportionately more severe, producing disorganization to such a degree that persistent psychotic tendencies (*processes*) may be induced. The effects are far-reaching because the basic security of the child is threatened, and anxiety and its derivatives mount to high levels.

We have highlighted the effects of severe stress and the resultant induction of high degrees of anxiety, but we have not given much attention to the effects of milder degrees of these phenomena. Although the milder conditions are important, they are more significant for normal reactions and for theories of learning than for psychopathology. Various investigators have been experimenting with reactions of essentially normal subjects to milder forms of stress. The studies by Sarason and Mandler (1952b) have shown that with an "unselected" population of college students, those students who have a low level of anxiety tend to do better in test situations in which unanticipated stress is introduced, whereas those who are higher in anxiety level do better on the regular scholastic or course examination for which they were able to prepare. These studies point up the differential effects of degrees of anxiety. The effects of different kinds of defense mechanisms in handling anxiety also have been explored (Waterhouse and Child, 1933). Additional studies by Eriksen (1954) and by Lazarus et al. (1952) have contributed further to our understanding of the differential effects of anxiety and have shown, in addition, that there may be different kinds of anxiety for different kinds of situations.

Cattell (1957) worked intensively on the problem of the measurement of anxiety for a number of years, using factor analytic methods of investigation. He developed a questionnaire method of measuring anxiety (called the *IPAT Anxiety Scale*), as well as laboratory methods of measuring anxiety. He summarized much of his thinking in a speech delivered in January, 1957. He believes: "that there is indeed a single factor in the realm of anxiety manifestations. . . . This functional unity called the *general anxiety factor* is also shown to be distinct from neuroticism and from the stress reaction, though it tends to be significantly correlated with the former." Cattell also has shown that what he calls anxiety state (and what we have called objective anxiety or reaction to stress) is subject to a specific stress situation, whereas general anxiety is a persistent characteristic of the person, operating at a continuous level within that person. Cattell's position is, in general, consistent with our own. We differ from him mainly in our specific analysis of the cause of anxiety (he postulates five or six possible sources of anxiety), and in our conclusions that anxiety at the latent, or symbolic, level may not be measurable by the same means as other manifestations of anxiety (especially overt anxiety). Nevertheless, his experimental studies have extremely important implications that have stimulated considerable research.

We now may pull all this material together and summarize our own position. In doing this, we wish to remind the reader that our summary is essentially intended to provide a frame of reference and stimulate further critical thinking.

We have defined anxiety as a condition in which the child is unaware of the source of intense emotional reaction, apprehension, or dread. In any given response, however, there may be an admixture of this type of *objectless* anxiety and *objective* anxiety (or fear). Each child has a persisting anxiety level that tends to remain more or less constant over a period of time, unless increased by severe trauma or decreased by some benign or favorable factor (such as psychotherapy). Anxiety of the objectless variety has a highly significant effect on the ego, depending on the age and condition of the child when it is developed and on the intensity level of the anxiety, among other conditions. Small amounts of anxiety that can be dealt with successfully lead to strengthening of the ego's functions. Large amounts of anxiety tend to overwhelm the ego, produce some persistent damage to its functioning, create the need for certain defensive maneuvers to reduce the tension level, and produce symptomatic derivatives. There probably is an optimal level of anxiety for effective functioning and effective learning.

Thus, we may conceptualize three levels of anxiety: a normal level, which facilitates learning and adjustment; a lower than normal level, which has little or no effect on adjustment; and a pathological level, which produces more or less persistent maladjustment, rigid and stereotyped behaviors, poor learning and adaptation, and pathological defenses and symptoms. In addition to having an effect on the emotions (the *affective* behavior), pathological amounts of anxiety disturb the *cognitive* (intellectual) processes and interfere with smooth and effective motor behavior.

Besides the individual's characteristic, or chronic, level of anxiety, we must consider two other general factors. One is the relative and sudden increase or decrease in anxiety (particularly an increase), which may be produced by some ego-involving stress (which is subjectively perceived as threatening). Such rapid changes in anxiety level tend to produce the effects that we attribute to pathological anxiety. The other factor that must be considered is the nature of the defenses that have been developed to deal with anxiety. The more immature these are, the less satisfactorily will the anxiety be controlled.

Basic, or objectless, anxiety may be characterized as either security anxiety or separation (or *rejection*) anxiety. As noted above, either type of basic anxiety, in intense amounts, is conducive to some degree of maladjustment. In separation anxiety, the earlier psychological model of basic anxiety, anticipation of losing support or being rejected by an important love object tends to bring on feelings of catastrophe. Security anxiety, or apprehension about being mutilated or destroyed, is a second model of anxiety, associated with later forms of interpersonal experience. These two basic forms of anxiety proliferate, as the individual matures and differentiates, into many subsidiary forms, the characteristics of which may be greatly influenced by cultural factors.

ANXIETY AND THE RETARDED CHILD

The retarded child, like all other human beings, experiences anxiety for the basic reasons that we have discussed above. It can be expected that problems of *security* and *separation* will be especially important for such children. It is our contention that retarded children are, in general, more prone to develop intense anxieties than other children, although the manifestations of such anxieties at the behavior level may take different forms than with children of normal and superior intellectual development. For example, tendencies to *characterological behavior* (that is, persistent life styles) involving loss of attention and interest in the intellectual world, loss of interest in many forms of social interaction, decrease in use of intellectual capacities for abstract thinking and for fantasy creation, decrease in use of verbal skills for interpersonal communication, and increase in use of motoric skills, as well as passive-oppositional orientation to the world, may be more common manifestations of continuing, intense anxiety in retarded children.

The proposition that retarded children experience more anxiety than other children generally is supported by research evidence. This is certainly true for overt, or manifest, anxiety—in other words, anxiety that is consciously visible to others and that is experienced by the child as apprehension of an immediate situation. Anxiety concerning tests is an example. Consciously experienced anxiety in relation to immediate learning situations of other kinds is another example. Silverstein (1970) finds that, quite generally, retarded individuals have higher levels of anxiety than do nonretarded individuals. We shall later review in some detail two studies (Cochran and Cleland, 1963; Malpass et al., 1960) that clearly demonstrate that mentally retarded children show more manifest anxiety than normal children. In studies such as these, manifest anxiety usually is measured by a questionnaire in which respondents state how they feel at a given time in their life. The evidence indicates that retarded persons experience and are aware of anxiety in greater amounts than persons with superior intelligence.

The evidence is not as clear-cut or convincing with respect to covert and basic anxiety. In fact, there is some evidence that basic anxiety, sometimes termed *general anxiety* to distinguish it from more specific anxiety (like test anxiety), is not greater in retarded persons than in normal persons (Sarason, 1959). However, it is evident from the research that has been published that it is more difficult to measure covert anxiety than overt anxiety, in general, and that the results of the usual tests of covert anxiety have doubtful validity when the tests are administered to retarded groups (Sarason, 1960).

The retarded child with a high anxiety level may pay a double penalty. Hutt (1947) conducted a study to ascertain the effects of stress (generated by the frustration of failing successive items on the standard intelligence test) on obtained IQ score. Dividing the subjects taking the *Stanford-Binet Intelligence Scale* into categories of adjustment level, and equating these categories in other respects (such as age, sex, and socioeconomic status), the examiners gave the test to half of the subjects by the *consecutive method* and gave it to the other half by the *adaptive method.* The essential difference between the methods of administration was the order in which the test items were presented. In the *consecutive method,* the items were given in sequence from the easiest level to the most difficult level, as in the standardized condition. In the *adaptive method,* the easy and difficult items were alternated. The administration of the items, themselves, was the same, whatever the method of administration. Since the consecutive method involved a succession of increasingly difficult items, it tended to increase the subject's frustration and anxiety. On the other hand, since the adaptive method involved the alternation of hard and easy items, it tended to minimize constant frustration and permitted a siphoning off of any anxiety that might be built up.

As was predicted, there was no difference between the average IQ scores obtained with the two methods in the category of highly adjusted children. However, the average IQ score obtained by less well adjusted subjects tested by the adaptive method was much higher than the average IQ score that was obtained by less well adjusted subjects tested by the consecutive method. In fact, the greater the degree of maladjustment the greater was the difference in average IQ scores obtained between the consecutive and adaptive methods. Moreover, when an external criterion of intelligence was used as a measure of the "true" intelligence, the results of the adaptive method correlated higher with this criterion than did the results of the consecutive method. The study demonstrated that frustration (and concurrent anxiety) can significantly depress the obtained IQ score. More than that, it showed that test anxiety can result in spurious scores in IQ that provide inaccurate prediction of later intellectual performance.

That covert anxiety may be directly related to mental retardation and that there may even be a significant causal relationship may be inferred from an intensive study of 172 children referred for evaluation because of suspected mental retardation (Garfield et al., 1961). In 15 percent of the cases, even after intensive study by relevant clinical techniques, no conclusive diagnosis could be reached. Moreover, of the total population, 18 percent were evaluated as not being mentally retarded.

Garfield and his coworkers are careful to point out that the interplay of diverse factors, especially emotional factors that may affect behavior and performance, makes the diagnosis of mental retardation in young children especially difficult. Judging from the evidence presented in this study, one could infer that a significant proportion of this population was suffering from emotional problems in which a major factor was covert anxiety, although the authors do not specify this as a probable condition. As we have noted earlier, if intense and continuing anxiety is present, and if it takes the form of characterological withdrawal and reduced interaction with the environment, one of the major consequences may be apparent mental retardation.

One worker in the field of mental retardation (Davis, 1961) has suggested that impairment in learning capacity may be attributed to psychological stresses associated with disturbed parent-child relationships. Davis cites evidence from learning theory experiments by Liddell and others, and from his reviews of the clinical literature. Other workers (Olshansky et al., 1962) urge the abandonment of the term *mental retardation* in favor of the term *culturally different* for children who do not have any known brain damage. The evidence and arguments amassed by Olshansky et al. suggest that not only may cultural deprivation contribute to retardation but it may contribute as well to covert and basic anxiety, affecting the child's basic security system and thus leading to persistent impairment of mental abilities.

Another type of evidence, admittedly indirect, bears on the effects of anxiety on the development of mentally retarded behaviors. This evidence comes mainly from experiments on the learning characteristics of the retarded. We shall discuss some aspects of this evidence in a later section of this chapter (see Anxiety and Learning), but we shall refer to three kinds of evidence at this point.

Zeaman and House (1962) focused on what they call an *attention theory* in relation to the learning of discriminations in simple perceptual tasks. They found that when retarded individuals are helped by some experimental procedures to maximize their attention (and they have shown that the retarded tend to be deficient in paying attention), they are able to learn even difficult perceptual discriminations much more effectively. Their studies raise the question, "What causes the attention difficulties in the first place?" Was the attention difficulty a result of the mental retardation, was it caused by the same factors that led to both retardation and poor attention, or was some other factor at work? In our view, it is possible to understand the decrease in attention as a function of persistent anxiety (although other factors also may be causative agents). Hence, training in attending, although effective, may be regarded as treatment of the symptom directly. It also might be possible to relieve the anxiety that is producing inattention and thus effect an even more significant improvement. In any case, Zeaman's findings are consistent with such a view.

A second aspect of this type of evidence comes from studies of how retarded individuals learn abstract concepts. It has been found repeatedly that such persons do much more poorly than normals, even when matched for mental age. Even more striking is the finding that this ability becomes progressively and relatively worse when the children are placed and continued in institutions for the mentally retarded (Badt, 1958). One may speculate about why this condition develops. Is it because the children are innately less accomplished in verbal, and particularly in abstract, thinking? This should not be true when they are matched with normal persons for mental age. In fact, the reverse should be found under such conditions, for when they are matched with normal children in mental age, they have lived longer and should therefore have had more learning opportunity to acquire abstract concepts. We suggest, instead, that cultural deprivation and the general withdrawal that persistent anxiety breeds, in many instances, lead to decreased need for the use of verbal communication and abstract thinking.

A third line of evidence results from studies on "need to achieve" and "expectancy of failure." Such behaviors are the result, no doubt, of a complex of factors, but a central aspect is the anxiety generated by frustrations and failures first in social adaptation and later in cognitive demands and tasks presented by school situations that are too difficult for the retarded (see the case of Helena). Jordan (1972) has shown that retarded children have lower needs to achieve than do the nonretarded. A series of studies (MacMillan and Keogh, 1971; Gruen and Zigler, 1968) have demonstrated that mentally retarded children have a greater expectancy of failure than children possessing higher levels of intelligence.

These lines of inquiry need further clarification and verification. The strong implication is that anxiety has a powerful effect on modifying performance downward when the level of anxiety is excessive or when anxiety becomes a characteristic feature of the personality. Remedial efforts may be directed to the consequences of such conditions by attempting to improve attention, or by conditioning the need to achieve in a positive direction, for example. On the other hand, they may be directed to preventing the development of excessively high levels of anxiety in the first place, or of reducing such levels once they have developed. Probably both types of approach, in coordination, will result in the best remedial program. We shall discuss the relative merits of each approach and the appropriate use of each in later chapters on intervention, learning, and therapy.

One other general implication of the diverse effects of excessive anxiety in the development of retarded individuals has to do with the kind of self-concept they tend to develop. Both analytically oriented theorists (Sternlicht, 1975) and behaviorally oriented theorists (Garrison, 1975), despite differing underlying conceptualizations, agree that the nature of the self-percept of the retarded person depends more on the social experiences they have than on the level of their cognitive development. Although extreme degrees of retardation may contribute to poor self-regard, it is the deprivation in positive social experiences and the frustration that schools and institutions create, rather than the level of mental age, that are correlated with low self-esteem. Central to such maldevelopment is the experiential base of anxiety created by discrepancies between the *slow development* of an individual's skills and an environment that requires functions of which the individual is still incapable. A frequent consequence is the frustration of basic needs. Anxiety thus is seen not as a *necessary characteristic* of retardation but as a *consequence* of inappropriate or ineffective social milieus.

A significant amount of research now supports these formulations. Thus, Zisfein and Rosen (1974) found that self-estimates of self-concept were independent of IQ. Similarly, in a series of studies Guthrie and coworkers (1961, 1964) found that positive self-attitudes were derived from experiences in cooperative, socially approved behaviors whereas negative self-attitudes were derived from failures in interpersonal peer relationships. Gorlow, Butler, and Guthrie (1963) concluded that "ideals for the self arise early in the development and are generally resistive to change." Zigler (1966) concluded that the mentally retarded learn to anticipate failure and resign themselves to lower degrees of success. Miller and Gottlieb (1972) in an experiment designed to predict affect after task performance found that the mentally retarded tend to attribute negative feelings to others while they attributed positive feelings to themselves; normals demonstrated just the reverse relationships. Peters et al. (1974), in a four-year study involving adult-led recreation groups, found that EMR children scored lower than normal children on: interest-participation versus apathy-withdrawal. These findings suggest that it is not the inherent nature of mental retardation per se that produces these negative characteristics in aspects of the self-concept, but rather the frustrating experiences to which they are exposed.

ANXIETY AND DEFENSIVE BEHAVIOR

There are two general ways in which one can reduce anxiety. The more healthy method is to learn to cope with the conflict directly, making some appropriate, realistic, adaptive response to the situation and thus resolving the conflict. The other (less efficient and always relatively more pathological) is to use *defense mechanisms.* A defense mechanism is an indirect method of dealing with conflict. It does not resolve the conflict but, rather, reduces its severity. All children, so far as we know, employ both *coping behaviors* and *defense mechanisms* (as do all adults), but there is some evidence that retarded children rely less on coping behavior and more on defensive behavior than do normal children. Moreover, retarded children probably employ some types of defenses disproportionately more than do normals.

Every person would express biological drives quite directly (a) if physically capable of executing the behavior necessary for this expression (i.e., if maturation and learning enabled one to do so); (b) if opposing drives did not conflict; and (c) if no external factors (e.g., physical reality and cultural prohibition) inhibited their expression. However, some drives cannot be expressed directly because the child has learned to fear their expression through guilt or social value that has been interiorized. The retarded child who has been made to feel guilty because behavior does not meet familial or cultural standards is less likely to be able to express biological drives directly or in some appropriately adaptive manner than a child who has not experienced such psychological rejection. The retarded child, especially one with some general lag in biological development, also is less likely to be able to express drives appropriately in relation to the realistic difficulties involved in the external reality. Inappropriate expression of drives may occur not only because the child's sensorimotor development is inadequate to the task at hand, but also because the child has not acquired the cognitive, or intellectual, means of interpreting external reality accurately or responding adequately to its complexities.

A child in conflict attempts to produce some compromise solution through the use of various psychological defenses. Both the conflict and the use of defenses consume psychic energy. The greater the intensity of the conflict, the less energy is available for other purposes.

As we have said, in early infancy drives tend to be expressed quite freely. When the ego and superego begin to form and conflicts develop, the expression of a drive is changed—it is either blocked or altered in some manner. The reason for both the blocking and the alteration of behavior is the *anxiety* that has developed because of the conflict. Anxiety, then, signals conflict within the child, and because of that anxiety, the drive can be expressed only in a modified form. This is the basic function of psychological defenses: to change, in some manner, the way in which a drive is gratified.

The various ways in which drives are expressed, blocked, or modified are graphically represented in Figure 7.1.

Let us assume, for example, that the drive seeking expression is hostility of the child toward the mother. In condition A, neither ego nor superego structures have been established; hence, there is no internal barrier to the free expression of the hostility. It is permitted direct gratification. (For example, the child may bite mother.) In condition B, ego and superego structures have been established, so the direct expression of hostility is blocked. (The child might think, in effect: "Mother is bigger than I am and will punish me if I am hostile toward her"; or, "Mother will not love me if I am hostile.") Since the drive is not permitted direct expression, the child experiences anxiety. Even the hostile thought itself may be blocked, and the child may only be aware that he is anxious. In condition C, the drive is again blocked, but only temporarily. Anxiety is experienced and a psychological defense comes into automatic operation. The drive is then permitted expression in an altered form, and some or all of the anxiety is discharged. For example, the child may express hostility toward a substitute person or object in place of the original object of the hostility. The child might throw a doll on the floor instead of biting or injuring the mother. In this way, by using a defense, the child reduces his conflict and maintains a minimal tension level—that is, does not become too anxious.

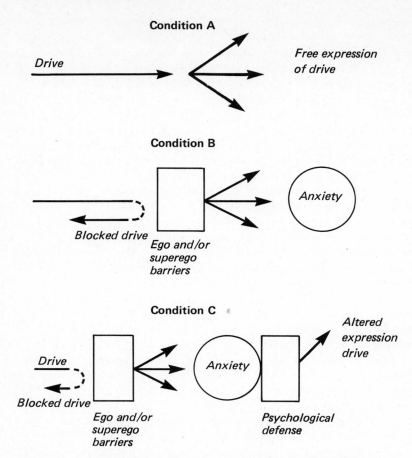

FIGURE 7.1.   Expression of Drives and Operation of Psychological Defenses

Major Defense Mechanisms

We now will discuss some of the more common defense mechanisms. Every child employs ·each of these defenses at some time. However, some children characteristically employ some of these defenses in preference to others. Some defenses, as we shall see, are more likely than others to produce serious types of behavioral maladjustment if employed as the preferred pattern.

Repression. Repression is one of the earliest and most prevalent defenses used by the child. It is an unconscious forgetting, which makes the child unaware of internal drives. Not only may a drive itself be repressed, but events and feelings associated with a drive may also be shut out of consciousness. We all have had the experience of not being able to recall a well-known fact or name. That is an instance of repression. Repression probably occurs as soon as there is even an immature differentiation of the ego from the id.

Denial. Denial is another very primitive way of dealing with unpleasant or psychologically painful realities—by denying their very existence. If a situation or object does not exist, then it cannot possibly be a threat to the child. If we observe a child closely, we may see the mechanism of denial in operation. The child may simply assert that a given situation or present objective does not exist. At a more primitive level, the child may close his eyes and not "see" the object or situation that is painful. When the ego is poorly developed or when the young child is unable to escape physically from a painful object or situation in the external world, he may use denial as a means of avoiding psychological pain. Repression and denial are closely allied defenses.

Isolation. Isolation is another very primitive and infantile defense. It is the process of separating the emotional components of a drive from their ideational representations in conscious thought. Thoughts then may be experienced because their emotional aspects are stripped away. A child may, for example, experience the thought "I am going to kill you" without any psychological discomfort because the emotional aspects of the wish have been blocked off. The impulse is no longer threatening.

Undoing. In the mechanism of undoing, the child does something that is *symbolically opposite* of what would be done if the drive were to be directly expressed. Because of its symbolic nature, the act of undoing may appear to be the execution of an act like the drive itself, but its meaning in the unconscious is, nevertheless, the opposite. To ward off the impulse, which is felt as painful, the child tries to "reverse the field," to undo the act that permits expression of the impulse. For example, as an extreme instance, a boy who had an impulse to raise the skirts of girls and examine their genital organs would usually go to bed and sleep, thus *undoing* his impulse to observe sexual organs. If this defense is used by the child, he finds it necessary to repeat the undoing act constantly in order to reduce the anxiety that he would otherwise develop.

Introjection. This defense mechanism has its origin in infancy. Its function at that time is the avoidance of undue tension provoked by external prohibitions or frustrations. When direct expression of the infant's drives is prevented, the threat of the opposing person (or situation) appears to be very great indeed. Since the child depends on this person (usually mother) not only for affection but for existence, the child experiences intense conflict between a need to express drives, on the one hand, and a fear of disapproval by mother, on the other hand. To solve this dilemma, the child resorts to introjection, or *taking in,* of mother's wishes—that is, acts as if he, and not mother, disapproves of the expression of the drive. By this process, the child avoids some of the anxiety, since it now appears to him as if *he* does not want to do what the mother forbids.

The process of introjection has been preceded by the infant's experience of *taking in* other, more literal, aspects of environment. For example, in the very act of being nourished, the infant has learned to take in food. This is the prototype of the later mechanism of introjection. The infant gradually learns to take in not only food but also the prohibitions of mother—and later of other important adults. The child learns to behave as they expect it to. Besides internalizing prohibitions, the child takes in some of the positive characteristics of the important adults in life. Through introjection, the infant identifies with the important people around—feels as they do and behaves as they do, to a certain extent.

Reaction Formation. Reaction formation is a defense that produces behavior exactly opposite to that demanded by the unacceptable drive. It always involves repression of the drive seeking expression. For example, a person with strong hostile drives acts very passive and docile by developing a reaction formation against his hostility; or a child with "dirty" impulses (that is, impulses that appear to him to be dirty), such as sexual impulses or an impulse to play with his feces, may respond, instead, by being excessively clean, often going to extreme lengths to achieve such a condition.

Projection. In projection, the child attributes her own unacceptable traits, impulses, and ideas to another person or to other people. Projection, one of the early defenses of the child, is the opposite of introjection. In introjection, the child takes into herself certain traits; in projection, the child externalizes her unacceptable traits. Such a defense is normal only during the period when the ego structure is weak and poorly formed or during periods of extreme stress. When the ego develops to the point at which reality is perceived accurately, the use of projection as a defense is usually considered abnormal or psychopathological. As an example of this mechanism, we can consider hostility again. The child may deal with this unacceptable impulse by projecting it on another person and feeling that that person, rather than she, is hostile. She then reacts to the attributed hostility of the other person.

Regression. In all the defenses previously listed, the ego actively participates. In regression, however, the ego experiences the phenomenon passively. In regression, the child resumes a previous mode of behavior when conflicts or frustrating situations cannot be resolved by the ego. For example, the child may return to thumb-sucking or enuresis (bed-wetting) when conflicts occur. (This often happens to young children when another child is born into a family.) Regression is more likely to occur when the child has previously been *fixated* (or traumatized) at a certain level and so has overlearned the modes of behavior prevalent at that time and has not been able to mature adequately to higher modes of behavior.

Sublimation. Of all the defense mechanisms, sublimation is the most mature. (In fact, some workers do not classify this behavior as a defense.) In sublimation, in contrast to the other defenses, the drive is fully discharged, but its goal is so changed that it is discharged in a socially acceptable manner. Sublimation therefore makes a change in the *object* of the drive. It is used only when there is no great amount of repression. The ego must be sufficiently well developed to make and accept the change in object of the drive. For example, as adults, we often sublimate sexual drives through our vocational activities, reading of poetry, dancing, and the like.

To illustrate some of the differences between the various defenses discussed, Table 7.1 summarizes some of the behavioral reactions to hostility. The behavioral reactions listed are, of course, not the only ones possible; they are merely representative types of behavior that *may* be shown by the child in each type of defense.

Defense Mechanisms in Mental Retardation

We have discussed defense mechanisms in general and have pointed out the characteristics of the most common mechanisms. Our discussion applies to the defensive reaction developed by the mentally retarded child as well as to those of the normal child. However, because of more severe problems and lower capacity to tolerate stress, the retarded child's anxieties are more readily aroused, and the child has more need to engage in defensive reactions. He uses the *same* defensive mechanisms as do all other children, but there are some points of difference.

In the first place, the retarded child cannot as readily use those defenses that depend on a more mature level of ego development. In general, he tends to use primitive defenses most readily. Not only does his ego fail to reach as high a degree of maturation as that of the more normal child, but it also matures at a slower rate. The extremely primitive defenses of the personality thus persist much longer in the retarded child than in the more average child. We tend to expect certain forms of behavior from an infant but are intolerant of the same behavior when it is shown by an older child. We are not overly concerned by thumb-sucking in a one-year-old child, for example, but are highly concerned when this form of behavior is shown by a ten-year-old. The adult's intolerance and disapproval of the child's behavior increases the child's anxiety level, which leads to further maladaptive behavior by the child.

Another major point of difference is in the rigidity, or persistence, of the defensive mechanisms employed by the retarded child. The more average child,

TABLE 7.1.   Defensive Reactions to Hostile Drives

Defense	Behavioral Reactions
Repression	Total unawareness of hostile feelings.
Isolation	Expression of "I'd like to kill" without any emotional reaction.
Undoing	Giving money to a charity.
Introjection	Behaving like the person toward whom the hostilities are directed.
Reaction formation	Showing "love" toward the person toward whom the hostilities are directed.
Projection	Seeing the hostilities as directed toward himself by another person.
Regression	Bed-wetting or thumb-sucking.
Sublimation	Shooting a cap pistol or bow and arrow at a target.
Denial	Saying: "I don't feel angry. He doesn't do anything to make me angry. Everything is fine."

provided she does not suffer from an emotional problem, has a relatively fluid defense network. Her defenses are employed in accordance with the requirements of the particular situations in which she finds herself. She switches from one to another with no great difficulty. The retarded child, however, does not as readily vary defenses as the situation changes.

Retarded children show a preference for such defenses as denial, introjection, regression, undoing, and repression. To a lesser degree, they use projection, reaction formation, and isolation. Sublimation is very difficult for them to achieve.

Our discussion up to this point has been based on extensive clinical observation and study of the effects of therapeutic intervention with mentally retarded children. Therefore, our findings are more theoretical than empirical. We think, however, that our inferences are profoundly significant both for understanding the retarded child and for planning education and training. Only in recent years has any experimental study been given to the many aspects of this problem, and we are just beginning to understand the issues involved.

In a previous chapter, we discussed the development of a perceptual style (adience-abience) and noted that retarded individuals are more likely to develop abient perceptual patterns than those endowed with higher cognitive abilities. However, the development of such patterns of perceptual defense is not inevitable, nor is it impossible, if very difficult, to reverse. As we shall see, with the provision of appropriately stimulating and challenging behavioral experiences, especially early in life, such perceptual maldevelopment, like other forms of inappropriate defensive behavior, can be counterbalanced and modified.

There is some support for our general thesis that deprivation leads to ineffective defenses and impaired functioning. For example, Baumeister et al. (1963) have shown that the structure of intellectual abilities is different in retarded children than it is in normal children. Retarded children show a factor that these authors call "concentration," which significantly affects their scores on the *Wechsler Intelligence Scale for Children* (see chapter 11). What they mean is that these children are weak in attention to such a degree that their general intellectual performance is thereby significantly impaired. This finding has been confirmed by Tillman (1965), who found that older subjects showed a factor he designated "freedom from distractibility," which was unique to retarded children. He found that retarded children were, in fact, easily distracted—even though they tended to persist .with the same task unless distracted by new stimuli. In other words, like Baumeister, he noted that retarded children are unable to attend appropriately to relevant stimuli and therefore show impaired functioning on intelligence tests. We shall.comment later on this attention factor but note, at this point, that it is consistent with the position that retarded children have unique defense characteristics.

There have been relatively few studies of the defense mechanisms of the mentally retarded child. Stephens (1953), who studied the defensive reactions of mentally retarded adults, suggested that their primary defense is *denial*. He stated that they are unable to accept the reality of their retardation. (But this may be because they are not helped to do so.) The concept of retardation tends to be forced on the retarded child by society, through the experiences of early childhood, which in effect are socially alienating and serve to lower self-esteem. In general, the retarded individual perceives himself as odd and queer and becomes fearful of "defectiveness." This is a function of the way others perceive him. He tends to incorporate the feelings of other persons toward mental retardation, so he often ends up with a fear-ridden image of himself. Stephen stated that such a person uses the defense of *identification*. (We prefer to label this process *introjection* and to call its product, or resultant, *identification*.) Stephens pointed out that the retarded child has strong feelings of inadequacy from which he tries to escape. In order to deal with these feelings of inadequacy, he identifies with, and clings closely to, other people. He unconsciously selects someone with whom he has contact. This process eventually precipitates him into difficulties, since he identifies (or attempts to incorporate) ego ideals that are far beyond his level of attainment. We have referred to the review of research on this subject by Zigler (1965). There is evidence that retarded children tend to be *outer-directed* rather than *inner-directed;* that is, they tend to be governed more by external cues for their behavior than by internal values or motivations.

We may cite the case of Johnny, discussed in chapter 1, to illustrate the use of psychological defenses in mental retardation. Johnny used several defenses in attempting to cope with his emotional problems. The most striking of these was regression: after the birth of his siblings, Johnny began to creep and crawl again and later began to soil and wet himself. There also were indications that Johnny was attempting to deny threatening situations. He would put his head on the desk and withdraw completely from the too-difficult academic work. Such behavior also is suggestive of attempts at isolation and repression. Johnny also appeared to have introjected attributes of his third-grade teacher, with whom he had had good interpersonal relationships.

Perhaps our greatest problems in dealing with the defense mechanisms of the mentally retarded child lie in the area of attempting to reduce the *necessity* for the child to employ psychological defenses constantly. This requires an adequate program for the child, an educational program for the public at large, and psychological treatment or guidance for the parents or caretakers. Special programs of training or behavioral modification have been shown to influence significantly the nature of defensive behaviors of the retarded person. For example, Carson and Morgan (1974) were able to modify defensive and severe patterns of food aversion in a profoundly retarded female. Hall et al. (1973) showed that they were able to extinguish behavior in group settings through the use of positive and negative reinforcement procedures. Webster and Azrim (1973) used methods of "required relaxation" in modifying adaptive-disruptive behavior. They report obtaining almost complete reduction in self-injury, screaming, physical aggression, tantrums, and the like in eight retarded adults. And, we have noted previously the work of Chasey et al. (1974), in which it was found that programs of physical training in motor control resulted in improved self-images in institutionalized mentally retarded children. Improved body control seems to be especially important for retarded children, both in infancy and early childhood, when so much of perceptual behavior depends on body control. It also is important in adolescence, when discrepancies between cognitive development and more rapid physical growth cause confusion in the self-concept and reinforce defensive behavior. Cobb (1961) pointed out years ago that adolescence is a particularly difficult adjustment period for retarded persons and that appropriate training could help ease and improve this adjustment.

A subject that requires considerable additional research is the effect of defensive behavior on cognitive and intellectual performance. We have maintained that severe and continued anxiety leads to the development and persistent use of undesirable defensive behavior. What is the effect of this behavior on intellectual development? Clinical evidence, as well as research evidence, suggests that it can distort intellectual development considerably, and that withdrawal from intellectual pursuits may be a primary consequence in some cases.

A study by Silverstein and Mohan (1963) lends additional support to this thesis. They evaluated the intellectual behavior of fifty retarded patients in an institution by means of two types of intelligence tasks: the *Object Sorting Test* and the Similarities subtest of the *Wechsler Intelligence Scale for Children*. (See chapter 9 for a discussion of such tests.) The patients were about thirty-six years of age, on the average, and their average length of institutionalization was about fifteen years. Their intellectual behavior was analyzed in terms of two dimensions of conceptual behavior: *public-private* (which refers to the degree to which the concept employed is accepted by the community); and *open-closed* (which refers to the number of attributes by which a concept can be defined). These dimensions may be thought of as defining the degree of *concreteness* (or specificity) of thinking and the degree of *abstractness* (or generality) of thinking. The study showed that the thinking of these retarded persons was both *private* and *closed,* whereas other studies have shown that the thinking of normal people is both *public* and *open.*

Unfortunately, all types of mentally retarded adults were included in the sample of retarded persons. This makes the meaning of the results less clear. Nevertheless, the findings suggest that retarded persons, at least those who have experienced lengthy institutionalization, may have become relatively more withdrawn and more concrete-minded as a defensive maneuver. One wonders how they might have developed intellectually had they had different kinds of learning and adjustment experiences!

Coping Behavior

Coping behavior is behavior that enables the person to master the external world. As the child encounters external obstacles to the satisfaction of inner needs, he is at first frustrated, but then he learns to deal with his needs by mastering or appropriately circumventing the obstacles. When coping behavior is successful, internal drives are not blocked, but find relatively direct expression in some appropriate and realistic manner. In the process of learning such behaviors, the child not only builds up a complex array of personality attributes that give him flexibility and adaptability, but also gains in *self-regard.* Coping behavior may be employed in combination with defensive behavior, but the healthy personality is relatively rich in coping methods and uses defense mechanisms relatively sparsely. Some examples of coping behavior in normal development include: crying, boasting, and day-dreaming (Menninger et al., 1963).

In a fascinating and detailed account of the development of coping behavior in a group of children, Lois Murphy (1962) found that such behaviors were related to some types of early learning experiences. For example, gratification of oral needs in infancy was correlated with accuracy of perception, sense of self-worth, and ability to control the impact of the environment. On the other hand, unfavorable experiences in infancy were correlated with poor coping behaviors, including criticalness of people, a tendency to become fatigued, and decreased perceptual clarity.

We do not have evidence of the effect of early experiences on people who are born with retarded biological capacities or who function in a retarded capacity during early phases of their development. We do not know precisely how retarded people differ in coping behavior from normal and superior people. And we certainly know far too little about the possible interrelationships of early experiences and the development of coping behaviors in different kinds of retarded people. The facts, however, that many retarded individuals experience more than the usual share of reality frustrations and that the majority of them experience moderate or severe cultural deprivation in early childhood suggest that they are less likely than normals to develop good coping behaviors. Their inability to cope, in turn, would lead to more need for defensive behavior and to less adequate development of inner potentialities.

ANXIETY AND LEARNING

We have noted previously that moderate degrees of anxiety may facilitate simple learning tasks but that severe degrees of anxiety are likely to have disabling effects on learning, especially on complex learning activities. In chapter 9 we deal extensively with the general adjustment effects of intense and persistent anxiety. In this section, we wish to emphasize the specific effects of anxiety on learning, especially on school achievement.

Studies, such as the one by Wiener et al. (1960), have shown that there is a negative correlation between level of manifest anxiety and educational achievement as measured by a standardized achievement test. Other studies, such as the one by Jordan and DeCharms (1960), have suggested that retarded children have proportionately less motivation to achieve (i.e., a lowered aspiration level) than children of average intelligence. These and related studies suggest that one important variable producing proportionately less effective learning in retarded children, less even than their mental age level would indicate, is the presence of persistent anxiety. We are not suggesting that other variables may not contribute an even greater amount to their decreased ability to learn, or that high anxiety is necessarily the only or fundamental cause of reduced learning capacity. The problem of impaired learning ability is far more complex than that.

Other studies suggest that retarded children have reduced ability to attend and to discriminate—a loss that is disproportionate to mental level (Zeaman and House, 1963). The interesting feature of this theory is that it suggests (and there is some evidence to support the theory) that retarded individuals, despite the inauspicious circumstances of their early lives, are not lacking in their ability to learn to discriminate, but they need far more time and training *to begin to learn*. Once their learning begins, it proceeds rapidly. We shall point up some of the implications of this viewpoint for learning and educational programs in chapter 13. At this time, it is important to emphasize that if sufficient and appropriate practice in learning to learn is not given, the retarded child not only becomes frustrated by experience but also *learns not to learn*. This viewpoint is consistent with Hebb's theory of mental development (1949), which suggests that the infant needs a continuing input of perceptual experience so that the central nervous system (particularly the reticular brain stem formation) can build up appropriate integrations of *cell assemblies* (or functional pathways of neural excitation) for subsequent development to occur. If such experiences are not available during this critical period, later development may be seriously and, perhaps, irreversibly impaired.

It also has been demonstrated that the performance of both organic and familial retarded individuals is characterized by disproportionately high rigidity (Shepps and Zigler, 1962). This finding indicates the prior presence of persistently high anxiety levels, which may have contributed to impaired learning ability. It also has been demonstrated that we can reverse some of the factors that adversely affect learning capacity and give the behavioral effect of retardation (sometimes a pseudo-effect) (Kass and Stevenson, 1961). Training that emphasizes improved attention and improved discrimination and offers reinforcement for correct performance (especially when carefully graded to the abilities of the subjects) significantly increases learning performance (Clarke and Cookson, 1962).

Thus, we are able to support the general hypothesis that for a considerable portion of at least nonorganic cases of retardation, high anxiety experienced over a long period of time adversely affects learning performance and learning potential, as well as such skills as ability to attend and to perceive accurately. We also are able to support the hypothesis that for cases such as these, techniques and environments designed to reduce anxiety and to provide compensatory retraining experiences and reinforcement of appropriate responses may considerably improve both the short-term and the long-term learning abilities of retarded individuals. As we shall see in later chapters, schools and institutions responsible for the training of retarded children must carefully evaluate the personality difficulties of the children (determining the nature of, and causative factors in, the anxiety reactions when they are present) and provide specific remedial educational programs or therapeutic programs to correct the difficulties. We appreciate the complexities of the tasks and of the additional knowledge we must gain in order to maximize such efforts. Even though progress and improvement are almost impossible for many retarded individuals, sometimes even slight improvement may increase our motivation and sustain us.

The generalizations that have been offered are further limited by the fact that there are many kinds of learning. For some forms of learning, anxiety may have little effect except for the general effect of decreasing the motivation to learn and the consequence of a general expectancy of failure. For other forms of learning, the effects of anxiety may be more specific and more devastating. Berman (1975) reviews much of the research on the learning problems of the retarded pupil and demonstrates both the "general learning defect" of the retarded, which we believe, in large measure is attributable to early frustrations in the learning situation with consequent development of excessive anxiety responses, as well as the great range in modifiability of learning abilities of the retarded, depending on the appropriateness of the kinds of instruction that are provided. We shall comment on these issues in later chapters.

— 8 —

The Structure of the Personality

Our previous discussions have demonstrated that each individual behaves in ways that are characteristically different from those of other individuals. This statement holds true in all ranges of intellectual ability and in all ranges of social adaptation, although there are signifiant differences between *groups* of individuals who differ in gross intellectual level or social effectiveness. Mentally retarded children, *differ as a group* from children at higher levels of intellectual and social efficiency in some important personality characteristics, but they also are similar in other characteristics. Thus, we need to know what some of these general personality differences may be and we also need to know what some of the similarities are.

We shall shortly begin our attempts to define *personality* and to see how it is assessed. We shall learn that there are characteristic ways in which an individual behaves so that, often, we can predict how the individual will behave in a variety of situations. In order to understand how best to plan intervention and education for an individual, we must know some important features of that individual's make-up: general personality characteristics as well as specific abilities and disabilities. Without such knowledge, we would be in the position of a plumber who is trying to fix some leaky pipes. The leaks might be due to deterioration in the whole system so that merely fixing specific leaks would not solve the problem. The leaks might be due to excessive pressure in the system so that reduction in pressure might help solve the problem. Or the leaks might be due to faulty joints which therefore, could be corrected at those specific points. An accurate assessment of the source of the difficulty is indispensable if corrective efforts are to be most helpful.

The characteristic *constellation* or configuration of traits that define how an individual characteristically differs in behavior from other individuals is our first approximation to define that individual's personality. Many individuals have personality constellations that seem to be dominated by one or two features, such as excessive timidity, excessive fearfulness or anxiety, or excessive aggression. When this is the case, the optimal approach to assisting such a person would be to modify this excessive tendency. This might involve a direct "attack" on that aspect of behavior or it might involve an "attack" on the sources of the abnormal trait. Whether one approach would be more effective would depend on both the cause of the problem and its interrelationship with other factors. Both treatment approaches might be equally effective, depending on the nature of the personality constellation; in other instances, one approach might prove more effective.

When an individual shows significant impairment in the ability to deal appropriately or effectively with the demands of reality, as is often the case with the mentally retarded, it may be that the individual has insufficient intellectual ability to understand or master these demands. In such instances, simplifying environmental demands or providing intensive training in order to improve the individual's effectiveness may be the approach of choice. When the individual shows gross impairment in social adaptiveness, this area may be targeted for improvement. When the individual demonstrates specific disturbed behavior in speech, in attention span, or in toilet habits, focus on these specific behaviors may be warranted. However, if there is some general personality problem, such as extreme passive oppositionalism (see case of Helena in chapter 7), or extreme anxiety, or extreme dependency, it would seem wise to attempt to understand the cause(s) of the problem as well as the specific symptoms that are present.

The personality of the mentally retarded individual is, therefore, of critical importance in designing any plan for education and treatment. In fact, the personality of the mentally retarded may be the central feature of the disability. At other times, it may be less important in the individual's total repertoire of behaviors. Emotional maldevelopment may grossly impair an individual's ability to meet the demands of daily living. It may be the decisive factor in impaired intellectual performance. It may be responsible for ineffectiveness in social adaptation. It may be manifest in low self-esteem, low level of aspiration, low level of expectation of success, and impaired efforts at sustained effort. It also should be emphasized that it is not only the child who shows overtly disturbed behavior, such as antisocial behavior, excessive crying or depression, and the like, who may have a personality problem, but that the child who is excessively compliant, socially withdrawn, or placid also may be equally disturbed in personality adjustment.

This chapter, therefore, will first discuss definitions and conceptions of personality and then the concepts of homeostasis and conscious and unconscious processes. We then will consider personality traits and present evidence concerning personality structure.

THE DEFINITION OF PERSONALITY

Thus far, we have been using the term *personality* without specifying precisely what it means. Although many attempts have been made to define personality, few have received wide acceptance. In part, such a confused state of affairs is a result of insufficient clinical and research evidence. Nevertheless, the majority of workers in the field today would find the definition proffered by Gordon Allport (1961) reasonably acceptable. He states:

Personality is the dynamic organization within the individual of those psychophysical systems that determine his characteristic behavior and thought.

Note that the *inner* determinants are specified to be *psychophysical,* and not merely physical or psychological. This implies that personality is determined by the interplay of the child's constitutional characteristics with experiences. The resultants (or the personality) may be thought of as *characteristic,* or relatively persistent and stable, qualities.

Some workers, however, think of personality as more than that which exists "within the skin" of the individual. They define it in interpersonal terms, specifying the *interacting* and *reciprocal* nature of the phenomenon. Heider (1958) exemplifies this approach. He defines it this way: ". . . the person is located in the complicated causal network of the environment. . . . Close relations across a distance exist . . . between thoughts, wishes, emotions, and sentiments of one person and those of another person." Figure 8.1 illustrates this conception.

This approach to the definition of personality has some important advantages, the most important of which may be that it leads to a search within the environment, as well as within the individual, for conditions that influence behavior. In Figure 8.1, the organism is represented by the inner circle and the relevant environment is represented by the outer circle. The organism's personality is represented by his responses 1, 4, and 6, which are influenced by internal factors A through G interacting with external factors 2, 3, and 5. The mother's frustration at her infant's relatively slow development may have a pronounced effect on the infant, who is given excessive or too little stimulation and responds even more "differently" as a consequence. A study by Baer et al. (1967) illustrates the important effects of such shaping influences on exceptional cases. The workers found that behavioral similarity becomes self-reinforcing.

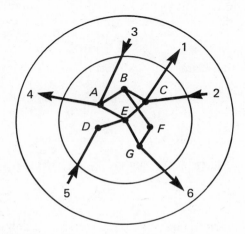

FIGURE 8.1.   A Field Conception of Personality

A modern definition of personality by Kagan and Havemann (1972) emphasizes the realms of behavior that are involved. They suggest that personality comprises "... the total pattern of characteristic ways of thinking, feeling and behaving that constitute the individual's distinctive method of relating to his environment." They emphasize the importance of considering the *pattern* of behaviors rather than the discrete and specific behaviors alone.

It also is necessary to distinguish between *character* and *personality*. Character is generally utilized by psychologists to connote the ethical or moral aspects of the behavior, whereas *personality* connotes the characteristics without any moral evaluations.

THE SEE-SAW

Physiologists have been concerned with the regulatory mechanisms of the body for a long time. Claude Bernard published his important research in 1859. He described the internal environment of living cells, pointing out that the body made continual and automatic efforts to remain constant despite the changing external and internal environmental forces. It became evident that the physiological processes of the human being tended to compensate for any changes in the steady states of the organism caused by changes in external or internal forces. This point of view led Cannon (1963) to the formulation of the principle of *homeostasis*. He described the self-regulating physiologic processes of individual tissues, organs, and organ systems. It was clearly evident to him that the organism tended to maintain its natural organic states. Homeostasis, in Cannon's formulation, referred to compensatory reactions undertaken by the organism after the disturbing stimulus situations came about. This tendency to compensate, innate in the organism, is a function of the autonomic nervous system. Behavior of the person, according to Cannon, is directed either toward getting rid of disturbing forces or toward prolonging or reviving what the person perceives as agreeable stimulation. Homeostasis refers to the first of these two possible behavioral reactions—getting rid of unwanted pressures.

More recent work by Richter (1942; 1943) has substantiated the earlier hypotheses of Cannon. Of most importance is Richter's finding that even when the simple physiologic regulators of the body are experimentally removed, the organism will attempt to maintain homeostasis by changes in the behavior of the *total* organism. The homeostatic tendency thus is a function of the entire organism, and not just of one part. One of Richter's observations will serve to illustrate this point. An animal living in a region deficient in salt will (1) migrate to a salt lick or (2) increase activity in the adrenal cortex with a resultant decrease of salt loss in the urine. An animal whose fodder contains too much salt will (1) decrease its total food content, (2) increase its excretion of salt by drinking large amounts of water, or (3) decrease activity in the adrenal cortex with a resultant increase of salt loss in the urine.

The tendency of the organism to strive continually to preserve its physiological status quo thus has been clearly demonstrated. It is not surprising, therefore, that we find the homeostatic principle being applied to psychological functions. As Fenichel (1945) points out:

Mental functions should be approached from the same angle as the functions of the nervous system in general. They are manifestations of the same basic function of the living organism—irritability.... Stimuli from the outside world or from the body initiate a state of tension that seeks for motor or secretory discharge, bringing about relaxation.

The human being learns to tolerate a particular level of psychic tension, or irritability. As long as that tension remains at a fairly constant level, the person is in a comparatively pleasurable state. However, if an internal or external stimulus increases the tension level, then the person strives to regain the former level. Activities are therefore constantly directed toward an attempt to remove forces that increase tension states. The aim, it is important to note is *not* to eliminate *all* tension but to *preserve* the level of tension that is characteristic for the particular person.

This homeostatic process is illustrated in Figure 8.2, which represents the hypothetical anxiety-tolerance (tension-tolerance) level of a person.

In A, the anxiety-producing forces are dealt with by the defensive reactions of the child, who is quite comfortable with the anxieties experienced. He has anxieties, but they are not so great that he feels uncomfortable.

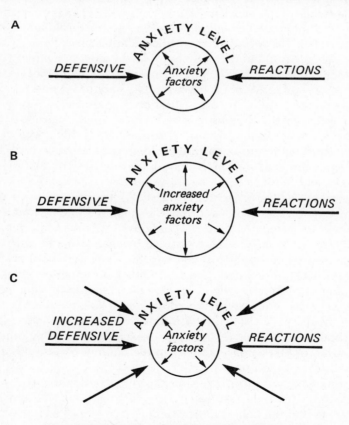

FIGURE 8.2. **The Homeostatic Process**

In B, the familiar anxiety-provoking factors of level A have been augmented by an additional factor—for example, a situation in which the child feels rejected. The anxiety level then increases beyond the point of comfort and tolerance. The child then attempts to defend against the pain of this increased anxiety.

In C, the defensive reaction (for example, an increase in hostile and aggressive behavior) has been strengthened so that the anxiety level is again reduced to one that is comfortable to the child.

As used in psychology, the homeostatic hypothesis has taken on a much broader meaning than that originally implied in the physiological applications of the concept. It is concerned with the *entire* behavioral reactions of the person. It applies to both the physiological and the psychological aspects.

There is another important aspect of homeostasis that we should consider. A person never achieves a complete condition of rest; rather, there is a continuous instability to which the person reacts by striving to return to the original condition. The person may almost achieve that state, but then there is a further imbalance. The homeostatic reaction, therefore, is a continuous *striving* for maintenance of the most comfortable psychic tension level. A perfectly stationary condition cannot be achieved during the life of any organism, either physiologically or psychologically.

Maze (1953) has emphasized some important points concerning the concept of homeostasis. He stresses the complexity of the process, deploring the fact that too often we refer to only its steadiness or its restorative aspects. He feels that we do not remember that homeostasis is not the *cause* of balance in various physiological or psychological functions, but the *effect* of various specific processes.

The mentally retarded child, like all other persons, also strives to maintain a status quo. He strives to rid himself of unpleasant forces and pressures, and, perhaps more than the normal child, is particularly resistive to changes in his status. This is partly because he perceives change as more threatening—and the unknown as more dangerous. He clings tenaciously to previously learned patterns of behavior and reactions; they have controlled his anxieties in the past, so they are comforting and reassuring. This leads to a tendency toward rigidity and persistence of established behavioral reactions. Because of generally lowered capacities to deal with change and make the necessary adaptations, the mentally retarded child approaches new situations very cautiously and adapts to them with great difficulty.

LEVELS OF MENTAL LIFE

In order to obtain a better understanding of the overall psychological characteristics of a person, normal or retarded, it is essential to have some knowledge of that individual's personality organization. With that knowledge, we are better able to characterize that person and, therefore, to predict behavior.

We are prone to describe or evaluate a person on the basis of consciously motivated behavior. That aspect of behavior is most visible to others; therefore, it is likely to impress us most. But a person's conscious mental life is only one aspect of mental functioning. The total mental life comprises much more than conscious experiences. Most of us are aware of this fact, and the term *unconscious* (or *subconscious*) appears frequently in our daily vocabulary. It has been demonstrated that mental processes take place at different levels within the personality. Freud described three major levels of mental phenomena: (1) the conscious, (2) the preconscious, and (3) the unconscious. The conscious level consists of the mental activity of which we are aware. The preconscious level refers to mental experience that can become known to us when we shift our attention to it. It is the background of conscious mental activity. Thus, if I wish, with a little or great effort I can recall the author of *Dangerous Corner*—it was in my preconscious thought. Material is at an unconscious level when it is highly resistant to conscious recall. It can only be recalled through special methods such as hypnosis and psychotherapy. Ordinarily, the person has no conscious awareness of its existence.

The Conscious Level

We have stated that the conscious level of the personality is that part of mental life of which the person is aware. It usually offers no serious threat to the person and does not produce severely painful psychological reactions. The conscious mind contains thoughts that form rapidly from moment to moment and from situation to situation. The conscious aspects of mental life are those that the person has developed to meet the demands of the external world and its realities. However, the total content of our conscious life is not confined to our sensory perceptions of our experiences and our relationships to the outer world. In addition, it is made up to a large extent of *derivatives* of the unconscious level, which force themselves into consciousness in a disguised, often symbolic, manner.

How we perceive reality is determined in part by unconscious factors. A person tends to avoid perceiving, or to distort in some way, situations that are threatening or unpleasant. Research has indicated that a person may either avoid a threatening situation or be *overly vigilant*. In the latter case, the person tends to be unduly sensitive to potentially threatening situations.

The conscious level of the personality is *only one* important aspect of mental life. And it is *not* the aspect that is of the greatest importance in the determination of human behavior.

We may explore the contents of consciousness through the process of introspection, that process in which we turn our thoughts inward and reflect on inner events. Not only may the contents of the conscious thus be scrutinized readily, but they also may be easily verbalized (i.e., we can tell them to others).

The Preconscious Level

There are some aspects of mental life of which we are consciously aware only at certain times; their availability to consciousness fluctuates. The part of mental experience that can become conscious only through special effort is called the *preconscious*. It has more of the characteristics of the conscious than of the unconscious. In fact, the preconscious does not differ markedly from the conscious except that it is not part of our day-to-day awareness.

The Unconscious Level

The third level of mental life, the unconscious, is crucially important.

The unconscious has, of course, no actual physical existence, and it cannot be located in either an anatomical or a physiological sense. It is a theoretical construct—a concept. By using the concept of the unconscious, we are able to integrate and better explain the large masses of apparently unrelated data we may gather about a person. We cannot see the unconscious. It must be *inferred* from the observed behavior of the person. The conscious and preconscious may both be verbalized through introspection by the person, but unconscious material is *inferred* by another person from the actions and verbalizations of the first person.

Phenomena of the unconscious level may be readily demonstrated by several methods (see Brenner, 1973). Freud described some of these. The following are some of the major indications of the operation of unconscious processes. When a person is *hypnotized,* she may be given the specific suggestion to perform a certain act after she has awakened. She does so without awareness of the fact that she had previously been given instructions to do it. *Dreams* are representatives at a conscious level of unconscious material that is too threatening to be consciously accepted by the person. *Slips of the tongue* usually are manifestations of internal (unconscious) conflicts. Sudden appearance of *ideas* or solutions to problems are indications of unconscious activities. During *psychotherapy,* long buried (repressed) conflicts and traumatic episodes emerge.

The unconscious has many unique qualities: (1) It has no awareness of *time* sequence. (2) It has no understanding of deprivation or *negation*. (3) It completely ignores all social, moral, and ethical considerations; it is *amoral*. (4) It may be completely *irrational,* and ideas that are mutually exclusive exist without contradiction. (5) It functions at an *infantile* level, and its contents are infantile.

At this point we may ask, What is the content of the unconscious level of mental life? Primarily, it consists of those thoughts, wishes, and needs of the infant and very young child that were never consciously experienced. Many of these remain at an unconscious level and are never known. Secondly, the unconscious is composed of previous conscious experiences that were extremely painful to the child and caused a great deal of psychological discomfort. In order to protect oneself against the pain of these experiences, the child "pushed them back" to the unconscious level. The process whereby painful material is thrust back to an unconscious level is termed *repression* (see chapter 7).

Factors in the unconscious are not merely passively present but are constantly seeking discharge and are partially responsible for all forms of a child's mental and motor activities. Let us examine a simple illustration from everyday life in which the unconscious determinants are not at a very deep level. A man comes home following a day's work. He is very irritable and, without any apparent reason, argues with his wife. He criticizes the dinner and the behavior of the children and is hostile in general. If we reviewed his activities throughout the day we might find that he had been severely rebuked by his superior. He might have felt the criticism to be unwarranted and felt very hostile toward his boss. However, since one usually cannot express hostility directly toward one's boss, this man unconsciously expressed hostility toward his wife and children.

The behavior of young children toward their school teachers also furnishes us with a clear example of the presence of unconscious determinants of behavior. Children often behave toward their teachers in the way they feel inwardly toward their mothers.

When a situation is repressed, only some aspects of the original situation are not consciously experienced. The emotions that were part of the situation constantly strive for expression, becoming attached to other situations that may be consciously known to the child. The emotion of the repressed material is thus experienced, but its source is not known to the person.

The mental life of a person is thus much richer and more extensive than one would infer from investigation of its conscious elements. It should be emphasized that a tremendous amount of activity is continually going on at an unconscious level and that unconscious reactions exert tremendous pressure for expression at all times. When unconscious drives are discharged, they are expressed in distorted and symbolic ways, so their origins remain hidden from the conscious awareness of the person.

All behavior contains some unconscious determinants. The number varies within the same child from situation to situation and from time to time, as well as varying from one child to another. Probably the greater part of mental life and activities is at an unconscious level. We may think of the total personality structure as being somewhat similar to an iceberg, with only a small part above the surface (conscious awareness). Most of it, like the greater part of the iceberg, lies beneath the surface and is hidden. The quantitative relationship between the conscious, preconscious, and unconscious levels is diagrammatically illustrated in Figure 8.3.

The unconscious plays a highly significant role in our everyday relationships with other people. The unconscious of one child may react on the unconscious of another, with the children not being consciously aware that such

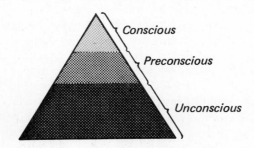

FIGURE 8.3. The Three Levels of Mental Life

subtle interactions are occurring. For example, we ourselves may have violent likes or dislikes on our first encounter with another person. We may feel comfortable with some people and very uncomfortable and anxious with others, without knowing just why. These are indications of the influences of unconscious factors in our interpersonal relationships. The concept of the unconscious is one of the cornerstones of our modern system of psychopathology.

Mental processes operate at all three levels in the retarded child. However, because of the child's impaired functioning, such a child tends to react more to the pressures of unconscious motives than the average child. There is a great difficulty in holding back unconscious drives. Behavior tends, at times, to be largely determined by unconscious needs. Often, the retarded child will engage in a form of behavior that is unexplainable to the observer; that is, it apparently is not in accord with the situation in which the child finds himself. The retarded child thus is more prone to engage in impulsive or insufficiently controlled behavior. However, if we spend enough time with the child and make a determined effort to try to understand his behavior, we can help him make a better adjustment.

Although we have no evidence that the unconscious is essentially different in the mentally retarded child than in the nonretarded child, the manner in which it is controlled is different. In the mentally retarded child, unconscious motivations tend to emerge more readily in overt behavioral reactions, and they govern much more of behavior. Much of the evidence for the conclusions we have offered is derived from data obtained in psychotherapy with retarded children; these data are discussed in chapter 16. In psychotherapy, we sometimes learn that the retarded child's apparently inexplicable behavior is governed by motives of which the child is not aware. Some cases of highly impulsive and erratic behavior become understandable and modifiable once we ascertain what the unconscious motivation is.

TRAITS AND STRUCTURES

When an individual responds, she behaves in a particular manner to some particular situation. We might attempt to characterize her in terms of all of the particular responses made in a lifetime or over a considerable span of time, but that would be almost impossible, and we would still be left with the problem of *categorizing* the individual in terms of *clusters* of behavior.

One way of dealing with this difficulty is to try to extract some of the characteristic ways in which an individual responds over a number of situations. These characteristic ways of behaving are commonly called *traits*. A *trait*, then, is a relatively persistent way of behaving across a number of different, but related, situations. It is a higher order of organization of personality than the specific behavior. But traits do not exist in reality; rather, they are abstractions that are inferred from selected observations of behavior. For example, we may say, in describing a person, that she is *honest*, or that she is *persistent*. What we really mean, however, is that in certain situations in which we or others have observed that person, her behavior has been honest or persistent. The behavior of the person, and not the person, thus led us to believe that she was honest or persistent. Since she was behaving honestly or persistently, *she* might, by inference, be characterized as honest or persistent.

Generally speaking, there are three major ways in which we can characterize a person by a certain trait. We may do so from *what* he does, *how* he does it (or the manner in which he performs the behavior), and *how well* he does it. In all of these instances, we infer the trait from samples of behavior that we, the observers, note. Of course, it is possible for a person to rate himself on various traits. But whether it is the result of self-ratings, ratings by others, or scores on a test, the trait is an inference derived from some sample of behavior.

Another problem concerns the number and nature of traits that might be used in describing the total personality. Some careful, rigorous workers in the field of personality believe that a great number of such trait-names is needed. For example, Allport and Odbert (1936) found that nearly 18,000 terms used to describe people were insufficient to account for all of the subtleties of human personality. The philosophy of their approach to personality description has been termed *idiographic*, meaning that each person represents a unique constellation of innumerable qualities. At the other extreme are psychologists who prefer to categorize people into *types*, or a few very general clusters. In between are those who believe that a relatively small number of traits may be used in adequately describing each person in the population. Although there are scientific grounds for preferring one system over another, the basic differences in the kinds and number of traits that can be employed is largely a matter of the philosophy one adopts towards personality evaluation rather than of scientific criteria, for one can make out a good scientific case for each of the three major approaches.

In relatively recent years, a number of workers, using the statistical method known as *factor analysis,* have attempted to characterize the personality structure in terms of *factors,* that is, statistically derived clusters of traits or scores that have a great deal in common. The factors suggested are then organized into what is called the *personality structure.* Thus, there is a hierarchical organization from specific responses to habits to traits to trait-clusters, or factors (sometimes called *primary traits*), to personality structure. Figure 8.4 illustrates this scheme.

We shall discuss some of the proposed trait-clusters, or factors, in a later section, but at this point we wish to comment further on the values and limitations of such an approach to the description of personality organization.

One value of factor analysis is that it enables us to assess the personality with an economy of trait-clusters. Another is that factors can be objectively derived from test questionnaires or from self-ratings with statistical rigor, and they can be subjected to further experimental study. Still another advantage to this method is that the generality of the derived factors can be studied in different populations, so it is possible to tell whether the same or different factors can be used in describing divergent populations.

This last advantage also is a limitation, since recent research has failed

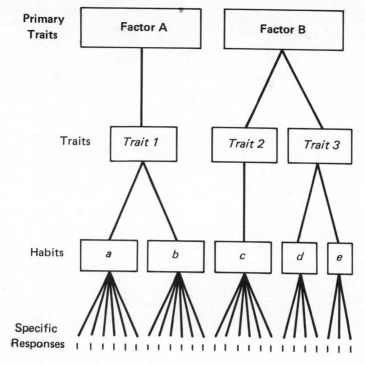

FIGURE 8.4.   Schematic Illustration of Personality Structure

to develop a list of factors acceptable to most workers. There are many reasons for this, but one is that since the factors depend on the measurement of traits, and since self-rated traits are of doubtful validity in some populations (this is especially true of retarded individuals), they can hardly be used to make intergroup comparisons. Moreover, rating of subjects by observers as a basis for deriving factors has also very serious limitations. For example, in one study (Borg and Hamilton, 1956) in which instructors were rated by their students in a variety of instructional situations, the ratings only correlated between the levels of .13 and .19 with ratings obtained in the same situations from other instructors, teacher peers, self-ratings by teachers, and ratings of performance behavior in test situations.

Such low correlations suggest that very different things are being measured by the various sets of ratings and that rating scores are therefore of dubious value. As we shall see, some workers have devised other methods to overcome this difficulty. When traits are derived from carefully constructed test questionnaires of personality, the problems of cultural bias, level of intelligence, deliberate falsification by the respondent, and sundry *halo* effects (effects produced by general bias of the respondent) all affect the validity of the findings.

It usually is assumed by trait theorists that traits remain stable over time, but this assumption has been challenged on two fronts. Longitudinal studies (even with college students who may be expected to have more stable dispositions than younger, more rapidly developing persons) indicate that primary traits do change (Stewart, 1964). Even more pertinent is the finding that traits depend on the *environmental constancies* that nourish them (Chein, 1972). This point leads to the most serious deficiency of *trait theory,* in our opinion.

The so-called primary traits can be an artifact of the tests from which they are derived and the particular population used in the sample. Thus, for example, Norman (1969) is critical of many studies purporting to find an invariant (constant) structure in such traits. A number of workers have shown, as we shall see, that the so-called trait factors are different in a retarded population than in an average or superior population. This means that traits do not exist in a vacuum; they vary with varying circumstances, which help determine whether a trait will emerge at all, how strong the trait will be, and what other traits will accompany it.

Finally, it has been argued that the meaning of any trait depends on its place in the total constellation of traits of any given person. At the extreme, this difficulty would mean that the values (or weights) assigned to traits would be as variable as the individuals to be evaluated, and therefore there could be no consensus. In other words, the dynamic meaning of a trait may vary markedly, depending on the way it is used. Thus, fantasy can be used constructively by the healthy, creative person. But the same amount of fantasy in a very disturbed person could lead to withdrawal from reality and immersion in pathological or delusional thinking.

FREUD'S CONCEPTION OF PERSONALITY STRUCTURE

Freud suggested that three distinct functional aspects of the personality could be hypothesized: (1) the *id,* (2) the *ego,* and (3) the *superego.* All of these functions are interdependent, yet each has specific characteristics of its own. Freud's basic conceptualization offers an explanation of many aspects of human behavior.

Since knowledge of the structure of the personality is essential to an understanding of both normal and mentally retarded children, we shall consider in detail the characteristics of the id, ego, and superego. We shall then discuss the relationships among them. We shall emphasize that their proper development is essential to the achievement of integrated capacities for functioning as a healthy person. Regardless of the degree of intellectual potential with which a person has been endowed, it cannot be used adequately unless there has been an appropriate development and integration in these aspects of the personality.

The Id

Id is a Latin term, which can be roughly translated into English as *it.* The id is the basic and central core of the personality of the individual.* It is the

---

*Although we speak of *the id,* and later of *the ego* and *the superego,* we do not imply that they are things or entities. *The id* is simply an abbreviated way of saying "the organized system of unconscious drives."

source from which all the psychic energy of the child is derived. It is the basis of all the inborn instinctual forces. For example, all of the sexual drives stem from the id. The instinctual forces of the id, like all biological drives, tend to be expressed unless inhibited or modified.

Id forces tend to be experienced as pleasurable. Like the unconscious, the id is amoral—its expression does not involve any sense of right or wrong. Since functions of the id are, by definition, unconscious, they are not constrained by concepts of time. The id also is alogical and is *not* susceptible to the impact of logical arguments or processes. Although the id shares the characteristics of the unconscious, the id and the unconscious are *not* synonymous. The id is only one part of the total unconscious processes of the individual. Put another way, we might say that all id processes are unconscious, but the unconscious is not all id.

The personality of the newborn child is motivated primarily by id forces. It has not developed, as yet, those attributes (*structure*) that the maturational process will produce. It is from the id that all the other elements of the personality structure later evolve in accordance with maturational processes that are *common to all persons*. These processes will be discussed in terms of the gradual evolution of the ego and superego from the basic core of the id.

The Ego

The id is the innermost layer of the personality. As the child's psychological maturation proceeds, a second type of structure gradually develops out of the basic id core. This new portion of the personality relates id forces to the outside world. For example, there may be social-cultural-religious prohibitions against the unrestricted expression of sexual impulses. Each child must learn to inhibit or modify many of the id's impulses. In short, the child must learn to mediate the "demands" of the id and the requirements posed by the world. The personality structure that does the mediating is known as the ego. The functions of the ego, therefore, involve perception of the requirements of the world and the mediation of impulses with external values. For example, the child may wish to engage in some biological need, such as to urinate, and might urinate whenever and wherever he pleases; but through development of ego functions, he learns to delay his urination or to urinate in appropriate places.

According to psychoanalytic theory, therefore, there are two major ego functions: (1) to express impulses originating in the id, when feasible; and (2) to modify expression or inhibit expression of such impulses so that they are socially acceptable. With further development of ego functions, the child also may learn to modify external conditions so as to gratify biological needs more satisfactorily.

Ego and id functions are, however, never completely separable. Although in theory these are two separate "structures," their functions overlap and interact. As the child develops, however, the ego becomes the internalized representative of the external world, thus making possible more mature social adaptation.

Since an appreciation of the world of reality depends on various sensory processes (such as visual and auditory), the development of ego functions is dependent on perceptual development. And, as we have seen, mentally retarded children often are retarded in perceptual development. Hence, they tend to develop more slowly in aspects of ego growth than do the nonretarded.

The ego structure of very young children is rudimentary and cannot cope adequately with id impulses. Thus, the behavior of the very young child is largely dominated by instinctual drives, which tend to be expressed in an uncontrolled manner. Emotional reactions, in particular, are not effectively under ego control at this stage of development (temper tantrums, for example, are common). As maturation proceeds, perception of external requirements becomes more accurate and ego functions become more dominant. In the mentally retarded child, the slow and inadequate development of ego functions produces poor control over impulses, inaccurate evaluations of reality, and inadequately integrated behavior.

In contrast with the failure of the id to perceive and respond to such features of the "ordered" world as time sequences and spatial arrangements, the functions of the ego enable the child to begin to deal with these and other aspects of reality. Development of the ego also assists in the learning of *right* and *wrong* and thus contributes to the development of moral values.

Operations of the ego must constantly adjust to pressures from three major sources: (1) forces of the id; (2) external factors; and, (3) the superego.

Fenichel (1945) describes the archaic, or primitive, reactions of the infant exhaustively. He suggests that the child's perceptual processes are very hazy. Objects and persons are not sharply distinguished, and visual images tend to be large and inexact. The perceptions of the various sense organs tend to overlap, creating a confused total perception. The most primitive of the perceptual processes is dominant—the kinesthetic (bodily movement) perceptions. The primitive perceptions of the infant are influenced by two additional factors. First, the child is physically small in relation to the outer world. This modifies, by contrast, what it perceives. Just imagine, for example, what our perceptions would be in a world where we were surrounded by smoke-spouting giants, 25-foot chairs, and towering objects whose summits we could only dimly perceive! Secondly, the child tends to see the world either as a provider, satisfying wants, or as a terrible threat that constantly seeks to annihilate it. The child cannot distinguish between the *self* and the *not-self*. The child does not know what is *inside* and what is *outside* self. Rather, the child attempts to differentiate at first between states in which it is in greater tension and states in which tension is much less.

The ego develops in part because the needs of the child are not immediately satisfied. The occurrence of deprivation, in certain areas, is automatic in the lives of all children, and will occur to some extent regardless of the promptness or extent of parental activities. No matter how quickly the need for nourishment is satisfied, there exists a period in which some time elapses between the experiencing of the need by the child and its actual gratification and resultant lessening of tension. Because of this time interval during which heightened tension is experienced, the child gradually becomes aware of the presence of an external source that satisfies needs. The child begins to be aware of external reality—perceives that he has needs that he cannot gratify by himself. The ego evolves as the child meets partial deprivation, or delay in gratification of basic needs. If one could automatically take care of all the needs of the newborn child, providing satisfactions immediately, the child would be exceedingly slow in developing an ego structure. Actually, the concept of reality that the child develops is concurrent with the development of the ego structure. To have a strong ego structure, the child must have a full awareness of outer reality, an awareness of the forces of the outer world as they affect the individual. It is only through a long, gradual maturational process that the child finally becomes aware that there are forces in the outer world that are beyond control and that do not lie within the self.

At this point, some of the implications of these formulations should be mentioned. The child's first conception of reality is in terms of mother (or mother substitute) and her behavior—the child and mother are one as far as the child is concerned, and not separate. It is only gradually that the child begins to see that mother is an object who is entirely separate from self. Sullivan (1947) states that during the first year of life the child knows only momentary states of consciousness. It makes no distinctions in either time or place. Later the child begins to perceive the mother. Spitz (1946) investigated the first smiles of babies and found that they were elicited only by human faces or masks of faces. By the age of eight months, children began to differentiate new from known faces.

Thus, infantile ego functions are extremely weak, both in relation to control of forces of the id and in relation to the external world. Normal ego development takes time and the mastery of some frustration. If the child is too severely deprived or frustrated, the development of ego functions is delayed or distorted. Hartmann et al. (1947) feel that the best situation is one in which the mother gives the child a great deal of indulgence and a small amount of deprivation. As we shall see, both Freud and Piaget emphasize the value of some degree of deprivation and "challenge." Eventually, if the child is to become well-adjusted, it must learn to substitute future for immediate gratification.

The infant, and even the child, does not easily give up the belief that it is omnipotent and the center of the universe. A child hangs on to this belief tenaciously, but must finally face the fact that the self is not omnipotent. Many are the devices that the child creates to maintain the fiction of omnipotence, only to have to give up this fiction, bit by bit, as reality forces these concessions.

If we observe the behavior of young children, we can readily find examples of their longing to control reality by maintaining infantile omnipotence. We can find many additional examples in our folklore and fairy tales (remember "Rumpelstiltskin"?).

Many writers have stressed that there must be gradual opportunity for the child to experience a delay in gratifications of needs. If, however, the frustrations that the child undergoes are too severe, then an incomplete and immature ego structure may result. (See Hartmann, 1950; Spitz, 1950; Rank, 1949.)

The ability to postpone immediate gratifications and to tolerate the resulting tensions is only gradually mastered. In order to achieve this mastery, there must first be an adequate control of the muscular and motor components.

The child must learn to walk, talk, and control its own bodily functions. In addition, the child must learn to test reality. That is, it learns to anticipate the future in imagination, testing, in a very small way, what might happen in the real world. Bowlby (1953) puts this excellently when he states:

> As our personality develops we become less and less at the mercy of our immediate surroundings, and the ways in which they affect us, and become more and more able to choose and create our surroundings, and to plan ahead, often over long periods of time, for the things we want. Amongst other things, this means we have to learn to think in an abstract way, to exercise our imagination and to consider things other than just our immediate sensations and desires. Only when he has reached this stage is the individual able to control his wish of the moment in the interests of his own more fundamental long-term needs. One expects the child of three, or even five, to run into the road and seek his ball—at those ages he is still largely at the mercy of the immediate situation. As he grows older, however, he is expected to take more things into account and to think ahead. By ten or eleven he is capable of pursuing goals some months distant in time. At sixteen or eighteen the more developed boy or girl is able to perform great feats of abstraction in time and space. This is the process whereby the individual frees himself from slavery to his instincts and urge for immediate pleasure, and develops mental processes more adapted to the demands of reality.

The development of the ego structure thus is a long, arduous, and gradual process, and an adequate perception of reality depends on it. However, the primary components of ego structure, although modified to some extent in later years, are usually well established by the time the average child reaches the age of five or six years.

There has been a great deal of experimental study of ego phenomena and ego development since 1945, and many extensions of Freud's concepts of the ego have been proposed. A few of the major innovations will be of particular interest to the student of the retarded child.

It has been learned that the infant's omnipotence has to be subordinated to the tests of reality. How does this come about? The infant is required to adapt its behavior to the needs of the culture and the subculture in which it lives. Parents no longer minister to helpless needs with complete disregard of their own wishes. Instead, as the infant's motor, emotional, and intellectual growth permits, it is urged, coaxed, cajoled, and taught to begin to behave differently to conform to parental expectations. The parent judges the infant's readiness for these changes by the kinds of behaviors of which it becomes capable. Such behaviors may involve the infant's emotional interest in external objects, beginning perceptions of other people as being different from self, and (especially) beginning differentiation, in rudimentary language symbols, of self from others (Gesell and Ilg, 1974).

The pressures of the culture, as expressed usually through the demands of the parents, cause the infant to become aware of some of the limits of potency. The infant's ego now begins to experience some traumatic devaluation as the sense of omnipotence diminishes. The child's ego can suffer severe, even irreparable, damage if this early series of crises in ego development is not weathered successfully.

One of the important early signs of the process of self-devaluation, and the defense against it, is the emergence of negativistic behavior (Aushbel, 1950). In the healthy parent-child relationship, some negativistic behavior is tolerated, and the child is not overly traumatized by rejection if he does not conform immediately. In this relationship, the child learns that he is loved and accepted for what he is, and he receives additional affection as he learns to conform to some parental expectations. Such a relationship enhances the development of healthy ego functions. It marks the early stages of volitional activity by the young child.

The mutually satisfying parent-child relationship leads to the child's *identification* with the parent, through which the child can share in the parent's power and prestige and thus assuage the loss of infantile omnipotence. Further, as Erikson (1956) puts it, "The fate of childhood identification, in turn, depends on the child's satisfactory interaction with a trustworthy and meaningful hierarchy of roles as provided by the generations living together in some form of family."

For the retarded child, this early period of ego development is especially fraught with perils. Since, to begin with, a retarded child is likely to be slower in motor, mental, and social development, the child may be severely frustrated or frustrated unnecessarily early, since behavior does not conform to the norms expected in his culture. The mother may experience frustration, too, as she waits expectantly for her child to begin to learn the things other children the same age have already learned, and finds that her child does not. She may become overprotective or rejecting as her own anxieties mount. As Ausubel (1952) points out, the lack of a reciprocal and mutually trusting relationship between mother and child may produce severe ego deflation, as well as unnecessary loss of self-regard. In the retarded child, the effect may contribute to withdrawal from adequate interaction with the environment, slowing up of the process of mental growth, and increasing frustration in many or all spheres of interpersonal relationships. Thus, what might have been a mild or even a transitional, retardation in development may become a severe, chronic disturbance.

Traumatization of the ego during early childhood is likely to affect the rate and course of language development, in particular. Retarded language development, in turn, may contribute to a loss in ability to develop a sense of personal identity and proper autonomy, since language plays such a large role in that development (Erickson, 1956). The cumulative effects of this possible course of development may be very great indeed. This kind of phenomenon may also explain why retarded children typically do much more poorly on mental tests involving verbal capacity than on tests not involving this ability. (See chapter 9 for further discussion of such tests.)

The crises in ego development are particularly striking in infancy and early childhood, but they also may occur during other years, especially during adolescence when new identity roles are being learned and when matters of sexual identity, vocational goals, and further differentiation from the family become important. Each of these crises is especially difficult for the retarded child because of inadequate ego capacities and because of society's likelihood of rejecting (or at least not accepting) the individual for not conforming to its standards.

The Superego

As the child continues to mature, a further modification of the existing personality structure develops. This development involves ethical, social, and cultural values. It is referred to as the *superego*. Just as the functions of the ego are derived out of id functions, so, too, are the functions of the superego derived out of ego processes. Moreover, development of the superego can, in turn, modify some ego functions. This occurs chiefly through the creation of a strong sense of guilt within the child.

Popularly, the superego has been termed the *conscience* of the individual. In one way, we may regard the superego's function as that of a watchdog—constantly warning: "This is not permissible." When its warnings are unheeded, we are automatically punished by feeling guilty. This feeling of guilt is unconscious to the extent that we often are unaware of its true source. The superego is unconscious to a greater extent than the ego, and it is beyond the direct control of conscious and ego activities. The superego is more perceptive of, and reactive to, the id impulses than is the ego. The superego permits the expression of some id drives and causes the suppression of others. The mature ego of the human being tends to remain under the domination and control of the superego. The id is *instinctual,* the ego is concerned with reality factors, and the superego is concerned with the social, cultural, and ethical values of the particular society in which the child happens to be reared.

The superego structure stems from the relationships of the child to the parents—from the corrections, the taboos, and the *don'ts* of the parents. The child is punished by the parents for some activities and is praised for others. The mother may be very demanding, or the father may be very dominating; or, on the other hand, they may be passive and dependent. These and other personality characteristics of the parents are absorbed by the child, that is, he takes into himself (he *interiorizes*) the prohibitions and the general standards and ideals of the parents themselves. The child wants his parents to love him, and he feels that they will do so if he does what they want him to do. For these reasons, the child adopts the standards and basic values of the parents for himself. In this way, the attitudes of society and the culture are made part of the child, and social adaptation becomes possible.*.

The basic fear of all young children is that they will lose the love of their parents or parent surrogates. When the superego structure is more completely formed, this basic fear becomes, instead, fear of loss of support of the superego. In other words, the older child (and later the adult) is still fearful of losing the support and love of the parents, but the parents are now symbolically *inside* rather than *outside* of himself. As Freud stressed, the individual will behave toward the superego in exactly the same way as toward the parents, for getting along with one's superego as an adult is just as important as getting along with one's parents as a child. Getting along well with our superego and complying with its demands gives us a sense of relief and a feeling of well-being. Refusing

*For an extended discussion of this process, see M. L. Hutt and D. Miller, (1949).

to comply with our superego's demands makes us feel guilty and remorseful. There is a direct relationship between the strictness of the parent and the strictness of the superego. If the parent, for example, was extremely punitive or very harsh and hostile toward the child, then it is probable that the superego of the child will be extremely harsh and punitive.

Bowlby (1953) points out that it is the awareness of things that please and displease the persons around us that gives rise to conscience (superego). He, like Freud, stresses the role of the mother in its formation. She acts *for* the young child, getting the child's way for him and making adaptations to the demands of other people. She provides for the child in all ways, and she acts as his personality and conscience. As the child grows older, the mother transfers these roles to him. If the child's relationships with the mother are unhappy, the superego will not develop adequately.

Interrelationships of Id, Ego, and Superego

The interrelationships among the id, the ego, and the superego constantly change during the development through which we all pass. For this reason, we must regard the complex interplay among them from the standpoint of several different time levels. What would be true of their interrelationships at age three would not be true at age sixteen.

At birth, as we have stressed, there is only id. During infancy, the first-formed ego structure is necessarily weak and is completely overwhelmed by the demands of the id. As the ego matures, it becomes stronger, until it succeeds in controlling and modifying the basic id drives. A balance is finally achieved between id and ego forces in the healthy young child. At early adolescence, the uneasy truce between the two is broken; first the id then the ego forces prevail in a see-saw sort of fashion. In the normal child, the ego finally is able to deal effectively with the forces of the id.

The primitive superego at first allies itself strongly with the ego in inhibiting id impulses and cannot be too clearly distinguished from the ego itself. The developing superego is at first extremely rigid and punitive, but gradually it becomes more and more permissive. However, at about puberty in most children, the ego and superego finally become completely differentiated.

Figure 8.5 schematically illustrates the relative strengths of id, ego, and superego at various points in the normal maturational process.

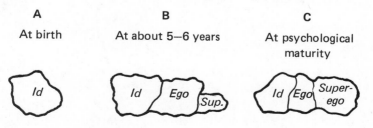

FIGURE 8.5.   Development of Id, Ego, and Superego

In A, at birth, the id is all-powerful and neither ego nor superego structures have developed to exert any pressures or determine behavioral reactions. In B, at about five or six years of age, id forces are still powerful, but the ego has developed and exerts considerable control, whereas the superego is still relatively weak. In C, at maturity, ego and superego are fully developed so that all components are in harmony.

The ego and superego are very much alike in that both are based on the individual's relationships with the external world of reality. However, since the superego is latest in time of development, it stands in closer relationship to the outer world—particularly to its social and cultural attributes—than does the ego.

The relationship of the id, ego, and superego to each other—as well as their relationship to the conscious, preconscious, and unconscious aspects of mental life—is diagrammatically represented in Figure 8.6.

Other Theories of Personality Development

There are many other theories of personality development and the emergence of personality attributes. It would take us too far afield to consider each theory separately. Each theory offers some valuable contribution to our understanding of processes of development and of relevant factors. Some theories, like social learning theories, help to explain better than Freud's the development of such attributes as social attitudes and moral attributes of the individual. Our concern, however, has been with basic dynamics that help explain personality functions and their significance for the mentally retarded, and Freud's theory of ego development seemed most salient.

However, we should like to cite, briefly, a theory concerned with *self-*

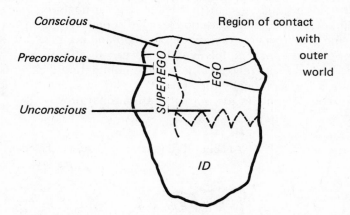

FIGURE 8.6.   Topographical Relationships of Id, Ego, and Superego (W. Healy, A. F. Bronner and A. M. Bowers, *The Structure and Meaning of Psychoanalysis.* New York: Alfred A. Knopf, 1930, p. 56).

actualization, since we find that mentally retarded individuals so often are grossly deficient in this regard.

Maslow (1954) proposed such a theory and subsequently expanded it on the basis of empirical investigations (1970). This theory posits five levels of needs that operate in a hierarchy. The lowest and most basic level consists of physiological needs (hunger, thirst, and sex). Above this, in ascending order, are: safety needs, belongingness, esteem (prestige and self-respect), and self-actualization. Individuals who develop in deprived or non-supportive and non-stimulating circumstances rarely are able to rise above the levels of physiological and safety needs, perhaps finally attaining some satisfaction of needs for belonging. One can infer that many mentally retarded, in current society, never attain adequate development and satisfaction of needs for esteem and self-actualization.

EFFECTS OF RETARDATION
ON MATURATION
OF PERSONALITY STRUCTURES

We now will discuss the relationship of retarded intelligence to the maturation of the personality.

The mentally retarded child does not have *different* id drives from other children. There may be differences in the amount of psychic energy present, but there has been no demonstration of qualitative difference in basic needs between retarded and nonretarded children.

The general development of the ego in the retarded child probably follows the same general principles of maturation that apply to all children. However, there are highly significant specific differences in ego phenomena between children of inferior and children of average intellectual potential. In the previous discussion, it was noted that ego development was dependent to some extent on the development of sensory mechanisms. Consequently, the development of adequate speech patterns, muscular reactions, and perceptual processes is of great importance in enabling the child to obtain a valid grasp of reality factors and to deal with them. Because these mechanisms develop more slowly in the mentally retarded child, the development of the ego also is delayed, and it finally attains a relatively inferior level at maturity. Understandably, the mentally retarded child experiences great difficulties in ego functions. The retarded child can respond best when dealing with immediate and concrete experiences; the retarded child has difficulty in responding adequately when the problems are more remote or abstract. Events that are removed from the child in either time or space are exceedingly difficult to grasp.

The retarded child's relatively immature ego makes it difficult for her to control or modify id drives in accordance with the demands of reality. She tends to express such drives in an uninhibited manner, and her controls tend to remain infantile and relatively ineffective. For example, sexual needs tend to be expressed directly, either toward other individuals (as in excessive sexual curiosity) or toward the self (as in excessive masturbatory behavior). Aggressive drives, similarly, may be expressed without adequate control or direction—impulsively or inappropriately. The inadequate ego thus proves to be ineffective in two general ways: (1) it cannot control id drives and (2) it cannot realistically assess the demands of the external reality. The ego's inadequacies prove to be a source of considerable difficulty to both the child and the people responsible for the child's behavior.

In addition, the relatively weak ego of the mentally retarded child makes it difficult for her to learn to substitute future gratifications for immediate pleasures. She wants things right now—not tomorrow or the day after. Since the retarded child cannot plan ahead very well, she remains pretty much at the mercy of the situation in which she finds herself and thus is unduly influenced by environmental forces that she cannot control. The retarded child's retarded capacity for abstract thought, retarded capacity for inner creativity and imagination, and inability to take a number of things into consideration simultaneously make the child a slave to instinctual drives and wishes. In brief, she has great difficulty in learning to master reality adequately.

The mentally retarded child's inadequate and confused perceptual and intellectual abilities make it very difficult for her to develop a clear self-image and to differentiate her own needs from the demands of reality. The child therefore continues to be overdependent and only with great difficulty succeeds in making even an elementary emotional separation of self from parents. Depending in part on the nature of early home care, the child tends (in later life) to see the entire world as either a place that is excessively threatening or a place that exists primarily to gratify personal needs. The first of these defensive alternatives is more probable because most mentally retarded children by their very nature endure excessive deprivations.

Children with underdeveloped ego structures also tend to have severe emotional problems. Therefore, they often get into severe difficulty with other people in various social situations. The resulting conflicts further accentuate their emotional problems. Of particular importance are the reactions of the child's parents (particularly the mother) to weak ego functions. (See chapter 10.)

The superego of the mentally retarded child, like the ego, matures slowly. Even when it has developed to its maximum capacity, it tends to be quite immature and at times infantile. It tends to be structured in terms of absolutes (everything is either all good or all bad, all right or all wrong, and so on). As a result of the absence of the finer variations, the primitive superego structure tends to be either excessively permissive or excessively severe. The mentally retarded child thus tends to accept, to a great extent, the direct prohibitions of the parents—the *good* and *bad* valuations that are placed on behavioral reactions—or to rebel excessively against such prohibitions. Parental prohibitions also tend to remain externalized—that is, a particular action is taboo and not undertaken because of the perceived fear of an external person, not because of internalized and integrated needs. Since growth in the superego is, in part, a result of the awareness of things that please and displease the persons around us, the mentally retarded child, because of an inadequate perception of the results of behavior, is unable to develop a mature social conscience—or a mature superego.

There is another important aspect of superego functions. We all have some desire to achieve—to attain success in some activity. We aspire to a particular level. This aspirational level is, in part, a function of the superego—the inner representations of the parents. The mentally retarded child often aspires to a level that is beyond his ability to achieve. The disparity between the aspirational level and the achievement level leads the child to form a poor opinion of himself—he blames himself because he cannot succeed. This results in a generalized lowering of self-esteem, with attendant emotional problems and maladaptive behavior.

Klein (1944) pointed out that the superego of the young child is much harsher and more cruel than that of the adult, and it completely dominates the ego:

> But in the young child we come across a superego of the most incredible and fantastic character. And the younger the child is, or the deeper the mental level we penetrate to, the more this is the case. We get to look upon the child's fear of being devoured, or cut up, or torn to pieces, or its terror of being surrounded and pursued by menacing figures, as a regular component of its mental life; and we know that the man-eating wolf, the fire-spewing dragon, and all the evil monsters out of myths and fairy stories flourish and exert their unconscious influence in the fantasy of each individual child, and it feels itself persecuted and threatened by these evil shapes.

The mentally retarded child suffers from the cruel domination of this primitive type of superego much longer than the more average child, whose maturing ego fosters the development of a more benign superego.

The child of inferior intellectual capacities thus is more at the mercy of his id strivings, which are not adequately controlled by either ego or superego forces. This child also is more controlled by external forces, to which he reacts in an immature manner. The reactions to his behavior by society (particularly the persons close to him) further aggravate his emotional problems, and the task of adjustment is made more difficult.

SOME OF PIAGET'S CONTRIBUTIONS

We have previously referred to some of the conceptions provided by Piaget. Although his concern was primarily with the process of cognitive development, he was well aware that experiential and emotional factors influenced such developments. Piaget's work may be regarded as supplementary to that of Freud and other psychoanalytic authors. An excellent exposition of Piaget's findings is provided by Flavell (1963).

As we noted previously, Piaget proposed four stages of intellectual development: sensorimotor period, preoperational thought period, concrete operations period, and formal operations period. He believes that development through each preceding period is necessary for subsequent development in later periods. Some workers, after reviewing the evidence, maintain that this developmental sequence is invariant and essentially unaffected by external factors (Laurendeau and Pinard, 1962). Others (Woodward, 1961; Breger, 1974), including us, suggest that that position has not been proven, especially in the case of the mentally retarded, and that there is both clinical and experimental evidence indicating that external factors may be important.

Long before the average child reaches the stage of formal operations and the attainment of abstract, conceptual thinking, he proceeds through the previous stages, in which he acquires certain *learning schemata*—a complex integration of more or less specific behaviors providing a strategy of dealing with the worlds of internal and external stimulation. Of particular importance to us at this point is the nature of these experiences during the sensorimotor period, roughly the first two years of the child's life. Reflexive behavior is dominant during the first month, but then behavior is rapidly modified by the infant's experience, and more coordinated behavior emerges. Between the fourth and eighth month the infant shows evidence of having internalized some of the external phenomena in his world, and he now behaves with intentionality toward these external objects. Later in the first year, he clearly demonstrates *means-end relationships;* that is, he uses what he has already internalized to explore his world in new, as well as old, ways. Experimentation is more markedly shown during the next half-year so that by one and a half years of age the child normally shows much evidence of *curiosity about his world.* During the last half of the second year, he manifests the rudimentary beginnings of reasoning with symbols or logic rather than simply using trial and error. Thus, the basic foundation of cognitive development is laid during the first two years of life. *It appears to be dependent on the opportunities for receiving appropriate stimulation under conditions of emotional security.*

Research evidence seems to indicate that children with relatively lower intelligence proceed through the same process and same stages as those with relatively higher intelligence, although there is considerably more variability in the patterns of development among the lower intellectual levels (Woodward, 1961; Osler and Fivel, 1961; and Inhelder and Piaget, 1958). Put another way, those who are lower intellectually need more time and practice to develop, but given the necessary time and practice, they are able, except when very inferior, to acquire the same conceptual schemata. The implication is that the relatively slow learner can develop mature conceptual development given sufficient time and practice. This implication, while not proven, is sufficiently important to warrant extensive experimentation. It also has become evident that severe emotional disturbance, especially autistic behavior (a psychotic condition in which the child shows extreme withdrawal from interaction with the environment), can profoundly impair conceptual development; but there is evidence that intensive conditioning can do much to alleviate or correct maldevelopment (Sarason et al., 1960; Finch, 1960). Thus, once again, we are faced with the conclusion that experience, emotional state, and intellectual development are interdependent.

FACTORIAL STUDY OF PERSONALITY

A number of workers have attempted to develop a conception of personality structure by means of factorial analysis of ratings, test data, or performance. As indicated in an earlier section, such analyses attempt to extract the least number of trait-clusters, or factors, necessary to account for the intercorrelations among the several traits or test measures employed. We cannot go into the technical procedures involved in factor analysis, but a brief summary of some of the main ideas may be helpful.

In factor analysis, the investigator starts out by applying a fairly large number of allegedly well-validated tests to a representative population of subjects. The intercorrelations of these tests are then calculated. Then, by one of a number of statistical techniques, the smallest number of factors necessary to account for these intercorrelations is extracted, and the *loading* (or weight) for each factor is obtained. Usually, these factors do not account for all of the intercorrelations (or, more technically, the *variance* in the data), and the unaccountable data are considered to be due to unreliability of the measuring instruments, errors in sampling the population, and error from other sources.

The final task, once the statistical factors have been selected, is to name them. This is a subjective process, depending, in part, on the names already given to the tests making up the test battery, the apparent similarity of various tests making up the greatest loadings on each factor, and the investigator's own preference for nomenclature. It should be clearly recognized that the statistically derived factors are abstractions derived from data; in fact, they may even be artifacts of the data—due to cultural bias that predisposes people, for example, to answer tests or to rate others in conventionally approved ways. One investigator (Vernon, 1950) has even gone so far as to say, "Factors should be regarded primarily as categories for classifying mental or behavioral performances, rather than as entities in the mind or nervous system."

The vast majority of work done with factor analysis methods has been performed on adults, and within this population the preponderant sampling has been college students—a captive audience and therefore easily tested or rated. This kind of bias limits the generality of trait-clusters that have been proposed, although, in recent years, increasing attention has been given to younger populations and to other kinds of samplings.

As we noted, there is incomplete agreement on the most general factors in personality derived by factor analysis, and many psychologists are completely unwilling to accept even the most agreed-on findings as relevant or significant. We believe that such an attitude is inappropriate, for, despite their limitations, factor analytic methods remain a powerful tool, and the findings from such methods still can be subjected to experimental and clinical analysis. At least, their findings need to be considered seriously.

Guilford (1959) has summarized the findings of various factor analytic studies of personality, and we shall follow his summary in sketching some of the most significant findings. He includes findings relating to somatic, aptitude, and temperament characteristics and to hormetic disposition (motivational traits) in his compendium of personality structure, but we shall confine our discussion to the dimensions of temperament, since they are most relevant to our purposes.

Guilford divided the temperament factors into three major groups: *general, emotional,* and *social.* Then, within each group, he proposed five subcategories. Let us consider the *general* group of factors first.

A general factor that has been very widely studied is *inferiority feelings.* Since this is a clearly bipolar factor (not all factors are), Guilford calls it *confidence vs. inferiority feelings.* This factor has been found in populations of normal and abnormal adults as well as in children. Qualities described as belonging to the negative end of this trait-cluster include egocentricity, discontent, and guilt. Guilt is an inextricable part of the attitude of inferiority. Retarded children rarely exhibit feelings of inferiority, as measured. Whether this finding is an artifact of the test instruments or is basically true remains to be determined. However, it has been shown that feelings of inferiority are related to the *discrepancy* between the child's home conditions and the child's attitude toward these conditions (Ackerson, 1943).

Another of the widely accepted general factors is *objectivity vs. hypersensitivity.* The negative pole of this dimension, *hypersensitivity,* often has been linked with Jung's concept of *introversion.* This end of the dimension has been found more frequently in the population than the other end. Hypersensitive people recoil from reality. They tend to be egocentric and easily upset. They worry over humiliating experiences. At the extreme, they have paranoidal thoughts and feelings (such as, "people are watching me," and "they can read my mind").

A third general factor is *alertness vs. inattentiveness.* Guilford defines this dimension as ". . . a matter of keeping in rapport with the environment versus being inattentive or absentminded." The factor refers to spontaneous attention rather than directed attention. From what we already know concerning the attention difficulties of retarded children, we should expect them to cluster at the inattentive pole. It would be interesting to determine how much this factor is a consequence of the condition of retardation and how much it contributes to retarded functioning.

Among the factors in the major emotional group, *cheerfulness vs. depression* is particularly important for our purposes. The negative end of this dimension is characterized by such descriptions as these: is emotional, is depressed, feels physically depleted, and has periods of loneliness. It has been found that pathological depression is *not* the same thing as *extreme depression,* as measured by this factor. Nor is *hypomania* (supposedly the opposite of pathological depression) the same as *cheerfulness.* This finding suggests that there are different levels, as well as different attributes, to the condition of depression. Indeed, other investigations of depression have indicated that this phenomenon is difficult to evaluate accurately by means of self-ratings or questionnaires because of the intense withdrawal and unwillingness to cooperate that severe depression usually involves. Depression in retarded children may be a significantly different kind of phenomenon than in normal children. Both clinical and experimental study of depression are needed.

Other emotional factors are *immaturity vs. maturity, nervousness vs. composure, stability vs. cycloid disposition,* and *poise vs. self-consciousness.* Not all of these factors have been extrapolated in all of the factor studies. The stability vs. cycloid dimension appears extremely well validated and has been demonstrated in both normal and abnormal populations. Again, we should emphasize that little is known concerning the relevance and significance of these factors among the retarded. When such findings are available, they will assist us in better understanding this group.

The factors in the social disposition group are most clearly related to specific environmental experiences of the individual. Accordingly, we should expect that retarded children would rate quite different from children of normal intelligence. Such factors as *ascendance vs. timidity, socialization vs. self-sufficiency, social initiative vs. passivity, friendliness vs. hostility,* and *tolerance vs. criticalness* are clearly dependent on previous conditioning and learning. The preconditions for the positions on these factors and the consequences of the phenomena should be of great importance in understanding, educating, and guiding retarded children especially. Such questions as, "Is timidity a consequence of retarded intellectual functioning and does it impair still further the retarded person's intellectual functioning?" and "Does passivity result from retarded functioning or is it a contributor to such functioning?" are highly important in any adequate psychological approach to the problems of retardation and the education and treatment of retarded pupils. Unfortunately, there is very little reliable information on such matters, and we must wait for future research to assist us in finding answers.

Cattell and others (see below) have attempted to develop a comprehensive description of personality by means of what is called *multivariate factor analysis.* By this is meant the use of a great many (rather than a few) measures of presumed personality traits in relatively large populations (mostly "normal" subjects). Such an approach uses more than, for example, one measure of anxiety and simultaneously uses more than one measure of some related phenomenon, such as learning, so that a broad spectrum of related behaviors and their measurements are simultaneously involved.

Based on these kinds of studies, Howarth and Cattell (1973) have reported more than a dozen source traits that are believed to account for a considerable degree of the variance responsible for differences between people in personality (defined as "that which enables us to predict what a person will do in a given, defined situation"). Moreover, the findings are based on a variety of types of data: questionnaires, direct observations of behavior, and ratings. We shall not attempt to report all of the findings or all of the factors; rather, we will describe a selected sample of the most important of them. In order of importance (in terms of accounting for their statistical significance) these factors are: *Affectothymia vs. Schizothymia* (easygoing, adaptable, etc., versus obstructive, secretive, etc.); *Intelligence; Ego Strength vs. General Emotionality; Excitability vs. Insecurity; Dominance vs. Submission; Surgency vs. Desurgency* (cheerful, joyous, etc., versus pessimistic, seclusive, etc.); *Superego Strength* (persevering, responsible, etc., versus fickle, immature, etc.); *Parmia vs. Threctia* (adventurous, gregarious, etc., versus shy, withdrawn, etc.); *Premsia vs. Harria* (demanding, impatient, etc., versus emotionally mature, independent minded, etc.); etc. This sampling will give the reader some conception of the kinds of factors that have been extracted. Some factors are given "technical" names in order to differentiate them more easily from terms in common usage that might be defined or conceived differently. It will be noted that many of the basic factors that have been discovered have much in common with conceptions developed by Freud and others as also being basic. The advantage of the multivariate method rests primarily on the empirical and demonstrable qualities of the designated factors.

Cattell, however, has gone beyond the measurement of source traits. He also has investigated and developed measures of motivational factors, called ERGs. The ERG is defined as "a source of reactivity or energy." At least nine such ERGs have been found, and five of them, which are most replicable, are: mating ERGs; assertiveness ERGs; fear ERGs; narcissism ERGs; and pugnacity-sadism ERGs.

There are other findings in Cattell's work, but perhaps of greatest importance in the practical sphere is that tests have been developed to measure the phenomena, as defined; in time, the utility of such tests in prediction and in intervention can be properly assessed.

As yet, the findings derived from factor analytic studies show no clear picture of what levels of the personality are being tapped, although Cattell believes they do, nor do we know what the putative interrelationships of such levels might be. Still less do we know of the possible interaction of the several factors. Although these are still virgin fields for investigation, we must note that factor analytic research is a fruitful approach, and that there is no essential antagonism between it and clinical methods for the study of personality structure. In time, a rapprochement of the two methods may be possible, and a higher order of understanding of people may well emerge.

Closely related to the factorial approach in the analysis of personality is the longitudinal study of temperament and development reported by Thomas and Chess (1977). Although this study focused on normal children for the most part, intensive analyses also were made of 52 mentally retarded children in the IQ range of 50 to 75. The children ranged in age from 5 years to 11 years, and 44 of these children were involved in a six-year follow-up study. Based on an interactional concept of the nature of human behavior that stipulates that behavior "is typified by reciprocal stimulative relationships" and that these relationships change "progressively under the influence of intimate interrelationships of factors of maturation and of experience," they found nine categories of temperament that were needed to describe an individual's temperament. These are: activity level (mainly motor activity), rhythmicity (predictable vs. unpredictable functions), approach-withdrawal (initial response to new situations), adaptability (to new or altered situations), threshold of responsiveness (intensity level of stimulus needed to evoke discernible response), intensity of reaction, quality of mood, distractibility, and attention span and persistence.

In an early study of these 52 children, all of whom were living at home, Chess and Korn (1970) found that 31 had a behavior disorder (based on psychiatric and other data). Of these, 19, or 61 percent, had three or more of the signs of the "Difficult Child" syndrome—a syndrome indicating disturbed behavior based on the ratings on the *Temperament Scales*. Moreover, it was found that the more signs of the "Difficult Child" syndrome a child had, the more likely he or she was to have a behavior disorder. Chess and Korn concluded that "retarded children with even mild manifestations of the Difficult Child temperamental constellation are especially vulnerable to the development of a behavior disorder." They further noted, "The demands for socialization of the Difficult Child appear to intensify the stresses to which the retarded child is especially subject."

In a six-year follow-up of 44 children from the original group, similar relationships were found between frequency of signs of the "Difficult Child" syndrome and behavior disorders. Although retarded children were found to display more of the "Difficult Child" signs than the comparison "normal group" studied, the difference in frequency of signs was not statistically significant.

The general significance of the findings as they relate to the retarded child is that there is a tendency for such children to *develop* more than normal unfavorable temperamental characteristics, but what is particularly significant is that these retarded children, already *vulnerable* because of their condition and circumstances, are even more likely than normal children to suffer more adverse effects from such temperamental qualities. An interesting finding related to the significance of qualities of temperament was that obtained by Sameroff (1974), who studied a group of infants and very young children in terms of intelligence and temperament. He found that ". . . if one wants to predict an infant's IQ score at 30 months of age from a child's behavior at four months of age, a much more reliable prediction can be based on his temperament than on his intellectual functioning." One finding on which this conclusion was based was that the correlation between the children's *Difficult Child Temperament* score at 4 months of age and their Bayley IQ scores at 30 months of age was $+.49$, whereas the correlation between the children's Bayley IQ scores at these ages was only $+.18$!

OTHER PERSONALITY CHARACTERISTICS OF RETARDED INDIVIDUALS

Some research evidence points up the importance of personality considerations for the retarded. We have indicated that, in general, the retarded child's personality development may be expected to be slower than that of more average peers. Bialer (1961) has shown that the motivational system (see Cromwell's position, chapter 13) is, in some important respects, correlated with mental age development. This same study indicated that more mature conceptualization by the child leads to an orientation that events in the child's life are controlled more by self (so-called internal locus of control) than by outside events (external locus of control). Since retarded children are less mature conceptually than their average peers, we would expect them to be more easily motivated by external events in their lives, such as a teacher's praise or expectations by their peers. However, motivations are notoriously complex, and other factors than those studied also may be important. What is significant about level of conceptual maturity is that the conceptually mature child will tend to persist in long-term tasks and do better than a less conceptually mature competitor (Northcutt, 1963). Motivation also is affected by failure of the child and its effects on self-image. There is evidence that those with lower levels of self-image tend to have a lower aspiration level and do not strive as hard as others do.

It is very difficult to evaluate the effects of various cultural and educational experiences on the self-image, or self-concept, of the retarded child. As we shall see in Parts IV and V, the attitudes of society and the experiences retarded children have in school or in institutions—as well as the reflected attitudes of their parents, siblings, and peers—greatly influence that aspect of development. Educators have argued for decades about the effects of special-class placement (segregation) on the child's personality. It is extremely difficult to separate the effects of such placement from other factors, such as prevailing attitudes toward the retarded and toward the importance of academic achievement. In general, it has been found that the lower the level of a child's cognitive development, the lower the acceptance of the child by others and the lower the self-concept of that child. (Schurr et al., 1970). Efforts have been made to counteract such adverse characteristics in the retarded by limited intervention programs. For example, in one study some retarded children put on a carnival with their nonretarded peers (Rucker and Vincenso, 1970). It was found that these retarded children became better accepted by their peers for a time, but one month later this effect had disappeared. In short, it is possible to obtain some improvement by short-term intervention, but it doesn't solve the fundamental problems.

In later chapters, we will review the research on the various effects of intervention programs and other habilitative approaches and evaluate their effectiveness.

— 9 —

Problems of Adjustment

In this chapter, we will discuss the maladaptive behavior of the mentally retarded child. We will first discuss some of the general characteristics of maladaptive behavior, then some of the specific behavioral disturbances. Our emphasis will be on the emotional trauma to the child and the psychopathological behavior that may result.

MALADAPTIVE BEHAVIOR

Children, as well as adults, often engage in behavior that is in some way disturbing to themselves or to other persons. For example, persons often develop symptoms, such as gastrointestinal reactions, palpitation, and other anxiety reactions; negative and hostile behavior; and poor interpersonal relationships. We call such forms of behavior *maladaptive behavioral reactions,* since they interfere with adequate adjustment. They are not the usually accepted ways of behaving. It is important to recognize that the maladaptive behaviors of mentally retarded children *are not the primary result of their retarded intellectual capacities. Rather, they are the result of incomplete or distorted personality functions associated with mental retardation.* It is, of course, true that the inferior intellectual capacities of the mentally retarded child make it much more difficult to achieve a high degree of success in many areas (such as academic or vocational areas), but intellectual factors play a *secondary* rather than a *primary* role in the production of maladaptive behavior.

Blatt (1958) reported finding marked personal and social adjustment difficulties in noninstitutionalized mentally retarded children. Such problems are not, as some persons believe, manifested only by those children whose retardation is sufficiently severe as to require institutionalization. This finding was confirmed in a study reported by Kern and Pfaeffle (1965). The fact that retarded children so often manifest maladaptive behavior is not indicative of any indigenous condition; rather, it is a reflection, in part, of the social and other difficulties we confront them with. Slower mental development and frustrations in meeting the demands of improperly organized school programs often contribute to maladaption.

Rather than saying: "Billy is a mentally retarded child and therefore shows this or that disturbance in behavior," we should ask instead: "What disturbances in psychological growth, which may be associated with retardation, have led to the production of Billy's maladaptive behavior?" The significance of this point of view cannot be overstressed. It leads to a program of positive action, such as consideration of possible methods of treatment for the mentally retarded child. Such an approach, of course, is not directed primarily toward raising the intellectual capacities of the retarded child, but, rather, toward the removal of his emotional conflicts and the development of more adequate patterns of behavior—in other words, enabling him to live a happier and more productive life.

We also should like to reemphasize that the mentally retarded child shows *no* behavioral reactions that are not also shown by the child of normal intellectual capacities. The essential difference between the two is that the mentally retarded child is *more prone* to show maladaptive behavioral reactions, and that such behavior tends to *persist* over a much longer period of time than that of the more normal child. This conclusion has been demonstrated by many research studies. McLachlan, for example, found that the emotional needs of mentally retarded children were the same (qualitatively) as those of normal children. In particular, McLachlan (1955) pointed out that the retarded child:

1. Needs recognition. He, like all children, has a self that needs satisfaction.
2. Needs to be protected from, on the one hand, and prepared for, on the other, those situations whose demands too often exceed his capacities.
3. Must be given adequate outlets for his tensions.
4. Must be recognized as having many assets. These should be carefully evaluated so that they can be developed most profitably.
5. Needs careful explanations of his problems at various maturational stages.
6. Has a family, and this family as well as the child needs attention.

McLachlan feels that the degree of the retarded child's emotional stability is more dependent on his methods of responding to social situations than on his intellectual level.

Gorlow, Butler, and Guthrie (1963) studied the correlates of the self-attitudes of retarded children. They administered the *Laurelton Self-Attitude Scale* to 164 institutionalized retarded girls. The scores were then related to a number of measures of various traits, such as achievement, intelligence, early experiences, and personality functions. It was found that there were statistically significant correlations between self-acceptance and measures of intelligence, school achievement, and success in the institution training program. However, *despite the fact that the correlations reached statistical significance, they were very small indeed, indicating that the child's acceptance of herself was a function of other factors in addition to intellectual level per se.* This finding is substantiated in another study by Gorlow and his coworkers. It was found that the girls who were separated from their mothers at an early age had a more negative self-image than did those who were separated at a later age. It is our contention that the emotional characteristics of the retarded child are functions of factors other than intelligence alone, and that they are primarily the consequences of early child-parent relationships.

This point of view is supported by evidence derived from studying the responses of mentally retarded children on projective tests. (See discussion of projective tests in chapter 11.) In one study, Beier and his coworkers (1951) investigated the fantasy life of mentally retarded children by means of the *Thematic Apperception Test*. On this test, the child is instructed to make up a story about a picture. The investigators compared the stories of retarded children with those of normal children in regard to two major characteristics: (1) the psychological aspects of the themes expressed and (2) the environmental aspects of the stories they created. Marked similarities between the two groups of children were found in both of these areas. It was the feeling of the investigators that differences in the intellectual capacities of children do not contribute significantly to their emotional needs, although they do affect some other aspects of the child's test functioning. The themes of the retarded group of children were less aggressive than those of the normal group. The retarded group was more preoccupied with themes of self-accusation, rejection, and problems of socialization. The retarded children were more concerned with family relationships than were the normals, and were much more preoccupied with their own perceived "badness."

Beier and his coworkers also observed that the emotional feelings of retarded children came out very directly, almost as "if social learning had not provided the mental defective with techniques for dissembling." It is our judgment that these differences are not the *direct* result of the defective intellectual capacities of the retarded child, but, rather, the result of the child's experiences in relating to others—both in the family and in society in general. They are the result of emotional problems stemming indirectly from an inferior level of functioning. They may be changed by ensuring adequate social and learning situations for the child and the child's family. (See chapters 12 and 13.)

Two other general issues should be noted. The first concerns that aspect of adjustment referred to as *adaptive behavior* (see chapter 3). The question is: Is adaptive behavior a single unitary factor or is it a multivariate factor (that is, Does it consist of a number of elements?)? Research has shown that, like intelligence, adaptive behavior consists of a number of components. The pioneering research in this field has been done by Nihira (1969). Using a checklist of observable behaviors, he made a series of studies of retarded children and adults. He found that three important factors contribute to adaptation: personal independence, social maladaptation, and personal maladaptation. The last factor is not, perhaps, as clearly delineated as the first two. The checklist has been found to be particularly useful in differentiating severely maladaptive persons from mildly maladaptive ones. The findings clearly reveal how widely different in maladjustment mentally retarded people are. (See also Nihira and Shellhaus, 1970.)

The other issue relates to the effect of intervention programs in reducing aspects of maladjustment. On this subject, apart from therapeutic and behavior modification programs, the evidence is far from complete. As we have shown in the previous chapter, short-term experimental procedures are likely to have short-term effects. In a study done by Lilly (1971) on children in the upper grades of elementary school, it was shown that providing paired and shared experiences (for example, making a movie) for unpopular and popular children produced improvement in acceptance of the unpopular children, but the effects were only temporary. We shall discuss this issue more fully later.

We will view the maladaptive behavior of the retarded child from the same perspective as that of the more normal child, seeing it as the result of disturbances in the same developmental processes that are reacted to in the same manner by all children. There are some differences between the normal child and the retarded child, such as the excessive persistence of behavior in the retarded child, and there are some differences in their developmental processes. These special problems will be discussed in detail later in this chapter.

Rather than dealing with the maladaptive behavioral responses of mentally retarded children as a single group, we will divide such children into three subgroups based on chronological age: (1) infancy and early childhood (from birth to about six years of age); (2) late childhood (from six to about puberty); and (3) puberty and adolescence.

PROBLEMS IN INFANCY AND EARLY CHILDHOOD

During infancy the mentally retarded child, like all others, relates primarily to parents and siblings. Interactions with people outside the home are at a minimum, so the interactions that occur between the child and the immediate family are of primary importance in determining behavioral reactions. Most parents show no great concern about the child's mental retardation during infancy, unless the child is markedly retarded. This is true, in part, because the gap between the retarded and the more normal child is not yet great enough to be easily perceived. Sociocultural factors have not yet had an opportunity to make their impact easily evident in the child's behavior, and the personality structures in both the retarded and the normal child have not differentiated to the point at which marked differences are evident. In most cases, however, the parents *are* somewhat aware that the retarded infant is slower in many aspects of development than is the normal child, and they may develop some mixed feelings toward the child. When these feelings develop, they usually involve rejection of the child (often unconscious) and frustration because of its limited abilities.

The mentally retarded child usually shows delayed speech and walking. The child has difficulty in *visual-motor* functions—that is, it is hard to coordinate muscular activities with vision and to manipulate objects accurately. Later, the child has great difficulty in feeding himself. It is very difficult to tie shoelaces and to perform similar complex motor activities. The parent often expects too much from the child during this period, and as a consequence, the retarded child begins to see himself as inferior and inadequate.

Weaning presents many problems, and it is difficult for the mother to get the retarded child off the bottle. There are many reasons for weaning difficulties. The mentally retarded child may have overly strong needs to retain oral satisfactions and is not apt to give them up as readily as the more normal child. The retarded child has many oral conflicts that are not yet adequately resolved and so is more strongly fixated in this phase. Further, even the physical task of manipulating a spoon is often too difficult. When the process of weaning is apparently achieved, the child still shows many residual characteristics of oral behavior. The retarded child may continue to suck fingers, for example, or chew clothing, put objects into his mouth, or bite himself or other persons. Often he will show marked needs for affection and will cling tenaciously to other people. Frequently the retarded child will want to be held, lying quite passively while this need is gratified.

Toilet training also is a difficult process for the retarded child. The child's fixations at the oral level make it more difficult to cope with the problems of the anal level. It is difficult to understand what mother expects, and often he is not biologically mature enough to establish adequate bowel control. This may frustrate mother, and her negative reactions emotionally traumatize the child.

As the child approaches school age (kindergarten), retardation becomes more and more apparent, and the difference between his capacities and those of the more normal child becomes more discernible. In play activities, for example, he begins to become more and more isolated and feels rejected *outside* as well as *inside* the home.

In general, the period of early infancy is one of extreme *biological dependency* for all children. Their very lives depend on adequate gratification of their biological and physical needs. They are unable to move readily from one place to another, and they are unable to gratify their hunger and thirst needs by themselves. Similarly, they are unable to gratify their psychological needs. Although this is true for *all* children, it is particularly significant for mentally retarded children, since they remain in a condition of biological and psychological helplessness for a longer period of time.

The retarded child often develops *depressive reactions* (Menolascino and Egger, 1978). The development of such reactions is in large measure due to inadequacies in biological maturation and in the relationships of mother and child. That a good relationship is of extreme importance in the healthy emotional development of the child has been emphasized by Ribble (1943). Her studies clearly indicate that without adequate mothering, children lag far behind in both psychological and physical development. This has been demonstrated by many studies of rejected children (such as those placed in institutions). Bakwin (1942), in describing such cases, noted that:

A striking feature is their failure to gain properly despite the injection of diets which in the home are entirely adequate. Infants in hospitals sleep less than infants who are at home, and they rarely smile or babble spontaneously. . . . Infections of the respiratory tract which last only a day or two in a home often persist for months in a hospital. Return home results in a defervescence within a few days and a prompt and striking gain in weight.

He also lists other reactions, such as apathy, poor appetite, or too-frequent bowel movements.

Spitz (1948) has perhaps contributed more than others to our understanding of this problem. The institutionalized children he studied engaged in an excessive amount of autoerotic play over a relatively long period of time and were generally emotionally retarded. He noted that they cried a great deal, had immobile faces and expressionless eyes, and showed unusual positions of the fingers and hands. Spitz stresses that the absence of maternal care and love may be responsible for severe psychological and physical retardation and illness of the child. Recent studies of institutionalized children corroborate this conclusion (Baldwin, 1955; Hunt, 1969; Blatt and Kaplan, 1966).

Mohr and his coworkers (1955) studied a group of children with *psychosomatic* involvements (physical symptoms due to psychological factors). On the basis of their results, they offered the following as tentative conclusions:

1. During the first year of life, any noxious stimulus, physical or psychological, tends to produce a generalized response. It follows that even minimal traumata have generalized effect and are experienced as traumatic, impeding functional growth and integration, during this age period.
2. Traumatic experience of any sort, during this very early age period (under six months), can be responded to only at the level of physiological, or somatic response. . . .
5. Psychologically, noxious or traumatic stimuli in early infancy evoke reactions of physiological disturbance; only with maturation can these responses become more differentiated and object-directed. Anxiety initially stems from the disintegrative connotations of the noxious stimulus. Later, guilt feelings and fear of retaliation or punishment play their role, e.g., after establishment of object relationships.

It is likely that rejection is more apt to occur in a retarded child than in a more normal child because of the retarded child's persisting dependency needs, mother's lack of understanding of the child's problems, and mother's emotional reactions to deficiencies. Because mothers of retarded children may often unconsciously reject them (and may even separate themselves physically from their children), the mothers may fail to provide adequate or consistent mothering. When such a situation develops, the children are more likely to become depressed.

Occasionally, the retarded child develops *convulsive seizures.* Such seizures may result from organic brain damage, but they frequently occur when there is no known organic injury. A convulsive seizure is a symptom of some underlying disturbance and may stem from any one of many causes. For example, it may be the result of some minor infection, or it may result from severe emotional tension. However, apart from specific central nervous system involvements, infants can develop seizures because of their general low threshold for irritability. Such seizures do not necessarily predispose the infant to epilepsy or chorea in later life, nor do they necessarily persist. Only when the condition is severe or prolonged or is complicated by serious infection do convulsions have important consequences, by themselves, for the behavioral adjustment of the infant. The seizure may be more significant for the subsequent personality development of the infant than for the reaction itself. Because of the instability of the retarded child and the increased potency of the emotional trauma to which he is subjected, seizure reactions are more common for him than for normal children. The attitudes of the parents, and their reactions to convulsions in the retarded child, are important in dealing not only with the child but also with siblings and peers, who, by their own anxiety reactions, may affect the retarded child's behavior. When seizures do occur, careful medical and psychological consultation should be available in order to determine the cause(s) and to provide appropriate guidance for the child and the family.

Another behavioral reaction of the mentally retarded child is the tendency to *repeat the speech* of an adult. This is a fairly common characteristic of the group. An example of such speech behavior follows:

Mother: Put the spoon back.
Child: Spoon back.
Mother: That's not nice.
Child: Not nice.
Mother: Don't talk like this.
Child: Like that.

This type of repetition of speech is known as *echolalia.* Psychologically, it is similar to other types of *repetitive, imitative behavior.* For example, the child may repeat the actions of parents, mimicking their behavior in walking or in other physical activities. This type of repetitive behavior is known as *echopraxia.* We often see echolalia and echopraxia in average children during infancy, but when they occur and persist in the retarded child, they are likely to add to other adjustment problems. This type of behavioral pattern often can be ameliorated by the use of drugs (Menolascino and Egger, 1978) or by behavioral modification methods (see chapters 13 and 14).

Both of these reactions indicate that the ego of the child is still immature, and that the boundaries between the *self* and the *not-self* have not fully developed. Objects (including persons) are not yet clearly perceived for what they are, and so may appear to be frightening. Since retarded children develop their ego skills more slowly and less adequately than average children, they may exhibit repetitive behavior for much longer periods. Moreover, retarded children use such behavior to form a closer relationship with an adult. Both echolalia and echopraxia may be viewed as infantile forms of identification—the retarded child is unconsciously trying to identify with the adult by doing the same things the adult does. These behaviors also may be regarded as attempts to master threatening stimuli—another indication of the immature ego strengths of the retarded child.

The personality development of the retarded child can be significantly influenced by parents and by other people close to the child. Cromwell (1961a) has suggested seven fundamental principles for fostering healthy development. Since it is believed that they provide the best possible growth-stimulating environment for the child, they are presented here in detail.

1. Positive reinforcement will increase the possibility of a particular behavioral reaction's occurring. Negative reinforcement (currently termed aversive conditioning) will decrease such a possibility. This means that wanted forms of behavior should be praised whenever possible.
2. If the child is to develop a more goal-directed than avoidant form of behavior, then more positive reinforcement than aversive conditioning should be provided. That is, more "praise" than "punishment" should be meted out.
3. The reinforcement should be as immediate as possible.
4. The parent is, of course, not always able to administer reinforcement whenever it is appropriate. But this does not necessarily mean that its efficiency in maintaining a particular form of desirable behavior is impaired.
5. Whenever possible, the reasons for the reinforcements should be verbalized to the child.
6. It is important that the parent be consistent in the administration of reinforcements. (Do not punish tomorrow what is praised today.)
7. Positive reinforcement should be administered to the child regardless of whether or not it is specific to the behavior that the child is displaying. As a result, the child himself learns to regard himself as a worthwhile person despite a particular behavior. Cromwell feels that this principle is the most important of all.

We believe that Cromwell's seven points are applicable to the fostering of the development of all children. They are, however, of particular importance in the personality development of the retarded child.

PROBLEMS IN LATER CHILDHOOD

During the period of later childhood (six to fifteen years of age), the gap between the mentally retarded child and the child of higher intelligence becomes more evident. During this period, factors in the total home situation have a more clearly demonstrable effect on the child's social behavior, and social and cultural forces outside the home become increasingly important.

Compared with children of average or above average intelligence, retarded children in this age span show the same frequency of maladjustment or a higher frequency. For instance, Chazan (1964) reported finding depression, hostility toward adults, inhibitions, and symptoms of emotional tensions in noninstitutionalized, mildly retarded children of school age. He had used the *Bristol Social Adjustment Guide* to evaluate their behavior. He found that more than one-third of the educationally subnormal children that he studied were maladjusted, and that their rate of maladjustment was significantly higher than the 12 percent rate that was characteristic of a control group.

During the period of later childhood, the parents have an increasing awareness of the deficiencies of the child and begin to react emotionally to this awareness. Often the parents develop severe conflicts about the retarded child, and these are reflected in their behavior toward the child. Their feelings may involve either conscious or unconscious rejection of the child, or both (see chapter 10). As many authorities have pointed out, parents of normal intelligence usually are rejecting parents to their mentally retarded child. Since parents usually regard the child as an extension of themselves—indeed, too often *as themselves*—the fact that the child is retarded is a severe blow to their own narcissistic picture. They often feel: "How could I have produced this?" and begin to wonder about their own adequacy. As Foale (1956) has pointed out: They "regard unconsciously the mental defective as a reflection against their creative forces."

The guilt feelings of the parents over their rejection of the child may rise to serious proportions, and they then tend to react overprotectively toward the child. As a consequence, the retarded child often is not even permitted to learn to do the many things that she could do, and so functions below the level of already limited abilities. The child is likely to be aware of, and sensitive to, the feelings of the parents, even though they do not verbalize them; the child reacts to *all* the behavioral reactions of parents, not only to their verbal expressions. What the parents *do* often is of more importance than what they *say*.

The presence of siblings within the home may greatly complicate the problems of the retarded child. Often, siblings develop feelings toward the retarded brother or sister that are similar to those of the parent. They may be overprotective or unwittingly become critical or rejecting of a retarded sibling. They may resent the special attention she is receiving. Like their parents, they may develop feelings of guilt or shame because there is a retarded child in their family.

The parents are greatly concerned over the sibling relationships. They fear that the younger siblings will pick up the characteristics of the older retarded child, or they fear that the retarded child will embarrass the siblings. Often, of course, these fears are rationalizations or projections of the parents' own feelings.

The parents' concern about the effect of their retarded child's behavior on siblings as well as the defensive behavior and feelings of the siblings may complicate the adjustment problems of the retarded child. The child is confused and bewildered and feels rejected. She is not sure how much she is to blame; she is not sure how to react. Thus, no part of the family climate is conducive to the full development of the capacities that the retarded child *does* have. Rather, the climate has two negative effects: (1) it inhibits psychological maturation in all areas and (2) it complicates the normal problems that every retarded child has.

At the same time, during this period of childhood, social and cultural forces outside the home begin to have important impacts on the retarded child. In school, the inevitable unfavorable comparison between the child's abilities and those of other children is constantly present. If placed in a regular class, the retarded child has great difficulty in academic work, particularly in reading, and is soon given differential treatment in the classroom. The teacher begins to notice the child's difficulties and brings the facts of retardation to the attention of the child's parents. Other children perceive the differences between themselves and the retarded child and are quick to point out deficiencies to her.

The retarded child is likely to become a scapegoat for the jests of other children and the butt of many jokes. Other children displace their own negative feelings upon the retarded child since she is weaker than they are, and often serves as an object of their hostilities, fears, and anxieties.

The retarded child begins to perceive that she is different from other children and becomes aware of many of her own limitations and disabilities. She therefore tends to perceive herself as someone who is "bad" or "no good." The child's attempts to relate to other children often are rebuffed; she is the last one chosen for games (if she is even permitted to play at all), and when permitted to join a group, is criticized (either explicitly or implicitly) for ineptness. The retarded child is usually aware of, and sensitive to, the differential classroom treatment. Her self-esteem thus suffers many blows, and security status is constantly threatened.

Neighbors often show irrational attitudes toward the retarded child. Bob is a dull boy, they say, and they fear that if they allow their children to play with him, their children will be affected adversely. They may be afraid that their Todd will become like Bob, or that Bob will lead him into doing bad things. They also may fear that Bob actually will harm their Todd physically. They may have such mental stereotypes concerning mentally retarded children as these: retarded children are sex fiends; retarded children are delinquents; retarded children are sadists. Although such attitudes are beginning to die out (chiefly through the corrective efforts of enlightened parents of retarded children), they are still far too prevalent.

As a consequence, most life activities of the retarded child become colored by the child's inability to achieve success. Jordan and DeCharms (1960), for example, have explored the drive for achievement in retarded children. They compared the achievement motive of forty-seven mentally retarded special-class children with the achievement motives of forty-two mentally retarded children who were not special-class children and sixty normal children. It was found that although the need for achievement was not specifically related to intelligence, in general, the mentally retarded children expressed less need to achieve than did children of more normal intelligence. Jordan and DeCharms attribute this difference to probable differences in child-rearing practices, particularly to the experiences that retarded children are subjected to by their parents.

No specific evidence was offered to support this inference. It may be that the parents of retarded children have a different set of expectations of their offspring than do parents of normal children. In effect, according to Jordan and DeCharms, retarded children receive less training for independent functioning in early childhood; consequently, in later years they are less motivated to strive to achieve than are children of normal intelligence. Jordan and DeCharms also found that the special-class retarded children showed less fear of failure than did the non-special-class children, suggesting that the special class may offer many more benefits to the retarded child, in addition to providing for more adequate academic achievement.

The retarded child begins to be exposed to the attitudes that will frequently be directed toward him throughout his life—he is rejected and then seen as an *isolate.* These attitudes were, of course, present during early childhood, but they are far more important during later childhood because the retarded individual then interacts with more persons, his sphere of activities is enlarged, and social and cultural factors play a more significant role in his life.

Another special problem of the retarded child is that of play activities. All children need play experiences. Their emotional growth is facilitated through such activities. Mentally retarded children are in more need of play activities than average children, but they are the ones who are often deprived of such experiences, both at home and elsewhere.

Mentally retarded children are physically able to play with toys during the period of early childhood. Most of the toys that are readily available, however, are inappropriate for their immature emotional and intellectual levels of development. As pointed out by Benoit (1955), the toys designed for normal children usually are not suitable for mentally retarded children. By the time they are mature enough to use the toys, the children are too large and strong for them and they break the toys too easily—or they use the toys as instruments of destruction. Since they are older and bigger than children who are their mental equals, they do not care to play with "baby" toys. As Benoit points out, retarded children want to be like their peers; they wish to be accepted by them and wish to imitate them. They tend to resent "kid stuff" and reject the toys that are appropriate for their intellectual age but inappropriate for their chronological age.

Specific intellectual disabilities may make participation in many games and use of many toys completely out of the question for the retarded child. The child may not be able to read, so the usual books of early childhood are out, as far as he is concerned. Paper-and-pencil activities tend to be beyond the child's capacities, and any game that depends on reading, writing, language abilities, imagination, or complexity is too difficult to enjoy. As Benoit stresses, many adults apparently have an *attitude of helplessness* toward teaching games to mentally retarded children, but play can be one of the "principal vehicles of stimulation" for such a child. The more such a child is stimulated through senses, the more total growth is encouraged. Benoit feels that the mentally retarded child does best in physical games—those that use the larger muscular systems. He also believes that such children do best in group games that are essentially realistic; that is, those that do not involve too much fantasy.

Many attempts have been made to provide adequate play experiences for the mentally retarded child. The Play Schools Association has been a pioneer in this area. Cleverdon and Rosenzweig (1955), who have described the program of this association, point out that it has tried for years to develop work-play programs for all children, since *all children have a right to play.* The focus of such programs for retarded children is on the promotion of social adaptability. Cleverdon and Rosenzweig believe that work-play programs stimulate dramatic expression, gradually increase differing kinds of play activities, are adaptive with respect to the retarded child's size and mental capacities, and help to develop significant skills and attitudes.

The significance of *appropriate* play activities for retarded children in terms of developing assertive and constructively adaptive behavior traits cannot be overestimated. Peters and associates (1974) completed a study of adult-led recreation groups in which retarded and nonretarded children were observed over a four-year period. Although they found no significant difference between the two groups in measures of cooperation-compliance vs. anger-defiance, they found that retarded children rated significantly lower on the dimension of apathy-withdrawal vs. interest participation. This finding is important in that it confirms the frequent tendency of retarded persons, in the face of their many reality-based frustrations, *to adjust by withdrawal and regression* rather than by assertion and growth. We shall have more to say about this pattern of adjustment in later sections. At this point, our emphasis is on the constructive use of appropriate play activities and programs.

During childhood, the problems of the intellectually retarded child become increasingly acute. Conflicts continually grow more severe, and psychological defenses need to be constantly maintained. The widening gap between self and other children of the same chronological age leads the retarded child to perceive self as a social outcast and of no worth to family or society. It is no wonder that profound behavioral disturbances frequently occur. The retarded child is denied the usual childhood experiences—what other children *casually accept* is not for the retarded child. No close childhood friendships, group activities, shared experiences, and successes for which praise is given. Rather, the retarded child is constantly reminded of worthlessness and weaknesses and has feelings of futility and rejection. This child is truly a Jonah—a social outcast—and rarely has any feelings of belonging to a social group.

Even though this state of affairs does usually occur, it *does not have to occur.* This development is not an inevitable correlate of the child's mental retardation but the result of numerous unfortunate reactions to the retardation—the reactions of the child, the reactions of family, and the reactions of society and its institutions.

During the period of childhood, the retarded child gradually becomes more socialized. He begins to learn to take care of many personal needs, to acquire some skills in communicating with people, and to acquire some information about himself and the world around. He also manages to learn how to gratify some needs while conforming to the demands of the world of reality. Some of these increments of growth are due to the general maturational process. Many more are dependent on training and special opportunities for practice. These are referred to as *learning.* Although learning depends on intellectual capacities and adequate opportunities for acquiring skills, it also requires something more. It also depends on *the emotional climate* in which the learning takes place. The retarded child thus is at a disadvantage in all areas: mental capacities are at a lower level; the child is given few appropriate, specialized opportunities; and the emotional climate to which he is exposed is not conducive to effective learning (except perhaps in a negative sense).

Retarded children, as a group, are certainly not as happy as they might be. As Morris (1955) has pointed out, their need for "contentment, security, and a dignified nonpressure existence is continually disrupted by a demand to achieve and conform." Parents seem always to be pushing the child, and they often resist recognizing the fact of retardation. Thus, the child too often is denied the usual experiences of childhood. As Morris states: "Most rights of retarded children as human beings are confiscated, and they are deprived of the respect and mastery of their own simple wishes."

Our review thus far of the many factors in the external environment that contribute both in amount and in quality to the kinds of frustrations that the retarded tend to experience and that lead to undesirable traits of personality and social behavior can be buttressed by many research studies. Significant samples of such studies, and their findings, will now be adduced.

Webster (1970) points out that evidence indicates that retarded individuals have more than ordinary difficulty in adaptation due to restricted and inadequate ego development. Harter and Zigler (1974) demonstrate that mastery of appropriate tasks leads to pleasure, and that the greatest pleasure results when tasks are "optimally challenging." A series of studies (see, for examples, MacMillan and Keogh, 1971; and Gruen and Zigler, 1968) have concluded that retarded children have greater expectancy of failure than normals, due in large measure to being asked to do what they have not been prepared for or are not yet ready for. Zigler also has shown that retarded persons tend to be outer-directed as a consequence of the environmental experiences to which they have been exposed. Balla et al. (1974) and Yando and Zigler (1971) have demonstrated that the retarded child is most outer-directed when given cognitive tasks that are difficult. Silverstein (1970) has indicated that retarded persons consistently have greater anxiety than other groups. And Brown and Jones (1970) have found that retarded adolescents were more frequently retarded than normals as judged by the *Bell Adjustment Inventory*. Kirkendall and Ismail (1970) replicated this finding with preadolescent boys and girls.

Other studies have found that, in general, the retarded tend to be more impulsive and less inhibited in their behavior than normals (Epstein et al., 1975; Levine, 1976). These workers also note that such behavior can be modified by the appropriate behavioral methods of training. Levine notes that inhibitory control "is an important parameter along which intelligence may be ordered."

We have referred to studies of the self-concept of retarded individuals in previous chapters and, in general, have found that retarded children tend to have inferior self-concepts. Frequently it is alleged that placement in special classes has caused, or contributed to, such inferior self-concepts. Such a conclusion is strengthened by the findings of studies such as that of Zisfein and Rosen (1974), which show that estimates of self-concept are independent of IQ. Later, we will review the possible effects of placement in special education classes and in institutions on the self-concept.

Maladaptive Behavioral Reactions of Childhood

Mentally retarded children react to the impact of emotional stresses in the same general manner as the more average child, although, as noted previously, they tend to be less able to tolerate anxiety and stress because of their relatively slower maturation. Their egos are affected in varying degrees by emotional trauma. Sometimes only a slight disturbance in ego function may result from the emotional stresses encountered. Such moderate ego disturbances result when there is a relatively mild degree of trauma. The consequent disturbances in the behavior then tend to be of short duration (*transient*) and capable of being remedied (*reversible*).* These behavior reactions are known as *transient, adaptive problems in behavior.* If, however, a child experiences more severe trauma, then there may be a disturbance in the growth of the ego, and although the ego may remain essentially intact, the child's total capacity for effective adjustment is impaired. The reactions of such a child are termed *persistent, nonadaptive problems ·in behavior.* If the trauma is severe enough to produce disintegration or fragmentation of the ego, then profound disturbances in behavior may result. The consequent psychopathology is severe, and the process of recovery, even with intensive psychotherapy, is very difficult and slow. Such reactions are known as *extreme, persistent, nonadaptive problems in behavior.* Mentally retarded children may develop behavioral reactions at any one of these levels, depending on the strength of the emotional trauma to which they are subjected and the stage of development of their egos at the time of the stress. We shall discuss each pattern of reaction in turn.

Transient, Adaptive Problems in Behavior. The mentally retarded child is readily affected by environmental stress. (By *environmental stress,* we mean all factors that are external to the child.) The retarded child finds it difficult to adapt to sudden changes in the environment, such as a shift in school, meeting new or strange people, and a new sibling. In addition, the child finds it very difficult to adapt to cultural demands. Many transient, adaptive behavioral reactions may result. The more usual of these are discussed in the following paragraphs. It should be emphasized that the retarded child's reactions are similar to those of average children, only they are *more likely* to occur in the retarded child because the world tends to be such a frustrating place.

Reactions of *excessive aggression* may be shown. In such reactions the child may bully younger children and may, at times, hurt them. In this respect, the retarded child behaves like an average child with excessive aggression. He may become disobedient and defiant toward parents and be cruel to animals. He may break things, even if he harms himself as a result. He may use obscene language. The child may lie, cheat, steal, and be untrustworthy in general. Such reactions are not the result of the mental retardation *per se,* but of the emotional trauma that may be encountered as a result of it.

On the other hand, the retarded individual may react with patterns of *excessive timidity.* He may be very shy and bury his head in mother's skirts when meeting strangers, or he may show asocial forms of behavior when in the presence of other children or adults. Such a child tends to react with excessive daydreaming and often seems to be remote and "far away." He may refuse to play games. Often, he will not be interested in other persons and will wander away by himself.

*For a more complete discussion of the classification of behavioral reactions of children and of the concepts of personality disorganization and their relations to critical periods of development, see Hutt and Gibby (1959) and Hutt (1977b).

The retarded child, especially if severely or profoundly impaired, may have *habit* disorders. This child persistently reacts to emotional stress with *enuresis* (bed-wetting). He may wet or soil his clothing during the day (*diurnal enuresis*) or only at night (*nocturnal enuresis*). He may show an excessive amount of thumb-sucking or nail-biting. He also may have feeding problems, such as refusal to eat certain foods or even refusal to eat at all (*anorexia*).

Often there is an increase in *masturbatory* activities. Masturbation often is resorted to by the child as a means of *discharging tensions* without any *conscious* sexual connotations. Rather, the act of masturbation provides a measure of pleasurable gratification. (Unconsciously, of course, sexual gratification may occur).

Quite frequently the retarded child will react to stress situations with regressive forms of behavior. For instance, it is not uncommon for a teacher to remark that: "Johnny could do really well last month. He know his letters and could read some words, but he can't do nearly as well now." Or the mother might say: "I thought that Joe had gotten over those tantrums that he used to have, but now they're back again." Complaints of the recurrence of more infantile forms of behavior—such as eating problems, soiling of clothes, and speech disabilities—are frequently encountered. Such forms of behavior may indicate that the child is reacting to a stress situation through the use of regressive defenses. In such an event, a detailed study should be made in order to determine the specific environmental or situational factors that precipitated such a maladaptive behavioral response, since it may result from one of many varied causes.

Barsch (1960) studied the regressive behavior of a group of brain-injured children. He stated that it is very difficult for the brain-damaged child to establish stable perceptions. Consequently, such a child may see the entire world as chaotic, and the tolerance level for stress situations is characteristically low. Barsch's observations are important, since severely and profoundly mentally retarded children often have mild brain damage (minimal brain dysfunction). Barsch believed that the child experiences stress whenever forced to restructure or to reorganize a percept, a task that is difficult for the brain-damaged person.

It appears from Barsch's study that any changes in the child's world requiring restructure of the old and familiar environment may result in stress and subsequent regressive behavioral reactions. Further, Barsch found that regressive behavior due to stress may be shown at any age level. To the mentally retarded child, as Barsch points out, "little things may be very important."

These are merely some of the ways in which the retarded individual may respond to the stresses of the environment. Menolascino and Egger (1978) present an excellent summary of the most recent findings relating to retarded, brain-damaged individuals. Usually, no serious emotional disturbance is involved if brain-damage is not responsible for the stress. We have not listed all of the forms of temporary disturbance in behavior that may occur. There are so many diverse forms that to list them would be in effect to catalogue almost all types of behavior of children. We have noted a few of the more common behavioral reactions in order to illustrate transient and adaptive problems. However, in considering these ways of behaving, we should remember that it is not possible to judge the significance or the degree of disturbance on the basis of symptoms alone. Each form of maladaptive behavior cited may, in fact, also be associated with more severe ego destruction. If it is, then more severe psychopathology is involved. The following sections discuss some of these more severe forms of disturbance. It will be noted in each case that not the symptom, but the severity of ego disturbance, is crucial.

Persistent, Nonadaptive Problems in Behavior (Primary Behavior Problems). The term *primary behavior problem* has been used traditionally to describe most types of psychoneurotic behavior in children. It is preferable, we believe, to the phrase *psychoneurotic reaction,* because most reactions of children that fall in this category are not as clear-cut or as systematized as are the corresponding reactions of adults. We have suggested, in another context (Hutt and Gibby, 1957), reasons for a substitute phrase (or category): *persistent, nonadaptive behavior.* This new phrase seems, to us, to help differentiate such reactions more easily from the "transient, adaptive," and from the "extreme, persistent, and nonadaptive" reactions.

Mentally retarded children may react to the emotional stresses that impinge on them by developing a *psychoneurosis.* A psychoneurosis is a continuing reaction to a basic conflict between the unconscious wishes of the person (the id strivings) on the one hand, and the forces that attempt to prevent such gratifications (ego and superego) on the other. In this type of *solution* to a conflict, there is no essential destruction of the child's ego structure. As we have stated elsewhere, ". . . a psychoneurosis is a *continuing* disturbance in the integration of the personality resulting from the conflict of drives within the individual and manifesting itself in tension states, impaired functioning, and symptomatology." (Hutt and Gibby, 1957) The psychoneurotic reactions shown by the retarded child are similar to those shown by nonretarded children, except that they are not as well delineated and are more diffuse. They also tend to be more *directly* shown in behavioral reactions. (It is in these ways also that the psychoneurotic reactions of the child of normal intelligence differ from those of the adult.)

A frequent problem in mentally retarded children is *reading disability,* which is *likely* to be part of a psychoneurosis, or primary behavior problem. The act of reading is so complex that it is sensitive to the impact of many factors. In discussing reading disability as a persistent, nonadaptive behavior, we would like to make clear what we mean by *reading disability.* We should distinguish between two forms of reading difficulties, *reading retardation* and *reading disability,* which often are confused with each other. Reading retardation means that a particular child's level of reading is below that expected of an average child of the same chronological age. An eight-year-old child who reads at a seven-year level is said to have a reading *retardation.* This child may or may not have a reading *disability,* however. We are using the term *reading disability* to indicate something else—that the child's ability to read is *below the mental age level.* A ten-year-old child with a mental age of eight years and a reading level of six years has a reading *disability.* If the reading age is not lower than the mental age, the condition is not called a reading disability.

Reading disability thus is a phenomenon in which the *actual* reading level is below the child's *potential* reading level as determined by mental capacity. This relatively new concept emphasizes the discrepancy between *potential* and *actual* reading skills and, in so doing, also emphasizes the great number of causes that may be responsible for this difference.

Since *reading capacity* is a function of the intellectual level of the child, all mentally retarded children are retarded in reading. However, not all such children *need* to show reading disabilities, although far too many do. Reading disability is *not* a function of intellectual level; rather, it is the result of many factors, including physical defects or diseases, inadequacies in the child's learning experiences, and disturbances in the child's social and emotional adjustment. We are particularly concerned with this last factor, since we now are considering reading disability as a psychoneurotic reaction of the retarded pupil.

If the underlying cause of the mental retardation is a neurological condition, and it has involved sensory mechanisms (such as hearing or sight), then, of course, we may expect a reading disability in addition to the generalized reading retardation. Children of more average intelligence learn to adapt more readily to sensory deficiencies, so they often show no significant reading disability, particularly if given special attention. The retarded child cannot meet these deficiencies as readily, however, and the disability is more apt to occur, to persist, and to be more serious.

That factors in the emotional and social adjustment of the child are important in the etiology of reading disabilities has been established by many studies. When the act of reading arouses certain symbolic reactions (such as fear of looking, repression of the impulses involved in curiosity, feelings of guilt, and repressed aggression), blocking in the area of reading may be very severe.

Any one of a number of emotional problems may contribute to reading disability. Examples of these would be fear of competition from classmates, strong sibling rivalries, fear of social situations, repressed hostile feelings toward authority figures, ambivalent reactions toward the teacher, fear of rejection, anticipation of failure, and greatly lowered self-esteem. Any factor that affects the social and emotional adjustment of the child might produce or enhance a reading disability.

The mentally retarded child is particularly prone to such a condition. This child generally has a markedly low estimate of self and fears competition with the more average children in the schoolroom. Furthermore, attempts are often made to teach the retarded child to read long before she is ready to profit from exposure to such a process. This leads her to react negatively to the entire reading process and makes learning to read much more difficult. Indeed, at times, it is necessary to devote considerable effort to a reeducative attempt in order to undo the harm that such premature attempts usually cause. Reading, to the retarded child, is a tangible indication of retardation. It interferes with almost all other school activities and is a badge of inferiority. Reading becomes emotionally laden with displaced conflicts; therefore, it often is overvalued by the retarded child—and also by the parents.

The mentally retarded child also is prone to other types of

psychoneurotic involvements. He may develop *acute anxiety states*. Usually these are accompanied by feelings of depression or some physical complaints (stomach ache, pains in the side, etc.). These anxiety states usually center around the child's feelings of rejection—by parents or teachers or by another significant adult. The retarded child fears losing the love of an important person (usually the mother). The child may experience nightmares, horrible dreams of being pursued by a giant or being run over by a car or being hurt or mutilated in some other way. The basic core of the anxieties of the retarded child is fear of rejection—and there are many instances in reality to support such feelings.

An important study by Malpass, Mark, and Palerma (1960) confirms our clinical impression that the child of lower intellectual capacities may develop strong anxiety reactions. These investigators administered the *Taylor Manifest Anxiety Reactions Scale* (as revised for ten- to twelve-year-old children) to forty-one children in an educable mentally handicapped group, to fifty-three children institutionalized in a state school, and to sixty-three normal children in the same schools as the group of educable children.

It was concluded that the *Manifest Anxiety Scale* differentiated between the educable mentally retarded children and the institutionalized children. The educable retarded children were less anxious than the institutionalized children. But, in addition, it was found that both groups of retarded children were significantly more anxious (as measured by the *Taylor Manifest Anxiety Scale*) than were the normal children.

The presence of severe anxiety inhibits the adjustment of the retarded child in many significant ways. For example, it has negative effects on the child's relationships with parents, siblings, peers, and others. In addition, anxieties may hinder academic progress. A study by Wiener and his coworkers (1960) bears on this point. In this research, the correlates of anxiety were studied in a group of fifty-two mildly retarded teenage boys. It was found that poor academic achievement was significantly related to high test anxiety, and that a high level of anxiety prevented the mildly retarded child from achieving academic success at a level commensurate with ability. It was felt that psychotherapeutic measures designed to reduce severe anxiety might be effective in promoting the academic progress of the child.

Extreme, Persistent, Nonadaptive Problems in Behavior. The emotional maladjustment of the mentally retarded child may be so severe as to result in considerable disintegration of the ego. If this occurs, then the child's already lowered capacities for dealing with reality suffer further impairment. The child loses touch with reality and shows even more social inadequacies. There are even further reductions in outside interests, which in any event are limited, and abilities to relate to other persons decrease. The child may show many forms of pathological behavior, such as hearing voices or seeing people who are not actually present (auditory or visual hallucinations).

Such forms of extremely disturbed behavioral reaction in children have been termed *psychoses*. The most common form is *childhood schizophrenia*. Fortunately, however, it is a relatively infrequent condition. We do not understand it too well and it is very difficult to treat. It also is known by other names. Kanner (1972) has termed one form of childhood schizophrenia *early infantile autism*. In this form, the child seems withdrawn and unable to relate to other persons from the beginning of infancy. As early as 1866, Séguin (1907) pointed out that children sometimes develop a psychotic-like reaction. Other investigators since that time have devoted attention to such reactions of mentally retarded children and have attempted to describe and to understand their behavior. The term *pfropfschizophrenia* has been applied to ego disintegrative reactions in mentally retarded persons, but this term is not commonly used.

Although it occurs infrequently, the problem of infantile autism is important. Its etiology is still unsettled, but adherents of each of the opposing views (genetic-neural versus environmental) are convinced of their own position. The possibility that environmental factors are important is evident from the devastating effects that traumatic experience can have: severe withdrawal and impairment in mental functioning. Bettelheim (1967), who espouses the environmentalist position, offers dramatic and detailed evidence (drawn from his experiences at the Orthogenic School of Chicago) that (1) it is the very young child's inability to cope effectively with frustrating experiences that is at the root of the autistic withdrawal; and (2) this style of withdrawal is a consequence of extreme and unbearable anxiety. Although he recognizes that infants differ in temperamental qualities, and some are much more sensitive than others, he believes that these reactions of the infant result from infant-parent interactions, rather than some prenatal or congenital condition.

On the other side of the controversy is, for example, Rimland (1964), who recognizes that the evidence is not clearly conclusive but believes that biological factors are responsible for infantile autism. He feels that there is evidence that an impairment in the reticular formation of the brain stem, associated with perceptual disability, is responsible.

Schizophrenia also is one of the most common forms of mental illness in adults. In this disorder, the balance between the id, ego, and superego forces is upset. The several components of the personality do not work together in harmony. Thought processes are illogical and not well integrated, and the person's moods and emotions often are inappropriate to the present situation. There are acute disturbances in the total integration of thinking, feeling, and behaving. Perceptions of reality are distorted and contact with reality often is lost. True schizophrenia usually is a long-lasting chronic disorder that assumes many forms and is difficult to treat.

Childhood schizophrenia differs in many respects from the schizophrenic reaction shown by adults. There are many reasons for this. Because the ego of the child is not as well developed as that of the adult, and because the child's language and speech functions are not as complex, the manifestations of the child's breakdown are very different. However, despite these differences, children do show severe behavioral reactions, characterized by chronic and severe loss or impairment of ego functions.

Whether or not it is really correct to call these severe ego disturbances of the child *schizophrenic,* such disturbances involve the child's whole way of life. Such a child has many unique characteristics. There is typically a withdrawal of interest from the outside world, often accompanied by an increasing seclusiveness—that is, a tendency of the child to want to be alone and not be "bothered" by people. There is a decrease in emotional reactions. The emotions shown tend to be rigid in expression, and often they are not appropriate to the situation. (For example, he may laugh in a situation in which tears would be more appropriate.) There are many severe disturbances in the child's thinking processes. These may be bizarre, and *hallucinations* (faulty perceptions, such as "seeing things") and *delusions* (faulty and morbid thinking, such as a belief that people "are going to kill me") may be shown. There may be many disturbances in the vegetative nervous system, resulting in such reactions as "cold" extremities, excessive perspiration, and insensitivity to severe changes in temperature.

The specific cause of childhood schizophrenia is still a perplexing question. It also is questionable whether all of these types of reactions constitute one or many types of disorder. Some people believe that the reaction is inherited or is due to internal physiological causes. Others believe that environmental conditions surrounding the child are primarily responsible. In any case, the evidence does *not* indicate that any significant changes in the brain tissue cause this condition.

There is considerable evidence to indicate that the nature of the child's experience in *interpersonal relationships* is important. The child who develops a schizophrenic pattern of behavior has not developed an *adequate* and *consistent* relationship with other people. This difficulty is clearly related to the home situation, in which *inconsistent* and *pronounced maternal* rejection are commonly found. The mother of such a child usually is overprotective, oversolicitous, aggressive, and—most important—highly *ambivalent* toward the child. (That is, she unconsciously vacillates in her attitudes toward the child, being overly punitive at one time, overly permissive at another, and the like.) Nevertheless, the specific cause of the disorder is still undetermined.

Many attempts have been made to treat such children. At one time it was thought they would not respond to treatment, but today the attitude is one of cautious hopefulness. There appears to be a difference in the extent of recovery that is related to the type of onset of the disorder. Those children who develop the condition more suddenly (for example, directly after an acute psychological trauma or after a severe infectious disease) respond better and more rapidly to treatment than those children in whom the onset is slower and more gradual (Bettleheim, 1967).

When children of average or superior intelligence develop childhood schizophrenia, infantile autism, or some other form of psychotic disturbance, they may behave as though they are mentally defective. They are unable to use their mental capacities, and they show retarded thought processes and sluggish emotional reactions. However, impaired mental functioning due to psychoses is an entirely different condition from mental retardation, although the diagnostic differentiation may be difficult to make. The psychotic child *appears* to be mentally retarded. On the other hand, it is possible for a mentally retarded child to develop a psychotic type of reaction, in general, or a form of childhood schizophrenia, in particular. That child is *both* mentally retarded and psychotic.

Benda (1952) feels that childhood autism is a *symptom* that indicates the inability of the child to establish satisfactory contact with the environment. There may be several underlying causes of the autism. These, according to Benda, include (1) injuries to the central nervous system, especially those due to asphyxiation; (2) severe psychogenic factors, such as severe rejection or severe grief reactions due to loss of a beloved person; and (3) childhood schizophrenia.

We have previously noted that the etiology of infantile autism is disputed, with adherents of both the environmental and genetic positions. With increasingly sophisticated diagnostic methods and more precise approaches to the research problems, it has become more likely that there is a polygenetic basis underlying most cases, if not all. Such genetic determinants may not be the only percursor of infantile autism, but may be a *necessary precondition*. Studies of twins strongly support this position. For example, Ornitz and Ritvo (1968) found in their study of monozygotic twins that both members of pairs of such twins, with one exception, developed infantile autism. On the other hand, it is rare for dizygotic twins to be concordant for this condition. Moreover, an epidemiological study (Ritvo et al., 1976) of seventy-four autistic patients compared with seventy-four children hospitalized for other neuropsychiatric disorders reported that there were no significant differences in average parental age, at the time of the patient's birth, educational level, family income, social class indices, or *distribution from expected populations frequencies*. This latter finding is emphasized since some authorities have suggested that parents with better education and intelligence take better prenatal and postnatal care of their children so that their autistic children survive, whereas parents from lower social classes do not provide such intensive care and their autistic children die before or shortly after birth. In addition, Ritvo et al. have shown that autistic children "have an increase in biogenic amine, serotonin, and platelet cells in their blood," thus indicating a profound biological disturbance. Nevertheless, such findings only demonstrate that there are likely to be underlying genetic and biological determinants to the development of autism, and not that these are sufficient to cause the condition. In short, autistic children have a high *vulnerability,* which predisposes them in this way, but other conditions may contribute to the maldevelopment.

Although appropriate pharmocological treatment may be necessary, psychological methods of treatment also may be helpful. Bettleheim uses intensive individual and milieu treatment in his program. On the other hand, behavioral methods of intensive conditioning, especially operant behavior modification, (see chapter 16) can be helpful, as Metz (1965), Ferster and Simmons (1966), and Lovaas et al. (1967) have demonstrated. Such behavioral approaches can lead to modification in motoric, perceptual, and other primary behavior forms, and these, in turn, can lead to improved social adaptation. It is not as yet clear how long such improvements will last, but they are conducive to improved functioning. Later, we will see how such methods can similarly improve the behavioral reactions of even profoundly retarded children.

The behavioral reactions of retarded children with severe ego damage differ from those of more normal children to some extent. Such retarded children tend to engage in either too little or too great an amount of activity. They are depressed and melancholic or they are given to temper outbursts; they are given to stupor or to rage; they are apathetic or excitable. The most prevalent picture of a mentally retarded child with severe personality involvement, however, is one in which there are severe withdrawal symptoms (*catatonia*) and numerous odd, or queer, mannerisms.

The phrase *primitive catatonic psychosis of idiocy* has been applied to the psychotic state shown by some mentally retarded children. Psychosis in retarded children tends to differ from that in children with higher intelligence. It is manifested more in *motor* behavior in the retarded, whereas it is manifested more in *symbolic* behavior in the other children. Symbolic behavior requires higher levels of intellectual functioning.

MacGillivray (1956) has added to our knowledge of psychoses in mental deficiency. Based on a review of the literature on the subject and his own studies of psychotic children who were mentally defective, he concluded that such types of psychotics were likely to display catatonic-like behavior—that is, behavior characterized by withdrawal and reduction in activity. He noted that psychotic children who were average or above in intelligence showed a greater variety of specific, differentiated forms of psychoses, whereas psychotic children in the mentally defective range were more apt to display diffuse, ill-defined, and nondifferentiated forms of psychoses. Like other workers, he found that there were special difficulties in treating psychoses in mentally retarded cases, one of these being the great difficulty in learning about their thought processes.

But Wolfensberger (1960) does not agree with the contention that it is more difficult to communicate with the mentally retarded schizophrenic child than with the schizophrenic child of more normal intellectual capacities. He believes that the retarded child is unable to create a personal high-level symbolic world and has limited informational resources. Consequently, withdrawal from the outer world is more difficult for the retarded child than it is for the nonretarded schizophrenic child. Wolfensberger believes that because the retarded schizophrenic child is unable to remove himself from the symbolism of his cultural group he may be approached and treated more readily by the therapist.

All schizophrenic children communicate through nonverbal behavior (one of the many "currencies of psychotherapy"), but this is particularly true of the child who is, in addition, retarded. Such a child communicates essentially through nonverbal symbols, such as patting or touching part of the body, grimacing, and gesturing. One additional factor facilitating communication, according to Wolfensberger, is the contention that the retarded child is less capable of creating an extensive fantasy world. His psychotic state is characterized by brief episodic periods of disturbance. As a result, he remains more exposed to reality, which facilitates the processes of communication and psychotherapy.

We realize, then, that a child may be mentally retarded and psychotic at the same time, but too often such a multiple diagnostic evaluation is not made. Menolascino (1965) studied thirty-two mentally retarded children who were considered psychotic. The group included twenty-two boys and ten girls. The median age was 4.4 years for the boys and 5.2 years for the girls. The psychiatric diagnoses of the group were as follows: two cases of early infantile autism, six cases of childhood schizophrenia, one case of pfropfschizophrenia, and twenty-three cases of chronic brain syndrome with a psychotic reaction. Menolascino points out that usually the young mentally retarded child is viewed essentially as an emotionally immature child, hardly capable of maintaining any marked behavioral deviation. He states that this raises some very basic questions. Are primitive behavioral patterns invariably the result of conflict-induced personality fixation or regression? Has the child displayed a lack of progression rather than some degree of regression? Did the family psychopathology cause the child's behavioral symptoms, or was the family psychopathology a reaction to the child's personality changes from an ongoing disorder of the central nervous system? Menolascino, then, is concerned with the differential diagnosis of the psychotic reactions of childhood. He feels that it is necessary to stress the need for specific diagnostic classification of the psychotic reactions in infancy and early childhood so that treatment and prognosis may have universal meaning to clinicians in the field. We would like to stress that the diagnosis of the psychotic elements present in a basic framework of mental retardation is exceedingly difficult to establish, requiring the highest degree of clinical acumen.

PROBLEMS IN PUBERTY AND ADOLESCENCE

Puberty is certainly a critical period for the mentally retarded child, as it is for all children. The retarded child has had numerous problems throughout childhood, but puberty brings additional stresses that create even more difficulty in adjustment. Unfortunately, insufficient research has been done on the behavioral maladjustment of adolescent retarded children. But neither have we explored as fully as we might the problems of the child of average intelligence, so perhaps this lag is understandable. The research that has been conducted on retarded adolescents has served to point up our lack of knowledge. For instance, an excellent review of the research on the social and emotional adjustment of mildly retarded children and adolescents has been prepared by Gardner (1966). He concluded, contrary to a number of statements appearing in various texts and review articles, that very little was known concerning the type and frequency of occurrence of behavioral adjustment problems among the mildly retarded. Gardner also concluded that there was no suitable evidence in any published study to indicate that the adjustment level of special-class children was superior to that of retarded children attending regular grades.

We believe that there have been some promising approaches. Spivak (1967) attempted to develop a reliable means of describing the problem behavior patterns of mentally retarded adolescents. The subjects were 644 children between the ages of thirteen and eighteen years, including children with severe psychotic disorders as well as those who had been diagnosed as mentally re-tarded. The mean IQs of the various diagnostic groupings ranged from 62 to 107, thus reflecting a wide range of abilities. Each youngster was rated by a trained rater on a behavioral rating guide, and the resulting data were then studied by factor analytic methods. Nineteen factors emerged from the study. These are summarized below:

1. *Unethical Behavior.* This was found to be related to IQ.
2. *Poor Emotional Control.* There were marked differences in the groups here, with the schizoid groups obtaining lower than normal scores on the control factor, indicating emotional underactivity. The scores tended to decrease as the in-telligence quotient dropped.
3. *Defiant-Resistive.* No relationship was demonstrated with IQ. (The correlation was .02.)
4. *Heterosexual Interest.* Scores increased with increase in IQ.
5. *Need Approval-Dependency.* The scores on this factor decreased with IQ.
6. *Physical Inferiority-Timidity.* This factor was not related to IQ.
7. *Negative Identity.* This factor was unrelated to IQ.
8. *Untidy-Uncleanly.* Scores tended to decrease with increase in IQ, but no signifi-cant relationship was demonstrated.
9. *Schizoid Withdrawal.* The score on this variable decreased as IQ increased. A significant relationship was demonstrated. (The correlation was .20.)
10. *Poor Coordination.* There was a definite relationship with IQ, with the score decreasing with increase in IQ. (The correlation was −.15.)
11. *Incontinence.* The scores were unrelated to IQ.
12. *Poor Self-Care.* A significant relationship was found, with the self-care score decreasing with increase in IQ. (The correlation was −.15.)
13. *Emotional Detachment.* This factor was found to be unrelated to IQ.
14. *Bizarreness-Cognition.* This factor decreased with increase in IQ. (The correla-tion was −.17.)
15. *Bizarreness Action.* This factor was related to IQ, with a lower bizarreness score accompanying a higher IQ.
16. *Anxious-Self-Blame.* The factor score was higher in brighter youngsters. (The correlation was .23.)
17. *Persecution Feelings.* The factor score was higher in females than in males and decreased with an increase in IQ.
18. *Paranoid Thinking.* This factor was unrelated to IQ.
19. *Inability to Delay.* Girls as a whole tended to achieve higher factor scores than boys, but the scores were not related to IQ.

Spivak and Spotts (1965) conducted a somewhat similar study. Although this research was done on children during the latency period (the period from about six to twelve years of age when sexual curiosity tends to be repressed and superego functions become more prominent), it is directly relevant. The follow-ing major factors were found in this study:

1. Autistic Withdrawal
2. Social Need Dependency
3. Incontinence
4. Pathological Use of Senses
5. Poor Coordination and Body Tonus

6. Messiness and Sloppiness
7. Pronounced Confusion
8. Inadequate Need for Dependence Mastery
9. Unresponsiveness to Stimulation

Spivak and Spotts felt that one major contribution of their work was that it presented a refined, descriptive system based on the overt symptom behavior of mentally retarded children. The fact that these findings replicated previous studies tends to indicate that the scale has some measure of reliability. The validity of the scale, however, has not been established.

In the following sections, we will discuss first the general problems of the retarded adolescent, then turn our attention to two specific types of problems: sexual maladjustments and aggressive behavior.

General Adjustment Problems

The period of puberty ushers in sudden changes in both physical and psychological areas. There are rapid physiological changes, among which increased hormonal activity is especially important. Secondary sex characteristics develop and require, of themselves, new psychological adjustments by the child. In the boy, for example, the growth of pubic hair and facial hair makes his image of himself (his *self-percept*) different. In the girl, the beginning of menstruation and the development of breasts assume similar importance.

From the psychological standpoint there are important problems during puberty. The increased sexual drives and the great importance attached by society to the development of secondary sexual characteristics makes unusually difficult the readjustment of the mentally retarded child, whose capacity for understanding and dealing with these phenomena is limited. It is difficult for the child to know how to handle increased sexual excitement. Many former conflicts are reactivated by this sudden upsurge of sexuality. The retarded child may now be regarded as more of a man or woman by society, yet be totally unable to accept the responsibilities of this new role. The weak ego of the retarded child is not strong enough to cope with it, and the child is, therefore, frequently overcome by strong emotional states.

The gap between the retarded child and other children of the same age widens during puberty and is more and more evident both to others and to the self. The child is less able to interact socially with children in the same age group, is not a part of their closely knit interest group, and is, in general, not accepted by them. *They* go on to high school, with its plethora of activities, while *he* remains behind. The children of more average intelligence are concerned, during puberty, with their future life plans and vocational goals, whereas the retarded child is still struggling to master the rudiments of social adjustment. In academic areas, the differences between others and the retarded adolescent are now very pronounced and quite obvious to all. Younger siblings have begun to catch up or pass in school, and this creates additional emotional burdens. The child sees self more and more as a defective person, and the self-percept of being worthless and unfavorably unique is reinforced.

Ringness (1961) has investigated some of the differences among the self-concepts of children of low, average, and high intelligence. He compared forty children whose *Wechsler Intelligence Scale (WISC)* scores were between 50 and 80 with forty children whose IQs were between 90 and 110 and with another forty children whose IQs were higher than 120. He obtained measures of the self-concept in the following areas: success in learning arithmetic, English, spelling, and writing; reading ability; acceptance by parents and adults; success in sports and game activities; leadership of peers; and intellectual abilities. He found that the mentally retarded youngsters tended to *over-estimate* their successes more than did the average or bright children. The brighter children tended to rate themselves as more capable than they were.

The retarded children generally had a much less realistic picture of themselves than did either the average or the bright children, and their self-ratings were significantly less reliable. The findings of this important research study indicate that mentally retarded children, as compared with other children, have a less well formulated self-concept, are less reliable in their test results, and differ more in diverging from reality in the image they hold of themselves.

In puberty, the retarded individual tends to be subjected to overt rejection on all sides — by social institutions, by the family, by neighbors, and by other children. There is scarcely a single area in which rejection is not pronounced. Friendships, especially with children of the opposite sex, are difficult to establish, and the lack of heterosexual relationships makes the task of dealing with increased sexual drives more difficult for the adolescent to handle. The retarded child usually does not have a friend of the opposite sex, and therefore meets further frustration in dealing with sexual drives. There are fewer parties, dances, shows, or dates to provide the normal outlets for these needs. Unless the child is indeed fortunate, he is relegated to the category of undesirable, to the portion of humanity that is shunned and is better off (from the standpoint of the rest of society) when not seen or recognized. Adolescents are ruthless when they deal with deviants of normal intelligence in their own group — they are (partly because of projection of, and reaction formation to, their own fears) even more so in their treatment of the mentally retarded child. They simply do not want a retarded adolescent cluttering up their activities. At best, such a child is ignored.

Trippe (1959), in an excellent article, has discussed the social psychology of exceptional children in general. He makes the point that when the goals of success, prestige, and status are held as desirable for all members of society, then considerable deviant behavior may result if the means of obtaining such goals are not available to the individual. He further states that our contemporary American culture seems to hold promise of success for all people, yet many groups in our society do not enjoy equal opportunity to obtain adequate recognition and reward. According to Trippe, it is very rare that a person with little formal education or inadequate economic resources achieves social success, despite the widely held belief in our society that success is open to all. The deviant behavior that then results comes about, not because the members of the groups are (exceptionally) biologically different, but because, as Trippe puts it, they are responding normally to unique conditions. We feel that this point of view is especially important.

At puberty, then, the retarded child becomes a still more serious problem to parents. They now have to grapple with a new group of questions, including the very pressing one of pre-vocational training. The question, "What is Johnny going to do?" assumes tremendous practical significance. Then, too, they react emotionally to the constantly increasing gap between their child and the children of the neighbors. In turn, their own emotional reactions affect their relationship with their child.

For these reasons, the mentally retarded child may show unusually severe behavioral reactions during puberty, even more severe than those shown by the child of more average intelligence. This is demonstrated in a study by Foale (1956) on the incidence of psychoneuroses in mentally retarded children. He pointed out that while only 6 percent of normal adolescents develop psychoneurotic reactions, 12 percent of mentally retarded adolescents show such personality involvements. In reviewing the need for psychiatric/psychological care of such retarded individuals, Wortis (1977) also emphasizes the relatively high frequency of their severe behavioral reactions.

The emotionally disturbed and retarded adolescent may show any of the maladaptive behavioral responses discussed in the preceding section on childhood. In addition to the constant educational problems of such a child, two additional specific types of problems are of special importance during puberty. These are the problems of sexual and aggressive maladaptations.

As we have pointed out, the retarded adolescent has extreme difficulty in dealing with the increase in sexual drives that occurs during puberty. Primarily, the adolescent has difficulty in attaining an adequate sexual role, and one may wonder whether or not such a role is ever achieved by the retarded child. Biller and Borstelman (1965) studied the relationship of the intellectual level of the mentally retarded child to the degree of sex role development. The subjects were eighty-seven institutionalized retarded children, ages seven to fifteen years, with no serious motor handicaps. The Draw-a-Person Test was administered to these children, and a measure of congruence between the sex of the child and that of the initial figure drawn was determined. It was found that boys and girls in the educable retarded range were more likely to draw a figure of their own sex and had more appropriate sex role preference scores than the children in the trainable retarded range. The data indicated that retarded children with mental ages below six had less definitive sex role development than did those with a higher mental age. However, it also was concluded that the usual procedure of evaluating sex preference in retarded girls by the same measures used for boys was not valid, and the authors recommended the development of separate measures of femininity.

The maladaptive sexual reactions of the retarded child may take a number of different forms, but they may, in general, be placed into three categories. There may be (1) a significant diminution of sexual interests and activities, or (2) an excessive increase of sexual interests and activities, or (3) the development of perverse forms of sexual behavior.

Diminution of Sexual Interests and Activities. The increase in intensity of sexual drives that occurs during puberty results in the production of tremendous anxiety in all children. The mentally retarded child has similar reactions, since there is no difference in the basic sexual characteristics from the child of more average intelligence. However, because of the retarded adolescent's severe fixations at earlier developmental levels, he has a limited number of defenses with which to cope with all types of stress situations, and so has severe difficulties in dealing with increased sexual drives. When sexual excitements are aroused within him he may feel guilty and remorseful and, in some way, dirty. When guilt feelings occur, all sexual impulses then tend to be repressed, and as a consequence, the retarded adolescent withdraws more and more from all external activities and interests. More infantile defenses tend to be used; those of denial, repression, isolation, reaction formation, and projection are dominant.

When the previous history of the retarded child has been one of severe inhibition or repression of interests and behavior by the parent, then it is to be expected that the child will tend to curtail *(inhibit)* the expression of increased sexual drives. For example, an inhibiting parent might be overly concerned with the child's masturbatory behavior and deal very harshly and punitively. As a result, the child would tend to overly conform to most parental and societal demands in later life (because of a severe superego). The child also would tend to see his own inner drives as unacceptable and, therefore, inhibit their expression.

Increased Sexual Interests and Activities. As we have seen, many mentally retarded children have strong fears and anxieties concerning their own adequacy as people. Such anxieties frequently lead to an *increase* in the child's sexual activities. This increase may be regarded as an attempt, through compensation, to remove fears and to prove adequacy to the self. For this reason, sexual excitement itself, rather than the derivation of pleasure from being able to relate to another person in a heterosexual situation, becomes the end goal. In such a case, the need for sexual gratification tends to distort all the other interpersonal values and needs of the child. Increased sexual activities assume importance because they help avoid feelings of loneliness, offer consolation following disappointments, and, in general, serve as a way of escape from conflicts and frustrations.

An increase in sexual activities may be manifested in different ways by the child. There may be an increase in masturbation. There may be increasing manipulatory and exploratory activities with children of either the same or the opposite sex. There may be a seeking for frequent direct sexual intercourse. The retarded child frequently does not understand the nature or consequences of the sexual act — the child's store of sexual information is scanty and usually faulty. As a result, the child too often contracts a venereal disease; a girl may also become pregnant. The mentally retarded child needs to be given information about sexual activities at a level that can be comprehended, but this information in itself will not serve to reduce the intensity of sexual activities.

Perverse Sexual Behavior. If the infantile aspects of the sexual drives persist, as they are likely to do in the retarded child, then the child is apt to engage in some form of *perverse* sexual behavior. A perversion is a form of sexual behavior in which pleasure is derived from some *partial* aspect of the sexual act—it is an *infantile* form of sexuality. Probably all human beings use such forms of infantile sexuality in the heterosexual behaviors that precede sexual intercourse (*foreplay*). Used then, however, they are not perversions, for they are part of the *movement toward* the final goal of sexual intercourse. The partial acts are perversions only when they are goals in themselves. Because of the fixations and conflicts characteristic of the mentally retarded adolescent, the adolescent is more prone to show such forms of behavior than is the more average child. It should be stressed that the retarded adolescent does not engage in a perverse activity because of conscious or deliberate choice; rather, he is compelled to obtain sexual gratification through the perversion.

There are many forms of perversions. *Homosexuality* is a frequent form. It involves the choice of a sexual partner of the same sex as the *preferred* object in achieving sexual satisfaction. Sometimes the sexual interest is displaced from the genital organs to some other part of the body or to some object. This is a form of perversion known as *fetishism*. The *fetishist* derives major sexual pleasure from looking at, thinking about, or touching the object to which the sexual interest is displaced. Common fetishes are shoes, stockings, underwear of the opposite sex, jewelry, hair, feet, and ears. *Voyeurism* is a sexual perversion in which the desire to *look* has replaced the desire for normal sexual gratification. *Exhibitionism* is another form of sexual perversion. In this type of behavior, the compulsive need to expose one's genital organs to other persons has become the method used to achieve some degree of sexual release. The perversion in which the mouth replaces the genitals as the primary zone for sexual satisfactions is known as *fellatio*.

None of these forms of sexual perversions are unique to the mentally retarded adolescent. All may be, and frequently are, manifested by the adolescent of average (or above) intelligence (Kinsey et al., 1948). Sexual perversions involve the use of sexual modes that *were* appropriate during earlier, formative years, before adult sexuality developed. In a perversion, what was formerly a part—often an unimportant, incidental part—of infantile sexual behavior has replaced the normal, genital sexual outlet appropriate for the more mature person.

There is considerable misunderstanding in our society of the nature of sexual adjustment and maladjustment. Deviant forms of sexual behavior tend to be automatically labeled *bad*, but they often are merely arrested or retarded forms of sexual behavior. Sometimes they are simply culturally deviant behavior, that is, deviant from the prevailing cultural mode. Perversions in retarded children are frequently of this type. Mentally retarded children, even when they reveal perversions, are *not* necessarily fiends. Rather, their sexual behavior usually reflects their more infantile level of development and their emotional retardation in general. Often they *will respond* to psychotherapy and develop more appropriate social forms for gratifying their sexual needs.

Many of the sexual maladjustments of the mentally retarded child stem from inadequate information and lack of appropriate sex education. The more normal child learns much about sexual matters from peers at a relatively early age, but this informal learning is not so common for the retarded child. Furthermore, in many instances, even though a formal program of sex instruction is provided, the retarded child, because of his condition, often is unable to understand the symbolism and language in which sexual information is usually couched. As a result, this child is either ignorant of many sexual matters or has a store of faulty and sketchy information. Hence, it is becoming more evident that the mentally retarded child (boy or girl) should be taught fundamental sex facts at the level appropriate to age and degree of retardation.

Many factors concerning the sexual adjustment of retarded children deserve special emphasis. In the first place, it is becoming increasingly recognized that among the retarded, as well as among normals, our schools tend to show a bias in favor of males, treating them more beneficently, offering them more special programs, and providing them with better facilities for recreational outlets. Cegelka (1976) did a systematic study of sex role stereotyping and found that: there was a bias in favor of males, they were given more admissions to special programs, offered more program offerings, and their programs received better evaluations. Cegelka concludes that retarded females therefore are doubly handicapped!

Abelson and Johnson (1969) studied the adjustment of institutionalized retarded persons. From a large number of cases, they selected those who were exclusively heterosexual. (They also studied those who were exclusively aggressive.) They found that such individuals usually were well adjusted and were capable of a number of socially acceptable behaviors, even more often than those with higher intelligence. In short, even under conditions that were not the most favorable, retarded persons were capable of good sexual and social adjustment.

Finally, a problem of special interest in recent years is that of sexual molestation of minors by adults. The data on this problem are not adequate, but from clinical and other investigative reports, it would appear that retarded persons, more often than the nonretarded, are selected as targets for such "seduction" by adults because they are more suggestible and are, therefore, more easily influenced to agree to such behaviors. Schools and communities should be especially alert to such problems since they tend to occur in cycles.

Aggressive Behavior

Rebellion against authority figures is quite characteristic of the adolescent. It is not psychopathological in itself; rather, it is a normal attempt by the adolescent to develop initiative and independence. When it takes extreme forms or persists over a long period of time, however, it is likely to be psychopathological. When rebellion results in the breaking of laws, apprehension by civil authorities, and conviction, it is termed delinquency. Research evidence does not confirm the belief that mentally retarded children are predisposed to delinquent and criminal behavior. Levy, for example, studied the relationship of mental retardation to criminal behavior. He found the rate of mental deficiency in the population of a state penitentiary to be approximately the same as that in the general population of the United States. He concluded that mental deficiency per se did not play such an important role in the causation of criminal behavior as had formerly been assumed.

Retarded children, like other children, sometimes will engage in delinquent behavior. Often they are not aware of the consequences of this behavior—often they are oblivious to the fact that they are breaking some particular law. (Rather than being called *immoral*, this behavior should be called *amoral*.) Then, too, impulses are not as readily controlled and tend to emerge in an impulsive manner. Further, when retarded children become involved in some delinquent act, they do not have the capacity to cover up or to get away and are more readily apprehended. It is surprising, therefore, that the popular stereotype of the mentally retarded child as a delinquent is not more closely approached in fact. It would seem that many more such children would be likely to engage in poorly controlled, amoral behavior (which looks delinquent to the observer), and that they would be apprehended more readily. We can only surmise that the frequency of such behavior is kept within average levels by compensating factors such as the close supervision of parents and other adults and the tendency of retarded children to be conformists because of their previous experience in being supervised.

Since frustration is one of the primary causes of aggression, it is not surprising that the retarded child frequently may manifest aggressive behavior, since he is presumably subjected to so many more frustrating situations than is the child of normal intelligence. Forbes (1958) has elaborated this point in some detail. She points out that the normal child begins to work with symbols, "the tools of our modern day civilization," at a much earlier age than does the retarded child. As a consequence, the retarded child cannot experience pleasure in competition with other children, since it is not possible to win. The retarded child then reacts with aggressive behavior designed to "keep his rivals away." Sibling rivalries and aggression toward other children are then commonly manifested.

The problems stemming from frustration are intensified as the child approaches adolescence. As Forbes indicates, ideals are ordinarily developed by the normal child at about age eight. But the retarded child probably never completes that part of development adequately. Also, in our culture, a child learns to achieve recognition by producing things and by being industrious. If incapable of such acts, then the retarded child feels inadequate and inferior to other children. Particularly in the case of the mildly retarded child, the perception of the difference between self and peers is not acute until approximately the high school level, when the discrepancy in abilities is clearly obvious, and the mildly retarded child learns that the tasks easily accomplished by other adolescents are beyond personal ability. This child may then regress to earlier stages of rivalry and manifest aggressive behavior.

When the retarded child is in an academic situation in which the work is beyond achievement level, he is constantly exposed to frustrating situations that foster aggression. In many instances, the transfer of the child to a special class may dramatically reduce the incidence of overt aggressive and hostile acts, since the stress situation to which the child is exposed is alleviated. But such a transfer in itself may not result in the desired alteration of behavior. There are levels of performance even within the special class, and the child may perceive his level of achievement as still being inferior to that of the other children, resulting in feelings of frustration. That was the case with Bill:

Bill, a fourteen-year-old boy of borderline intelligence, was transferred to a special class following repeated school failures. His academic achievement was far below the level at which he could be expected to achieve, and as a result, the work given to him was below that of all the other children in the room. Bill began to bully the younger children and began to show many primitive rage states. He would destroy their belongings, break their pencils, tear up their papers, and the like. At times, his rages were almost uncontrollable, and he would physically attack the other children with his fists or even with articles of furniture. Fortunately, the teacher soon acquired insight into Bill's problem and began to look for particular assets that could be stressed. She felt that Bill had (comparatively) good visual-motor coordination and that he was more comfortable working alone than with a group. Accordingly, she gave Bill the job of preparing scrapbooks to be used in the science and social studies units, and he worked on these for a period of time without any stress being placed upon formal academic work. The entire class then used the scrapbooks that Bill had prepared. The overt aggressive and hostile behavior did start to diminish, but it was many months before Bill was able to relate adequately to the group.

Even when the child is removed from the pressure of the normal classroom and adjusts adequately to the program of the special class, the frustrations may be maintained by pressures from many different sources outside the classroom. One source of pressure may be the parent, who mistakenly views the special class as a place where the child's academic achievement is to be accelerated. Such a class often is seen by the parent as a tutorial class, in which the child is to be given special help in reading, arithmetic, and other academic subjects. The parent then berates the child for not making the progress expected. An example of this type of situation follows:

Johnny is a twelve-year-old boy of borderline intelligence. As would be expected, his academic progress was poor, and he consistently failed all academic subjects. The child was finally placed in a special class some distance from his home, and the mother was required to drive the child to and from the school each day. This gave her ample opportunity to see the teacher, and her invariable complaint was: "I can't understand what is wrong with that boy. I do everything for him, I even bring him here so that he can get special help, and he isn't doing better in his work than he was last year. The reason I bring him here is because there are only fifteen children in the room, and he can get special help. There's no reason why he shouldn't be able to go faster than he is."

Frequently, frustration stems from the retarded child's inability to cope with the reactions of more normal children in the neighborhood. Even though the child relates quite well to classmates in the school situation, the child may be unable to relate adequately to more normal children outside the classroom, which offers some measure of protection. The special class is only one part of his life, and the children with whom the child relates during the school day are usually not those with whom he comes in contact in the evening, on weekends, or during school vacations. This fact often is overlooked.

The best way to deal with aggressive behavior is to explore the possible frustrating situations to which the mentally retarded child is exposed, and then attempt to alleviate them by altering or manipulating them. But in many instances, despite such attempts, the aggressive pattern of behavior may persist. In such an event, attempts should be made to alleviate the undesirable behavioral reaction by some form of psychotherapeutic intervention. (See chapter 16.)

The question might be raised whether an increase in acting out behavior characterized by hostile and aggressive impulses is accompanied by an increase of fantasy dealing with aggressive themes. A very interesting study was conducted by Sternlicht and Silverg (1965) who explored the relationships between fantasy aggression and overt hostility in mentally retarded adolescents. The subjects were sixty moderately retarded male and female adolescents between the ages of twelve and seventeen whose intelligence quotients ranged from 50 to 69. They were dichotomized into two matched groups of thirty each (fifteen males and fifteen females) who differed in overt aggressive behavior. The first group was characterized by extreme acting out, hostility, and destructive behavior. The second was a non-acting out group that manifested docile, conforming behavioral patterns. The groups were individually matched in terms of age, intelligence quotient, sex, ethnic origin, and length of institutionalization. The *TAT* test was given to both groups of subjects. Fantasy aggression and punishment scores were derived for each subject by two raters who worked independently, without knowing the identity of the individuals or groups. The two sets of scorings correlated .97, indicating a high degree of inter-judge reliablility. There were no statistically significant differences between the acting out and the docile institutionalized mentally retarded adolescents in terms of their *TAT* fantasy content, their fantasized aggression or punishment scores, or their mean number of words per *TAT* story. In this study, then, acting out, aggressive behavior did not mean that the retarded child had an increased amount of fantasy centering around aggression. The study deserves replication and extension to other populations.

A GENERAL STATEMENT ABOUT
PERSONALITY DISTURBANCES
IN THE RETARDED

Our review of the available literature indicates that there is a higher incidence of personality aberrations among mentally retarded children than there is among children of more nearly average intelligence. There has been considerable disagreement about the reason for this, and perhaps the most acceptable explanation has been offered by Hirsch (1959). He believes that the mentally retarded child does not function in accordance with the same set of principles applicable to the child of average intelligence, and the need systems of the retarded child also are different. Hirsch states that people believe that a retarded child is "less sensitive to hurt, less responsive to disappointment, and not in need of gratifications which come with the knowledge that one's efforts are appreciated." This belief is not valid. To Hirsch, the essential differences between the retarded child and the normal child lie in the fact that the ego structure of the retarded child is less mature, so behavior tends to be more maladaptive. The retarded child's ability to obtain gratification and ability to meet environmental demands are reduced; therefore, this child needs to depend more on support and help from other persons. If the persons around are supportive and helpful, then the child will probably make an adequate emotional adjustment. But if they are not, then the child will not be able to cope with basic needs. Hirsch concludes his excellent discussion with the point that when the demands made on the retarded child are confusing and beyond his ability, then he may show an increasing variety of symptoms and maladaptive behavior. That is essentially the viewpoint that we have emphasized throughout this book.

Adolescence is a period of shifting values, one in which the child is required to move from the dependent status of childhood to the more independent status of adulthood. It is difficult enough for the normal child to achieve such a new role, but it is much more difficult for the mentally retarded child. If the period of puberty is described as a period of storm and stress for the child of average intelligence, as it often is, then it could well be termed a typhoon of cataclysmic proportions for the retarded child, particularly for the one who lacks adequate guidance. The degree to which such a child manages ultimately to resolve the conflicts that are reinforced and initiated during the period of puberty is not a function of retardation per se; rather, it is related to basic personality characteristics and the help received.

– 10 –

Family Problems and the Influence
of Parents

We have seen that what happens to the infant after birth is significantly influenced by the behavior of its caretakers. Often the influence of these caretakers can determine whether or not the infant develops retarded behavior; by the same token, this influence can contribute to corrective measures and to positive experiences that increase the infant's capacity to cope and to develop more effectively. In addition, the reactions of the caretakers or parents as well as the other members of the family can influence the developing patterns of behavior of the infant, and later the child. Moreover, these members of the family group experience problems of their own in dealing with the retarded child and the attitudes of members of the community to the child. Thus, a whole complex of factors impinge on the developing child and on the family.

In this chapter, we shall attempt to elucidate the nature of these problems and factors; we will begin our discussion of methods of coping with them more effectively. We should point out, at the outset, that until quite recently little attention was given to the problems of the parents and especially to the issue of assisting the parents to cope, not only with their own emotionally loaded reactions to the problems of a retarded child in the family, but also more particularly to help them provide effective care and training for the retarded individual. In some measure, this neglect stemmed from difficulties in recognizing the presence of retardation in the infant and young child, except in cases with profound or obvious symptoms of retardation. As methods of early detection of mild and moderate retardation developed, more attention was given to programs for training parents so that they might be more effective in dealing with their retarded youngster. It has only been in very recent years that adequate preschool programs for such youngsters were developed and even more recently that parents were provided with special training so that they, and not only the schools and professional personnel, might assist in training and corrective measures.

In the report of The President's Committee on Mental Retardation: the Known and the Unknown (1976), recommendations were made for improving *preventive measures* before conception, during pregnancy, and at delivery. Before conception, improved genetic counseling, counseling with respect to timing and spacing of pregnancy, improved nutrition for women of child-bearing age, and immunization were recommended. The recommendations for the pregnancy period included protection of the mother and fetus against disease, adequate nutritional care, adequate medical supervision during pregnancy, the use of amniocentesis to determine the condition of the fetus in high-risk mothers, and parental choice in determining termination of pregnancy. At the time of delivery, the recommendations included appropriate medical supervision in the hospital, screening for conditions causing mental retardation, protection of Rh-mothers with gamma globulin, and intensive care of children who were born ill or prematurely.

An adequate program for training mothers *after the birth* of a retarded child is at least equally important. One example of the possible effects of such a program is the work of Heber and Garber (1971) and of their associates in reducing the effects of socio-cultural mental retardation. This program, begun in 1967, first attempted to identify high-risk mothers in Milwaukee, Wisconsin. They selected a group of infants with IQs assessed to be below 80 and provided intensive training and counseling for a subsample of this group. The mothers were given academic education, vocational training, counseling, and assistance in providing increased stimulation for their infants. This group of infants was compared with a control subsample of infants from the same population some twenty-four months later. At that time, the average IQ of the experimental group was about 120 whereas that of the control infants was about 95. At forty-two months after the study program was initated, the respective IQs were 127 and 90. Thus it was demonstrated that appropriate training of mothers of potentially retarded infants could have a significant and lasting effect on cognitive development of "high-risk" children.

In this chapter, we will consider some of the issues that have been raised, the nature of the underlying problems, and some methods of coping with them.

PATTERNS OF PARENTAL REACTIONS TO MENTAL RETARDATION

The presence of a mentally retarded child in a family unit has far-reaching effects. At the periphery of the circle of which the child is the center are the effects of retardation on society at large, which ultimately has to bear responsibility for the child's management and treatment. At the core are the tremendous impacts made by the child's condition on parents and siblings, and these effects indeed may be catastrophic. Nor should it be overlooked that the reactions of the family and society in turn affect the retarded child.

It may be stated categorically that parents of mentally retarded children are likely to show some significant emotional reactions to the fact that their child is retarded. Such reactions vary in degree and quality from one parent to another, depending on a multiplicity of intricate and closely interwoven factors. They also vary from one time to another in the life span of a given parent. For instance, the emotional reactions of the parent when first aware of the degree of the intellectual deficit of the child may be somewhat different from those manifested ten years later. Or the pressure of the stress situations to which the parent may be subjected by the retardation of the child may increase and become more devastating over time.

A study bearing on these points was reported by Kenney (1967), who studied mother and retarded child relationships. She compared four groups of mothers with respect to their levels of ego development and their authoritarianism in child-rearing practices. The groups consisted of mothers of children who were (1) educable and adjusted in school; (2) educable but maladjusted in school; (3) nonretarded and adjusted in school; and (4) nonretarded, but maladjusted in school. The *Authoritarian Family Ideology Scale* (the AFI factor of Loevinger's *Family Problem Scale*) was used to measure the degree of control that the mother exerted in her child-rearing practices. Loevinger's ego development concept was used to rate responses to a sentence completion test in order to measure the mother's level of ego development. In addition, a single-page sentence completion test composed of fourteen items was used to explore further personality characteristics of the mother. The intelligence quotients of the children were measured by individually administered intelligence tests (either the *Stanford-Binet* or the *Wechsler Intelligence Scale for Children*). The children's degree of adjustment was determined by teacher ratings on a four-step adjustment scale. No statistically significant support was found for the general hypothesis that mothers with adjusted children, irrespective of the intelligence quotient of the children, would have higher levels of ego development than mothers of maladjusted children. However, it was observed that the mothers of adjusted retarded children had higher levels of ego development than did those of any of the other groups. It was concluded that mothers of adjusted children were less authoritarian than were the mothers of the maladjusted children. It had previously been held by some authorities that the mothers of retarded children were more authoritarian than were the mothers of normal children, but this hypothesis was not upheld by the study.

Kenney concluded that mothers of maladjusted retarded children tended to be less mature and had lower levels of ego development than did a matched group of mothers of maladjusted nonretarded children. This would imply that a mother's ability to understand and accept a retarded child relates to the development of her own personality as she deals with the varied stress situations that the introduction of a deviant child into the family inevitably brings. According to Kenney, *coping* is a very complicated process, in that the *developmental* sequence of stress situations that is experienced is *cyclical*, but the *effect* on the mother's internal personality structure may be both *cyclical* and *cumulative*.

From our knowledge of the developmental sequences in children, it seems reasonable that the stress experienced by the mother of a preschool retarded child is quite different from what she will experience during the child's adolescent years. How the mother experiences and deals with these shifting stresses, then, is largely dependent on her own ego development. The presence of a retarded child is an unusual stress situation for any mother, and it may stimulate her further growth in personality or it may contribute to her regression. As Kenney points out, it would be of inestimable value to those of us who counsel mothers and their retarded children to know much more about the dynamics of the strong mother who has been able to help her retarded child adjust maximally to the shifting stresses that are imposed on the child growing up in the community. Such knowledge would assist us in counseling the "weaker" mother and her child.

It should be emphasized that, as we have indicated in previous chapters, retarded children tend to develop more slowly in many personality attributes than children with higher levels of intellectual capacity and present many personality features that pose difficult problems for their families. Webster (1970) made an exhaustive study of characteristic personality attributes among moderately retarded children. It was found that they tend to show "characteristic postures" in their "interpersonal transactions." The most prominent of these were: nonpsychotic autism (or selective isolation), inflexibility and repetitiveness, and simplicity of emotional life. Such characteristics make them more vulnerable to the usual emotional stresses that all children encounter and can greatly aggravate the problems with which the family has to deal.

Like any other human being, the retarded child does not live in a vacuum. The retarded child needs, as do all persons, close emotional relationships with others — and these relationships must be satisfying and stress-reducing if the child is to achieve maximum potentialities. The relationships between the retarded child and parents are of great importance. If the parents manifest negative personality reactions to the child's deficient abilities, then it becomes more difficult for wholesome relationships to be established. The greater the negative emotional reactions of the parents, the less likely it is that the child will achieve the level of emotional maturity he is capable of attaining. Negative reactions of the parents, thus, can adversely affect the full maturational development of the retarded child.

Other concomitant effects also are important. In many instances, the emotional reactions of the parent lead to the child's own personal dissatisfactions and personality maladjustments. The child may develop severe anxieties, and other undesirable behavioral reactions may occur. For instance, marital difficulties may arise, ranging in depth from minor irritations to complete disruption of the family unit. Thus, the parental reactions to mental retardation are important, not only for the welfare of the child, but also for the welfare of the parents themselves and the entire family group.

Considerable attention has been devoted to study of many aspects of the retarded child, but very little has been given to study of the emotional reactions of the parents. This is unfortunate, since the welfare of the child depends, in large measure, on the well-being of the parents; in general, "as the parent goes, so goes the child."

We now will consider characteristic reactions of parents and families of retarded children. First, we will present representative case material. Next, we will discuss some typical, broad patterns of parental reactions and some specific personality reactions. Finally, we will present methods of coping with parental maladaptive behavioral reactions.

Illustrations of Differing Parental Reactions

Some characteristic and important reactions of parents of mentally retarded children are summarized in the following three cases.

The Case of Ann. This case illustrates positive, constructive attitudes of parents who are accepting of the problems of their child:

Ann is a borderline retarded child, approximately ten years of age. She is currently attending a private day school for academically disabled children. Prior to special-class placement, Ann's first-grade teacher observed that she was not making adequate progress, and, on recommendation of the school principal, she was referred to a psychologist for evaluation. The psychological examination indicated that Ann had a verbal IQ of 76, a performance quotient of 81, and a full-scale quotient of 78 on the Wechsler Intelligence Scale for Children. On Form L of the Stanford-Binet she achieved an IQ of 79. The psychologist noted, on the basis of interviews, case history material, and projective tests, that Ann did not show any severe emotional disturbance, and he felt that the test results were valid indicators of her retarded intellectual capacities.

The results of the evaluation were discussed in detail with the parents, the school principal, and the teacher. Following these conferences, attention was devoted to planning Ann's academic program. Since no facilities for a specialized academic program were available in the public school she attended, it was recommended that Ann attend a private day school where the currculum could be tailored to meet her unique needs.

Both of Ann's parents expressed the desire for continuing counseling and guidance by the psychologist. The mother, in particular, felt that she needed help. She stated: "I find myself wanting to do too much for Ann. I know that she can do many things if I let her, but I have to be careful that I don't step in too often and not let her make her own mistakes so that she can learn. Then, too, I find myself feeling very sorry not only for Ann but for myself too, and I think I want to wrap her in cotton wool. I know that I baby her, and give her too much attention. This isn't right, either for Ann, for myself, or for her brother and sister.

"Of course, I love Ann, and her happiness is very important to me. But I think I should love her in the same way that I do the other children. I need help on this."

Ann's mother accepts the degree of retardation Ann manifests. She perceives that Ann has many limitations, but she also perceives that Ann has many assets. "I feel that it is my job to see that Ann's potentialities are developed just as far as possible, but, at the same time, I don't want to put pressures on her to do things that she simply can't do."

At home, Ann is encouraged to mingle freely with all guests and to participate in all family activities. These are not tailored necessarily in all instances to Ann's capacities, and she always participates in all family vacations, outings, and trips. As far as possible she does what other members of the family do, and she is encouraged to be an individual in her own right.

Ann's father is able to see many of the ways in which he reacts emotionally to Ann's retardation. He said: "I've had some difficult times about this. I've overlooked a lot of things in Ann's behavior that I really shouldn't have. I let her get away with things that I should have corrected. For example, at one time she didn't do anything around the house. This was largely because I felt sorry for her and didn't feel that she could do things. But now she straightens up her room and helps her mother with the dishes and some housework. She got her own way in a lot of things, but now she knows what is expected of her and I try to make certain things stick." The father has set limits for Ann, so that she knows what is reasonably demanded of her, and she is expected to conform to certain rules and regulations.

Ann's mother and father attend social events and parties in the neighborhood and hire a babysitter to sit with Ann and the two younger children. At first they had a great deal of trepidation about this. "We were really afraid to go out, and we found ourselves pulling away from our friends. We were getting to be social hermits, and our lives were getting very narrow. But we realize that we have our own lives too, and it wasn't the best thing for Ann or for us to just sit around at home."

Both parents are concerned about Ann's future, but they realize that they cannot solve all the problems that may arise in the years ahead. As Ann's father said: "I think about what Ann is going to do when she grows up. At first, I felt that everything was hopeless, but I see now that she can do many useful things and that there is a good possibility that she will get married. I used to lie awake nights and worry about what the future holds, but this is foolish. My wife and I should be concerned with what we can do at the present time, and take things as they come, with some planning, of course. But our job right now is to give Ann the best program and handling that we can, so that she will be better able to take care of herself years from now. I wanted Ann to go to college, I guess, and I still have some feelings about that. And I realize that high school is out of her reach. However, there are a lot of things that she can do, but it was hard for me to give up my first ideas about what Ann could do. We should love Ann for what she actually is, and not fool ourselves with the picture we have inside ourselves of what we want Ann to be like."

Ann's mother had a clear insight into the nature of Ann's retardation. She sought competent guidance to help her solve the complex problems with which she was faced, and she accepted the counseling she received. The mother was aware that Ann had severe disabilities, but she was able to see that Ann also had many assets. The mother's degree of insight into her own behavior and feelings was surprising. She perceived that she wanted to protect Ann, and she tried hard to keep her from suffering either psychological or physical hurt However, she realized that her own tendencies toward overprotection would not benefit Ann and might, in fact, be detrimental to her intellectual and emotional maturation.

Ann's parents fully accepted her as a person in her own right and were able to acknowledge her as a full member of the family group. They were not ashamed of her intellectual disabilities, but encouraged her to participate (to the appropriate degree) in all family and many social activities.

Ann was not allowed complete license to act as she wished. Rather, the parents set limits on her behavior, as they did for the other children in the family, and Ann was not permitted any special privileges or given favors out of a sense of pity, a feeling of shame, or a feeling of guilt. Standards of behavior (realistically determined) were set for Ann, and she was expected to be a contributing member of the family (she was assigned tasks in the household and had definite regular chores for which she was held responsible).

It is noteworthy that the parents were not overly anxious concerning their social relationships and did not perceive Ann's disability as being detrimental to themselves. They participated freely in community social affairs and were secure enough to trust Ann with a neighbor's daughter who acted as babysitter. The parents perceived that they also were individuals and that they had needs and obligations toward each other as husband and wife. Ann did not, therefore, dominate and control the total family behavior.

Rather than being concerned about Ann's distant future, the parents realistically attempted to resolve her more immediate problems. They perceived that education is for the present and not always designed primarily to meet future life problems. They were, of course, concerned about Ann's eventual life as an adult, but not overly so. Consequently, they were primarily concerned with her present-day problems, growths, and adjustments. They perceived that concern with these would make Ann more secure in the future. Ann is indeed fortunate. Her parents were mature persons who were well able to cope with the problems she presented, and they did not develop any serious emotional problems of their own.

The Case of Bobby. The parents in this case did not perceive the difficulties of their retarded son, and they had limited insight into his problems:

Bobby is an eleven-year-old boy who has experienced difficulty in school ever since he entered the first grade. The school records show that, on Form L of the 1937 Stanford-Binet test, he achieved an IQ of 79. This test result has been confirmed on numerous occasions throughout his five years in the public school.

Bobby failed the first grade, and at that time the parents were advised by the school principal that he was a very slow learning child who would be likely to experience difficulty througout his academic life. Special class placement was recommended.

Mr. Smith, Bobby's father, became very indignant and aggressive when told that Bobby could not keep up with the class. He stated that there was nothing, in his opinion, "wrong with the child," and that he was not retarded in any area. "There is absolutely nothing wrong with Bobby. The trouble is that there are too many children in the classroom, and he just doesn't get the proper kind of teaching. It's no wonder he can't read."

The following year, in opposition to the recommendation of the principal, Mr. Smith secured the services of a tutor, in order to "teach Bobby how to read." After a three-month period of little progress, the tutor discontinued her services. Another tutor was employed, and again little headway was made. At the end of his second year in the first grade, Bobby was "socially promoted" to the second grade, but still was unable to do adequate academic work.

Both parents frequently visited the school and talked with the teachers and principal. They complained and found fault with the school in many areas. They also stressed vehemently that Bobby's problem was due to his lack of interest in school work and that he "really didn't try." Great pressure was placed upon Bobby at home; the mother constantly had the child read to her and the father drilled him in simple arithmetic operations.

This type of dissension continued throughout the third year of school, when Bobby was again "socially promoted" to the third grade. This school year was characterized by a large number of visits to various clinics and physicians. First, Bobby was taken to a reading clinic, and a thorough evaluation was conducted. The parents were advised that Bobby could not be expected to read much beyond the level he had attained, and the degree of mental retardation present was interpreted to the parents. In light of the retardation, Bobby was not accepted for remedial reading by the clinic, and the parents were advised that he could not profit from remedial reading but was more in need of a total specialized academic program.

Bobby saw various medical specialists for eye, ear, gland, tonsil, neurological, and metabolism examinations. The results of all of these examinations were essentially negative, but the parents still could not accept Bobby's limitations. They still sought a specific cause for his inability to achieve in school, a fault which could then, in some way, be treated miraculously.

Meanwhile, the school reports concerning Bobby's poor adjustment continued to mount. Bobby was constantly in difficulties with the teacher, in that he was becoming aggressive and hostile in the classroom. He fought constantly with the other children and frequently kept the class in a turmoil. Currently, the principal is seriously considering whether Bobby should be permitted to attend school next year.

The parents continually discuss Bobby's scholastic disabilities with the neighbors. They complain about the school program and its functions to all who will listen, expressing hostile feelings toward the teachers and the school administrators. Also, the parents point out the tremendous efforts that they have made in attempting to "find out what is wrong with Bobby," and complain that no one as yet has been able to give them any satisfaction or to do anything about his condition. The neighbors do not relish such discussions and are reluctant to invite Bobby's parents to neighborhood social events. There has been a gradual process of diminishing social interaction, which has been accelerated by the increasing reluctance of the parents to accept such invitations when they are forthcoming.

Bobby's parents present a much different picture from those of Ann, in that they were unable to accept his limitations. Rather, they perceived them as shameful and derogatory and tried to disguise their true nature from Bobby and other people. They attempted vainly to find some external cause for Bobby's shortcomings. They blamed the school and even blamed Bobby for being a "lazy and uncooperative" child. The parental pressures on the child to achieve were tremendous, but they only served to aggravate an already serious situation.

The desperate attempts of the parents to discover a specific remediable cause of the mental retardation are evidence of the needs of the parents to disguise the nature of a situation that they were totally unable to accept. Their reactions imply that they perceived Bobby's disability as threatening to themselves, and that they had a deep sense of shame. In effect, Bobby was thoroughly rejected by the parents, although they, of course, did not accept this implication of their behavior.

The parents consistently rejected the counsel that they sought initially. They refused to accept the recommendations of either the school principal or the reading tutors who attempted to work with Bobby. They were seeking some sort of magical cure, and they expressed the neurotic hope that time would solve the problem. "In the end everything will come out all right." Thus, these parents were clearly emotionally unable to cope with the problem of Bobby's mental retardation. The conflict within their own personalities also is reflected in the disturbance in their social relationships. The anxieties engendered by their reaction to Bobby spread to many of their social interactions, and, as a result, they tended to isolate themselves from other people.

It is not surprising that Bobby began to develop unacceptable patterns of behavior in school. The basic pattern of rejection by the parents, as well as the increased pressures to which he was subjected, caused him to find an outlet in his hostile feelings and aggressive reactions not only toward his classmates but also toward his teachers. Bobby suffered, but so did the parents. They were under considerable stress and showed many symptoms of severe anxiety. Their relationships with other people suffered, and even their feelings toward themselves began to show change. Life began to be more and more miserable for everyone concerned.

The Case of Jeanne. This case material illustrates the development of some serious adjustment problems in both the father and the mother of a retarded child:

Jeanne is a seven-year-old girl. She was referred to the school psychologist for evaluation when it became clear to her first-grade teacher that she could not begin to do the work of her grade. Toward the end of the school year, Jeanne could not write her name or read at pre-first-grade level, and she had few numerical concepts. On the Wechsler Intelligence Scale for Children she achieved a verbal IQ of 62, a performance quotient of 68, and a full-scale IQ of 66. These test scores were in agreement with similar IQs achieved on Form L of the 1937 Stanford-Binet Intelligence Test and on the Arthur Point Scale of Per-

formance Test. *A reading readiness test indicated that Jeanne was far from ready to begin her reading experience. Further evaluation indicated that she had exceptionally poor visual-motor abilities. The personality evaluation indicated that she was a very immature child who clung to childish ways of behavior and was very much threatened by her school experiences. It was felt that she was unable to profit from the experiences of the first grade and that, rather than being retained in the first grade, she should be transferred to a special class for retarded children.*

The results of the evaluation were discussed with the father and mother at a conference attended by the school principal and Jeanne's teacher. The results were catastrophic! Jeanne's father became highly insulted at the possibility that his girl was a mentally retarded child. He stated (or, rather, shouted): "It's just an impossibility! No one in my family has ever been accused of being dumb. I got good grades all through school, and all of the children did. My father is a successful businessman, and my mother is a college graduate too, so this thing is absolutely absurd! The whole family is bright, and so it just can't be! If there were someone in the family like that it would make more sense, but there just isn't anyone who didn't get along in school."

Jeanne's father also presented a large number of reasons to "explain" why she could not achieve in school. He stated: "I know that she hasn't been doing her school work properly. But I also know why she doesn't. The whole trouble is because of her mother. Her mother just babies her all the time. She takes her part when I tell Jeanne it's time to do her homework, and many times when I tell her to do something that she doesn't want to do then her mother always steps in and sees that she doesn't have to do it. Just the other night, I sat down and gave her some simple addition in arithmetic to do. She couldn't even add 8 and 6 right. So, I told her she couldn't watch television any more or go out and play until she could do all her arithmetic correctly. Then the very next night, when I came home from work, I found Jeanne outside playing. I grabbed her up and was going to give her a few slaps but her mother interfered again. She says that the girl is trying hard and doing as well as she can, but I don't see that at all. What she needs is somebody to sit down on her very hard and see to it that she does her work. The way her mother handles her she never will get anywhere. Jeanne's got the idea now that she can just slip by and not do a thing, and that if I try to make her do anything, she can go to her mother and get her own way. But that's going to change. From now on I'm going to put my foot down and see to it that she does learn. I think that you are making a big mountain out of a molehill. You're making a problem where there really isn't any at all!"

In regard to Jeanne's low test scores he stated: "There's lots of people that just can't do well on a test at all. I had trouble with tests too; I knew the stuff, but when I used to take a test I wouldn't do too good. It's the same way with Jeanne. I know that she can do a lot better on things than she did on the tests. She probably didn't want to try anyhow, so they don't mean too much."

Jeanne's father refused to consider the possibility that Jeanne would do much better if placed in a special class. He felt that such a course of action would be shameful to the entire family. "What in the world would I tell my relatives if you did that? They would think that she was a real dummy or something. How could I explain it to them and what would all the neighbors think about it? That's out!"

Upon being informed that Jeanne just could not do the work, he said that he would employ a tutor in the summer months so that Jeanne could be promoted to the second grade at the beginning of the next school term. At a second conference Jeanne's father still maintained the same opinions. He said that he had *"been sitting down on Jeanne,"* and that he felt she was making some progress.

Following the second conference, Jeanne's mother visited the school by herself, and talked to the principal. She said that she knew that Jeanne could not possibly keep up with the work of her grade. She said that Jeanne was crying a great deal and that it was difficult to *"get her off to school"* in the mornings. The mother stated that she and her husband were in frequent disagreement over ways to handle Jeanne. She also said: *"It seems that we are always fighting about something. It has gotten so bad that I hate to see my husband come home in the evening. He is grouchy, and he is always complaining about things. Our whole family is entirely up in the air. He finds fault with everything I do, and it seems that he is always picking on Jeanne."*

The emotional reactions of Jeanne's parents were maladaptive. The father, in particular, could not accept the reality of Jeanne's retardation, tending to view her limited capacities as a reflection on his abilities. He reacted toward Jeanne with strong hostility, blaming her for her inability to achieve. As the situation became progressively worse, he began to displace his feelings on his wife.

Feelings of guilt and shame were pronounced, and Jeanne's father was particularly concerned about the attitudes and feelings of his neighbors, which he perceived as being derogatory to the family. The father's reactions only tended to make the situation deteriorate even more, since he insisted on placing pressures on Jeanne to achieve at levels completely beyond her capacity (the pressures of extra tutoring, lengthened study periods, and the like).

This case also illustrates the beginnings of the breaking up of the family unit. There were increasing disagreements between the parents, with the father blaming the mother for Jeanne's shortcomings. Neither the mother nor the father had insight into the fact that their problems did not stem from their relationship to each other but, rather, from their continuing frustration in being unable to cope with the stress of Jeanne's problems.

We have chosen to illustrate a variety of reactions of parents whose children had borderline or only mildly retarded cognitive capacity. It well can be imagined that, given the personality constellations of these particular parents, such reactions might be expected to be more exaggerated and, in some respects, quite different if the children were moderately, severely or profoundly retarded. Severe parental reactions may be anticipated if, in an otherwise "normal" family, a child is born who is so severely handicapped that constant medical and special care are needed, even for survival of the child. Reactions also will differ if there are some gross physical abnormalities in the child. But, to a large measure, the basic personality constellation of the parents, and their knowledge about mental retardation as well as their moral attitudes, will determine much of the nature of parental reactions and subsequent behavior.

We also should emphasize at this point that much more than the degree of cognitive impairment in the child contributes to parental reactions. Whether the infant is happy, shows "good" interpersonal behavior, shows adaptability in learning to manage bodily functions, and constantly requires attention to needs can also be highly significant. The whole range of social skills of which the child becomes capable not only should be taken into consideration by professionals who evaluate the relative degree of his retardation, but also are significant in determining how parents react and what they expect from their child. In the cases we have provided, we have not given much consideration to such factors either in evaluating the nature of the retardation or the nature of parental reactions. Nor have we discussed the value of assessing the personality and other characteristics of the parents. However, as we shall see in later chapters on assessment, intervention, treatment, and education, this complex of factors must be carefully considered in both evaluation and training of both the child and parents.

Dynamic Considerations

As we have seen from the preceding cases, there are many different ways in which parents can react emotionally to the fact that their child is mentally retarded. They are difficult to define and isolate, but it is our conclusion, based on our clinical experience, that the patterns of parental behavior may vary from a constructive form of adjustment (such as a realistic acceptance of the child's condition) to a destructive, maladaptive form of adjustment (such as rejection or denial of the retardation). Thurston (1960) developed a useful scale for evaluating a parent's attitudes. It uses a sentence completion form consisting of forty questions.

The multitude of individual parental reactions may be grouped into a number of major categories of behavior, according to the type of acceptance of the child's retardation. In one categorization scheme, Kanner (1953) states that the parent may react to the stress situation of the child in one of three major ways. The parent may *accept, deny,* or *disguise* the child's mental retardation. (Parental reactions to retardation are categorized in this manner for didactic purposes only. Each parent reacts in a unique manner to the stress situation created by the child's retardation.) We shall consider typical parental patterns of behavior in the following paragraphs.

The Accepting Parent. A parent who is constructive and adaptive maturely acknowledges and accepts the reality of the child's disability. Such an acceptance of the child leads to many positive benefits for both the child and the parent, as well as for the family unit and, in the last analysis, for society as a whole. The parent eventually comes to a full acceptance of the child and loves the child *as the child is.* The parent does not attempt to substitute a fantasied picture of the child for the way he is in reality. The parent clearly perceives his role as a parent and recognizes that he has an identity of his own that must be preserved. Therefore, the accepting parent deals with the problems of the child in a realistic manner and does not make a slave of himself in his relationships with the child. He assumes responsibility for the many other roles demanded by society, such as father, husband, breadwinner, and companion.

An accepting parent has no undue anxieties about his own needs and capacities or about the disabilities of the child. His behavior is essentially problem-solving. Like all other persons, he may have anxieties from time to time, but essentially they are *object* anxieties. They are based on particular situations that cause difficulties, and since the cause of the anxiety is thus known, it is dealt with in a rational, problem-solving manner. Such objective anxieties are in contrast to the *objectless* anxieties that the psychoneurotic person experiences, in which the feared situation is not consciously known.

The parent who reacts to anxiety positively is able to accept an unpleasant reality situation that is possibly quite threatening. This acceptance is by no means easy; its achievement depends on the psychological maturity of the parent and on appropriate guidance. It may be postulated that logical thought processes are inhibited to the degree that the personality structure of the parent is psychoneurotic, so the perception of the reality situation also is distorted. Psychoanalysts have pointed out the prerequisite for logical thinking. They believe that such thinking demands a strong ego that is able to postpone immediate gratifications, control basic drives adequately, and judge reality in accord with its experience. Thus, if the parent is not psychologically mature enough, full acceptance of the child becomes difficult indeed.

However, the acceptance of the reality situation by the parent is not an all-or-none affair; a parent's reactions may fall at any point within a *wide range* of the total scale of adjustment possibilities. As we shall see, the attainment of a high degree of reality perception based on acceptance of the mentally retarded child comes about as the result of a gradual process of growth within the parent. (Fortunately, it may be fostered by proper learning and guidance experiences.)

Thus, the parent initially may rank at the lower end of the scale of acceptance of the child, but through appropriate growth experiences may acquire more insight and understanding until reaching a much higher and more mature kind of acceptance. In addition, the full acceptance of the situation is not only logical or rational; it is also *emotional*. A concept or situation may be accepted intellectually, but be completely rejected emotionally. For instance, a parent may react in a manner similar to this:

John's mother stated that she was well aware that her seven-year-old son should be encouraged to do things for himself to the extent that he was able. As she said: "It is in this way that he will grow." Yet, in discussion it was learned that the mother completely dressed the child each morning and usually accompanied him to school. The reason she gave was: "John has such a tough time."

At one level, the mother was aware of John's needs, but emotionally she was unable to behave toward him in a mature and growth-stimulating manner.

The accepting parent, then, needs to be aware of the nature of his own emotional relationships to the retarded child. The parent must be aware of what *needs of his own* are threatened by the child's condition and must be aware of the extent to which these needs determine his own behavioral reactions.

One of the primary goals in the counseling and guidance of parents of mentally retarded children is to develop full acceptance of the child, both emotionally and intellectually. Such acceptance leads to many beneficial results. First, the child is made more secure in relationships with parents. As a consequence, the child is likely to be more secure in relationships with other children and with the world as a whole. The child's percept of self is more positive, and the child is stimulated to achieve maximum growth in all areas. The demands the child makes on parents and others tend to be more realistic and pertinent, and the child is better able to achieve potential growth levels.

Second, the parent reaps many direct benefits. The parent's own self-percept also is more positive, and he too is more secure in relationships with the family, with other people, and with the world in general. Energy is not consumed in dealing with neurotic, internal problems in regard to the retarded individual; consequently, it can be used to deal with other important factors. The parent is able to work more adequately and can form more adequate and satisfying social relationships. Marital discord and strife are not so apt to occur, and greater satisfaction can be achieved in marriage and family life in general.

The Disguising Parent. Another major category of parental reactions to mental retardation includes modes of behavior that attempt to *disguise* the child's condition in some manner. Such attempts are made not only to hide the child's condition from other people, but, more important, to hide it from the parents themselves. In general, the disguising parent does perceive, to some extent, that there is "something wrong" with the child. But she is unable to recognize or admit that the child's inability to perform tasks that are ordinarily done by other children of the same chronological age is due to limited intellectual capacities.

As Kanner (1953) points out, the disguising parent searches very hard for some reality factor to which the child's retardation may be attributed. Consequently, medical consultations may be frequent. At one time or another, for instance, the child's condition may be attributed to "bad tonsils," or "infected teeth," or "dietary insufficiency." The child is given one medical examination after another, each time with the hope that a specific remediable cause for the retardation will be discovered and corrected.

In many instances, the parent may see the child as being at fault. In such an event the child may be seen as lazy, uncooperative, "not wanting to try," or punitive to the parents. For instance, Mr. Roe stated:

"Bob is just plain lazy. He could do much better if he tried. He goes to school and just sits there, and doesn't want to get anything out of it. If he would get it into his head that he has to do better, he would — that's his real trouble — he just doesn't want to learn." This despite the fact that Bob has an IQ in the low sixties, and that several attempts had been made to interpret the situation to Mr. Roe.

Here is another example of attempts to disguise the child's condition:

"Jack has some real problem somewhere. We thought sure that it was his eyesight that was the trouble. We took him to an eye doctor, and he found that Jack really had a severe astigmatism in the right eye. He prescribed glasses, and Jack has been wearing them now for about six months. His school work hasn't improved very much, though, so there must be something else wrong. We have made an appointment to get his hearing gone over, and he is to be seen in about two weeks."

Frequently the child's academic disabilities are attributed to inadequate instructional methods. The parent is able to see that the child is seriously retarded in school and, possibly, may even acquiesce to the placement of the child in a special class. But the disguising parent is unable to accept the real function of such a class. Shortly following such a placement, the parent may begin to make strong demands on the child for academic progress. The parent may frequently visit the school and complain to the teacher about the child's progress. Such behavior indicates the parent's misperception of the situation. Despite being told that the special class is designed to meet the unique needs of the retarded child, the disguising parent may see it as essentially a tutorial or remedial class, where the child will receive instruction so as to quickly bring him to the academic level of more average children. These feelings are clearly demonstrated in the following example:

Joe is a ten-year-old boy who is of borderline intelligence. Following consistent failures in the regular grade, he was transferred to a special class. After about six months in the class, the parents visited the school and talked with the teacher. His father stated: "Joe isn't doing any better than he did in the regular class. He still isn't able to read. I don't know why. He is over here with you and there are only twelve children in the class. With all that attention he should be making good progress. In his other class there were over thirty children, and he did not get the attention that he needed. But now, with just a few children, he should be able to learn much faster. I don't see why his reading hasn't improved."

The Denying Parent. A severe emotional reaction to the stress situation resulting from the mental retardation of the child is shown by the type of parent who feels the need to deny, both to others and to himself, the reality of the child's disabilities. This mode of defense is called *denial*. It is said that the ostrich, when faced with a threatening situation, attempts to avoid it by burying its head in the sand, as though blocking out the visual perception of the situation is enough to remove the threat itself. But even though the ostrich buries its head and so does not see the danger, it is still vulnerable (and even more so!) to the threat. It is still very much exposed!

The defensive behavior of the ostrich often is manifested in the behavior of children. Frequently a child, when exposed to a threat of some sort, will shut his eyes or cover his eyes with his hands to avoid seeing the threatening object or situation. Symbolically, the same type of reaction is shown by the parent who denies the reality of the child's retarded condition. The parent does not, of course, close his eyes, but he does avoid perception of the actual reality of the situation. In effect, the person believes: "What I refuse to see does not exist." This type of behavioral reaction was shown by Mr. White in discussing the problem of his son, a mildly retarded child.

"There's nothing at all wrong with Jack. This whole thing is just a passing phase in his growth. I had a lot of problems when I went to school too, but I got over them in pretty good shape. I had a rough time until I was about fourteen years old, then I straightened out and didn't have any more real trouble. Jack will do the same thing. One day he'll wake up and then go ahead. So why make all this fuss about this thing? It isn't going to do any good to hold him back in school again. I'll talk to him, and next year he'll get along fine. I don't see anything at all to get worried about, and I can't understand why you seem to think that it's so important."

Attempts to deny the mental retardation of the child are by no means rarely encountered. The use of this psychological defense is not a deliberate or planned, conscious reaction by the parent but, rather, an automatic, unconscious reaction to a stress situation. The particular defense used is a function of the general maturity level and life history of the individual, and, as we have seen, the more immature the parent, the greater the stress of the situation and the more extensive the defensive reactions and consequent maladaptive behavior.

Characteristic Personality Reactions of Parents

The parent may react in a variety of ways to the stress situation resulting from the child's retardation. As we see, parental reactions are functions of many complex interacting variables and are unique to the particular parent. But some general parental reactions are encountered so commonly that they warrant detailed attention. These include distorted perceptions of the capacities and qualities of the child, rejection tendencies, marital discords, narcissistic involvements, unwarranted ·reactions to the community, and feelings of guilt about the mental retardation. These specific psychodynamic problems are discussed in the following pages.

Distorted Parental Perceptions. It is not unusual to find that the parent of the retarded child is unable to perceive the reality of the child's retardation. The parent often sees the child as being quite different from what he actually is. As a consequence, many family problems arise. In a symposium (Symposium, 1953) it was concluded that parental difficulties in dealing with retarded children included (1) setting of unrealistically high goals for the young child; (2) overprotection of the child; (3) overindulgence of the child; and (4) maladjustment of the parents, manifested in alcoholism or emotional disturbance. It was found that the most frequent stumbling block in attempts to deal with these problems was the unrealistic perception by the parents of the child's disabilities.

Many studies have demonstrated that such faulty parental perceptions may occur. For example, Schulman and Stern (1959) conducted a study of parents' estimates of the intelligence level of their retarded children. They asked fifty parents to estimate the developmental age of their retarded children before psychological tests were administered. These estimates then were compared with the obtained intelligence test scores. They found that the mean obtained IQ was 55.5, and that the standard deviation was 16.6. The mean estimated quotient was 57.2, and the standard deviation was 17.4. Thus, there was *no* statistically significant difference between the two mean scores. Four parents overestimated the intellectual level of the child by more than 20 points, and seven parents overestimated the IQ by 15 points or more. Twenty-three parents overestimated the IQ by an average of 12.6 points, and nineteen underestimated it by an average of 10.7 points. The correlation between the actual obtained IQ and the estimated quotient was +.67, indicating that the two measures were moderately correlated.

This study is limited in the sample studied and the factors that were evaluated. As other studies also have shown, the parents of retarded children, as a group, are quite aware of the disabilities of their offspring. Too often the generalization is made that the parents are unaware of the child's intellectual retardation. Studies do not support such a generalization. Although parents, *as a group,* are quite accurate in their assessment of the degree of mental retardation, there is considerable variation from one parental estimate to another. Some parents *underestimate* the child's capacities to a marked degree, whereas others *overestimate* the intellectual level. The degree of insight into the extent of the child's deficits will thus vary significantly from one parent to another.

Meyerowitz (1967) also studied parents' "awareness" of mental retardation in their children. His total sample, consisting of the parents of 186 children entering the first grade of public schools, was composed of three groups of 60 families. Children in the control and experimental groups had Binet IQs ranging from 60 to 85 and had been placed in either regular or special educational classrooms by random assignment. The criterion group, selected on the basis of family socioeconomic matching, had IQs of 90 to 110 and attended regular classrooms. Each family was interviewed three times during a two-year period: the first interview took place about one month after the child had begun school, the second interview was at the end of the first school year, and the third interview was at the end of the child's second school year. The interview focussed on questions relating to the parents' awareness of the retarded abilities of the child.

Meyerowitz noted that the parents thought that their retarded children responded "obliquely" and immaturely to their environment, and he interpreted such observations as signifying parents' awareness of the child's retardation. Parents also expected their children to complete fewer years of formal schooling. However, the parents made no implications about the limitation of the children when they attained adulthood. The parents' professional and occupational expectations for their retarded children were not found to be statistically different from those held by the matched criterion group for their children.

Parents of retarded children who were placed in special education classes manifested greater awareness. But despite the special-class placement of these children, 55 percent of the parents were judged to be unaware of the retarded capacities of the youngsters.

At the end of the first and second years, the parents were asked to compare their children with other children on six academic dimensions. The criterion parents responded in a significantly different manner from the parents of the retarded children, but the control and experimental groups were not differentiated statistically from each other. More than one-fourth of the parents of children who had been in special-class training for two years persisted in responding that the child was "better" than other children in academic skills. At the end of the first year, these parents also compared their children with other children in social areas of functioning and did not perceive any differences. It appears that the unaware parent effectively rejects the communications of the school, apparently viewing them as being based on inapplicable values and standards.

Meyerowitz raises serious questions about the value of special-class placement, by itself, in benefiting the parents' socialization. He also feels that there are many instances in which negative effects may occur in the child's socialization as a consequence of special-class placement. He believes that the retarded child is placed in "a vortex of conflicting assessments," and he pleads for shared values that ultimately would lead to greater education efficiencies. We believe that shared values would produce more veridical attitudes in both parents and their children.

A related issue is whether fathers are more realistic in their appraisal of retarded children than mothers. Evidence seems to indicate that fathers do tend to be more realistic, as a group, but the studies did not examine sufficiently wide samples or control adequately for "contaminating" factors. In one study, for example, Capobianco and Knox (1964) attempted to evaluate parents' estimates of the mental level of their retarded child. They found that fathers were, indeed, more accurate and that mothers tended to overestimate the mental level slightly.

It is important to emphasize that the parents' attitudes in evaluating the mental level of their retarded children are a very complex phenomenon and depend on many factors, as Kramm (1963) was able to show. The most important variable affecting evaluation was the size of the family, but other factors, such as amount of education, religious belief, and chronological age, also were involved. Thus, we must wait for more comprehensive studies to provide a more definitive understanding of this issue.

Some attempts have been made to relate the parent's estimate of the intellectual ability of the child to various specific attributes of his own. Such attempts have not, in general, been successful. An example of such a study is that conducted by Ewert and Green (1957). They explored relationships between the mother's ability to estimate the age level of the child's behavior and the mother's personality traits. They made the fundamental assumption that the accuracy of the mother's perception of the retardation of her child was, to some extent, a measure of her acceptance or rejection of the child's condition. The validity of this assumption was not demonstrated in the study. They also obtained data on fifty retarded children who did not have any serious physical pathology and on fifty who had organic brain lesions. In each instance, the mother was asked to estimate the age level at which the child was currently functioning. That age was then transformed into an estimated IQ for comparison purposes.

Ewert and Green then divided the mothers into two groups: mothers whose estimates were within 15 points of the obtained IQs and mothers whose estimates were more than 15 points (or more deviant) from obtained quotients. The two groups were then compared by certain personality characteristics. Ewert and Green found that the presence or absence of physical anomaly in the retarded child was not related to the validity of the estimate, nor was the sex of the child. It is not surprising that there was no relationship between previous psychological evaluation and correctness of the estimate. There was a slight tendency for a more correct estimate to be made for the younger children, but this was a trend only. Neither educational level nor the occupation of the father was related to the validity of the estimate. The significant relationship demonstrated was with the educational level of the mother—the higher her educational level, the more accurate the prediction.

It should not be concluded that no psychological factors are related to the accuracy of the mother's prediction of the intellectual abilities of her child, since it may well be that important variables were not explored in the Ewert and Green study. For instance, other personality characteristics of the mother (such as her dependency needs, hostile and aggressive impulses, and need for dominance) may determine the accuracy of her perception of her child's limitations.

Another such study is that of Worchel and Worchel (1961), who explored aspects of the parents' perceptions of the child. They asked parents from twenty-two families with at least one retarded child to rate the child on several different variables. It was found that the parents rated the retarded child less favorably on many personality traits than they did their nonretarded children. Further, the retarded child was seen as deviating more from the concept of an ideal child than was the nonretarded one. Worchel and Worchel interpret their findings as indicating that there is a greater degree of parental rejection of the retardate child than the more average child.

Zuk (1959a) has studied *autistic* distortions in parents of retarded children. (Autism, according to Zuk, is the process that causes a person "to see what he wishes to see.") He formed two groups of retarded children, one without significant motor impairment and the other with serious motor disabilities. The parents were then asked to give information about their child, and this was compared with information gathered by more objective means. Zuk found that the information furnished by parents of the children without motor disabilities had a high degree of autistic distortion, whereas that furnished by the parents of the children with motor disabilities was not found to be as highly distorted.

Zuk feels that a more realistic perception of the child's disability is held by the parent when there is a motor disability present, since the perceptual ambiguity is less in such an instance. He states that "the realistic process" operates in a stronger manner when objective evidences of the child's lowered level of functioning are manifested. Further, Zuk states that the unconscious wish for normalcy held by the parents of the retarded children with motor disabilities lacked an external factor to which it could be attached and so be reinforced. The same unconscious wish for normalcy of the child was present in both groups of parents, but the parents of the motor-disabled children had less opportunity for conscious expression of the wish.

The concept of autistic distortion has been investigated further in other research studies. Boles (1959), for example, compared the attitudes and personality characteristics of mothers of cerebral palsied children with those of the mothers of normal children. He concluded that mothers of handicapped children tended to overestimate the capacities of their children. It appears that children who are handicapped both physically and intellectually are more likely to be rated unrealistically than are less handicapped children, and that younger children are more likely to be rated unrealistically than are older children.

Children readily adopt the attitudes and feelings of the parents (identification) toward the mentally retarded child. This is illustrated by the experiment conducted by Caldwell and Guze (1966), who were primarily concerned with investigating the adjustment difficulties of the parents and siblings of institutionalized and noninstitutionalized retarded children. They compared the adjustment patterns of the mothers and siblings of 16 institutionalized children with those of the mothers and siblings of 16 noninstitutionalized children. No important differences were found between the mothers of each of the groups. However, the siblings of an institutionalized child felt that it was much better that the sibling was away from home, whereas the siblings of a noninstitutionalized child felt that it was much better that the child was at home. Caldwell and Guze stated that, without exception, the siblings of retarded children mirrored the attitudes of their parents, and that they molded their value systems to conform to the family *status quo*. This is another reason why it is so important that the parents realistically perceive the assets and liabilities of the retarded child.

Parental Reactions of Rejection and Hostility. It is apparent that the emotional maladjustment of the parent is reflected in the parent's behavior toward the retarded child. In many instances, this behavior is essentially rejecting. But, as Fried (1955) points out, the rejecting parent is unaware of the child's hurt sensibilities. Fried feels that the parent tries to adopt patterns of rigid and persistent discipline and training at home because he feels that such actions will help the child. The parents cannot see that they block off the possible fantasy life of the child and lead to the development of many severe emotional disturbances. For instance, a rejecting parent frequently has great concern over the sexual development of the child, but this concern is essentially a projection of personal sexual fears and disturbances.

Because the parent's rejection of the child is frequently unconscious, the parent is not aware of the basis of personal feelings toward the child; consequently, the parent experiences severe conflicts. These, of course, depend on the parent's own personality characteristics. If the parent is an anxious person, the added anxiety brought about by the relationship with the child may precipitate a severe psychoneurotic reaction. This conditon would again react in a circular fashion on both the child and the parent.

At times, parents reveal hostility and aggression. Hurley (1967) explored the relationship between what he called *parental malevolence* and children's intelligence. His sample consisted of 206 girls and 245 boys and all members of their families. This sample constituted about 55 percent of all third-grade children enrolled in public and private schools in a rural New York county in 1960. This county was described as a "rather typical United States rural county." An objective scale administered to the parents was scored for punishment, judgment of punishment, aggression, and rejection. The intelligence level of the child was assessed by means of the 1957 *S Form* of the *California Test of Mental Maturity.* The independent interview responses of the parents were then correlated with the intelligence test results. It was concluded that the degree of parental malevolence and the child's IQ were negatively correlated, that the mother-daughter pair showed the highest correlation between parental malevolence and the child's IQ, and that parental education and socioeconomic status account for little of the relationship between parental malevolence and child's IQ. However, the relationship between the child's IQ and parental malevolence is somewhat greater for parents having less than a high school education. Hurley concluded that parental malevolence is related to the level of the child's intelligence. He suggests that less intelligent children might elicit more malevolent behavior from parents than do more intelligent children. He tends toward the viewpoint that more ambitious, upper-class parents experience greater frustration and manifest greater malevolence towards slow-learning children than less ambitious and less educated parents.

Marital Discord. Marital difficulties often arise because of parental anxieties. Each parent may blame the other for the child's condition and behavior (either consciously or unconsciously), and they may displace some of their feelings toward the child on each other. In addition, the restrictions that the parent may perceive in social interrelationships may result in further hostility and anxiety. These also may be displaced on the other marriage partner, producing further marital discord and occasionally resulting in a needlessly broken home. (For a discussion of the problems of the family, in toto, see the later section on General Family Problems.)

There is ample evidence that a severely mentally retarded child may disrupt the integration of the family. Farber (1959) has developed two scales (the *Index of Marital Integration* and the *Sibling Role Tension Index*) by means of which the extent of the disruption may be explored. He concluded that marital integration is affected negatively by the presence of a severely mentally retarded child within the family structure. He also found that the role tension of the siblings was higher when the retarded children were kept at home. Interestingly, there appears to be a differential sex response to the presence of the retarded child, with the oldest female sibling being more adversely affected than the oldest male sibling. It appeared to Farber that the emotional needs of the siblings should be considered when counseling parents of retarded children. Fowle (1968) reached the same conclusion in her study of the effect of the severely mentally retarded child on the family. This problem is too often overlooked in the counseling program.

Further evidence on this issue has been provided in an extensive study of two groups of families: one group consisted of 150 families whose severely retarded children lived with them; the other group consisted of 100 families whose children had been placed in an institution. The families were thought by Tizard (1964), the major investigator in this study, to be representative of families living in London, England. Some of the major findings were that (1) families who kept their retarded children at home experienced more problems than those whose children were institutionalized; and (2) the problem of retardation tended to lower the quality and standards of life in the home significantly. Tizard believes that families with retarded children living at home are "heavily penalized" even when they receive assistance from welfare agencies. Other research has indicated that this penalty is far less significant for families who are better off economically.

The mentally retarded child, particularly at a young age, does demand more than the usual amount of attention and care. It is usually the responsibility of the mother to provide this. However, the father may often resent the fact that his wife pays more attention to the child than she does to him, so he tends to react with hostility toward both his wife and his child—toward the wife for rejecting him, and toward the child because of demands on the mother. Such a reaction is more apt to occur when the husband is immature and infantile.

Narcissistic Involvements. All parents tend to see a great deal of themselves in their children. They tend to see the child as an extension of self and displaced on the child many of their own feelings and needs. Too often the parents are so closely identified with the child that they cannot see the child as having any separate existence as an individual. When the child does something that is approved, the parent takes pride in the performance, and when the child fails at a task, the parent feels undue grief and anger.

For example, Johnny brings home a poor report card from school. The parent who overly identifies with his child may feel aggrieved because he perceives the failure as his own—it is *he* who has failed and not the child. It is *he* who is responsible for the poor grades. The problems of the parent are foremost in such instances, not those of the child. The parent has a picture of himself—a self-image—that is confused with that of his child. Thus, any blow to the child—and shortcoming, failure, or censure by other persons—is perceived by the parent as a blow to himself. It is a blow to his narcissistic pride (self-love). When the child is diagnosed as mentally retarded, then such a parent feels that he himself is in some way being described in a derogatory manner.

Dependency Reactions. In some instances, the parent may be a dependent person who leans very heavily for emotional support on other persons. The presence of a retarded child often serves to intensify such dependency. It might well be that before the birth of the retarded child, such a parent's psychological defenses were relatively adequate in dealing with dependency conflicts. However, the retarded child needs to lean more heavily on parents than normal children do and must lean for a longer period of time. The retarded child *demands* a great deal from the parents. This demand on the dependent parent to give more than he is able often precipitates further conflict within the parent, and the dependency needs, which otherwise would be handled marginally, break through, frequently with catastrophic results. Severe emotional reactions and maladaptive reactions by the parent may then be expected. In a similar way, other problems of the parent may be aroused by the problems of the retarded child. For example, the weaning or habit training of the retarded child may serve as a trigger to the parent's own severe dependency problems in these areas and re-arouse problems that were, up to that point, controlled in a relatively adequate manner.

The parent of the retarded child also is prone to a continual fear that tends to increase the parent's dependency. Even though the child may be making good progress, maturing both physically and psychologically as well as can be expected, the parent is faced continually with the reality of the child's limitations. The parent then begins to wonder: "What will happen to my child when I am no longer here to help?" This type of fear is persistent, constantly plaguing the parent. Some relief follows when the parent realizes that the child can profit from vocational training, can be helped to become self-supporting, and that continuing help from social agencies probably will be available. If the fear is too persistent and too anxiety-producing, then the parent will need some form of treatment to alleviate these anxieties.

Reactions to the Community. Parents react emotionally not only to their retarded child, but also to the community's perception of, and reaction to, the problem of mental retardation. As pointed out earlier, society has many stereotyped attitudes and prejudices about mental retardation, and the parents, being members of society, often are affected by them. Consider, for example, Mrs. Brown's feelings about her son:

Mrs. Brown brought her five-year-old child to the clinic for examination. She said: "You know it is very hard for me to do this. I knew that there must have been something wrong with him even when he was a little baby, but I did not want to really find out. People have a lot of ideas about retarded children, and I didn't want them having them about my boy. But then I found out that there were a lot of other children like this, and I talked to some of the other mothers and I decided to bring him in. I still feel awful funny about it, though, and I don't want other people to know. I guess it can't be helped, though, and you can't hide it all the time."

Let us look at a similar reaction to social forces, as expressed by Mr. Smith:

"All right, I can see that the boy is a retarded child. But what in Heaven's

name am I going to tell the neighbors? They have been asking me what is wrong with him, and some of them know that I brought him in for examination. Now I'm not going to tell them that he is a retarded child—they have too many funny ideas about that. Don't you have some other kind of name that you can tell me, then I'll give them that instead? It's none of their business anyhow, but I've got to tell them something. You've got to live with people, you know."

As Weingold and Hormuth (1953) so clearly point out, the presence of a mentally retarded child accentuates the personality problems of all members of the family. The attitudes of the parent are, in part, reactions to the fact that he is often rejected by the various community groups of which he is a member. Group pressures, whether real or merely perceived by the parent, often force the family to withdraw from their normal social contacts. The family tends to become isolated. Because of this increasing social rejection and isolation, the parent then tends to focus intently on every minute activity of the child. This increased attention to the shortcomings of the child further serves to accentuate the personality difficulties of both parent and child. The final result is an increase in the parents' feelings of shame and guilt and the development of attitudes of rejection and overprotection toward the child.

Guilt Feelings of Parents. Frequently the parent of the mentally retarded child feels that the child's condition is due, in some way, to some past action of his own. Such a reaction stems directly from the parent's guilt feelings, which may be aroused by the disabilities of the child. As we have seen, guilt is a special form of anxiety stemming from overly strong superego factors. It is generally directed by the person toward some past actions. "I have done something wrong," or "What I did was not right." The person who constantly feels guilty has a lowered self-percept and tends to see himself in an unfavorable light. When guilt feelings are strong, the person feels insecure and unprotected. In short, *self-esteem* is lowered. The greater the existing guilt feelings of the parent, the more readily the parent tends to blame himself for the disabilities of the child.

A guilt-ridden parent asks, in effect: "What have I done to deserve such a terrible thing?" or, "What sin have I committed to be punished in this way?" He may berate himself and constantly ruminate over events in his past life in an attempt to uncover his defection or sinful behavior. Very often no specific act is discovered. But often some "wrong" act is seized on and made the focus of the guilt reaction. The following statements made by parents are illustrative:

It is my fault that my child is retarded. It is a punishment on me for giving up my religion. When I married my husband I changed faith, and this is my punishment for sinning.

This is all my doing. Before I was married I ran around a lot, and twice I had premarital sexual relationships. I always felt very badly about that, and now I have to pay for what I did.

Human nature being what it is, everyone has had experiences about which some degree of shame or guilt is felt. Consequently, such experiences are easily remembered and may then serve as the focus of the guilt reaction aroused by the presence of the retarded child.

Laufer and Denhoff (1957) have explored the genesis of the guilt feelings of parents of retarded children. They state that, normally, childhood is a period of disorderliness and disorganization in any event. But if the child is mentally defective, his behavior may become unbearable for the parent. Because of the mental defect, the child has a low degree of frustration tolerance and, consequently, makes a poor response to mother. The mother's percept of the child then becomes distorted by her own feelings of inadequacy, since she cannot placate or satisfy the needs of the baby. These feelings of inadequacy are then displaced onto the father and other members of the family. According to Laufer and Denhoff, a vicious "cycle of childhood" ensues, and a behavior problem develops with the family as "parental guilt displaces dislike and overprotection superimposes itself on realism."

Murray (1959), in her moving discussion of the needs of the parents of retarded children, is deeply concerned with the theological conflicts that so often arise. She states that death, physical illness, loss of job, and economic insecurity are familiar to every adult and are accepted as being within the realm of possibility. But the presence of a retarded child often places the parent "outside the providence of God's mercy and justice." If such parents have been reared in a puritanical environment, then they are overwhelmed by guilt. Murray feels that any event that destroys or permanently damages one's concept of a "loving and merciful God" presents a problem that must be resolved by skilled help. We have repeatedly noted such feelings in our clinical treatment of parents of retarded children.

Throughout the ages, concern with sin and guilt has been inextricably interwoven with the basic tenets and concepts of all religious creeds. For this reason, the religious background of the parents may be an important factor in determining the degree to which they accept or reject the retarded child. Zuk (1959a) has explored this hypothesis in studying the relationship between religious factors and the role of guilt in the parental acceptance of the child. He studied the religious backgrounds of seventy-six mothers of retarded children and compared them with various measures of acceptance of their children. The results of this study showed that mothers of the younger children were more accepting of the child's disability than were the mothers of the older ones. As Zuk points out, this is a somewhat characteristic parental reaction, since initially it is not the child but, rather, the diagnosis of mental retardation that is rejected.

Zuk (1959a) found significant differences in the degree to which Catholic and non-Catholic mothers accepted their retarded offspring: the Catholic mothers were more accepting than the non-Catholic mothers. Zuk offers the hypothesis that Catholic mothers are given greater emotional support by their religious faith, in that they are explicitly absolved from parental guilt in the birth of a retarded child. As a result, the Catholic mother is less subject to the process of searching self-examination that often results in feelings of guilt. Zuk states that she accepts the fact that the child's condition was the "result of a decision made by a high spiritual authority," and this enhances the possibility of her accepting the child. Such a point of view, according to Zuk, also is embraced by the Hutterites, who do not socially reject the defective, but, regardless of the child's age, view him as a child who is incapable of sinning and therefore attains automatic salvation.

It should be noted that other studies have not found the same types of relationship between religious affiliation and degree of guilt about, or acceptance of, the retarded child (see Saenger, 1960). Many factors besides religious affiliation affect these attitudes (for example, intensity of religious beliefs and educational and intelligence level of the parents). Nevertheless, the parents' religious beliefs, insofar as they are related to their feelings of guilt about the retarded child, must be considered by the counselor, as Stubblefield (1965) so well documents.

In light of the available evidence, it seems reasonable to assume that the religious background of the parent may have a considerable bearing on the acceptance of the retarded child. It may be concluded that if the religious background predisposes the parent to a feeling of personal sin and guilt, without explicit absolution, then it is likely that the parent will experience guilt related to the birth of the child. The greater the feeling of guilt is, the greater will be the difficulties of the parent in fully accepting the child, and the more probable it is that intrafamily problems will arise.

Development of Insight

There appears to be a developmental process through which the parent usually passes before adequately recognizing and accepting the problems of the child. Rosen (1955) points out that there is a pattern of growing comprehension as the parent gradually becomes aware of those problems. He postulates five levels in this process. There is, first, a phase of *awareness,* when the parent perceives the child as being different in some way from other children. The mean age of the child at the time of this perception is about two years and eight months. This is followed, when the child is about five years of age, by *recognition* by the parent that the child is retarded. Following such a recognition of the problem, the parent seeks anxiously for the *cause* of the retardation. More than half the mothers in Rosen's study felt that there just *had* to be a specific physical basis for it. Next, there is a phase in which the parent seeks a *solution*—the parent takes the child from person to person, talking to all who are perceived as possibly being of help. Finally, there is the phase of *acceptance,* when both the child and the child's problem are accepted by the parent. The progression of the parent through these phases is not automatic. The adequate growth of the parent—and it is really a process of growth—depends not only on the basic emotional maturity of the parent, but also on the guidance that the parent receives in coping with the problems involved.

We have pointed out many of the more *usual* emotional reactions of the parent to the retarded child, but there are many other *possible* reactions. However, the point of primary importance is that *the emotional reactions of the parent of the mentally retarded child are essentially a function of the parent's own personality characteristics.* As Morris (1955) points out:

> To some the mentally retarded child comes as an additional family member, to be loved and cherished, subject to the same privileges and restrictions as his siblings, geared to his sameness and differences. To others, he comes as a pawn or added burden in interpersonal conflict.

Our contention that the optimum development of the child is related to the growth of the parent is substantiated by the findings of Cashdan and Jeffree (1966), who studied the influence of the home background in the development of severely subnormal children. This was a rather small study in that it included only ten children, but the findings are suggestive. The mean mental age of the group was 5.5 years, with a mean chronological age of 11.5 years. These children were matched roughly for socioeconomic background with a group of ten 5.5-year-old children of normal intelligence who were attending regular school classes. The mothers were interviewed, and the data were then analyzed under a number of headings, covering parental attitudes towards the child and social stimuli and opportunities afforded to the child. These factors were then rated. Three tests were then given to the children: tests involving nursery rhymes, games, and adult activities. It was concluded that there were no significant differences between the scores of the two groups of children in either language or general stimulation. However, it was believed that some of the characteristics of subnormal children, both at home and in training centers, which are ordinarily attributed to their subnormality, actually stem from a variety of deprivation experiences to which the children are subjected. Cashdan and Jeffree (1966) feel that better counseling of parents and more intelligent educational procedures help to alleviate at least the secondary handicaps of the severely retarded child. Specifically, they feel that such characteristics as withdrawal, behavioral rigidity, and poor language development frequently may be due *not* to the primary mental handicap, but to the circumstances of the children's upbringing by their parents. We agree with their conclusion.

It thus is evident that the emotional problems of the parents must be treated, since the well-being and emotional maturation of the child depend to a great extent on the child's relationships with the parents. Cianci (1953) has pointed out that only a very small percentage of all retarded children are placed in either state or private residential schools. It has been estimated that only ten percent are so placed, which means that *ninety percent of retarded children are cared for at home.* Their future psychological growth is thus dependent to a great degree on the care, training, and emotional climate provided within the home by the parents. Parental emotional reactions are, therefore, of paramount importance, since they can seriously interfere with the proper emotional development of the child.

SOCIOLOGICAL ASPECTS OF
FAMILY PROBLEMS

In recent years, increasing attention has been given to the effects of interaction between the retarded child and the family. Farber (1960) has examined this problem from a sociological viewpoint. In a series of studies, he has concep-tualized the sociological characteristics of families, showing how these characteristics interrelate and affect each member of the family. When the fam-ily discovers that their child is retarded, particularly if there are physical symp-toms that can be regarded as *stigmata,* the family experiences what Farber terms a *tragic crisis.* It is emotionally traumatic, and the family senses it as a bereave-ment. This is sometimes followed by a continuing state that is termed *role organization crisis.* In this condition, the family fails to adopt suitable strategies for dealing with the problem in a realistic manner and fails to develop suitable roles for the several members of the family. In general, the *tragic crisis* reaction is more typical of families of high social and economic status; the *role crisis* is more typical of families of low social and economic status. Families with crisis role organization who have a moderately or severely retarded child are more likely to institutionalize the child if there is marital discord, overcrowding in the family, family disintegration, and lack of professional support than if these stresses did not occur (Braginsky and Braginsky, 1971).

Farber (1960) also asserts that when families develop any one of the three strategies for dealing with the problem of the retarded child—*child-oriented, home-oriented,* or *parent-oriented*—there is generally some degree of marital disintegraton. If the child is moderately or severely retarded, disintegra-tion is more likely to occur when the child lives at home rather than when placed in a residential facility or institution. Of course, as we have pointed out above, other variables, such as religious persuasion, economic status, and number of siblings, affect these results. Farber (1959) and Farber and Jenné (1963) suggest that female siblings are more affected by the presence of a retarded child in the home than are male siblings. When there are good, supportive, professional guidance services available to the family, and when financial support is ade-quate, family problems are reduced or minimized.

A PERSPECTIVE CONCERNING PARENTS AND FAMILIES WITH RETARDED CHILDREN

Although we have stressed the probable emotional impacts of the presence of a retarded child, especially a severely or profoundly retarded one, on the parents and their families, we should also be cautious not to overem-phasize the character of these problems. Many parents are, at first, shocked by the unexpected presence of a retarded child, showing what Menolascino (1977) calls "the novelty shock." The families may feel the disruption that may follow for a time, but many parents are able to react rationally, maturely, and construc-tively—given time and, especially, given appropriate information, guidance, and support in dealing with the problems. Although it is true, as Schild points out (1971), that parents often use denial as a defense against their anxiety in finding that they have a retarded child, such denial may operate only for a time until the parents can learn to adapt to the situation. In this process of constructive adap-tation, the parents need *accurate information* about what the nature of the child's limitations are; what the *immediate prospects* are for the development of the child; *information, support,* and *training* in dealing with the child; and *comprehensive planning for the immediate medical and educational needs* of the child. The mature parent usually is able and willing to participate effectively in such a supportive program.

It may be true that in dealing with the families of retarded individuals, some, perhaps many, professionals have ignored the "reality aspects" of the problems confronting the parents (Baker, Heifetz, and Brightman, 1973), and have overemphasized the emotional aspects of the reactions of families and parents. Too often, professionals, including teachers and physicians as well as psychologists, have been uninformed concerning the precise nature of the retardation or of the possibilities for rehabilitation, training, and education of the child. As Sarason (1974) points out, such professional orientation may add to the professional's feelings of "presciousness" or importance, but it does a great injustice to the retarded child and his parents.

Too often, professionals evaluate the retarded child's problems inadequately, and too often dire predictions are made covering the entire lifetime of the child. Similarly, the parent's emotional reactions too often are seen as only inappropriate and pathological. Both types of errors do not serve the needs that are present. Assessing the precise nature of the retarded child's impairment and assets, as well, has become increasingly more sophisticated in recent years and has led to better programs for training the parents as well as for training the child. In any case, prognosis is hazardous, at best, and can best be utilized in prescribing measures for the immediate future rather than for the lifetime of the child. Helping both the child and parents with appropriate strategies with the current situation, and especially, with specific training procedures, sometimes can be remarkably effective. On the other hand, professionals should not neglect the emotional needs of the parents, as well as the child while offering only behavioral modification programs for treating the child. In this, as in most matters, a balanced perspective is needed.

TREATMENT OF PARENTAL AND FAMILY PROBLEMS

Emotional problems in parents of retarded children are so common that we may safely state that *all* parents of retarded children need some help in order to deal with their own problems, let alone those of the child. To begin with, we should not overlook the elementary *fact* that parents of retarded children often hold attitudes toward them that are widely divergent from reality. This disparity is well illustrated by the study completed by Condell (1966), who explored parental attitudes of sixty-seven parents towards their mentally retarded children through use of the *Thurston Sentence Completion Form.* It was clearly demonstrated that not only was there a marked divergence from reality in the attitudes of the parents towards the retarded child, but there also was a marked discrepancy between the opinions of persons working professionally with the mentally retarded child and the opinions verbalized by the parents themselves. It is our conviction that all parents should receive frequent and continuing opportunity to discuss their problems with appropriate professional personnel so that they may realize that their problems are not unique but common to most parents of retarded children. However, in light of the findings of the Condell study, we should be aware that the parents of the mentally retarded child may not regard the child in the same manner as we do, and that determining their individual attitudes is a fundamental part of the counseling process.

The emotional problems of parents fall into two major categories. The first group of parental reactions stem from a lack of adequate knowledge concerning the retarded child. Parents need to know a great deal about the condition of mental retardation; too often they have a large amount of faulty information that needs to be corrected. If there are no deep-seated personality changes in the parent and no severe maladaptive behavioral reactions, the parent essentially needs a very carefully designed *educative* program (or guidance). At the same time, of course, attention must be paid to the parent's feelings and emotional reactions. In the second broad type of parental reactions, the parent does develop significant personality changes and resultant maladaptive behavior. The parent may, for example, develop a severe psychoneurotic reaction. In such an event, an educative or guidance approach is not adequate to help resolve his problems. More intensive help, such as that offered by psychotherapy, is needed. We now will discuss each of these major treatment approaches.

Parental Training, Education, And Guidance

Our discussion in this section will focus first on general issues concerned with counseling parents, and then on training parents during early intervention in infancy and early childhood. In the next section, we shall deal with more specific therapeutic procedures. We shall postpone to Part V discussion of education of parents during the school years.

Most educated parents have some knowledge or easily acquire some knowledge about mental retardation once they are faced with the problems of a mentally retarded child in the family. Various associations of parent groups provide programs of information and discussion that can provide significant informational input and emotional support. Unfortunately, such information and support are not as readily available to less educated parents and to parents from lower socioeconomic strata and from ethnic minorities. For these groups, special out-reach programs are necessary to provide the needed information and guidance. Here, we will discuss some types of early intervention programs, and in later chapters we will discuss other special programs for parents of school-age retarded children.

It should be recognized that any parents with a retarded child face the "unknown." Even with the best of programs for guiding parents and for providing special training, the parents find much that is "unknown" about their particular child. In the first place, as we emphasize throughout this book, each retarded child is unique, despite many commonalities with other retarded children. In the second place, the course of development of the retarded individual is, to a considerable extent, unpredictable. In the third place, the possible effects of special training for the retarded children are quite variable for different children in different families. Hence, there is always a great "unknown" area for each child.

Since we usually fear the unknown, one major objective of educating and guiding parents is to impart both general knowledge about retardation and specific knowledge about the particular retarded child in order to increase accuracy of understanding and thus relieve unnecessary stress. This process is not simply an intellectual excursion. It also intricately involves the emotional attitudes and needs of the parents. Hence, professionals who offer guidance for parents should be sensitively alert to the necessity of meeting these emotional needs of the parents as well as of supplying specific information and training procedures. On the informational side, such books as the one by Issacson (1974) can be very helpful. But since each parent will tend to read such books with selective interest and biased views, thus distorting the meaning of the information to try to meet internal needs as well as the child's needs, the professional who is assisting the parent should be alert to the kinds of distortions the parent is making and should try to deal with them in a supportive and "corrective" manner.

However, it must be noted that the professional also is not without personal biases and needs. Too often, the professional tends to be overly authoritative in attempting to hide personal insecurities in dealing with the practical management problems of the retarded child or the parents. The professional then may overgeneralize about the child's limitations, offer unnecessary long-range predictions, and sometimes provide an unrealistic projection of the child's potential or of the child's irreversibly unfavorable condition. The professional reacts to the anxious, insecure, and "threatened" parent who makes demands that he is unable to deal with comfortably by becoming more assertive and authoritative. The parent who does not conform to these needs of the professional is then seen as "neurotic" or, at least, negativistic. As Heifetz (1977) states, "Professional ignorance all too often quickly reifies the child's 'untreatability,' increases parental frustration and sense of helplessness, and ultimately legitimizes the need for psychotherapy. . . ."

The educative process should be initiated as soon as feasible following the diagnosis of mental retardation. Such an action helps to prevent excessive and undue anxieties in the parent and reduces the probability of subsequent severe emotional reactions. Rose (1958) has found that uncertainty about the child's future has a severe impact on the mother-child relationship. He states that any problem resulting in uncertainty about life or death or about normal or defective capacities influences a mother's feelings toward her child. Once such a suspicion is aroused, she *must* know. The longer time it takes her to find out, the greater is the internal conflict.

A similar point of view is expressed by Denhoff (1960), who studied the emotional reactions of parents of exceptional children. Denhoff concluded that the mothers of children who learn about the condition of their offspring early tend to be more free and easy about the child. On the other hand, the mothers who learn about their children's disabilities later, because they are milder and less obvious, are more difficult to treat.

Morris (1955) has pointed out that there are many levels within a counseling or educative process that may be offered to parents. He postulates four such levels, based on the emotional reactions of the parents. At one level is the *emotionally mature* parent who has accepted the reality of the child's retardation. However, even such an accepting and understanding parent needs continual help in redefining the child's needs and his own objectives in dealing with the problems of the child and himself. The parent needs guidance in dealing with specific events, such as problems of adolescence and vocational training. At another level are the parents of the pseudoretarded child, who usually are faced with the results of a very *poor parent-child relationship*. Then, there are the parents who experience great difficulties in their management and treatment of the child because they *lack knowledge* concerning the effect of lowered intellectual capacities on behavior in general. Finally, there are the parents who *exert pressures* on the child to force the child to perform at levels that are beyond his capacities of achievement. The extent and depth of the educative program provided for the parent will depend on the problems that each parent presents.

But, regardless of the level at which the counseling or educative process is undertaken, the needs of the parent and the child must be kept paramount. Too frequently the needs of the counselor intrude into the situation, and then it is highly probable that a more serious situation will arise. In many instances, the counselor, motivated by personal anxieties, is unable to communicate the reality of the situation to the parent. In fact, the counselor may be carried away by personal feelings of omnipotence and may seriously minimize the extent of the actual defect of the child. An example of this follows:

Joe was referred to the school clinic for psychological evaluation following a history of failure in the first and second grades. After extended study, it was evident that he was a child of borderline intellectual capacities. This information was imparted to the school principal, acting as a counselor, who assumed the responsibility of interpreting the findings to the parents. But the parents were told, in effect: "Joe is a slow-learning child. But he will probably be able to do his school work if he gets a lot of special help. We will make arrangements to do this next year." The principal told the clinic staff: "I think Joe might get along next year a lot better than he did last year. I hate to give up on a child, and I think I should make an all-out attempt to work with him next year before I tell the parents that they have a retarded child. You don't want to rush these things." Fortunately, it was possible for the school counselor to intervene and give Joe's parents a realistic appraisal of his abilities.

Zwerling (1954) states that persons dealing with the parents of retarded children often are prone to make three major errors: (1) delaying definition of the problem; (2) encouraging parents' false hopes for the recovery of the child; and (3) offering too much direct advice.

What are some of the more common educative needs of the parents?

Many persons have attempted to spell them out in detail, but such needs vary in accordance with the characteristics of individual parents (Hutt, 1977b).

Kanner (1961) states that the parents of retarded children have five "curiosities," which should be answered straightforwardly, without evasion. Their questions cover these subjects: (1) diagnosis of the child's condition; (2) etiology of the retardation; (3) family structure; (4) prognosis and future guidance of the child; and (5) therapeutic planning.

Parents themselves have indicated what they feel their needs are, and Murray (1954) has summarized them. The points she has stressed are somewhat different from those ordinarily emphasized by many guidance authorities, but we have observed them quite commonly in our clinical practice. According to Murray, the most pressing needs of the parents of retarded children are (1) an acceptance of the fact that the child is retarded; (2) a solution of the financial problems involved, in order to use available income intelligently in relation to the child; (3) an easing of the emotional tension resulting from carrying a burden that cannot be shared with other people; (4) a resolution of the very · severe theological problems that usually arise; (5) some answer to the need for lifetime care of the child; and (6) a way of dealing with the problems stemming from inept, immature and ill-timed professional advice. The parent must learn to sift the wheat from the chaff.

According to Murray, the chief need of the parent is continuing and adequate counseling at various stages in the child's life. She points out that an adequate guidance program enables the parent to find answers to individual problems, which, of course, benefits the child, in turn. Some of the more important concerns are presented in the following paragraphs.

Etiology of Mental Retardation. The parents need to be given a thorough understanding of the etiology of mental retardation. As we have pointed out, lack of understanding promotes the development of feelings of shame and guilt in the parents. Further, it frequently leads to disturbances in the social relationships of the parents, causing them to withdraw from groups, activities, and interactions.

Capacities of the Child. The parents should be made to understand that regardless of the treatment program developed for the child, probably no startling changes will occur in their child's abilities to function in many different areas. They should be aware that the child will mature gradually over a period of time, but that at best, many abilities may be below those of the average person. Both the limitations and the assets of the child should be explained to the parents so that total planning can proceed in a more realistic manner. The parents should have a clear idea of what may reasonably be expected of the child. The need for a detailed, complete, and continuing assessment of the child's capacities should be stressed.

Family and Social Relationships. The relationships of · all family members with the retarded child should be discussed with the parents. The effect on the siblings should be stressed. Relationships of the child with neighbors and social groups also is an important topic. The parents should have opportunity to discuss the cultural stereotypes of the mentally retarded child and be aware that they themselves often share such attitudes. There should be discussion of the feelings of the parents toward the attitudes of neighbors and other persons with whom they interact.

Emotional Needs of Parents. Great stress should be placed on discussing the emotional reactions of the parents themselves. Often, parents lack insight into their own conflicts, so this area needs to be handled very delicately. The parents should be brought to an awareness of their own particular psychological defenses and helped to grow to the point at which they accept both the child and their own emotional reactions to their child. This involves a very careful study by the parents of their own particular way of life; that is, how the retarded child influences their life and actions. It is important that there be thorough clarification of the role of the parents in the etiology of the child's condition so that their fault-finding and guilt reactions will be alleviated. The parents should see that they are not alone; many other persons have problems similar to theirs. They should be encouraged to interact with groups of such parents. The parents should know that help is available from many sources if they wish to avail themselves of it. Further, there should be development of the point of view that seeking for help is not an indication of weakness of the parents, nor does it necessarily indicate that they are emotionally disturbed. (Many parents do not discuss their problems or seek help for such reasons.) Rather, they should be helped to see that if they perceive and acknowledge their problems, and then do something about them by seeking help, both they and the child may profit. Seeking help is, therefore, an indication of a maturing point of view and an indication that the parents are not continuing to deny their problems (as well as those of the child). It may be helpful for the parents to meet with other parents who have retarded children—with "pilot parents"—in groups such as the Association for Retarded Citizens has organized.

Emotional Characteristics of the Child. The parents must be given a thorough knowledge of how the personality of the child develops and what the child's unique needs are from time to time. This will enable to parents to anticipate future problems of the child so that the problems will not be as serious as they otherwise might be. It also will help them to deal with their problems in a less anxious manner. This entails understanding that intellectual functioning is but one aspect of the total personality of the child, and many other factors are important in determining the child's total adjustment patterns. The parents should learn about the various unique problems that the child will encounter at different developmental levels and should be aware of the ways in which these problems may be handled.

Treatment Procedures for the Child. The parents should know how mental retardation may be treated, and what the limitations and expectations of treatment programs are. This means that (1) their own role in the treatment of the child should be made very explicit; and (2) they should be informed of all available community resources and how they may be used.

Problems in Deinstitutionalization. As we will see in later chapters, there is tremendous pressure to deinstitutionalize all, or at least most, individuals who are presently in institutions for the severely and profoundly retarded. Whether and to what extent it is feasible and effective, from the individual's viewpoint, to remove such individuals from institutions is a highly complicated problem. Whether improved institutional care can provide most effectively for a segment of the retarded population is still another issue. These and related issues, as well as the kinds of effects, both favorable and unfavorable, that some institutions create need to be considered carefully, dispassionately, and in the light of the best available evidence.

At this point, our focus will be on the problems that deinstitutionalization create or include. Our specific emphasis will be on the issues that confront the parents and the home. Before the advent of social pressures to deinstitutionalize individuals, deinstitutionalization occurred because the individual had made sufficient progress to merit such a change, or because there was a change in parental attitudes or abilities in coping with their retarded child, or because new facilities for the care of the retarded individual become available in the community, or for other reasons.

We have previously cited conclusions from the *President's Committee on Mental Retardation: Report to the President* (March 1976a), which characterized the "central custodial institutions" for the retarded as "overcrowded, dehumanizing repositories of a quarter of a million disabled human beings." At least some of these institutions, however, did eliminate impossible burdens for parents, and did provide better adjustment for at least some of the severely and profoundly retarded, including services that were not available in the home or the community (Sontag, 1977). Returning such individuals to the home or the community does not inevitably provide improved conditions unless adequate programs for effective care and training are available and unless parents are properly assisted in reassimilating the retarded child. As Scheerenberger (1974) notes, deinstitutionalization without such appropriate programs and facilities can lead to even more restrictive conditions than were present in the institutions.

The return of the retarded child to the family group following a period of institutionalization is not a simple matter. Complex interrelationships are involved, and many latent conflicts, attitudes, and behavioral reactions of parents and siblings become reactivated. It must be recognized that the original decision to institutionalize the child was, in part, the result of the interaction of many significant personality functions of the family group. To return the child to the family situation without resolution of some of the negatively loaded factors, which may never have been verbalized let alone resolved, is in many cases not prudent. An important contribution to this problem is the study completed by Mercer (1966), who evaluated the patterns of family crisis related to reacceptance of the retarded child who returns to the family group. She correctly points out that the nature and severity of the crisis a family endures during the period preceding institutionalization of a retarded child are likely to have a lasting effect on the family and its willingness to reaccept the child into the family circle.

Mercer studied a group of patients who had been released to their families from a public hospital for the mentally retarded and had not been readmitted to any other institution for the retarded at the time of her study. A matched group of subjects who were residents in the hospital at the time of the study was selected as a control group. Age, sex, intelligence quotient, and length of hospitalization were held constant across both groups, and the subjects were matched for ethnic status. Members of the family were then interviewed to determine their perception of the severity of the problems prior to admission of the child to the institution. Mercer concluded that two patterns of crisis were distinctly discernible. She stated that subjects still in the institution had frequently produced a severe pre-institutional crisis. The heavy burden of caring for the child had been superimposed on interpersonal problems, such as behavioral acting out and structural stress in the family. This *crisis configuration* made such stringent demands on the physical and emotional resources of family members that they agreed that institutionalization was the most equitable solution for the crisis. When this pattern had prevailed, the retarded child remained in the institution. By contrast, the pre-institutional crisis of released subjects had included behavioral acting out and structural stress in the family, but it had seldom involved excessive demands on other family members for physical care. Almost one-half of the families of the children discharged were either divided on the issue of institutionalization or were unanimously opposed to such a course of action. Institutionalization was *not* regarded by the family as a legitimate resolution of the crisis.

Mercer suggests three possible interpretations of her results. One concentrates on the intensity of stress, and she refers to it as the *additive hypothesis*. This explanation proposes that the family social system is able to absorb only a limited amount of deviant behavior and still maintain its integrity as a functioning system. When the tolerance limits of the family are exceeded by having the problems of physical care added to interpersonal tensions and structural stress, the crisis is resolved at a high level of consensus by institutionalizing the "offending member."

The second hypothesis is that the crisis varies the *congruent-incongruent dimension*. Mercer states that the performance of individuals in any social system occasionally varies from the norm. As a consequence, there develop within the system certain expectations about the *ways* in which the behavior of members is likely to deviate and the *extent* to which it is likely to deviate.

When the behavior of a member does deviate markedly, but in a fashion that is consonant with the family's expectations of the kinds of deviations that can be anticipated, it produces a crisis that is congruent with family expectations. A congruent crisis has three attributes, according to Mercer. First, it is in a sense expected because the pattern of deviation is one that the family would have reason to suppose it might sometimes face in raising a child. Second, it is experienced relatively frequently by other familes in the social milieu. Since other families have similar problems, the family experiencing a congruent crisis does not feel stigmatized by its difficulties and does not strain to evaluate the events in terms of its own acceptance of feared responsibilities. Finally, those undergoing such a crisis are guided towards socially acceptable resolutions by cultural solutions developed by the many people who have had similar experiences.

An incongruent crisis, on the other hand, is one in which a family does not anticipate what is going to happen to it. It is a crisis that few if any other persons in its social world have experienced. Mercer feels that the families of the released subjects have experienced an incongruent crisis. In most cases, they described a pattern of problems that are similar to the kind of problems any parent might have in raising children. Conversely the pattern of crisis described by the families of the nonreleased subjects included problems that a parent does not ordinarily expect to have to overcome in raising a child. Examples of these are heavy financial expense, extensive medical care, constant supervision, epileptic seizures, and exhaustion of the mother. The crisis pattern is incongruent with expectations. As Mercer points out, few other families have these kinds of difficulties, and the family must consequently rely on emergent strategies.

Because the incongruent crisis pattern is relatively rare, there is high consensus among family members that a crisis does in fact exist and that it demands an extraordinary solution: institutionalization. Once a child is institutionalized after an incongruent crisis, the decision is less likely to be reversed than in cases involving congruent crises.

Mercer's third explanation of the findings suggests that time is the critical variable: some crises are *time-bound* whereas others are not. Perhaps the family can "wait out" some types of crises, but not others. This third interpretation by Mercer hypothesizes that the pattern of crisis experienced by families who reaccept their retarded child is more time-limited than the pattern experienced by families who do not reaccept their child. The aging of the child or changes in structure of the family may ameliorate interpersonal conflicts and structural stress. Thus, the reacceptance of the retarded child may result primarily from the passing of such a crisis. In such an instance, institutionalization may have served to tide the family over a difficult period.

Parental Treatment through Psychotherapy

The parent's emotional reactions to the retarded child may be so severe as to result in a psychopathological reaction. However, the *primary* cause of such a parental reaction is not the condition of the child per se; rather, it is the severe problems of the parent. The added stresses to which the parent is subjected and the additional problems created by the child intensify existing anxiety and precipitate severe emotional problems. It might well be that without the added stresses caused by the child, the parent might have been able to defend himself enough to hold the psychopathological reaction in abeyance. But the more conflicted and unstable the parent is (because of internal problems), the more apt that parent is to react in a maladaptive way to the additional problems created by the child. The degree and severity of the resultant emotional reactions of the parent are proportional to the parent's emotional instability. The most usual maladaptive reaction is the development of a psychoneurosis, but a psychotic reaction may occasionally develop. (See chapter 9 for a discussion of the characteristics of psychoneuroses and psychoses.) An example of a psychoneurotic reaction in a parent of a retarded child follows:

Mrs. Doe, the mother of a severely retarded girl, developed extensive symptoms. She complained of many gastrointestinal disturbances: "I throw up just about every morning, and I get cramps real often." She also had difficulty in going to sleep at night, and often had nightmares about being run over by a car. At times she got dizzy: "It's just like I was going to faint, and I get shaky and weak and feel that I'm going to pass out. I don't, though, but I feel like I'm going to faint." She had many conflicts concerning her own abilities and capacities, and the psychoneurotic symptoms she presented were related to her relationships with her parents during childhood. The responsibilities of caring for her retarded daughter served to revive and intensify her own conflicts. She responded fairly readily to psychotherapy, her anxiety symptoms disappeared, and she adequately assumed the responsibilities of caring for and relating to her child.

A person developing a psychoneurotic reaction like this usually cannot be adequately treated through education or guidance alone. Such a person needs treatment specifically directed toward relieving the basic emotional problems. Such treatment is known as *psychotherapy.*

The parent may be given guidance and education on the problems involved in mental retardation, either individually or in a group with other parents who have similar problems. If the parent has severe emotional reactions, individual sessions may be more desirable at first. In our experience, we have found that group sessions are highly effective for educative and guidance purposes. Such groups provide the parent with an opportunity to interact with other persons who are experiencing the same difficulties; they provide the parent with an opportunity to identify with a group; they serve as a clearinghouse where valuable procedural methods may be passed along from parent to parent and where experiences may be shared; and they enable the parent to gain a sense of positive achievement and hope from association with others. We have held group sessions on a once-a-week basis, each session lasting for approximately one hour. The group is most effective when it is not too large (that is, not more than ten persons and probably not fewer than five or six). We also believe it is important to provide the parents with an opportunity for individual sessions in addition to the group sessions. We now will discuss individual and group psychotherapeutic approaches. (Psychotherapy is discussed further in chapter 16.)

Individual Psychotherapy. Individual psychotherapy is, as the name implies, a form of psychotherapy in which just one person is seen by the psychotherapist at one time. (This is in contrast to *group* therapy, in which the therapist deals with several persons at one time.) Many misconceptions are commonly held about psychotherapy. One is that the therapist "finds out what is wrong" with the client (or patient) and then tells the patient "what to do about it." Although there may be some therapists who operate that way, such behavior is not common. Another misconception is that the therapist can "make the patient over"; that is, can change the patient at will. But in psychotherapy, as in most other forms of learning, the patient's motivations and active effort and cooperation are important factors in psychological growth and resultant change. Moreover, psychotherapy is not a process in which the therapist's will is pitted against that of the patient; it is a *joint* undertaking by both therapist and patient. There also is the misconception that only "crazy" people or psychoneurotic persons receive or ask for psychotherapy. Yet, more and more people, such as college students and industrial workers, to give merely two examples, are increasingly seeking psychotherapeutic help, although they may not be suffering from any recognizable psychiatric disorder. They may seek such help simply to improve their overall emotional adjustment in an effort to live richer and fuller lives. In fact, this last statement describes one of the general aims of psychotherapy.

There are many aims of psychotherapy. The specific aim in a given case, of course, will depend on the problem for which the individual seeks help, the circumstances of that person's life situation, the nature of personality structure, and the kind of help that the person wishes to have. These are factors that are dependent on the person who comes in for help. The aims of psychotherapy also will depend on the training and the personality of the therapist; the time and energy available in a given case; the therapist's estimation of possibilities for, and dangers of, change in the patient, and the therapist's estimation of how much help, as well as what kind of help, seems advisable. Thus, in a given instance with a given therapist, there still may be considerable variability in the selection of the aims of psychotherapy.

In general, however, psychotherapy seeks to help a person to achieve at a more adequate level and to improve adjustment. Sometimes this may mean only the elimination of a symptom or a reduction in its severity, although an evaluation will have to be made of whether or not the person will profit or lose by such a modification. (Symptom removal without consideration of its meaning and cause can be quite dangerous.) The aim may be to help the patient achieve better insight into personal conflicts and their causes, in order to lessen their severity. Another aim of psychotherapy may be to help the patient become less sensitive to or less disturbed by, conflicts and symptoms. This may mean that the patient learns to tolerate the symptoms and to live more effectively even though the problem remains unchanged. (For example, this is sometimes done in certain cases of homosexual reactions.) The aim may be, again, to offer emotional support to the patient during critical periods in life and thus enable the patient to master a painful situation. The most ambitious aim of psychotherapy is a reorganization of the total personality so that the patient is eventually freed from all major conflicts and can lead a more spontaneous and effective life.

We may ask how these aims can be achieved. In order to answer this, we must know something about psychotherapy. Psychotherapy is a process of self-realization. In emotional maladjustment, unconscious factors have too great a role in the determination of behavior. By this, we mean that the ego is overwhelmed, or its functions have been interfered with by forces over which it has lost some control. Self-realization implies that, in the course of psychotherapy, the patient becomes more aware of these unconscious determinants of behavior, perceives himself differently as a result, and then begins to change the means and goals of adjustment. The patient can then be freer to lead a well-disciplined life in which he uses his capacities in a more spontaneous manner. This process of self-realization goes on between two people, the subject and the psychotherapist. The major "currency" of this interaction is *verbalization;* that is, the patient talks, telling about himself, complaints, feelings, and the like. There are other currencies; the motor behavior of the patient (since the patient may communicate thought and feeling by gesture, movement of the body, postural tonus and adjustments, and other means); the forms (as distinguished from the content) of communication (since attitudes may be revealed by making "slips of the tongue," coming late or missing an appointment, being unable to think of anything to say, and saying things in unusual ways); and even the unconscious communications between the patient and the psychotherapist.

There are many unique characteristics of the therapist as distinguished from all other persons to whom a person may go in the search for help. The therapist is not a moralist; she does not presume to function as a superego representative of society. Unlike parents, teachers, friends, or other people, the psychotherapist does not judge the "goodness" or "badness" of the person. Instead, the therapist tries to understand, accept, and help the patient to a more effective emotional adjustment. Moreover, the therapist retains her own integrity as distinct from that of the patient. This means that she does not become confused in the role; she does not permit private problems or conflicts or value systems to obtrude themselves into the therapeutic situation. The therapist attempts to help the patient *differentiate* himself more adequately from the roles of parents, siblings, peers, and superiors. She enables the person to *become himself* more fully.

At base, psychotherapy involves a relationship between two or more individuals in which the client (or patient) learns to modify some aspect of behavior. In working with parents of the retarded, learning procedures frequently involve helping the parent cope more effectively with the retarded child. In such situations, the parent can be helped to deal more effectively with the child through the use of training procedures for the child, while being supported emotionally and educationally in coping with personal "internal" problems (Jefrey et al., 1977; Schopler, 1977). Explicit behavioral modification techniques sometimes can be employed in helping the parent to modify his own behavior, and thus can contribute to the child's growth (Baker, 1977).

Psychotherapists tend to operate within the framework of their own psychotherapeutic schools or theories. Such therapists tend to practice client-centered therapy, psychoanalytic therapy, neopsychoanalytic therapy, transactional analysis, and behavior modification therapies. Other therapists see the need of using those aspects of the theory and method of different schools in their attempt to mold the therapy to the particular patient and the patient's current needs (Hutt, 1977a). We shall discuss major aspects of these and other approaches in chapter 16.

All psychotherapists attempt to establish an *emotional relationship* with the patient in treatment. This sometimes is referred to as *rapport*, an intense relationship in which the patient becomes emotionally involved, not only in the therapeutic task, but also with the therapist. The therapist offers *emotional support* to the patient and helps the patient feel understood and accepted. In all forms of psychotherapy, the patient becomes *identified* to some extent with the therapist and takes in many of the therapist's attributes (either consciously or unconsciously). All forms of psychotherapy involve and encourage the *release of emotional tension*. To some extent, all psychotherapists *interpret* the patient's behavior. Through such interpretation, they develop *emotional insight* into the subject; that is, they help the subject understand the complexities of the emotional and intellectual causes of his reactions. Finally, all psychotherapeutic approaches attempt *integration* of the personality.

In treating the parent who needs psychotherapy, both the goal and the therapeutic approach will vary with the specific nature of the problems involved. Generally, however, the treatment is directed toward relieving the problems of the parent that the child *precipitated* but did not *originate*. As the parent responds to psychotherapy, relationships and reactions toward the child will change. This change will, in turn, initiate a change in the adjustmental and behavioral reactions of the child. The effects of psychotherapy thus are much broader than those occurring in the parent, since they spread to the child and to other members of the family.

Group Psychotherapy. Group therapy includes any organized program of psychotherapy in which more than one person is treated simultaneously by one or more psychotherapists. In most group therapy approaches, the therapist behaves as she would in individual therapy, except that she has to deal with several persons at one time. Emotional experiences and the gaining of emotional insights are stressed, and there is active interaction between members of the group and the therapist.

The purposes of group therapy are varied. It was at first thought that group therapy could produce only minimal changes in adjustment. For some time, it was thought to be a palliative measure only and was considered by many persons a supplement to individual therapy. The purpose of group therapy was, simply, to treat large numbers of persons more economically than could be done by individual therapy. As group therapy became more widely used, it was believed that the method was applicable to only certain types of people, such as those in need of socialization experiences, or those who found individual therapy to be too threatening. Some group therapists believed that psychotic persons could not be helped significantly by group therapy. However, there now is evidence to lead us to believe that all types of persons can profit considerably from group therapy if the nature of the group and the competence of the therapist are appropriate. Certainly parents who develop emotional problems usually can profit readily from such a therapeutic approach. The aims of group therapy may vary. Some group programs may be aimed at symptom relief only, whereas others may be aimed at deep reconstructive therapy.

Modern approaches view group therapy as a process of dynamic interaction between the therapist and group members, as well as among the members themselves. They stress the importance of the emotional reactions between individual group members, and the therapist interprets the behavior (both words and deeds) of the participants in much the same way as in individual psychotherapy.

We have found group psychotherapy to be an effective method of treating the emotional problems of the parents of retarded children. Of particular importance are the interactions that take place among the parents themselves and the support they offer to each other, which, of course, do not occur in individual psychotherapy.

Group therapy differs from usual group education. The primary purpose of the educational group is to induce changes in the parents by imparting information, even though the emotional reactions also are considered. Primary attention is not paid, as it is in group therapy, to the resolution of the personality problems of the parent, since the parent in such a group should not present sufficient psychopathological reactions to warrant such an approach. The parent who does is in need of psychotherapy. Whether or not a parent is in need of group guidance and education or group psychotherapy depends on the nature and extent of the psychopathology he shows. The determination of the treatment program for the parent thus demands that the psychologist (or other professional therapist) must carefully assess not only the problems of the child, but also those of the parent.

Family Problems Difficult of Resolution. As we have repeatedly stressed in this chapter, the emotional adjustment and the consequent behavioral reactions of the young retarded individual are determined, to a significant degree, by the nature of the parental relationships, particularly by the child's relationships with the mother. If such interactions are not wholesome, then the adjustment of the child may be affected in an adverse manner. The President's Panel on Mental Retardation (1962) focussed on several highly undesirable patterns of maternal behavior that directly affect the welfare of the child. As previously discussed (see chapter 8), any separation of the child from the mother, regardless of the reason, is important, in that it may induce severe emotional reactions, usually characterized by depressive and somatic symptomatology. One of the categories that characterize the separation of mother and child has been termed the *Unavailable Mother* pattern by the Panel. In this category are mothers who must work to support the family and therefore are unavailable to their young children.

Another type of mother (unfortunately, too often encountered) is the one who is unable to meet the emotional needs of the child because of her own problems. She is herself emotionally unstable. According to the President's

Panel, such mothers would include those who are extremely possessive or lethargic, deeply depressed, highly rejective, or mentally ill.

A third type of maternal behavior is that of the parent who, in the words of the Panel, produces the *Battered Child Syndrome*. We share the dismay of the Panel that this is: "an incredible occurrence in our society—various injuries to young children, including brain damage, resulting from frequent or severe beatings on the head by parents or others who care for small children." We do not know the incidence of this type of abuse of the child by the parents, but we know from our clinical experience that such cases are by no means rare.

To these three severe patterns of undesirable maternal behavior we should like to add a fourth. Frequently, a parent of the retarded child also is mentally retarded herself, and so may be unable to deal effectively with the child's needs. Sometimes she is even unable to provide the child with the absolute necessities of life. Of course, in such instances, psychotherapy or educational guidance will be of limited value.

Thus, in some cases, the problems of the parents may be too severe to be ameliorated by any type of usual psychotherapeutic approach. In many cases, the most appropriate solution (and indeed, perhaps the only humane one possible) may be to remove the child from the situation that is so deleterious to the child's welfare. Placement in a foster home or in an appropriate institution may then be warranted. Such action may prove to be best not only for the welfare of the child, but also for the welfare of the parent, and for society.

PART
III

MEASUREMENT AND EVALUATION

– 11 –

Psychological Assessment
and Evaluation

In this chapter, we will discuss some of the major problems concerned with psychological measurement and evaluation and will provide examples of tests and procedures that may be used in these processes. Our focus, of course, will be on the assessment of retarded individuals, with major emphasis on the mildly and moderately retarded. The problems of assessing the abilities of severely and especially of profoundly retarded persons are enormously complex; proper assessment of such individuals, especially in respect to cognitive functions and possible brain damage, usually require highly trained and skillful professional persons or preferably teams of such persons.

It is extremely important for all individuals who work with retarded persons to have some degree of sophistication concerning the problems of assessment. Even if some of these individuals are not called on to administer such tests or to interpret the results, they are, nevertheless, asked to use the results in their educational programs. Yet without an adequate understanding of the values and limitations of such tests, effective use of the results is limited or even distorted. Moreover, there are many kinds of testing procedures that the teacher is called on to employ in the work of evaluating status and progress, and so the teacher often is required to construct or use tests of specific functions for such purposes.

THE FUNCTION AND MEANING OF
INDIVIDUAL ASSESSMENT

It is appropriate, at this point, to ask the question: What are the objectives of the assessment of the characteristics of the mentally retarded child? In the first place, the *assessment* of such a child or the *evaluation* of the findings derived from assessment procedures, should give us information about the ex-

tent of the assets and deficits. (In the case of Johnny Jones detailed in chapter 1, the evaluation indicated that he was a child of subnormal intelligence, but not so inferior as to require segregated placement. Data also revealed the extent of his deficits in academic work.) In the second place, the assessment should furnish information about the qualitative aspects of the deficit and its emotional consequences. (Johnny had very poor memory and could not concentrate. He was functioning below his age expectancy in academic work. He had many emotional problems, such as hostilities toward his siblings and ambivalent feelings toward his mother.) In the third place, the assessment should determine the *reasons* for the mental retardation and the emotional maladjustment—the basic *why*. (In Johnny's case there were no definite indications of the primary cause of his intellectual deficit. However, physical illnesses, school problems, and home relationships were found to be of importance in the production of Johnny's maladaptive behavior.)

The case of Henry Distal, presented in chapter 1, illustrates each of these three considerations in the evaluation process. Henry's deviant cultural and familial background required the use of nonverbal tests, particularly tests of perceptual-motor performance, to provide the assessment data necessary for valid evaluation. Some of the possible reasons for Henry's poor academic achievement and for his behavioral difficulties became more understandable as a consequence of an appropriate assessment program.

There is considerable disagreement about what constitutes an adequate assessment program, and some psychologists even question the value of evaluation. For instance, Dunn (1968) believes that assessment has probably done more harm than good, since it has resulted in disability labels and it has led to the grouping of children into homogeneous school classes on the basis of these labels. He pointed out that the diagnosis has rarely been done by a multidisciplinary team. The purpose of the multidisciplinary team approach is to look at the complete child, yet, as Dunn indicates, too often the outcome has been merely to label the child mentally retarded, perceptually impaired, emotionally disturbed, minimally brain damaged, or the like. It is Dunn's belief that the team doesn't go beyond establishing that there is something wrong with the child or justifying a recommendation for placement in a special class. He concluded that assessment results in "digging the educational graves for many racially and/or economically disadvantaged children by using a *WISC* or *Binet* IQ score to justify the label of mentally retarded." This term then becomes, according to Dunn, "an all destructive, self-fulfilling prophecy." He advocates the abandonment of the use of such diagnostic practices and disability labels.

Dunn also made the telling point that the expectancies of teachers influence pupil progress. As he pointed out, when a child is labeled handicapped, the teacher's expectancy for that child to succeed is reduced. Dunn suggested that we do away with many existing disability labels and the present practice of grouping children homogeneously by these labels into special classes. Instead, we should try to keep slow-learning children more in the "mainstream of education" by having special *educators* serve as diagnostic, clinical, remedial, resource-room, itinerant and team teachers, consultants, and developers of instructional materials and prescriptions for effective teaching. He suggested that this approach would require a revolution in much of special education.

Dunn also stated that the usual tests of cognitive development, such as the *WISC* and the *Binet,* are of little use except in providing baseline data on the level at which a child is functioning. In place of these psychometric tests, diagnostic educators would rely heavily on a combination of various tools of "behavior shapers and clinical teachers." He contemplated a program in which the first step would be to make a study of the child to find out what behaviors the child has acquired along the dimension being considered. Next, samples of a sequential program would be designed to move the child forward from that point. The method by which he could best be taught the material would also be determined, so the instructional program itself would become a diagnostic device. Dunn viewed this diagnostic procedure as the best available, since it would enable one to assess the problem points of the instructional program against the assets of the child continuously.

Weiner (1967) suggests that the traditional clinical approach to the evaluation of mentally retarded children has been intended to serve three objectives. These are (1) the determination of intellectual status, which usually is expressed in terms of classification or degree of developmental retardation; (2) the projection of a theoretical pace of the future course of intellectual development; and (3) an estimate of the child's educability derived from conclusions based on the two preceding criteria. Weiner points out that the type of assessment that he proposes does not result in scores that can be manipulated mathematically. However, it does yield information that is of substantive assistance in describing the status of the child more fully, in providing a basis for selecting and directing the course of development, and in indicating the dimensions of the child's educability.

Weiner indicates that assessments of educability are integrated observations about the total development of the retarded child. First, rather than traditionally considering level in terms of age or grade equivalences, he would describe level in terms of degree of difficulty or complexity, which are functional descriptions. Second, the assessment of educability should include observations about *rate,* which refers to the time required to attain a particular level or to achieve a specific amount of gain. The activity rhythms of individual children and each child's rate of change need to be considered. Third, the assessment of educability also should include an evaluation of *range,* which Weiner uses in "its territorial" rather than in its statistical sense. One needs to know the array of learning opportunities, as well as the quality of the child's response to them. Further, the efficiency of the program needs to be evaluated. Here one would look for behavioral adequacy as expressed in economy and accuracy of performance on specified tasks. Weiner feels that determination of the degree of efficiency in a broad range of socially and educationally meaningful tasks is a better basis for the assessment of educability than is reliance on an arbitrary IQ score. Weiner points out that we should observe not only how children approach a task that has been selected for them, but also whether and how they select tasks for themselves, how they initiate and execute tasks they have chosen, and whether they experience satisfaction in their choice. We are inclined to agree with Weiner, who feels that it is unlikely that the preparation of a worthwhile descriptive report on the intellectual and educational status of a mentally retarded child will ever be a simple or easy assignment. We would like to offer for serious consideration his conclusion that "assessment is not a calling for the professional or nonprofessional dabbler or for anyone who wants to succeed without really trying. The useful extension of our knowledge of children beyond the pedestrian boundaries of psychometric and educational test scores can be accomplished only by the meticulous attention to the small diagnostic truths."

What Does a Test Really Measure?

We fully share the concerns of Dunn and Weiner. However, to dismiss the use of some tests because their use has sometimes or even often been abused is not only to miss the major issue that is involved—and thereby possibly add to our difficulties rather than to correct them properly—but also to fail to come to grips with the essential and central problem in any attempt to test and evaluate. These issues have to do with the questions of *validity* and *reliability* of measurements of any nature, which we shall presently discuss in detail. To illustrate the significance of these issues, let us examine some of the legitimate furor that has been raised about intelligence testing.

The November, 1977 issue of the APA *Psychology Monitor* (APA *Psychology Monitor,* 1977a) contains a report of some of the proceedings in a class action trial, *Larry P. v. Riles.* This action has been pending in the Federal District Court in San Francisco for six years. The case involves the allegation that six black elementary pupils had been improperly diagnosed and placed in EMR classes as a consequence. It was claimed that the intelligence tests that were used to diagnose these children as mentally retarded—the *Stanford-Binet,* the *Wechsler Intelligence Scale for Children,* and the *Leiter Intelligence Scale*—were culturally biased against nonwhite minority children, and when the children were retested by members of the Bay Area Association of Black Psychologists with assessment methods designed to reflect the children's cultural and language experiences, their scores improved substantially. In a preliminary finding. Federal District Judge Robert Peckham, expanding his earlier 1972 ruling, ordered a statewide moratorium on IQ tests for evaluating minority students.

The possible implications of this trial, which is likely to proceed to the Supreme Court for final adjudication, go far beyond the proper or improper use of intelligence tests. In our opinion, there is little doubt that current standardized intelligence tests are clearly biased in favor of white, middle-class individuals. There is no doubt, too, that many minority individuals—not only blacks—have been improperly "diagnosed" with such tests and have been judged to be far less capable than they really are. But the tests, and not only intelligence tests but all standardized and nonstandardized tests, are not really the culprit! Tests are simply a means—albeit imperfect—of evaluating some behavioral phenomenon. It is the users, or rather the misusers, of tests, who should be on trial! To understand this assertion, let us examine more critically what tests measure.

A test is simply a device for obtaining a measure of some behavioral attribute, (such as intelligence, spelling ability, motor dexterity, or amount of aggressiveness, for example). A *standardized test* is a device that has been developed through research and experimentation and has been "normed" to provide defined standards for a given population. Both nonstandardized and standardized tests involve attempts to provide more objective evaluations of the behavior in question than a rating by an observer; that is, by a teacher, a psychologist, or an experimenter. Standardized tests have been developed to provide a more accurate assessment of the behavior in question through such procedures as more adequate *sampling* of the phenomenon (to secure an adequate sample of the behavior), more *objective scoring* of the behavior or responses (to reduce subjectivity of the evaluation), more *valid samples* of the defined behavior (to reduce the influence of irrelevant factors), and more *adequate standards* (to provide norms for comparative purposes). These are laudable goals with which no reputable psychologist would quarrel. However, many reputable psychologists would quarrel with *the uses to which tests,* and especially standardized tests, *are put.* But the same psychologists also would note that other means of evaluating some aspects of behavior have their own peculiar problems and difficulties. Let us first look at some of these problems of more informal assessment.

If behavior is assessed by informal means, such as by observing the behavior while it is being performed in a real-life situation, and even if the observer is a trained observer, there are likely to be many pitfalls. For one thing, the sample of the behavior that is observed may be inadequate. This is true because the individual might behave differently on different occasions due to changing circumstances, and thus obtaining an adequate sample of the behavior in all circumstances might be quite impractical. The test, and particularly the standardized test, attempts to define the circumstances so that they can be replicated and the test findings can be comparable. Another problem of the observer evaluation is that the observer may easily be biased, and therefore perceive and evaluate improperly what is being observed. Put in another way, two observers noting the same behavior might easily make differing judgments about that behavior. And, finally, the observer would be unable to provide adequate standards or norms by means of which to evaluate properly what is being observed. Thus, for example, a teacher-observer, whose experience had been only in observing very superior pupils, would be unable to evaluate adequately the behavior of very retarded pupils. This teacher's "subjective norms" would be too high! These are only a few of the major limitations of observer evaluations.

On the other hand, tests have been employed as if no subjective evaluation and no clinical judgment needed to be involved. A test may yield a score or a profile of scores, and the tester might assume that "a score is a score is a score." Nothing could be further from the truth. A test, no matter how well standardized, *always involves several critical assumptions,* and these assumptions *always need to be carefully evaluated.* Let us examine these assumptions.

(1) A standardized test assumes that the individual taking the test has been exposed to the same or essentially comparable conditions to which the population on which the test was standardized has been exposed. At best, this assumption is only approximated when the individual being tested has had learning opportunities that are at least roughly comparable to the standardization population. Since there always are differences in such background experiences, sometimes minor and sometimes critical, the score on the test always must be regarded as a *measure of current ability* obtained under specified learning opportunities, and not as a measure of capacity. In the case of individuals from backgrounds with some degree of deprivation (culturally, linguistically, or in social stimulation), or some degree of deviation from the standardization population, the score on the test will necessarily reflect these differences in background experiences. Hence, at the least, any score on an intelligence test, or on any standardized test, should be *evaluated carefully* in the light of discrepancies in prior experience between the standardization population and the individual in question. This cannot be done without knowledge and evaluation of the relevance of such experiences and their possible impact on the test score. Clearly, in the case of minority or divergent cultural groups, this assumption is critical and needs very special evaluation.

A number of studies have documented the significance of differences in social-cultural experience on cognitive style and intellectual performance. One of the most interesting was a comparison of Guatemalan village children and middle-class children from Buffalo, New York (Meacham, 1975). These five- to seven-year-old children were compared on memory tasks involving either place or object. Meacham was careful to utilize objects and places of hiding that were appropriate to each culture so thay any differences that were found in differing memory abilities would not be attributable simply to unequal exposure to these aspects of the experiment. It was found that the Guatemalan children performed better at place recall than object recall, whereas the Buffalo children performed equally well at both memory tasks. The differences in the two cultures thus were reflected in differential performance on these tasks.

(2) Performance on a test is *always* affected by various personality and motivational factors. The degree of this effect may vary in significance from individual to individual, and from circumstance to circumstance, but it is always present. Hutt (1977a) has demonstrated the nature and effect of some of these factors, as have others. Let us cite the more important of these, particularly as they relate to the evaluation of retarded children.

(a) Performance on a test is a function of the degree of motivation shown by the subject. Retarded individuals in particular, as a result of numerous frustrations of the past, may have developed an aversive attitude toward almost all kinds of testing. They approach the test with lowered levels of aspiration, may make minimal efforts to succeed with the task, and often are content to accomplish far less than they may be capable of.

(b) The level of anxiety related to test performance may be unusually high in some individuals. Consequently, they may approach the test situation with considerable apprehension and may do less than they are capable of.

(c) The level of general adjustment may easily affect test performance. As Hutt (1947) and others have shown, the pupil with poorer general personality adjustment tends to perform below maximal level on intelligence tests in which the items are organized by age level as a consequence of the frustrations that the test situation provides.

(d) Individual testing, and even group testing, is affected by the nature of the interpersonal relations between examiner and examinee. Such factors as discrepancies between examiner and examinee, like social status, skin color, and sex, have been shown to affect test performance.

These and other factors influence the test results. Their possible effects on the test score always need to be considered in interpreting the test findings.

This last point needs emphasis — it is critical in the assessment of intellectual functions. Various factors tend to depress the functioning (and hence the scores) of some individuals, particularly the retarded. Among these factors are: an atypical and abnormally low level of motivation; poor habits of attending; poor persistence at tasks; previous inadequate experience with the "materials" of the test (language and symbols, for example); and, personality factors such as excessive anxiety, oppositionalisms or noninvolvement). Consequently, the behavior or score on the test may be more a reflection of such factors than of the true capacity of the individual.

As we have indicated, the test score too often is assumed to reflect the true ability or capacity of an individual without appropriate and careful consideration of relevant background factors. Since these may significantly affect performance on the test, the sophisticated examiner will attempt to determine how and under what conditions performance may be improved. Hutt (1977a) has suggested an "experimental-clinical" procedure. Briefly, in this procedure, each of a number of factors that might have contributed to unfavorable performance is evaluated. The examiner tests out the relevance of each factor by systematically varying test stimuli or test conditions. Hutt also has termed this procedure "process testing" to contrast it with the usual "static testing." A recent development along such lines, in which learning experiences are designed and their effects measured, has been developed by Feuerstein (1978). He and his collaborators have had considerable success in evaluating learning potential using a test-train-retest procedure in a series of operations utilizing standard materials.

(3) The competence of the examiner both in administering the test and in evaluating the results is an important factor in evaluating test findings. It usually is assumed that the examiner "knows his business" and administers the test properly. This assumption often is violated in practice. Although the examiner may administer the test in accordance with the usual "standard" conditions, such conditions may not be appropriate in an individual case. For instance, the problem of gaining and maintaining adequate *rapport* is an art that some testers fail to master. Moreover, when examiners are under the stress of examining large numbers of individuals, insufficient care may be taken to administer the test effectively.

The problem of interpreting the test results is even more difficult. Such issues as the relevance of the test norms for a particular case, the pattern of performance on the items of the test, and the influence of extraneous factors on test performance all must be considered when evaluating the test score or the test profile. Often, the examiner must possess some knowledge of how and to what extent physical handicaps and personality disturbances may affect test performance and must know how to evaluate such influences.

This discussion has been intended to demonstrate that the *interpretation* of a test score, no matter how valid a test or an observation may generally be, is a highly critical issue. In short, a test can do no more than provide data that then must be evaluated, in the individual case, in terms of all the relevant factors before the significance of the findings can be interpreted. A good test measures performance in some defined domain under certain conditions, but the measure can have no valid meaning unless all of the conditions we have noted are carefully considered.

A Pluralistic Assessment Model

One issue highlighted in the *Larry P. v. Riles* case is that the well-known intelligence tests are biased against subcultural and minority groups and biased in favor of middle-class, white groups. We have discussed many aspects of this problem in chapter 2. Dr. Jane Mercer, in her testimony in the California trial, criticized the inapplicability of the norms on these tests since they were based on the dominant Anglo culture in this country; she stated: "[The assumption is] that we have essentially a homogeneous society in which the dominant culture is an American version of the Anglo culture, and that other migrant groups . . . have melted into the melting pot" (*APA Psychology Monitor,* 1977b). She disputes this view (and previously had offered considerable evidence to justify her position) and believes instead that since people in this country live in quite differing cultures, with quite differing developmental experiences, tests, therefore, and special tests designed to evaluate intelligence level should be tailored to these differences. She has proposed a pluralistic model for test evaluation in which multiple norms for people with different sociocultural backgrounds would be available and for test procedures and content that would be geared to these differing cultures.

Mercer has described her assessment approach in an article by Soeffing (1977). This approach is known as SOMPA (System of Pluralistic Assessment); the research being conducted in constructing the assessment measure was funded in 1970 by the National Institute of Mental Health. The aim is to develop norms for representative samples of four cultures in California: blacks, Chicanos, Latinos, and Anglos. Seven hundred individuals from each of these cultures, a total of 2100 people, in the age-range from five to eleven are being evaluated. The procedures in the initial standardization involve an interview with the mother or principal caretaker and two test sessions with each child. These procedures yield: a sociocultural index, an adaptive behavior inventory, and, a health inventory and an impairment inventory. The individual tests that are administered are: *Physical Dexterity Battery;* the *Bender-Gestalt Test;* and, a version (in the native language) of the *WISC-R* (*Wechsler Intelligence Scale for Children,* revised). Based on the data obtained by these procedures and these tests, normative data will be established separately for each of the four ethnic groups. Then on the basis of a statistical method known as multiple regression, in which each score is given proportionate weight within each subpopulation according to its degree of contribution to the criterion (a measure of learning potential), a total score is derived. Thus, this research attempts to make appropriate allowance for the differences in background experiences of each culture instead of comparing each culture with the Anglo norm.

It is clear that this ambitious project should yield "more valid" and "more discriminating" scores for each of the four subpopulations, since the scores will be "weighted" separately in terms of the relevant cultural patterns. Better prediction for each group should therefore result.

However, there are several basic problems with this approach. In the first place, it assumes that each subculture is homogeneous, just as was previously, and incorrectly, assumed that the entire American culture was homogeneous. In the second place, it assumes that each subculture is representative of that subculture throughout America—that is, that blacks in California are identical to other blacks in other parts of the country, that Chicanos in California are also similarly identical to other samples of Chicanos, and so on. Such an assumption certainly is not supported by available evidence. If this is the case, then new normative data and new regression equations will have to be determined for many samples of each subculture.

Finally, and most important, this approach assumes that *each member of a particular subculture (even within California) is a replicable member of all members of that culture.* Even if the subculture is *relatively* homogeneous, the relative weight of each factor in the assessment will surely differ for different individuals. They cannot be entirely similar in the kinds of factors that we have suggested are critical in determining test scores: similar stimulation patterns in the home, similar degrees of motivation, similar linguistic experiences, similar personality adjustment, similar reactions to frustrations, and so on. Thus, although measurement and prediction for the group, as a group, may be improved, the problem in each individual case will remain essentially the same: test results will require an evaluation in each case of those special characteristics that may invalidate the weights assigned, in general, to the group.

Let us posit an extreme example of this problem in order to highlight the issue: If a child has a severe convulsive disorder that affects his motivation and his performance on most test procedures, then how will the weights assigned to his particular subpopulation, say the Chicanos, be applicable? We are left, therefore, with the ultimate issue in all individual testing: the relations of the idiosyncratic features of the individual's developmental experience in the light of his present idiosyncratic current status to the meaning of the test score or test pattern. This issue cannot be disregarded whether the assessment is made by standardized individual test or by ratings based on observations of current behavior. If it is, gross disservice may be done to the individual just as it has been done to the group.

These analytical observations about the nature of assessment should not be used to make us discard our many valuable testing instruments, but to help us use them more effectively. Standardized tests can be used properly *if their limitations as well as their values are appreciated.* Assessment involves more information than the standardized tests provide. To use such tests properly, the psychologist must analyze the performance that generated the end product (i.e., the score), determine what factors influence the score, and examine the specific nature of the variability of the performance that led to the score. Too often, however, administrators allow too little time for the psychologist to do this kind of careful analysis and probing. In addition, many psychologists are inadequately trained, or are too insensitive to the factors involved, to be capable of making appropriate analyses. And, finally, other *observers* (for example, the teacher, the school nurse, and the remedial or special teacher) are not used adequately in the total evaluation process.

It now should become obvious that assessment means far more than the mere administration of psychological tests and the determination of the level of mental functioning. It involves an exploration of many aspects of a child's life to determine the nature of the problem, the reasons for it, and the prospects for dealing with it. Assessment involves a detailed study of the *whole* child. It should indicate, insofar as possible, the etiologic and precipitating factors underlying the child's mental retardation, and it should describe the specific level at which the child functions. It should be concerned not only with the child's deficiencies, but with assets as well. Further, assessment should include a *prognosis* (prediction of the future development of the child) and should lead to helping the child to adjust adequately.

The intricate process of assessing the retarded individual involves several major areas of investigation. These include (1) personal history, (2) physical condition, (3) adjustmental characteristics, and (4) psychological characteristics. We shall discuss each of these major areas in turn.

Personal History

A complete assessment and evaluative study of a mentally retarded child necessitates the compilation and evaluation of many types of background data. There should be a summary of the child's physical history, including such items as the nature of the birth process; developmental phenomena, such as walking, speech, and dentition; illnesses and surgical operations; and reports of laboratory findings. These data should preferably be compiled by a physician or medical specialist. A detailed social case history also should be obtained, including a description of the child's social environment both inside and outside the home. It also should include an appraisal of the types and amounts of "learning opportunities." It should evaluate the personality characteristics of the parents and the problems they manifest in dealing with the child, stressing both parental liabilities and parental assets. It should stress the characteristics and interrelationships of the child's family structure. Of particular importance in the social case history is an evaluation of the attitudes and emotional reactions shown by the members of the family toward the child—specifically, how they react to the child's mental retardation. Further, there should be an *adjustmental history* giving a detailed picture of the child's adjustment to various situations throughout life. The social and adjustmental case histories usually are compiled by a social worker.

Physical Condition

In addition to historical data concerning the child's past life, data about the child's current status are necessary.

The total assessment should include, when appropriate, a detailed medical examination of the child. This entails the referral of the child, in some instances, to various medical specialists so that an evaluation may be made of the effects, if any, on performance and behavior. For example, referral to a physician specializing in the treatment of *glandular* difficulties (an *endocrinologist*) might be necessary. A complete neurological examination by a *neurologist* might be required to explore the possibility of any central nervous system involvement. There may be a need for further detailed examinations, such as X-rays of the brain or other organs (by a *radiologist*), studies of the brain waves (which may reveal the presence of some organic brain pathology) by means of the *electroencephalograph* (commonly called the *EEG*), or additional laboratory examinations. Physical assessment also should be made of the child's motor skills, both during play and during other activities, to ascertain how well coordinated the child is in the use of large and small muscles.

Adjustmental Characteristics

The total assessment should include a summary of how the child is *currently* adjusting, emphasizing both assets and liabilities. This phase of the evaluation asks such questions as: How is the child relating to members of the family? How well is she doing in school? How does she get along with playmates? What kinds of activities does she engage in? What are characteristic defenses? The summary should cover the entire range of the child's behavior, including relationships with adults, with peers, and with the community. These data usually are secured by either the social worker or the clinical psychologist from interviews with the parents and other persons having contact with the child, as well as from the child, when possible.

Psychological Characteristics

It is important that the assessment of the retarded child include a detailed evaluation of psychological characteristics. This portion of the total assessment process is based on psychological tests and interviews. To be adequate, the psychological evaluation should cover many areas, including (1) intellectual capacities, (2) personality characteristics, (3) academic abilities and disabilities, and (4) special skills and interests. We shall present a brief introductory discussion of these problems and then devote the remainder of the chapter to a more detailed analysis of the specific methods used to explore each of these areas. The psychological evaluation is done by a clinical psychologist.

Intellectual Capacities. It has been suggested that there are essentially two approaches to evaluation of intellectual functions. In the first, one makes an inventory of the factors that might interfere with receptive and expressive behavior and then, in light of these, infers from the performance of the retarded child the underlying potentialities. In the second, the process is reversed. We start with the performance and evaluate the factors that might have lowered the level of the performance. In practice the clinician uses both approaches. This often requires an extensive battery of tests to cover a variety of situations and behavioral capacities.

The evaluation of the retarded child's intellectual capacities should include an estimate of his general degree of deficit and of his assets and liabilities. A child is not necessarily equally retarded in all intellectual functions, and an evaluation of his unique pattern of abilities is helpful in guiding him more effectively. For example, some retarded children are more seriously handicapped in their capacity to deal with verbal material than they are with concrete objects and situations; others are equally handicapped in both areas. Such specific intellectual functions as verbal skills, nonverbal skills, memory (auditory and visual), general comprehension, capacity to integrate and synthesize experience, and capacity to deal with reality should be assessed.

The psychological evaluation of a mentally retarded child often is a complex process. It is complicated by the fact that, in many instances, the child is unable to express himself adequately and to relate to others in the testing situation. The child often manifests both receptive and expressive difficulties in communication. An adequate psychological assessment must involve *not only* an evaluation of the current intellectual performance of the child, but also (at least equally important) an estimate of the child's intellectual *potentialities*. Such evaluations in cases of suspected mental retardation are made difficult not only by communication difficulties of the retarded child but also by perceptual, motoric, and cultural limitations.

Personality Characteristics. A careful evaluation of the personality characteristics of the retarded child is highly important. In order to provide the best possible program for the child, we need to know the maturity level of the personality; the level of ego development; the nature and strength of conflicts; the characteristic psychological defenses; and, the degree to which psychopathological reactions are present. This part of the assessment is significant in suggesting leads for treatment and in estimating current prognostic limits. Such a personality evaluation is particularly difficult with the retarded individual, but it is essential to adequate planning of the treatment program. It usually is done by a clinical psychologist, a psychiatrist, or both. The teacher can contribute significantly to this evaluation by providing observations of the child's behavior.

Guthrie et al. (1963) have discussed the problems involved in assessing the personality dynamics of retarded children. They point out that at best it is an uncertain undertaking, because the majority of assessment procedures use some form of verbal report from the child who is being evaluated. Further, they state that the experiences and the perceptions that the retarded child offers tend to lead the psychologist to infer a rather simplified pattern of dynamics in which the mechanisms are not as elaborate as those in children of higher intelligence. They point out that the clinical reports dealing with the dynamics of mentally retarded children stress such characteristics as dependency, hostility, and negativism. Retarded children, according to Guthrie et al., have a very limited ability to say *how they feel* and *what they think;* therefore, the reports based on their verbal descriptions may be misleading at times. Consequently, the model that is currently used in reporting personality evaluations, since it has been developed from normal subjects, may *not* be applicable to verbalized productions of retarded children. Guthrie et al. believe that the psychologist must infer the specific dynamics that are being evaluated from other sources of information.

We agree that the psychological tests, scales, and assorted techniques used to assess personality variables have been developed primarily for the evaluation of the normal child, and they have been applied, in most instances, only secondarily to the evaluation of persons with severe intellectual handicaps. Gallagher (1959) has discussed this important consideration. He points out that even though there are many instruments for the assessment of personality factors, very few are easy to apply and to interpret in the case of the mentally retarded child.

Gallagher has reviewed the shortcomings of various types of techniques of personality assessment as applied to retarded children. *Self-reports,* or methods involving questionnaires—as exemplified by the *California Test of Personality* and by the *Rogers Test of Personal Adjustment*—are, in his opinion (and ours), not satisfactory. Such methods require at least a third-grade reading level, require that the child be perceptive of his own inner feelings, and require that the child report his own feelings truthfully. Gallagher indicates that the mentally retarded child is inadequate in at least two of these aspects.

Most *projective* methods also are difficult to apply to the retarded child. The responses of such a child sometimes are influenced more by environmental events that immediately precede the testing session than by basic internal needs. Thus, the reactions of the retarded child are curtailed and determined by the child's *time-bound* and *situation-bound* behavioral tendencies.

Further evidence supporting the hypothesis that the mentally retarded child tends to react to projective test material in terms of immediate environmental stimuli rather than in terms of deep inner dynamics is found in a study by Matthews and Levy (1961). They gave the *Children's Manifest Anxiety Scale (CMAS)* to thirty institutionalized children who were mentally retarded, in a test-retest experiment. They also administered a specially designed response-set scale prior to the second administration of the *CMAS*. They found that the *CMAS* scores were influenced by response-sets as well as by situational and capacity variables, and they concluded that the *CMAS* was not an appropriate instrument for evaluating the institutionalized retarded. Cromwell (1961b) has provided an excellent discussion of the values and shortcomings of projective and other types of personality assessment methods for evaluating retarded children.

Observational methods have value, but most methods that are currently in use leave much to be desired. The same objections that were raised to projective tests are applicable to observational techniques. Gallagher proposes (1959) that observers be trained to match the child to behavioral descriptions related to significant stages of personality development. These matchings would be based on the types of relationships the child forms with others in the environment. They would include (1) isolation tendencies, (2) dependency reactions, (3) omnipotence feelings, (4) imitation of adults, (5) identification with adults, (6) imitation of peers, (7) identification with peers, and (8) self-determination behaviors. Gallagher's proposal, even though the mechanics and rationale have not been developed, does have merit in that it would tend to provide a dynamic description of the personality characteristics of the mentally retarded child.

Academic Abilities and Disabilities. A part of the total assessment program includes an evaluation of the academic skills of the child. Such questions as the following are important: How well does the child read? Can the child write? What are arithmetical capacities? Particularly important is the question of whether the child's academic achievements are at a level commensurate with intellectual capacities. (We saw in chapter 9, for example, that children often fail to read at the level they are capable of attaining.) Further, the evaluation of academic abilities and disabilities should stress skills in which the child has a relatively high degree of proficiency. (One child in a group of retarded children won an elementary school spelling contest!) The assessment also should include a prediction of the highest academic level the child is likely to attain. (Such predictions should never be regarded as final, but only as best possible estimates.) The more detailed the analysis of academic skills is, the more likely is it that it can be used to specify the particular learning experiences that are needed.

Evaluation of Special Skills and Interests. As we have pointed out, the retarded child is a unique individual. He often has relatively high degrees of skill in specific areas (e.g., mechanical skills, skill in cooking, skill in performing various industrial tasks, and [less frequently] skill in some academic area), as well as various deficiencies in others. It is important that these be explored and evaluated as the child gets older so as to provide for more effective guidance. His vocational aptitudes as well as vocational interests need to be assessed, and information about his motor skills in general should be gathered. Usually the psychologist performs this part of the assessment.

Integration of Material

A wealth of material from many different sources and specialists is required before adequate planning can proceed for a specific child. After this material has been accumulated, it must be integrated to provide the most reliable representation of the particular child. Such an integration is best accomplished through interaction of, and discussion by, the specialists involved in the child's total assessment process. (See the discussion of the team approach in chapter 15.) It requires the united efforts of the physician and other medical specialists, the clinical psychologist and other psychological specialists, the social worker, the teacher, the learning specialist, the parents, and all other persons who can contribute to a better understanding of the child.

An example of how such materials are integrated is furnished by the case of Bobby, which follows. This material is presented in summary form, and although the dynamics are interesting in themselves, they will not be discussed at length. The case material presented is intended to serve primarily as an illustration of the need for integration of all available information in the evaluation of a child thought to be mentally retarded.

Bobby was referred to the clinical psychologist for evaluation, since it was thought that he was a mentally retarded child. At the time of referral he was sixteen years of age, and history material had been obtained by the social worker and physician. The social worker stressed the fact that Bobby's home environment was particularly undesirable. He lived with his mother in a small structure that was described as "substandard" housing. Bobby had been excluded from school at six years of age, after attending less than a week, because he had been thought to be a "feeble-minded" child. There was no record of any psychological evaluation of Bobby at that time, and no specific reasons were given for arriving at the conclusion that he was mentally retarded. He had not attended school at all since his exclusion. His appearance was very unfavorable—he was very dirty and unkempt when first seen. The results of the detailed medical examination conducted at the time of referral indicated no specific physical defects other than a general condition of malnourishment. Bobby played very little with other children and spent almost all of his time at home. He had no close companions and knew only a few children living in his immediate neighborhood. Bobby did not belong to any group of children. For instance, he had never attended Sunday School or any church or Scout activities and had never engaged in any other organized group activity. There were no siblings. The father had deserted the mother when Bobby was approximately one year of age. His mother was felt to be an ineffectual person who did not have the capacity for providing adequately for Bobby.

The Wechsler-Bellevue Intelligence Scale was administered to Bobby by the clinical psychologist. He noted that Bobby's results on the various subtests of this scale showed that his stock of everyday information was extremely poor and that his comprehension of daily events was impaired. Memory functions, as tested, were poor. Bobby did, however, have the capacity to relate events to each other. All of his verbal capacities were at a much lower level than his nonverbal (performance) capacities. His performance on such nonverbal tasks was, however, considerably below those of an average child of his own chronological age. It was observed that he had some insight into his disabilities, and when he made an error he was aware of "something being wrong," and he tried to correct it. On the basis of these results alone, it might be concluded that Bobby was functioning at a mentally retarded level. However, it was recognized that a test such as the Wechsler-Bellevue might be inappropriate for a child who had never attended school, so further evaluation of his intellectual capacities was conducted through appropriate analysis of the projective tests that were administered. (See later section for discussion of characteristics of such tests.)

Bobby did extremely poorly on all the standardized tests of academic achievement that were administered. His achievement was consistently below that of a first-grade child. He could not read a single word, and he could neither write nor print his name. Even though he could count from 1 to 10, he could not write any number or perform even the most elementary arithmetical operations.

The projective tests of personality (such as the Rorschach, the Hutt Adaptation of the Bender-Gestalt, and Draw-a-Person) that were administered indicated that Bobby was a very tense and anxious child. He perceived the world as a hostile and severely threatening place. Bobby felt rejected and worthless—no good to himself or to anyone else. Further, he passively accepted himself as worthless. What little aggressive reactions he did show were turned inward on himself rather than outward against the world.

The total picture was one of severe deprivation in all areas—emotional, physical, and social. Yet, despite the extremely harsh childhood experiences that had left deep impressions on Bobby, it was evident that the ego structure (that is, his ability to perceive reality accurately, his awareness of his impulses, and his ability to integrate his needs in terms of his social world) was relatively intact. He still had good potentialities for forming positive relationships with people once his initial fears of being hurt were allayed. However, his conflicts were severe and numerous. Bobby attempted to deal with them through withdrawal and repression.

In the light of the evidence it was concluded that Bobby was not mentally retarded but, rather, pseudofeebleminded. At the time of examination he was functioning at a mentally retarded level, but this was because of the extreme deprivations that his history indicated he had experienced in so many areas, and not because of any innate intellectual deficit.

Keeping in mind the general principles we have discussed in the foregoing pages, we shall now discuss the primary characteristics and functions of intelligence tests in general, then consider methods of evaluating intellectual and related functions. Next, we shall discuss methods of assessing personality characteristics and social factors. Finally, we shall discuss techniques of evaluating academic achievement and vocational aptitudes. At all times we shall stress the need for integration of all aspects of the retarded child.

THE PRIMARY CHARACTERISTICS AND FUNCTIONS OF PSYCHOLOGICAL TESTS

The psychological test has come to be regarded, unfortunately, as both an "indispensable" and "self-sufficient" tool in the diagnosis and evaluation of mental retardation. In particular, the value of intelligence tests has been overemphasized. They have been used, in too many instances, as the sole diagnostic instruments for the evaluation of retardation. We have seen, however, from the preceding material, that an adequate evaluation of a retarded child involves much more than the information obtained through the administration of a psychological test or even a battery of such tests. No psychological test should be used as the sole basis of diagnosis of retardation (or any other psychological condition, for that matter).

Despite the overemphasis on the psychological test, it is of considerable value in many ways: (1) it is an aid in the establishment of a valid diagnosis of mental retardation; (2) it provides for quantitative and qualitative evaluation of the degree of retardation; and (3) it is an aid in the assessment of the retarded individual's skills, assets, and deficiencies in many areas, such as academic, social, intellectual, emotional, and vocational.

In our present consideration of the characteristics and functions of psychological tests, we will first consider what they purport to do in general. We then will discuss the ways in which they are constructed.

The General Functions of Psychological Tests

The fundamental purpose of any psychological test is to measure some human trait—to attempt to put into figures or to categorize in some other way a particular psychological characteristic of the individual. From one point of view, such a device may be regarded as being analogous to a yardstick or to some other tool by means of which we make various physical measurements. However, although they both measure something, there is an essential difference between a psychological test and a yardstick. With the yardstick we measure a property of an actually present physical object—an object that can be handled, felt, and seen. With a psychological test *we attempt*, in most instances, to measure intangible attributes of a person. Therefore, we must use *indirect methods*, such as those used to measure the intangible qualities of physical phenomena (for example, the strength of a magnetic field and the strength of an electric current). The intangible quality being measured cannot be directly perceived; rather, it is inferred through the responses made on specially designed instruments. Its presence, as well as the degree of its strength, can *only be inferred from the observed reactions on the measuring instrument*. This is particularly true of psychological traits—the strength of the trait that is measured is inferred from the reaction to the test (*instrument*). In general, the more intangible the particular thing we attempt to measure, the more difficult it is to construct an instrument through which we can accurately make such a measurement. For example, it is relatively more easy for us to measure the length of a table top than it is to measure the amount of radioactivity in the atmosphere. It is even more difficult for us to measure accurately the intensity of any particular psychological characteristic of the individual.

All types of measurement, physical as well as psychological, must be done with a standard measuring instrument so that our measurement is meaningful. In the National Bureau of Standards, in Washington, D.C., there are very carefully perserved standards of length or weight for a foot, a yard, an ounce, a pound, a pint, a quart, and the like (or, in the metric system, gram, kilogram, and so forth). These are the prototypes on which our everyday measuring instruments are based. Our everyday yardsticks and rulers are made to approximate the size of the basic standards as closely as possible. Because of the existence of the standards, we have no doubt about the exact length of an inch, a foot, or a yard.

Of course, these particular standards were first determined in a rather arbitrary way, but once determined they have been rigidly maintained.

Just as standards had to be developed for the measurement of physical characteristics, standards had to be developed for the measurement of various psychological characteristics, such as intelligence. The standard for the measurement of such characteristics is the test itself. In the same manner that we apply a yardstick to an object to measure its length, we may apply a psychological test to an individual to measure the strength of a particular psychological trait.

We cannot use a standard developed for the measurement of one characteristic to measure another. For example, we cannot properly measure the distance from point A to point B with a voltmeter. The standard must be applicable to the particular situation for which it is being used. This also is true of any psychological measurements that we wish to make. *The psychological test must be specific to the trait that we wish to measure.* We cannot use a test (or standard) developed for measuring reading ability to determine intellectual level. Each psychological standard (or test) must be carefully developed to measure *validly* what it is supposed to measure, and it must be *selected* by the examiner for use only in situations in which it is *properly applicable.*

We should bear in mind, thus, that psychological tests are standards that are applied to individuals or groups in an attempt to measure some specific trait or some group (*cluster*) of traits. From one point of view, a psychological test therefore may be regarded as a standardized situation to which an individual is subjected. On the basis of performance, the individual may be compared with peers, and the strength of a trait may be estimated.

Construction of Psychological Tests

We shall discuss several aspects of psychological test construction: (1) reliability, (2) validity, and (3) standardization procedures.

Reliability. We stated earlier that our standards for physical measurement were precisely constructed and very carefully maintained. We try to be as sure as possible that they will not vary from one time to another. This is necessary so that repeated measurement of the same thing by the same standard under the same conditions will give us the same results. We wish to be sure that our measuring instrument measures *consistently.* If the obtained measure varies from one time to another, while the thing measured does not, then the measure is relatively worthless. If we measure a table top today and find it to be 5 feet 2 inches long, and measure it the next day and find it to be 5 feet 6 inches long, then one or more of the following three things may have happened: (1) the table top may have changed in length; (2) the standard that we are using may have changed; or (3) we may have incorrectly used the standard. If we can rule out incorrect use of the standard and the possibility of any significant change in the size of the table top, then the discrepancy in the measurements must be due to variability within the measuring instrument. We may conclude that the instrument does not measure *consistently* what it purports to measure. The degree of consistency of measurement by a test is referred to as *reliability*—the higher the reliability of a psychological test, or any other standard, the more consistently it measures a particular trait.

The reliability of a test is not an all-or-nothing matter; that is, a psychological test is not either totally reliable or totally unreliable. It is a matter of degree. A test must be reliable enough, however, to measure an aspect of human behavior with reasonable accuracy. If an intelligence test, for example, yields markedly discrepant scores from one day to the next, then we must be skeptical regarding its reliability (provided, of course, that it is administered properly and that there is no corresponding change in the person tested).

The reliability of a test may be determined in many ways. One method is to administer two alternate (and equivalent) forms of the test to the same person and see how closely the measured results agree. Another method is to retest the same person with the same test within a short interval of time. A third way is to divide the test into equivalent halves, and check one half against the other by giving both to the same person. (In this method we treat the single test as if it were two tests, using a procedure that is similar to the first method.)

In order to obtain a measure of the degree of reliability of a test, we may give the same test to the same group of people on two occasions within a short time interval, or we may give the same group two alternate forms of the test (or split-halves of the test) at the same time. Then we may correlate the results to determine the degree of reliability. (i.e., the *correlation coefficient*).*

If the same test is given twice, we keep the interval of time short to be sure that the individuals do not change in the meantime. The more nearly the two sets of measures agree, the more reliable the test is and the higher the correlation coefficient.

There are other statistical methods of measuring the reliability of a test such as the *standard error of measurement,* and *confidence intervals*. These are measures of the precision of the obtained score or of the amount of error in the score that may reasonably be expected.

Validity. We have stressed that a test should measure consistently what it purports to measure. It is equally important that a test measure *validly* what it purports to measure. A measure of height should actually measure height, not weight or any other dimension. A test of intelligence should measure intelligence and not, for example, reflect the amount of educational experience to which a person has been exposed. This implies that a psychological test should be con-

Correlation refers to the relationship between two variables. If one variable changes in exactly the same degree as the other, the two variables are perfectly correlated. There is a constant relationship between the diameter of a circle and its circumference, for example. Traits may be *positively* correlated (that is, as one variable increases so does the other) or *negatively* correlated (one variable decreases as the other increases). A perfect positive correlation is expressed by the *correlation coefficient* + 1.00, and a perfect negative correlation by the coefficient − 1.00. A total lack of correlation is expressed as 0.00. Human traits are seldom perfectly correlated, but lie somewhere between + 1.00 and − 1.00. The greater the relationship between two traits, the higher the correlation coefficient (either positively or negatively).

structed for a particular purpose. In the same way that a measure of length (a yardstick) cannot be used to measure weight, so a test purportedly measuring a certain personality trait cannot be used to measure some other trait. If a test measures adequately what it purports to measure, then it is said to be a valid test.

Like reliability, validity is not an all-or-nothing affair. A test is usually not perfectly valid, but it must be a sufficiently valid psychological measure for the purpose for which we wish to use it.

The validity of a test may be established by determining how well the test performance correlates with criteria that we have sufficient reason to believe are functions of the trait to be measured. (See Anastasi, 1968, Cronbach, 1970.) For example, tests of intelligence usually are checked against, or *correlated* with, the following kinds of criteria: (1) known groups of individuals (such as superior or mentally retarded); (2) scholastic grades and cumulative scholastic records; and (3) judgments and ratings by teachers.

Cronbach and Meehl (1955) point out that three major types of validity studies of psychological tests usually have been employed. *Predictive validity* refers to studies in which the experimenter administers a test, obtains measure on appropriate criteria, and determines the correlation between the psychological test score and the criterion score. On *concurrent validity* studies, the test score and criteria scores are obtained at the same time. *Content validity* refers to studies in which the test items are shown to be adequate samples of the attributes of the person whom the researcher is measuring. As Cronbach and Meehl point out, however, it is very difficult at times to establish adequate criteria with which to correlate the test. This is true when we deal with such a general characteristic as intelligence, and even more so when we deal with personality characteristics. To deal with such a situation, Cronbach and Meehl propose a fourth type of validation approach, called *construct validity*. It involves an acceptance by the researcher of an operational definition of what he wishes to measure, since the criteria themselves are inadequate. As we have pointed out, we have great difficulty in setting up adequate criteria of intelligence. Thurstone (1952) noted that it has been the custom to define the validity of an intelligence test in terms of its correlation with some outside criterion, but he feels that this approach alone is too coarse and should be considered obsolete. He feels that the validity of a test that measures intellectual functions should be determined by criteria of internal consistency—that is, how well the test items relate to each other.

Standardization Procedures. It is obvious from the foregoing discussion that any psychological test can only be as useful as its standardization permits. As an example of standardization procedure we shall review the method by which the *New Revised Stanford-Binet Tests* (see Terman and Merrill, 1937, 1960) of intelligence were originally developed. Our presentation of the standardization of these tests is considerably simplified. However, the following condensation will indicate the complexities of the problem.

First, a great many intelligence test items were examined, and a list of such items was drawn up. These items were then screened on the basis of their practical applicability and their known correlation with various other measures of intelligence. The most promising of these items were then selected on an *a priori* basis for preliminary trial. They were administered to approximately 1,000 subjects, but not all items were given to each subject. On the basis of statistical findings, each of the items was then assigned to a particular chronological level (or level of intellectual difficulty). The best of these items then were selected according to the following criteria: (1) the apparent validity of the items; (2) the ease and objectivity of the scoring of the item; and (3) such practical considerations as the time necessary to administer the item, the subject's interest in the item, and the need for including a variety of types of items in the final test. (About 30 percent more items were included in the provisional scale thus established than were included in the final scale.) The next step was to train examiners to administer the provisional scale properly. They were given two months of closely supervised training.

Great care was given to the selection of the children (the standardization population) on whom the test was to be standardized. All subjects of the first standardization were *American-born, white children*. In order to ensure proper geographical distribution, children from seventeen different communities of the country were selected. Rural as well as urban children were proportionately included. A tabulation of the socioeconomic levels of the children's parents was made, and the population was matched with that taken from a census report. Care also was taken to use a representative sample of both preschool and older children, since such children were not randomly available. A total of 3,184 subjects was used in the first standardization of the test.

Following this preliminary part of the standardization, the least satisfactory test items were eliminated, and the test blanks were rechecked by the various examiners for accuracy of scoring. The test items that were retained then were statistically reexamined and given their final age placement according to difficulty. Reliability and validity studies were conducted. (These are still being continued with the present scales.) Thus, the standardization of the *New Revised Stanford-Binet* involved (1) selection of suitable test items; (2) perfection of methods of administration; (3) adequate sampling of the population for standardization purposes; (4) determination of the test norms; and (5) continuing studies relating to the reliability and validity of the test. This simplified account gives evidence of the variety of procedures and the great amount of labor involved in the standardization of the psychological test.

A few comments may be relevant in order to emphasize some of the critical issues presented earlier. This original intelligence scale, as well as the later revision in 1960, certainly reflects the great care and effort that went into their development. Nevertheless, the *norms* of the test are based on *selected strata of our society*. Thus, any individual who is from another sector is being compared with those of this sector. To the extent that these different sectors reflect differences in language, cultural experience, and educational experience, the test results are necessarily biased to the extent that such factors influence the test results. And, as we have seen, such differences can be very significant.

The other point that needs to be underscored is that even though the *test is standardized, the testing of an individual can never be standardized,* no matter how faithfully test directions are followed. Individual testers use varying methods of developing rapport, administer the test items in their own, unique style, and respond to the examinee's test answers in differing ways. On the other side of the picture, the examinee may differ from the norms of those who were used in the standardization procedure in terms of such variables as motivation in taking the test, reactions to failure, and interpersonal behavior, quite apart from cultural differences. Thus, although a test may be very well standardized, the test data that are actually obtained never really are; they *always* need to be interpreted.

ASSESSMENT OF INTELLECTUAL FACTORS

There are several types of tests for determining the intellectual capacities of children. We shall discuss some of the more widely used of these tests in the following pages.

Intelligence Tests

First we shall briefly discuss the early history of intelligence testing and then discuss some specific tests. The term *mental test* was first used in American psychological literature by Cattell (1890). At that time, Cattell was interested in determining the intellectual capacities of college students. The tests he devised and employed involved, predominantly, sensory and perceptual functions, such as vision, reaction times, and memory. This was in keeping with the emphasis placed on such functions by psychologists at that time. It was thought that tests of such functions would provide measures of the individual's intellectual capacities. This approach was criticized by Binet and Henri (1895), in France, who felt that measures of sensory and perceptual functions were not adequate indices of intellectual capacities. Their belief was shared by other psychologists.

In 1904, the Minister of Public Instruction in Paris became concerned about children who were not responding adequately to instruction in the public schools, and he appointed a commission to study the matter. This Commission included Binet and Henri. As part of their attack on the problem, they devised an intelligence test in an attempt to classify the children according to their capacities to learn and to profit from classroom instruction. Although they included some sensory and perceptual items in their test, they stressed language items. This first scale was modified by Binet and Henri in 1908 and was further modified by them in 1911. The test was first used in America by Henry Goddard at the training school for mentally retarded children at Vineland, New Jersey. The most widely used early American revision of the Binet test was published in 1916 by Terman and Merrill. Thus, the modern intelligence testing movement is about seventy years old.

The changes that have occurred in the concepts of intelligence and intellectual functioning have made it necessary to revise our thinking concerning intelligence tests. As we have indicated, it is essential that cognitive abilities be assessed in the best possible manner. There is considerable doubt, however, whether our present instruments (intelligence tests) really do the job that we would like them to do.

Gallagher and Moss (1963) have discussed some implications of the more modern concepts of intelligence as they pertain to the evaluation of mentally retarded children. They state that four major generalities regarding measures of intelligence are commonly accepted. We summarize these as follows:

1. It is agreed that intelligence test scores are not too stable in children. They may fluctuate widely during the first ten years of a child's life. (It is the experience of Hutt and Gibby, supported by research studies, that the greater the maladjustment of the child, the greater the likelihood that there will be significant variability in intelligence test scores.)
2. The same intelligence tests measure different cognitive functions at different ages.
3. Each test measures only a small part of the complex phenomenon we call intelligence. There are (as we shall see later in this chapter) many intelligence tests, each purporting to measure various abilities and cognitive functions. But these tests tap only a portion of the total number of cognitive abilities of the child. It may well be that some of the more important and fundamental factors are as yet unknown and therefore are not evaluated by our present instruments.
4. Intelligence tests have three major functions that often are confused with each other. These are (1) to predict school performance; (2) to determine the patterning of abilities in a given child; and (3) to provide information leading to clarification of the child's problems.

Since the time of the Binet tests, many different types of intelligence tests have been developed for use with children. They may be classified as follows: (1) individual tests, (2) group (paper and pencil) tests, (3) verbal tests, and (4) performance tests. Each of these will be discussed in the following sections.

A given intelligence test may be an individual verbal test, an individual performance test, a group verbal test, or a group nonverbal (or performance) test.

The particular intelligence test should be carefully selected so as to correspond to the developmental experiences of the child. Any interpretation of a test depends on its particular characteristics as well as those of the child who is being tested. When told of the results of an intelligence test, we must always ask: "What type of test was administered?" and "Was this type of test suitable for this child?"

Individual Intelligence Tests. As the name implies, an individual intelligence test is a test that has been developed for administration to only one person at a time. This type of test usually provides us with the best possible estimate of the child's intellectual level. Since the examiner has to interact with only one person, he can form a suitable relationship with the child during the period of test administration and can provide suitable motivation for the test.

Because the examiner is able to make more valid observations of the child's reactions and behavior, he is better able to interpret the test results. In the optimal situation the examiner who administers the test also should be selected so that, by virtue of ethnic-social background, that examiner is most likely to promote maximum rapport with the examinee.

Group (Paper-and-Pencil) Tests. Group intelligence tests are designed to be given to a number of children simultaneously. A class of children or an entire small school, for example, may be examined at the same time. This type of test has the advantage of being a considerable time-saver, since test results may be secured for a group of children in the same length of time it would ordinarily take to secure results on one child by means of individual examination. However, group tests do not permit the examiner to make extensive behavioral observations of each child. Opportunities for developing and evaluating interpersonal relationships are not as adequate as in individual examinations. The results of a group test are, in general, not as valid as those obtained with an individual intelligence test. The greatest value of group tests is their use as a general screening instrument to determine the possible need for more detailed assessment of certain children.

Paper-and-pencil tests consist of a series of questions or tasks that are printed on paper. This printed material is given to the child, who is required to perform the task or answer the question by writing on the test blank. Instructions, however, may be given orally by an examiner. Most group tests of intelligence are paper-and-pencil tests. The content of such tests may involve either verbal or performance skills.

Verbal Tests. Verbal tests require the use of language by the child. Such tests may be of the individual or group variety. The questions require language comprehension, and the child responds verbally. These are examples of verbal test questions: "If you bought nine cents' worth of candy and gave the clerk a dime, how much change would you get back?" "When is Lincoln's birthday?" There are many types of verbal items. For example, they may deal with reasoning capacities ("What makes a sailboat move?"), with memory ("Repeat after me: I saw a pretty little dog on the street"); and with verbal proficiency ("What does *scorch* mean?"). The use of such tests presupposes that the child has had the average exposure (for a child of that age) to language experience and has no auditory or speech difficulties that would significantly affect the test results. If these assumptions are not correct, a verbal test is not applicable and will not yield a vaild measure of intellectual capacities.

Performance Tests. Performance tests are nonverbal and do not require any significant use of language by the child. In many tests of this type, instructions can be given in pantomime. The familiar formboard, in which the child is required to place differently shaped blocks in their proper holes, is an example of a performance test. Tests of this kind are useful in a variety of situations. The child's background may have been so impoverished that he did not have ade-

TABLE 11.1. Illustration of Calculation of MA

Year Level	No. of Items Passed	MA Credits
8	all (basal age)	8 yrs. 0 mos.
9	5	10 mos.
10	4	8 mos.
11	3	6 mos.
12	0	0 mos.
		MA = 10 yrs. 0 mos.

quate experience with language; he might have come from a foreign country; or he might suffer from auditory or speech defects that impair responses on verbal tests. In such cases, a performance test may give a more valid estimate of the child's intellectual capacities than a verbal test. Obviously, performance tests should not be used if the child has physical or sensory defects (such as a crippled hand or extremely poor vision) that would significantly impair test performance. As in the case of the verbal tests, performance tests may be either individual or group tests, but, as might be expected from the nature of such tests, most are devised for individual administration.

The results of many studies show that performance tests do not correlate highly with verbal tests of intelligence. Thus, it may be said that verbal and performance tests do not measure the same kinds of intellectual functions. Each type of test contributes uniquely to the assessment of the intellectual capacities of the retarded child.

Mental Age Concept

Items on an intelligence test may be arranged (*ordered*) according to their difficulty. For example, we could group several test items that could be successfully completed by average ten-year-old children but not by average eight-year-old children. In theory, we might expect that an average ten-year-old child would be able to pass all items at the ten-year and lower levels and would fail all items above the ten-year level. However, that is not the case. A ten-year-old child with average intelligence usually is able to pass most of the items at the ten-year level, may fail an item or so at lower levels, and may pass an item or so at higher levels. Thus, as illustrated in Table 11.1, this child's test results add up to a total mental age of ten years. This fact is illustrated with successes and passes on the items of the 1960 edition of the *Stanford-Binet Intelligence Scale*.

We should be very careful to understand the *meaning* of a given mental age (MA). If a child of eight has an MA of ten years, it does not mean that this child is exactly *like* an average ten-year-old child. Because he may not have had some experiences appropriate for the test, because of emotional factors, and because of certain maturational factors in which children differ, an eight-year-old child with an MA of ten is different from both a ten-year-old child and a twelve-year-old child, each with an MA of ten years. An MA of ten years simply means that, on a particular test, a child achieved successes that are achieved by average ten-year-old children. Similarly, if a child of eight years achieves an MA of six years, it does not mean that she is exactly *like* an average six-year-old child. It means that the child achieved, on that test, successes that are ordinarily achieved by the average six-year-old child. Therefore, we cannot evaluate mental age by itself—we must consider it in relation to the chronological age of the child.

One convenient way of expressing this relationship is through the use of the *intelligence quotient (IQ)*. This quotient expresses the ratio of the mental age to the chronological age *(CA)* of the child. It is calculated by means of the following formula:

$$IQ = \frac{MA}{CA} \times 100$$

(The quotient is multiplied by 100 to eliminate the decimal point.) Thus, if a ten-year-old child has an MA of ten years, he has an IQ of 100. If a twelve-year-old child has an MA of sixteen, he has an IQ of 133. If a ten-year-old child has an MA of seven, he has an IQ of 70.

Thus, children with the same mental age may differ widely from each other and do not necessarily function in the same way. A child with a CA of eight years and an MA of ten years differs from a child with a CA of twelve years and an MA of ten years—the former child is *brighter*. The IQ thus may be considered an index that expresses the brightness of a particular child.

Objections to the Mental Age Concept

As we have implied in the previous discussion, the mental age concept has certain limitations. The most general limitation is that the mental age is an *average score* obtained on test items from various age levels. Therefore, the MA does not completely and accurately characterize the mental ability of all persons whose average score is the same. (This limitation applies to all averages.)

David Wechsler (1944) offered another objection to the use of the MA as a basis for obtaining the IQ. He points out, and in our opinion quite rightly, that the use of MA limits the possible range of scores that may be made on a particular intelligence test. One reason for this, as many studies have shown, is that, on the average, MA scores do not continue to increase with increasing chronological age. A person sixty years of age obviously does not have an MA of sixty years, even if average in intelligence. If the test is too easy, then the top MA obtained on that test will tend to be too low. *Mental age is only a score.* If the test on which it is based is an easy one, then subjects will tend to achieve the maximum score at a lower age (on the average) than if the test is a more difficult one. On the easier test, therefore, a high MA may not be indicative of the person's true intellectual capacities. Such a score may be misleading. Wechsler offers the example of an individual who achieves an MA of twenty years on a test. This score can be interpreted as (1) the average mental age of a person twenty years of age, or (2) a score higher than that of the average person but expressed in terms of mental age. Since there is a point at which MA scores cease to increase with increasing chronological age, Wechsler feels that the MA cannot be adequately used to define levels of mental ability beyond that point.

Wechsler also objected to the use of the CA as a divisor in computing an IQ. He stated that the CA also is a score—it is the number of months a person has lived. It may be worthwhile to quote Wechsler's argument:

> An intelligence quotient is the ratio between a particular score which an individual gets (on a given intelligence test) and the score which an average individual of his life age may be assumed to attain on the same test, when both scores are expressed in the same notation (e.g., in terms of months and year). The usual formula:

$$IQ = \frac{MA}{CA}$$

should be really stated as follows:

$$IQ = \frac{\text{Attained or actual score}}{\text{Expected mean score for age}}$$

According to Wechsler, then, the intelligence quotient defines *relative* intelligence. It has been assumed by many authorities to be largely constant, but, as Wechsler stresses, many studies indicate that it does not remain constant when extreme groups (such as bright or retarded children) are studied, although it does tend to remain *relatively* constant for children ranking at about an average level.* He also points out that, in practice, we cannot use the person's actual CA as the denominator in arriving at the IQ—rather, we must use the CA beyond which MA has been demonstrated *not* to increase (for the particular test). When we use a fixed denominator for ages beyond that point, then we assume that mental ability is constant with increasing age after the critical level is reached. When this procedure is followed we actually are comparing individuals not with those of their own age group but, rather, with a highly selected group, probably of superior persons. We thus are computing what probably is an *efficiency quotient* rather than an intelligence quotient. To summarize, Wechsler objects to the usual practice of using the MA in arriving at the IQ on the following grounds: (1) The IQ is not equally constant in all ranges of intelligence; it is relatively constant only around the average range. (2) The IQ is not constant for all ages, because a linear relationship between MA and CA is not maintained. (3) IQs computed for adult subjects are really efficiency quotients.

In the standardization of his own intelligence scale, Wechsler eliminated the use of the MA but retained that of the IQ. However, on his test the IQ merely defines a person's relative position in the particular group with which that person is being compared (his own age group). The IQ is computed by directly comparing the number of points achieved on the test with a distribution

---

* See discussion of constancy of intelligence quotient later in this chapter.

of the scores achieved by the standardization group of the same age. Wechsler feels that this is a much more adequate procedure than the use of the MA in arriving at the IQ because (1) it does not require assumptions about relationships between mental and chronological ratings of growth; (2) it does not require that we use any fixed average adult MA, as each age defines its own denominator; (3) the IQs obtained have some meaning at all age levels; and (4) the obtained IQ retains the only important meaning of an intelligence quotient—as an index of relative brightness.

Some Individual Intelligence Tests for Children

Many intelligence tests have been constructed during the past several years—far too many to review in detail in this volume. However, we shall review several of the most important and most commonly used individual intelligence tests. The ones that we shall discuss are (1) the Terman-Merrill revisions of the *Stanford-Binet Scales* (essentially verbal), (2) the *Wechsler Intelligence Scale for Children*—Revised (combining both verbal and nonverbal scales), (3) the *Wechsler Preschool and Primary Scale of Intelligence,* (4) the *Peabody Picture Vocabulary Test,* (5) the *Porteus Maze Test,* and (6) the *Standard Progressive Matrices Test.*

The Stanford-Binet Scales. The original Stanford revision of the *Binet-Simon Intelligence Test* (developed by Terman) was first published in America in 1916. It continued to be the most widely used individual test of intelligence until *new revisions of the scale* by Terman and Merrill, first published in 1937, gradually took its place. As pointed out by Terman and Merrill, the revision was necessary because most psychologists who had been using the original 1916 scale felt that (1) it did not provide adequate measures of intelligence at either end of the scale (at either the very young or the adult levels); (2) it was inadequately standardized; (3) no alternate form was available for retesting purposes; and (4) many items on the 1916 scale had become dated. For these reasons, among others, Lewis M. Terman and Maud A. Merrill undertook the tremendous task of constructing what amounted to two entirely new tests of intelligence. The two forms of the test were different in specific content, but equivalent in "difficulty, range reliability, and validity." Terman and Merrill called the first form *Form L* and the second, *Form M.* They believed that these new scales covered a wider chronological age range, were more adequately standardized, provided a richer sampling of abilities, and had more rigidly defined procedures than the 1916 scale. Both revisions used the basic assumptions of Binet's mental age scale of measuring intelligence.

Each form contained a total of 120 test items. (The earlier form of the test contained 90 items.) Each form of the 1937 scale extended from the two-year level to the Superior Adult III level, so it is applicable to individuals ranging in age from early childhood to the adult level. The items are arranged, or grouped, by age levels. The test items, of course, increase in difficulty from one year level to the next.

In 1973, a further revision of the *Stanford-Binet Scales* was provided (Terman and Merrill, 1973) in which the best items from the previous L and M forms were selected and up-dated. New norms, including revised IQ tables obtainable directly from standard scores and percentile rankings also were provided.

Table 11.2 presents a representative list of types of items from the 1960 revision of the *Stanford-Binet Scale*. It also indicates the number of months of credit that is given for successfully passing the items.

In administering the test, the subject is given items from the several levels to establish a *basal age* (the highest level at which all items are passed) and a *maximal age* (the lowest level at which the subject fails all of the items). All of the items at the intervening year levels also are administered. Credit (in terms of mental age) is given for each of the items passed. These partial credits then are added to the basal age as was indicated in Table 11.1.

It is assumed that the child taking the test would have passed all items below the *basal age* if they had been administered, and similarly, it is assumed that the child would have failed all items above the *maximal age*. However, if there is an unusual pattern of responses or if, for some other reason, the examiner suspects that these assumptions are not valid in a particular case, items above the maximal or below the basal may be administered.

As we have noted earlier, Hutt (1947) has demonstrated that children with poor adjustment tend to be unduly handicapped by the standard procedure of administering the items of the test from the lower levels at which all items are passed to the highest level at which all items are failed. The major reason for this unfair effect with such children appears to be their relatively greater unfavorable reaction to frustration than is the case with well-adjusted children. The significance of this frustration factor is especially relevant for retarded children. In their comments about the Hutt proposal (that of *adaptive testing* rather than *consecutive testing*), Terman and Merrill state (1960, p. 48): "The *adaptive method* of alternating hard and easy tests suggested by Hutt seems to us to offer inadequately demonstrated advantages to offset the complications introduced by so many individual variations." Quite apart from the fact that subsequent research has confirmed Hutt's findings (see Frandsen, McCullough, and Stone, 1950; Carter and Bowles, 1948) and leads to more valid results (Watson, 1951), Terman and Merrill's assertion seems to be specious for several reasons.

First, Terman and Merrill's assumption that the "standardized procedure" provides the same conditions for all subjects taking the test can easily be shown to be false. Even when two subjects are given precisely the same subtests over the same year levels, *they do not have equivalent experiences with test materials.* They may, for instance, pass or fail different items of the several subtests and therefore have differing amounts and kinds of test experience. More typically, two different subjects who attain the same MA, may, as we have shown previously, derive this total MA by different combinations of items passed at different age levels.

Second, "the complications introduced by so many individual variations" are already present in the standard procedure. Even Terman and Merrill (1960, p. 48) state: "The accepted practice is to limit changes in test order to *practical* requirements of testing. Thus, it is sometimes [sic] advisable, in order to secure the child's effort when a certain type of test . . . is found to arouse resistance, to *shift* [our emphasis] to a more agreeable task." In fact, as any ex-

TABLE 11.2 Representative Items from the 1960 Terman-Merrill Revision of the Stanford-Binet (Form L)

Year Level	Number of Items	Credit for Each Item (Months)	Representative Item
II	6	1	A card with pictures of common objects is shown. The child is asked to identify the objects.
II-6	6	1	The child is asked to repeat a series of two digits.
III	6	1	The child is asked to copy a circle.
III-6	6	1	The child is asked to tell about a picture.
IV	6	1	The child is asked to name objects from memory.
IV-6	6	1	The child is asked to discriminate similar and dissimilar pictures.
V	6	1	The child is asked to define words.
VI	6	2	The child is shown pictures of common objects with parts missing. He is asked to name the missing parts.
VII	6	2	The child is shown pictures depicting absurd situations. He is asked to recognize the absurdity.
VIII	6	2	The child is asked to define a series of words.
IX	6	2	A series of absurd situations is related, and the child is asked to identify the absurdity.
X	6	2	The child is asked to repeat a series of six digits.
XI	6	2	The child is asked to define abstract words.
XII	6	2	The child is asked to repeat a series of digits backwards.
XIII	6	2	The child is asked to repeat sentences.
XIV	6	2	The child is asked to reconcile words with opposite qualities.
Average adult	8	2	The subject is asked to give the difference between pairs of abstract words.
Superior adult I	6	4	The subject is asked to give the similarity between pairs of words.
Superior adult II	6	5	The subject is asked to reconcile pairs of words that have opposite meanings.
Superior adult III	6	6	The subject is asked to explain proverbs.

344

perienced clinical psychologist can attest, it is precisely those children from disadvantaged cultures and with emotional disturbances who require adaptions in the testing procedure (see Carter and Bowles, 1948). Thus, "complications" are present in all test situations and particularly in atypical situations—and it is for these situations that *adaptive testing,* following some simple *principles* rather than mechanical *format,* is recommended.

Third, and most relevant, if the aim of intelligence testing is to obtain the most adequate assessment of current intellectual functioning, then the empirical question is: "Which procedure produces the most valid results?" We, and others, have demonstrated that for the maladjusted individuals, adaptive testing does precisely this. One highly significant finding is that, in the case of maladjusted children, the MA obtained with *adaptive testing* correlates more highly with the vocabulary level than does the MA obtained with *consecutive testing.* The vocabulary level on the Stanford-Binet is the best single predictor of the total MA on that scale. That is why we have questioned the "accepted practice." If that practice is better, where are the data to support it?

The latest revision of the Binet test by Terman and Merrill was published in 1960, and a revised manual for administering and interpreting the results was published in 1973 (Terman and Merrill, 1973). The 1960 revision retains the essential characteristics of the preceding *Stanford-Binet* tests, but incorporates in one form the most valid subtests from Forms L and M of the 1937 scales. The latest test is called the *L-M Form.* The criteria for selection of the test items were (1) increase in percent passing at a given age (or mental age) and (2) validity, which was determined by biserial correlation of the item score with the total test score. Some subtests were found to have changed in difficulty since the time of the original standardization, and these were either relocated at a more appropriate age level or dropped entirely.

Previously accumulated standardization data showing the distribution of IQs by age on the 1937 scales demonstrated that the obtained IQs showed atypical variability at certain age levels. In the 1960 revision, Terman introduced conversion tables to correct for such atypical variability, so the average mental age derived by use of the L-M form of the scale more nearly corresponds to the average chronological age at each age level. Therefore, the IQ is, in effect, a standard score that is more directly comparable for all chronological age groups. Revised IQ tables were provided in 1972.

Cronbach (1970) has summarized the following shortcomings of the 1937 *Stanford-Binet* scale: (1) The scores on the *Stanford-Binet* do not reflect native capacity; they are affected by previous educational experiences. (2) The subtests are essentially verbal. (3) There is evidence to indicate that cultural differences affect the test scores. (4) Scores at different levels represent different mental abilities. (5) The varying standard deviations affect the various IQ distributions. (6) The scores are affected by emotional involvements. (7) Specific mental abilities cannot be defined by use of the test.

Although these criticisms were aimed at the 1937 revision of the Binet scales, they apply just as well to the 1960 revision, since the materials have not been modified. Despite these significant limitations, the *Stanford-Binet* test is one of the most widely used tests of intelligence. The clinician deals with its weaknesses by also employing other tests, which are designed to measure the areas in which the Binet is inadequate.

Hoefstdetter (1954) performed a factor analysis of the items on the *Stanford-Binet*. It was found that the test does measure a general factor (called "Manipulation of Symbols") above four years of age. Below two years of age "Sensori-motor Alertness" is a highly significant factor, and from two to four years "Persistence" is a critical factor.

The L-M form of the *Stanford-Binet* has been used extensively for the evaluation of retarded children, and some validation studies have been published. A typical study is that of Rohrs and Haworth (1962), who compared the 1960 Binet test with two older intelligence tests: the *Wechsler Intelligence Scale for Children (WISC)* and the *Goodenough Draw-a-Man* test. The primary purpose of the study was to determine the degree of agreement between the 1960 *Stanford-Binet* and each of the other two tests. But in addition, Rohrs and Haworth attempted to determine the degree to which the Binet test scatter pattern served to differentiate familial from organic brain-damaged mental defectives.

A total of forty-six subjects were studied; of these, twenty were diagnosed as *familial* and twenty-six as *organic*. The mean IQ for the familial group was 61.05, while the mean IQ for the organic group was 61.15. The mean age of the familial group was 12.5 years, and that of the organic group was 12.4 years. For the group as a whole, the mean IQ was 61.12, with a standard deviation of 5.45; the mean age was 12.5 years, with a standard deviation of 1.98; and the mean length of institutionalization was 3.28 years.

Rohrs and Haworth found, for the total group, that the mean *Stanford-Binet* IQ was 56.91, the mean *WISC* IQ (Full Scale) was 52.76, and the mean *Goodenough Draw-a-Man* IQ was 56.46. The difference between the *Stanford-Binet* and *WISC* IQs was found to be statistically significant, whereas that between the *Stanford-Binet* and *Goodenough* quotients was not significant. It also was concluded that the scatter patterns on the L-M form of the *Stanford-Binet* test did not differentiate validly between the familial and organic mentally retarded children. Similar results have been reported in other studies.

In an excellent review of the use of Form L-M of the *Stanford-Binet* with retarded individuals, Himmelstein (1968) found that this instrument showed substantial relationship with other tests of intelligence. It is a good predictor of social maturity, of learning, and of some specific attributes of intelligence for the retarded individual.

The Wechsler Intelligence Scale for Children — Revised. As pointed out in the previous section, the *Terman-Merrill* tests are based on the mental age concept, and the test items are grouped at their appropriate levels. Since each year level includes different test items, the items given to a particular child will vary with chronological age and intellectual capacities. Thus, test items given to an average ten-year-old child are different from those given to an average eight-year-old child, although there may be some overlap at the upper extreme of items for the eight-year-old and the lower extreme of items for the ten-year-old. The *Wechsler scale (WISC–R)* (Wechsler, 1974) is constructed in an entirely different manner. Each child is given the same test items regardless of mental or chronological age; there are no groupings of items according to year level. The child is given credit for each item passed. The score consists of the total weighted credits earned on all subtests (the raw subtest scores are converted into weighted scores, and these are totaled). This total weighted score is converted directly into an IQ by means of tables for each chronological age group. The younger the child, the higher the IQ allotted to a particular total weighted score. A ten-year-old child achieving a total weighted score of 80 thus would score a higher IQ than a twelve-year-old child achieving the same score.

The *WISC-R* is divided into two major sections: (1) a verbal scale, yielding a verbal IQ, and (2) a performance scale, giving a performance IQ. Scores on both sections are combined to get a full-scale IQ. Each section consists of five subtests plus a supplementary (or alternate) subtest. However, unlike the previous edition of this test (Wechsler, 1949), it is now recommended that verbal and performance subtests be administered alternately. The subtests of the *WISC-R* are the following:

Verbal Scale:

Information. The child is asked questions to tap his fund of general information.
Similarities. The child is asked to indicate how paired objects are similar.
Arithmetic. The child is asked to solve mentally some arithmetic problems.
Vocabulary. The child is asked to define, in his own words, a number of words.
Comprehension. The child is asked to deal with problems involving common situations.
Digit Span (Supplementary). The child is asked to repeat a series of numbers and also is asked to repeat a series of numbers backwards.

Performance Scale:

Picture Completion. The child is presented with a series of pictures each of which has something missing. He is asked to state what is missing in each picture.
Picture Arrangement. The child is asked to rearrange each of a series of mixed-up pictures so that they are in the correct, temporal order.
Block Design. The child is given a series of problems involving colored blocks and asked to reconstruct a design shown on the test card.
Object Assembly. The child is asked to assemble pieces (like in a jigsaw puzzle) so as to construct the appropriate object.
Coding. The child is asked to complete sheets according to a code consisting of various symbols.
Mazes. The child is asked to complete a series of mazes on paper.

The *WISC-R* is designed for use with children from six through fifteen years. This revision was completed in order to provide more up-to-date content than the previous edition of the test and to provide a better normative sample. The 1974 edition is based on a stratified sample of children, including both black and other nonwhite groups as well as whites, in the same proportions as those reported in the 1970 U.S. census. The standardization population consisted of 2,200 subjects.

Both the original 1949 version of the *WISC* and the present revision, the *WISC-R*, differ in several important respects from the *Stanford-Binet Scales*. In the first place, the *WISC-R* discards the concept of MA entirely, since Wechsler believes that this measure has several inherent difficulties: similar MAs of children with differing CAs mean different things; the IQ derived from the usual formula involving the MA as the numerator and CA as the denominator is not equivalent for differing CAs and differing IQs; and, the problem of defining the adult norm or adult MA is confusing because of problems with the nature of the mental growth curve (Wechsler, 1974). The IQ is calculated directly from the test score by means of tables based on the variability of scores at the age of the examinee. Although this solves some of the issues that Wechsler has raised, the unavailability of the MA score limits the usefulness of the test score in terms of educational planning since the MA is an indicator (if not an entirely adequate one) of current, general learning potential.

The major differences in content of the Wechsler from the Binet type of scales are that (1) all of the subtests are given to all examinees, thus making scores more directly comparable, and (2) verbal and performance tasks are given equal emphasis. These characteristics make the test especially valuable in clinical diagnosis and in clinical predictions.

We should emphasize again, that despite the *representativeness* of the sample on which the test was standardized, the problem of *evaluating* the meaning of the test score for persons with differing personal-social-cultural background experiences is not thereby solved. In evaluating the meaning of the findings, careful analysis must be made of the possible impact of such factors on the test results.

Statistical analysis of the *WISC-R* for reliability revealed that the split-half correlations, usually between scores on even and odd items, with an N of 200 for each age group between 6 years 6 months and 16 years 6 months were: .94 for the verbal scale, .90 for the performance scale, and .96 for the full scale. The test shows good internal consistency. Wechsler also presents stability coefficients over an interval of about one month for six selected age groups, the total N being 303. These correlation coefficients are of about the same order as the test-retest coefficients, confirming the test's reliability. Nevertheless, Wechsler reports mean gains on the second IQ scores over the first IQ scores as: 3½ points for the verbal scale; 9½ points for the performance scale; and, 7 points on the full scale. Thus, there clearly are important practice effects that should be taken into account if a child is retested.

Validity of the *WISC-R* is based primarily on the validation studies done with the original scale. In addition, correlation coefficients were obtained for four groups of normal children, fifty subjects in each group, with the Stanford-Binet IQ. In general, the two tests correlate about .73 in terms of IQ. Similar results are reported by Zimmerman and Woo-Sam (1972). Thus, although the two scales show a substantial amount of correlation, they are by no means equivalent. The reported correlation indicates that the commonality is only about 53 percent.

More data on these and other features of the statistical qualities are currently available for the earlier version of the test than for the present version. We turn our attention to such findings now.

Thorn, Schulman, and Kasper (1962) have reported on the reliability and stability of the *WISC* when used with retarded boys. They studied a group of thirty-nine mentally retarded boys, whose chronological ages ranged from eleven years to fourteen years eleven months. The range in verbal IQ for the group was 49 to 79, the range in performance IQ was 33 to 87, and the range in full-scale IQ was 36 to 69. Thorn and his co-workers retested their subjects with the WISC after a three- to four-month interval. They reported the following test-retest correlation coefficients: full-scale IQ, 95; verbal IQ, .92; performance IQ, .89. They also reported that the test-retest correlation coefficients for the subtests of this scale were highly reliable. It may be concluded that *under the conditions of this study*, the WISC was a reliable intelligence test for mentally retarded children over a short period of time.

Baumeister (1964) has provided us with an excellent review of the use of the WISC with mentally retarded children. This test is very widely used for the assessment of mental retardation. However, as Baumeister states, it was not designed by Wechsler to test severely retarded persons, since the lowest obtainable full-scale IQ score is 46. This *floor* effect, aside from lowering the reliability of scores at the low extremes, represents a severe limitation in measurement. In an effort to overcome this effect, Ogdon (1960) has extrapolated the full-scale IQ downward.

Baumeister has provided a summary of the correlations reported for the WISC with other intelligence tests in the appraisal of retarded subjects. His results are reproduced in Table 11.3 (p. 352). Baumeister concluded that even though the floor effect does affect the reliability of the lowest scores, the WISC IQ scores of persons who are not severely retarded appear to be reasonably stable and reliable. However, he notes that there are some indications that scores on the performance subtests of this scale are likely to be influenced by practice. He finds that the WISC score probably can be used to predict school achievements in both verbal and manual learning with some validity. He also feels that it will predict a *Stanford-Binet* IQ quite well.

However, there are some objections to the use of the WISC and WISC–R as diagnostic instruments with retarded children. Cultural-familial and undifferentiated retarded children score higher on the performance scale than on the verbal scale, whereas brain-damaged subjects appear to perform comparably on the two scales. Baumeister indicates that although pattern analysis based on variability among the WISC subtests is of limited value, factor analytic studies suggest that qualitatively, retarded and normal children perform differently on the WISC.

Davis (1966) studied the internal consistency of the WISC with the mentally retarded at three different levels of functioning. He used a total of 142 subjects, who were divided into three groups: borderline, mildly retarded, and moderately retarded. There were fifty subjects in the moderately retarded group, with a mean chronological age of 12.92. There were fifty subjects in the mildly retarded group, with a mean chronological age of 11.86. There were forty-two subjects in the borderline group, with a mean chronological age of 11.17. The WISC was administered individually to each subject, and odd-even reliability coefficients were computed for nine of the subjects, as well as for the verbal, performance, and full-scale IQs. All of these subtests were corrected by means of the Spearman-Brown formula. Davis concluded that the intelligence scores showed a satisfactory degree of reliability and internal consistency at the three levels of retarded functioning displayed by his subjects.

Alper (1967) analyzed the use of the *Wechsler Intelligence Scale for Children* with institutionalized mentally retarded individuals. His study was based on 713 mentally retarded institutionalized children in fifteen different institutions in various areas of the country. Only complete *WISC* protocols of non-psychotic children from 5 years 1 month to 15 years 11 months in age were evaluated. One of his major hypotheses was that the subtest scores would not contribute equally to the total IQ score for mentally retarded children, as it was assumed they would for a sample of normal children. He concluded that "inequality rather than equality is the rule in regard to the contributions of the various subtests." It appeared that four of the subtests (comprehension and similarities among the verbal tests, and picture completion and object assembly among the performance tests) were contributing disproportionately to the total weighted score.

A second area of investigation dealt with sex differences on the various subtests. It was found that male subjects made higher mean scores on the subtests than did females; therefore, they made higher IQ scores. The IQ scores of the males were approximately 8 to 10 percent higher than those of the females. Additional statistical analyses revealed that sex was a differentiating factor on *all* of the subtests (the males obtaining higher scores) except similarities and coding. Males and females performed equally well on the similarities subtest, but females scored significantly higher on the coding subtest.

A third area of study was the relationship of variability in the subtest scores to the total IQ score. The results indicated that mentally retarded children scored higher on performance items than on verbal items. An examination of the verbal and performance IQs indicated that the performance scale IQs increased at a more rapid rate from level to level than did the verbal IQs. Alper noted four general findings relating to correlation of subtest with global IQ scores: (1) arithmetic correlated lowest with verbal scale IQ; (2) vocabulary correlated highest with verbal scale IQ; (3) coding correlated lowest with performance scale IQ; and, (4) object assembly correlated highest with performance scale IQ.

Since some retarded individuals show hearing impairment, Neuhaus (1969) developed a technique for presentation of the *WISC* performance subtest to children with profound hearing losses. The usual instructions are given in pantomime regardless of the child's ability to read lips. Since many children are unable to comprehend the directions for the picture arrangement test, in which they must put cards together to form a concept sequence, he developed special pictures to illustrate to the child how the picture arrangement task is to be completed.

Many investigators have been interested in developing a short form of the *Wechsler Intelligence Scale for Children* to reduce the time involved in the assessment process. Finley and Thompson (1958) developed a short form that, they report, correlates highly with the full *WISC*. Kilman and Fisher (1960) applied this abbreviated scale to the evaluation of both brain-damaged and familial retarded children. They examined 145 retarded children between the ages of eight and sixteen, then divided them into three groups: an undifferentiated group, with 70 children; a brain-damaged group, with 44 children; and a familial group, with 31 children. When the full-scale IQ was calculated by prorating the obtained short-form scores, there were no significant differences between the full- and short-form IQs. The authors reported the following correlations between short- and full-scale IQs: for the total sample, .87; for the undifferentiated group, .91; for the brain-damaged group, .80; and for the familial group, .80.

Short forms of intelligence tests do have some value. But an intelligence test should not be regarded as an instrument designed only to yield a score. One does not give any intelligence test merely to obtain an IQ. *The test provides an opportunity to interact with the child and to observe that child's behavioral reaction over a period of time.* Any reduction in test material thus reduces the interaction potentials between the examiner and the child. Further, the *WISC* provides a variety of different tasks through which various functions can be assessed. Any short form of the test reduces the amount of the total information available to the clinician for evaluation. Since the evaluative process should be as complete as possible, the use of a short form of an intelligence test is difficult to condone in the evaluation of a retarded child. It defeats the purpose of an adequate evaluation and has little place in the total assessment process if the results are to have value for the individual.

Table 11.3 summarizes some of the research findings with the *WISC*.

The Wechsler Preschool and Primary Scale of Intelligence. This scale (Wechsler, 1967) was developed for use with children under the age of 6½ years. Since the publication of this instrument, the range of the Wechsler scales reaches from early childhood through adulthood. Its use in the examination of younger retarded children seems valuable. However, the norms of this test, like those of most other intelligence tests, are not adequate for severely retarded children. As we noted earlier, Ogdon (1960) attempted to overcome this deficiency on the *WISC* by developing prorated scores. Silverstein (1969) used a similar method to extend the applicability of this new scale to lower intelligence levels. However, he agrees with Wechsler that an IQ score should *not* be calculated when the child does not score above zero on at least two of the verbal and two of the performance tests.

The Peabody Picture Vocabulary Test (PPVT). This test was developed by Dunn (1959) to assess the intellectual capacities of handicapped persons. Essentially, it is a modified picture vocabulary test. The subject is required to point to the best picture in each set of four possible responses or to say the number of the best picture in response to the stimulus word. One hundred and fifty picture plates are included in this test. The test is not timed, and it can be administered to the usual subject in ten to fifteen minutes. Designed to test the physically or verbally handicapped subject, it is of particular value in assessing the intellectual potentials of individuals who have difficulties in a prolonged testing situation.

TABLE 11.3 Studies in Which the WISC Has Been Correlated With Other Intelligence Tests in the Appraisal of Retarded Subjects

Investigator	N	Subjects Description	Age	IQ	Test	Correlations FS	VS	PS
Sloan & Schneider (1951)	40	Familial & Undifferent.	13.5	58	Arthur Performance	.79	.47	.83
Alper (1958)	30	Institut. Brain-Damaged or Familial	13.6	54	Arthur Adaptation of the Leiter International Performance Scale	.77	.40	.79
Condell (1959)	22	Chippewa Indians	10.3	..	Draw-A-Man	..	..	.57
Rohrs & Haworth (1962)	46	20 familial 20 organics	12.5	53	Draw-A-Man	.46	.28	.53
Warren & Collier (1960)	49	Institut.	12.1	61	Draw-A-Man	.43	..	..
Dunn & Brooks (1960)	56	Educable	12.75	66	Peabody Picture Vocabulary	.61	..	..
Kimbrell (1960)	62	Educable	13.8	..	Peabody Picture Vocabulary A —Form B—	.30	.43	NS
						.41	.41	NS
Reger (1962)	25	Institut.	9.9 to 14.6	..	Peabody Picture Vocabulary	.60	.60	.55
Condell (1959)	22	Chippewa Indians	10.3	..	Ammons Full Range Picture Vocabulary	..	..	.04
Warren & Collier (1960)	49	Institut.	12.1	61	Columbia Mental Mental Maturity Progressive	.68	..	..
Malpass, Brown, & Hake (1960)	104	56 Institut. 48 Pub. Sch.	11.7	65	Matrices	.51	..	..
Stacey & Carleton (1955)	150	Undifferent.	7.5 to 15.9	68	Colored Progressive Matrices	.55	.54	.52
Vanderhost, Sloan, & Bensberg (1953)	38	Undifferent. Institut.	15.1	62	Wechsler-Bellevue	.72	.54	.77
Condell (1959)	22	Chippewa Indians	10.3	..	Stanford-Binet (1937)	..	..	.57
Nale (1951)	104	Institut.	8.9 to 15.9	58	Stanford-Binet (1937)	.91	..	..
Sloan & Schneider (1951)	40	Familial & Undifferent.	13.5	58	Stanford-Binet (1937)	.49	.75	.64
Stacey & Levin (1951)	70	Institut.	11.9	66	Stanford-Binet (1937)	.68	.69	..
Sandercock & Butler (1952)	90	Institut.	13.0	58	Stanford-Binet (1937)	.76	.80	.66
Rohrs & Haworth (1962)	46	20 familial 20 organics	12.5	53	Stanford-Binet (1960)	.69	.72	.50
Webb (1963)	20	Negro Educable	15.7 (WISC) 17.1 (WAIS)	68	Wechsler Adult Intelligence Scale	.84	.80	.91
Webb (1964)	32	Educable	14.3 (WISC) 16.9 (WAIS)	67	Wechsler Adult Intelligence Scale	.91	.87	.83

352

Many studies have explored the relationships between the *PPVT* and other measures of the characteristics of the retarded child. It has been demonstrated that the *PPVT* correlated highly with measures of academic performance. For instance, Wolfensberger (1962) correlates *PPVT* scores with academic achievement scores, using sixty-one subjects with a mean age of 18.12 years and a mean *PPVT* mental age of 6.80 years. The obtained correlations between the *PPVT* scores and scholastic achievement scores were .52 with reading, .33 with spelling, and .35 with arithmetic. He concluded that the *PPVT* correlated significantly with measures of academic achievement.

Mein (1962) correlated the *PPVT* with the *Stanford-Binet* intelligence test. Eighty institutionalized subjects with a mean mental age of 58.7 months were studied. Mein reported a correlation coefficient of .71 between the two tests, and it may be concluded that they were moderately correlated with each other. However, this degree of correlation indicates that considerable discrepancies do occur in the results obtained for some individuals with these two tests.

Budoff and Purseglove (1963) investigated the reliability of the *PPVT* with mentally retarded children. They administered the tests to a group of forty-six retarded children on two separate occasions, one month apart. The same examiner administered both tests to each subject. A reliability coefficient of .80 was reported for the total sample. However, when the total sample was divided into high- and low-IQ subjects, the reliability coefficient for the low-IQ group was found to be moderately high, but the coefficient for the high-IQ group was found to be quite low. Budoff and Purseglove concluded that the usefulness of the *PPVT* in assessing the intellectual capacities of high-grade institutionalized delinquents is questionable.

Burnett (1965) studied the interrelationships of the *Peabody, Wechsler-Bellevue,* and *Stanford-Binet* tests with educable retarded children. He found a significant, but only medium, degree of correlation of the *Peabody* with the *Stanford-Binet* and *Wechsler-Bellevue* IQs. The correlations between the *Wechsler-Bellevue* IQs and the *Stanford-Binet* IQs were much more substantial. Burnett felt that the correlations of the *Peabody* with the *Wechsler-Bellevue* and the *Stanford-Binet* IQs probably were reduced because of the restricted range of intelligence and the age of the sample used. IQs obtained with the *Peabody* scale were found to be significantly higher than those obtained on both the *Wechsler-Bellevue* and the *Stanford-Binet* tests. Nevertheless, he felt that the *Peabody* test was a useful screening device for measuring the intelligence of emotionally disturbed, educable, mentally retarded adolescents.

These and other studies of the *PPVT* raise some important doubts about whether the results of this test are equivalent to those of other standard intelligence tests. Only within limited ranges of intelligence is this test as useful as the others. It may be regarded as a supplementary test that has special utility, especially for persons with limited verbal abilities.

A special problem of the *PPVT* must be borne in mind. It appears that the level of perceptual development is significantly related to *PPVT* scores (Allen et al., 1965). Hence, the IQ estimates based on this instrument may be misleading, especially in the case of mentally retarded individuals. When the perceptual development of a retarded person is disproportionately poor for both chronological age and mental age, the *PPVT* underestimates the individual's IQ. Similarly, when a retarded individual's perceptual development is significantly higher than mental age, the *PPVT* overestimates intellectual ability.

The Porteus Maze Test. The *Porteus Maze Test* consists of a series of increasingly difficult printed mazes that are given to the child to solve in an individual test situation. The mazes were developed by S. D. Porteus (1915), who worked with mentally defective children in Sydney, Australia, in 1913 and published the results of his work in 1915. The maze test has been used extensively since that time in evaluating the intellectual functions of mentally retarded children.

Porteus (1959) maintains that traditional psychological concepts of intelligence omit consideration of the child's *planning ability* as an essential component of intelligence. This ability, he states, includes *"prevision and prehearsal"* as necessary factors in the attainment of a goal. Porteus maintains that planning and foresight have been considered nonintellectual factors instead of fundamental components of all intelligent behavior. These two functions are supposed to be tapped by his maze test, which provides, according to Porteus, a better estimate of the social adjustment of the mentally retarded individual than does a test of intelligence like the *Stanford-Binet.*

There have been numerous studies on the validity of the *Porteus Maze Test.* These have been reviewed by Porteus (1959). An example of a study relating to the predictive value of the test is the research completed by Dentler and Mackler (1962), who studied the relationship of *Maze* scores to certain "functioning abilities" of retarded children. They stated that both the *Wechsler Intelligence Scale for Children* and the *Stanford-Binet Intelligence Test* measure functions that are essentially verbal. Further, both tests tend to ignore cultural, maturational, and situational factors. On the other hand, the *Porteus Maze Test* is more abstract and nonverbal, so Dentler and Mackler investigated the relationships between *Porteus* scores and measures of specific behavioral functions. The *Porteus Maze Test* and tests of language, social maturity, and accuracy of immediate surroundings were administered to twenty-nine institutionalized mentally retarded children. The mean chronological age of the subjects was 9.61, with a range of from 6.6 to 12.8 years, and the mean mental age was 5.5 years. Dentler and Mackler reported that the correlation between the *Porteus Maze Test* and the accuracy-of-the-surroundings test was .66, for the language test it was .71, and for the social maturity test it was .64. They concluded that the *Porteus Maze Test* was of value in predicting specific functional abilities of the retarded child. We agree that the *Porteus Maze* is an excellent supplementary instrument for assessing the capacities of the retarded child because it taps important functions not measured by either the *Wechsler* or the *Binet* type of intelligence tests.

The Standard Progressive Matrices. The revised form of this test consists of two major parts: the *Standard Progressive Matrices* (Sets A, B, C, D, and E) and the *Colored Progressive Matrices* (Sets A, AB, and B) (Raven, 1960). This is a unique type of test that may be especially useful for evaluating retarded children. Each of the tests is designed to test a restricted range of mental development. The *SPM* Sets A and B, plus the easier items of Set C, are in the range of most mentally retarded individuals. Each set consists of twelve plates and supposedly measures conceptual development. Subjects are asked to show the relationships between geometrical designs. Verbal responses are not required. The *CPM* provides vividly colored materials that are of interest, and pertinent, to children up to about eleven years in development.

Raven does not think of this instrument as a conventional intelligence test but rather as a test of observational and reasoning abilities. As such, the test supplements the IQ score and merits consideration. Scores on this test have fairly high correlations with such tests as the *WISC* for normal children (Malpass, et al., 1960). However, the correlations for retarded children are considerably lower. For them the correlations of *WISC* and *SPM* are generally reported to be in the .50 to .60 range (Stacey and Gill, 1955). Nevertheless, the validity of *Matrices* scores (especially on the *CPM*) for retarded children is presumed to be fairly good (Orme, 1961). Many clinicians seem favorably disposed to this instrument.

Tests for Infants and Very Young Children

The psychological tests discussed in the previous section were not specifically designed for use with very young children or infants. With the exception of the *Terman-Merrill,* they are more properly applicable to children of about school age and higher. The psychological examination of the infant poses unique problems that are not as pertinent in the examination of the older child. The infant cannot talk and is physically immature. The infant's visual-motor functions also are immature. Usually another person needs to be present during the examination to hold the infant. Because of social and emotional immaturity, an infant needs the presence of a familiar person—usually mother. Further, the infant cannot comprehend verbal instructions. For these reasons, the tests and scales developed for the infant are based essentially on sensory reactions and rudimentary motor skills.

The Gesell Developmental Schedules. Probably the best known and most widely used instrument for the psychological evaluation of infants is the *Gesell Developmental Schedules.* Gesell and his co-workers (Gesell, et al., 1949; Gesell and Amatruda, 1949) at Yale University developed a number of such schedules. They were standardized on infants as young as four weeks of age. They are unique in that Gesell conducted longitudinal studies; that is, he followed up (through retesting) the *same* group of children over a period of time. The schedules provide a means of evaluating the levels of behavior of the infant in four major areas:

1. *Motor Behavior.* Here both gross and fine motor reactions are evaluated. (How does the infant sit? Does he walk or creep? Does he reach for objects? Can he manipulate objects?)
2. *Adaptive Behavior.* This portion of the schedule is concerned with visual-motor reactions and solution of problems. (How does the infant react to the ringing of a bell or to a dangling object?)
3. *Language Behavior.* This area refers to all means of communication, in-

cluding reaction to attempts to communicate by others. (What changes occur in facial expressions, posture, gesture, and the like?)

4. *Personal-Social Behavior.* This involves the infant's reactions to the particular
social environment in which he is reared. (How does he play and feed? What
are his toilet training responses? Does he smile? How does he respond to other
persons?)

In administering these schedules, the essential role of the examiner is to
present test objects and to evaluate the responses made by the infant. In interpreting the nature of the infant's development, the examiner uses data obtained
through interviews with the parents (usually the mother).

These schedules, unlike the previously discussed tests, do not result in a
single score or IQ for the entire test. Rather, each of the four developmental
areas is evaluated by the examiner, sometimes on the basis of subjective
judgments, and a *developmental age* (in months) is assigned to the infant's performance in each. This is done by comparing (on a subjective basis) the infant's
reactions with the norms for infants and children at ages 4, 18, 28, and 40 weeks,
and at ages 12, 18, 24, and 36 months. In this way, the extent of the child's retardation may be estimated.

The Cattell Infant Intelligence Scale. Cattell (1947) has developed a
downward extension of *Form L* of the *Terman-Merrill Scales.* Included in this extension is material from *Form L* of those scales, selected material from the *Gesell
Development Scales,* and new test items devised by Cattell. The revised scale extends from a low chronological age of two months to a high age of 30 months.
The test items deal chiefly with perceptual and motor reactions. The scale yields
an IQ that is supposed to be comparable to that obtained on the *Stanford-Binet.*

Many other intelligence and developmental tests have been devised for
use with infants and young children. Characteristics of several of these are summarized in Table 11.4.

ASSESSMENT OF PERSONALITY
AND SOCIAL ADJUSTMENT

As we have noted, a very important part of the task of assessing the
mentally retarded child is the evaluation of personality characteristics. We first
will discuss the general characteristics of psychological tests designed for this
purpose, then consider some specific personality tests.

Characteristics of Personality Tests

Personality tests are designed to explore the emotional and adjustmental characteristics of the child. Like intelligence tests, they may be either
group or individual in nature. In general, the group forms of personality tests are
not suitable for administration to retarded children. One reason for this is that
the group type of test is not as valid as the individual type. The statements made
previously about group intelligence tests apply equally well to the group forms
of personality tests. In addition, most group tests assume that the child can read

TABLE 11.4.   Representative Intelligence Tests for Younger Children

Test	Age Range	Method of Reporting Results
California First Year Mental Scale	1 to 18 months	MA, IQ, and Standard Score
Cattell Infant Intelligence Scale	2 to 30 months	MA and IQ
Gesell Developmental Schedules	4 weeks to 36 months	Developmental age for each area evaluated
Gesell Preschool Schedule	15 months to 6 years	Developmental ages
Kuhlmann-Binet (1939 revision)	4 months upward	IQ
Merrill-Palmer Scale	24 to 36 months	MA, Percentile, Standard Score
Minnesota Preschool Scale	3 to 5 years	C-Scores
Northwestern Infant Intelligence	4 to 36 weeks	IQ
Oseretsky Tests of Motor Proficiency	4 to 16 years	Motor Age
Valentine Intelligence Scale	2 to 8 years	MA and IQ

adequately; therefore, the test items often are beyond the comprehension of the retarded child. Some persons have attempted to administer such tests to nonreading children by reading the test aloud to them and then writing down the children's responses, but such an approach is unsatisfactory, and it is unlikely that the results obtained in this manner are valid representations of the retarded child's personality characteristics. We prefer to use tests designed for individual administration that do not depend on the reading and writing abilities of the child.

Hutt (1945a) has indicated that personality tests may be *structured, partially structured,* or *unstructured* in form. The psychological tests previously discussed were, in general, highly standardized approaches to the measurement of the intellectual capacities of the child. The test tasks were specifically validated against various criteria of intellectual functioning and yield numerical scores that are considered to be indices of intellectual abilities. In general, intelligence tests, such as the 1960 *Stanford-Binet* and the *Wechsler,* are *structured.* The test material has clearly apparent meaning, and the task to be performed is delineated as clearly as possible for the subject—the subject is told as precisely as possible what to do. An *unstructured* test is one in which the test material is ambiguous and does not require a specific response by the child. The possible responses are almost unlimited. Unlike the response to the structured task, a response on this type of test is not considered either right or wrong; rather, it is evaluated by the examiner to obtain insight into the personality structure and functioning of the child. The task given to the child in an unstructured personality test, in contrast to that typical of the intelligence test, may be comparatively vague and nonspecific. *Unstructured* or *partially structured* personality tests are known as *projective tests*. We believe that they are among the most valuable of all types of personality tests.

Characteristics of Projective Tests

We have noted that on intelligence tests the child is given a highly specific task that requires a specific response scorable as right or wrong. On projective tests the task is less specific; in fact, the child is asked to place a personal interpretation on the test material. There are no right responses. The child thus projects his own unique perception of the material and organizes his responses in a unique manner. His responses are functions of his total personality.

Sargent (1945) points out that the stimulus situation in a projective test has different meanings to each subject, depending on the subject's particular personality characteristics. It is chosen because of this ambiguity, not because the experimenter has arbitrarily decided that it should have a particular meaning. As Sargent further points out, projective methods seek to uncover the underlying determinants of mental life. Let us consider a very simple illustration (not part of a test) of how an individual may impose private meaning on a stimulus. Let us look at the relatively simple pattern in Figure 11.1 and then ask ourselves the question: "What does this look like to me?"

FIGURE 11.1.   An Unstructured Stimulus

Many possible responses might be made, of course. The figure might look like seven dots, a triangle, a wedge, a piece of pie, a flock of flying geese, an Indian teepee, or any number of other things. No one of these responses is a "correct" response; on the other hand, no one is a "wrong" response. Rather, the response is evaluated on the basis of many factors, including the total personality characteristics of the individual making it.

Rapaport (1946) pointed out that projective procedures are procedures in which the "subject actively and spontaneously structures unstructured material, and, in so doing, reveals his structural principles—which are the principles of his psychological structure." According to Rapaport, the use of a projective technique assumes that the examiner is seeking something of which the subject is unaware, otherwise the subject could be asked about it directly. Projective techniques, therefore, are *indirect questions,* and the responses to them are *indirect answers.* Rapaport stresses that in projective tests *all* aspects of thought processes (as well as emotional factors) come into play. Hence, such tests are extremely valuable in the psychological evaluation of a child. They help us in arriving at a *dynamic* interpretation of the intellectual functioning of the retarded child that is unlike the more static measures of intelligence tests (Rabin, 1968).

In our view, projective tests have an important place in the total evaluation of the retarded person. If evaluated improperly, however, they are particularly hazardous for retarded children, especially severely retarded children. The results of these tests require skillful analysis by a highly competent clinician who is experienced in working with the retarded. They cannot be evaluated properly without a thorough consideration of all of the factors that might influence the results: the individual's life history, motivation for the testing, physical and sensory limitations, relationship with the examiner, and skills in communication. Nevertheless, such tests often give us insight into the dynamics of the individual's behavior without which we might easily misinterpret overt behavior.

Some workers in the field have rejected the use of projective tests because of the limitations we have noted and have suggested the exclusive use of checklists of observable behavior for personality evaluation. Although such checklists can be of great value, they can only tell us what is on the surface. What is underneath may be very different and can astonish us at times. We may gain glimpses of extreme, but covert, withdrawal, or we may see evidence of creative thinking in a timorous, frustrated child who is fearful of failure on objective tests.

Bell (1948) has discussed the broad theoretical foundations that underlie the use of projective procedures. These, in summary form, are as follows:

1. The personality of an individual is not static but, rather, dynamic. It changes and fluctuates and is modified by passage through time. The projective test reflects these dynamic qualities.
2. The personality, even though it fluctuates, is still relatively structured. As Bell stresses, the structure of the individual is developed by the particular range of physiological, psychological, and physical-social-cultural influences that are brought to bear on him. These forces produce a dynamic and evolving, but nevertheless structured, unit.
3. The personality structure of the individual is revealed in behavior, since behavior is functional. Our behavior reflects the relationship between the demands of the self and those of the situation in which we are involved. It is, from one point of view, an adaptation of the personality to the complex interaction of internal and external forces.
4. Personality is not a shallow surface phenomenon; it has depth. The surface reactions shown by the person are manifestations of the deeper forces within, many of which are hidden from the person himself and from others. (They exist at an unconscious level.) The projective techniques explore these deeper layers of the personality.

Some Projective Tests

We now will discuss some representative projective techniques that are useful in the evaluation of mentally retarded children. We shall not, at this point, deal with the specific contributions of these techniques to the development of theories of the psychopathology of intellectual deficit; rather, we shall describe the techniques and discuss their applicability.

The Rorschach Test. Of all the projective techniques, the *Rorschach* is probably the best-known and most widely used test. It consists of a series of ten cards, on each of which is printed an ink blot design. In fact, the test is often referred to as the *ink-blot test.* Some of the designs are colored, and some are in black and white. Psychologists had been using ink blots for a number of years prior to the advent of the *Rorschach Test* in order to investigate such traits as imagination (Tulchin, 1940). In 1911 Hermann Rorschach, a Swiss psychiatrist, began to experiment with the use of various relatively unstructured designs in order to develop a psychodiagnostic method of assessing mental illness. He first published his techniques and results in 1921 (Rorschach, 1921). Many revised editions have been published since that time in many languages (see Rorschach, 1942; Goldfried et al., 1971), and the *Rorschach* technique now is used internationally.

The administration of the *Rorschach* is relatively simple. Each *Rorschach* card is given in turn to the subject, who is instructed to look at the card and to tell the examiner everything that she sees. This part of the procedure is known as the *free association.* All of the subject's responses are recorded exactly as they are given. Usually the total time required for the whole card, and the time elapsing between the presentation of the card and the initial response, are recorded. Following the presentation of the last card, the examiner returns to the beginning of the series and again presents each card in turn to the subject. The examiner now questions the subject about each response in order to learn what areas of the blot were used in the response and what characteristics of the blot determined the response. This procedure, known as the *inquiry,* is difficult because the examiner must not suggest any way in which the subject should respond.

The responses (free association and inquiry combined) are then scored by the examiner. This is a complex process involving four major categories of scoring, as follows:

1. *Location.* What area of the design is used? Does the subject use whole blot, a large, obvious area, or a small, rare, minor section of the design? Does the subject use the white spaces of the design?
2. *Determinants.* What characteristics of the design determined the response? Some of the major determinants are form, color, shading, texture, vista, and movement. If multiple determinants are involved, which are primary?
3. *Content.* What is the content of the response? Is it, for example, animal, human, anatomical, or geographical? There are many content categories.
4. *Popularity or Originality.* Is the response one that is usually seen by most people, or is it a highly original one that is rarely given?

Each response is scored for each of these categories. Symbols are assigned to the various aspects of the response to facilitate scoring—a kind of shorthand notation. In the location category the symbols are the whole blot, W; the white space, S; a large, obvious area, D; and a minor area, Dd. The major

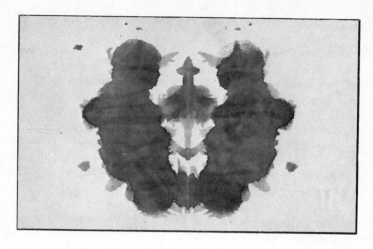

A Rorschach-like blot.

determinant symbols are: color, C; shading, Y; vista, V; human movement, M; form, F; and texture, T. The form response is further scored as good form (F plus) or poor form (F minus), depending on whether or not it is appropriate to the area of the blot used. The content categories are abbreviated (such as A for animal, Ad for part of an animal, H for human, and Hd for human detail). Some examples of *Rorschach* responses and their appropriate scorings are shown in Table 11.5

   After each response has been scored, the scores are totaled and analyzed. The tabulation of scores is referred to as the *psychogram*. Many ratios of total score categories are computed. Then the psychogram and qualitative aspects of the test performance are interpreted. The interpretation of a *Rorschach* record (the *protocol*) is a very complex and difficult process, and the

TABLE 11.5   Rorschach Responses and Their Scoring

Card No.	Response	Location	Determinant	Content	Original or Popular
III	Blood—it is red like blood	D	C	Blood	
VI	A bear rug—it is shaped like one and it is shaded light and dark just like one too	W	FY plus	Ad	P
VII	A woman dancing—she is shaped just like a woman	D	M plus	H	
IX	A man's head—it is just shaped like a man's head —nose here, mouth here, shape of head here	Dd	F plus	Hd	

value of the final report depends greatly on the skill of the psychologist using the technique.

The Rorschach technique was originally standardized on adults, but has been extended downward to be applicable to young children (Ford, 1946; Ames et al., 1971). The same cards are used as stimuli, but the norms and standards, of course, are different from those for adults. An extensive bibliography of research and areas of use of the *Rorschach* may be found in the volume on projective techniques by Goldfried et al. (1971).

The *Rorschach* enables us to assess basic personality characteristics of the retarded child, and this aids us in understanding the child's emotional assets and liabilities. But because it requires extensive use of language, its use with the lower levels of retardation is limited.

Holtzman Inkblot Technique. This test was developed to overcome some of the criticisms that were leveled against the Rorschach Test, such as the complexity of the scoring methods and the relatively low reliability of some of the test factors. The Holtzman Technique utilizes two series of test cards, 45 cards in each series, with a practice card for each series. The subject is asked to give only one response to each card, and only a simple inquiry is conducted. Scoring is based on twenty-two variables but other scores and qualitative analyses are also available. Statistical analysis has shown that six "personality dimensions" account for most of the variance in scores: perceptual maturity and integrated ideational activity; perceptual sensitivity; psychopathology of thought; perceptual differentiation; a complex involving reaction time, rejection, and animal content; and, a residual factor consisting of penetration, anatomy, and sex.

Split-half and test-retest reliabilities for each of the Holtzman test variables have been reported and vary from rather low levels (correlations of .45 and .51) to fairly high to very high levels (from correlations of .70 up to .97 and .98 for others). A number of studies reported by Holtzman (1968) have reported fairly good differential diagnostic possibilities for a number of pathological conditions, such as brain damage, schizophrenia, and personality disturbances. Thorpe and Swartz (1965) analyzed developmental age differences in a population of 586 normal subjects ranging in age from five to twenty years, suggesting the value of this test in evaluating perceptual aspects of development. Although there has been little reported research use with retarded subjects, the test appears to have considerable value in developmental studies of mildly and moderately retarded children. The relative objectivity in scoring and the rich projective sample of behavior that the test provides should make it especially useful in evaluating the effects of various intervention and training programs.

The Thematic Apperception Test. The *Thematic Apperception Test* (also known as the *TAT*) is a projective technique developed by Morgan and Murray (1935). It consists of a set of thirty pictures. Some of these are designed to be used for both men and women, some for men alone, some for women alone, some for boys and girls, some for boys alone, and some for girls alone.

Each picture selected by the examiner from the total set is shown to the subject, who is instructed to tell a story about the picture. The subject is asked to tell what is happening, what led up to the scene pictured, and how he thinks the story will end. In other words, he is asked to give a past, present, and future for each picture. The subject also is instructed to tell what the people in the story feel and think. In dealing with retarded children, of course, it is not always possible to get such completeness.

Each story is recorded in as complete detail as possible and is then analyzed by the examiner. Murray originally analyzed the stories according to these five major characteristics:

1. *The Hero.* This represents the subject and reflects the subject's personality characteristics.
2. *The Needs of the Hero.* These are representative of the needs of the subject.
3. *The Presses.* These are forces that either hurt or help the hero. They are the external forces that are brought to bear on the hero.
4. *The Thema.* This may be roughly regarded as the plot of the story.
5. *The Outcome.* This refers to how the story is ended. For example, is it pleasant or unpleasant?

The *Thematic Apperception Test* is a method for the exploration of the fantasy of the child. Basic to the clinical use of the technique is the hypothesis that the individual makes use of material from his own unique personal experiences in making up the stories. Both conscious and unconscious determinants are present, and thus the child's personality dynamics may be inferred from the stories that are constructed.

Like the *Rorschach,* the *TAT* requires that the examiner be highly trained and experienced in the use of the technique.

Bergman and Fisher (1953) found the *TAT* to be useful in diagnosing and understanding the dynamics of the mentally retarded child, as well as in facilitating psychotherapy.

Thompson and Bachrach (1951) have introduced color in the *TAT.* Some studies have shown that retarded children respond more readily to such color. Lubin (1955) studied the performance of a group of retarded children on the colored *TAT.* He found that their productivity increased; they produced a larger number of themas on the colored than on the noncolored test. It was hypothesized that the use of color tended to make the picture more *reality bound* and facilitated the identification of the child with the picture. (There is still considerable controversy regarding the effect of color on the validity of the derived measures.)

The original *TAT* was felt to be applicable to persons seven years of age or older. However, there have been special forms of the test developed for various age groups. Symonds (1948) has constructed a test for adolescents, in which the pictures represent situations that are thought to be pertinent to teenagers. Bellak and Bellak (1950) have constructed the *Children's Apperception Test.* This test employs situations concerning animals rather than people. The rationale for this is that children between ages of three and ten years probably would tell more clinically useful stories in reacting to pictures involving animals as the central figures than to those using human beings.

Many clinicians do not accept this hypothesis. In a review of the literature about the *Children's Apperception Test,* Budoff (1960) concluded that previous research had, in general, failed to support Bellak's hypothesis. He then proceeded to explore experimentally the hypothesis that children with a young mental age would identify more readily with animal rather than human figures since such children were essentially very concrete thinkers. Budoff (1963) used twenty-three first-grade students with *Otis Alpha* IQs ranging from 70 to 91 and with chronological ages from five years one month to seven years of age.

He then divided the total group of subjects into two subgroups. The first, the borderline group, was composed of twelve subjects, who ranged from 70 to 78 in IQ and who had a mean mental age of four years five months. The second subgroup was composed of eleven subjects, with a range in IQ of from 87 to 91 and with a mean mental age of five years eight months. Budoff then administered the *CAT,* omitting a card depicting bears in a cave (card 5 of the *CAT*). Following this, he administered a revised *CAT,* in which the animal figures were replaced with human figures. Both forms of the *CAT* were administered within a two- to three-week interval.

Budoff used two measures to compare the test responses. The first was a word count of all the words in the body of the story made up by the child, and the second was a *transcendence* level score, which was a measure of the number of comments made up about the picture other than those of pure description. The interjudge reliability for the word count score was 1.00, and that for the transcendence level score was .83. The scores thus were highly reliable. Budoff then compared the performances of both groups of subjects on both measures for each of the *CAT* tests. It was found that Bellak's hypothesis was not substantiated, and that the retarded children did not respond more to the animal than to the human figures. Rather, *exactly the opposite situation prevailed.* The children gave *longer and more imaginative* stories to the human cards than they did to the animal cards. This finding was contrary to what had been expected, but was in accord with our clinical experience.

The Michigan Picture Test. Like the *Thematic Apperception Test,* this test is based on responses to pictures. It is unlike the *TAT* in several respects, however. First, it is specifically designed for children in the age range of about eight to fourteen years. This means that the pictures were selected to be appealing and relevant for this age group, and the methods of analysis are applicable to this population. Second, the pictures were selected, on the basis of extensive clinical and experimental testing, to tap common conflict areas. For example, one picture depicts a family at breakfast, and another shows a group of boys walking along a country road. A third feature of this test was the development of a number of objective and easily scored measures that would yield general and specific measures of personality reactions. Still another feature was the provision for flexible testing procedures: there are four *core pictures* that serve as a basic set of testing materials applicable to all subjects; there also are pictures for boys only, some for girls only, and some for both sexes, all or some of which can be used to explore specific conflict problems that may be of interest in a particular case.

The total set of materials includes sixteen pictures and a comprehensive manual discussing the theory, standardization, administration, and interpreta-

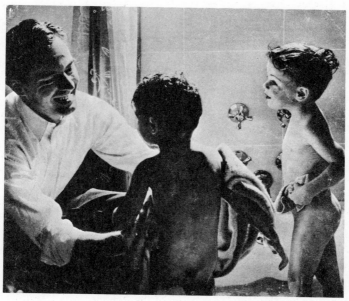

Two pictures used in the Michigan Picture Test. (Courtesy of Michigan Department of Mental Health)

tion of the results. The test can be given individually or in groups (although *group* testing is not applicable to retarded children). It yields a *tension index,* based on relatively simple scoring that a clerk can be trained to do. The score provides a general measure of the degree of maladjustment. There also are norms for specific types of personality measures. Moreover, the responses can be scored and evaluated clinically in the same ways that the *TAT* responses are analyzed. All in all, the test should prove very useful in a variety of situations calling for the assessment of mentally retarded children.

The Blacky Test. Another projective test that is useful in exploring the personality characteristics of children is the *Blacky Test,* devised by Blum (1950). This test is composed of a series of eleven cartoons, depciting a dog named Blacky in various situations. Blum created the test primarily to investigate

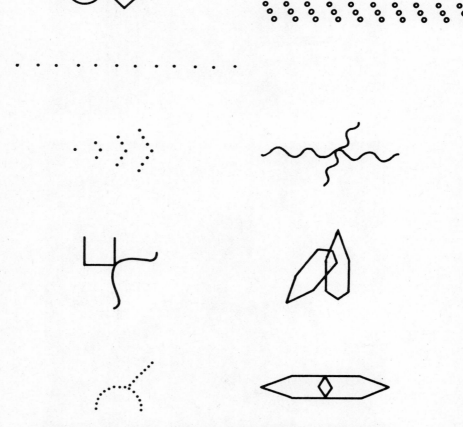

FIGURE 11.2   The Hutt Adaptation of the Bender-Gestalt Test. (This illustration has been reduced by about 45% from the
original size.)

Freudian hypotheses relative to the psychosexual development of the person, but it has since been used to explore the major psychological defenses. We can illustrate the nature of the test by describing one of the cards: Blacky's tail has been placed on a block of wood, and a large knife hovers over the tail. (This card would presumably elicit the castration anxieties of the child and reveal the characteristic ways in which he deals with them.)

The child is given the cards one at a time. He is required, first, to make up a story about the picture (somewhat similar to the *TAT* procedure), and then is required to answer specific questions about each card. This test is valuable for assessing mentally retarded children, since it provides useful information about the children's motivation, anxieties, and preoccupations.

The Hutt Adaptation of the Bender-Gestalt Test (HABGT). The *Bender-Gestalt Test* consists of nine relatively simple geometrical designs, or gestalt figures, ranging in maturational level from about three to twelve years. Bender (1938), who introduced this test in its present form, adapted the figures from the work on visual perception by Wertheimer (1923). The figures were drawn freehand by Bender and had certain irregularities in drawing, as well as structural differences from the Wertheimer figures. Hutt (1969), therefore, provided a new set of figures based on his own clinical experience and more accurately reflecting the principles developed by Wertheimer. These figures are shown in Figure 11.2.

The *basic administration* of this test is simplicity itself, since all that is required is to ask the subject to copy each figure as it is presented. The child, drawing freehand, uses paper and pencil in copying the figures. The visual and motor abilities necessary to perceive and copy these figures are dependent on the general rate of biological maturation. Hence, the drawings may be evaluated for general maturity level. As will be seen in our later discussion of this test, evaluations of mental maturity may be derived from scores on this test, which are closely correlated with other measures of general mental development.

This test is particularly useful for assessing the retarded child's development for several reasons, as Hutt (1977a) indicates. First, it is largely independent of cultural deprivation and linguistic skills. Second, it is highly useful in assessing the presence of organic or neurological dysfunctions. Third, it can be used to evaluate the presence of emotional disturbances. For these reasons, the test is now widely used in the differential diagnosis of suspected cases of mental retardation.

This test is particularly important for assessing the perceptual motor performance of retarded children, since perceptual motor behavior is highly correlated with learning performance and with general intelligence at lower levels of intelligence. When used as a test of perceptual motor performance, only the basic administration, or *Copy Phase,* is required. The many ways in which this test can be of value in assessing retarded children is discussed in detail in the 1977 volume by Hutt. In addition to the manual provided by Hutt, two other manuals (and additional figures) are supplied in the work of Koppitz (1963, 1975) and of Haworth (1970), who offer scoring methods and norms. Haworth's norms go as low as four years of age. Thewatt (1963), using Koppitz's scoring method, was able to show fairly high predictive ability with children manifesting learning disabiities. Hutt as well as Koppitz has demonstrated the test's usefulness in the differential diagnosis of neurological disabilities.

Hutt (1945b) introduced the usefulness of the test as a projective device. Its projective features can be emphasized by explaining the method of administration. After the *Copy Phase* has been completed, the subject's drawings are withdrawn and the subject then is asked to "do something else with these drawings." He is asked to change them in any way he wishes so as to "make them more pleasing to [himself]." This is called the *Elaboration Phase*. Finally, the subject is asked to look at both the original cards and his modifications of them and to tell what each "reminds [him] of." These methods, it is believed, yield rich clinical data and can reveal conflict areas, degree of emotional disturbance, and the like. Other methods of administration, also useful for specific purposes, are described by Hutt (1977). Hutt and Gibby (1970) have prepared an Atlas that presents detailed methods of scoring the test, as well as many examples of records of various psychiatric and retarded conditions.

Tolor and Schulberg (1966) published an extensive review of the work with the various forms of this test and have shown many of its useful applications. Recent research studies have shown the special advantages of the Hutt Adaptation. In a research and training program with deaf-retarded children conducted by the Mental Health Department of the State of Michigan, the findings from the Hutt Adaptation were very helpful in predicting development and providing guides for training (Hutt and Feuerfile, 1963). Some children who appeared to be severely retarded were found to have potential for better learning.

Hutt (1969, 1977a) has developed two objective measures that have been applied in various research studies. One of these is a 19-factor score of psychopathology. The other is a measure of adience-abience, which appears to be relatively resistant to change and which predicts capacity for profiting from a variety of learning experiences.

The two objective scales developed by Hutt have been applied in a variety of situations with varied populations. Both the *Psychopathology Scale* and the *Adience-Abience Scale* have been shown to have high test-retest reliability over short and long intervals.of time with normal and disturbed children and adults (Hutt and Miller, 1975; Hutt and Miller, 1976; Hutt and Dates, 1977). These studies also indicated the separate usefulness of the two scales in differentiating retarded from nonretarded individuals as well as normals from disturbed individuals. Another study (Hutt, Dates, and Reid, 1977) offers evidence concerning the predictive value of the scales with a group of delinquent boys.

A unique feature of the *HABGT* is its possible use in differential diagnosis, especially when organic brain damage and/or mental retardation is suspected. The method, called *experimental-clinical analysis,* enables the examiner to obtain significant data in assisting in such differentiation (Hutt, 1977a). Another method of great value in a practical sense is the method of *Configurational Analysis* (Hutt, 1977a). This method offers a relatively quick and simple means of "spotting" cases in which severe pathology or organic damage is present. Such individuals then can be given more intensive analysis and study. These and the other characteristics of the test make the instrument and its scale particularly useful for individuals with disadvantaged cultural and educational experiences who may show far greater potential than is evident in the customary linguistic tests that are employed for intellectual and personality evaluation.

Pacella (1965) studied the use of the *Bender-Gestalt Test* in the diagnosis of mentally retarded children. He felt that there was evidence that a single *Bender-Gestalt Test* was not sufficient for satisfactory quantitative evaluation of visual-motor functioning in mental retardates. Accordingly, he compared organic and nonorganic mentally retarded individuals on three successive trials of the *Bender-Gestalt*. His subjects were two groups of hospitalized mentally retarded persons between the ages of twelve and thirty-five. Twenty-two were diagnosed as suffering from brain damage. Of the twenty-two controls, fifteen were cultural-familial mentally retarded. Both groups were given three successive trials of the *Bender-Gestalt Test*. Tests were scored on the *Pascal-Suttell* scale. The results indicated that even though there was no significant difference in accuracy scores between organic and nonorganic mentally retarded individuals on the first and second trials of the *Bender-Gestalt,* the difference was significant on the third trial. Neither group exhibited significant improvement in accuracy or speed over the three trials, but the nonorganic group showed a tendency to improve on both variables, whereas the organic group tended to improve only in speed. Pacella suggests that for some mentally retarded individuals, visual-motor abnormality is a learning deficiency for which they may compensate through repetition, but for others, it is a manifestation of a relatively enduring structural impairment that is not easily overcome by learning.

The *Bender-Gestalt Test (BGT)* has been found to be very sensitive to changes in the child. For instance, positive personality changes due to psychotherapeutic intervention and negative changes due to increased pathological states are reflected by corresponding changes in the child's *BGT* protocol. An example of this phenomenon is furnished in a study by Krop and Smith (1969). They were interested in teaching visual-motor skills and determining whether there were concomitant changes in the *BGT* protocols from pre- to post-experimental conditions. Their main hypothesis was that visual-motor skills could be taught and could then be applied outside the classroom situation. But their experiment also provided a good test of the sensitivity of the *BGT* to change in the individual. After a psychologist administered the *BGT* to one group of children, teachers gave them special training in the drawing of geometric figures for a period of thirty minutes daily for twelve weeks. They were taught to associate the design with its name, and emphasis was placed on accuracy, neatness and discrimination between the figures. The teachers were unaware of the purpose of the visual-motor training and did not see the Gestalt reproductions. Two other groups were similarly tested, but did not receive the training. They received, instead, the regular special education class program. Following completion of the experimental program, all subjects were given the *BGT* again. The two sets of tests were scored and compared. The results indicated that although the performance of mentally retarded subjects improved significantly from participation in an educational program, even greater improvement resulted from a period of special instruction on the drawing of geometric designs. It was concluded that this study provided further evidence of the usefulness of the *BGT* in reflecting growth in developmental skills.

Tests of Social Adaptation

We have previously discussed some of the tests and some of the problems in evaluating social maturity and social adaptation. We now will present and discuss two of these tests in greater detail.

AAMD Adaptive Behavior Scale. There are two versions of this scale: one developed with and for institutionalized mentally retarded individuals (Nihira et al., 1974), and the other, an adaptation for elementary school children (Nihira et al., 1976). The two versions are alike except that in the public-school version the items that were inappropriate for school settings were omitted. In that edition, norms are available for grades 2 to 6. In the earlier version, norms are available for both children and adults.

Whatever else enters into the level and pattern of social adaptation, it is clear that the nature of social experience is *situation-specific* to a large extent; that is, social behavior is highly dependent on the specific types of social training that an individual is given. Hence, any measure of social adaptation is likely to vary with varying circumstances. Consider, if you will, what differing experiences in the social domain are present in such diverse cultures as aborigines, Japanese natives, and people living in the Arctic regions. For these reasons, a measure of social-adaptive behavior must be carefully interpreted with proper evaluation of the possible effects of the background experiences on the score or scores. Similarly, predictions based on such a measure have only limited generalizations.

Nevertheless, since adaptive behavior must be taken into account in any analysis of retardation, such measures are indispensable both for practical and theoretical reasons. The *AAMD Adaptive Behavior Scale* was carefully and extensively evaluated and provides one of the best current measures of such behavior. Its goal is the measurement of "effectiveness of an individual in coping with the natural and social demands of his or her environment" (Nihira et al., 1974). It consists of two parts: Part I is based on a comprehensive review of existing behavior scales in the United States and Great Britain and attempts to *rate* many aspects of current social-adaptive behavior; Part II was "designed to provide measures of maladaptive behavior related to personality and behavior disorders."

Items for the scale were selected and evaluated on the basis of three criteria: (1) inter-rater reliability, (2) effectiveness in discriminating among *institutionalized* retarded persons, and (3) discrimination among adaptive behavior levels "while the variance due to measured intelligence was controlled."

Part I has ten sections: *Independent Functions* (8 items), including eating, toilet use, care of clothing, and the like; *Physical Development* (2 items) involving sensory and motor functions); *Economic Activity* (2 items) involving the handling of money and shopping skills; *Language and Development* (3 items); *Numbers and Time* (1 item); *Domestic Activity* (3 items), including cleaning activities and kitchen duties; *Vocational Activity* (1 item); *Self-Direction* (3 items) measuring initiative, perseverance, and use of leisure time; *Responsibility* (1 item); and *Socialization* (1 item). It is stated that ratings on the items of this part, as well as of Part II, can be done by people without special training, but the ratings must be based on *observed behaviors* with information from persons who "spend the greatest number of waking hours with the individual."

Part II consists of fourteen sections, all but one of which relates to maladaptive behavior. They include such areas as *Violent and Destructive Behavior, Antisocial Behavior, Withdrawal,* and *Self-abusive Behavior.* The fourteenth section deals with *Use of Medication.*

Norms are provided for each of eleven age categories, and percentiles are available based on 496 residents of retarded institutions. The authors assert that factorial analysis results in three dimensions of the scale: personal independence, social maladaptive behavior, and personal adaptive behavior.

A number of statistical studies of properties of the scale have shown that interjudge reliability for sections of Part I varies from .71 to .93, with a reliability for all of Part I of .86 (N = 138). The reliabilities in interjudge ratings for Part II vary from a low of .37 to a high of .77, with a reliability for the total of .57. Another study (N = 531) showed that Part I discriminated various levels of adaptive behavior quite well, but that Part II showed only moderate success in such discrimination. This is not surprising, since Part II has a total reliability of only .57, indicating a commonality between interjudge ratings of only about 33 percent. In our judgment, this level of reliability is unsatisfactory for individual diagnosis. Still another reported study indicated that when retarded children and adolescents were offered an operation-oriented set of experiences over a two-year period, the ratings changed significantly.

Thus, although the scale offers some promise, it also has severe limitations. It cannot be used for predictive purposes. It is highly dependent on the special circumstances of the individual. Part II is of questionable value due to low reliability. Part I is fairly reliable *provided the raters have adequate access to relevant data.*

Balthazar Scales of Adaptive Behavior. Another highly interesting set of adaptive scales for severely and profoundly mentally retarded subjects that is suitable for use in institutional settings are the *Balthazar Scales of Adaptive Behavior* (1973, 1976a). These scales, developed over a number of years of try-out and research study, provide measures of "functional independence" and of "social adaptation." As Balthazar states (1973), "the behaviors represented by the BSAB-II *must be interpreted in terms of the subjects' environment.* . . . Comparison or matching of subjects under *differing* conditions should be avoided" [our emphasis]." This is clear acknowledgment of the point we made previously that the measures tend to be, in part, situation-specific. Another feature of both scales is the emphasis placed on obtaining *pre-baseline studies*. These studies by the rater are intended to familiarize and acquaint the rater with the subjects. The rater also is urged to participate in conferences during which she can receive and impart information about the subjects, thus adding to the rater's knowledge of the subjects and insuring more reliable ratings.

The 1976 version of Scale I, for measuring functional independence, consists of three subscales: *eating* (with five major subclasses of eating skills, including dependent feeding, finger foods, spoon usage, fork usage, and drinking); *dressing* (including shoes, socks, undershirt, etc.); and, *toileting* (including behaviors involved in daytime and nightime bladder and bowel functions). The 1973 version of the adaptive scale (BASB—II) comprises eight social categories: *unadaptive self-directed behaviors; unadaptive interpersonal behaviors; adaptive self-directed behaviors; adaptive interpersonal behaviors; verbal communication; play activities; response to instructions;* and, *checklist* items. After pre-baseline data have been obtained, coded, and scored, individualized programs may be developed to stimulate improvement in independent and adaptive behavior as well as to reinforce behaviors already available.

Balthazar reports interjudge reliabilities, utilizing four raters, in evaluating the reliability of an earlier version of Scale I (Balthazar and Stevens, 1969), with coefficients ranging from .841 to 1.000, as well as "proportions of agreement" for raters using the 1976 version. For Scale II, reliability was evaluated in a study by Naor, Rocca, and Balthazar (1972). In general, quite satisfactory degrees of both intrajudge and interjudge reliability are reported for both scales.

The scales are suitable for children and adults. A number of manuals are provided for supervisors of training programs, for raters, and even for parents, teachers, and home trainers (Balthazar, 1976b).

Assessment of the Self-concept

The self-concept of the retarded child is fragile indeed and is easily shattered by the impossible demands placed upon it. Failure only engenders further failure and ultimately may result, particularly in the case of the mildly retarded child, in a very negative self-image. Goldstein (1964) has developed the *Illinois Index of Self-Derogation (IISD)*, a scale for determining the attitudes of the child toward self. This scale has undergone three revisions and has been standardized on a population of 120 children with intelligence quotients between 60 and 85, as well as on 160 children of average intelligence. It yields a score that equates with the child's self-concept. This is a promising instrument, but it needs further clinical validation.

Gibby (1964) has developed a scale that is useful in many clinical situations: the *Intellectual Rating Scale (IRS)*. It attempts to measure the reality of the child's self-concept, the perceptions of the child by significant people in his life, and the discrepancies between the child's self-perception and the perceptions of these significant others.

ASSESSMENT OF ACADEMIC ACHIEVEMENT
AND VOCATIONAL APTITUDE

Assessment of the retarded child's academic achievement and vocational and interest aptitudes also is necessary. We shall discuss each of these areas briefly in the following sections.

Assessment of Academic Achievement

For both educational planning and appropriate guidance, it is important to know the level of the retarded pupils academic abilities, in general, with the extent to which academic achievement is commensurate with intellectual capacities. (See discussion of reading retardation and reading disability in chapter 8). We should know, for example, how well the child can read or use simple number skills and what the specific disabilities are in these and other skills. Levels of achievement in the traditional scholastic subjects are evaluated by means of *achievement tests.* These usually are paper-and-pencil tests that may be administered as either group or individual tests. In addition to the general achievement tests, there are other tests that evaluate specific disabilities in a given academic subject (*diagnostic achievement tests*). Another type of test is designed to assess the readiness of the child to be taught to read. Tests of this type are known as *reading readiness tests.*

Achievement tests are designed to measure the child's skills in one or several academic subjects. There are achievement tests in reading, arithmetic, spelling, writing, geography, and other subjects. They are not intended to serve as predictive tests (that is, to predict the future achievement of the child) but, rather, to indicate the level at which, and types of skills with which, the child is functioning at the time of the test.

The results of achievement tests usually are expressed as *grade norms;* that is, the child's achievement on the test is expressed in terms of the grade level to which it is equivalent. For example, Jeanne, a twelve-year-old child, may have a third-grade reading level, fifth-grade spelling level, and fourth-grade arithmetic level. Some tests have norms for a variety of skills within the same subject. For example, a reading achievement test may have norms for reading vocabulary, general comprehension, and rate of reading.

Diagnostic tests do not measure primarily the achievement level of the child. Rather, they are designed to help the teacher discover the child's particular disabilities in a given subject. For example, an achievement test in reading indicated that Ellen was reading at a level below that expected from her mental age. A diagnostic reading test, administered by the teacher, revealed that Ellen had little ability in the use of phonics. A program designed to deal with this diability was then planned for her.

As pointed out, achievement tests have been developed for all academic subjects. We shall discuss, first, the various types of achievement tests, giving some representative samples, and then examine some of the tests that are devoted to the assessment of specific aspects of reading.

Achievement Tests. Achievement tests may be designed to assess the child's abilities in a single subject or to assess the child's achievement in a group of subjects. The latter type is known as an achievement test *battery*. The *Stanford Achievement Test* (Kelley, et al., 1953) was one of the earliest batteries of achievement tests. First published in 1923, it was revised in 1929, 1940, and 1953. The present battery consists of five equivalent forms of the test, so frequent retesting of the same child is possible. It covers academic achievement in grades 2 to 9. Many different norms are available for the interpretation of the test results. The child's achievement may be interpreted in terms of age and grade norms or in terms of percentiles for each grade for each of the various subjects.

Another achievement battery is the *Metropolitan Achievement Tests* (Hildreth et al., 1948). It covers the range from the first grade to the first half of the ninth grade. Still another battery, the *California Achievements Tests* (Tiegs and Clark, 1951) covers grades 1 through 13. This test differs from the *Stanford* and *Metropolitan Achievement* batteries in that it is concerned only with the basic academic skill subjects. It purportedly can be used as a diagnostic instrument to detect specific disabilities within a given subject.

An excellent general achievement test for reading was developed by Gates and MacGinitie (1965). There are four forms of the test: *Primary A* for grade 1, *Primary B* for grade 2, *Primary C* for grade 3, and *Primary CS* for grades 2 and 3. A, B, and C measure vocabulary and comprehension; CS measures speed and accuracy. The 1965 edition of this test, standardized on 40,000 pupils in thirty-eight communities, provides standard scores, percentile scores, and grade scores. Gates and MacGinitie also have developed a *Readiness Skills Test* for children below the first grade. It contains eight subtests and is administered in four half-hour sessions.

Diagnostic Reading Tests. These tests provide diagnostic evaluations of the child's reading abilities. (See the later section on Criterion-Referenced Testing.) They purport to reveal areas in which the child has specific disabilities. Examples of such tests are the *Gates-McKillop Reading Diagnostic Tests* (Gates and McKillop, 1973), the *Gray Standardized Oral Reading Paragraphs* (1915), and the *Durrell Analysis of Reading Difficulty* (1937). The *Gray* test is concerned with the child's oral reading abilities from grade 1 through grade 8. The *Durrell* diagnostic test is designed to be used in grades 1 through 6. It evaluates oral reading, silent reading, recall of material read (both orally and silently), speed of recognition of words, writing, and spelling.

Reading Readiness Tests. We often wish to know whether a given child has reached the level at which she is *ready* to learn to read. Reading readiness implies that the child has appropriate social and communication skills, an adequate vocabulary, sufficient use of oral language, and no severely handicapping perceptual or motor problems. This readiness may be evaluated in part through the use of *reading readiness tests*. These tests measure such areas as simple number concepts, word meaning, information, knowing the use of objects, and copying. Examples of such reading readiness tests are the *Metropolitan Reading*

Readiness Test (Hildreth and Griffiths, 1949), the *Monroe Reading Aptitude Test* (1935), and the *Betts Ready to Read Battery* (1934). Such tests may be given by the teacher or by a clinical psychologist.

Linguistic Abilities. Many new methods have been developed to assess aspects of the complex faculty known as linguistic ability. One of these, more conventional than the others, is the *Illinois Test of Psycholinguistic Abilities.* This test, developed by Kirk and McCarthy (1961), and revised by Kirk, McCarthy, and Kirk (1968), consists of nine subtests, as follows: auditory decoding, visual decoding, auditory-vocal association, visual-motor association, vocal encoding, auditory encoding, auditory-vocal automatic maturation, auditory-vocal psycholinguistic maturation, and visual-motor psycholinguistic maturation. Some aspects of the validity of this test appear to be well established, but others are still questionable (McCarthy, 1965). The test has been found to be useful in evaluating specific communication skills of the retarded child as a basis for remedial programs.

Other approaches are based on language sampling procedures (i.e., sampling of observed language behavior). The *Parsons Language Sample* (Spradlin, 1963) was specifically designed to evaluate two areas: vocal and non-vocal. Based on a system developed by Skinner (see chapter 16), observational samples of primitive language behavior are made in a variety of situations. Another system that has been found valuable is that developed by Johnson and co-workers (1963). Small objects and books are used to get the child to respond to oral questions. Tape recordings of the responses are made and analyzed.

Assessment of Vocational Aptitudes and Interests

The aptitudes of the retarded child must be assessed to plan the child's total program adequately. *Aptitude tests* differ from achievement tests in that aptitude tests attempt to *predict* the future performance of the child in vocational areas, whereas achievement tests measure scholastic abilities at the time of testing. Aptitude tests have been developed in many areas: musical, artistic, clerical, motor, and mechanical. For the sake of illustration, we shall discuss the last two areas only, since they have more general significance for the vocational guidance of the retarded child.

Assessment of Motor Aptitudes. Tests of motor functions center around two major functions—*speed* of motor responses and *coordination of muscular reactions.* Examples of tests designed to explore motor abilities are the *O'Connor Finger Dexterity Test* and the *O'Connor Tweezer Dexterity Tests* (1938), the *Crawford Small Parts Dexterity Test* (1949), and the *Purdue Pegboard* (Tiffin, 1948; Tiffin and Asher, 1948), and the *Bennett Hand-Tool Dexterity Test* (1947). Many other tests in this area have been devised, but these will serve as samples.

In the *O'Connor Tests,* the child is required to insert small pins into holes. In one of the tests, the insertion is done directly by hand; in the second, it is done with a small pair of tweezers. The *Crawford Test* uses a similar procedure. The subject first uses a pair of tweezers to insert small pins into a series of holes and then places a small collar on the end of each of the pins. Further, the subject is required to screw small screws into holes with the aid of a screw driver. The *O'Connor* and *Crawford* tests involve small muscle coordination and skills. The *Purdue Pegboard* evaluates gross and fine manual dexterity. It requires the insertion of pins in small holes (first with each hand separately, then with both hands) and the assembly of a series of pins, collars, and washers. The *Bennett Test* attempts to measure ability in the use of common hand tools, such as a wrench, and also is concerned with coordination and skill in the manipulation of objects. The child is required to take apart and reassemble a series of nuts, bolts, and washers.

It should be noted that all of these tests involve specific motor skills. Studies have shown that even though such tests appear to be reliable, they have low validity in general. They serve to give us only a rough idea of the abilities of the retarded child and cannot be used to predict vocational success accurately for a given child.

Tests of Mechanical Aptitude. The so-called *mechanical aptitudes* include such capacities as motor skills, perceptual capacities, comprehension of spatial relationships, reasoning about mechanical relationships and processes, and speed of motor responses. Many mechanical aptitude tests involve the manipulation of actual objects, and others are written tests.

Examples of mechanical aptitude tests are the *Minnesota Spatial Relations Test* (Patterson et al., 1930), the *Kent-Shakow Industrial Formboards* (1928), the *MacQuarrie Test for Mechanical Ability* (1943), the *Stenquist Mechanical Aptitude Test* (1923), and the *Bennett Mechanical Aptitude Test* (1948).

The *Minnesota Spatial Relations Test* is based on form and space perception. It is made up of four formboards, each having 58 differently shaped inserts. The subject is required to insert the pieces into the board as rapidly as possible. The *Kent-Shakow* formboard consists of a formboard with five recesses. There are a series of eight blocks to be inserted into each of these, each succeeding series of blocks being of greater difficulty. It is apparently a test of motor speed, of motor dexterity, and of capacity in dealing with spatial relationships. The *MacQuarrie* test consists of seven subtests: tracing, tapping, dotting, copying, location, blocks, and pursuit. It attempts to measure spatial relationships and motor skills. The *Stenquist* test is a mechanical reasoning test. The subject is required to assemble a number of common objects, such as a mousetrap, electric bell, and door lock. The test was developed during the first World War, but has been restandardized and is now known as the *Minnesota Mechanical Assembly Test* (Paterson et al., 1930). The *Bennett* test evaluates the subject's understanding of mechanical processes. It is a paper-and-pencil test.

All of these tests are applicable to the older retarded child and may be of some help in vocational guidance and counseling.

PROGRAM EVALUATION AND
CRITERION-REFERENCED TESTING

In this section, we will discuss some other approaches to testing and evaluation. In the first approach, the actual curriculum is so arranged that each step in progress can be monitored and evaluated while the appropriate skills are being taught. Based on experience with similar programs elsewhere, the personnel in Wayne County, Michigan in 1976 developed a program called "Steps: Structured Training and Evaluation of Performance System." A number of "terminal objectives" for appropriate pupils are defined, and the "steps" deemed appropriate to reaching this objective are described. Although it is believed that approximately four to six months are required to reach the objective, it is recognized that the time required will vary with the individual learner. The several skills are evaluated in terms of: A. Maintenance Objective; B. In Process; C. Achieved; and, D. Not Achieved. One other category of evaluation is offered, specified as Other, meaning that the achievement of the designated objective may be unrealistic or impossible.

"Steps" are provided in the following areas: Cognitive, Affective, and Psychomotor. In all, more than 200 "steps" are described. Examples in the Cognitive area are: the learner reacts to auditory stimuli; the learner shows understanding of verbal direction; the learner uses oral language to obtain wants; the learner holds pencil/crayon in fist and makes marks 100 percent of the time; and, the learner demonstrates the use of protective/directive word. In the Affective area, the following examples may be indicative: indicates awareness of person in proximity; maintains appropriate social distance consistently; performs assigned responsibilities. Examples from the Psychomotor area are: uses toilet when taken; turns faucet in drinking fountain and drinks at the same time; runs 600 yards in 2:30 (boys) or 2:47 (girls).

Such a program can have great value to the teacher in monitoring progress and in suggesting additional needed training for the pupil. It should be obvious that many of the items that are grouped under a given heading have little in common, as for example, "performing assigned tasks" and indicating "awareness of person in proximity." One therefore should not take the area headings too literally. It also is clear that, despite care taken to define each "step" there is considerable room for interpretation of the meaning of the behavior or of its evaluation, and that inter-rater reliability may not be as high as one would prefer.

Another example of program evaluation is provided by Hagedorn et al., (1976). This program deals with evaluation of the effectiveness of community mental health centers; we therefore defer discussion of it until chapter 16, in which we elaborate on problems of mental health and psychotherapy.

Barrett (1977) provides a systematic account of applications of behavioral analysis to programs for remediation and for procedures to evaluate changes in behavior. She recommends continuous, direct recording and measurement of the evoked behavior, the utilization, where possible, of mechanical recording devices by the observer, and both intermittent and continuous recording of behavior. When such approaches to measurement are applied in a specifically designed behavioral management program, even severely disabled persons, it is alleged, often can make significant progress. As we shall see in our later discussion of educational methods, behavioral management involving sequentially planned contingencies together with behavioral measures specifically designed to evaluate changes in behavior can be very helpful.

Emphasis on criterion-referenced testing has been increasing in recent years. According to Gorth and Hambleton (1973), "A criterion-referenced test is one that is deliberately constructed to yield measurements that are directly meaningful in terms of specified performance standards." Such tests can be most useful for dealing with specific learning situations. They may be constructed by the teacher, under the guidance of experts in test construction, or they may be constructed by the experts and are available commercially. No matter how valid a general, standardized test may be, it leaves out what the individual teacher dealing with an individual class or child needs to know: very specific information concerning performance in specific situations. Criterion-reference tests are useful, also, in evaluating the effectiveness of instruction. In diagnostic-prescriptive teaching situations (discussed in chapter 15), the teacher wishes to know not only the level of performance, but also the specific skills and disabilities that a child manifests. Hence, such hand-tailored tests are an indispensable part of the assessment process. However, such tests must meet the same requirements of reliability and validity that all good measuring instruments should possess. Teachers need training, therefore, in constructing appropriate tests (usually called *norm-referenced tests*) so that in addition to meeting the specific requirements of a specific teaching situation, they contain the relevant content and predictive characteristics that are needed. This is not a simple task.

Vocational Interests. Studies have shown that vocational success is, in part, a function of the individual's interest in the occupation. If the retarded individual's interests are not congruent with the work situation, then that individual will have less chance of achieving success in that vocation. Since an individual may have aptitude in a given area but have relatively low interest in that area, information relative to aptitudes should be supplemented by information relative to vocational interests.

Many tests have been devised to explore vocational interests. An example of such tests is the *Thurstone Interest Schedule* (1947), for ages nine to sixteen and adults. Detailed references to this and other more recent interest tests may be found in Buros's yearbook (1965) of mental measurements.

Such interest tests are valuable in developing a vocational program for the average child, but it is our opinion that they are not particularly applicable to the retarded child. This is true, in part, because the reading level of the retarded child is not high enough for the reading content of the tests. Further, the tests deal with situations that the retarded child usually has not experienced. For these reasons, the results of vocational interest tests are not sufficiently valid.

One approach to this problem is that of Parnicky and his coworkers

(1965), who are aware of the difficulties involved in evaluating the vocational interests of mentally retarded persons. They agree that standard vocational interest tests are not directly applicable to retarded subjects. For example, the *Strong Vocational Interest Blanks* and the *Kuder Preference Record* require reading ability and comprehension far beyond that achieved by even most mildly retarded individuals. Further, the objection can be raised that these instruments concentrate on job areas and levels for which the retarded child cannot realistically aspire. Consequently, Parnicky et al. developed the *Vocational Interest and Sophistication Assessment Test.* Two versions of this test were developed. One covers a range of specific occupations considered feasible for retarded persons; the other covers such general preferences as working with one or more in a group, being supervised or unsupervised, working outdoors or indoors, doing heavy work or light work, and working with the same sex or with the opposite sex. The test is still relatively new and is in need of further validation and reliability studies. However, preliminary reports indicate that the test is valuable for assessing the vocational interests of the mentally retarded adolescent.

We have found that observational data and interviews can be valuable in vocational guidance. The child should be provided with a variety of occupational experiences. Reactions and feelings can be explored through discussion and through observation of behavior. The findings then can be integrated with vocational aptitudes and other characteristics. As we have noted previously, there is a wide range of occupations in which a retarded child can succeed. The vocational adjustment of the retarded child is discussed in detail in chapter 15. The exploration of interests is an important part of the assessment and guidance program. As we shall see, it is a continuing process that starts at an early age. It continues beyond adolescence and needs to be highly integrated with the child's total program of education and guidance.

ASSESSMENT AS A CONTINUING PROCESS

The material presented in this chapter reveals the wide range of assessment procedures and techniques that can be applied to the retarded child. It also emphasizes the need for the services of a wide variety of specialists. However, not all of the assessment procedures discussed are applicable at the same time. For example, we do not need to evaluate the mechanical aptitude of a six-year-old retarded child.

Assessment should be viewed as a continuing process, in which certain attributes of the child are evaluated as the needs arise. All too often, a child is given an intelligence test, and if the IQ is found to be low, the child is placed in a special class for retarded children. The likelihood is then great that he will remain in such a class for the remainder of school attendance. Such a practice is tragically based on the mistaken idea that a single test, at a given time, can predict the static (or unchanging) development of the child. But the retarded child is not a static organism; every child is constantly evolving, particularly if given adequate growth-stimulating programs (see chapter 15). The retarded child is in need of continued reappraisal in light of constantly changing patterns of abilities and emerging capacities. Therefore, regular and frequent reevaluation should be carried out. In this *longitudinal* reassessment, the observations by the teacher of the actual adjustment and achievement of the child are crucial. In addition, retesting with standardized tests of mental capacities, restudy with personality tests, and reinterview by the psychologist or psychiatrist are needed. It is only with this kind of continuing reassessment that the most effective educational and mental health programs can be charted.

PART
IV

INTERVENTION, TRAINING, AND SCHOOL PROGRAMS: ISSUES AND SOLUTIONS

– 12 –

Intervention and Training
in the Preschool Years

We will now begin to consider in a more systematic manner some of the problems, methods, programs, and possible consequences for dealing with the prevention of mental retardation, the improvement in functioning of the mentally retarded, and provisions for humanizing the life circumstances of those with mild to profound degrees of such retardation. In this chapter, we shall focus our attention on problems and issues that characterize the preschool years.

PROGRAMS OF INTERVENTION

We already have discussed some of the early and pioneer efforts that were directed toward improving the behavioral effectiveness of preschool children (see chapter 5). The first phase of such work focused on the improvement of both "normal" and subnormal individuals, mainly but not exclusively in nursery school situations. Research studies based on such programs, which usually offered limited but increased stimulation in school settings, seemed to demonstrate that intellectual functioning and educational attainment could be improved both for short and long periods through improvement in the educational experiences of preschool youngsters. We also indicated that the research findings frequently were disputed by adversaries who pointed to shortcomings in experimental design or to inadequate criteria of improvement, or both.

The second phase of such studies involved the so-called Head Start Program. This program consisted of projects funded mainly by federal grants to improve the educational functioning of preschool youngsters from disadvantaged homes. Numerous projects throughout the country were hastily initiated, most of them in the 1966–1967 period, and were offered to children from disadvantaged homes. Most of the enrollees were in the four- to five-year age range. Many of the programs were never adequately organized, many involved inadequately

383

trained personnel, and many did not plan any appropriate research evaluation. As Payne and Mercer (1974) point out, the initial expectation that spectacular results might be achieved by such programs was soon dissipated and a period of skepticism followed. By 1969, a more sophisticated approach to such programs was usually present, however. Personnel were more carefully screened and selected, educational curricula were better prepared, and more sophisticated research designs were employed. Some programs for infants also were developed. Cicerelli (1969) and others prepared reviews of the best of these programs. In general, evaluations of the findings were found to be encouraging by many analysts. Caldwell (1970) offered a rationale emphasizing the importance of intervention in infancy, rather than delaying training until later childhood years, and others soon noted the importance of actively involving the parents in programs for their own education and their assistance in the training of their youngsters. Although a great deal of effort went to waste in these early Head-start programs, the great potential values also were recognized.

The third phase of the development of intervention programs, which emphasized training during infancy with high risk families, thus was ushered in.

Early Intervention Programs

The importance of early intervention programs, *when properly planned and implemented,* cannot be overemphasized. There are several reasons for this assertion. In the first place, as Bloom (1964), who reviewed the evidence, showed, intelligence tends to become stabilized very early (by about four years of age). What this means is that, barring highly intensive efforts in later years, the rate of intellectual growth tends to remain fairly constant thereafter. In the second place, the attitudes toward achievement and effective social intervention have, by this time, become fairly limited in cases in which low levels of environmental stimulation and support have been characteristic. And, in the third place, significant deficits in basic sensorimotor skills, in language and communication, and in general fund of information have become prominent by this time and make later adaptation to formal school instruction much more difficult and failure-prone. Hence, as the programs we shall review have demonstrated, appropriate and continuing early intervention can not only forestall such developments, at least to a large extent, but also can make much more effective later programs of special training and education.

We shall review several early intervention programs and suggest the inferences and conclusions that may be drawn from them.

The Carolina Abecedarian Project. This program was begun in 1972 and initial results have been reported by Ramey and Campbell (1977). On the basis of various criteria, 87 families were selected as being "high-risk" families. They were offered inclusion in the program and their new-born children and the families were assigned to either an experimental or a control group. Eighty-six of the families agreed to participate in the program. The target children were randomly assigned to one of these groups. The experimental children began to participate in a day-care facility at between six weeks and three months of age. Both the experimental and control groups received the following services: (1) Family support social services including goods, services, or guidance were supplied on the basis of requests from parents or on the basis of routine visits. (2) Nutritional supplements were provided to both groups. The experimental group received the bulk of nutrition at the day care center, and the controls received an unlimited supply of free formulas. This was done "to control for the effects of nutrition on development." (3) Medical care was provided for both groups. (4) Transportation was provided to and from the project to all participants. (5) Mothers of all participants were paid for nonmedical evaluations.

Although Ramey and Campbell do not describe in detail in this initial presentation of results the specific nature of the program that was offered to the experimental group, they note that this group, in contrast to the control group, was given various "experiences in physical and motor development, perceptual and cognitive development, language development, and social development."

Preliminary findings are presented chiefly for the area of cognitive development over the period from birth to eighteen months (*Bayley Scales of Infant Development*), and at twenty-four and thirty-six months (*Stanford-Binet, Form L–M*). The numbers of children included in the analysis of Bayley scores at eighteen months were 55, and 28 on the Binet scores at twenty-four and thirty-six months (since only those numbers of children had reached these respective age levels).

The chief findings are striking. (1) On the Bayley scores, the experimental group of high-risk children (from poverty backgrounds) maintains a consistent pattern of *average mental development* through eighteen months of age (mean IQ's are in the 100 to 105 range), whereas the control group *drops in mental development* from about 100 to slightly below 90. The difference is highly significant statistically. (2) On the Binet scores these differences tend to be increased: at twenty-four months, the experimental group's mean IQ is 93 whereas that of the control group is 82; and at 36 months, the respective mean IQs are 97 and 81. (It should be noted that the norms on which the Binet IQs were obtained were derived from the 1972 data on this test and represent IQs that are approximately 10 points lower than IQs based on this test with earlier norms. If the thirty-six month IQs were transmuted in terms of the earlier norms, the respective IQs would be approximately 107 for the experimental group and 91 for the control group.) In any case, there is a 16 point difference between the two groups at thirty-six months. (3) An item analysis based on seventeen items from the Bayley scale revealed a difference of 20 percent or more on eleven items in favor of the experimental group. A similar item analysis on the Binet items (forty-two items) showed that the experimental group was superior on seventeen items, whereas the control group was superior on only one item (repeating digits), but the findings on that item appeared to be unreliable. (4) No sex differences were found for any of the comparisons.

Ramey and Campbell believe that their results indicate that "our early intervention is preventing early and progressive developmental retardation." We concur that the evidence seems to favor this conclusion. The conclusion is strengthened since the control group was not left entirely to its own resources, as is usually the case in research of this kind, but instead was offered some kinds of significant support (nutrition, medical assistance, and other support). They also believe that "language differences between the groups is a plausible major factor in accounting for group differences." Although we concur that this is a plausible major factor, analysis of their evidence suggests that perceptual-motor differences is at least equally plausible as a major factor, since their item analysis revealed that on the Bayley and Binet scales a total of eleven items in the perceptual-motor domain accounted for significant differences between the groups. Of course, any analysis is limited by the restriction in types of items present on the measuring instruments; if other instruments were employed, other differences might have been demonstrated. Finally, we should add that the role of the parents in this program was not assessed in this report, and we shall have more to say about this in our later discussion.

The Milwaukee Project. We have referred to this study in previous chapters and now will discuss it in greater detail. The Project, begun more than ten years ago, is highly significant for several reasons. In the first place, the program involved mothers as well as target children in terms of intensive training and support. Secondly, there were attempts to individualize the training for each child and for each mother in terms of idiosyncratic needs and assets. Thirdly, extensive and sophisticated measures of behavioral functions were obtained during the extensive experimental period. And, fourthly, follow-up data have been collected and will continue to be collected.

Various reports of methods and findings are available (Heber, Dever, and Conry, 1968; Heber and Garber, 1971, 1973, 1975); we shall select data and findings from a recent report on several aspects of the research (Garber and Heber, 1977). The Milwaukee Program had found that it was possible to identify "high-risk" families by selecting children whose mothers had IQs below 80. (Being from a disadvantaged economic home was not, by itself, sufficient to determine the probability of being "high risk!") Heber and Garber had learned that offspring from both seriously disadvantaged socio-cultural background and mothers with IQs below 80 declined markedly in IQ level during the period from infancy to maturity.

A research program was begun with forty families, each of which had a mother with a WAIS IQ below 75, from an economically depressed area in Milwaukee. Half of the families were assigned to an experimental group and half to a control group. None of the children had significant birth anomalies. The two groups of children did not differ in early birth measures. The experimental group was offered a six-year program involving vocational and social training for the mothers and an elaborate educational program in a neighborhood center on a daily, year-round basis with a staff of teachers and paraprofessionals. The program for the experimental mothers first involved training in job skills, reading skills, and home management.

Both experimental and control groups were assessed at six months on the Gesell Developmental Schedule, and later assessed at 18 months on language functions, and assessed again at 24 months with the Cattell, Stanford-Binet, and learning tasks. When the children had reached 30 months, child-mother interactions were assessed, and at 36 months additional language tests were employed in evaluating the children.

Highly significant differences were found between the experimental children and their mothers, on the one hand, and the control group on the other hand. The "experimental" mothers became more self-confident and became more responsive with their children (both verbally and nonverbally). In contrast, the "control" mothers were low in self-confidence and were relatively nonresponsive in interactions with their children.

The differences between the two groups of children were even more striking. The experimental group showed enthusiasm and conscientiousness in tackling problem-solving tasks and used "strategy" behavior, whereas the control group were passive, lacked enthusiasm, and were unable to learn problem-solving skills.

Another important finding was that even though "experimental" mothers tended to become more responsive and interactive with their children, *not all of them did*. Garber and Heber conclude that it is a mistake to treat all families alike, as if poverty and low IQ were sufficient to characterize them and the family processes that were ongoing. They point up the need of developing more effective methods for rehabilitating some of these mothers.

Further analysis of findings on the *WISC* beginning at four years and continuing to nine years revealed that the experimental group attained an average IQ about 20 points higher than the control group and that they were able to maintain this difference over the years until the (then final) testing at nine years. Although both groups showed some decline in IQ after school age was attained, the experimental group maintained an IQ slightly above 100 on the average whereas the control group had an IQ of about 80. There was almost no overlap in IQ between the two groups. Further, it was found that differences in language skills between the two groups were approximately two years, and these differences favoring the experimental group persisted at least until school age.

One additional finding, obtained in the follow-up phase of the study, was that the experimental group of children exhibited "behavior problems" in school. Garber and Heber suggest that this is due to their confidence and ability in using language skills with which the schools have difficulty in coping. It also is probable that much more than language skills is involved. Perhaps the experimental group had learned to express themselves much more freely in many behavioral areas as a consequence of their enriched and "free" experimental program, and the school was unable to cope with this degree of freedom in children.

Although we have presented only some highlights from the findings of the Milwaukee Project, some points deserve emphasis. The first is that early and appropriate intervention, including both mothers and their children from high-risk areas, can produce significant differences in behavior and ability in both, and the children seem able to maintain their improvement over some period of time. Second, not all mothers from disadvantaged socio-cultural sectors are "high-risk" mothers; a low IQ in a mother (or other low cognitive and social skills) also is important. Third, there are important individual differences in mothers as well as in children coming from high-risk populations, and differential treatment is necessary if programs of intervention are to be most effective. Finally, far more than cognitive and adaptive skills are the outcomes of such intervention programs, significant as these may be. There are highly important changes in self-concept, self-confidence, and in many types of attitudes that can have profound effect on later behavior and adjustment.

The Family-Oriented Home Visiting Program. Our third illustration of early intervention programs focuses on helping mothers with their young children and enlisting fathers whenever possible. This program is in its early stages and final results are, therefore, not available; the program is based on previous findings (Gray and Klaus, 1970; Gilmer, Miller, and Gray, 1970), which attempted to assess the effects of participation by the mother in programs for intervention for low-income families. It had been found that even though involvement of the mother "did not increase the children's performance on tests of intellectual ability or language" (above that of intervention without training of the mother) for older siblings, it did produce such increases for younger children (infants 8 to 18 months) which were maintained for a period of two years after intervention but which were not significantly different from a control group (in a follow-up evaluation). It was believed that training during the period of infancy, which did produce remarkable if temporary gains, may have served the mothers well during the period of infancy but served them less well during the toddler period. Hence, a continuing program for the mother (and the father as well), aimed at producing parents who become more effective teachers and programmers in improving the educational potential of the home, may be highly important.

The program involved weekly visits in the homes for nine months, and monthly visits for half of the families for the following years, and a randomized control group which did not receive such visits.

Gray (1977) reports positive changes in the mothers as more effective change agents were produced. Mothers improved the stimulus potential of the home, as contrasted with the control group, and maternal teaching style also was significantly improved. The "experimental" children were significantly superior also, as toddlers, on a test of receptive language and on an intelligence test at a later time. The gains, while significant but modest, seem to indicate clearly the possible effects of improving parental management with children from low-income groups.

Intervention for Children with Biological Disability. Our fourth illustration focuses on a program not for children from disadvantaged homes but for children who "have suffered adverse prenatal, intrapartum, or neonatal biological events" (Parmelee, 1977). It has been shown that "the risk or the severity of possible developmental disability for these infants cannot readily be predicted by the occurrence of any single hazardous prenatal, intrapartum, or neonatal biological event." (Parmelee and Haber, 1973; Sameroff and Chandler, 1975; Broman, Nichols, and Kennedy, 1975; and Hutt, 1976). Many infants with

TABLE 12.1.   Infant   Assessment   Procedures   for   the   Nine-month Cumulative Risk Score*

1. Obstretric complication scale.
2. Postnatal complication scale.
3. Newborn sleep polygraph for assessment of state organization.
4. Newborn neurological examination.
5. Newborn visual attention assessment.
6. Three months sleep polygraph.
7. Four months Gesell test of infant development.
8. Four months visual attention assessment.
9. Four months pediatrics complication scale.
10. Eight months exploratory behavior assessment.
11. Eight months hand precision and sensory-motor schema assessment.
12. Nine months Gesell test of infant development.
13. Nine months Casati-Lezine assessment of sensory-motor cognitive development.
14. Nine months pediatric complication scale.

*Reproduced from: Parmelee, A. H. Planning intervention for infants at high risk identified by developmental evaluation. In Mittler, P. (ed.) *Research to Practice in Mental Retardation,* Vol. I. Baltimore: University Park Press, 1977. Reprinted with permission of Peter Mittler.

such brain damage either suffer only transient brain insult or are able to compensate even for demonstrable brain injury. Hence, Parmelee et al. (1976) devised a comprehensive assessment procedure for infants that would yield a cumulative risk score. Table 12.1 presents the items of this procedure.

Several features of this "risk score" may be noted. It provides for assessment and evaluation in several areas that are regarded as critical for effective behavioral development; i.e., general physical, neurological, sensory, motoric, attention, and social interactions. Scales such as this are more likely to be effectively predictive since they take into account a number of important parameters of development. By the same token, it should be noted that a total score does not necessarily reflect adequately the relative importance of the several dimensions for every infant; i.e., a particular impairment may be more significant in one instance than in another. Another feature of the "score" is that it is *cumulative over time* (a nine-month period). Several measures that are obtainable at or near birth are derived later, when they are relevant. Finally, it should be noted that measures of the several dimensions are replicated at different ages, so that changes in the developmental rate can be reflected as the infant develops. To some degree, this assists in providing more accurate predictions since the "score" takes into account differential rates of development for each individual.

In this program, the major aim is to maximize effective and constructive interactions between infants and their families and environment. It has been learned that during the weeks and early months following birth of preterm babies, mothers and the families are most concerned about the physical welfare of the children (Brown, 1976). The program therefore involves assisting the mothers (and others in the family) with difficult problems involving feeding, crying, and the like. Toward this end, a nurse and a physician are assigned to each family to provide emotional support as well as specific help with these early physical problems. This nurse-physician team begins to work with the family while the mother and infant are still in the hospital and then continues contact immediately after discharge from the hospital through phone calls and home visits.

A major aim is to help reduce parental anxiety and confusion about how to deal with the infant. Monthly visits to the home continue from four to nine months. In the latter part of the first year, attention is focused on educational intervention, using the data from the cumulative risk score. Families, and especially mothers, are assisted not only in providing effective help for the infant, but also in dealing with "interferences" that the infant's condition imposes on family interactions. Utilizing criteria outlined by Bromwich (1976), the mother is helped to obtain more pleasure in dealing with her infant by learning what to expect, to help train the infant more adequately, and *to obtain pleasure rather than frustration from the interactions.*

Findings from this type of program should be of considerable help, not only with families whose infants suffer from biological impairment, but also with families from high-risk sectors who need specific techniques for rehabilitation, stimulation, and training.

The Perry School Study. Our fifth illustration involves a longitudinal study of 58 children who attended an experimental preschool program in Ypsilanti, Michigan and compares them with 65 children, equivalent in IQ, ethnic origin, socioeconomic status, and sex who did not attend the program. The children in the experimental program attended preschool for a two-year period (except for thirteen, who attended for only one year) for five days per week during the regular school year. The program involved "individualized support of a child's cognitive development by the teaching staff" and weekly home visits (Schweinhart and Weikart, 1977).

The major characteristics of both the experimental and control groups were: low *Stanford-Binet* IQ scores (ranging from 50 to 88), black ethnic origin, and low socioeconomic status (57 percent of the families in the experimental group were on welfare). The area in which the study took place (Ypsilanti, Michigan) has had a history of low academic achievement. Among the tests that were administered, in addition to the *Stanford-Binet* (which was administered as a pretest and at the end of each school year through the fourth grade), were: the *WISC* (given at the end of the eighth grade), the *California Achievement Test,* the *Peabody Picture Vocabulary Test,* the *Arthur Adaptation of the Leiter International Performance Scale,* and the *Illinois Test of Psycholinguistic Abilities.* The curriculum utilized was progressively modified with experience and is described in a book by Weikart et al. (1971).

Findings have dealt with intellectual performance, achievement in academic subjects, and vocational adjustment. Our immediate concern is with the findings concerning the first two categories. Insofar as intelligence, as measured, is concerned, the preschool experimental group achieved a mean IQ that was 12 points higher than the mean of the control group during the preschool period. By one year after preschool, the difference in means was only 5 points. By the end of the third school year there was no difference in mean IQ score, and this lack of difference between the groups was maintained thereafter. However, a surprising finding is that the mean IQ score tends to drop consistently for both groups between the fourth and eighth grades. Schweinhart and Weikart suggest that this drop may be an artifact resulting from the change in tests used from the *Stanford-Binet* to the *WISC,* but the data supplied by them does not warrant this conclusion since the major drop in IQ score for both groups occurs before the fourth grade, when the *Stanford-Binet* was still utilized. Rather, the drop in IQ score could more readily be explained by the lack of an educationally and environmentally stimulating environment, which is characteristic of that community.

The results in terms of achievement, as measured by the *California Achievement Test,* are somewhat different. By the end of the first grade, there was a slight difference in achievement in favor of the experimental group. This difference is maintained and becomes significantly greater after the fourth grade. By the eighth grade, the experimental group achieved significantly higher grade equivalents on each of the three major divisions of the *CAT:* reading, language, and arithmetic. In absolute terms, however, both groups are below their actual grade placements, the experimental group having an average achievement at about the fifth-grade level, and the control group having an achievement slightly below the fourth-grade level.

Weikart and co-workers believe that "the advantages imparted by preschool formed a supportive basis for later academic achievement." This may be true, but the data do not strongly support such a proposition. Although significant gains in IQ were reported during the preschool period for the experimental group, these were not maintained later, and the significant differences in achievement of the two groups did not become manifest until after the fifth grade. These complex and differing patterns of developmental change are not explicable entirely in terms of the differential preschool treatment. Other factors, not detailed or evaluated in the study, may have contributed to the inconsistencies in the findings.

ISSUES AND IMPLICATIONS

Our review of these five significant, illustrative programs for early intervention, as well as our review of other pertinent research, enables us to formulate several major issues and possible resolutions.

1. It now has been well documented that developmental retardation may result from deprivation in early years due to faulty nutrition, inadequate stimulation, and improper or ineffective training procedures. Deprivation may produce impairment in cognitive, social adaptive, and motivational aspects of behavior (Yarrow, Rubenstein, and Pederson, 1975). Although some children are able to overcome the handicaps from such deprivation due to their own

resources or later intervention in schools and "therapeutic agencies," the risk that developmental retardation will persist and even increase is very great.

Early detection of such potentially depriving circumstances is, therefore, imperative. In the past, such detection was difficult because indices for evaluation were lacking or inadequate, as well as because financial resources to initiate and maintain detection programs were limited. Resources are still limited although becoming more readily available, but intervention programs have reached only a very small fraction of high-risk populations. Moreover, high-risk families do not come only from families suffering from poverty. Other factors, such as low IQs of the parents, poor educational-cultural backgrounds of the parents, the low stimulus potential of the family and social environment, and the lack of concern or motivation of the parents in coping with cognitive and developmental problems of their children also are significant. Effective programs must be *community-based* and must coordinate the resources of the various, relevant agencies in the community.

2. A significant number of potentially retarded children come from premature births and related complications. Such infants may suffer impairment in their early days due to physical inability to adapt and thrive as well as due to the emotional disturbance in their parents and their parents' inability to cope effectively with the condition of their infants. Intervention in such cases must involve the hospital team while mother and child are still in the hospital and must provide continuing follow-up, support, and guidance during the following months. Brain damage in such infants may be only transient or may, in other cases, be compensated for. Brain damage, in any case, *does not inevitably lead to developmental retardation.*

Hospital-based programs are essential for such cases, with subsequent coordination provided for continuing intervention by appropriate agencies. The myth that brain-damaged children will necessarily be handicapped for their remaining years must be dissipated. Although children with severe brain damage may suffer irremediable consequences, many of these cases can profit tremendously from intensive rehabilitation. Many "irreversible" cases turn out to be reversible. Important as biological defect may be, the psychological consequences are also critical and need to be attended to.

3. Some mothers and some families do not volunteer for help in intervention programs, and some do not respond to offers of remedial help. This poses a serious moral problem for society. The conflict involves the *rights of children versus the rights of parents.* This conflict usually is faced only in cases in which there is obvious and serious abuse of the infant; society (and the courts) then may take some decisive action to save the endangered child. However, there probably are many other cases in which mild neglect or milder forms of physical-social deprivation seriously and adversely affect the development of the child. We need more effective laws and procedures for dealing with these cases. The rights of parents should not interfere with the rights of their children to develop normally and maximally.

4. There has been some debate concerning the significance of critical periods, and especially early critical periods, in the pace of development of the child. Although few conditions are entirely irreversible, sufficient evidence has

been accumulated to demonstrate that critical periods do exist and that deprivation and/or trauma during these periods have devastating effects on subsequent development of the individual.

As both Piaget and Freud have argued, and many others have demonstrated, conditions of "early bonding," the development of basic trust, the development of adequate sensori-motor skills, and the stimulation of communication and language development are profoundly important for subsequent development. Early intervention programs must take these findings into account. The emotional needs of the infant are paramount. In addition, appropriate programs for sensori-motor stimulation, perceptual-motor training, language training, and training in social adaptation are necessary. In general, structured programs, rather than more haphazard programs, have been found to be most effective.

5. The evidence clearly demonstrates that there are huge individual differences among retarded children, and that retarded children have important assets as well as deficiencies.

Careful and continuing diagnostic assessment by appropriate specialists with differing professional skills is needed to plan *individualized programs* for each retarded or potentially retarded youngster. Assessment should lead to programs tailored to each individual's needs and be revised in the light of emerging developmental data.

6. Available evidence indicates quite clearly that under effective conditions, intervention for the mothers of high-risk children contributes significantly to the improved developmental functioning of these children (Bronfenbrenner, 1974). The mother is important in stimulating the child's development and in preventing arrest or regression of such development. There is limited evidence concerning the effectiveness of the father in early intervention programs, and of the role of the whole family in such situations. Nevertheless, both research and clinical evidence favor the proposition that the whole family is affected by high-risk and seriously retarded youngsters.

Programs of intervention therefore should attempt to involve the entire family through effective guidance and training procedures. Although the mother may be critical in this process, the contributory functions of other members of the family should not be neglected. Research is needed on both the significance of such family contributions and on the effects on the family of such interventions.

7. As in all matters involving relatively large segments of the population, the cost factor is highly important. We do not have much data on cost-accountability and cost-effectiveness of various programs. Such data are urgently needed not only if efficient use is to be made of our resources, but also if the possible benefits to society, as well as to the affected individuals, are to be assessed properly and utilized for more effective intervention.

Although humanitarian considerations must be given priority, there should be no conflict between improved cost-effectiveness and social consequences. Toward this end, all programs should build research appraisal of such factors into the design of their research and training programs.

PART
V

EDUCATION: OBJECTIVES, METHODS, AND THERAPY

– 13 –

Education and Training in the School Years: Problems, Issues and Programs

The three major goals of the President's Committee on Mental Retardation have been summarized by Krause (1977), executive director of the Committee: "1. to reduce the occurrence of disability from mental retardation; 2. to promote human services that will enable retarded persons to achieve their potential *in the most normal, least restrictive setting possible* [our emphasis]; 3. to help retarded persons achieve the rights of full citizenship and public acceptance." We have dealt with aspects of the first goal in previous chapters. In this chapter, we will discuss major aspects of the last two goals as they relate to education in the school years, leaving to the next chapter a discussion of the issues involved in institutionalization and deinstitutionalization. We have underlined a portion of goal number 2 in order to emphasize an issue that has been much debated, sometimes distorted, and sometimes ignored.

FEDERAL LEGISLATION AND SCHOOL POLICY

We can trace the major initiation of current and developing programs for education in this country to the opening sentence in the 1962 President's Panel on Mental Retardation, which states: "Every human being has potential for useful activity." This report also alleges: "Modern science and action by our social institutions have demonstrated that many of them [retarded individuals] can become self-supporting and self-reliant if provided adequate education, rehabilitation, and training services including counseling, guidance, and placement." Thus, the broadly conceived goals of education embraced both vocational adequacy and self-reliant behavior.

By 1965 the movement toward normalizing and mainstreaming most, if not all, retarded individuals was well under way, although the means for implementing such programs had not yet been provided. The emphasis, which first was on providing new programs for children in the preschool years, soon became the integration of retarded persons into the mainstream of educational settings throughout the school years. In that year, Mackie (1965) reported that about 390,000 children were enrolled in special classes and that provisions for such classes in preschool, elementary, and high school programs were available in most major cities. But by 1972, the arguments against placement in special education classes had reached a crescendo and many legal battles proclaimed that retarded children were being deprived of their constitutional rights to "equal educational opportunities" and their parents were being deprived of their rights to participate in the decision to place their children in special programs or to place them in regular classes (Institute for the Study of Mental Retardation and Related Disabilities, 1972). Moreover, some leaders in education of the retarded voiced strong objections to any special class placements. One of the foremost spokesmen in this area, L. M. Dunn (1968) had stated: "Separating a child from other children in the neighborhood—or removing him for therapy or special-class placement—probably has a serious debilitating effect upon his self-image."

In 1970 the National Association for Retarded Citizens prepared a position paper (NARC, 1970; promulgated in 1972). It required that *no child* [sic] be classified as mentally retarded unless evaluated by an *evaluation team* composed of qualified "diagnosticians." The rush was on to develop alternatives to special education classes, and to move toward *normalization* and *mainstreaming* of retarded children into regular classes, with some provision for special training when needed. We shall have much to say about these developments later in this chapter. Various plans were developed to provide for such mainstreaming, but the goal was to move retarded children into an integrated educational class with normal children (Beery, 1972).

The year 1975 was a landmark in sustained efforts, culminating in Public Law 94–142. This federal law was the result of several refinements of the Education of the Handicapped Act. It was passed in the House of Representatives by a vote of 404 to 7, and in the Senate by a vote of 87 to 7! It was foolhardy to vote against a law which was so humanitarian. It was signed into law by President Ford on November 28, 1975, although he stated (White House Press Release, December 2, 1975): ". . . this bill promises more than the Federal Government can deliver and its good intentions could be thwarted by many unwise provisions it contains." The provisions of this law are so far-reaching and its possible consequences are so great that we shall consider its provisions in some detail.

The provisions of PL 94–142, becoming effective with the start of fiscal year 1978, are aimed at providing a free public education for *all handicapped children* (including the retarded) between the ages of three and eighteen years by September 1978, and for all handicapped individuals between the ages of three and twenty-one years by 1980. In order to accomplish this, the bill provides "full fundings" so that states will receive "entitlements" based on the number of handicapped children actually receiving services. An escalating clause for funding provides more than 300 million dollars by 1977–1978 and more than 3 billion dollars by 1982. In order to receive funding, the state must file a state plan that includes provision for full educational opportunity for *all* handicapped children; a date by which the state intends to accomplish a plan for *full services*—not later than September 1980; assurance of due process procedures and nondiscriminatory procedures; a program to identify, locate, and evaluate all handicapped children; a description of the kind and number of facilities, personnel and services; a program for development of personnel; assurance that handicapped children will be *educated with normal children to the maximum extent possible; written communication* to the parents (or surrogate parents) *before* the child is placed in any programs; assurance that the program for each child is *individualized* to meet the child's condition and needs [our emphasis].

We have emphasized several portions of the provisions of PL 94–142 in order to highlight them. These provisions are critically important and, no doubt, will be interpreted by various individuals and educational organizations in differing ways. We can anticipate that the interpretation and application of the provisions will be tested in the courts and in other arenas. What, for example, is the meaning of "full service"? How will it be checked and evaluated? What, specifically, is meant by the provision that handicapped children will be educated with normal children "to the maximum extent possible"? This provision already had been interpreted in differing ways (see Schippes and Kenowitz, 1975), and already is causing great concern among educators and parents. Does it mean that all retarded children, regardless of the extent of and severity of their difficulties and handicaps, will be "mainstreamed"? We will discuss this problem in a later section of this chapter on Implications. What will be the nature of the "individualized" program? Will it become a "face-saving" device engaged in to meet the letter, but not the spirit, of the law? How will it be accomplished?

PL 94–142 has other provisions and involves other implications. In order to provide the services that are required, it is obvious that extensive in-service training programs for personnel will be required. A pool of 121 special education administrators predicted (Schippes and Kenowitz, 1975) that by 1988 teacher education would be shifted from the universities to local school systems and teacher associations. Such a shift could have very far-reaching consequences—not all necessarily favorable. The same pool of experts predicted that by 1995, *all* exceptional children would be receiving educational services that transcended state and district boundaries and provided for *uniform* educational opportunities. The experts also predicted that there would be regional resource sharing and greatly increased institutionalization of handicapped individuals with a corresponding increase in public school programs. It was also believed that there would be a great increase in instructional technology, including mobile vans, instructional media services, and individually prescribed instruction.

Even before PL 94–142, many states had begun to implement some of the provisions that were later included in this federal law. Among these was the insistence on a Placement Team that would obtain the necessary diagnostic data for each child and meet to discuss plans for that child. It is anticipated that in the future, such teams will include both regular and special education teachers as well as administrators. The parents or "care givers" of the child also will attend the appropriate meeting of the team; in many states, they already do. In some school districts, specialized school personnel also will attend (or have already begun to do so) including school psychologists, social workers, remedial or resource teachers, and the like. The Team concept is meant to insure full and adequate consideration of each child's needs, proper evaluation of available data about the child, and alternative methods of providing appropriate educational training, due process in arriving at decisions, and systematic review of placement and program at least annually.

Placement teams are a costly and sometimes cumbersome means of developing educational plans for each handicapped child. With experience, and with research evaluation of their effectiveness, their effectiveness can be improved. As we pointed out in chapter 11, however, too often some team members do not make a significant contribution to its effectiveness and others are insufficiently trained to do a valid job of evaluating the evidence. For instance, some school psychometrists who function on some school teams as clinical psychologists do not properly evaluate their psychological test findings, and others who attempt to contribute to an anlysis of learning difficulties or methods of instruction are inadequately trained to offer appropriate recommendations. In addition, some teachers, purporting to evaluate psychological abilities or findings, are not qualified to do so, and yet they attempt to provide diagnostic appraisals or evaluate test findings. Such types of members of the Placement Team are not only "dead weight" but also contribute by their sheer numbers to inadequate evaluation or recommendation. Thus, although the team concept probably is an important one and can contribute to more adequate and more effective evaluations, it must not be taken for granted that this is necessarily the case. Moreover, candid and frank evaluations of the actual abilities of the team members also are necessary so that the "democratic process" does not become a hoax.

THE ROLE OF SPECIAL EDUCATION AND SPECIAL CLASSES

Before we consider in some detail the rationale, methods, and effectiveness of mainstreaming and normalization, let us first review the history of special education, its values, and its limitations. A brief history of special education will help us to gain perspective.

The Early History of Special Education

The history of special education programs for the mentally retarded in this country is only a little over 100 years old, and the history of special educational classes for such children in the public schools is even shorter, the first one reportedly having been established in Springfield, Massachusetts, in 1897. Prior to that, various sporadic efforts had been made, especially in Europe, to deal with the problems of the retarded. It will be helpful to see how the present programs of education gradually came into being.

The attitude toward mentally retarded persons in ancient times can best be characterized by the use of the then prevalent term *idiot* (from the Greek, meaning *peculiar*). This attitude was deprecatory and hostile. Gradually, a more tolerant attitude developed. During the medieval period it was highly ambivalent, ranging from amused tolerance to hostility and persecution. In the thirteenth century, the first colony for retarded individuals was established in Belgium. In later centuries, other custodial places were sometimes established, but almost never for training purposes.

The modern period in the education of retarded individuals had its beginnings in the work done in the retraining of the blind and the deaf. Various attempts were made in the eighteenth and nineteenth centuries to teach persons who were severely deprived in these sensory areas, and a great deal was learned about special methods and techniques suitable for their education. It was on the basis of these prior experiences that the now-famous experiment was conducted by Itard on the so-called Wild Boy of Aveyron in 1798.

This eleven- or twelve-year-old boy, discovered in southern France, behaved like an animal. He wore no clothes, walked on all four limbs, was unable to speak, selected his food by smell, and was largely uninhibited in his behavior. Itard, who was a physician in an institution for the deaf in Paris, thought that the boy's condition was essentially the result of his severe social-cultural deprivation and that intensive sensori-motor training, stimulation of his social needs, and tutoring in language and thinking would overcome his socially derived handicaps and enable him to function in a normal manner.

Itard devoted five years of extremely intensive tutoring to this boy, but finally gave up in severe disappointment when the boy *failed to respond according to Itard's expectations*. That his efforts were not entirely unsuccessful may be seen from the facts that the boy learned to read a little, he could recognize many objects, he became socialized to a great extent, and he seemed to improve in many aspects of his thinking processes. Itard was even commended by the French Academy of Sciences for his contribution to educational methods. He was able to demonstrate that even a profound mentally retarded person could profit considerably from an intensive program of *individually tailored educational stimulation* by the so-called *clinical method*. Perhaps his greatest contribution, however, was in stimulating others to develop and try out special methods for training and educating mentally retarded individuals.

One of Itard's pupils (Séguin) developed his methods more explicitly. In 1837, Séguin opened the first school in Paris for the education of mentally retarded children. Later he came to the United States and helped to organize special institutions for such children. He emphasized the importance of neurophysiological training: muscle training (especially of the hands), sensory training (including discriminatory exercises in audition and vision), speech training, and writing and reading. He provided individualized programs adapted to the specific needs of each child. Later, followers of Itard and Séguin developed special educational methods based, in large part, on this earlier work, making adaptations in both materials and methods of instruction. Almost all of them focused on the pedagogical rather than the medical problems involved in training mentally retarded individuals.

The work of these early pioneers led to the establishment, in 1832, of the first state-supported institution for the handicapped, the Perkins School for the Blind, in Massachusetts. Some three years later, New York State followed with its own experimental institution, now known as the Syracuse State School. But it was only in the last few years of the nineteenth century that public school classes specifically intended for retarded children were established in the United States.

It was in the public schools that significant shifts in educational philosophy, as well as in pedagogical methods, were introduced. Hungerford and his co-workers (1952) have reviewed the major shifts in the basic educational philosophies for retarded children. At first, the objective of educational programs for retarded children was to relieve the stress on normal children and their teachers by removing retarded children from regular classes and placing them in a special class. This approach, called a *relief philosophy,* entailed a negative attitude and pessimistic expectations toward retarded children. Later, the concern was that the retarded children should be happy. They were placed in a special class so that they would not have to compete with normal children and suffer unnecessary frustration. This has been termed the *happiness philosophy,* but it involved a negative and sterile orientation, in that it suggested little more than removal from a frustrating situation.

The next phase, termed the *salvage philosophy,* emphasized the teaching of academic skills, sometimes at a watered-down level, but more often at levels beyond the children's actual capacity to achieve. In any case, excessive emphasis was placed on the need to achieve. There followed a compensatory reaction, embodied in the *handiwork philosophy,* in which stress was placed on manual activities. The implication was that retarded children *could not learn from books but could learn to do things with their hands.*

The *modern philosphy* emphasizes the worthwhileness of each child. It assumes that the child can become a contributing member of society. Although it accepts the essential dignity of the child as a human being, it recognizes that the retarded child lacks certain skills and talents. Education represents an attempt to evaluate carefully the specific capacities of each child and to assist in developing them to the highest degree of which that child is capable. It attempts to be both humane and realistic. It often emphasizes the vocational goals of the educational process.

Special Classes—History

In the United States, the main approach to the treatment of mentally retarded children in the public schools was the provision of special classes. At the end of the first decade of this century, ninety-nine cities had such classes.

After that there was an ever increasing number of special classes, except during the period of the great depression in the 1930s. By 1963, it was estimated that some 390,000 children were enrolled in special classes (Mackie, 1965). Currently there are provisions for preschool, elementary, and high school retarded children in most major cities.

The intent of special classes was to provide specialized instruction with specially trained teachers and with smaller class enrollment than in regular classes. Although there were many advantages to such placement, personal, social, and legal objections to the programs soon arose. On the personal level, it was charged that placement in special classes produced undesirable effects by labeling the children and imposing limits on their growth. On the social level, it was claimed that segregation not only produced stigmatization but also caused inferior competencies in socialization skills. On the legal level, it was claimed that retarded children were being deprived of their constitutional rights to "equal educational opportunities" and that their parents were being deprived of their right to participate in the decision to place their children in special programs. Moreover, in some legal cases it was held that many minority children were improperly classified as mentally retarded and placed in special classes for the retarded on the basis of intelligence tests that were standardized and biased in favor of middle-class whites. Case law on this matter began in 1967 when, in the famous *Hobson v. Hanson* case, Judge Shelly Wright held that "the tracking system of educational placement in Washington, D.C., was illegal since it was in violation of the equal protection clause of the U. S. Constitution." This finding was upheld in the U. S. Circuit Court of Appeals in 1968. There are four legal issues: (1) educational testing does not accurately measure the learning ability of the child; (2) the administration of these tests may be performed incompetently; (3) the parents are not given adequate opportunity to participate in the placement decision; and (4) special educational programming is inadequate and placement in these classrooms causes irreparable harm.

A disproportionately large share of children labeled mentally retarded and placed in special classes came from minority groups and low socioeconomic levels; in many instances their poor performance on standardized tests and in academic skills was a result of inadequate cultural-intellectual stimulation, lack of English-language experience, or both. Therefore, the legal implication (Lang, 1973) seemed to be as follows: "Because the students' interests seem to outweigh the disadvantages to the school system of holding hearings, it seems probable that procedural protection will be required for minority children facing placement into EMR [Educable Mentally Retarded] classes." These considerations led to the NARC position paper of 1972, noted previously.

Special Classes — Issues and Evidence

As we have seen, the traditional twentieth-century method of providing a program for the mentally retarded child has been to place the child in a special class for such children. The objectives have been to provide specially trained teachers; to reduce the class size so that more individualized instruction can be provided; to provide appropriate materials and methods for education; to reduce the traumatic and failure experiences of retarded children by taking them out of competition with more superior learners; and to provide guidance and training, especially in the pre-employment years, so that retarded children can more readily find and retain employment. Many educators feel that special classes are effective in reaching toward these goals, but others are critical of the effects of segregation. There also is the serious concern that such placement keeps children from normal social interactions with a representative cross-section of their peers, thus further limiting the development of appropriate social competencies. Finally, there is evidence that many children, because of their ethnic and cultural backgrounds or because of emotional or behavioral disturbances, are being improperly classified as retarded.

These charges are serious. Some of them undoubtedly stem from the limits on what can be done to improve the functioning of the retarded. Others are directed to inadequacies in the training of the special teacher rather than to the programs themselves. Others, still, are more concerned with the idea of *labeling*, with its unfortunate consequence of diverting attention from the great variations in specific learning aptitudes among retarded children.

What is the answer to such problems? Undoubtedly, there will be many answers, some of which have nothing specifically to do with the concept of special-class placement. For example, whether individual differences in learning patterns are given adequate attention and appropriate remediation has little to do with placement *per se;* rather, methods of assessment may be improved and instruction may be individualized no matter what the placement may happen to be. Many proposals have been offered, some of them extremely creative. We shall examine a sample of such proposals, but we must note that the final answers concerning their relative effectiveness still await much more effective research and follow-up studies. Special classes continue to be used in many communities, but many safeguards are employed to assure that children are not improperly selected for such placement.

Early Research Evidence. As a result of early research studies dealing with the effects of special-class placement, many educators believed that such placement tended to produce poorer academic achievement for retarded pupils and poorer social adjustment. On the basis of these conclusions, quite apart from the charge by Mercer and others, many children from minority cultures and from poor socioeconomic backgrounds were improperly classified as mentally retarded and inappropriately placed in special education programs; and educators, as well as parents, clamored for abolition of special classes and for intergration of retarded children into regular classes. Let us examine some of this early evidence.

In an often-cited study by Johnson (1950), it was concluded that children who are kept in regular classes tend to show a better social adjustment than children placed in special classes. Although Johnson recognized that many variables in this study were uncontrolled, other educators overlooked this and generalized the finding that special-class placement was *the responsible factor* in producing such poor adjustment.

A very extensive study was completed by Thurstone (1959). Thurstone investigated a population of 1,273 educable retarded children, comparing those who had been placed in regular classes with those who had been placed in special classes. The children, ranging in age from about nine to fifteen years, were compared on individual and group intelligence tests, on achievement tests, on gross motor functions, and on sociometric tests. After one year in their respective placements, retarded children who had been placed in regular classes were superior to those in special classes on all measures except arithmetic. After two years in the respective programs, those with IQs in the range of 60 to 79 showed no significant differences on any of the measures, but those with IQs in the range of 50 to 59 and in special classes were superior to those in regular classes on all measures except arithmetic. Thurstone also found that, as a group, retarded children placed in regular classes were more socially isolated and more socially malajusted than those in special classes.

A study on the possible effects of *early* versus *later* placement was done by Warren (1962). An experimental group of twenty-four EMR children was compared on a variety of tests of intelligence and achievement with a control group, who were eligible for special class placement but retained in regular classes for a year. The groups were matched roughly on a sociometric measure and equated on sex and on measures of age, intelligence, and numbers of years in school. The two groups did not differ significantly in achievement as a consequence of the type of placement. However, Warren found, contrary to expectations, that EMR children who were placed in special classes at an earlier age were superior in self-acceptance than those placed at later age. It was thought that children who were placed at later ages had already begun to see themselves as "failures."

A more specific study on the effect of age of placement in special classes on self-concept was undertaken by Mayer (1966). The study involved 100 children divided into subgroups of: early placement, middle placement, and late placement. Age of placement was not found to be significant in producing differences on two tests of self-concept.

Other early studies also found that retarded children profited more from placement in special classes than in regular classes. For example, Kern and Pfaeffle (1965), comparing three groups of EMR, 31 in each group, who were placed, respectively, in segregated schools for the retarded, special education classes in public schools, and regular classes in public schools, found that the children in the special schools had the highest overall adjustment scores whereas those in regular classes had the lowest scores. The test used to measure adjustment was the *California Test of Personality*. One may criticize the validity of this test for this type of population, but the findings are *not* suggestive that special class placement has a negative effect. Goldstein et al. (1965) conducted an interesting study with children randomly assigned in the first grade to special or regular classes. The research population of 129 children had Binet IQs ranging from 56 to 85. Over a four-year period, it was found that: (1) there was no significant difference in the groups in gain in IQ; (2) on measures of sociometric behavior in the neighborhood, special-class children exceeded regular children in freedom of interaction and in originality; and, (3) the mothers of children in regular classes tended to view their children with less derogatory attitudes than those with children in special classes.

There have been only a few studies on the effects of placement with trainable mentally retarded children (TMR). We shall summarize only two of these as fairly representative. A study by Cain and Levine (1963) was fairly comprehensive and sophisticated. It involved 182 children with an average IQ of 37, an average MA of about 3.2, and an average age of 9.4. The study focused on the relative effects of institutional versus community placement of these children. Although not directly relevant to the problem of special class placement, the design of the study permits some evaluation of the effect of type of schooling. The study compared four conditions of training: (1) children living at home and attending public school; (2) children living at home and receiving no schooling; (3) children living in institutions and attending classes there; (4) children living in institutions but receiving no schooling. On a test of social competence (Cain-Levine Social Competence Scale), both groups living at home showed significant improvement in social competency. There was, however, no significant difference between the two home groups. Both institution groups decreased in the measure of social competence, and there was no significant difference in amount of decrease between these two groups. And, finally, both home groups did significantly better than both institution groups. The factor of home placement, and attendant home experiences, thus appears to be the significant factor in determining development in social competence as measured.

The other study, by Peck (1960), attempted to investigate the effect of type of placement on intelligence and social adjustment of very low IQ children (IQs between 25 and 50). There were only 30 children in the study, ranging in age from six to twelve years, but a single curriculum was provided for all of them over a two-year period. Nine of the children were in public schools, 6 were in a private agency, 8 were in institutions, and 7 were at home. On a measure of intelligence (Stanford-Binet) and a measure of social maturity (Vineland Social Maturity) there were no significant changes. However, on ratings by their teachers on social adjustment, self-care, language, and the like, the three classroom groups made significantly more progress than the group that remained at home. The rating scales are, of course, suspect since their degree of reliability and the possible bias of the raters are unknown. The suspected devastating effect of institutional placement was not, however, demonstrated. Apart from the small numbers involved, the fact that there were no evaluations of the quality of the instruction and training suggests the findings must be considered speculative.

More Recent Research Evidence. We now shall sample some recent research studies and examine their findings. On the whole, these studies were better designed and directed to more significant issues than the earlier ones.

A critical study by Monroe and Howe (1971) analyzed the effects of length of time in special classes on social acceptance of EMR children. The population studied was in five junior high schools, and the duration of their experience in special classes varied from one to three years. The seventy boys involved in the study were between thirteen and sixteen years of age and their IQs were 54 or higher. Based on a scale of social acceptance, it was found that there was a significant effect of length of time in the program on degree of social acceptance. If placement in special classes contributed to lower social acceptance, it was believed that length of time should have had a deleterious effect. It was found, however, that the degree of social acceptance was a function of socioeconomic status!

In a study published one year later (Goodman, Gottlieb, and Harrison, 1972), forty educable retarded children (twenty males and twenty females) were evaluated to determine the effects of segregation versus integration into regular classes. These children also were compared with children of average intelligence. Although it was found that EMR children were rejected more frequently than non-EMR children, regardless of the type of class placement, segregation did not add to the kind of stigmatization, as might have been anticipated. Of special interest was the finding that younger non-EMR children were significantly more accepting of younger EMR children than they were accepting of older EMR children.

Lewis (1973), employing a population from twenty-six school districts, conducted an evaluation of four school environments for EMR children. The children were six to about eleven years of age. The numbers in each type of school environment were relatively small (they varied from ten in one category to twenty in two other categories), but they were comparable on important variables that might affect the criterion variables: physical development, self-concept, achievement, and attitude toward school. The school environments that were compared were: I. a self-contained, nonintegrated environment; II. placement in a regular class, although children were eligible for special education; III. special class placement plus a high degree of integration; and IV. resource room placement but enrolled in regular classes. The findings indicated that there were no significant differences: (1) among the groups in self-concept; (2) in achievement as measured by the Metropolitan Achievement Test; and, (3) in attitude toward school. However, it was found that Group I was lower on measures of physical development, adaptive behavior, and socialization.

Another significant study was that reported by Bruininks, Rynders, and Gross (1974). This involved relatively large numbers: 65 mildly retarded elementary school children, and 1,234 nonretarded children in regular classes. The retarded children were either in urban or suburban settings; the respective average ages were ten and eleven, and the respective average IQs were 75 and 69. The retarded children in urban schools were found to be significantly *higher* than the nonretarded in terms of acceptance by their peers, but the retarded in suburban schools were significantly *lower* than the nonretarded. These differences held, however, only for same-sexed individuals. When the data for the sexes were combined, there were no significant differences. This study suggests that the total social setting (in this case, urban versus suburban) is a critical factor in the degree of social acceptance versus nonacceptance, and that the sexual identity (and the factors that go along with it in our culture) also can play a decisive role.

Our sampling of studies surely does not indicate that special class placement, per se, is always the decisive factor in producing the deleterious effects that have so often been alleged. In the first place, the effect of special class placement cannot be determined apart from the social climate that prevails. Moreover, the attitudes of teachers, of other school personnel, and of parents cannot be disregarded. If we tend to regard mental retardation in negative terms, it is likely that the class placement will, itself, have little relative effect on such attitudes. In the second place, the kind of teachers who are involved in special class programs, their relationships with other teachers and with administrative personnel, and their integration into the total school program — in terms of decisions, activities, and the like — easily can make a decisive difference. And, of course, the outcomes of such special education programs — whether, for example, they lead to better achievement of the retarded or to their increased employability — also can be quite significant. In short, the problem is highly complex, and it is relatively easy to find data to support any position on the issues to support one's prejudice if one disregards these complexities. Too often we have blamed special class placement when it was the lack of adequate training for some of the special class teachers, or lack of support for their programs, or other social and political considerations that really were at fault.

Nevertheless, there were sufficient data to show that many retarded pupils were being stigmatized, that many were poorly or improperly educated, and that many, as a consequence, were unable to find suitable employment. Moreover, it had become increasingly clear that the usual intelligence tests, and particularly the verbal intelligence tests, were heavily biased against individuals from lower socioeconomic sectors and from some minority, ethnic backgrounds. Mercer (in Soeffing, 1977) has stated that "Tremendous cultural biases exist in the IQ test." We could not be in more complete agreement although we do not concur with some others who seek to abolish the use of intelligence tests (see chapter 11). Considerations such as these led the Missouri Conference (Meyers, 1971) to express by majority sentiment that it strongly favored the return of the mildly mentally retarded to regular classes. Others questioned the advisability of such a move unless or until other issues were dealt with adequately, such as what the basis might be for any school grouping, whether regular class teachers have the appropriate skills for teaching retarded pupils, and whether they were receptive toward them. The issue of "labeling" often was employed to support the stigmatizing and other unfavorable effects of special class placement, even though Jones (1972) clearly pointed out that even though children do not like being called mentally retarded, the research data do not "support the detrimental effects hypothesized for labeling."

The rush was on to "mainstream" all mentally retarded children, except, perhaps, the most severely retarded and those with very severe physical handicaps. Let us turn our attention to this movement, reserving until later a more incisive consideration of underlying issues and implications.

MAINSTREAMING: OBJECTIVES AND PROGRAMS

The challenges to special education programs, led by Dunn in 1968, and legitimately reinforced by minority groups who wished to have their retarded children "decertified" (i.e., no longer labeled "retarded" and restricted to placement in special classes), led to the movement known as mainstreaming. Although efforts in this direction were made prior to this, broad scale implementation of mainstreaming began in 1971. As Meisgeiger (1976) puts it, this movement "advocates the rights of all children to acceptance within the school program regardless of how they may deviate from 'norms' in appearance, performance, or behavior." The aim was to provide the *least restrictive educational environment* for the retarded so as to maximize learning while, at the same time, to provide for presumably more nearly normal social adaptation with peers and, later, with society. Over the years, a variety of programs for mainstreaming had been developed to meet these aims. As Deno phrased it (1973), "If the goal is broader learning opportunities for handicapped children then it is not enough to tinker just with the special educational system." Although some were cautious about this new and revolutionary approach and requested a moratorium of massive and radical changes, others were impatient with anything less than total mainstreaming of all retarded children (Heller, 1972).

The "tinkering" referred to in the previous paragraph consisted of various attempts, short of massive mainstreaming, to improve special education and instruction for retarded pupils. One attempt involved the approach known as *diagnostic/prescriptive teaching*. This approach is basically founded on Skinner's theoretical model of operant conditioning (see chapter 14). The learning task is defined in terms of both specific elements that are lacking and needed for progress, and in terms of the rate at which learning is to proceed. In brief, this approach involves a careful and detailed diagnostic analysis of the learning task, selecting target behaviors that are to be modified, and then monitoring progress as the learner proceeds in mastering the required skills. The teacher focuses objectively on the required performance, specifies the individual steps necessary to obtain the objective, reinforces the learning that does occur with some appropriate reward, modifying the steps as required, and continues with this procedure until the desired response has been firmly established. We shall discuss later some of the values and problems in this approach (see chapter 14), but may point out that this approach, requiring highly individualized programs of instruction for each child and for each objective, is both time-consuming and requires expert diagnostic appraisal.

An example of a plan for diagnostic/prescriptive teaching is furnished by Prouty and McGarry (1972). Eight steps are involved in their procedure, somewhat as follows:

1. The child is referred to the diagnostic/prescriptive teacher (DPT).
2. The DPT observes the child in the regular class.
3. The DPT confers with the regular classroom teacher to plan time periods in which the pupil will come to the DPT for diagnostic teaching.

4. Diagnostic teaching, in small groups, is used to assess the child's specific needs and strengths.
5. The DPT writes a report containing an educational prescription involving specific materials and techniques of instruction.
6. There is a prescription conference with the regular classroom teacher involving demonstration teaching by the DPT and modification of the prescription, if needed.
7. The DPT offers a demonstration in the regular class.
8. There is a short-term follow-up through visits by the DPT to the regular class.

There are many possible advantages to plans like this. The demonstration-sharing of problems and skills of the DPT and the regular classroom teacher can be very valuable for both parties. The barriers to communication between special teacher and regular teacher tend to be reduced. The individual tailoring of instruction also can be most helpful. Not only may the child receive improved instruction, but he may also be able to return to the regular class, at least part of the time. However, there are still many questions to be answered about this plan: Will the retarded child be able to maintain himself in competition against the mainstream? Will the child feel more, rather than less, stigmatized if he finds he is falling increasingly behind? Will this specialized approach be consistent over the entire school program so that the child is not suddenly set adrift if he begins to display increasing problems of personal and educational adaptation?

To test the appropriateness and effectiveness of diagnostic-prescriptive teaching in the area of molar behavior, a critical study was performed by Sabatino, Ysseldyke, and Woolston (1973). This study involved 106 educable retarded children who were first tested in cognition (*WISC*), visual perception (*Bender-Gestalt Test*), perceptual integration (*Birch's Auditory-Visual Integration Test*), audition (the *TAP* test of auditory perception), and academic achievement. From this population, 36 *audiles* and 36 *visiles* were selected who were, respectively, at least one standard deviation above the means of the entire group on audition and visual perception. Each subject was then randomly assigned to one of three treatment groups. Each group contained 24 children. In phase 1 of the study, group 2 served as control, while groups 1 and 3 were given training in audition for 10 weeks, half an hour per day, in a resource room. In phase 2, groups 1 and 3 served as controls, and group 2 was given training in perception. It was found that all three groups improved on all visual and auditory measures. However, they did *not* improve in reading achievement.

Assuming the results of this study are valid, as indeed they seem to be as far as they go, several important questions are raised. It is clear that specific behaviors can be improved under conditions of tailored, fractionated instruction. The basic question, however, is whether there was too much fractionation; i.e., should the more global aspects of learning have been taught as such? Another question is, What constitutes a significantly important molecular aspect of behavior? Still another is, How do such molecular units become integrated into molar aspects of behavior? These issues are pursued in detail in two articles by Mann (1970, 1971).

We have argued the merits of individualized instruction, and they seem firmly established. The merits of diagnostic-prescriptive teaching, especially as a cure-all, have not been so firmly established, although the case for this approach is appealing. Ysseldyke (1973), in reviewing the evidence for diagnostic-prescriptive teaching, states: ". . . the goal of aptitude-treatment interaction is identification of significant disordinal interactions, better personological variables (IQ, specific abilities, . . . background variables, and so-forth), and alternative treatments," but, he adds, "there is little empirical support for the concept" of diagnostic-prescriptive teaching.

Another approach that has been employed in order to achieve more effective learning is that of *programmed instruction*. (See Razik, 1971, for a bibliography on this subject.) Although similar in some respects to diagnostic/prescriptive teaching, this approach emphasizes a group-instructional program in which each learner may proceed at his own rate, "through a predetermined sequence of learning materials" (Malpass, 1967). Teaching machines are commonly used in connection with this method of instruction. The assumption, of course, is that there is a fixed, predetermined sequence in the learning that is applicable to *all children*. This assumption has been challenged by many workers and is especially questionable in the case of retarded children, who may have special handicaps and special limitations in appropriate skills or knowledge. What is really individualized in this approach is the *rate* at which progress is made. Especially with teaching machines providing preselected sequences and checks for the correct responses, the amounts of practice and rate of progress can be individualized for each child. Hence, although programmed instruction has its important place in teaching the retarded, it has yielded to diagnostic-prescriptive teaching, which is more specifically tailored to each child's unique pattern of abilities and disabilities. According to J. L. Evans (1962), the following five principles are used in this approach: (1) progress is from easy, small steps to harder items; (2) the child responds actively; (3) the learner knows immediately whether his response is accurate; (4) the program is self-pacing; and (5) the program is revised on the basis of the learner's performance.

In individual behavior modification and in diagnostic-prescriptive teaching, both the *content* and the *rate* are individually tailored and modified.

Mainstreaming, in contrast to the "tinkering" approaches we have illustrated, attempts to provide a much more comprehensive adaptation of the *total learning experience* in which assimilation into the normal educational grouping is achieved. It is designed, as Begab (1977) phrases it, to remove the dissatisfactions with special education programs and to eliminate the alleged detrimental effects of labeling. Kolstoe (1977) has summarized six basic allegations (or assumptions) concerning the unfavorable effects of special education, as follows: (1) it is unnecessary since mental retardation, which is most noticeable during the school years, disappears in the adult years; (2) labeling the child by placement in a special class is deleterious; (3) placement in a special class increases the child's negative self-concept; (4) segregated classes are fruitless; (5) teachers of special classes contribute to the self-fulfilling prophecy of low achievement; and, (6) special classes are not needed since general education can deal adequately with individual differences in regular classrooms. Kolstoe disputes the validity of each of these allegations, citing evidence that illustrates this. For instance, regarding the first allegation, evidence from Kennedy's study (1965) shows that in England, in a follow-up analysis lasting from 1948 to 1960 of 256 retarded children with IQs in the 50 to 75 range, compared with 129 nonretarded children, the retarded were still inferior. This study is believed to be critical since the groups were matched on age, sex, ethnic background, religion, and father's education. Kennedy concludes: "Thus when retarded are compared with peers who differ only in IQ, it appears they are no more adequate as adults than they were as students in school."

Each of the other allegations is similarly disposed of as inaccurate. Labeling is thought to be insufficient, by itself, to account for poor self-concepts. To the charge that segregation does not produce any significant gain in either academic performance or, later in employability, evidence from two well-controlled studies are offered in rebuttal. The study by Goldstein, Moss, and Jordan (1965), to which we have previously referred, indicated that when children with similar IQs were randomly assigned to either regular or special classes, there were no significant differences, after a period of four years, in either academic achievement or in social knowledge. And a study by Chaffin et al. (1971) is cited to show that with equated groups, a workstudy experience in special education compared with a nonworkstudy group in regular classes revealed that the former group resulted in a 94 percent employment record whereas the latter group resulted in a 68 percent employment record. These and other studies seem to indicate that special education, if not better, is at least as good as regular class placement, in general; and in some areas, special education is clearly superior to regular class placement for retarded pupils.

We have presented considerable evidence to indicate that the case for mainstreaming is not as clear-cut as many advocates would like to believe. However, the general "push" to improve the lot of the retarded, the apparent limitations in the effects of special education in producing some desirable (if, perhaps, unattainable) goals for all retarded individuals, the fact that many pupils from minority groups and groups with low socioeconomic status were invalidly thought to be retarded and placed in special education classes, and above all, the democratic ideal of treating all children equally in terms of education opportunities—all of these factors led to the general trend to mainstream all mild and moderate cases of mental retardation.

An excellent description of the elements involved in mainstreaming is provided by Birch (1974). There are eight elements in all that may be paraphrased as follows. (1) All handicapped children should be assigned, from preschool through the secondary grades, to a regular class. (2) The regular classroom procedures should be adapted, and the content of instruction modified, to meet the needs of handicapped children. (3) Handicapped children who may need special learning situations must, nevertheless, be assigned to regular classes for at least half of each day. (4) There should be special educational support systems, including the special education teachers as team members. (5) Regular and special education teachers should cooperate in developing schedules, school assignments, and the like. (6) Special education teachers should help regular classroom teachers in these assignments. (7) Removal of children for special services should occur for short periods and only when absolutely necessary. (8) Identification of children should be based on educational needs rather than on categories or severity of the problem.

In order to initiate mainstreaming, it was recognized that extended programs of orientation, education, and training were needed for both administrative and teaching personnel, and should, hopefully, involve the parents and the community. However, such preparatory steps were not always provided; sometimes the mainstreaming program was imposed from above, at the state or county level, without such discussion and preparation. Sometimes, the financial backing needed for revising the educational plan and obtaining needed personnel and training resources, was not provided. At other times, the special personnel required, such as consulting teachers, learning specialists, school diagnosticians, and curriculum experts were not available. But, above all, mainstreaming required intensive planning and cooperative efforts by all concerned parties. Toward this end, suggestions and manuals were offered by various bodies. A good example of a "practical guide" for implementing mainstreaming was provided by Paul, Turnbull, and Cruickshank (1977). This manual stresses the need of discussion with both abetting and opposing personnel, including teachers, parents, principals, and specialists. It emphasizes the need of developing positive attitudes in such personnel *before* the program is implemented. It *requires* that all education personnel receive in-service and continuing education. And it views mainstreaming as involving complex changes in the entire educational system "affecting both normal and handicapped students."

Before considering some models of mainstreaming programs, let us examine in more detail some of the needed services.

The vast array of services needed for the mentally retarded was charted as far back as 1962, in the program reported by the President's Panel. (See Table 13.1.) It will be noted that services are proposed from the infant level through the older adult level. To these may be added service to the pregnant mother and her family. In recent years, many or most of these services have been centered in the school system and school building. Even the infant is brought in for observation and training, and the mother can participate fully in observing her infant and reporting on events in the home. It will be noted that such an orientation removes the major responsibility for assessing and training the child from the hospital to the school, although, of course, hospital facilities and medical personnel are used whenever circumstances require them.

The program in Wayne County, Michigan (including Detroit and the surrounding areas), illustrates the trend toward channeling assessment and training efforts through the school system. As a result of the Mandatory Education Act, which requires the provision of education for the handicapped from infancy through adulthood, a vast program of services was developed by the Intermediate School District of Wayne County, with local schools and school districts pooling their resources whenever needed. In 1973, some $32 million was allotted to this program for approximately 32,000 individuals in Special Educa-

TABLE 13.1. Areas of Direct Services for the Retarded[1]

Life stage	Components of special need						
	Physical & mental health	Shelter nurture protection	Intellectual development	Social development	Recreation	Work	Economic security
Infant	Specialized medical follow-up Special diets, drugs or surgery	Residential nursery	Sensory stimulation Home training Environmental enrichment				"Disabled child's" benefits
Toddler	Home nursing Correction of physical defects Physical therapy	Child welfare services Foster care Trained baby sitter	Nursery school				
Child	Psychiatric therapy Dental care	Homemaker service Day care Short-stay home	Classes for slow learners Special classes—educable Special classes—trainable	Religious education	Playground programs Scouting Swimming		
Youth	Psychotherapy	Boarding school	Work-school programs Occupational training Speech training	Social clubs Youth groups	Day camps Residential camps		
Young adult	Half-way house Facilities for retarded in conflict	Guardianship of person Long-term residential care	Vocational counseling—Personal adjustment training	Marriage counseling		Sheltered workshops Selective job placement Sheltered employment	Total disability assistance Guardianship of property Life annuity or trust Health insurance
Adult		Group homes Boarding homes	Evening school	Social supervision	Bowling Evening recreation		
Older adult	Medical attention to chronic conditions						Old age assistance OASI benefits

Reproduced from: *The President's Panel. A Proposed Program for National Action to Combat Mental Retardation.* Washington: Sup't. of Documents, 1962, p. 76.

1. Not included are diagnostic and evaluation services, or services to the family; the array is set forth in an irregular pattern in order to represent the overlapping of areas of need and the interdigitation of services. Duration of services along the life span has not been indicated here.

414

tion. The program provides services for all retarded children, from the severely retarded to the mildly retarded, as well as for children with other types of handicaps. Included are school programs for temporarily hospitalized children, work with infants in the home and school, an *early intervention program,* and an *outreach program.* All of these activities and services are monitored through an Educational Planning and Placement Committee.

School programs also are using *teacher aides* and *peer-teaching.* Teacher aides are parents or other adults who assist in providing the supervised individualized training that is necessary. In peer-teaching, children who have learned a skill demonstrate and teach it to other retarded children. According to Craighead and Mercatoris (1973), such peers may be used in limited roles, primarily as reinforcing agents for specific target behaviors in experimental settings. They believe that in this limited role the children "are effective behavior modifiers."

As yet, relatively little attention has been given to research on the needs for structure in the classroom or on the types of environment that are needed. It has been shown that appropriate structure in the classroom can assist greatly in producing improvement in both achievement and behavior, even in the case of brain-injured and hyperactive children (Cruickshank et al., 1961). And even earlier, Bettelheim (1950) demonstrated clinically that the total environment and the control of behavior were influential in modifying the behavior and adjustment of severely emotionally disturbed children. The physical arrangement of the room, the types of limits and controls that are used, and the physical relationships of children and teachers can, over a period of time, influence behavior and achievement.

A good example of research on the effects of the physical environment on various aspects of behavior is that by Levy and McLeod (1977). This study was done with thirty-seven severely and profoundly retarded teen-aged and young adult females. It dealt with some problems and some aspects of behavior that are less frequent in moderately retarded children and adults and that are highly infrequent in mildly retarded individuals. The research focused on the effects of changing the environment from a hall (used for a variety of individual and group activities) with ceramic floors and walls and containing twenty-five plastic chairs, three tables, and some balls and toys (brought into the room occasionally), to a large group area. This area was carpeted and contained a carpet-covered pyramid. It also had a small area devoted to small group activity and provided for privacy, when needed. The small area contained learning modular booths, buzzer-reinforced shape matching, as well as a booth for subject-activated music, and a sound activated sound light-box. A punching bag also was available. Using both electronic and personal recording of behaviors, baseline measures of these behaviors were obtained first, and then were compared with similar measures obtained after the change in environment. The authors found that the changed and enriched environment "succeeded in: reducing neutral or stereotyped activity; increasing purposeful movement; eliciting new patterns of space utilization; and supported learning activities."

Although the study made no effort to evaluate the effect of specific

Learning to play helps to develop social skills, as well as coordination. Sports and games also make children more aware of their bodies. (Photos by Michael D. McCoy)

aspects of the enriched environment, and although a number of other relevant variables were possibly uncontrolled (as, for example, possible changes in attitudes and behaviors of personnel in the program), it seems clear that the new environment probably had a highly significant and positive effect on important behaviors.

The total program in the school must provide resources, flexibility, individualized instruction, and systematic reevaluation. Figure 13.1 is a schematic design for such services in the school. The elements of this chart have been drawn from ideas and plans previously discussed in chapter 11 and in this chapter.

The child will be referred directly into the regular classroom if there are no obvious difficulties. If difficulties are obvious, the child will be referred directly into the resource room. If the child has problems in the regular classroom, she may be transferred into the resource room. The resource room is used for such activities as observation, diagnostic-prescriptive teaching, assessment, and demonstration teaching. From there, the child may be placed in the special class (with only limited visits to a regular class) or in a regular class for trial placement on a full-time or nearly full-time basis with limited visits to a special class. In either case, the plan provides for retransfer to other units in the

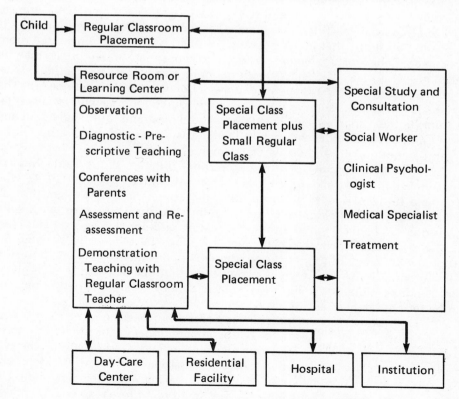

FIGURE 13.1   Flexible Planning and Placement Program

plan. Sometimes, referral for special study may be recommended, with movement back into the appropriate unit. In very severe cases, transfer to day-care,
residential, hospital, or institutional facilities may be needed. But even here, provision is made for rerouting whenever it can be done. Two basic elements of this
design are its flexibility—so that no long-term commitment in placement need
be made—and its provision for committee evaluation (not shown on the plan).
The appropriate personnel and the parents are involved in committee evaluations.

Additional Examples of Mainstreaming Programs

To illustrate the variety of plans developed to accomplish the purpose
of mainstreaming, let us describe briefly some of these plans. One of these, conducted by the Board of Cooperative Educational Services in suburban Buffalo,
New York (Reger and Koppmann, 1971), employs resource rooms or a resource
center. By 1971, this program involved nine school districts with a total of
twenty-three resource rooms. The plan includes a Child Evaluation Center using
the services of teachers only. The referred child is seen for three days by the staff
of the center, then the staff spends a day with the classroom teacher reviewing
the results of the assessment. Later, a day is spent on follow-up visits with the
classroom teacher. A unique feature of this program is that parents are encouraged to participate fully, observing all aspects of the evaluation process. If
the evaluation shows that it is necessary, the child is placed in a resource room
in regular school. At the elementary level, no more than fifteen pupils may be
placed in such a class. The child spends no more than half a day at a time in this
room; the rest of the time is spent in a special or regular class, as needed. The
regular-class teacher is supposed to view the resource room teacher as a special
assistant. In the resource room, specially tailored programs, both individual and
group, are designed for each child. Emphasis is placed on "rather basic
perceptual-motor skills and similar fundamental areas."

The other example of a resource room program is the Santa Monica
Madison School Program, in California. Hewett and co-workers (1974), who
developed this program, feature the following aspects in their design. If at all
possible, the child is first assigned to a regular class for a period of two weeks.
This is done to help the child establish a feeling of belonging to a regular class
with his own regular classroom teacher, to allow the teacher to become ac-
quainted with him, and to give the teacher an opportunity to evaluate how well
or how poorly he fits into various activities of the regular class. If such placement is not possible, the child is kept out of school during this period until he
can be referred to the resource school program.

The resource school program is housed in three adjacent rooms, with
doors permitting direct access from one room into either of the others. The three
rooms actually occupy the space of two regular classrooms. One of the two
smaller rooms, called Pre-Academic I, is a classroom for twelve children who
need special instruction. Its staff consists of a teacher and a teaching aide. The
other two units are Pre-Academic II, a very small room for six to eight children,
where specialized preparation for the work of Academic I is offered, and

Academic I, the largest of the three rooms, in which a simulated regular classroom is maintained for about twelve children. These two units are serviced by a teacher and her teaching aide.

A child who cannot function in the regular classroom is assigned full-time to Pre-Academic I and given special training according to specific needs and strengths, usually in some reading activities, some basic arithmetic skills, and perceptual-motor skills. However, the child can move to Pre-Academic II or even to Academic I for some activities, and finally to Academic I for most or all activities. Flexibility and participation by all of the children in the program in some common activities are encouraged. The curriculum is further dictated by a general plan designed by Hewett involving three functions: (1) pre-academic and academic skills; (2) varied instrumental settings (the *conditions* of learning); and (3) incentives to motivate the child (the so-called *consequences*). When the child is ready, he is scheduled for regular-classroom activity part of the time or all of the time; his regular seat is kept for him in that room during his enrollment in the resource program. Careful observations are made of performance and progress, and both social behavior and academic achievement are monitored.

It will be noted that such a program requires the investment of additional space, additional facilities, and additional personnel if it is to work effectively. It fosters minimal deprivation of normal social contact with regular classroom pupils. There is a danger, however, that some parents may get the idea that their retarded child will become normal in all respects, academic and social. Of course, this is not the intent of such programs—only more effective academic, social, and vocational learning. Care must be taken in such programs to avoid flights of fantasy, while encouraging the most constructive conditions for improved learning and adjustment.

In brief, other examples of mainstreaming programs are the following. Buffmire (1973) reports on the Rocky Mountain Regional Resource Center. This is a so-called statistician model that involves modeling methods (see chapter 14), class screening, observation, individual planning, program evaluation, diagnosis, instructional and interaction skills, evaluation of interventions, and data collection. Research is built into the program. Frankel (1974) describes a plan built on the diagnostic-prescriptive model of training. A Houston plan reported by Meisgeiger (1974) emphasizes the retraining of regular classroom teachers so that they can work more effectively with handicapped children.

These and other plans have shown much ingenuity and creativity and have been designed to maximize interactions of retarded children with all other children. But what are their merits, and what are the issues that still need to be faced? We now turn to those matters in the next section.

ISSUES AND IMPLICATIONS

Our review of problems, evidence, and programs enables us to highlight several critical issues and to examine some of the implications. We shall attempt to focus on what seems to us to be the most critical problems. Doubtless, other people will have different perspectives.

1. The most central theme in all of the recent developments is the *right of every individual to obtain full and equitable opportunity of developing his or her abilities to the maximum so as to enable him/her to lead a more effective life.* Toward this end, various proposals have been made to insure an educational environment and educational training that are *least restrictive* and *most conducive* for individual growth. Whether or not current mainstreaming programs are the final answer is surely debatable. The intent, to promote adequate social opportunities for interaction with all peers, is laudable. The intent, to provide better opportunities for learning, is both laudable and necessary. However, mainstreaming is not necessarily the Garden of Eden nor are special classes the abode of the Devil. It is not necessarily their inherent natures that cause such attribution of opposite and extreme evaluations as we have witnessed. Rather, it is how such programs are conducted, the methods of selection and assignment of pupils, the characteristics of the teaching personnel, the methods of instruction, and the content of the curriculum that constitute the core of what makes for effective educational opportunity and training.

Ziegler and Hambleton (1976) have demonstrated that removal of retarded children from special education programs into a regular elementary school did not produce any significant differences in thirteen kinds of interactions that were measured in comparison with a matched group in a school for retarded children. The subjects of the study were "trainable" mentally retarded children. However, Ziegler and Hambleton argue that the changed environment for the "experimental" group did provide a more normal environment. That may be so, but the question is whether a normal social environment, which may be needed, is enough! The learning needs of many retarded children, especially those with severe handicaps, cannot be expected to be met in the regular classroom. As Smith and Arkans (1977) phrase it, "The requirements for a severely or profoundly retarded child would necessitate unrealistic attainment of near normalcy." We would add that the special methods and intense, individualized instruction that many retarded pupils need cannot be most effectively met except in an educational setting that deliberately attempts to provide for these needs.

In some measure, the arguments have been confounded by the lack of differentiation of the culturally handicapped retarded, many of whom—with adequate early intervention programs and with more adequate assessment—would never have been classified as retarded, but only as *deprived,* and the genetically handicapped whose attainment is thereby limited. The former group can, with effective training and guidance, more appropriately move into the mainstream in all or most activities. The others may never be able to adjust to the requirements of a "normal" educational environment. Instead, they need opportunity for social and other kinds of interactions in the areas in which they are capable of making both an effective adjustment and significant contributions. Although the mental age does not describe adequately all aspects of learning potentials, it is quite clear, for example, that a fourteen-year-old child with an IQ of 50 and an MA of seven years cannot be expected to adjust to a classroom setting for regular classroom children, with MAs of 14 or higher, in which the academic content and the rate of learning are totally beyond the capabilities of the retarded pupil. However, with more flexibility in educational programming, the fourteen-year-old retarded pupil can, in many instances, interact in those areas in which this pupil is capable of "holding his/her own." Such areas may include social events, athletic events, special projects involving many levels of mechanical and motoric skills, and the like.

2. Special education classes can provide educational experiences that are most effective for individualized and special needs of the retarded. As Valeutti (1969) puts it, "Regular classroom teachers who have not compliantly completed a specialized training program cannot be expected to teach these incoming exceptional children effectively . . . often their attitude is derogatory." Moreover, they cannot be expected to have the time to devote their efforts to the special needs of the retarded individual. The special education teacher has the training and the interest to provide such services. Although these teachers may need more effective training than they have previously been given, it is they rather than the regular classroom teacher who can profit most from such training.

MacMillan, Jones, and Aloia (1974) have reviewed the available research evidence concerning the effects of special versus regular class placement of retarded pupils and have concluded that children placed in special classes generally have a better social adjustment than the others. If retarded pupils are offered additional help as needed in resource rooms, with consulting and helping teachers, and in other specialized services, and if provision for social and other types of interaction with the "mainstream in school" is provided, special education placement may be most effective.

3. The issue of "categorization" or "labeling" has received widespread and critical attention. Labels have been adjudged to have caused irreparable damage to the self-concepts of retarded pupils. Our review of the evidence suggests that it is not the label, per se, that has done the damage, but the derogatory attitudes toward the label that schools and communities have displayed that may be decisive. Some form of categorization is necessary; indeed, it may be inevitable. Some types of categorization may be derogatory (as is the case with labels such as "idiot" and the like which carry a clearly derogatory attribute), and some types may be inadequate or inaccurate. Yet labeling is one way of providing a message that people in that general category need some special assistance or have some special requirements. However, as we have stressed throughout this book, any label or any type of categorization does not indicate the unique assets and requirements of a particular individual. *A category is only a first means of approaching the problems of how best to provide the services needed in a given case.* Much more is necessary.

Hobbs (1975) has reported that a group of experts found that categorization had been a means through which needs could be identified and funds allocated. (Many states require such categorization.) However, the experts also believed that the available simplified classification systems "obscure both the uniqueness of individual children and the similarities of children assigned to various categories." We are in complete agreement! The experts have proposed that a standardized profile system be developed to describe individual children more adequately, taking into account a broad variety of physical, intellectual, and social characteristics, and the like. Some states have developed such systems. It should be clearly recognized, however, that even the best of profile systems will not accomplish the desired ends, even though the substitution of profile systems can be employed instead of an over-all classification as a means of allocating funds for needed services. The assumptions involved in profiling may not always apply to the individual child—just as the assumptions involved in any measuring device may not always apply. Moreover, adequate diagnostic appraisal and evaluation will still be needed (see Issue #4 below).

In short, more adequate statements of assessment of abilities and needs can lead to more refined and more effective systems of subcategorization. Such efforts can be helpful. Proper and careful assessment of each individual is still necessary, however.

4. There is a clear need for careful and continuing assessment of each retarded individual. We have reviewed the problems involved in assessment in chapter 11 and need not recapitulate them here. Let us emphasize, however, that assessment always requires critical and clinical evaluation of *why* the individual responds as he does as well as *what* the nature of his response is. Moreover, assessment requires an appraisal of *how* and *under what conditions* improvement may be expected, with subsequent evaluation of the nature of the change and the conditions that lead to change. Such assessment is a *continuing process* in which further recommendations for guidance and training may follow from the past history of development and current assets and liabilities. Such types of assessment require adequately trained personnel—both teachers and specialists—and adequate funding, if they are to be effective.

Recent developments have offered some promise that more effective assessment methods may be developed. As examples of such developments we may cite the recent publication of tests for early developmental abilities described in chapter 12. Babab and Budoff (1971) have prepared a "learning potential" test that seems to contribute to the prediction of improvement in academic skills beyond that of the conventional intelligence test. In a recent study, Babab (1977) demonstrated that "improvement in reasoning ability during the eight-month period [of the study] was a positive function of the children's learning potential." Hutt (1977) has developed a measure of "adience-abience" that seems to have considerable promise in predicting some types of behavioral change.

5. There is an urgent need to improve teacher training and teacher in-service training for services to the retarded. At various points throughout this book, we have discussed some of these needs and some of the suggested innovations. However, it is clear that the specialized personnel involved in work with the retarded need the *active assistance and understanding* of all other school personnel. The regular classroom teacher, especially when mainstreaming is attempted, needs to know more about the work of the specialized personnel, needs to contribute actively both in attitude and resources, and must participate in some of the programs for all pupils at the appropriate levels of instruction. Similarly, administrative personnel need to be fully informed of programs for the

retarded and need to contribute through active support of such programs. On the other side of the picture, the professional personnel who are asked to assist in specialized programs (psychologists, psychiatrists, social workers, and the like) need to learn more about the details and possibilities of specialized programs as well as to learn how to translate their findings and recommendations into specific methods for effective training.

6. Parental involvement and consent are a necessary part of school programs for the retarded children. More than participation in decision making in terms of school placement and programs is needed. Many parents can become active allies of the educational process, but they need guidance and instruction. They also need to be aware of current limitations of the child so that false expectations are not raised and then crushed. To provide for effective involvement of the parents, a comprehensive "out-reach" program is necessary. The boundaries between school, home, and community, which are so often employed to block effective communication and cooperative participation, need to be breached. There is room for creative efforts to broaden the base of the educational undertaking so that needed services are provided and cooperative attitudes are developed.

7. The whole community is involved in the educational undertaking, especially for retarded pupils. Too often it was believed that the "school knew best" or that the school should be left to its own devices. Although the technical aspects of providing education experience must be the province of those who are trained for it—the school personnel—the aims of the educational program and the means to implement them must be the province of the entire community. Federal agencies and state agencies may provide the financial resources (or some of them) and the general guidelines for education, but effective education cannot function without the direct involvement and input of those who must deal with the product. There are special problems in this regard at the several stages of educational training. For example, at the preschool level, participation by community agencies, such as community centers, churches, and hospitals, may be particularly relevant. At the adolescent level, the businesses and factories in the community may become part of the in-service training and employment of retarded individuals. At every level, community involvement can be a great asset if integrated effectively through planning and programming.

8. Research on programs, methods, processes, and outcomes is still urgently needed. Although research studies seem to have been more effectively designed and administered in the past decade than ever before, only the surface of the multitudinous problems has been scratched. Recent publications (Mittler, vols. I and II, 1977; and Begab and Richardson, 1975) have sketched some of the contributions and findings of individual and project research efforts. Much has been learned and some of it already has been applied both in terms of new programs and new practices. However, as with all research, the more that is learned, the more problems are opened up to investigation. It should be noted that such research programs on problems of the retarded have applications far beyond the area of retardation, although that, in itself, can be far-reaching. They also contribute directly and indirectly to such issues as: the nature of cognition; the

nature of social development; the nature of the learning process; the effectiveness of certain methods of instruction; and, the nature of environmental-genetic interactions. It is to be hoped that we can retain an inquisitive and open mind to the complexities of the issues in all of these problem areas and continue our search for critical factors.

— 14 —

Institutionalization and Deinstitutionalization

In previous chapters, we have discussed some of the relevant evidence on the effects of institutionalization of the retarded. Many studies have shown that institutionalized retarded individuals, especially the severely and profoundly retarded, suffer decline in cognitive ability, show poor academic attainment relative to their ability, and make inadequate social adjustment even within their restricted environment. We have cited the surveys that have revealed horrendous conditions that exist in some state institutions for the mentally retarded, with extremely poor physical conditions, poor nourishment, and sometimes inhuman treatment. Moreover, as Begab (1975) has stated, institutions offer limited opportunities for self-determination or decision making, thus producing inhibition in many aspects of personal growth. Nevertheless, not all institutions are uniformly bad, not all are nonstimulating for growth, and not all are unmindful of the rights of all human beings to some degree of privacy, individual decision making, and opportunities for self-betterment. In institutions, as among people, there are marked individual differences!

In recent years, the trend toward deinstitutionalization, or *normalization,* has become extremely strong. PL 94-142, which provides funds for improved education and training, also proclaims that all handicapped children between three and eighteen years of age shall be provided with a free public education by 1978, and that all in that age range plus those in the range up to twenty-one years shall have such free public education provided by 1980. In 1971, the President announced the goal of returning half of all institutionalized retarded individuals into community settings (Braddock, 1977). The National Association of Superintendents of Public Residential Facilities, at that time, defined deinstitutionalization as consisting of three goals: (1) prevention of institutionalization admission; (2) return of institutionalized patients to the community; and, (3) establishment and maintenance of "a responsive residential environment." Wolfensberger (1972), who is one of the most outspoken advocates of both deinstitutionalization and normalization, defines the principle of normalization as: "Utilization of means which are culturally *normative as possible,* in order to establish and/or maintain personal behaviors and characteristics which are culturally *as normative as possible* [our emphasis]." He argues that normalization refers not to treatment but to the services, situations, and attitudes that will bring about humane care of the mentally retarded.

Both proponents and opponents of deinstitutionalization recognize that neither institutionalization nor deinstitutionalization, by itself, offers a complete solution to the problems of the retarded individuals especially of the severely and profoundly retarded. In order to understand some of the central issues and proposed plans for their solution, let us first take another look at the history of institutions for the retarded and at the changing objectives and programs that they have provided.

THE DEVELOPMENT OF INSTITUTIONS FOR THE RETARDED

Residential facilities for the most severe cases of mental retardation—then called "idiots" and "feebleminded"—began in the mid-nineteenth century in this country. The first one was organized in 1848. More than twenty facilities had been established before the turn of the century. The pattern of objectives and organizations for these early institutions was quite similar to that of the asylums for the "insane," which preceded them. Residents were drawn mainly from the economically disadvantaged population and often were severely maladjusted in the social sphere as well as severely handicapped in the physical sphere. Often they were the "rejects"—abandoned by their families and by their communities. Nevertheless, the orientation of the institutions was therapeutic and optimistic. Royfe (1972) points out that the directors of these early institutions believed that many cases of severe retardation were the result of extremely poor social environments and that, therefore, providing a good therapeutic environment in an institution and good physical care could do much to produce improvement in both physical development and intellectual functioning.

At the same time, mental retardation often was confounded with insanity or psychosis. Thus, the first annual report of the Pennsylvania Training School stated "that in nearly all of the less-marked cases of idiocy, the mind may be so far improved as to be pronounced sane, and that the individual may be trained to such skill as to enable him to support himself . . . " (Royfe, 1972). The institutions were well-built, provided good physical arrangements for the "inmates," provided extensive programs for educational and vocational training and retraining, and encouraged inspection of their facilities. Data indicate that many residents of these institutions were returned to their homes or communities (Wolfensberger, 1969; Tyor, 1972).

It should be noted that considerable and significant research was generated by the personnel in state and other large residential institutions. Such research was facilitated by the belief that many retarded individuals could improve in many aspects of their functioning if given appropriate care and training. Moreover, the institutions housed many individuals who could be observed, studied, trained, and evaluated. Some institutions, such as the Vineland Training School in New Jersey, not only conducted considerable research, but also published their own research journals. Thus, a great deal of highly useful information was acquired.

However, the therapeutic and training functions of the large institutions were replaced by focus on custodial care. By the beginning of the twentieth century, this shift in emphasis had become quite evident. The courts were referring large numbers of "retarded" children for placement in institutions, not so much because the children were retarded, but because they were antisocial or because their disturbed behavior could not be tolerated in the community. During periods of economic hardship, many families sent their children, especially those who were having severe educational or social problems, to institutions. Social workers who could not find acceptable homes for retarded individuals often referred them to institutions. Thus, both the numbers and varieties of types of individuals placed in institutions increased. At first, many administrators of institutions for the retarded resisted placement of many people who had been assigned to the institutions for custodial care and behavioral rehabilitation. Later, the emphasis came to be that of increasing the size of the institutions so that larger numbers could be accommodated. At the same time, insufficient funds were provided for personnel, although relatively more funds were provided for buildings. The quality and training of personnel suffered as a consequence. The change is described by Lazerson as follows: "Originally work [in the institutions] was to be moral and educational. . . . With the emergence of a custodial ideology, work came to be justified more for its aid in producing institutional self-sufficiency than individual self-sufficiency" (Lazerson, 1975).

In time, many, but by no means all of the institutions became "warehouses" for the retarded—the most profoundly handicapped and the most socially maladjusted and deprived. Some institutions, through insufficient funds or insufficient care, deteriorated to the point at which subhuman conditions were permitted to develop. Court actions and federal legislation sought to "correct the abuses." National attention was spotlighted on many deplorable conditions existing in some institutions. The cry became "abolish the institutions" or "normalize all inmates by returning them to their community." Institutionalization was attacked as being necessarily depriving, degrading, and even immoral.

As one example of flagrant abuses that developed in some institutions, largely as the result of inadequate numbers and inadequately trained personnel, we can cite the situation in Michigan. As a result of protests and charges by parents and by concerned professionals, some intolerable conditions were exposed in one state institution for the mentally retarded. In 1978, the Governor appointed a special committee to investigate conditions. It was found that some personnel were totally untrained and unsuited for their work. Also found were cases of severe physical abuse, sexual assault on some inmates, and even neglect with respect to basic conditions of nourishment and physical care. Many staff members, however, were competently trained and had valiantly sought to correct or improve conditions, but their pleas were lost in the administrative morass that had developed. The superintendent resigned and more than twenty staff members were dismissed—some charged with neglect, abuse, and immoral behavior.

Conditions such as these dramatized the need to deinstitutionalize many patients in such institutions and called for drastic action to improve the selection and training of personnel, to institute effective training and educational programs, and to provide more appropriate conditions for social and interpersonal experiences.

The sweeping generalizations to the effect that institutionalization was, by its inherent nature, inhuman, inappropriate, and ineffective led to a clamor for its total abolishment and for the normalization of all institutionalized individuals. Deinstitutionalization had become an end in itself!

SOME FACTORS FAVORING INSTITUTIONALIZATION

We have indicated that some individuals profited from institutionalization, even if they subsequently were returned to their homes or to some community setting, and that others required some form of institutionalization because of their special needs. In addition, there were other factors that seemed to favor institutionalization in some instances. Let us now examine the arguments and evidence for institutionalization before considering the criteria and values of deinstitutionalization.

Larsen (1977) has summarized the arguments in favor of institutionalization (not necessarily in favor of very large institutions) as follows: (1) Institutions eliminate impossible burdens for some parents. These burdens may involve the financial cost of special services and medical care, intensive supervision that may be impossible to provide or may detract from attention needed for other members of the family, and emotional trauma produced by some cases with severe physical handicaps and extreme stigmata. (2) Some handicapped individuals can adjust better to special settings with peers of their own kind. They may need special physical equipment and may need to interact with others at their own levels of social and intellectual competence. (3) Some severely/profoundly handicapped are so different that the public will never accept them into the mainstream. Although this argument may have been factually accurate in the past, there is no inevitability that such mainstreaming cannot occur. Much depends on education of the general public with respect to the true nature of the handicaps of such individuals as well as their possible contribution to society. Much also depends on the general social climate of the times; when the public is experiencing severe economic or social distress or is perceiving such distress even when it is exaggerated by the emotional uproar of the times, it tends to find a "scapegoat." The severely/profoundly retarded then are seen as "dangerous," or "too burdensome," or totally incapable of maintaining themselves in the mainstream. (4) Institutions are not *inherently* bad, and instead can be good places for effective development. As we have noted, institutions vary. Some provide good care and stimulating environments. Some provide much better environments than the very deprived and impoverished homes from which the individuals came, or than some foster homes can provide. Clarke et al. (1958) were able to show that institutionalized children in England did receive good stimulation and did show gains in cognitive development. (6) It is impractical to provide in the community the extensive educational, medical, and social services that some retarded require. This argument is likely to be especially relevant for severely/profoundly retarded who live in rural or impoverished areas. (6) It is less expensive to serve large groups of handicapped individuals in institutions than in dispersed settings. (7) Community services are just as restrictive as institutional services. The last two arguments, especially, can be seen to be a problem in logistics. When arrangements that improve the economy and the availability of services are such that only large institutions can provide them, then those arguments will hold up. However, this is not to say that this is the inherent nature of the matter.

An interesting analysis of the attitudes of parents toward the issue of institutionalization has been provided by Payne (1976). These attitudes were elicited by means of a questionnaire sent to 500 randomly selected parents whose children were in institutions in the state of Texas. At the time of the survey, there were limited, alternative facilities for these institutionalized children and only a few small, group homes. There were 150 responses to the questionnaire. The mean age of the individuals who were in institutions was twenty-one years, with a range from two to fifty-eight years. The mean length of institutionalization was 9½ years. And, most interesting, the mean distance from the institution to the home of the parents was 132½ miles! The responding parents felt that "almost all mildly and moderately retarded persons could live in small group homes," but had "no opinion" that, given adequately trained staff the profoundly retarded could be cared for in such small homes. Further, the parents agreed that: (1) large institutions offer some advantages; (2) institutions should be continued; (3) there may be some value in small group homes; (4) *parents should have the right to decide which type of placement their children should have;* (5) large institutions were better because they provided a place *that was permanent,* and one in which the retarded *could stay after their parents died.*

Two characteristics of this survey should be emphasized: it took place in a state in which distances from home to institutions were very great; and, alternative means for caring properly for some of the retarded had not been developed adequately at the time. Nevertheless, the findings suggest that deinstitutionalization by fiat will not provide universally affirmative responses.

There are other critics of deinstitutionalization and the ways in which the normalization principle are being interpreted and applied. Mesibov (1976) argues that the normalization principle involves assumptions that are not supported by the research data. One such assumption is that normalization will cause society to respond more favorably to those who had been stigmatized previously. Mesibov cites studies by Goodman et al. (1972) and by Gottlieb and

Siperstein (1976) in opposition to this assumption. Another basic assumption is that the norms of society should be made the standard of acceptable behavior. This assumption rejects the value of atypical behavior. Mesibov claims that alternative methods, other than simply deinstitutionalizing individuals, are available, such as developing a "humanistic approach" as advocated by Mahoney (1975), developing an ecology that fosters positive self-feelings, and utilizing "needs assessment" (Browder, Ellis, and Neal, 1974) to develop effective service systems within a given setting. Smokoski (1971), supporting some of the positions taken by Mesibov, has asserted that the normalization principle has been used to mask the real differences between the retarded and the normal and to overemphasize the similarities.

Two exhortatory and emotion-laden articles have been offered by Burton et al. (1977) and Roos (1977). Burton et al., in an article titled "For sale: The state of Alabama," argue that recent court decisions (notably *Pennsylvania Association v. Commonwealth of Pennsylvania,* 1971) and federal legislation will "bankrupt the various states affected" since the public schools, in Alabama, for instance, would require more than an additional $2 million. They plead instead for the *elimination* of large institutions and for "more efficient community programs." In rebuttal, Roos, speaking for the National Association for Retarded Citizens, states that a recent survey by the Accreditation Council of Facilities for the Mentally Retarded (1975) indicated that 79 percent of the institutional administrators responding felt that their facilities could meet the new standards by 1977, and Roos adds that federal financial assistance, including redistribution of funds from other programs to programs for the mentally retarded would help. Roos argues: "The important issue raised, then, is whether constitutional rights of citizens should be blatantly violated on the basis of financial and/or public opinion considerations." Roos maintains that not all institutions need to be, or should be eliminated. Instead, small institutions, say with fewer than 150 residents, could be one viable alternative.

SOME FACTORS FAVORING DEINSTITUTIONALIZATION

We already have seen that complete elimination of all institutions for the retarded is not the inevitable answer to the problems of very large or poorly administered institutions. Nevertheless, it is clear that there are countless residents in institutions who could be better served in alternative settings and for whom normalization would provide immense benefits. It should be noted that normalization does not require that all individuals be completely assimilated in the mainstream of society. This, in itself, would insure cruel and inhuman conditions for many. *Federal and state policies call for "as near normal as possible" conditions.* Deinstitutionalization without adequate regard either for the realistic limitations of the handicapped or for the provision of adequately developed, maintained, and monitored alternative services can lead to even more restricted conditions for the handicapped (Scheerenberger, 1974).

Our review of the evidence suggests that several factors favor deinstitutionalization for many, perhaps most, of the institutionalized retarded.

1. The public clamor for deinstitutionalization often is primarily based
on humane considerations. (Other considerations include fiscal costs and inadequate personnel.) Central to such humane considerations are the opportunities
that community living provide for integration into the mainstream of all activities, greater freedom of choice for the individual, and more opportunity for
establishing at least a somewhat independent life-style.

2. Prevention of institutionalization, with many concomitant benefits,
can reduce the incidence of those in institutions if early detection and remedial
services are provided. Long-term institutional care thus can be avoided. We have
shown that such early intervention programs, *properly conceived* and *properly
administered,* can have both significant short-term and long-term positive effects. A highly useful sourcebook of available and needed community resources
is furnished by Abt Associates (1974).

3. The great variety of individualized services needed for training and
educating the retarded are more readily available in schools and community
agencies than in institutions. Good residential care has been provided, for example, in Israel with adolescents. Utilizing a creative test for assessing cognitive
modifiability, Fuerstein and Krasilowksy (1972) first induced social regression,
which was thought to be a prerequisite for effective re-identification, and then
provided exercises in cognitive functioning. They reported consequent gains in
intellectual functioning and in peer relationships. Small residential units are
especially useful for such programs.

4. Parents, foster parents, and other surrogate caretakers in homes or
small residential units can provide not only the warm and intimate relationships
of a "home atmosphere" but also the continuing and consistent care needed for
long-term intervention and consistent training. Research evidence, which we
have cited, indicates how effective such "parental" care, under conditions of
good supervision and instruction, can be.

5. The great variety of social experiences that can be available in community settings usually are lacking in institutions and are difficult to duplicate in
such institutions. Interpersonal experiences with less handicapped or normal individuals can become available in communities and can lead to the development of interests, activities, and abilities that would not otherwise be possible.

6. Many severely/profoundly retarded individuals show gains in many
areas of functioning when residential facilities are provided with effective programs (Martin et al., 1972; Favell et al., 1976; Townsend and Flanagan, 1976).
Such programs can involve short- or long-term leaves from the institutions as
well as permanent deinstitutionalization.

7. Core areas for consideration are the mildly and moderately retarded
individuals who have been institutionalized because of personality or antisocial
behavior problems. Placement in a good foster home or in smaller residential
facilities can provide more appropriate means of correcting such behaviors.
Although it is recognized that, in the past, many attempted placements out of institutions resulted in failure (Windle, 1962), such placements were not ade-

quately planned nor were adequate treatment programs made available for the individuals. Personality and antisocial behavior problems often require both individual and group therapeutic care as well as gradual reintegration into normal patterns of social behavior. Careful, individual assessment of liabilities and assets is essential for planning such treatment. Therapy plus involvement in small-group living can then provide needed rehabilitation. In any case, placement in institutions has, in the past, been conceived of more as a punitive measure than as a corrective measure. Many such maladjusted individuals were never properly diagnosed in the first instance and many were not necessarily retarded, but were maladjusted and impaired in their functioning. Some may have needed intensive in-patient psychotherapy in hospital units or clinics for a time, whereas others may have needed placement in appropriate foster homes accompanied by supportive services for them and their foster parents.

These and other factors favor the deinstitutionalization of many retarded individuals and can serve to prevent institutionalization for others. A fraction of the population of retarded individuals may need institutionalization for a short time. And then there is the remaining proportion, especially of the profoundly retarded and physically handicapped, who may require long-term institutionalization. Perhaps the goal of deinstitutionalizing at least one-half of the population of institutionalized retarded is too optimistic. Only further experience in extended efforts to find appropriate alternatives will enable us to find an accurate answer. However, even for those who require long-term institutionalization, enriched opportunities for some normalization experiences, even if transient, may be possible, and improved care and training also can be provided.

ISSUES AND SOLUTIONS

A major issue is providing humane and effective care and training for all of our citizens, including the profoundly retarded. Very large institutions, by their very nature, make personal and individualized care difficult to achieve. Probably much smaller institutions or independent units of, say, no more than 150 residents as part of a larger institution, may be more effective. A redistribution of specialized services also may be required so that medical care and special physical and rehabilitative care may become more readily available. In many areas, such plans may involve a central unit serving the local area, with nearby hospital and special therapy and social service units available as needed. In other areas, other arrangements may be necessary because of the wide dispersion of the population.

Another issue is providing adequate assessment and training programs from infancy through adulthood. Programs for supporting and training parents—if they are cooperative—and instructional programs in the community agencies and schools also are needed. Such programs require the availability of adequately trained personnel. Universities, research centers, as well as programs within the agencies and schools, can help to provide needed training and effective evaluation of outcomes.

A critical issue if deinstitutionalization is to produce effective results is the development of adequate alternatives—properly designed, properly maintained, and properly supervised. Small residential facilities, hostels for older retarded persons, good foster care homes, community villages, and part-time "leave" from institutions are some alternatives. Programs in the schools, both preschool and other school programs, need to be adapted so that effective mainstreaming becomes more nearly possible for many. At the same time, more research is needed to specify more precisely what the negative and positive factors are in all of these alternatives, including the institutions themselves.

Undoubtedly, at the extremes, IQ does make a difference in whether deinstitutionalization is possible (McCarver and Craig, 1974), but other factors such as disposition, nature of specific abilities and limitations, and the like also are significant. The nature of the preparation for deinstitutionalization is, as we have shown, also critical. Thus, we can see that the *evaluation of the individual,* in depth, followed by a carefully designed and effective program of training, is a central ingredient of child care and placement.

– 15 –

Educational Objectives and Methods

We now will turn our attention to the many complex problems of designing appropriate educational objectives, selecting and implementing educational methods, and assisting the retarded individual to attain an adequate degree of personal and vocational competence. In the next chapter, we will consider behavioral and other psychotherapeutic approaches for minimizing maladjustment and assisting the individual to maximize effectiveness.

The general goal of education and training should be *the maximum development of the particular individual's competencies in order to insure a productive and satisfying life style.* Although this objective is not essentially different for the retarded than for the more normal individual, we have tended to restrict maximum development of the retarded by: (a) not understanding and accepting the individual's capacity for growth; (b) not providing sufficiently adequate and extensive training from early childhood through adulthood; and, (c) not recognizing adequately the vast amount of individual differences among retarded individuals at all levels of retardation.

We therefore shall wish to consider in detail the specific nature of the objectives of education for the retarded, the nature of their learning characteristics, and the kinds of technical procedures that may be employed to stimulate growth and development. We shall see, later, how intimately related are processes of maladjustment and their amelioration to the processes of education. Behavioral modification and psychotherapeutic intervention too often have been divorced from the educational process, whereas, they are in fact an essential part of that total process, sometimes assuming greater significance and at other times being less conspicuous.

GENERAL OBJECTIVES IN THE EDUCATION
OF THE RETARDED

Although there is no clearly established consensus among the general public concerning the general objectives of education for retarded pupils, educators and scientists concerned with these problems seem to be emphasizing certain goals. We shall discuss some of the most important of these objectives.

Self-actualization

Present educational philosophy emphasizes the maximization of each individual's potentials as they are uniquely manifested. The outcome of any process that maximizes the self-actualization of children will necessarily be different for widely differing levels of retardation. But in all cases, education should attempt to stimulate the maximum development of abilities and skills of which the individual is capable. One of the major difficulties in realizing this objective in education is that it requires very careful and detailed assessment of the individual at many points in development and *adequate evaluation of all the relevant factors*—physical, emotional, intellectual, and social—that may affect (especially adversely) development. It also requires intensive individualized training and teaching.

This objective in the education of the retarded child is not different from that proposed long ago by the Educational Policies Commission (1946) as the first of four general objectives for normal children. For the retarded, however, its attainment is far more complicated. As we have noted throughout this book, retarded children are more likely to have been blocked in their development because of special physical handicaps, subcultural conditions in the home, and emotional withdrawal, among other conditions. By the time such children reach school, their own expectancies, as well as society's expectancies of them (as reflected in the school's orientation and evaluation of them), may very well have been considerably lowered.

Such children therefore need not only intensive assessment, but also *continuing* assessment in order to discover possible assets that adverse experiences may have covered or inhibited. They need special attention to satisfy their need for acceptance by teachers, peers, and others. They also need a school climate that is both accepting and appropriately stimulating. In some cases, they may need highly individualized programs of training, guidance, or psychotherapy.

Some research studies have shown that, generally speaking, retarded children have more fear of failure than normal children. Other studies have shown that children who are placed in special classes feel less rejected than those who are placed in regular classes. In all of these studies there are significant individual differences. Hence, no matter what type of program is planned for retarded pupils, the worker must evaluate the kinds of progress of which each child is realistically capable and help each child maximize such progress.

Personal and Social Competence

Personal and social competence includes both the ability to maintain effective relationships with peers and others and the ability to maintain an internal harmony within oneself. Thus we are referring to *interpersonal* relationships as well as to *intrapersonal* adjustment. These related objectives are combined here for several reasons. First, intrapersonal adjustment is markedly dependent on interpersonal adjustment, as we have shown elsewhere in this text. Second, it is universally recognized by authorities that one of the school's functions is to foster social competence, but it is not so widely accepted that the school also has a basic responsibility in the sphere of personal adjustment. Yet, if the two are so inextricably linked, how can we attain one objective if the other is neglected? Third, the retarded child has unique problems in personal adjustment—some of them unnecessary consequences of society's unfortunate attitudes toward the child—so special emphasis needs to be placed by the school on the simultaneous and complementary processes leading to overall general social competence.

Lloyd M. Dunn (1963) pointed out that the goals for the trainable retarded have to be somewhat different from those for the educable retarded. Since, as he stated, the trainable retarded will not be able to live independently as adults, their education programs must stress "the development of minimal skills for living and working in sheltered environments." The educable retarded, however, will be able to make an independent adjustment and will be able to maintain themselves effectively in the community. Numerous studies have shown that most retarded individuals are able to adjust at least reasonably well when conditions are favorable. As Kirk (1962) put it, ". . . the educable retarded are able to adjust to society and lead a normal life in the community if the social conditions of the community are conducive to their adjustment."

The school must make special provision to teach personal and social skills to the retarded, not only because of their retardation, but also because they are often socially and culturally handicapped by their home and community environments. Even when they do not suffer such social privations, the attitudes of their school peers as well as school personnel may make the attainment of social competence a more difficult task for them than for others who are more nearly normal. In general, the greater the degree of mental and social inadequacy, the greater the emphasis must be on teaching simple social skills and adjustments as a basis for effective relationships within the environment. For the trainable retarded such skills must include self-care, methods of communication, eating habits, and personal cleanliness.

Readiness for Academic Training

In addition to meeting the general objectives of education for the retarded, we also must consider the preparatory skills in which so many of these children are lacking. Indicating that "there is no preferred curriculum for mentally retarded children which is agreed upon by educators," Smith (1971) nevertheless suggests three main objectives for such a curriculum: (1) to provide a general fund of information; (2) to develop personal, social, and vocational skills so as to make retarded individuals occupationally self-sufficient; and (3) to develop adequate interaction with the environment. But to accomplish these ends, readiness training is required in the preschool years and in the early years of elementary school. Some of the specific skills noted by Smith are visual and auditory discrimination; visual and auditory memory; separation of a figure from its background; and association among stimuli. These are, of course, basic perceptual and memory skills. Other areas of readiness include small motor movements (such as cutting, sorting, and tracing); large motor skills; meaning of the spoken word and of the visual stimulus for the word and expression of ideas, concepts, and procedures. Personal readiness skills include toilet care, control over emotions, and development of "comradeships."

Another approach in developing readiness skills is proposed by Junkala (1972). He proposes a systematic approach to *task analysis,* especially at the primitive levels of learning. In the domain of cognition, two separate but related tasks are *coding* and *perception.* The teacher's task is to determine whether either or both of these skills is lacking. For example, the child may be unable to recognize and sound the *b* in *boy* and *bug.* The task, then, is to teach the specific abstract code for this letter by offering sufficient examples at the same level of complexity. But the problem may not be coding; it may simply be perception. This requires *identifying* a stimulus rather than *abstracting* it. The task, then, is to teach the perception of the stimulus. This requires exercises in recognition of the stimulus at an appropriate level of complexity. Sometimes, however, the problem is conceptual. This involves the learning of *meaningful relationships.* Thus, in *task analysis,* assessment of the specific skill that is lacking leads to a precise set of learning experiences at the particular level of difficulty appropriate for the particular child. If the level of the task is too difficult, as it so often is when specific analysis is not employed first, the teacher then selects tasks at a simpler level.

Development of General and Special Skills

Many retarded children will be able to learn to read reasonably well and to do simple computational work, but others will be able to make only minimal progress. Similarly, many retarded children will have little difficulty in communicating, but others will have considerable difficulty. Not only will there be significant differences in skills and abilities between educable and trainable retarded children, between mildly retarded and severely retarded children, for example, but there also will be considerable variability within each group. Taking into account these significant differences, the educational program must provide *appropriate* academic training for each child, as well as special training for any child who needs it.

In general, retarded children will need training in specific activities that normal children do easily or learn spontaneously. They need highly specific training in habits of safety, habits in motor and sensory behaviors, habits in the arts and crafts, and the like, as well as more general work habits such as attention, persistence in working at a task, and avoidance of being distracted and of distracting others. The particular pattern of general academic and specific skills taught, as well as the teaching *emphasis* and the *sequence* in which the skills are taught, will have to be geared carefully to the special needs of the particular class and the particular children in it. A number of guides for preparing such specialized objectives offer the teacher considerable help in planning a suitable course of study for the group under consideration. (See Thiel, 1960; Barrett, 1977.)

It should be emphasized that when children entering school or preschool programs have had limited experience in language, communication, sanitation, and interpersonal skills, they will need considerable training in these and related skills before they can make significant progress in more advanced skills. To train such children successfully, the teacher must arouse and maintain their interest while meeting all their psychological needs, especially their great need for acceptance.

Vocational and Economic Competence

Whether a retarded child is expected to live in complete or relatively complete economic independence when he has completed his training or whether he is always expected to live under sheltered and dependent conditions, a major objective is the attainment of some degree of vocational competence and economic productivity. The accumulated evidence has shown that a far higher proportion of mentally retarded persons is able to become productive and work in gainful occupations than was previously suspected (see chapter 9). The whole trend in dealing with this population has been towards placement in, and involvement with, society in normal patterns of employment, rather than toward institutionalization and a welfare status. As suitable training programs have developed at both elementary and secondary school levels, increasingly larger percentages of the mentally retarded have become part of the nation's work force. Retarded persons are capable of performing many complex manual and technical operations if they are given appropriate training.

In general, the higher the mental level of the child, the higher the complexity of vocational training that is possible. It must be remembered that factors other than mental ability enter significantly into the kind of work a person is capable of performing under reality conditions. The economic status of the community at the the time of possible employment is one such factor (Heber and Stevens, 1963). The social skills—especially ability to get along with others and to take and follow directions—constitute another.

Some attention has been given to the factors affecting the retarded child's choice of vocation and to success in vocational choice when leaving school. Gorelick (1963), for example, was particularly interested in studying aspects of what she termed *vocational realism*. She described three fundamental levels of vocational planning by the retarded child: realistic, unrealistic, and no planning. Her subjects were 886 tenth- to twelfth-grade mentally retarded children with intelligence quotients between 46 and 79. A semi-structured interview was used to determine each child's vocational plan and knowledge of the job requirements of the plan. The interview was designed to secure information regarding the child's family background, school program, and work experience. Post-school interviews were conducted with 149 of the subjects. At the time of these interviews, 38 percent of the subjects were unemployed, 38 percent were employed, and 24 percent were not working but were engaged in further schooling or miscellaneous community activities.

It was found that 67 percent had held at least one job since leaving school. The school dropout was found to have had less employment success than the person who had completed the school program that had been planned for him. Gorelick found significant sex differences on the employment variables, in that the females had held fewer jobs, had worker fewer hours, and had earned less money than had the males. She concluded that the retarded child who had a realistic plan during school was not more successful in obtaining post-school employment than was the child with an unrealistic plan or no plan. However, on all measures of employment success, the child with a realistic plan maintained a middle position. The hypothesis that the mentally retarded child with formal work experience in high school would be more realistic in planning was partially confirmed, but it was true only of those children who were employed on off-campus jobs, or who were employed independently of the school.

In the light of her findings, Gorelick questions the validity of the generally accepted belief that mentally retarded children must be realistic about their job plans. For example, she wonders whether urging the retarded child to become a dishwasher results in great realism or in a poor self-concept. She also wonders whether giving the retarded child a true understanding of inabilities would diminish motivation and result in more marked feelings of inadequacy and hopelessness. Her findings are not definitive, but she raises questions that indicate the need for still further exploration.

Vocational training not only enables retarded individuals to participate meaningfully in society, but also leads them to a higher self-regard and contributes to their improved social adjustment. Vocational training can include, besides specific occupational skills, many social skills such as punctuality, courtesy, cleanliness, and reliability. Some studies have indicated that traits such as these are of primary importance in getting and holding many types of jobs.

One of the most intensive follow-up studies of retarded pupils who had been enrolled in special classes (but who had not necessarily been given specific and continuous vocational training) (Charles, 1953) found that more than 80 percent of the "graduates" of the special-class program (in Lincoln, Nebraska) were gainfully employed. Although most worked as laborers, some held much higher-level positions, including managerial positions. A few even maintained expensive homes. Charles also found that more than half of the men had been involved in some law violation, but *none* had committed any serious offenses, the usual offense being a minor traffic or civil infraction!

Although not all follow-up studies paint such a favorable impression as this one, the general finding is that a mentally retarded person, except at the lowest grade, is able to hold a job as well as the rest of the population during times of reasonably good or very good employment and is essentially a good, law-abiding citizen.

For the interested reader, several recent reviews of the vocational adjustment of retarded persons and the relatively good results that can be achieved with good vocational training followed by in-service or on-the-job training are worth more detailed study. (See Browning, 1974; Gold, 1973; and Cobb,

1972.) We concur with the evaluation provided by Halpern, Browning, and Brummer (1975), who state: "The extraordinary success of recent vocational efforts for the severely retarded brings into question the traditional view that vocational abilities are extremely limited in this population."

More research is needed on the nature of the vocational task that retarded persons are asked to master, rather than simply on the nature or degree of retardation, in order to maximize the effectiveness of vocational training. More study also is needed on effective means for placement and for counseling after placement in an effort to insure vocational success over longer periods of time.

QUALIFICATIONS OF THE TEACHER

As we have seen, the role of the teacher in the education of the retarded child has become ever more critical as well as ever more complex. In addition to knowledge of the formal subject matter that the teacher teaches, he or she must possess many special skills. There is a limit, however, to the number of pedagogic and psychological areas in which the teacher can become skilled. We cannot expect the teacher to fulfill the special roles of psychologist, social worker, medical specialist, and resource person as well as that of pedagogue. The problem, then, is to determine what minimal combination of skills, attitudes, and knowledge he or she must possess to provide the individualized, effective training that the diverse needs of retarded children require. And, given this base, there is the further problem of how to provide trained specialists whom the teacher can call on when technical skills are required. There is no simple solution to these problems—either in terms of cost or in terms of available personnel—but some solution must be found to provide for effective education.

Hurley (1974) has described the kinds of special skills the modern teacher of the mentally retarded must possess. He refers to these skills as "supportive knowledge," suggesting that at least minimal competency should be attained in these areas. The first of these areas is knowledge of child development, which implies knowledge of the *sequence* in which abilities develop. A second area is knowledge about *learning* (its principles as well as research findings), including knowledge of programming, sequencing, and methods of presentation. A third area is *sociological knowledge,* including information about the effect of cultural and ethnic differences. A fourth area is *behavior management,* including behavior modification techniques. These areas of knowledge also include knowledge about, and skills in, maintaining attention, developing perceptual skills, and improving memory abilities, as well as knowledge about the role of language in cognition.

This summary indicates the breadth of training that the modern teacher of the retarded is expected to have. However, we should like to emphasize what we consider to be the most basic, underlying area of competence: *interpersonal skills.* Whatever technical skills may be required in the teaching situation, the teacher-student encounter involves human interaction. We have learned from research on therapeutic intervention and from operant conditioning methods in behavior modification that techniques will only be effective in the long run when the relationship between teacher and student is one of trust, respect, understanding, and warmth. The child must feel that he is loved and respected, that his needs are understood, and that the teacher is sympathetic to his problems. In the process of interaction, the teacher presents a model from which the child learns in many concomitant and covert ways. The child becomes more motivated to learn, and anxiety in learning situations is decreased. The child acquires a positive self-image. All of these outcomes are aspects of the affective dimension of learning and of teaching. Morse (1970), in discussing the responsibility of schools to children, stresses that "teachers in the best schools are trained to be *sensitive* [emphasis ours] to the covert as well as overt needs of the pupil. . . ." He also points up the need to train teachers to be aware of their own defensive reactions against the critical and aggressive behaviors that children direct against their teachers. In short, part of a teacher's fundamental training is to learn to understand the dynamics of children's behavior. It is especially important that when the teachers fail or feel thwarted, they become aware of how they react against "threats" to their integrity. Whatever merits there are in having competence in some technical teaching skill, the child cannot learn effectively, or make use of the learning in the long run, if he does not participate appropriately in the learning process because he is emotionally disturbed by the teacher's personality reactions. And even if the child learns some skill, at what price is that skill acquired if he loses self-respect or becomes more negatively oriented to his world?

The role of the teacher in the total emotional growth of a child is especially important with retarded children — the teacher serves as an additional parental figure. In the lower grades especially, the classroom teacher is a powerful figure to the child, one toward whom the child may develop intense feelings. The child tends to behave toward a female teacher the same as he does toward his own mother, at least in the prepubertal years. The child tends to identify with her, so she is likely to be an important influence in later superego development. Since the child learns many emotional habits from the teacher, she is likely to be an important positive or negative force influencing personality development. The following illustration will make some of these points more concrete:

A child who was in psychotherapy developed unusual insight into his relationship with his teacher. He had been rather withdrawn, but had made excellent therapeutic progress. As a result, he had begun to perceive his need to be close to his teacher and had begun to develop a good emotional relationship with her. The teacher was accepting of his needs for closeness to her, up to a point. The relationship between them continued to develop until the child finally reached a point at which he was able to express some of his hostility toward her in the classroom situation. (This was based on unconscious feelings the child had toward his mother, which were displaced on the teacher.) This was a good development for the child, but his hostile expressions resulted in a severe emotional reaction by the teacher. Because of her own emotional immaturity, she was made extremely anxious by the child's expressed hostility. Instead of perceiving and dealing with the problem as a manifestation of the child's growth, the teacher referred him to the principal for disciplinary action. This destroyed the relationship of the child with the teacher.

The nature of this child's family relationships was manifest in the school. The teacher was cast in the role of the mother, the principal (the authority figure) in the role of the father, and (although it was not brought out in the case material just presented) the child's classmates in the roles of siblings.

Even more than the average child, the retarded child tends to cast the teacher in a parental role, and the special-class teacher must be aware of this almost automatic reaction. The teacher also must be aware of his or her own emotional reactions to such a role and learn to accept these feelings as well as those of the child. The teacher must learn to understand how different children *perceive him or her* and how each child differs in basic demands of the teacher. Despite unique emotional characteristics and personal integrity, the teacher is a different person to each pupil, depending on each pupil's particular needs. The teacher must not only recognize the emotional demands made by the child and the feelings that each child displaces or transfers on him or her, but must also learn how to use the relationship that exists with the child to promote the child's emotional growth. This last point is crucial; not only must there be feeling for the child, but there also must be *adequate knowledge of what to do about it*. This demands that the teacher know something of personality dynamics, of child development, of human relationships and group structures, of personal, emotional needs and reactions, and of the basic elements of psychotherapeutic relationships. As Bettelheim says (1950), "Love is not enough." More than affection and good intentions toward the child are needed. Of course, it is basic that the teacher have feelings of warmth, acceptance, and love for the child, but without the technical know-how, the child becomes buried in a stickly morass of feelings of pity, which eventually may prove to be a detriment to growth.

There have been some very interesting studies of special-class teacher-child interactions. One of these, done by Harris (1955), was partly a methodological study in which three types of teachers' attitudes toward retarded children were explored: *persuasive,* in which the teacher feels and expresses understanding of the child's problems and returns kindness for negative behavior; *suggestive* and *rational,* in which the teacher attempts to objectify the pupil's behavior and find reasons for his own behavior; and *disciplining,* a more restrictive and punitive approach toward the child. Harris suggests that the special-class teacher should vary his attitudes in a deliberate manner, noting the effect of each approach on the individual child.

Kirk and Johnson (1951) summarized their position with respect to the best teaching approach to mentally retarded children in the statements that follow:

1. Teaching procedures should be organized in harmony with good mental hygiene principles.
2. The child's attention should be focused through positive suggestions and a positive classroom atmosphere of acceptable social behavior.

3. The retarded child should be allowed to plan activities within the range of his interests and abilities.
4. Techniques such as sociodrama should be used for the purpose of developing insights in practical life situations.
5. Self-determining activities should be organized to give children practice in the independent management of their affairs.

We agree with these statements wholeheartedly, but would stress that the basic function of the special-class teacher is to promote the total personal and academic development of the child. This entails attention to the child's emotional and behavioral adjustment as well as to the child's learning problems and needs.

THE NATURE OF LEARNING: CHARACTERISTICS OF RETARDED CHILDREN

The Variable Effects of Slow Learning Ability

We have stressed that the degree of mental retardation cannot be represented adequately by IQ alone. Children with the same IQ or MA scores vary significantly in many aspects of cognitive functioning and vary tremendously in most other factors associated with learning ability. Nor have we meant to imply in discussing the differential learning experiences or the different goals in education for the mildly to profoundly retarded groups that these groups have little overlap in learning level or characteristics. The fact is that there is tremendous overlap in the characteristics of these groups, and their separation for educational purposes does not mean that each child in one group is distinctly different from each child in the other.

Despite the obvious fact that the general rate of learning is related very closely to general intellectual level, there is considerable controversy concerning the *specific* aspects of the intellectual functions as they are related to specific aspects of the learning process. Zigler (1967) has maintained that the child's developmental level, which is measured by mental age rather than by intelligence quotient, determines the rate of learning. This point of view has been rejected by Weir (1967), who maintains that persons with similar mental ages but different intelligence quotients show different learning rates. According to Weir, persons with a higher IQ learn faster than persons of comparable mental age but with a lower IQ. Some studies have been designed to test which of these two viewpoints is more tenable. An example of such a study is that reported by Jensen and Rohwer (1968). They matched children with identical MAs but different IQs and gave them similar learning tasks. They found that children with higher IQs learned serial and paired-associate lists three to four times faster than retarded children, even though the mental age was held constant. However, their study has been criticized severely on methodological grounds.

It is now apparent that neither Zigler's nor Weir's position is fully acceptable. Additional research is needed to evaluate the many complexities of this problem. As Glass (1969) points out, fundamental differences between other basic conceptual approaches to learning and intelligence also need to be resolved. The reader is referred to an article by Zigler (1968) for more detail on these issues.

Our previous review of some experimental studies of learning characteristics (see chapter 7) indicated that in some areas, retarded persons functioned disproportionately below their own levels of general mental development. We highlighted the significance of anxiety in producing unnecessary impairment in learning. In turn, failure in learning tends to reduce aspiration level and, therefore, impedes subsequent learning still more. We also have emphasized the relative lack of sufficient incidental learning experiences of retarded children, especially in those coming from substandard or culturally deprived homes. All of these and other factors tend to combine to produce variable learning characteristics in children with the same level of general mental development. Not only do retarded individuals have different learning characteristics from children with normal mental development because of the difference in mental maturity, but retarded children also have *learned to learn* in quite different ways from each other.

Studies on *discrimination set* (Barnett and Cantor, 1957) and on *transfer of training* (Johnson and Blake, 1960) in retarded children indicate that although retarded children are likely to be different in these characteristics from children with higher IQs who are matched with them in mental age, the differences are *not inherent or immutable*. Slow learners seem to have developed different kinds of learning sets, expectancies, attitudes, and capacities for generalization than normal learners of comparable mental age because of different experiences during the learning process: more frequent failure, inadequate preparation, too rapid pace in learning, and lack of sustained attention. But when such factors are compensated for by proper remedial instruction, the learning characteristics of the retarded do change.

Unfortunately, not all characteristics of the mentally retarded child are entirely or readily susceptible to modification by educational methods. For example, Alley (1969) studied the effect of specific training in perceptual-motor performance with mentally retarded children. Alley was interested in possible improvement in concept formation. His experimental subjects were forty-eight educable mentally retarded children, seven years and five months to nine years and ten months of age, who were enrolled in special classes. The comparable control group contained an identical sex distribution. The experimental group was exposed to a systematic visual training program covering a two-month period. The control group, instead, spent school time in regular special-education classroom activities. Training was provided for the experimental group in five areas: (1) eye-motor coordination, (2) figure-ground relationships, (3) form constancy, (4) position in space, and (5) spatial relationships. The results were then analyzed by means of a covariance technique. Alley did not find any advantages in such a training program. There was no significant difference between the performance of children who received specialized training in perceptual-motor skills and the performance of those who had not received such training.

On the basis of known facts, we may offer the following general conclusions:

1. In most learning situations, retarded children learn less rapidly than do children of comparable chronological age but superior mental development.
2. When retarded children are compared with normal children of comparable mental age (and, therefore, of lower chronological age), the results are variable: the retarded are equally competent in some tasks, better in some, and poorer in others.
3. Retarded children, as compared with normal children, tend to be inferior in ability to attend, to remember, to discriminate, to transfer, and to conceptualize, even when the groups are equated for mental age, but these differences are probably less significant for new types of learning situations (like those studied in laboratory experiments such as those described by Johnson and Blake); moreover, these differences are not necessary, intrinsic concomitants of the phenomenon of retardation.
4. Slow learners, like all other learners, show marked variability in learning capacities, and their potential for specific learning situations must be assessed on an individual basis rather than on a collective basis.

LEARNING PROCESSES AND LEARNING PRINCIPLES

Thus far, we have discussed learning as if it were a unitary phenomenon and we have examined some of the findings concerning the variabilities of the learning of retarded individuals. But learning is *not* a unitary phenomenon; *there are many kinds of learning.* Moreover, although some learning theorists seem to proclaim that they have, at least, an understanding of all of the basic aspects of learning, the wiser theorists make much more modest claims. The fact is that our present theories of learning fall far short of explaining satisfactorily all aspects of learning, and they do not enable us to predict with precision what the outcomes of many learning experiences will be. Our present task is to gain a deeper understanding of some of these learning processes and principles so that we can provide better learning experiences for pupils.

Let us remember, first, that there is both conscious and unconscious learning. We often are unaware that we are learning something, as for instance when we "incorporate" values and attitudes of our peers or our parents without being aware that we are assimilating them. We learn self-concepts and we learn to have certain levels of aspiration. We learn to fear certain kinds of situations while becoming confident in others. Sometimes we learn only when we are properly motivated, whereas we also may learn without having much motivation. Some things are learned better when we have massed or intensive learning experiences, whereas other things are learned better when the learning experiences are distributed over time. There is immediate learning, but there also is "latent" learning and later performance in which the products of learning appear only after a period of time. These assertions are illustrative of the different forms of learning.

On the other hand, learning proceeds through a great variety of learning processes. Thus, the learning of perceptual or motor skills is very different, in terms of process, from the learning of concepts and strategies. There are forms of learning that are relatively simple, such as memorizing names or facts, but there are forms of learning that are highly complex, such as those involving inductive reasoning. From the Piagetian viewpoint, there are simple schemas, learned early in life, and there are complex schemas, learned later in life. Some learning results from the frequent repetition of an act, whereas other types of learning are inhibited when there is too much repetition. Bandura and Jeffrey (1973) have demonstrated, for example, that repetition without simultaneous (internal) coding by the learner does *not* result in improved retention, whereas repetition accompanied by coding is more effective. In short, not only does learning proceed through varying pathways, but it also proceeds through varying processes.

We cite these considerations not only to stress the complexity of learning but also to emphasize that, in some respects, learning is *task* (or task-type) *specific,* and that different individuals learn through differing types of experiences.

Before proceeding to examine the relevance of these problems to the learning of retarded individuals, let us briefly summarize some of the basic theories of how learning takes place.

Conditioning Theories of Learning

Conditioning theories of learning were first developed to explain the simplest forms of learning, especially to explain learning in animals. As we shall see, some workers in the field of psychology have suggested that conditioning is all that is necessary to explain all learning. We believe that this is an unfortunate generalization that does not do justice to known facts of learning. On the other hand, principles of conditioning are highly important in explaining many forms of learning.

There are two general types of conditioning theories: *classical conditioning* and *operant conditioning,* also known as *instrumental learning.* These two types of conditioning help to explain many forms of basic learning experiences.

The "father" of classical conditioning was the Russian, I. P. Pavlov. As he conceived (1927), it was possible to learn a new or *conditioned response* in place of or in addition to the original or *unconditioned response* that was formerly evoked by the natural or *unconditioned stimulus.* Working with dogs in his experimental laboratory, Pavlov was able to demonstrate that by presenting a ringing bell (or a light) at the same time the dog was fed meat, the dog learned, after a number of trials, to salivate to the bell whereas it formerly salivated to the meat. Thus a new circuit had been established, which can be diagrammed as in Figure 15.1.

Let us examine the model of learning presented in Figure 15.1 more carefully. In the first place, it is assumed that US, the unconditioned stimulus, (meat or, as in the actual experiments, meat powder) is a *natural stimulus* that biologically leads to salivation (UR), an unconditioned or natural response. By vir-

$$US \longrightarrow UR \qquad \left.\begin{array}{l} US \longrightarrow UR \\ CS \longrightarrow CR \end{array}\right] \text{(paired)} \qquad CS \longrightarrow CR \text{ (UR)}$$

US → UR	US → UR ⎤ (paired)	CS → CR (UR)
(meat) (salivation)	CS → CR ⎦	(bell) (salivation)
	(bell) (listens)	

FIGURE 15.1   Paradigm of Classical Conditioning

tue of a number of trials in which the US is paired (*chained*) with CS (the artificial or experimental stimulus), CS becomes able, by itself, to produce CR, the conditioned response to CS. But note that in our figure we also have included UR in the conditioned response. The dog has learned to salivate (UR) with the presentation of only CS, but the CR turns out *not* to be exactly the same as the UR. For one thing, the amount of salivation produced with the CS is less than that produced with US. For another thing, the UR originally included more than salivation (for example it also included chewing of the food), whereas the CR does not include chewing. There are other significant differences, as we shall presently see.

It also is important to recognize that Pavlov's experiments dealt with basic physiological processes that were, presumably, present from birth on. In the human being, and especially in the adolescent or adult human being, it is quite difficult to deal with an exclusively natural, unconditioned stimulus; a great deal of learning and conditioning already have occurred by that time and it is unlikely that we can find a completely natural US. Nevertheless Pavlov clearly established the fact that conditioning was a primary form of learning and that neutral stimuli could produce conditioned responses.

Finally, it is important to recognize that the learning or conditioning that occurs is more complicated than Figure 15.1 suggests. The original UR involved more than simply salivation; as we indicated, it also involved chewing. Moreover, the response to the food also involved other elements that were not the focus of the experiment, such as the time of the day (or the degree of hunger) when food was presented, and the nature of the relationship between the dog and the experimenter (or with other aspects of the experimental situation). In short, although attention was focused on the salivary responses, other responses also were occurring simultaneously. In later studies by Pavlov and his co-workers, it soon became clear that the CR was not only different from the UR in terms of the amount of saliva that was secreted, but that the CR also involved other elements in the response pattern, so that the dog might also become conditioned to the room in which the experiment occurred, the experimental apparatus, the experimenter who was performing the experiment, and so on. There was a *generalizing effect* of the conditioning procedure that included conditioning to many more elements than the CS, and the response involved far more than salivation. The complexity of even this simple situation is presented in Figure 15.2. As Figure 15.2 indicates, the stimulus and the response, both unconditioned and conditioned, really are *stimulus patterns;* that is, each is a complex pattern of a number of elements. This point is emphasized because even in this relatively simple learning situation, involving involuntary responses (sometimes called reflexes), *the affected behavior is always more than a single discrete element.* This conclusion will help explain some of the concerns that psychologists have with

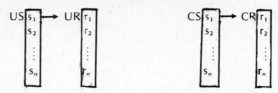

FIGURE 15.2.   The Complexity of the Classical Paradigm

all conditioning procedures, and especially, as we shall see, with procedures in which the subject is involved on an involuntary basis; more than the "target" behavior is likely to be affected.

It now remains to explain some of the other phenomena that have been discovered in the course of conditioning studies of the classical type. The first is the timing or *temporal pattern* involving the presentation of US and CS. The CS could, in theory, be presented before, at the same time as, or after the US is presented. These three conditions are called, respectively, *delayed, simultaneous,* and *backward* conditioning. A fourth type of condition (*trace conditioning*) is one in which the CS is presented and then removed before the US is presented. In general, it has been found that the simultaneous type of conditioning is most effective and that backward conditioning is extremely difficult. In usual practice, then, the CS is presented just before (less than five seconds before) the US is presented and then is continually present along with the US until the desired conditioning becomes established over a number of trials.

Conditioning to a chain of CS's also may be performed. In this type of conditioning, called *higher order conditioning,* after the first CS has produced the CR, a second CS may be paired with the first one, over a number of trials, until the second CS will evoke the CR. A number of such higher order conditionings may be completed. Sometimes such conditionings in the total chain occur inadvertently because they already are part of the pattern of the CS that is inadvertently introduced originally.

Another phenomenon is *generalization*. Once a CS ⟶ CR has been established, other similar stimuli may evoke the CR. Thus, with Pavlov's dogs, once the dog had learned to salivate to the tingling of a particular bell, bells with other timbre, pitch, or intensity also could evoke the CR. Hovland (1937) demonstrated that the greater the dissimilarity between the stimuli, the less effective they are in evoking the CR. In his work, Hovland used human subjects and employed an electric shock as the US in evoking galvanic skin responses.

Still another phenomenon is *discrimination*. In order to condition an animal or a human being to a specific CS, the subject is conditioned to a particular stimulus for which a reward or reinforcer is given. Then other but similar stimuli are presented, but on such occasions no reward or reinforcer is given. In time, the subject learns to develop conditioned discrimination among the several similar stimuli so that the conditioned response appears only with the specific CS that was rewarded.

Finally, a word should be said about *extinction* of conditioned responses. After a CS is able to produce a CR, the CS will tend to continue to evoke the CR for some time, even in the absence of the US. In time, however, unless there is reinforcement of the CS by the US, the CS no longer will evoke the

CR. Such extinction is a gradual process. However, it has been demonstrated experimentally that even when extinction has occurred, some *trace* or after effect remains. One way of demonstrating this is by showing that the subject can be reconditioned to the CS more easily.

Pavlov's explanation of learning involves a theoretical model that is similar to a switchboard. In this model, the primary elements are the S (stimulus) and the R (response), which become associated over time through some type of reinforcement. Other theorists who have contributed to this type of theory are Guthrie (1935), Thorndike (1911), and more recently, Hull (1952) and Spence (1958). These theorists have explored such additional factors in associative learning as the nature of reinforcement, the effect of exercise or number of trials, and the nature of the contingency between associated events in learning. The interested reader may find an account of these theories in Isaacson and Hutt (1971).

In some contrast to classical conditioning is *operant conditioning*. Although both methods of conditioning produce changes in behavior, operant conditioning can be utilized to produce *complex patterns* of *adaptive behavior*. In classical conditioning, on the other hand, the conditioned response does, indeed, change the behavior, but the change is internal and has no direct effect on the external environment. At the most, classical conditioning is adaptive only in the sense that the conditioned stimulus can serve as a signal or warning that prepares the organism for the conditioned response, which formerly occurred only to the unconditioned stimulus. Moreover, operant conditioning, or instrumental learning, can lead to highly intricate and complex behaviors through a process of *successive shapings*.

B. F. Skinner, more than any other psychologist, has explored the possibilities and elaborated the methods by means of which operant conditioning functions. The fundamentals of his approach were presented in his work *The Behavior of Organisms* (1938) and have been elaborated in other research papers and books. The most pertinent, in terms of our exposition are: *Science and Human Behavior* (1953), and *Beyond Freedom and Human Dignity* (1971). Skinner advocates the use of operant conditioning not only to change people for the better, so that they can function according to desired criteria, but also to change society for the better through shaping procedures agreed to by panels of "experts." Although operant conditioning can, in fact, be utilized to eliminate certain undesirable behaviors and substitute more desirable behaviors, it does not explain all learning and involves some great hazards, as we shall see. Nevertheless, utilized appropriately it can have great value in improving the functioning, especially for retarded and emotionally maladjusted individuals.

Skinner built on the prior work of others, notably of Thorndike, and later of Hull. He recognized that the laws of *trial-and-error* and of *effect* were important explanations of many forms of learning. The law of trial-and-error, more accurately termed the *Law of Exercise,* simply asserts that over many trials and errors, when a response occurs more frequently and more recently than any other response to a stimulus, that response will tend to occur more frequently on future occasions. Thus, in typical experiments done by Thorndike, an animal was given the opportunity to learn through many trial-and-error experiences the solution to some problem, and in time the animal learned that a certain response produced the solution. Thorndike added, however, that the *Law of Exercise* was insufficient to explain animal learning. His *Law of Effect* stated the response that is learned is the one that is rewarded by some satisfying result. In the case of animal experiments, food usually was the reward. Later, we shall offer some critical comment on these laws.

Skinner employed the so-called Skinner Box, an experimental apparatus in which the behavior of the animal could be monitored automatically as well as observed by the experimenter, to establish the "facts" of learning behavior. His favorite experimental animal was the pigeon. In the Skinner Box, the pigeon (a hungry pigeon) pecked aimlessly, in trial-and-error fashion, until he pecked at an illuminated window. A food pellet was then automatically delivered to the pigeon. Through successive experiences of this kind, the pigeon *learned instrumentally* to peck at the window to obtain food. Food was the *reinforcing* agent. Not only did this simple learning procedure produce efficient, learned behavior in obtaining food, but the method of reinforcement also could be used to shape highly complex behavior. Thus, for example, a pigeon could be trained to turn around by the method of *successive approximations*. This was done by reinforcing the first, small turning movement of the pigeon, *as it occurred,* by giving the pigeon a pellet. In successive learning trials, as the pigeon turned a little more, he was then given reinforcement. Still later, reinforcement was applied only after the pigeon had turned even more, until the pigeon had learned to turn completely around. The pigeon learned this procedure quite rapidly.

As with classical conditioning, similar principles were employed in explaining other aspects of operant conditioning. Thus there were principles of higher order conditioning, schedules of reinforcement, and methods of extinction.

Let us examine more closely some principles of operant conditioning and examine some typical experiments. In a book by Smith and Neisworth (1973), three classes of reinforcers are described. The first one is the positive reinforcer. When the response is forthcoming, the child is given a reward of some kind. The second is the negative reinforcer. For example, when Johnny is cranky, the experimenter may give Johnny another pleasant task in place of what he has been doing, thus avoiding the use of *aversive* reinforcement. The third class of reinforcers is punishment. The behavior is followed by an aversive event. For example, when Johnny rocks, he is told "Stop" or is punished in some way. Thus, it is held that these three classes of reinforcers tend to initiate desired behaviors or to cause undesirable behavior to be discontinued.

But initiated behavior can be extinguished before it is firmly reinforced if the usual reinforcer that has been used is withheld. Further, the pattern of reinforcement that is applied after a desired behavior is initiated influences the *duration* of the behavior. Reinforcers may be applied in a pattern of fixed ratios (e.g., the reward is given each time within five minutes after the behavior has been elicited); in a pattern of fixed intervals (e.g., after every fifteen minutes in which the behavior is exhibited); in a pattern of variable ratios (e.g., the reward is given every third time the behavior is shown); and in a pattern of variable intervals (e.g., the reward is given one time in every twenty minutes). These differing patterns have differing effects on the learning.

It is held that if unrelated, learned behaviors are linked together and reinforced consistently over time, they will finally become automatic and generalized. It is highly important to specify the precise behaviors that are to be modified. Thus, the statement that Johnny is hostile does not represent a *specific target* of behavior modification. Rather, the statement that Johnny kicks and that Johnny hits others gives more appropriate targets. Such targets are amenable to behavior modification, whereas the more general description of behavior as "hostile" or "aggressive" does not provide a sufficiently specific description for effective training.

Now let us look at some examples of typical experiments using principles of operant conditioning. We have selected examples of seriously disturbed behavior in order to highlight the effectiveness of this approach. One study deals with problems in toilet training and another with undesirable classroom behavior. However, the methods may be used with other forms of behavior and with various types of learning problems. In the first study, Hundziak et al. (1965) dealt with the establishment of toilet training in twenty-nine severely retarded boys from seven to fourteen years of age. The children were randomly assigned to one of three experimental conditions: (1) operant conditioning, (2) conventional toilet training, and (3) a control group (with no training offered). Groups 1 and 2 received similar training except that the former received positive reinforcement (these subjects were given candy after each act of defecation or urination in a commode). The control group did not receive any consistent toilet training. The findings of this study indicated that operant conditioning was superior to the other two approaches and that the acquired behavior transferred to other aspects of daily living.

In the other study, Giles and Wolf (1966) applied operant conditioning to five subjects who were incontinent and had other severe problems in bowel and bladder functions. They ranged in age from 6.8 years to 18.5 years, and they ranged in *Vineland Social Maturity* score from 14 to 24. All were judged to be severely retarded. The positive reinforcement procedures involved the presentation of candy and ice cream directly following all appropriate instances of toilet behavior, as well as more specific positive reinforcers related to the specific needs of each child. The latter included baby food, a hug, the words *good boy,* rides in a wheel chair, and the like. The authors also state that they introduced aversive stimuli following inappropriate responses, such as ignoring the subject, terminating meals, and retaining the subject in a crawl-pen. The findings indicated that all subjects were readily able to establish effective habits of toilet behavior. It was concluded that such *uniquely tailored operant procedures* were effective with these children, whereas general experience indicated that subjects with *Vineland* scores below 30 did not respond satisfactorily to traditional methods of toilet training.

Other studies indicate that with carefully programmed patterns of operant conditioning, even more complex behaviors can be successfully modified. Bijou and his co-workers (1966) have shown that instruction in the academic subjects can be more effective for retarded pupils when operant conditioning is used. Bijou's leadership in this area has had far-reaching effects on instructional efficiency. Perline and Levinsky (1968) demonstrated that operant conditioning could be applied to maladaptive behavior in severely retarded children. They worked with children ranging in age from eight to ten and in social scores from 22 to 38. The maladaptive behaviors were aggression toward other children, aggression toward the teacher, throwing objects, taking another child's property, and rising from the chair. The experimenters made use of *tokens* (in this case poker chips), which were subsequently exchanged for tidbits. Adaptive behavior was rewarded with tokens, and maladaptive behavior was punished by taking tokens away. In addition, some children were restrained by being buckled to a restraint post when they engaged in maladaptive behavior. The authors found that there was a significant decrease in all categories of maladaptive behavior for all four children.

These findings are fairly typical of the great many studies that have been reported. Behavior modification works! It also may seem very simple indeed. However, as we noted earlier, there are many cautions to be observed.

Let us now examine some of the issues that operant conditioning has raised. In our opinion, the foremost issue is the ethical one. Much has been written about this issue. Since individuals' behaviors can be "shaped" and even "shaped unwittingly," who is to decide what behavior is to be altered? On some matters, there is little controversy, such as when an individual's behavior is clearly destructive to others. However, the difficulty is that many forms of deviant behavior, which society does not accept simply because they deviate from the norm, are not necessarily destructive or even inappropriate. Some of our great "revolutions" in norms have come about precisely because someone dared to be deviant! Moreover, altering an individual's behavior without the individual's *informed consent* is a clear abrogation of individual rights. The literature is replete with examples of prisoners, school children, and others who have been subjected to operant conditioning experiments in clear violation of such rights.

At the level of theory and application are other critical issues. Although operant conditioning acts on performance, thus contributing to possibly better adaptive behavior, what precisely is a reinforcer? The typical answer given by the Skinnerians is that a reinforcer is that which reinforces. Put in more technical language, a reinforcer is an experience that serves to increase the frequency or probability of a desired response. This circularity of reasoning has been "clarified" by calling the reinforcing agent a "reward." There are several difficulties with this solution. One is that the expanded definition is simply an exercise in semantics: one word has been subtituted for another. Another is that the individual in the experiment has no choice over how he would wish to be rewarded. After all, people's motivations and values do differ. And, finally, the effect of a reward differs with different individuals. Recent experimental study has shown that the meaning and effect of a reward (or punishment) depends to a large extent on the subjective *interpretation* of the reward by the learner (not the experimenter) (Deci, 1975; Lepper and Greene, 1975) and of the specific kind of feedback that the reward conveys to the learner (Buchwald, 1969). In short, what is a reward to one person is not a reward to another! Thus, in the end, the nature of rewards and their possible effects is still an unresolved question.

One critical assumption about operant conditioning is that learning takes place via very simple stimulus-response connections. Such an approach has had very wide appeal. It seemed to indicate that in order to change behavior or performance, all one had to do was to define the behavior to be changed more precisely than had been done previously, and then arrange for rewards and punishments according to some simple formulae. Certainly such an approach is effective with many forms of behavior, especially relatively simple types of behaviors. However, as has been amply demonstrated in recent studies of learning, many complex cognitive operations intervene between stimulus and response. Schacter (1971) has shown that the subject attaches a label to what he experiences and then responds via emotionally experienced reactions to the label that has been attached. Modern psychologists view human beings as organisms that seek information, code it, store it, retrieve it, and employ it in some personally functional manner (Appley, 1971). It is no accident, then, that as psychologists began to experiment with more complex behavior, they (including the behaviorists) turned increasingly to considerations of covert symbols and imagery in trying to modify and predict changes in behavior (Mahoney, 1974).

Expectancy Learning

As many experiments show, much learning has little or nothing to do with reinforcement. One such instance has been termed *expectancy learning*, and we shall turn to this theory now. Tolman (1932, 1967) has been the chief architect of this theory. He has offered many and varied examples, from studies with both animals and men, that neither frequency nor recency accounts for many significant forms of learning. An individual may perform the wrong acts as frequently as the correct acts, yet he may learn the correct response nevertheless. Two studies will illustrate the accuracy of this statement.

A classical study reported by Blodgett (1929) investigated the learning of rats in mazes in which the goal (the desired response) was finding the food box. Three groups of rats were studied. In one, rats were permitted to find the food in the maze and permitted to eat for three minutes (i.e., were rewarded immediately). A second group was permitted to explore the maze for six days but were not fed. A third group was permitted to run the maze for the first two days without food, and then to run the maze with food as the reward on subsequent days. Despite the fact that the latter two groups did not receive any reward (food) during the initial days of the experiment, they were *immediately successful* in finding food (for the most part) on the very first trial when food was given. These rats were indistinguishable in behavior (the learning of the correct response) from the first group of rats by the second day after food was exposed. The results were interpreted by Blodgett to indicate that there was *latent learning* during the trials without food. In popular terms, groups two and three showed their learning of where the food was when food was actually available, but before this did not display what they had learned.

Isaacson and Hutt (1971) summarize a reported study that is even more critical. In this study, rats learned to run a maze and obtain food when hungry. Then cerebellar lesions were made to produce gross impairment in motor performance. The experimental question was: could rats with severe motor impairment still find their way to the goal (food)? In fact, they did! Tolman would thus argue that the rats could not have learned to solve the maze simply as a consequence of repeated motor responses but had learned a *cognitive map* of the maze and were thereafter able to find the goal by other means when motoric behavior was disrupted.

Tolman has suggested that to understand latent learning we must distinguish between "learning" and "performance." According to Tolman, reinforcement (whether reward or punishment) has differing functions for these two kinds of behavior. In learning, reinforcement helps the subject discover which responses are either rewarded or punished. Although reinforcement does not always operate in this manner, when it does, it assists the learner by helping him to develop a better cognitive map (or maps) through the functional addition of new information (Anderson, 1976). This type of learning *does not affect the probability that one will perform* a given act. Performance, on the other hand, is dependent on motivation and on a reward that is "wanted" at the time of the act. In short, we learn S $\longrightarrow$ S associations by contiguity of events and then, when it is relevant, we put this cognitive map to use when we are motivated to do so. A simple example may highlight this explanation. We may learn where a certain drinking fountain is because we have passed it a number of times even if we have never used it, but then when we are thirsty, we may perform the act of drinking at this fountain.

Tolman's theory of learning and performance is called not only expectancy theory but also a theory of *purposive learning*. Choice and purpose are highlighted in this theory. The implication to the teacher is that *more than rewards are necessary;* one must also utilize or improve the motivations that are relevant to the persons involved.

An illustration of the effect of choice in learning is provided in a study reported by Grigsby and Harshman (1977). Two matched groups of retarded pupils were compared in six areas of performance: self-help, communication, perceptual-motor-physical skills, personal-social, academic skills, and economic skills. The subjects were about fourteen years of age and had a mean IQ of about 50. One group shared responsibility for decisions in the teaching process whereas the other group did not but were taught by traditional methods. In five of the six areas the decision-involved group made significantly greater gains, and in the sixth area, the decision-making group was better although not significantly so. Although the numbers of pupils involved were small and the study needs replication, the findings are suggestive of the importance of utilizing pupils' motivation to maximize learning.

The issue of motivation in learning has assumed ever more complex aspects as it has been more extensively studied. Skinnerians assumed that motivation could simply be provided by the experimenter to reinforce a contingency: That which was reinforcing was motivating. We have commented on the dilemma such a conceptualization poses. More recently, some psychologists, taking their clues from Tolman's and other psychologists' concern about purpose, have attempted to define motivation more precisely. Some divide motivation into intrinsic and extrinsic rewards. Deci (1975), cited above, has found that sometimes extrinsic motivators actually reduce interest in learning and may decrease performance. Other psychologists distinguish between two types of reinforcement: the affective and the informational (Bolles, 1972). Each type of motivation may have differential results, depending on the task, the characteristics of the learner, and the way in which learning is measured. Thus, although much progress has been made since Tolman introduced his conception of purposiveness in learning, the complex issue of motivation has not been fully resolved.

SOME OTHER FORMS OF LEARNING: THEORIES AND FINDINGS

Now that we have reviewed the basic theories of learning, let us examine some other theories, methods, and findings.

Mediational Processes

Following from some of Tolman's observations, many learning theorists have analyzed so-called mediational processes in learning and their applicability to the retarded. An excellent review of such processes is presented by Borokowski and Wanschura (1974). They define mediators as follows:

> Cognitive structured learning (to be differentiated from rote learning) occurs when a direct association occurs between two events, together with some additional indirect association. The indirect association—perhaps a natural language associate—serves as a *chain* [our emphasis] or a bridge that links the two to-be-learned events more closely together. These indirect associations are commonly referred to as mediators.

This analysis of mediation is based on a presentation concerning thinking processes by Bourne, Ekstrand, and Dominowski (1971). Deficiencies in mediational processes are believed to occur when there is either a *production deficiency* or a *control deficiency*. In the analysis of mediators, the usual S $\longrightarrow$ R association is analyzed into S $\longrightarrow$ r $\longrightarrow$ s $\longrightarrow$ R, in which the internal stimuli and internal responses are seen as part of the total chain of learning events. When the implicit mediator, r, is not evoked by the S, there is a production deficiency; when s and r are present but are insufficient to influence R, there is a control deficiency.

Utilizing data from paired-associations in verbal learning, Borokowski and Wanshura are able to show that while normals are likely to show greater mediational facility, retarded individuals also are able to utilize this strategy. Moreover, the difference between normals and retarded persons is considerably larger for nonmediated learning than in mediated learning. Kendler (1972) highlighted the importance of mediational learning for many complex verbal tasks. Further, Jensen and Rohwrer (1963) were able to demonstrate that, contrary to prior assumptions, mental retardation and mediational deficiency are *not* synonymous. Jensen also showed (1971) that retarded individuals are not control deficient but production deficient.

Ross and Ross (1978) conducted a study with thirty-seven EMR children in primary special classes in which they evaluated the effect of mnemonic strategies in the learning of multiple-associated material. The three conditions of the study included the use of imagery in story and game programs compared with a rote learning group and a control group. All groups were comparable in age, MA, IQ, sex, socioeconomic status, racial origin, and number of years in school. Mneomnic training significantly improved the learning of multiple associates, and imagery training was clearly superior to rote training. Other studies have shown that retarded persons can utilize mediators in nonverbal learning when verbal mediators are introduced to assist in the process. Borokowski and Wanchura conclude "... retarded individuals can use mediators in a wide variety of contexts to aid PA learning." The significance of this conclusion is that if given adequate facilitative instruction, retarded persons can, through the means indicated above, significantly increase their learning capacities.

Strategic Behavior in Learning. This type of learning, like mediational processes, involves more than rote reproduction of learning materials. Meaningfulness, especially meaningfulness in relation to the goal or the activity that is relevant for the individual, builds up certain learning strategies that then transfer to other learning tasks. As Brown et al, (1974) phrase it, "... the conditions under which training takes place are of great importance." For example, Smirnov and Zinchenko (1969) demonstrated that children can better remember lists of things when they are asked to participate in activities that are interesting to them. They show superior performance in such activities than when learning the same lists by rote. And Ross (1971) indicated that long-term training with retarded pupils as part of a musical program produced successful transfer of training in complex strategies learned as part of the program. Combining the criteria of conservation training (*à la* Piaget) with training involving verbal rules, Field (1974) demonstrated that educable mentally retarded children with mental ages between about five and twelve years could learn better and more efficiently when given verbal rules to assist them.

Information Processing. Psychologists have been interested in how people receive information, store it, and retrieve it. Such skills are not entirely congruent with level of general mental ability. These sensory and related processes show considerable individual differences among all levels of intelligence (Hunt et al., 1973). Based in large part on the discoveries of Bruner (1964) and coworkers, it has been established that individuals can be trained, through subjective organization and reorganization, to recode stimuli so that larger amounts of relevant information can be processed, received, remembered, and retrieved. To facilitate such learning, environmental cues must be provided. Sitko and Semmel (1972) have shown that such cueing can help mentally retarded individuals to function more effectively in memory tasks.

The Self as a Change Agent. In all of the above varieties of learning experiences, little emphasis has been placed on the self as an agent in learning. The present brief introduction to this topic also will serve to introduce our next section on Imitation and Modeling in Learning. If the person utilizes her own antecedent behavior as a model that she can then alter or improve on, learning can be facilitated. Such use of the self as an object for self-study and change is discussed in an article by Mahoney and Mahoney (1976). They believe that self-monitoring can be profitably used in such areas as aggressive behavior, personal hygiene and academic performance.

The self as a change agent is only recently beginning to receive the critical attention it deserves in relation to learning problems. In this orientation, the self is seen as a theory (or a set of beliefs) one has developed about *one's self,* and this self-conception shapes our perceptions of external events. This conceptualization of the self is an emotionally toned, cognitive structure that has developed over the years (Kiesler, 1971). It is our belief, not yet supported adequately by relevant research data, that in the case of retarded persons, learning can be significantly improved if adequate attention is given to improving various aspects of the self-appraisal, such as self-esteem, self-confidence, and self-competence. These attributes of the self can only emerge out of a total learning climate in which the individual learns not only specific skills, but also learns that he is appreciated, is liked, and has value.

Imitation and Modeling: Observational Learning

Many aspects of learning, or of learning to learn, are significantly affected by the kinds of experiences to which children have been exposed, even if they are not given specific practice or reinforcement in performance of a particular behavior. As we have noted previously, these background experiences influence not only the development of attitudes, motivations, and values, but also the development of various specific behaviors. This kind of learning may be called observational learning, and it proceeds through the processes of imitation and modeling.

Some theorists distinguish between *imitation,* in which the child *consciously* or *deliberately* attempts to copy an example of behavior he chooses or is shown, and *modeling,* which may involve *no conscious* or *deliberate* attempt to conform to the example. In this sense, modeling is closer to *identification,* which we have discussed in previous chapters. But whether the behavior is deliberate or otherwise, observational learning can have powerful consequences. It seems clear that many of the differences we see in children by the time they arrive in school are attributable to differences in background experiences through which they have learned by observation. Similarly, many of the deficits in capacity to learn can be overcome or reduced through the provision of appropriate observational experience.

Bandura and his colleagues (1963) have contributed much experimental evidence and a theoretical explanation of modeling. Using live models as well as videotapes, Bandura (1962) studied various conditions related to the effectiveness of modeling in learning. It generally has been found that when children observe models who are rewarded for their behavior they are more likely to acquire that behavior than when the models are not rewarded or are punished. Bandura notes that other factors also may influence the learning of behavior through modeling, such as whether the model is prestigeful to the learner, whether the model is similar in important respects to the learner, and whether the learner is motivated to attend to the model. Many studies have been completed in which these findings have been replicated. For example, in one study in which models engaged in a wide variety of behaviors under conditions involving approval, disapproval, or no response to the model, children learned the behavior of the model only under conditions of approval (Geshuri, 1972).

Bandura's work has far-reaching significance for the classroom teacher in other respects. He was able to demonstrate (Bandura, 1965) the important distinction between the *acquisition* of behavior and the *performance* of the behavior. When, for example, children observe that the behavior of model is not rewarded, they tend not to perform that kind of behavior or to perform it less than children who have seen the model rewarded. But the children will still perform that behavior later if they are offered rewards for doing so. In short, they had acquired certain behaviors that they later performed. This is a highly important finding, for it shows that children *internalize potentials* for behaving in certain ways when later conditions reward them for such behaviors.

Another, more technical, aspect of the problem of imitation and modeling—one that relates to the issue of molecular versus molar units of learning—is *concurrent* and *serial* training. In the former mode, the learning experience contains the total molar unit that is the objective of the training; in the latter, the learning experience is fractionated so that some elements are taught first and others are taught later. In an experiment that is typical of the problem, Schroeder and Baer (1972) tested the concurrent versus serial method of operant training with retarded children in learning vocal imitation. This kind of experiment is important, for it helps us to determine whether the molecular or molar approach is more effective with specified kinds of material. In this study, two retarded children were trained with both methods. Under concurrent conditions they were trained with words and phrases *intermixed*. In the serial condition, each child was taught to imitate words and phrases separately. It was demonstrated that for this material the concurrent method was superior for both children. The study offers additional support to the research by Sabatino, Ysseldyke and Woolston (1973) described earlier (see chapter 13).

We have been considering the value of modeling as a method of teaching as if it occurs separately from other aspects of the teaching-learning process. However, we need to know far more about the combined effects of several factors operating together. What, for instance, is the relative value of modeling per se as contrasted with modeling when accompanied by verbal mediation (conceptual learning), and what are the results when there is verbal mediation without modeling? Yoder and Forehand (1974) attempted to answer these questions, using forty educable retarded children and forty nonretarded children, each group about half males and half females. The retarded group was about 12 years of age with an average IQ of 62, and the nonretarded group was about 6½ years of age with an average IQ of 108. Four experimental conditions were investigated: no modeling, modeling only, modeling plus low-meaning verbalizations, and modeling plus conceptual verbalizations. The material used came from the *Leiter International Performance Scale*. It was found that the retarded group took more time to complete the tasks. No differences were found among the low or simple items for the several conditions of the study, but on harder items, modeling produced fewer errors than no modeling, and the condition of modeling plus conceptualization produced significantly better performance on the harder items than any of the other conditions. Although the study failed to control for several possibly important items, such as level of mental maturity and previous learning experience, it is clearly suggestive of the value of mediational material for some kinds of learning.

Another example of a study demonstrating the value of combining learning methods was that done by Ross et al. (1973). In a five-week story, question, and game program with EMR children they found that "a long-time mediational strategy was effectively developed by observational learning as well as intentional training programs. . . ."

Special Learning Theories
Related to the Retarded

The past two decades, particularly, have been marked by numerous research studies related to special learning characteristics of the retarded. These studies have led to a number of theories. The work of Denny (1969), Ellis, Spitz, and Zeaman have been especially noteworthy. We shall discuss briefly some of the contributions of Ellis, Spitz, and Zeaman as special examples of research and theory on delimited aspects of learning. Denny's theory is especially interesting in terms of how he defines stimulus and response, but since it really is a variant of operant conditioning principles, we need not review it here. The reader who is particularly interested in elaborations of operant conditioning would profit from reading Denny's work as well as that of others to whom we referred in our prior discussion of Skinner's contributions.

Ellis was interested in short-term memory processes. Based on a series of studies with both normal and retarded learners, and following the lead of several prior formulations in the area of short-term memory, Ellis (1970) formulated his Multiprocess Memory Model. According to this model, incoming stimuli are processed via an attentional procedure by the individual, then are received through the *Primary Memory System,* which has limited storage capacity, and then are processed further through what Ellis calls *Rehearsal Strategies*. It is contended that verbal memory is limited by what the Primary Memory system can retain. This system can receive a great deal of information but can only retain a portion of it momentarily. Therefore, for memory to become more effective, it is hypothesized that through various rehearsal strategies, *Secondary* and *Tertiary Memory Systems* must be activated so that more material can be retained over longer periods. This additional storage processing can be facilitated by certain strategies of reinforcement.

Waugh and Norman (1965), whose theoretical propositions were used by Ellis, describes the Rehearsal Strategies as follows: there are "immediate or delayed, silent or overt, deliberate or involuntary" (actions) that are involved in recall. They add: "Obviously a very conspicuous item or one that relates easily to what we have already learned can be retained with a minimum of conscious effort." Thus, special methods are used to rehearse and store more effectively what is momentarily retained but otherwise, soon lost.

On the basis of his studies with retarded learners, Ellis concludes that there are several characteristics that can be used to increase the effectiveness of memory processing. The learner must be taught how to improve rehearsal strategies so that secondary and tertiary memory systems can be utilized to retain for longer periods what the primary system can only retain momentarily. He believes that for institutionalized retarded learners, the secondary system is deficient. On the other hand, such retarded individuals do not show deficiencies, in comparison with normals, in the primary and tertiary systems. He suggests that the retarded can be taught to use active rehearsal strategies. He also suggests that language deficiency of the retarded person contributes to poor rehearsal strategies.

Spitz (1973) also has studied the learning processes of the retarded, but has focused his attention on paired-associate learning. On the basis of many studies by Spitz and his followers, it is concluded that the retarded person is deficient in scanning ability (that is, in attending effectively to input materials) and is poor in selective organization of stimuli. Both input and retrieval tend to be chaotic. A major implication for the teaching of the retarded, therefore, is to apply the principle of redundancy at least 50 percent of the time; that is, to provide numerous paired inputs of a common element or concept to be learned in order to assure effective organization and subsequent retrieval. Thus to teach the conceptual relationship of, for example, clothing to specific articles of clothing, one can present in paired associate manner, a number of times, such associations as: coat-clothing; hat-clothing; blouse-clothing; shoes-clothing. Such redundancy facilitates learning and retention.

Zeaman (1973) has contributed to many aspects of the psychology of the retarded and we have discussed some of his work and that of one of his co-workers (House) in previous chapters. A general conclusion that his research has suggested is the need to improve both the attention and discrimination of the retarded learner. Two important dimensions in such an orientation are to include what Zeaman calls the learner's *dimension bias* in planning learning tasks, and to reduce the number of irrelevant dimensions while increasing the number of relevant dimensions in the tasks that are provided. These procedures are thought capable of reinforcing the relevant cues for the learner so that they are more distinctive; that is, can be discriminated more easily. The concept of learner dimensions is broader than the general concept of motivation. It refers to the qualities of stimuli or stimuli situations that already are of interest to the learner and for which the learner already has shown a preferential bias.

The implications for teaching that are based on the work of these researchers will be discussed more fully later in this chapter and in chapter 16.

APPLICATIONS: EDUCATIONAL METHODS

Let us now turn our attention to the problems involved in methods of teaching and special techniques that have been found valuable in work with retarded children. These problems are so complicated and diverse that we cannot expect to do full justice to all of the issues involved. Rather, we shall attempt to consider the more important central issues and illustrate some of the special methods, referring the reader to other sources of information that may be of interest. First let us turn our attention to the ubiquitous problem of individual differences among retarded children.

The Need for Individualized Instruction

By labeling some children mentally retarded, we often have limited their potential for growth in many areas. Apart from the stigmatization that such labeling may have produced, it has tended to make us overlook the great differences among retarded children. Educable mentally retarded children differ among themselves in the general degree of their cognitive and adaptive development; each child is a highly complex and uniquely differentiated individual by the time she reaches the preschool period. The same is true for trainable mentally retarded children. Children in the same general stage of maturity differ in such areas as capacity for auditory discrimination, capacity for visual discrimination, capacity to attend, capacity to communicate, ability to accept responsibility, and acquisition of social skills. Having failed to learn about these interindividual differences, we failed to capitalize on the unique strengths of each child. We also failed to give adequate attention to each child's unique weaknesses. Conversely, the more we learn about the specific behaviors of which an individual retarded child is capable or incapable, the more we can tailor the child's educational experience to that particular pattern of abilities and disabilities. We might add that even such categorizations as "perceptually handicapped," and "socially immature" are not helpful for educational purposes. The label "perceptually handicapped" may be accurate as a general assessment, but as an evaluation or diagnosis it is self-defeating, for it does not offer any direction to the teacher for correcting the condition.

Taking this example one step further, the label "perceptually handicapped" often implies that the child is suffering from some irreversible organic condition (i.e., has minimal brain dysfunction). Thus, the teacher (and the parents) may feel that nothing can be done about it. Quite the opposite may be true. According to Haywood (1966–1967), if a careful assessment is made of *the specific strengths and weaknesses in perceptual behaviors,* then a specific remedial program can be constructed that may lead to improved functioning in those areas of behavior. This assessment involves learning what specific perceptions the child can accurately make and under what conditions, as well as which perceptions the child cannot make and for what reasons.

One of the great virtues of behavior modification methods is that they stress the construction of a highly specific diagnostic profile for the individual. Although there are limitations to what behavior modification can accomplish, it does encourage specificity in defining the *targets in overt behavior that need to be modified.* Thus, as with diagnostic-prescriptive teaching (which we shall discuss later in more detail), the teacher can organize an appropriate program for a particular child at a given time and then alter the program, or parts of it, as the child progresses or fails to progress. All of this involves the best features of individualized, or individually tailored, instruction.

The need for individualized instruction has led educators to reconceptualize the organization of programs for the retarded. For example, Dunn (1973) has proposed what he has termed an "inverted pyramid plan" of educational organization. Dunn's plan involves eleven types of programs, forming an inverted pyramid. This plan provides gradients from the most segregated instruction at the bottom of the pyramid to the most integrated instruction at the top. At the bottom of the pyramid is *home-bound instruction* for the most severely handicapped, who require the greatest amount of segregation and the most individualized training program. Other programs range from *hospital instruction,* through *part-time special day-class instruction* involving considerable individualized instruction, through *regular-class instruction* including some special educational instruction, up to *regular-class instruction* using some special educational materials.

As illustrative of what may be accomplished in some cases with a highly individualized program of instruction, we may cite the remedial work done by Drash (1972) with a child who was retarded in speech and language.

The child was a 4½ year old black boy whose development in these areas was retarded by about two years. There were no known physical abnormalities. The parents were college educated. When initially tested, at the age of 4 years 7 months, he rated on the Revised Stanford-Binet *as follows: MA = 3 years 3 months; IQ, 67. On the* Peabody Picture Vocabulary Test *he rated even lower: Peabody age was 2.5 years; Peabody Quotient was 56. Three target areas of behavior were chosen for improvement: school achievement, speech and language acquisition, and measured intelligence on standardized intelligence tests. He was seen one time per week for a period of two years, and the Drash program for speech development was followed. The father was trained through observation of the initial training sessions, then he conducted reinforcement procedures at home for a period of two years.*

Assessment of this boy's behavior revealed the following at the initiation of the program. He could not speak in sentences, although he was able to imitate words consistently and accurately. He could name some objects and words, performing at about the three-year level. He could imitate, but only inconsistently, phrases of two, three, or four words. He had "no functional use of speech to communicate his needs." He avoided eye contact. (Drash feels that operant conditioning of speech proceeds more rapidly with eye contact.) He could sit in a chair but fidgeted for short periods.

The following procedures were typical of the training program. The child was shown pictures (for example, a boy riding a bicycle) and was asked, "What's that?" If he did not respond appropriately, the experimenter offered him a model, such as, "Boy riding a bike." When he was able to imitate the experimenter's model, he was given positive reinforcement (M & M candy) and was again asked,

"What's that?" To increase eye contact, the experimenter would say "Look at me" before presenting a picture. He was urged to sit in his chair and was given reinforcement when he did. He was taught twenty to twenty-five new words per training session.

The following results were achieved. On intelligence tests, the child attained an MA of 6.3 years with an IQ of 94 when he was 6 years and 7 months of age. When given the WISC at 7 years 2 months of age, he obtained an IQ of 107. He entered kindergarten at about 5 years of age. By the end of his second grade, he was achieving well in school, getting two A's two B's, and three C's. He showed normal attention and behavior.

These results are certainly impressive. Of course, many factors other than the operant procedures that were employed may have contributed to the improvement. The child was given far more attention than he had previously been given. The father may have spent more time with his child than had formerly been the case, and this may have contributed to a better relationship. Other factors in the child's personal, social, and educational experiences may have contributed their share to the improvement. Whatever the reason, the program achieved positive change in important areas, and the gross retardation, especially in speech and language, was overcome.

One also should add to these comments that there is a danger in this illustrative case. Not all retarded children can improve, and of those who can, not all can improve to this extent. Sometimes it is crucial to understand the etiology of the condition, for etiological factors cannot always be counteracted. Boundless optimism that any child can be helped in any area of deficiency is unwarranted and may result in shattering frustration to both the experimenter and the child. But attempts to improve functioning on an individualized basis, with careful attention to what works and what does not, often can produce significant gains.

Behavior Modification and Diagnostic-Prescriptive Teaching

In this chapter we introduced some of the basic concepts of behavior modification and in chapter 14 we discussed diagnostic-prescriptive teaching. Now, we should like to carry these concepts one step further by discussing how they may be applied to the practical task of teaching the retarded child. We shall illustrate these operations even more specifically when we discuss various aspects of the curriculum.

The principles of behavior modification, especially as they were developed by Skinner (1968), can be applied to learning in academic and non-academic areas such as social and adaptive behavior. Some target or behavior is selected (such as increase in sight recognition of words or increase in cooperative behavior in games), and the specific responses that are desired are selected and defined (usually arranged in sequential order from the simplest one to the most complex). Correctly completed responses are immediately reinforced by some appropriate reward (or token). If the response is not made, a model of the response may be offered by the teacher. The program is modified as the teacher observes what the child is capable of and incapable of. Finally, by continued specific reinforcement and by successive and more generalized reinforcement procedures, the learning sequence is firmly established. Diagnostic-prescriptive teaching makes use of the same principles of learning as they apply to educational content. We shall illustrate these principles shortly with an experiment on perceptual training.

As Skinner (1968) himself has pointed out, to answer these questions we must understand motivation, learning how to learn, and the values involved in learning, as well as how the learner proceeds from the simpler elements to more global elements. Skinner believes that his relatively (theoretically) simple procedure of behavior modification leads to such understanding. We believe the procedure may be necessary under certain conditions, but it falls short of explaining all of learning. Learning is, as seen in this and previous chapters, far more complex than Skinner suggests, and not all learning is currently specifiable under conditions of operant learning—nor may it ever be, for that matter. The personality of the teacher (or experimenter) has a subtle but pervasive influence on learning, as does the teacher's relationship with the learner. Factors such as these influence both the kind and the quality of learning, as has been amply demonstrated in a great many studies. Even a videotaped example of behavior can greatly influence the outcome of learning, especially when the video subject is receiving approval. Meichenbaum and Turk (1972) found that observing the models involved in the TV program "Sesame Street" produced considerable improvement in the *academic achievement* of disadvantaged children. These children watched this program frequently. Although they were originally lower in academic achievement than middle-class children, for example, they later surpassed middle-class children who watched this program only a little.

It also is important to recognize that, as Piaget has shown, there is an equilibration process in learning in which cognitive development results from the *dynamic* functioning of processes of assimilation and accommodation; that is, from previous exploratory activity, intrinsic motivation, and level of cognition already established in the individual. MacMillan and Forness (1970) point to the probable constriction "of learning, motivation and reinforcement to simplistic terms." They note the importance of factors such as anxiety, goal-oriented behavior, and attitudes in learning. In still another sophisticated review of the issues and findings, Bonneau (1974) points out that the individual has an *internal environment* through which he has "his own unique view of the world and determines his role in it." In other words, Bonneau emphasizes both the internal structure that the individual builds out of his own unique experience in life and the individual's decision of how he will react to life. His position is fairly well summed up in the belief that an "individual . . . [is] a gatherer, processor, and user of information rather than a *simple reactor* [emphasis ours] to external carrots, whips, and the stimuli associated with them." Bonneau also says, "It is recognized that there can be 'unconscious' and 'conscious' perceptions."

These are only a few of the basic considerations that have caused us to emphasize the complexity rather than the simplistic view of the total learning process. The good teacher will make use of the full knowledge of the rich resources of the unique human being and strive to apply this knowledge creatively in the learning situation.

DESIGNING BEHAVIORAL EDUCATIONAL OBJECTIVES

Before we proceed to an examination of more specific educational methods and materials, it remains to discuss the designing of the objectives of any educational program. We already have learned that it is important to specify both the immediate and the long-term objectives of subprograms of instruction. After the individual child's specific abilities and disabilities are assessed, it is well to write out the particular goals in behavior toward which the program will be designed. The assessment process is both *rigorous* and *continuing*. It is rigorous in that it requires in-depth study of the highly specific abilities in question (e.g., Can the child accurately perceive specific symbols or words? Can the child integrate these perceptions into larger units? Can the child communicate the perceptual response adequately? What kinds of errors does the child make? What kinds of behaviors is he now capable of? and, of course, How well motivated is he, or can he become, to try to improve his performance?) It is continuous because it is only in the light of progress or lack of it that modifications in both methods and objectives can be formulated.

McAshan (1970), who has published a simple but instructive book on the subject of designing such objectives, recommends *writing* the objectives to gain greater clarity and then revising them as necessary. According to McAshan, these factors need to be considered: (1) students differ in how they learn; (2) teachers differ in their self-percepts, teaching techniques, and relationships to children; (3) the ability of the teacher must be developed—it may be lost if procedures are too highly standardized; (4) writing individual behavioral objectives requires considerable technical knowledge and subject matter competency; and (5) objectives need to be reevaluated constantly to meet the specific needs of the student. These are important principles. The student can be directly helpful in assessing competencies and helping to revise objectives.

The Preschool Program

We already have discussed in the previous chapters some of the important considerations involved in *basic readiness*. Retarded children of all levels usually need additional time and additional experience in acquiring a fund of basic information about themselves, their immediate environment, and their peers. They also need to master rudimentary skills in simple motor coordination (so that they can begin to dress themselves, feed themselves, etc.), in simple sensory-motor adaptations (so that they can perceive and discriminate the forms of objects, perceive and name primary colors, trace lines and forms, and coordinate parts of the body more effectively), and in simple interpersonal relations (so that they can learn to wait their turn, cooperate with others in simple tasks, share experiences, and the like).

Since severely and profoundly retarded children are being enrolled in programs in the schools, the special kinds of experiences and skills they need and the methods of training in these areas are quite important for the teacher of the exceptional child. Moreover, many of these methods and materials are relevant for most retarded children at the preschool level, though the level of instruction and the specific content of the instruction may differ. Hence we shall first discuss some aspects of preschool education.

Much of the preschool instruction can be presented in the form of games and dramatizations. Such a technique is thought to be valuable because children are more likely to be motivated to participate actively in the lesson, rather than behaving passively, if they are playing and having fun. If such an atmosphere is combined with an individualized relationship between child and teacher (or aide), the resulting conditions help to foster security and reduce unnecessary and distracting anxiety. It also has been found that the use of music (Weber, 1966) and of psychomotor activities (much of it in the form of games) (Richardson, 1970) can be helpful.

Through a rich variety of educational experiences, the teacher can attain the specific objectives that are thought to be important as *readiness* for the more formal aspects of academic instruction. These objectives have been listed by Smith (1971). They include:

> visual and auditory discrimination
> visual and auditory memory
> separation of figure from background
> learning to associate stimuli
> small motor movements and dexterity (e.g., cutting and sorting)
> large motor skills
> memory of spoken words and visual stimuli
> expression of ideas and concepts
> location of objects in space
> labeling common objects, letters, numbers
> naming parts of the body
> toilet care
> willingness to attempt solution to problems
> control over emotions
> comradeships

This constitutes a list of "achievements" that frequently are taken for granted in the normal child, but detailed and sequentially reinforced training is necessary if they are to be mastered by the retarded child. As indicative of how much can be accomplished with programmed or diagnostic-prescriptive teaching, we cite the findings of a study of a Head Start program for children suffering from severe social, emotional, or language disabilities (Haring et al., 1969). In this study, twelve of the most severely disturbed children from twenty-five Head Start classes were selected for special training. Specific goals were designed for each child. Through graded, individualized programming, the children were taught discrimination of forms, colors, and letters by actual performance of specific behaviors accompanied by verbal responses. To build verbal responses in an effort to encourage language development, the teacher showed the child pictures and asked questions about them. The child was taught to respond imitatively with single words, at first; then to include subject, verb, and modifiers; and finally to respond with sentences. For example, a child might be shown a picture of a boy running. He would then be asked, "What is the little boy doing?" and be taught to answer, first, "run," then "boy runs," "boy running," "boy is running in the street," and, finally, "the little boy is running in the street." Periods of practice, varying for each child, ranged from five to forty-three days, and each child reached the behavior targets specified for him. Moreover, it was reported that these gains were maintained over a follow-up period of the study.

Methods Related to Perceptual-Motoric Training

Perceptual development generally proceeds at about the same rate as general cognitive development, so retarded individuals can be expected to be deficient in perceptual skills to about the same extent that they are mentally deficient (Liebowitz, et al., 1959). Retarded persons take longer than normals to develop perceptual meanings; their perceptual behavior tends to be more rigid (i.e., less spontaneous and adaptive), and as a consequence, they have greater difficulty in "erasing" perceptions (Spitz and Blackman, 1959). Retarded persons with brain damage have much more severe perceptual problems; they may have great difficulty in accurately perceiving even the simplest geometrical forms or in discriminating between somewhat similar forms. Hence, it is probably true that all retarded children would profit from special perceptual training, and the lower the level of intelligence and the more severe the brain damage, the more important such training would be.

We have learned that retarded individuals are not as severely retarded in motoric development as they are in cognitive development. However, they do have special problems in that (1) their motor development is generally slightly lower than that of normals; and (2) they have special difficulties in very fine hand-eye coordinations, such as those involved in finding a place in a book, selecting a detail in a picture, and dealing with moving objects. Therefore, they would benefit from motoric training, and such training can be helpful in other aspects of their learning and adaptation. Since motoric and perceptual training tend to complement each other, and since motoric development is basic to many aspects of perceptual development, we shall treat the special methods for their training together.

Perceptual-motoric training is, as can be inferred from what we have said above, especially important in the preschool and primary grade programs. It is probably more important for the trainable retarded than for the educable retarded. Along with training in these skills, training in attending, carrying out simple tasks, and following directions should be part of the total program.

Three basic aspects of perceptual-motoric training relate to perception of self, perception of space and form, and perception of time. In training the retarded in these three areas, physical movements of the body or parts of the body are very helpful for making the experience concrete and for reinforcing the learning. The use of music and of rhythmic activities through games and exercises can be helpful in perceptual development. And, as with all other basic learning for the retarded, reinforcement of the learning by means of multi-sense modalities should be constantly encouraged. An inherent feature of such training should be, as we have stressed previously, the enhancement of self-regard through pleasurable and successful activities.

A number of valuable principles have been developed in programs for such training:

1. The structuring of spatial perceptions can be greatly assisted by the manipulation of concrete objects. If the child is given objects to move about—to place ahead of, behind, below, or above something—especially in the form of games, the child is more likely to learn basic elements of spatial perception, and, at the same time, will begin to acquire conceptual terms that are basic in spatial perception. Usually, the teacher will start with simple objects, like blocks or balls, and try to keep the visual qualities (form, shape, and texture) constant while varying the spatial requirements of the activities.

2. To maximize attention and discriminal perception, it is wise for the child, and not merely the teacher, to feel and manipulate the object whose size or position he is exploring. Movement of the object by the teacher may be used to attract and hold attention, but manipulation of the object by the child is important in order to supply the child with concrete, vivid sensory experience.

3. The retarded pupil will respond to perceptual qualities before being able to respond to conceptual abstractions about these qualities. The child can be taught to match forms, colors, and sizes before being able to name the abstract qualities of the objects with these characteristics.

4. Along with principle number 3, the principle that each perceptual quality should be taught separately should be kept in focus. This means that differences in form should be learned with objects of the same size, rather than with objects differing in both of these characteristics.

5. The learning of perception can best proceed from the body outward to the external environment. The child should learn to distinguish the *body* from the *not body;* the child then can learn to distinguish parts of the body, as well as positions on the body; and finally can learn to distinguish spatial quality, form, and other qualities of objects around him. In the progression from *body* to *not body,* the child can learn to perceive important aspects of his body-image and to attach names to many aspects of the body.

6. The careful teacher will assess the specific perceptual assets and limitations of the pupils and then arrange activities designed to train the children in terms of these specific needs.

7. Some retarded children have special difficulties with axial orientation and with differentiation of figure and ground. They need special training to overcome these confusions.

8. Special training is needed in the perception of time, and such training is likely to be most efficient when linked with concrete representation of time. Time and space, and time and size, can be correlated both visually and

motorically by a variety of games in which these characteristics are concurrently present.

A special word should be said about discrimination learning, which has been given a great deal of research study since the 1960s. Discrimination is the ability to respond differentially to different stimulus situations, some very close perceptually and others not so close. In general, retarded individuals have been found to be inferior to normals in most forms of discrimination learning (Baumeister, 1967). However, some of this inferiority may be placed at the door of what Zeaman and House (1962b) have called the *failure set*. Retarded children, as we have emphasized throughout this book, frequently are subjected to failure experiences because the world, in general, and educational programs, in particular, tend to be geared to normals. Hence, their failure to learn to discriminate may, in some measure, be due to their expectancy that they will fail. However, improved methods of instruction may significantly improve retarded children's discrimination ability, thus assisting in other learning for which discrimination ability is a foundation. For instance, Sidman and Stoddard (1967) were able to secure improved discrimination by using what is now termed a *fading procedure*. In their study, they began with easy discriminations involving bright versus dark, then proceeded through form versus no form to circle versus elipse. Such procedures minimize errors and work well with retarded children.

We have stressed the need to provide experiences that integrate the diverse elements in perceptual training: the visual with the motoric; the visual-motoric with the verbal; the kinesthetic with the motoric and perceptual; and the like. An excellent summary of exercises and materials for such types of training is provided in the work of Wallace and Kauffman (1973). In part, they follow suggestions that have been tried out and tested by Kephart (1971), a leader in this field. They propose that the teacher carefully observe a variety of aspects of the child's perceptual-motoric behavior. For example, the teacher might observe how well the child can hold a pencil, can copy and trace, and what the level of motor coordination is. Then the teacher might observe whether or not the child shows reversals and can differentiate foreground objects from the background. An excellent checklist of skills that can be directly observed is furnished by Chaney and Kephart (1968). On the basis of such observations, followed as necessary by more formal tests, individually tailored programs can be devised for the child and for a group (Frostig and Harris, 1968).

Basic Readiness Skills

It may be assumed that the young retarded child has missed out on many normal experiences in preschool years, even when the home environment has not been a particularly deprived one. Because of retarded perceptual and motoric development, the child has not been able to profit as much as other children from the everyday experiences that youngsters have. As a consequence, the child's abilities to attend, to communicate, to understand language, to coordinate in physical activities, and to engage in creative thinking (especially in fantasy) are likely to be quite limited, and when the retarded child has additional physical handicaps, other special problems are created. The school program, therefore must focus on the development of a variety of basic readiness skills that can be taken more or less for granted in the case of the normal youngster.

The major portion of school time, both for the preschool program and for a year beyond that, will be spent on the development of these *readiness skills.* The aim at this level is to prepare the educable retarded child for later academic and prevocational training, and to help the trainable retarded child to become at least minimally self-sufficient, if at all possible.

There is controversy about how well retarded children can learn in comparison with normal children of comparable mental age (that is, younger children). Some researchers maintain that retarded children learn less well and forget more rapidly what they do learn. Retarded children are thought of, from this viewpoint, as having "leaky buckets." Although there is evidence to substantiate this conclusion, the reason for the finding may lie, not so much in the fact of mental retardation, as in the conditions under which the retarded usually learn. Because they need more time to master material than their normal peers, because they so often meet failure in a society geared for normals, and because their insufficient training in basic skills has left them unprepared to learn what they are exposed to, they tend to develop poor learning attitudes, and they also may forget more rapidly than they should.

Research indicates that retarded children can learn as well as normal children of comparable mental age, can retain as well, and can even transfer this learning to other related areas, *providing* they are not handicapped by poor learning of basic skills or by poor attitudes toward the learning task (Ellis, 1963). These findings suggest that retarded children need to be given ample time to learn — and even to overlearn — basic skills that are within their "current" grasp. For retarded children, as for normal children, the level of the learning must be geared to their current ability, the tasks must be presented simply, and the tasks must be *thoroughly mastered* (that is, *overlearned*).

All of these considerations point up the importance of sound training in readiness skills. What are some of these skills? First, *skills in controlling the body* should be taught, such as coordination in walking, drawing, eye-hand coordination, balancing, tumbling, and running. Studies have indicated that retarded children are one or more years behind the norms in both gross and fine motor coordination (Francis and Ravick, 1960). Second, as we have stated so often, retarded children need *intensive training in perceptual skills,* many of which normal children master incidentally through everyday experiences. They need training, therefore, in visual and auditory memory skills, in form perception, in the use of each eye as well as both eyes in looking at objects, and in focussing on details of visual objects. The teacher can provide a wide variety of games that emphasize the learning of these basic perceptual skills. A by-product of such activities, when taught properly, may be *learning to attend.*

Attending is such an important, fundamental skill that the teacher of the retarded must give special assistance to teaching it if other instruction is to be effective. Research has indicated that attention can be greatly improved, especially for the educable mentally retarded. As examples of such studies, we may cite those by Redd (1972) and by Ullman (1974). Redd trained two retarded

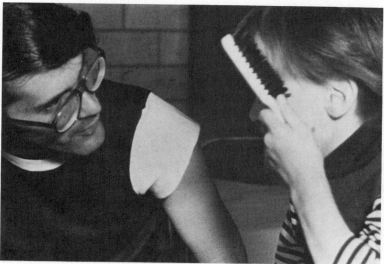

The teaching of the basic skills of dressing and grooming requires patience and detailed, repetitive instruction, but the rewards for both teacher and child are great: a more pleasing appearance for the child and improved self-esteem. (Photos by Michael D. McCoy)

children, using three methods of reinforcing correct responding: no reinforcement, noncontingent reinforcement, and contingent reinforcement. (See section on Behavior Modification Approaches to Therapy later in this chapter.) The essential difference between noncontingent and contingent methods was that in the former there was no immediate reward for correctly responding, whereas in the latter, there was an immediate reward to reinforce the response. Redd found, as had previous researchers, that only contingently reinforced tasks improved attentive, ongoing behavior. The implication of this study is that teachers wishing to foster improved attention in retarded children should consistently reward attentive behavior immediately on its appearance.

Ullman was interested in breadth of attention and in retention. He employed 100 children in his study, both educable retarded and trainable retarded, with an average mental age of six years. He also employed average children, at the same mental age level, as controls. His findings are of considerable significance. Degree of retention showed a relationship to IQ, but even though the IQ level of the educable retarded children was about 40 points below that of the average children in the study, the children were not significantly different in their breadth of attention as measured. On the other hand, the trainable group, which was only about 10 IQ points lower than the educable group, differed markedly in attention from both the educable and the average groups. The study needs replication, of course, and other tests of attention may reveal different results, but if these findings hold up, they may indicate that difficulties involving attention span may be a special characteristic of severely retarded children only. The study further implies that any attentional difficulties in the mildly retarded group should be corrected fairly readily with proper training.

In view of the well-demonstrated finding that degree of attention is related to efficiency of learning, it seems clear that special training in this skill is of considerable importance as part of readiness training.

Then, of course, special training is needed in *basic language skills:* vocabulary, simple sentence structure, articulation, and asking and answering questions. Retarded children also need training in *basic number concepts:* size, shape, numbers, and simple adding and subtracting. And, finally, they need to learn basic *social interaction* skills: learning to listen, learning to communicate, learning to share and cooperate, learning simple forms of independence, learning to respect the rights of others, learning simple games, etc. Skills such as these not only provide a foundation for many other types of learning in school situations, but also help to improve the child's self-confidence and self-assurance, thus indirectly improving the child's aspiration level realistically.

An example of the special kinds of training required for retarded children is the learning of the *mediational aspects* of language. Various aspects of sentence syntax, such as prepositions, conjunctions, and verbs, significantly influence the course of sentence learning and of language development in general. When the retarded child is given special training in using such mediators, the learning of language is facilitated (Turnure, 1971; Turnure and Walsh, 1971).

An Effective Total School Program

We shall reserve for discussion in a later section of this chapter some of the specific plans for organizing education for the retarded child, but we would like to take a general look, now, at the overall school program. We have emphasized the importance of preschool education, especially for the educable retarded. Such training appears to be vital to the development of readiness skills, constructive attitudes toward school and learning, and self-attitudes that are both realistic and positive. *But a good beginning is not enough!* It is likely that the educational program will be more productive if the terminal goals are clearly perceived and implemented. Toward what end is the total school program geared? What can be expected of the educable retarded and of the trainable retarded?

Research evidence has made it abundantly clear that a large majority of the educable retarded can become entirely self-supporting, maintaining themselves effectively in the community, and that many others can become at least partially self-supporting if provided with some guidance and support during the early adult years. Some of the trainable retarded can become partially self-supporting, and most can learn to get along in their communities if provided with guidance and counsel following their formal school period.

If, therefore, two of the important goals of schooling for these groups are (1) vocational competency and (2) effective social living, the total school program should be organized toward these and related objectives. There are those who argue that such a program places too heavy a burden on the schools, but although the school's assumption of this burden would not be warranted for normal children, the retarded present a special problem: an effective program for retarded pupils cannot be provided by the home or by any community resource except the school.

Viewed from this perspective, the total school program should provide preschool preparation; training in basic readiness skills; preparation in academic skills related to specific current aspects of living and to prevocational training; vocational training and counseling; and post-school training, especially guidance. The program should span the chronological age range from five years through eighteen years, with follow-up facilities after this. (In some cases, training may begin at age four years.)

Thus, the program should be divided into five major phases: preschool, primary, intermediate, secondary, and post-secondary. The emphasis in type of training in each phase of the program should shift, taking into account both the physical and the psychological maturity of the student. The program should provide for considerable flexibility, since some pupils will be able to transfer to regular school programs, whereas others will need continued placement in some phase of the total special-education program. In general, however, placement in each phase should be governed, within the limits of mental maturation and acquired skills, by the chronological and physical maturity of the student more than by any other single factor. And effective mental hygiene for each pupil, in each phase of the educational program, should be a central concern of the teacher and the school.

Relating the School Program to Other Experiences

In some European countries, special boarding schools are being used for retarded school children, in the belief that special education in the normal school program is insufficient in both scope and intensity. In these programs, intensive training is offered during school hours *and* after school hours. Not only is educational training provided, but training in social skills, often by specially trained personnel, is also an *intrinsic* part of the program (Dunn and Kirk, 1963). Such programs have the advantage—whatever their disadvantages may be—of coordinating the total-life-experience of the child during the critical years of his training.

If, as present educational trends seem to indicate, we are to continue to provide special instruction only during regular school hours, we must be alert to the need for integrating and coordinating school experiences with the concomitant experiences the children are having at home and in the community. Otherwise, the possible gains achieved in school may be offset by antagonistic or traumatic experiences elsewhere. This lack of coordination of the school program with other experiences may be one reason for the lack of success of some of the special programs (Lewis, 1973).

At the center of these other-than-school experiences is the milieu of the home. When at all possible, careful and continuing relationships with the parents should be maintained by the school. Even when special classes for the retarded are quite small and the teacher has time to maintain regular, frequent, personal contact with at least one parent, the assistance of the visiting teacher or of the social worker may prove to be indispensable. The parents need to know the specific current goals of the school program in order to reinforce them with appropriate related experiences in the home and community.

This is not to suggest that the parents should be encouraged to teach their retarded child but, rather, that they should be encouraged to provide the kinds of experiences in the home and outside that may supplement those of the school. The parents also will need help in understanding their child more deeply and will need guidance in providing their child with appropriate school experiences. There also will be situations in which the parents will need guidance in finding additional help for their child—such as speech therapy, psychotherapy, and physical therapy—that the school may be unable to provide.

We should like to consider another important point. We have stressed that the general attitudes of society are significant factors in determining the behavioral reactions and personality growth of the child. What is so often overlooked in connection with this point is the fact that the *school itself* is a part of society and, therefore, shares the attitudes of the culture in which it is embedded. Moreover, the special class is part of a larger institution—the public school system. And within this system there are negative and even hostile attitudes toward mental retardation. Administrators, teachers, clerical workers, janitors, and all other personnel have attitudes toward the child that often reflect the unfavorable cultural stereotypes previously discussed. Further, other pupils may have similar unfortunate attitudes, and so do the *retarded children themselves*. There should, therefore, be awareness of these undesirable attitudes, and attempts should be made to provide for their modification. The special-class teacher needs to be one of the "spark plugs" fostering more positive developments. This responsibility often has been ignored. Just as attitudes within the family structure often hinder the total growth process of the child, so do attitudes of the school. But the school is a community, and as such, it should be used as a positive force in helping the child to achieve maximum self-actualization.

LANGUAGE TRAINING AND READING

We now will focus our attention on two broad areas of educational training: Communication Skills and Mathematical Skills. In this section, we will discuss training in linguistic skills and then consider recent findings on theory and methodology in the area of reading. In the next section, we will deal with the area of mathematical training. These are basic types of skills needed for all subsequent learning.

The communication arts lie at the center of a great many interpersonal skills. Thus, the proper development of communication abilities is a central task for the sheer mastery of *receptive* and *expressive* communication. They also are highly important because they are part of the essential base for "getting along with others" socially as well as on the job. They are basic, also, for the learning of abstraction and generalization, as well as for the learning of many academic subjects. Linguistic skills have been categorized into three major components: *receptive skills,* which include attending to and comprehending the linguistic communication; *associative skills,* which include relating ideas and symbols; and *expressive skills,* which include speaking and writing.

There are a number of standardized tests of linguistic skills, as well as of readiness for training in these skills (see chapter 11). We should like to call special attention to a test developed by Kirk, McCarthy, and Kirk, the *Illinois Test of Psycholinguistic Abilities* (1968 revision), which can prove especially useful to teachers of the retarded. This test provides measures of twelve aspects of linguistic ability, including all of the major components we have previously enumerated, and, therefore, is useful in planning remedial teaching, as well as in organizing lesson plans for the entire class. Another very useful set of material is supplied in the *Peabody Language Development Kits*. These kits contain materials for the four levels of language development from the kindergarten through the third grade. Each kit consists of 180 daily lessons and is designed to teach oral language on a global basis. Hence, when more specific molecular or fractionated aspects need to be taught, the kits would have to be supplemented by other materials and methods. However, they contain a rich source of interesting materials and methods that help develop memory, cognition, convergent thinking, divergent thinking, and evaluation.

Mental Retardation and Language Development

It is well known that language development is highly correlated with general intellectual development, as currently measured. Aside from the fact that this result is biased by the very nature of our intelligence tests, linguistic development is a necessary precursor for, and concomitant of, most kinds of abstraction and generalization. Hence, it is understandable that, in general, retarded children are retarded in language development. However, the rate of the language development of retarded children is disproportionately slower than the rate of their intellectual development. That is probably because the children are *disproportionately* handicapped by factors other than lowered intellectual maturation. It has been shown that language development is affected by many external factors, even though the general rate of maturation is centrally important.

In many retarded children, such factors as general cultural deprivation, little motivation in the home for the use of language, insufficient interpersonal stimulation, and insufficient or improper emotional stimulation combine to retard language development excessively. In particular, the development of speech in these children is excessively retarded, for the children may have various physical limitations and anomalies that hinder such development (Hull, 1963). It is clear that improvement in language ability positively affects intellectual development (Hunt, 1961), and that special programs of speech and language training in the early years may significantly improve speech and language development (Smith, 1963).

These considerations emphasize the importance of a solid program of language instruction for both trainable and educable retarded. Some of the training, perhaps most of it, will be provided by the teacher of the classes for the retarded, who will offer appropriate, enriched remedial programs of language instruction. Some of the training may be provided by a speech therapist, and some of it may require assistance by a specialist.

Special Methods of Language Instruction

Language instruction must play a pervasive role in all school instruction, but it is especially important in the preschool and primary grade education of the retarded child. Of central importance, perhaps, is the *climate* of the classroom, which should be structured so as to encourage communication. It has been shown that a classroom program fostering social communication may be even more effective in overcoming defects of articulation than is the usual program of speech therapy (Lassers and Low, 1960). Thus, the school program should be designed to encourage speech, listening, and associating. These activities should be encouraged, not only as part of the unit on speech, but also in connection with *all* school activities.

Listening requires that the child *learn to pay attention*. Special games and devices can be used to make the "detective" art of attending enjoyable and profitable. Through such activities the child's life-space may be expanded and involvement in activities may be increased.

It would be well to emphasize that *learning to pay attention* is a consequence of both maturity and training. The ability to selectively attend to relevant stimuli and to disregard or give marginal attention to irrelevant stimuli can markedly affect the progress of the child in learning linguistic and other skills. It has been demonstrated that appropriate selective attention, which contributes to the retention and integration of information, increases with age during the elementary years (Hayen, 1967). However, retarded children are inferior in selective attention and need special training to develop that skill (Gordon and Baumeister, 1971). It is believed that two factors contribute significantly to learning to pay attention: one is novelty; the other is the absence of distractors. The teacher can encourage attention by varying the stimulus conditions of learning so that the child's attention is maintained by the novelty of the task. Simple, constant repetition leads to loss of attention. The use of reading material (for example, the use of books without distracting pictures in the middle of the text) can help to reduce distraction. Attention is such an important prerequisite for effective learning that programs for mothers of retarded children have been developed to teach them to train their preschool children to focus attention (Santosefano and Stayton, 1967).

Speaking requires motivation to speak! Again, if the child is provided with interesting activities that hold the attention and is given ample opportunity and reward for talking about such activities, speaking can be greatly encouraged.

Learning to associate requires skillful direction by the teacher so that pupils are encouraged to think of similarities and differences. For instance, the right kind of questioning about daily activities may do much to foster the growth of associative thinking in the retarded child. The child also may engage in games that require following directions, to associating verbal cues with behavioral cues, and to analyzing simple problems. The use of multisensory stimulation in learning appears to be especially important in the language instruction of retarded pupils.

Now, let us look at some examples of activities and units of work that encourage the development of the language arts.

Self-expression.   Self-expression is useful in facilitating the maturation of mental development, as well as that of language development. Since spontaneity in self-expression leads to effective emotional behavior, it serves a very important function in the earliest aspects of language development. In one technique of initiating the development of self-expression, the teacher uses an event in the lives of the children to encourage them to talk.

For example, the children come to school when it is raining or snowing. This experience may be used to provoke many kinds of self-expression. The teacher can ask each child about experiences in coming to school in the rain or snow. How did the child prepare for coming to school? What special kind of clothing did she wear? What did the snow look like and feel like, and what did it make him think of? Then, too, children can be encouraged to make drawings about snow or rain: heavy or light snow; snow with strong winds; snow on top of a house; simple drawings of snow flakes; drifts of snow; and the like.

Self-expression along such lines eventually can lead to a unit about the snow or rain, once interest has been sufficiently aroused. For example, the unit might deal with the causes of snow, the effects of snow on life, or the seasons and snow. The unit then can become the base for learning new words, learning new expressive techniques—such as drawing, speaking, or play-acting—and for learning simple generalizations or abstractions. The unit also can lead, in the later primary grades especially, to reading materials that will be read by the pupil, the teacher, or both.

Self-expression can be greatly facilitated if appropriate materials are at hand. Water and sand, for instance, are particularly important at both the preschool and primary levels for retarded children. The simple materials, contained in basin and box, are unstructured enough to provide emotional release. They are unlikely to encourage feelings of frustration, since there are no standards of success that cannot be attained by the child. Such materials, which have long been used in child guidance clinics to encourage the expression of affect and underlying conflicts, also are effective in the classroom. They can be used in combination with simple objects such as blocks of wood, simple toys, sponges, and pails and shovels (Lowentend, 1960).

Other materials useful for self-expression include crayons and paints; finger paints; clay; construction toys; mosaics; blocks of wood; and simple, toy musical instruments. A useful book by Jackson and Todd (1950) stresses the general therapeutic aspects of play and self-expression.

Receptive Language.   We have repeatedly stressed the importance of teaching the retarded child *to attend* to various external stimuli. *Discriminal attention* is necessary if receptive language skills are to be learned. Most authorities agree that the retarded child needs concrete experiences to relate to receptive language learning. These experiences should include stimulation of all sensory modalities—auditory, visual, kinesthetic, tactile, and olfactory—so as to insure overlearning and provide rich associative meanings. But all of these experiences, no matter how rich and how vivid, will yield pitifully small returns in long-term learning unless the child also *learns to attend carefully* to the experience.

It cannot be taken for granted, then, that simply providing the experience will insure effective learning. But how can attention be fostered? First the child must be directly encouraged to attend, even if this means saying, "Look at me," or, "Watch my face while I speak." Then the presentation by the teacher must be *dramatic* and *vivid*. Great care must be taken to insure that the child fully comprehends what is said or done. This means proceeding very slowly, repeating important ideas or words, explaining carefully and fully, and constantly checking to insure adequate comprehension.

The teacher must give concrete illustrations, carrying out activities to give varied examples of the idea or concept being taught. It usually helps if the child is requested to *do something* to show that he really has understood, such as following a direction, obeying a command, or making something (a drawing or the like).

Kirk and Kirk (1971) list severel types of activities that are useful in developing language ability. These are (1) encouraging free expression about immediate experiences; (2) having children carry out instructions; (3) using pictures for purposes of discussion (later, stories and books may be used for the same purpose); (4) using trips and excursions to encourage discussion and to introduce new concepts; (5) re-telling stories; (6) using games, rhymes and riddles; and (7) giving exercises in classifying ideas and concepts ("What things do you eat?" "How many animals do you know?").

Before reading is begun in a formal way, the child must have an adequate store of these and other experiences in order to make reading enjoyable and meaningful. There are several good sources of additional suggestions for pre-reading programs (see: Garton, 1961; Karnes, 1968; Lerner, 1971). All that we can do in this short account is to emphasize some essential elements in the learning of receptive language as a base for such reading programs: (1) an adequate store of rich, vivid, meaningful experiences; (2) an adequate store of words and concepts; (3) the association of the linguistic concepts in various sense modalities; and (4) the appropriate habits of attending, discriminating, associating, and generalizing.

The formal teaching of reading should not be introduced until the child's linguistic readiness and visual-motor skills are fully adequate for that task. For most moderately retarded children this will mean that reading instruction will not begin until the chronological age of at least eight years and the mental age of at least six years.

Authorities differ considerably on the values of different methods of teaching reading to retarded children, just as they do concerning teaching methods for normal children. Present evidence does not clearly establish the superiority of any one teaching method over the others (see the section Theory and Methodology, below). It is generally agreed, however, that retarded children need much more repetition and guidance in the learning process, that special remedial methods are required in individual cases, and that special reading materials need to be used. Regarding the last point, it should be remembered that retarded children are chronologically older than normal children of similar mental maturity; hence their interests are different in many ways. Since reading materials should be geared to current interests, materials must be specially selected for the children. Some materials will have to be developed by the classroom teacher, who knows the children's interests.

Expressive Language. Expressive language includes speaking and writing, primarily. We have already discussed some of the values and methods of self-expression. In the preschool program and in the early phases of the primary grade program, free play, trips, rhythm games, and the like will prove helpful. To these may be added dramatic experiences, the use of music and musical games, and the use of arts and crafts. It has been found that, to a large extent, retarded children prefer to deal with concrete experiences they have had or are having in their homes and communities. Hence, such activities as housekeeping, simple cooking programs, and simple crafts programs may well be incorporated in the teaching units, especially as the children become older.

Retarded children will need special stimulation to become involved in some of these activities; they will need frequent repetition of the same and similar activities; and they will constantly need encouragement to complete even the simplest projects. Art work seems to attract such children to a high degree, probably because it can be engaged in with very little language and because some of it, like clay modeling and weaving, is concrete and appeals to motoric and visual senses. Such work can be truly expressive, and it can encourage oral expression. When children have acquired adequate skills in using art media, they can be given models to copy, such as bowls, simple figures, and place mats. With careful guidance they can acquire considerable skill and enjoyment and will be interested in talking about their products, thus finding new words to use and new concepts to explore.

It is entirely possible, and quite useful, to teach educable retarded children to write. Either the *cursive* or the *manuscript* method of writing may be employed. The manuscript method seems to be easier to teach because the individual letters are spaced and learned as separate units and because such writing is more closely correlated with printed reading materials. However, some authorities prefer the use of cursive writing, especially for brain-injured children, because of the greater ease in perceiving the word as a total unit (Strauss and Kephart, 1955).

The teaching of writing can begin with instruction in writing the child's own first name, an activity that interests children since it enables them to label their own work and their own property. Additional training in writing should probably be delayed until formal instruction in reading is begun at about eight or nine years of chronological age. Educable retarded children will be able to learn to write more readily at that age because their motoric development is not as greatly retarded as their intellectual development. The emphasis in teaching writing should be on *accuracy,* not speed.

Children will need instruction in correct posture for writing. Learning to write at the blackboard probably should precede writing at the desk, since accuracy can be more easily assured when the letters are large and the large muscle groups are being employed in writing. Paper with ruled lines (and even boxes), allowing much more space than is needed for normal adult writing, has been found useful. Children should be encouraged to write in rhythm in the early learning stages.

As many sense modalities as possible should be employed. Writing in trays with soft clay or feeling a model of a word in the clay may be used as one method of reinforcing the learning of writing. Similarly, having children feel and trace words that are raised above the surface of the material on which they appear can be quite helpful. One method that has been suggested is to make letters with sandpaper, paste the sandpaper words onto paper with a smooth surface, and have children trace the letters and words with their fingers. In all of the work with writing, the words that are learned should have meaning and be of interest to the child, and they should be related to other current interests and activities.

Reading: Theory and Methodology. As Blanton et al. (1976) state: Teachers "must . . . deal with research literature which offers . . . few definitive conclusions regarding the superiority of one method of teaching reading over the others." Perhaps this conclusion, with which we agree, may be true simply because reading is *a highly developed set of skills,* rather than a simple, basic skill, and hence such matters as prior language experience, prior skills in attending and perceiving, special areas of interest involving communication with others, and complex motivations are critically important. Certainly, the general intellectual level also is important, as research evidence indicates, but surprisingly, retarded children, as we shall learn, are in many instances capable of utilizing higher order processes as well as normals.

Insofar as research is concerned, a comprehensive study by Woodcock and Dunn (1967) offers confirmation that no one reading method is universally superior to all others for mildly retarded students. They compared six methods of teaching reading: language experience, basal reader, and programmed text (all using traditional orthography); programmed text and language experience; and basic reading approach (with initial teaching of the alphabet). Based on a two-year program, they found no significant differences among the methods on seven different measures of reading ability. Another study, by Dunn et al. (1967), which attempted to control for degree of teacher motivation, involved an intensive analysis of results and could find no significant differences among three teaching methods.

Studies in which retarded pupils were compared with nonretarded pupils have shown, as expected, that the nonretarded are superior in all phases of reading ability. However, Cawley, Goodstein, and Burrow (1968) have shown that there are significant differences between good retarded readers and poor retarded readers, just as there are such differences between good average readers and poor average readers. *Good readers,* both mentally retarded and nonretarded, were able to read at their own mental age level, whereas *poor readers* were some two or more years below their mental age level. In other words, poor readers, whether retarded or not, had poor reading skills. On the other hand, Levitt (1972) found that retarded pupils used fewer higher-order reading processes, but were superior to nonretarded in at least one higher-order reading process (utilization of multiple cue responses). This finding is significant since it indicates that degree of mental retardation and type of skill are not always congruent for all retarded pupils. As an example of this conclusion is the finding of Belch (1974), who studied the effect of higher-order questioning strategies with three groups of secondary EMR pupils. One group was given higher-order questions (asking the pupils to analyze, synthesize, evaluate, and apply what they had read). A second group was given lower-order questions, and a third group was asked no questions. Belch found that higher-order questioning raised comprehension scores. There was no significant difference between the other two methods.

Finally, let us examine the findings of Blanton (1974b) who made an extensive study of information processing and organizational abilities in written and oral connected discourse. A comparison of EMR with nonretarded children showed, as expected, that nonretarded children were significantly better on five measures of reading and listening comprehension. It was concluded on the basis of an analysis of all of the findings that retarded children do, nevertheless, "possess the competency necessary for recoding certain types of information *when environmental cues are provided that facilitate the use of higher-order organizational abilities* [our emphasis]." This does *not* mean that all retarded children can learn to read as effectively as nonretarded, but that, given certain kinds of teaching assistance, they can perform better than they could without such assistance.

Our review of the evidence indicates that no specific reading method has been demonstrated to be superior to others with retarded children. The evidence does show, however, that the reading of some retarded individuals can be significantly improved providing they are taught to overcome some deficiencies in input and storage of material and can learn to utilize certain strategies in organizing material so that they are more efficient in retrieval. We shall have more to say about learning and teaching implications in the final section of this chapter.

METHODS RELATED
TO MATHEMATICAL TRAINING

Almost all retarded children can learn basic numerical and mathematical concepts, and almost all will need some competency in these areas in order to function effectively in the community and on the job. Although research studies have indicated that even educable retarded children have far more difficulty with arithmetic reasoning than with arithmetic computations in comparison with normal children of similar mental age, these findings are not necessarily intrinsic to the problem of retardation, as such. Rather, they may reflect (1) *inappropriate teaching methods* used with the retarded and (2) *inappropriate pacing* of arithmetic teaching. One example of inappropriate pacing is the introduction of arithmetic reasoning before enough concrete, vivid arithmetical experiences have been used to develop basic concepts of space, size, and time. Another example is the teaching of arithmetic reasoning before the child's linguistic conceptual level is adequate to comprehend the necessary abstractions.

Trainable retarded children can learn basic quantitative concepts such as big and small, heavy and light, and tall and short. They also can learn to count sufficiently to handle small amounts of money, and they can learn to tell time (in many cases), remember street numbers, and tell their age.

Educable retarded children can learn all of the basic computational skills involved in adding, subtracting, multiplying, and dividing. They also can learn more difficult mechanical operations, depending on the level of their mental maturity. And they can learn many aspects of mathematical reasoning and generalizing if these are taught after the basic concepts and computational skills have been well overlearned and the children's mental growth has attained the appropriate level. Too often, mentally retarded children become phobic about arithmetic, especially about arithmetic reasoning, just as many normals do, because their experience in learning has been attended by too early abstraction, too frequent failure, and too much traumatization.

Research and teaching experience have shown that by using appropriate, vivid, meaningful material, basic numerical concepts can be successfully taught to trainable, as well as to educable, mentally retarded children. A number of excellent sources of materials and methods are applicable to these children (Smith, 1971).

Smith explains that mechanical, or rote, teaching of arithmetic skills was replaced in the 1960s by more personally oriented and more gestalt (or molar) concepts through the influence of Piaget and others. These are sometimes referred to as an *intentional program of instruction*. The program teaches the concepts of classification, seriation, combination, and conservation. There is an interlinking of meaningful experiences, modulated through verbal and motoric-perceptual behavior with basic mathematical concepts.

Peterson (1973) has described the total program in mathematics from the preschool level through the high school level, explaining the sequential and comprehensive learning experiences. Let us look at some examples of the content of this program. It is emphasized that *form* and *perception* are basic to later conceptualizations and skills. Beginning concepts emerge out of the child's experience with his own body: its parts and its movements. He learns he is small enough to crawl under some objects; he learns where he can jump and climb; and he begins to acquire a conception of his own size or the size of parts of his body in relation to the size of objects in space. He begins to learn the concepts of *near* and *far*. He learns to synchronize visual and motoric relationships.

Suggested activities include crawling through a tunnel; building with blocks; using the Kephart walking board; climbing and stepping through spokes of a ladder; using stepping tiles (arranged in varying patterns); using a coordination board; matching three-dimensional shapes; using discrimination cards; solving paper-and-pencil mazes; making peg patterns; and using punch-outs and "stic'ems." Such games and activities promote the learning of the fundamental visual and motoric patterns that underlie primary mathematical concepts. At the same time, vocabulary and number symbols are gradually introduced. Finally, cardinal and ordinal numbers are introduced through games and other activities. The former relates to the question How many?, while the latter refers to the question What position? On such bases as these, measurement and number operations may then be taught. Peterson lists sources of materials, most of which are quite inexpensive or can be developed by the teacher. Still later, more advanced aspects of mathematics can be taught. At the high school level, the educable retarded child can learn functional mathematics needed in prevocational training and in daily living.

A careful review of the research evidence suggests that several factors are highly significant in the learning of mathematics. Once one gets beyond highly specific skills that can be learned by rote, such as in basic computational skills, mathematics requires the mastery of conceptual and analytical abilities. Hence, the mental maturity of the individual and the individual's current interest in mathematical concepts as they pertain to problems of daily living are critical.

Closely related to this base is the base of learning in a *climate of emotional security*. Our review of the relevant research in previous chapters demonstrated the effects of failure experiences and anxiety on the learning process. The learning of mathematics is too often attended by failure experiences. One reason for this is that the child can easily tell whether or not he fails ("gets the wrong answer") in mathematics, whereas that is not so easy in other subjects. Care should be taken, therefore, to insure repeated success in learning mathematics and to avoid frustrating failure experiences.

Another reason for failure experiences in mathematics is that "correctness" is highly valued by schools and by society, and the retarded child already has learned that what he does often is not correct. The child's slow rate of mental maturation, poor habits of attention, and poor work habits (lacking accuracy and persistence) have combined to lower his expectation of success in mathematics and to increase fear of failure. For these and related reasons, the child can become phobic about mathematics, particularly when it involves abstraction, generalization, and transference of learning. When a child has special emotional problems, they complicate the learning of arithmetical and mathematical skills considerably.

There are some special problems in teaching mathematics to retarded children. As we have emphasized, one of the first problems confronting the teacher is to evaluate the readiness of the child for learning number concepts and, later, for learning basic arithmetic fundamentals. A number of publications provided by the Council for Exceptional Children will prove highly useful for such evaluation. In addition to the more formal methods of evaluating readiness by means of tests of general intelligence and of specific skills, the alert teacher can learn much about each child's specific assets and limitations by observing the child closely in the *informal situations* in the classroom that involve games and other activities requiring some degree of numerical conceptualization.

The basis for effective, primary conceptualizations of quantitative concepts lies in activities involving the perception of size, form, space, and weight. Color perception may be closely linked with these phenomena as a means of providing discriminatory and differentiating experiences. It may be well to emphasize again that the general principle in such teaching is to make the experience as precise and vivid as possible. The use of multisensory experience to reinforce and help generalize the learning also is highly important. (See the Cuisendire System, D'Amelio, 1971.)

Color dominoes and form dominoes can be profitably employed at later stages in the learning process to reinforce and to enrich the learning experiences. Later still, the concepts learned through such experiences can be applied in counting money, keeping time with music, counting the number of children in a game, doing art work, and performing various craft activities. These lead quite easily to activities and projects in which children, singly and in groups, can engage in useful, meaningful, and contextually relevant experiences.

During the later stages of the primary grades, or at the beginning of the intermediate grades, the learning of quantitative concepts is followed by the learning of the fundamentals of arithmetic and, later still, by the learning of mathematical thinking of a simple kind. There have been a number of studies of the psychological processes involved in the four fundamental arithmetical operations. Although the principles discovered in these studies are applicable to the teaching of retarded children, various adaptations in methods of teaching these skills will need to be made. Again, the principle that the learning must be immediately meaningful to the child has special relevance. Sheer drill in fundamental operations is likely to be ineffective. On the other hand, fundamental operations that are tied in with activities and projects arising out of the child's needs are likely to be reinforced much more rapidly.

It is also worth reemphasizing the virtues of using *concrete demonstrations* of the four fundamental operations with the retarded child because of the child's relative difficulty in generalizing and abstracting. Experiences in which the child adds things, subtracts things from a group of things, multiplies things, and divides things can be used repeatedly until the concepts are firmly entrenched. Counting blocks or marbles, dividing them into groups, putting a number of blocks together in patterns to demonstrate multiplication, dividing a cake among a number of children, or subtracting objects from a larger number in a pile as a result of losses in a game—these kinds of concrete demonstrations as part of on-going activities are useful.(See Smith, 1974.)

Only after these operations are understood at the concrete level is drill in the mechanics of the fundamental operations justified. And the drills themselves need to be motivated—so that the child actually can see and understand how much he can gain from acquiring these skills.

The teaching of arithmetic to the educable retarded at the secondary school level should be pointed toward the dual goals of helping the child to acquire the social skills needed for effective and relatively independent living in the home and in the community and preparing the child for some degree of vocational competence. In a useful guide for teachers of retarded children at the secondary school level, the Kansas City, Missouri, Public Schools (1959) have suggested that, "To live comfortably as an adult, one should be able to use money, make change, have a concept of time, the calendar, time tables, weights and measures, etc." They also suggest that training in skills makes the child a useful and contributing member of society.

The specific content proposed in this guide for children with MAs of nine years and up—a range in mental maturity that is reasonable for most educable retarded at the secondary level—is divided into four major areas. The first, dealing with arithmetical vocabulary, includes such concepts as *second, payment, annual weekly, F.O.B.,* and *depth.* The second, dealing with skills in the use of numbers, includes such concepts as continuous adding using thought problems; the meanings of fractions such as 2/3, 1/5, and even 7/8; complex multiplication skills, such as multiplying a three-place number with one or more zeros in it by a one-place number; and skills in division involving problems up to a three-digit quotient.

The third area, on the use of money, covers installment accounts, down payments, the skills in making change for $50.00 and $100.00, and the ability to pay utility bills and other bills. The fourth area, involving measurements, covers such items as concepts of weather (spring, summer, fall, and winter); ability to set a clock; ability to read train schedules; ability to read weather reports; ability to keep a graph of temperature; ability to measure in terms of pint, quart, and gallon; and concepts of ounce and 100 pounds. This sampling of content areas suggests the wide range of skills and concepts that focus on the practicable and useful, which are so important for these children.

In the teaching of numerical and arithmetic skills, as in the teaching of other academic areas, much effort has gone into *programmed instruction.* Such programs, very often using teaching machines, provide for very carefully graded and individualized learning experiences. The goal is to minimize errors and failure experiences and to maximize efficient learning. An example of the research that has been done to evaluate programmed arithmetic instruction is that reported by Blackman and Smith (1964). They found that programmed instruction was effective for retarded children. It provided significant gains over conventional methods of instruction, and retention of what had been learned was very good after a period of three months. There are many *pros* and *cons* concerning such programs, but the overall evidence is that they are a valuable contribution to the teaching of retarded children.

It should be noted that despite the most intensive efforts, mentally retarded children, and even educable mentally retarded children, may be expected to achieve below their own mental maturity level as they become older (see Goodstein, Kahn and Cawley, 1976). One can only speculate why this is so, but probable factors are relatively poor language and conceptual development, and relatively little need to use higher mathematical concepts in terms of vocational and daily experiences.

GENERAL IMPLICATIONS FOR LEARNING AND TEACHING

Now that we have reviewed the theories and research evidence on the learning of retarded pupils and have attempted to cull major empirical findings, we shall summarize the general implications for educational practice. This is a hazardous undertaking for several reasons. First and foremost, despite extensive research studies, our knowledge of the learning of retarded persons, in general, and of particular groups of retarded persons, is still quite limited. Moreover, since the retarded differ "so spectacularly" in abilities, interests, and patterns of behavior, generalizations can apply at best only to general classes of the retarded. In addition, it must be recognized that many research studies were conducted in other than "natural settings" (and many of the most significant studies were done in laboratories rather than in classrooms). Hence, the applicability of the findings is limited. Finally, teaching remains an art. So much of what goes on between teacher and learner depends on how sensitive the teacher is to the pupil, how adroitly the teacher applies methods and rewards, and how effectively the teacher evaluates process and outcomes, thereby further modifying her approach to the learning situation—so much of these and related matters influence the teaching procedures and teaching climate—that it is well nigh impossible to reduce teaching methods to a statement of mechanical procedures.

One implication of this assertion, on which we shall comment further in chapter 17, is that the training of teachers may require more than the learning of specific methods; it also may require observational learning (as, for example, by observing good teachers perform) during teacher training and during, later, in-service training.

Nevertheless, we can summarize some general principles that may be helpful. We shall do this by discussing several categories of teaching principles.

1. *Readiness to Learn.* For a child to learn most effectively, and to avoid the possible devastating effects of failure over periods of time, the teacher should evaluate the child's readiness for the proposed learning experience. Readiness involves having: (a) appropriate background experiences for the task (i.e., the child's previous experiences at home as well as in school have provided an adequate base in "knowledge"); (b) appropriate skills for the task (i.e., perceptual, motoric, linguistic, and social); and (c) appropriate schemata of cognitive organization (i.e., the child has developed the type of "formal operations—*à la* Piaget—to make the task feasible). Evaluation of such readiness is an essential part of the teacher's responsibility.

2. *Climate for Learning.* Learning proceeds most effectively when the "learning climate" is appropriate. Such elements in the "climate" as the atmosphere of the classroom (or other setting), the nature of the relationship between teacher and pupil, and the absence of unduly distracting influences need to be considered. Prior success in learning with an interested, perceptive, and rewarding teacher can be most important.

3. *Motivation for Learning.* Without motivation, learning is a hazardous undertaking; with motivation, learning is likely to be much more effective. Motivation for the task may already be present. If it is not, the teacher should seek to provide such motivation by relating the task to be learned to the child's current goals. Of course, success in mastering the task can become its own reward, but often learning is facilitated when additional rewards are appropriate. Evidence indicates that the reward should be "tailored" to the child's needs and interests. (See Reinforcement, below.) Purposive learning (*à la* Tolman) can be most effective.

4. *Diagnostic-Prescriptive Teaching Is Most Efficient.* With adequate appraisal of the learner's readiness and particular motivations, the learning task can be fitted to the current abilities and limitations of the learner. This requires careful assessment of the learner and analytic consideration of the principal components of the task. Moreover, diagnostic-prescriptive teaching requires monitoring of performance and modification of the learning situation accordingly.

5. *Active Learning Is Effective Learning.* As demonstrated by Piaget, Festinger and others, the child learns by actively searching, trying, moving, and doing, rather than simply by being passively taught. Tasks therefore must be organized so that they provide challenges that the learner is able to meet, and activity in performing such tasks.

6. *Individualized Learning.* Since each individual has a unique constellation of assets and liabilities, effective learning requires some degree of in-

dividualization. Whether instruction is by machine teaching or is otherwise programmed, or whether instruction is provided in a group setting, provision should be made for individualization of the instruction and individualization of the learning experience.

7. *Attention and Novelty.* Retarded children, especially, often lack adequate skills in attending. Often, specific practice in "learning to attend" is necessary. Novelty in the task or in the task setting contributes not only to motivation but simultaneously tends to increase skills in attending. Novelty may be combined with individualized motivation in terms of the learner's current interests and experiences by connecting the task to be learned to these interests and experiences. The content of the task thus can be "tailored" to individual learners. Other forms of increasing novelty have been presented in this chapter (à la Smith).

Recent studies have indicated that the factor of "novelty" can have high impact on the improvement of learning. For example, Greenfield (1976) evaluated the effect of novelty in a two-choice discrimination problem. The subjects were eight- to nine-year-old retarded pupils, with MAs from about three years to slightly less than six years. It was found that "MA dependent novelty-familiarity preferences could be influenced by novelty-familiarity redundancy training." The study suggests that the upper limits in learning of this kind can be significantly influenced by teaching strategies even with quite severely retarded individuals.

8. *Training in Discrimination.* Especially for the retarded, learning to discriminate is highly important. Teaching can proceed more effectively when irrelevant cues are reduced or eliminated and when relevant cues are presented redundantly. Care must be taken to insure that discrimination operates with 100 percent effectiveness (or very close to that level) before introducing similar, but otherwise confusing, elements in the learning situation.

9. *Strategies for Organization of the Learning Task.* Specific teaching of higher-order strategies can be taught to most mildly retarded and can be taught to many other retarded pupils who are below this level of adaptation. Such strategies can involve methods of processing input, methods of organizing such input, and methods of responding. (See mediational learning.)

10. *There Are Many Methods of Learning.* Conditioning of the classical type requires frequent reinforcement of "simultaneous" presentation of unconditioned and conditioned stimuli. Instrumental learning requires appropriate schedules of reinforcement, emphasis on generalization, and subsequent relearning. Modeling and observational experiences, especially in group settings, can be effective in learning attitudes, values, and "condoned" behaviors. Memory processes can be improved by means of strategies that reinforce secondary and tertiary memory systems. Scanning behaviors, to improve input of stimuli and more effective retrieval, can lead to more effective learning.

11. *Learning Can Be Applied.* When what is learned is put to use by the learner in coping more effectively with the environment, and when it is applied in vocational tasks for the older learner, especially under guided supervision, higher levels of learning may be accomplished.

– 16 –

Counseling and Psychotherapy

At various points throughout this text, we have emphasized the significant role of emotional factors and adjustment in the development of behavior and learning of the retarded. Too often, in the intense effort to find more effective techniques to improve learning, consideration of the importance of affect or emotion on learning has been neglected. And yet, emotions and their consequences are energizers of behavior as well as barometers of well-being. The problems of the retarded cannot be fully understood, nor can they be dealt with adequately, unless their adjustment is taken into account. And, as we indicated in chapter 10, the adjustment of their caretakers also is critical to the welfare and learning of retarded persons.

In previous chapters, we have discussed the values of genetic counseling, counseling of the parents during pregnancy of the mother, and counseling following birth of the retarded child. We also have presented evidence of the importance of counseling and involving the parents or caretakers in programs of early intervention, especially among disadvantaged families. In this chapter we will consider the significance of counseling and psychotherapy for the retarded child during the school years, counseling of parents during this period, and the role of the school and its personnel in the total mental health program for the retarded. First, however, we should like to present an overview of psychotherapeutic approaches and methods.

AN OVERVIEW OF PSYCHOTHERAPEUTIC APPROACHES

Psychotherapy, in the strict meaning of the term, is a technical skill utilized by psychotherapists who have had special and intensive professional training for this purpose. Its precise meaning has never been satisfactorily defined, but it refers to the methods by means of which an attempt is made to reduce or eliminate psychopathology or maladjustment or to improve the adjustmental affectiveness of the individual or group. Counseling is a closely related profession, so that sometimes one cannot find any meaningful distinction between it and psychotherapy, but it has also been applied to practices that relate to problems of daily living, to vocational and personal adjustment, and to career planning. Many of the methods used in both psychotherapy and counseling are practiced, with or without specific training, by teachers, parents, religious counselors, marital counselors, and the like, in helping individuals to cope more effectively with concurrent problems. When, however, the aim is to promote mental health, particularly with individuals who are suffering from some form of psychopathology, a professional therapist or counselor usually is needed—such as a clinical psychologist, a psychiatrist, a psychiatric social worker, or a marital counselor. Sometimes the professional assistance of other specialists is needed, such as a neurologist, or neurosurgeon, or a pediatrician.

As the reader will have gathered, psychotherapists usually are trained (and licensed or certified by state and national bodies) in a limited specialty within their own field. Thus, there are psychoanalysts, behavior therapists, gestalt therapists, group therapists, milieu therapists, psychopharmaco-therapists, and others. Unfortunately, most therapists tend to be trained in a particular "school" only and are thereby limited in applying the *appropriate combination of methods* that are most effective in a given instance. Research evidence has accumulated that demonstrates that even when the therapist applies a personal "brand" of psychotherapy, the therapist often is unwittingly utilizing procedures and factors that are beyond the defined scope of that "brand" (Klein et al., 1969; Lieberman et al., 1972; Hutt, 1977b). Some therapists, recognizing the inherent limitations of the approach of any one school, attempt to obtain training in other approaches. On the whole, however, most therapists favor a single therapeutic school and are unnecessarily defensive in justifying such an orientation (see Binder, Binder, and Rimland, 1976; Fix and Haffke, 1976; and Loew, Grayson, and Loew, 1975). Hutt (1977b) has presented a rationale and specific principles for adapting the basic principles of several schools of psychotherapy to the requirements of the particular case.

Psychotherapy involves an *interpersonal relationship* in which several factors tend to operate, such as providing empathic understanding, developing better insights into the causes of behavior, learning new strategies for coping, analyzing defenses and improving ego functions, providing a secure and warm climate for emotional learning, and providing models of behavior that the "patient" can internalize and utilize. Some of these same factors are present (or absent) in pupil-teacher interactions, child-parent interactions, and peer relationships although they are not systematically or explicitly employed according to therapeutic principles. But there are other *forms* of therapy apart from the classical model of patient-therapist interaction.

Group therapy has become increasingly popular over the past decades and now includes such diverse forms as encounter groups, marathon groups, and child-parent or parent groups. Particularly important is a form called milieu therapy (Sanders, Smith, and Weinman, 1967), in which either within an organizational setting, such as a hospital or school, or within a community setting, environmental conditions are so arranged as to exercise a helpful influence on the individual's personality functioning. The implications of effective milieu planning in school settings to promote mental health and effective learning have yet to be fully explored or implemented, yet, as we shall see, the lengthy experience of each child over many years in the school setting can have either a beneficial or malevolent effect in these areas.

It seems almost self-evident that all school personnel having responsibility for the mental health and learning of children should have some degree of sophistication with respect to therapeutic methods and school applications so that they can contribute to more effective interpersonal relations with pupils and their parents and so that they can provide appropriate conditions for learning. They also should be able to make at least a preliminary evaluation of the presence of psychopathology or disturbed behavior so that they can seek referral of the pupil, either within the school system or in external agencies.

MENTAL HYGIENE AND THE TEACHER

The mental health of the retarded child is a unique responsibility of the school, although this responsibility has often been neglected. It is undoubtedly true that frustration and failure in school work contribute to problems of emotional disturbance of the child; it is at least equally true that emotional problems contribute significantly to difficulties in school learning. The school must deal with these emotional problems to the extent that it can. The school cannot simply assume that each child will come to school with an adequate emotional adjustment; it must do its part to help prevent, to help ameliorate, and to treat such problems within the limits imposed on it by its objectives.

Although the school cannot be expected to offer psychotherapeutic help of a technical nature, it can provide a climate that fosters good mental hygiene, it can deal with intercurrent problems as they arise, it can correct some kinds of behavioral difficulties, and it can act as a resource agent in proper referral for specialized help when it is needed. Moreover, there are many aspects of behavior modification, applicable to both academic and social adjustment problems, to which the teacher can contribute directly. Even when the child is being seen in psychotherapy outside of the school, the teacher can play an important role in assisting improvement in adjustment.

We have previously listed and discussed the goals of education proposed by the Educational Policies Commission of the National Education Association. Although the basic objectives listed by the National Education Association are relevant for the retarded child, there are, nevertheless, large and real differences in what specifically can be accomplished for the retarded as opposed to the average or superior child. These differences are reflected in the more specific educational objectives of programs developed for the retarded child. As Kirk and Johnson (1951) point out, and as we have indicated, the retarded child is generally slower in most things than the average child. He does better in physical and social areas than in academic tasks. The retarded child has greater success in hand skills than in those functions that depend on academic training. Vocationally, he usually functions best at an unskilled or semiskilled job, rather than at a highly skilled job, although some retarded children often develop high degrees of skill in a particular area. For these reasons, we believe that the educational objectives for the retarded child should stress occupational and personal adequacy, as well as social competence. The educational objectives for the retarded differ from those for other children chiefly in that they focus more on specific and differentiated goals. This is because the retarded child is not as flexible in adjustment to life and cannot contribute to society as extensively as does the more normal child.

More specifically, the goals of the educational process of the retarded child should be oriented toward daily life activities. This principles should be applied in all areas of instruction. The child should be helped to develop habits of physical health that are directly relevant to the child's current status and capacity. Similarly, the teaching of basic academic subjects should center on their direct applicability in daily life. Stress should be placed on socialization experiences, on developing within the child understanding of the responsibilities of group living, and on ability to participate as fully as possible in community life. The mental health of the child should be fostered.

There is still another important objective in the total education of the retarded child. The child has to learn a realistic evaluation of his own limitations and assets in order to avoid continual frustration. If unrealistic aspirations are beyond the child's actual capacities, resulting frustration may lead to the production of severe anxiety. This problem presents special difficulties for the special-class teacher. The teacher must provide stimulation to enable the child to develop capacities as completely as possible, yet must not expose the child to situations that lead to frequent discouragement and frustration. The successful teacher must gauge the child's assets and liabilities accurately.

As we indicated in chapter 15, the teacher can be a good or poor mental hygienist. If the teacher's own personality problems or insensitivity to the needs of pupils is significant, the daily interactions with pupils will be, on the whole, negative rather than positive. The same kinds of interactions will likely occur in conferences with parents and with other school personnel. The child with emotional problems will tend to be either rejected or will receive many negative reinforcements in interpersonal situations. Referrals to other specialists within or outside of the school will tend to be done in such a manner as to cause further rejection of the child, or will be delayed unnecessarily.

On the other hand, the secure and well-trained teacher will not only apply modern methods of modifying behavior as well as emotional growth, but also will deal more efficiently with the daily problems of the child in constructive fashion, utilizing principles of operant conditioning and other effective interpersonal "therapeutic" methods.

The teacher also should work closely with the parents of the child, interpret the child's progress to them, help them to deal with their own problems, and suggest ways in which they can further the development of the child. The teacher forms the link between the home and the school. He is primarily responsible for stimulating the growth of the child in many areas. The general mental hygiene of the classroom is the teacher's responsibility, and this entails an understanding of the needs and capacities of each child. He uses the interactions of the children to enable them to understand themselves better, to foster ego development, and to stimulate the growth of social skills. It is also the responsibility of the teacher to pace the educational and vocational tasks set for the child in accordance with his abilities, psychological needs, and specific maturational level. The teacher has a direct therapeutic role. He continually interacts in both group and individual sessions, either on a formal or an informal basis, dependent on his training. It is for all these purposes that the teacher needs to know more about personality development, guidance and counseling techniques, and psychopathology.

Even when the treatment program is centered around somatic methods, the role of the teacher is vital. The teacher is in a position to observe the reactions of the child on a continuing basis and can evaluate the child's possible progress and behavioral change. All pertinent behavioral reactions of the child should be discussed by the teacher with the other team members so that the somatic method used may be adapted to the child's changing needs. The teacher also has to change the classroom program to correspond to such changes.

The following illustration of the teacher's role in the somatic aspects of the treatment program will illustrate one of the many ways in which the teacher's direct observation of the child's behavior can be helpful.

Jerry, a nine-year-old retarded child, was receiving medication daily (chlorpromazine). The teacher noted that he showed marked behavioral changes in his classroom behavior. Formerly he had been quite active and involved in all the class activities. Two weeks after his medication had been initiated Jerry was lethargic, appeared to be drowsy most of the time, and did not enter into the class activities. He "just sat." The teacher discussed these behavioral reactions with the child's physician, who then adjusted the medication to help the child maintain more alertness.

The teacher also can be of great help in the psychotherapeutic treatment of the child. He should consult with the psychotherapist to acquaint him with the progress and behavior of the child and to find out how the teacher himself can aid in implementing the goals of psychotherapy. For example, he might allow one child to lean very heavily upon him. For another child, it might be desirable that the teacher not permit her to be too dependent. Through discussing the progress of each child and being an active participant on the therapeutic team, the teacher can play a vital role in the therapeutic process.

PSYCHOTHERAPEUTIC APPROACHES

Many retarded children who have emotional problems that interfere with learning or adjustment can profit from psychotherapy; for some it is essential. As our case illustrations have shown, some retarded children need direct psychotherapeutic help so that they can eliminate serious conflicts in their emotional adjustment or can learn improved methods of coping and social adjustment. For such children, psychotherapy may be a requisite for more effective learning.

It has been assumed, erroneously, that the mentally retarded child is unable to benefit to any great extent from psychotherapy. Long ago, Sarason (1949) presented some of the reasons underlying this belief: the retarded child cannot tolerate strong emotional states; cannot view the behavior of other people in an objective manner; has difficulty in relating to other people; and cannot see the results of his maladaptive behavior. Sarason also believed that one of the reasons that the usual methods of psychotherapy are not effective with the retarded child lies in the child's inability to communicate verbally in an adequate manner with other people. The retarded child has difficulties in using language; he cannot generalize or readily express himself. Therefore, it is not surprising that the usual psychotherapeutic techniques based on verbal interactions are not very effective in his treatment. We agree with Sarason's feeling that the pessimism expressed concerning psychotherapy with retarded children has been based on theoretical deductions rather than on specific research considerations.

Abel (1953) also felt that one of the reasons it is believed that the mentally retarded child does not profit from psychotherapy is that the child does not have the degree of verbal understanding believed to be necessary for this type of treatment. Further, it is believed that the whole process of psychotherapy is colored by society's rejection of the retarded child. These beliefs are not necessarily valid, and many studies have shown that the retarded child *can* profit from psychotherapy (see Menolascino, 1977).

We believe that, in many instances, retarded children can benefit from both group and individual psychotherapy, as studies that we will cite clearly show. The "currency" of the psychotherapeutic situation is the interaction that occurs between the subject and the therapist, and interactions occur in many ways *other* than at the verbal level. For example, a child may communicate feelings and thoughts by postural adjustments, play activities, and drawing. Inability to verbalize may be a limiting factor in some phases of therapy, but it is not necessarily a complete block to all psychotherapeutic work.

Intelligence also is considered by many authorities to be significantly related to psychotherapeutic progress, and it has been stated that little progress in psychotherapy can be made by persons with limited mental capacities. For example, Rogers (1942) believed that the subject must have adequate capacities for dealing with life situations and must have at least dull normal intelligence to profit from psychotherapy. Fenichel (1945) stated that the mentally retarded person cannot profit readily from psychoanalysis, since the ego does not have the capacity to "face its conflicts." However, even though Fenichel ruled out the use of psychoanalysis with such persons, he thought that they might respond to psychoanalytically oriented psychotherapy. Psychoanalysis is a special form of psychotherapy that may not be applicable to all types of people. Whether psychoanalysis is, in fact, contraindicated for all mentally retarded persons is a moot question. In any case, other forms of psychotherapy have been shown to be effective.

Dynamic Approaches to Psychotherapy

We have been discussing psychotherapy from the more traditional and dynamic viewpoint, which includes psychoanalytic and client-centered (Rogerian) approaches, as well as other "uncovering" types of therapy. Such approaches have emphasized helping the individual to understand and accept himself more completely and to find new strategies for effectively coping with his internal and external problems. The approaches can be applied to individuals or groups. We now will examine some of the research and clinical evidence on the effectiveness of such approaches to psychotherapy.

Thorne (1948) reported on psychotherapy with institutionalized children. His approach involved complete acceptance of the retarded child, expression of emotional reactions, an attempt at teaching emotional controls, teaching acceptable ways of behaving, building up feelings of self-confidence, and training the child to seek help when faced with severe problems. He studied the therapeutic responses of sixty-eight retarded children. Of these, he felt forty-five improved, sixteen were unchanged, and seven were less well adjusted following the course of psychotherapy. Thorne concluded that retarded children *could* profit from psychotherapy. Of course Thorne's study did not utilize a control population and his results, therefore, are only suggestive.

Heiser (1954) studied fourteen retarded children who were given psychotherapy. They ranged in IQ from 44 to 75. The diagnoses varied: one was diagnosed as familial, six were diagnosed as organic, and seven were diagnosed as psychogenic mentally retarded children. Each child had from eleven to fifty-eight hours of psychotherapy. Twelve children improved in social behavior and in coping with the environment; only one of the organic and one of the psychogenic children did not improve. Heiser felt that psychotherapy definitely was of benefit to retarded children.

Menolascino (1977) has reviewed psychiatric studies of the retarded and finds that: (1) the severe and profoundly retarded individuals have a "high vulnerability" to emotional disorders; (2) mildly retarded individuals have a lower degree of vulnerability; and, (3) psychotherapy is effective in the whole range of retarded disabilities. A considerable amount of effort has gone into group therapy with retarded subjects. In group therapy, the therapist is able to provide assistance for a number of children at one time; hence, it has been presumed to be more efficient, when applicable, than individual therapy. Some of the research findings are of interest. Astrachan (1955) carried a number of mentally retarded females in group psychotherapy. It was felt that they responded to such treatment, and that group psychotherapy was particularly valuable to those who were passive or depressed or who had mild paranoid feelings. In particular, Astrachan reported that as a group, the subjects were better able to recognize their dependency needs following psychotherapy. There was a reduction in feelings of isolation, shame, and fear. Astrachan also felt that the subjects were able to solve many of their conflicts concerning authority figures and siblings.

Fisher and Wolfson (1953) treated twelve mentally retarded girls, ranging in age from ten to thirteen years, with group psychotherapy. They concluded that eight of these showed definite improvement in their behavior and attitudes. These workers felt that there was an initial shift from ego-centered behavior to in-group-centered behavior. Finally, the girls developed out-group-centered interests. They showed more alert attitudes and were, in general, more receptive to learning experiences. Fisher and Wolfson felt that the keynote to the success of their group psychotherapy was their permissive attitude. They stated that the group therapist should move slowly, and that the group members themselves would eventually show him their ultimate levels, which he should not attempt to exceed.

This permissive approach also has been stressed by Harris (1953), who dealt with mentally retarded children in classroom situations. He found that a permissive atmosphere produced good results.

Group psychotherapy has produced some positive results, but the techniques applied to retarded children differ from those used with children of average intelligence. For example, Sternlicht (1964) has indicated that the therapist needs to be quite active in a group psychotherapy program and that a totally nondirective or permissive approach, which is highly desirable in normal groups, is inappropriate for mentally retarded persons.

Fine and Dawson (1964) reported on a program of psychiatric treatment devised for mildly retarded adolescent girls and young adult women at the Sonoma State Hospital, California. They described the subjects of their study as girls who were behaviorally disturbed and hyperactive with a severe character disorder or a borderline psychosis. The group as a whole was noisy and aggressive; it was frequently necessary to place the girls in seclusion rooms. Very few of the girls were able to leave the unit and return to the community. Of the three or four who did leave, many returned because of a continuation of the disturbed behavioral reactions. Fine and Dawson selected fifty-six patients between the ages of fifteen and thirty who had IQs over 50 and showed an absence of severe physical handicap and an absence of intractable psychopathology. They arbitrarily divided them into seven groups of eight patients each. Each group met weekly for a one-hour psychotherapy session led by two counselors. During the first eighteen months of the active treatment program, thirty-seven patients were returned to the community. This was a highly significant increase over the number who had been returned prior to the initiation of the psychotherapeutic program. It was concluded that this group of mildly retarded girls benefited from this psychotherapeutic approach.

Slivkin and Bernstein (1968) successfully used short-term psychotherapeutic techniques for dealing with retarded adolescents. Their approach has been termed *goal directed*. The subjects of their psychotherapeutic groups were boys between fifteen and nineteen years of age. The intelligence quotients ranged from 46 to 78. There were eight children in a group, and the group met for a one-hour session weekly over a period of approximately nine to ten months. The therapist used a technique of expressive psychotherapy, focussing on present realities and on the underlying personality dynamics of the group members. The therapist played a very active role, which appeared to decrease the disorderliness that was manifested. Slivkin and Bernstein note that their methods of dealing with the group of retarded children, in almost the same way they dealt with groups of schizophrenic subjects, led to an extremely deep relationship between the group members and the therapists. They state that the therapist "serves as a bridge to reality, a teacher, an ego control system, and a model for identification, who helps restrain some impulses." Spontaneity of interaction was felt to be a crucial factor that furthered the progress of therapy. Evaluation of the progress made by the group indicated that group psychotherapy diminished hyperactivity in response to emotional stress and reduced the possibility of rejection of the individual by others. It was felt that short-term psychotherapy was of considerable value in the treatment of mentally retarded adolescents.

Sternlicht and Wexler (1966) also studied the possibility of applying psychoanalytic percepts in the treatment of mentally retarded children. In particular, they were interested in determining whether or not retarded persons could profit from the *cathartic* process. Catharsis, for the purpose of their study, was defined as "the reduction of tension through some form of related substitute activity." As the authors point out, this is essentially the classical Zeigarnik-Ovsianka effect: when a person starts a task, a tension is created within that person to complete the task. When the task is completed, the tension is discharged, and the person returns to a state of equilibrium. If the task is interrupted, the tension will remain, constantly seeking discharge. Tensions persevere, and their influence is widespreading, ultimately causing behavior that serves to reduce the tensions.

Sternlicht and Wexler studied ninety retarded institutionalized adolescents, ranging in age from twelve to twenty years. Their IQs ranged from 50 to 69. Three groups were formed, one experimental group and two control groups. Each group consisted of fifteen males and fifteen females. They were given six sensory-motor tasks of equivalent difficulty, three of which were interrupted prior to completion. The results of the study indicated that the Zeigarnik-Ovsianka effect was found to be operative with these mentally retarded subjects; that is, that an interrupted task would create a need for completion of the task. Sternlicht and Wexler concluded that intelligence, even as low as an IQ of 50, was not a factor in catharsis and that educable retarded persons could successfully engage in a cathartic process. Further, the most important element in the cathartic process appeared to be the resolution of the tensions created by an earlier frustration. This resolution could be brought about by means of cognitive activity relevant to the content of that frustration.

Not all attempts at dynamic psychotherapy with retarded children have been successful, and it is unfortunate that these attempts have not been extensively reported, for we can learn as much from our failures as from our successes. Vail (1955) has reported on his attempts to use group psychotherapy with mentally retarded boys. The group was composed of fourteen-, fifteen-, and sixteen-year-old boys, ranging from 35 to 70 in IQ. Vail stressed verbal techniques in his approach. Even though no significant improvement was shown by the group, Vail felt that, paradoxically, those subjects who had attended the fewest sessions showed the greatest amount of improvement. He drew an important conclusion from this unsuccessful attempt at group psychotherapy: the psychotherapist cannot be only a listener and observer, regardless of his sincerity; rather, he must be alert to provide repeated gratification of the needs of the subjects as they arise.

What, then, can be accomplished by dynamic psychotherapy with mentally retarded children? It is unlikely that psychotherapy will raise the innate intellectual capacities of retarded children (although it may enable emotionally disturbed ones to make more adequate use of their mental capacities). It will not transform them into intellectually normal children. However, it may enable them to solve their emotional problems and conflicts. It may help them to grow in desirable directions and alleviate many of their maladaptive behaviors. It can promote their adjustment in the community and help them to lead a happier and often more productive life, both in the present and in the future.

Behavior Modification Approaches to Therapy

In recent years, great interest has developed in the so-called behavior modification methods, which are being used with a great variety of patients. These methods have been applied to the mentally retarded, from the profoundly retarded and institutionalized person to the mildly retarded child in a school setting. The enthusiasm for these approaches has, at times, seemed boundless. Reported results of the application of these methods have been favorable. However, although behavior modification has considerable merit, it is not without its limitations and even dangers. Moreover, despite the often bitter arguments between the proponents of dynamic approaches and the proponents of behavioral approaches, these methods are complementary and not necessarily antagonistic. After all, behavior modification approaches and dynamic approaches are all attempts to modify behavior by applying learning principles to the behavior, but in different ways and with different assumptions.

We have previously discussed (see chapter 15) some of the basic principles that operate in behavior modification approaches, emphasizing the applications to the learning of retarded pupils. The same principles are applicable to the modification of many types of behavior (Kanfer and Phillips, 1970). As we shall see, operant conditioning, in particular, has had favorable outcomes in some types of severe behavior disorders, particularly disorders in which the behavior produces highly undesirable effects both for the individual and those in the individual's environment. Nevertheless, it must not be thought that it is simply the application of operant conditioning that produces the observed changes. Many other factors enter into the behavioral outcomes, such as the nature of the stimuli that are employed, the nature of the relationship between therapist and "patient," the kinds of inherent motivations that the individual brings into the therapeutic situation, and the verbal explanations (interpretation) that are offered. *It is not possible to apply operant conditioning to the human subject in quite as impersonal and "objective" circumstances as one would apply them to a laboratory animal.* Hence, it is still too early to state with confidence just how much of the change in behavior is due solely to the conditioning process. As Bergin and Suinn (1975) state, after an intensive review of recent studies in this area: "The foregoing accounts suggest that the supposed major differences between the behavioral and traditional insight therapies are not as great as was once believed, either in outcome or process." They add: "Behavioral methods are loaded with affective and cognitive variables of the same kind that dominate other therapies. . . . " And, based on intensive interviews with practicing therapists, Bergin and Strupp (1972) asserted that behavior therapists did, in fact, utilize many "dynamic" procedures that are foreign to behavior modification in its "pure form."

Nevertheless, there are several important advantages to the operant conditioning model of therapy. As Menolascino (1977) indicates, these methods focus on minute, descriptive aspects of the atypical or abnormal behavior, thus making for more accurate identification of the behavior to be modified; the behavior is defined objectively, the therapist is not confused by a general, categorical type of nomenclature, and the behaviors to be modified are ordered in terms of a hierarchy, thus making possible a systematic program for their modification.

The field of application of operant conditioning procedures and other behavioral modification methods has been greatly extended in recent years. Let us now look at some of these efforts. Azrin and Wesolowski (1975) succeeded in eliminating habitual vomiting in a profoundly retarded adult through self-corrections and positive practices. Calhoun and Matherne (1975), using varying schedules of "time-out" (after every second aggressive act of behavior) were able to secure significant improvement in eliminating aggressive behavior in a 7-year-old retarded female. Time-outs after every fifth aggressive act had no effect, thus suggesting the importance of the interval in such behaviors. O'Brien and Schofield (1975) evaluated the relative effects of positive and negative reinforcement on a manual dexterity task. The subjects were eighteen retarded individuals with a mean IQ of 68 and were living in a sheltered workshop. Positive reinforcement was found to be more effective than negative reinforcement. Edgar et al. (1975) employed relaxation methods combined with tension activities to reduce significantly accidental urination and improve significantly appropriate urination in twenty profoundly retarded subjects, aged four to twelve years. Daniels and Hansen (1976) used visual and verbal reinforcers and abstained from using "token reinforcers" in improving the work productivity of four mentally retarded subjects (mean IQ 59) over short periods of time. Snyder et al. (1975) reviewed five years of research with behavioral methods in language training for the severely retarded and concluded that such studies emphasized antecedent contingencies, used a broad range of reinforcers (mostly tangible reinforcers), and produced positive findings. Finally, various forms of behavior modification have been successful in treating autistic children—no mean feat. One of the earliest studies using operant conditioning with eight severely disturbed children was successful in "reversing" this condition in six of the cases (DeMeyer and Ferster, 1962). Later studies have shown similar results.

Thus, behavior modification works, and works with some very difficult problems. It can be employed by nonprofessionals under guidance. Its limitations and possible dangers should not, however, be overlooked.

Music Therapy

A field of special interest in the school setting is that of music therapy. Relatively few studies have explored the systematic use of music in therapy with retarded pupils, but the studies that have been reported have shown promising results. Knight and his co-workers (1957) pointed out some time ago that when properly used, music therapy can help the retarded to inhibit random muscular impulses. Furthermore, it increases the child's ability to shift more readily from one activity to another and provides opportunities for growth in group situations. Strauss and Lehtinen (1947) developed specific forms of treatment, particularly applicable to brain-damaged children, that can help to improve sensorimotor functions. Confirmation of possible improvement in perceptual-motor skills was demonstrated in a report by Retjo (1973). The subject was a seven-year-old boy with very poor auditory and visual perception. He showed significant gains in both language functions and perceptual-motoric functions in a six-month period through the use of combined piano and motoric activities. Still more recently, Dilea (1975) combined music therapy with token reinforcement in a group of sixteen children, aged thirteen to nineteen years, with IQs in the range of 60 to 70. After eleven weeks, there was significant improvement in appropriate behaviors and significant decrement in inappropriate behaviors.

Some Conclusions Concerning Psychotherapy

We may conclude from the available evidence that the mentally retarded child *can* profit from psychotherapy. As Wiest (1955) pointed out, the general goal of psychotherapy is not only to develop a fuller use of the child's capacities, but also to effect changes in the home or family situations. He stresses that education reduces the stigma of retardation. In part as a result of such educative and psychotherapeutic approaches, institutions for the mentally retarded are undergoing a slow change in their purposes and functions. Institutionalization for the moderately retarded child is beginning to be perceived as a temporary measure—as an aid to the child until he can be returned to the community. Wiest has developed a frame of reference for his therapeutic approach to the mentally retarded child. He points out that a child may be psychotic because he has never left an infantile state, and that, from one point of view, infancy is a state of psychosis. He feels, as we do, that the unconscious of the retarded child may be modified without verbal interactions, and that the retarded child can profit from psychotherapy. He stresses that it is possible to make reality so appealing to such a child that the child will grow toward it.

It also is evident that traditional psychotherapeutic approaches are not very effective when applied to the mentally retarded child and that new approaches are needed. The approaches that lean heavily on verbalizations and intellectual processes are probably not highly effective and cannot be used successfully.

The goals of psychotherapy with the retarded child need to be reconsidered. They need not involve complete reorganization of the total personality, nor is it likely that such reorganization is feasible in the vast majority of cases. The goals set by the therapist or the teacher must be realistic and readily within reach of the child's capacities.

AN EVALUATION OF SOME SPECIALIZED
TREATMENT METHODS

For some time, there was the hope that a *somatic method* of treatment would be found that would either elevate the intelligence level or produce startling changes in behavior. That hope has not been obliterated, but extensive efforts in this direction have generally been found to be ineffective. Some studies of the effects of specialized treatment methods reported striking results, but the results were found to be invalid: research methodology was inadequate or inappropriate criteria were employed. The results were of value only in cases (such as cretinism) in which a specific deficiency could be counteracted or corrected with medication. But in the vast majority of cases, especially in the category of familial retardation, such treatment was of no avail.

At one time a great deal of attention was given to the possible beneficial results of the administration of *glutamic acid.* It was believed that there was improved capacity for learning. Some experiments seemed to show that the use of this drug was attended by improvement in the learning rate of white rats (Zimmerman and Ross, 1944). There even were some indications that human beings showed improvements in scores on psychological tests. However, a thorough review of studies in this area by Astin and Ross (1960) led to the clear conclusion that beneficial results in the areas of intellectual functioning had not been demonstrated.

Many other drugs have been tried, including tranquilizers and sedatives. Some are helpful in reducing hyperactivity or controlling tension states, but none have produced any basic change in learning capacity or improvement in intellectual level. Among these drugs, *Chlorpromazine* and *Reserpine,* as well as *Ritalin,* were employed to control overactive behavior. They can be useful for that, but often the claims for them are highly exaggerated and other, more general, mental hygiene methods or methods involving psychotherapy or behavior modification are more effective in the long run. *Benadryl* has been widely used for reducing hyperactivity in mildly and moderately retarded children with considerable success in children under twelve years of age. For children older than twelve years, *Atarax* and *Vistaril* have had some favorable results (Menolascino, 1978). For more severe behavioral reactions, *Thorazine* and *Melloril* have been used with beneficial results. Sometimes the drugs have an immediate, temporary effect that enables children to become more amenable to certain training procedures (Rettig, 1955). However, there also is evidence that such drugs may cause *impairment* on tests of intellectual and psychomotor capacities (Kornetsky et al., 1957). They have not proved to be effective in the general treatment of mental retardation.

Louttit (1965) has reviewed the effect of energizers, or stimulants, on the performance of mentally retarded persons. He points out that the intellectual level of mentally retarded persons is unaffected by such stimulants as *Deanol, Metraxol, Piperdol,* and the amphetamines. He notes that all published research concerning the use of these drugs has indicated that they have not been effective in raising the level of performance. In summary, Louttit points out that "the search for magic bullets" to improve intelligence among the mentally retarded has been a long, discouraging failure. On the basis of all the evidence, it appears that the use of chemical agents is not generally effective in the treatment of mental retardation. Of course, some preventive treatment has been developed, such as the treatment for mental retardation involving the biochemical lesions that occur in phenylketonuria. However, one may conclude that no specific chemical ailment is involved and that no specific chemical treatment is effective for the large group of familial mental defectives that makes up one-third to one-half of the low end of the distribution of intelligence.

Excellent reviews of the use of various drugs in the treatment of mental retardation has been prepared by Wolfensberger and Menolascino (1969), and more recently by Menolascino (1978). They are very critical of studies purporting to assess the effect of drugs on mental retardation, since they believe that these studies, as designed, did not constitute an adequate, fair, and efficient test of the effects. In particular, they note that only short-term changes resulting from drugs have been evaluated, and long-term changes generally have been ignored. They believe that if the effect of drugs on the intellectual processes of retarded persons are to be properly assessed, the subjects must be mildly retarded children with mental ages of at least two to three years and with chronological ages at or below six years. Further, they believe that the sample should be heterogeneous in regard to etiological categories and free of secondary handicaps, and the subjects should be exposed to varying intensive environmental stimulation during the course of the experimental study. They proposed that the experimental variable in the study of so-called intelligence-enhancing drugs is not the drug itself, but, rather, the *interaction between the drug and the experimental situation.* The question to be asked is "What is the effect of drug X on what type of personality?", rather than "What is the effect of drug X on the general population?"

We have not attempted to review all of the other specialized methods of treatment. Although the final chapter in this area has not been written, we must recognize that there is no shortcut to effective, patient, long-term education and training, and that improvement in specific areas of functioning requires both education and guidance. We cannot assume that the simple administration of a drug can resolve the problems of learning or substitute for diligent and efficient methods of instruction. Nor can we expect to find some agent that will elevate learning abilities in all areas of functioning.

Our general conclusion concerning the use of drugs for the mentally retarded is consonant with that of Kirman (1975) who, after a review of studies in this area, concludes that apart from a *few, specific indications,* the use of sedatives and tranquilizers for retarded individuals should be seen as a "holding device" to enable a different system of management to be adopted. They can be helpful in, at least, temporarily reducing severe, disruptive behavior. Some can produce negative side effects, such as rapid elevation of blood pressure with *Ritalin,* drowsiness with *Benadryl,* and gastrointestinal symptoms with *Ritalin* and other drugs.

ISSUES AND APPLICATIONS: THE CONSULTATION MODEL

It is clear that the mental health of the retarded individual is an essential ingredient in any program for effective intervention. Both in the schools and in other settings, considerations of mental health should not only be given high priority, but specific means also should be available to implement such considerations. But one may ask how, with all of the demands placed on school personnel and the high cost of professional personnel, is this to be accomplished? We have attempted to indicate how mental health needs can become an *integral part* of the educative process. However, many pupils and their caretakers need more than this. Referral to a professional therapist is not the only or the most effective answer in all instances.

It is suggested that some of the school personnel, already present in the system, as well as personnel in other agencies for the retarded, can be used much more effectively than they are being used at present. For instance, many school and agency psychologists can be utilized more effectively if their functions are broadened so that they do more than administer and interpret tests, and do more than "sit in" at team meetings with other school or agency personnel. Frequently, and sometimes with additional training, they can *participate directly* in individual and group therapy meetings with parents or caretakers; become more directly involved in translating needs of the pupils into day-to-day programs which can be implemented by teachers, resource personnel, and the like; offer demonstration and case discussions of common mental health problems and their solution; offer group programs or mental health programs for the retarded pupils; and, supervise paraprofessionals in many of these programs. In such ways, their practical usefulness can be greatly extended.

Similarly, other specialized school personnel can be utilized more effectively. School (or agency) counselors, school social workers, helping teachers, and even some administrative personnel can devote some of their time to programs such as were indicated above. Some of them, too, may need additional training to improve their skills in this area. But such additional training can produce much greater dividends than simply attempting to obtain more highly specialized personnel.

All of the suggestions made above can be greatly facilitated, and teachers, too, can profit greatly from the effective use of *mental health consulta-*

tions. One model for such a program has been described by Farley and Blom (1976). This model involves the following elements:

1. Visits to the school and possible evaluation of the child.
2. Utilization of the case review method.
3. Consultation in terms of the system; i.e. definition of the problems in terms of the school setting.
4. Use of the consultant in teaching behavior modification.
5. Occasional direct treatment of the child and/or parent.
6. Teach school personnel such techniques as "life space"; i.e. sensitive, empathic listening.
7. Early identification of children at "high risk."

Farley and Blom's suggestions are well taken. Of course, other models and other circumstances requiring other models will need to be considered.

A special word should be said concerning the use of paraprofessionals in *therapy programs.* There is ample evidence that such personnel, when properly selected, given some training, and provided with supervision, can be highly effective in therapeutic programs. Rioch et al. (1963) demonstrated that, even with psychiatric, hospitalized patients, untrained married women, after being given short but intensive training, were able to be highly effective. As Rioch states: ". . . as therapists they have performed some useful service to patients during the past year, and none of them has done anyone any harm." In fact, as judged by a number of criteria, they performed as well as would have been expected from experienced professional therapists. A program reported by Cowen et al. (1972) utilizing college student volunteers and housewives as therapists, showed effective results over a period of time. In this program the subjects were maladjusted school children.

We can learn to be innovative in the use of existing professional personnel and in extending therapeutic programs with paraprofessional personnel under suitable conditions of training and supervision.

— 17 —

An Overview: Retrospect and Prospect

Now that the reader has journeyed with us through the long and complex story of mental retardation, we should like to offer some personal reflections concerning this problem. Our own long association with the problem has taken us into the consulting room with retarded children and their parents, into state and private institutions, into school systems in which we have had many conferences with teachers and administrators, and into the neighborhoods and homes from which these children come.

Over the years, we have seen enormous strides taken in the recognition of the problem, in the understanding of its complexity, in the increasing scope of programs that have been developed, and in the development of ingenious methods of training. The research literature has burgeoned, and clinical studies have become more sophisticated. Yet our sense of humility also has increased. For we have learned that, despite their general cognitive impairment, the mentally retarded are extremely complex and intriguing. Many show unusual abilities and aptitudes. Many have astonished us with their capacity for growth and achievement in a number of areas. But beyond this, they have revealed to us their full share of the common human attributes that we value so highly: capacity for persistence in the face of frustration and failure; loyalty in comradeship; joy in accomplishment; boundless trust in others; and, above all else, human dignity. We, the nonretarded, often have misunderstood them and maligned them. We have shunted them aside or treated them unfairly. At times we have abused them. And, as Farber (1968) has expressed it, we have regarded them as "surplus commodity."

The retarded often have reminded us of the deeper meaning of the phrase made so famous by the Declaration of Independence: "All men are created equal." The authors surely did not mean that all men are equal in ability or aptitude. Rather, they meant that all men have equal right to opportunity, equal right to respect, and equal protection of the law. Whether through ignorance or through intent, we have frequently denied the retarded their equal rights; we have denied them the opportunity for maximum development.

505

Work with the retarded also has reminded us that we have too often forgotten some of the basic values to which we give lip service. We tend to respect individuals only for what they accomplish rather than for what they are. Our society usually has translated *accomplishment* into being first, achieving the highest grades, or amassing the greatest fortune. In short, in our culturally jaundiced view, we have downgraded the basic qualities of "being human," and have upgraded "getting to the top."

The paradox is that even though society has asked us to give priority to being the highest achiever, it also has asked us not to be different. Group education—nay, mass education—has sought for excellence in the student population while deriding individual differences and clamoring for conventional behavior. We have acted as if it is sinful to be different, whether it is to be mentally retarded, economically poor, emotionally disturbed, or physically deviant. In our paradoxical search for the "best" while deriding the "next best," we have discarded those who failed to meet expectations. In the process, society's morality has been eroded. Human life and human values have been devalued.

The retarded, in posing problems for us, have helped us to reassess some central questions. Can we, while seeking to assist each individual to attain his or her own fullest, unique development, respect those who are deviant? Can we, while improving our methods of teaching and training, encourage heterogeneity and diversity rather than sameness? Shall we impose standards of achievement and social behavior or shall we encourage each individual to fulfill himself in his own, unique way? How can we learn to accept the retarded individual as a human being with inherent dignity and encourage him to develop his potential to the extent of which he is capable? Is our society able to find a respected place in its midst even for those who are unable to achieve as much as others? In answering these questions about the retarded, we also are defining the values by which we all live.

THE MENTALLY RETARDED AS A SURPLUS POPULATION

It is important to regard mental retardation as a problem in the organization of society rather than simply as a problem of differing levels of intelligence. The consequences of such a reorientation may have a major effect on how we deal with the problem. Although we have focused in this volume on the intra-individual characteristics of the retarded (that is, on the unique patterns of traits of each retarded person), we also have emphasized that the definition of retardation, as well as its social roots and its treatment, is a matter of general social orientation and values. We may take note of the comment made by John Gardner, when he was the Secretary of Health, Education, and Welfare, that we should "stop nibbling around the edges of educational problems and take a "'barracuda bite' at them." This view implies that a massive reorientation of the educational process is needed.

James J. Gallagher (1967), when he was Assistant Secretary of Health, Education, and Welfare, followed this orientation by proposing four major goals for special education: curriculum development for exceptional children by experts; adequate research programs; innovation in teacher training; and improved dissemination of findings and ideas. In 1966, three-quarters of a billion dollars was made available, through Title I, Public Law 89–10, for new programs for deprived children, including the retarded. Programs and funds were badly needed, but they did not face the broader issue of the meaning of mental retardation in our society.

From the perspective of the social scientist, mental retardation may be seen as a problem of "surplus population." As Farber (1968) states, "Modern society requires a surplus of persons to maximize the fit between persons and positions in the rational selection of personnel in economic, educational, political, and marital institutions." Part of this surplus is seen as coming from the mentally retarded. They contribute to the maintenance of the existing social structure by creating the need for special welfare and other institutions, by making possible the operation of certain social institutions, and by perpetuating social classes. According to this view, the mentally retarded are deviant and incompetent. Actually, however, they are capable of engaging in many tasks and activities from which they are restricted. However, amelioration of the status of the mentally retarded requires far more than improving their education and training. In fact, Farber proposes four broad progams that are needed to deal with the problem adequately. These programs are extensive in scope and deserve careful evaluation and implementation. Many elements of the programs have been proposed by others. In essense, these are the four programs.

Program I. Increasing the Adaptation of the Mentally Retarded. The first program is aimed at improving the efficiency of current and developing institutional or agency resources. This may be done through such steps as reducing the size of special classes or providing a better ratio of special educational personnel in relation to the number of retarded. As we have seen, with increasing allocation of funds, especially federal funds, much has been accomplished along this line. The efficiency of this program could be improved by improving the training of personnel and improving resource materials.

Program II. Improving Goal Attainment of the Family. The aim of this program is to improve the cultural and social milieu of the family. Parental education in child rearing and in child relationships, marital counseling, family counseling to help all members assess and deal with the effect of the retarded child on their patterns of living, and even financial assistance (e.g., an annual minimum income plan) are seen as being helpful.

Program III. Revising Institutional Arrangements. This level of programming is concerned with the improvement of institutions and with the child's integration into society. There have been proposals (Kirk et al., 1968) for *public guardianship, community centers,* and *sheltered workshops.* Aspects of such plans have been worked out in some detail. Some communities have acted on the proposal that the community center include a residential unit, a day school, a consultation unit, and a sheltered workshop. The residential unit could serve as a halfway house between the hospital and the home; it could be used for persons waiting for placement in a hospital; and it could help persons looking for a job. The day-school unit would serve those in the residential facility and those living at home. Its training programs would be aimed at the severely and moderately retarded child. The sheltered workshop, in addition to helping the retarded to find economically useful employment, would provide recreation, crafts, and social experiences. The consultation unit would act as a referral agency, as well as a direct counseling agency.

Program IV. Changing Societal Values. This program is designed to change public attitudes and values so that a person is valued for himself rather than for his "institutional efficiency." Its aim is the total incorporation and integration into the mainstream of society of the vast majority of the retarded population. This is no mean task; it involves political, financial, and moral considerations of the first magnitude.

Farber, with the coauthorship of Royce (Farber and Royce, 1977), has published an extension of his ideas concerning the need of society for a "surplus population." In his hypothetical example, the situation has become the year 2576, when as a result of great advances in genetics, in prenatal diagnosis, in medical techniques of remediation, in treating mother-child interactions, and in counteracting adverse cultural conditioning, " 'mental retardation' will be wiped out." It is the year of the 400th anniversary of the Savant computer implant. But, say Farber and Royce, "The successful remediation of mental retardation led eventually to a general inflation of intelligence in society, with the least intelligent persons still in a position of relative deprivation." The story may seem far-fetched—for who would dream that what we now conceive of as "mental retardation" could be completely eliminated—but the need of society for a new kind of surplus population would still exist. At least, say Farber and Royce, this need would exist so long as society does not deal with more general questions concerning upper and lower levels of functioning. However, we would argue that even though the problems of how society values persons with relatively inferior attributes are issues in themselves, they are far different than inability to take care of one's bodily needs, to manage one's life prudently, and to engage in fruitful social interaction.

No doubt some people who are genetically inferior will always be with us. Insofar as the problem of mental retardation is concerned, the elimination through prevention of prenatal hazards, the correction of reversible disabilities or their remediation, and the upgrading of the socially-culturally deprived can lead to a far better world for these individuals and their families. The problem that society then will have of dealing with the much smaller percentage of those who fall at the bottom end of the cognitive scale will be infinitely less difficult.

POLITICAL AND LEGAL ACTIONS:
ISSUES AND IMPLICATIONS

Since the 1960s, tremendous changes have been made in philosophy and organization of educational programs for the mentally retarded. Some of these changes were brought about by the direct and indirect actions of parents and parent groups, which influenced legislators and professional organizations. Others came about as a result of court decisons and legal battles. There is a revolution in educational thinking and planning, but the outcomes are far from being settled, and much controversy has been engendered. Moreover, some of the changes in society's attitudes toward the problems of minorities and the disadvantaged also have influenced changes in attitudes toward the retarded and the handicapped. Let us see where we have been and where we seem to be going.

Recent developments can be better understood in the light of past trends in programs for the care and guidance of children, which were promoted by action at the national level and often were promoted by the National Education Association. Of special import was the series of Conferences on Childhood called by a number of presidents. Theodore Roosevelt called the first White House Conference on Childhood. Even before that, he had organized the Children's Bureau (placing it in the Department of Labor). A plan was promulgated to call White House Conferences every ten years. The second White House Conference on Childhood was called by Woodrow Wilson in 1920. The third conference, convened by Herbert Hoover in 1930, had as its basic theme "Child Health and Protection." This conference produced the *Children's Charter,* which laid foundations for the rights and protection of children. This charter included a *Bill of Rights for Children* that described five basic rights of all handicapped children:

1. The right to as vigorous a body as human skill can provide
2. The right to an education so adapted to his handicap that he can be economically independent and have a complete life
3. The right to be brought up by those who understand him and consider it a privilege to help him
4. The right to be brought up in a world that does not set him apart
5. The right to a "life in which his handicap casts no shadow . . . "

The fourth conference, called by Franklin D. Roosevelt in 1940, had as its theme "Children in Democracy." The fifth conference, called by Harry S. Truman, was known as the Mid-Century Conference. The delegates planned a long-range program to extend over the next fifty years to provide more adequate services for children.

On October 17, 1961, John F. Kennedy, who had a personal interest in mentally retarded children, appointed the first panel on Mental Retardation, which presented its report in 1962. The Panel was composed of leading experts in many fields relating to mental retardation, who merged their specialized knowledge to consider all aspects of retardation together. Formerly, problems had tended to be considered in isolation from each other. The Panel gathered the information that was available on problems of retardation and offered general and specific recommendations. We already have cited some of the findings in chapter 1; later in this chapter, we will discuss some of the other findings and recommendations.

The parents of retarded children were to have the greatest impact on the education of the mentally retarded. Acting through their National Association for Retarded Children, both at the national level and in local chapters, they influenced legislators and legislatures to appropriate funds and to approve programs for establishment of educational facilities, training of personnel, and improvement of educational procedures. They helped to correct abuses that had existed for many years. With private funds, at first, and later with federal and state funds, they helped to establish *day-care centers* and provided for the replacement of many moderately and severely retarded children from state (hospital) institutions to *local residential facilities*. With the federal and local allocation of funds, local school systems increased the number of special classes for the retarded, increased the number of special teachers, and made many other improvements—most notably, perhaps, being the creation of *resource rooms* and *special learning centers*. Various national professional associations concerned with the problems of the retarded, especially the American Association on Mental Deficiency and the Council for Exceptional Children, greatly expanded their programs of support for research, conferences, seminars, and publications.

The passage of a number of Public Laws at the national level was of singular importance. A major breakthrough came with P. L. 85–926, in 1958, which authorized grants for developing professional personnel for the mentally retarded. There was a great need for such professional leadership, for without it methods and materials could not be developed. Some of the subsequent Public Laws include the following: P. L. 88–164, in 1963, provided funds for research and demonstration projects. It also offered additional assistance in the development of professional personnel. P. L. 89–313, in 1965, allocated federal funds to states to support state operated or supported schools for the handicapped. In 1966, P. L. 89–750 allocated funds for preschool through high school levels for the education of the handicapped. In 1969, P. L. 91–230, a very important law, made funds available on a comprehensive basis for many services for the handicapped, such as the establishment of training centers, the development of educational media, and the implementation of research. These laws benefited not only the mentally retarded and the handicapped but also the disadvantaged.

It may well be, however, that in the long run, actions brought before the courts by parents and interested organizations may have the most far-reaching effect. In court proceedings, interests of the disadvantaged and the mentally retarded often overlapped. A legal precedent was established in 1954 when the Supreme Court, in *Brown vs. Board of Education,* ruled that separate but equal school systems, which were used to separate blacks from whites, were not proper. This ruling established the legal foundation for many subsequent court actions on *dual systems* and on the *tracking systems* that not only separated the races, but also separated retarded and handicapped children from the mainstream of educational organization (Weintraub, 1972). The *Hobson vs. Hanson* case, to which we referred in chapter 11, was brought in Washington, D.C., in 1967 and was upheld in the U.S. Court of Appeals for the District of Columbia in 1968. It ruled that the tracking system used in Washington, D.C., was illegal, since it violated the equal protection clause of the U.S. Constitution. The issue was discrimination against blacks and poor children, but it led to many suits against the public schools for placing certain children in special classes for the retarded. Another case, challenging the use of the results of standardized tests as a basis for placing children in special classes for the retarded, was brought in 1970 before the United States District Court for the Southern District of California on behalf of nine Mexican-American students who had been given either the *Stanford-Binet Test* or the *WISC* in English (Ismard, 1972). It was argued that these tests were culturally biased, since they had been standardized on native-born Americans whose native language was English. By stipulation it was agreed by both parties to the suit that (1) all children whose primary language was not English had to be tested in their native language as well as in English; (2) Mexican-American and Chinese children who were in classes for the mentally retarded had to be retested in their primary language and had to be reevaluated on nonverbal tests; (3) misplaced children were to be given special attention in readjusting to regular classes; and (4) the state was to undertake the development of more appropriate intelligence tests.

Many cases claiming that blacks and disadvantaged children were being discriminated against were settled out of court. The following issues were involved:

I. Educational testing does not accurately measure the learning ability of the child;
II. The administration of these tests is performed incompetently;
III. The parents are not given adequate opportunity to participate in the placement decision;
IV. Special education programming is inadequate and placement into these classrooms causes irreparable harm.

Another type of case sought to improve the treatment of institutionalized mentally retarded children in the Pennhurst State School and Hospital in Chester County, Pennsylvania. This institution had a rated bed capacity of 2,126 but it had a resident population of 3,013, half of whom were over thirty years of age. The case was brought to the United States District Court in 1971. The outcome, as stated in the court's findings, was as follows: " . . . the Commonwealth of Pennsylvania may not deny any mentally retarded child access to a free public program of education and training . . . among the alternative programs of education . . . required to be available . . . placement in a regular public school class is preferable to placement in a special public school class and placement in a special public school class is preferable to placement in any other type of program of education and training" (Lippman and Goldberg, 1973). Thus, the Court's findings recognized that the issues transcended the specific school and hospital and were applicable to all mentally retarded children in the state. The influence of this case is apparent in subsequent attempts to improve conditions of living and training in state institutions and in the re-placement of many institutionalized children into residential facilities and community centers.

We have discussed (see chapter 11) the far–reaching implications of the class action that is pending in California and will undoubtedly be appealed to the Supreme Court. This case involves the whole issue of the role of intelligence testing in eductional decisions concerning retarded pupils and special education. The consequences for the construction and utilization of tests as well as for the conceptualization of congnitive functions have been discussed in that chapter.

In our judgment, the most far-reaching political action is that of P.L. 94–142, which also has been presented in previous chapters. The great sums of money that the federal government will plan to allocate for the handicapped ($3 billion by 1982) will require that each state wishing to receive "entitlements" present a state plan specifying such items as the kind and number of facilities, personnel and other resources to be made available, proper identification, location, and evaluation of the handicapped, and assurance that the handicapped will be educated with normal students. Not all states are accepting all provisions of this act. There undoubtedly will be continuing discussions concerning interpretations of the provisions of the law as well as modifications of the law. One major issue will continue to be how "handicap" is to be defined and measured. Many educational leaders have favored definition in terms of "services needed" rather than on the basis of "categories" of deviant behavior. Hobbs (1975) reported the recommendation of the experts that a standarized profile system be developed to replace categorization. Later, we shall comment further on the issue of "labels" and "categories."

Some of the possible effects of all of these court proceedings and political actions can be formulated as follows:

1. The process for evaluating children suspected of being mentally retarded (or of having a general learning disability) will be far less mechanical and far more critical than it has been.
2. The assessment process will consider background factors more deeply, especially language and cultural handicaps.
3. More weight will be given to current performance and ability in the classroom and to patterns of social behavior in natural settings.
4. When special placement is deemed necessary, it will be attempted on a trial basis, and revision of recommendation will be considered at regular, short intervals. "Because it is impossible to accurately predict the learning or behavioral ceiling for any child, no placement decision can be final (Mental Health Law Project, 1973).
5. Parental involvement will be required in all placement decisions affecting the child.
6. Team evaluations, rather than evaluations by professional experts only, will be the rule. The team usually will include teaching personnel, administrative personnel, the parent, and some professional assessment personnel.
7. Resources for flexible placement and individualized and remedial instruction will be greatly expanded, and movement toward mainstreaming as soon as possible, for as much of the school day as possible, will be attempted.
8. Impetus will be given to placement of severely retarded children in small residential facilities rather than large state institutions, and in community centers rather than residential facilities, whenever possible. Attempts will be made to incorporate the child into some form of public school program, at least part of the day.
9. Increased attention will be given to better professional training and in-service training of teachers of special education.

10. The program of education for the handicapped will extend from the pre-school level through the secondary school level.
11. Increased attention will be given to training parents in better home guidance for their children, as well as to involving them more completely in all aspects of the educational process.

LABELS AND CATEGORIES

We need not repeat our prior discussions of the arguments concerning the pros and cons of labeling individuals, nor review the indecisive evidence on this issue. Suffice it to say that (1) no label, no matter how sophisticated, can adequately describe a particular individual, and (2) it is not the label per se that is as decisive as are the conventional meanings attributed to it by society. Nevertheless, labels and categories have always been found necessary and useful for some purposes since some class actions and decisions are inevitable. It seems to us that a critical issue is providing a "label" when it is, indeed, indispensable that will not likely have negative implications or consequences, or at least will minimize such consequences.

One possible implication of our considerations is that *particular* labels always outlive their usefulness after a time, having acquired unfavorable connotations as knowledge about the underlying conditions improves. Hence, from time to time, the labels have to be changed both in order to render them more accurate and to divest them of their unfortunate "social loading." Another implication is to recognize that a label or category is only a rough and preliminary approximation of an individual's complex characteristics, and therefore it always should be followed by further and more detailed characteristics of the individual. Profiles offer one method of providing such additional details.

Nevertheless, since some forms of categorization will be found useful, we need to find categories that serve present knowledge and needs more effectively. Prior attempts such as the utilization of categories like *general learning disability* and *educationally handicapped* were aimed at serving such ends. Perhaps, however, in terms of our present technological and computerized age, we can designate labels or categories that have less pejorative qualities. For example, since the profoundly retarded, despite their varying individual characteristics, and in view of the evidence that suggests that most will require continuing care, support, and special training, could be categorized as L4 (designating a low expected rate of learning capability), or, L-4 736284, indicating both the general category (L4) and the values on a profile system. Such a nonsemantic designation might indicate that such an individual requires special provision for care and training, although the social and educational setting might vary depending on the individual's characteristics (i.e., his particular profile). Similarly, other levels of care and service, in which less support and specialized training might be involved, could be designated as L3, L2, and L1, respectively. Such a system also would eliminate the designation of either "mental" or "retarded," both of which carry unfavorable social connotations. This suggestion might also discourage the unnecessary connotation of "mentally retarded" for individuals who perform below average because of deprivations in social-educational experiences in infancy and early childhood, or because of linguistic handicaps, or for other, related reasons. The designations of L4 up to L1 could be utilized to represent the general levels of retardation described by the AAMD, but the criteria for inclusion in each of the categories could be periodically revised as new data accumulated and modification of criteria was needed. Additionally, the several items of the profile (the figures following the period after the general category) could be modified with further experience.

Our general point, however, is that *both* the category designation and the social attitudes of society need to be considered in any plan for identifying individuals needing specialized or supportive services. Efforts will need to be continually directed to both problems if more effective educational programming is to be stimulated.

More important than either label or category is the *service* that the individual needs. Toward this end, school programs need to become more innovative. (See later discussions of Normalization and Mainstreaming, and Orientation to the Future.) Newer types of programs such as programs with resource rooms and inverted pyramids, which have previously been discussed, have been developed and some have been found promising. But they are only "fillips" on the surface. Perhaps our concerns with the retarded will lead us eventually to much more basic reorganization of the educational structure. One set of proposals that seems to have considerable merit is that proposed by Sontag et al. (1977). They state: "Severely handicapped education represents one of three global instructional areas under a reorganization plan which would include early childhood education and general and special education as the other two areas." Then assignment of children to new areas would involve an evaluation of the child's "service requirements." The specific competencies of the teacher also would play a role in such assignment. Early childhood education would include training in basic skills such as self-help, motor skills, perceptual skills, communication skills, and the like. General special education would include preacademic instruction. As we indicated, this proposal seems to have merit, but I would argue that this kind of program could be extended to include education at all elementary school levels, for example, and all children—not only the retarded. Our current grade-level type of curriculum and our educational organization may be much too rigid. It should be possible to conceptualize an education program in which services are provided to all children in accordance with their needs, and with varying patterns of assignment depending on the profiles of skills of each child and the available school personnel. Such a type of educational organization also would make more readily feasible the mainstreaming of all children—a topic to which we turn next.

NORMALIZATION AND MAINSTREAMING

Our previous review of the issues and evidence concerning these topics indicated the many pros and cons that are involved. The *principle* of normalization does not require that we attempt to make all children normal; that is, that they should *all* participate and perform in *all* aspects of the educational program. Rather, it should mean: (1) that each child is assisted to attain *the maximum growth of which he or she is capable,* and (2) that no child is deprived of interpersonal experiences with the main body of school children *to the extent that that is possible.*

Normalization for some of the severely and, especially, for some of the profoundly retarded may be attainable only within restricted limits. Deinstitutionalization may be impossible for some who require intensive medical, rehabilitative or continuing custodial care. Still other retarded children may need special and intensive training that can best be offered in an institutional or special agency setting. There need be no opprobrium if such institutions are properly staffed, properly organized, suitably equipped and are appropriate in size and geographic location. Perhaps we can call them "havens," "retreats," "schools" or by other more positively toned names. Perhaps, as has been suggested, they can be organized to consist of inner, "small community" enclaves, rather than as huge and massive establishments. Perhaps children, who are able to, can spend some of their time outside of the agency, or the outside can be brought in by visits and programs that are pre-planned.

Both mainstreaming in schools and normalization or deinstitutionalization require more innovative planning and organization than we find at present. On the other hand, return to the community or return to the mainstream need not be an "all-time-thing" to accomplish their desirable objectives. We need to remind ourselves that "forcing" an individual into a situation with which the individual cannot (yet) cope may produce more difficulty than making some other type of accommodation. We should remember that, in the case of deinstitutionalization, failures are not infrequent (see McCarver, 1974; Peterson, 1977). For both deinstitutionalization and mainstreaming, adequate provision must be made in terms of facilities and programs as well as adequate assessment of the capabilities of the individual, with or without supervision, to "swim in the stream."

THE TRAINING OF TEACHERS

We have hardly begun to provide adequate training and in-service training programs for teachers who deal with the retarded, and we have done even less than that for "regular teachers" who must inevitably be increasingly involved in programs in which retarded pupils will function. In previous chapters, we cited some qualifications that are desirable for people who educate retarded children and children with other handicaps.

Let us speak frankly about some of the difficulties in providing such training. Our schools of education and other training agencies for teachers are presently ill-equipped to provide the needed training. They may be able to provide effective courses in child development, personality theory, philosophy of education, educational sociology, and training in research methodology. They can offer suitable courses on learning theory and the applications of such theory. However, many professors have never taught classes of retarded children, or have never dealt directly with school administrators. They are ill-equipped, therefore, to provide suitable models of teaching procedures and interpersonal relations with retarded pupils. They may have limited skills in demonstrating specific remedial teaching procedures. Of course, practicum and internship can be made part of the training programs. For effective learning of specific teaching methods, however, it might be better to employ expert teachers of the retarded to teach and to offer demonstrations as a regular part of the training program. In short, direct observation of skilled teaching and apprenticeship training with selected teachers of the retarded might be much more helpful. Other means of improving the effectiveness of the training programs may be employed, such as videotape lessons and discussions, and "laboratory" sessions. Our main point, however, is that there should be intensive upgrading of the applied aspects of teacher training by all means available.

Model programs of in-service training also are needed. Such programs might include demonstration teaching involving the "team approach" including the utilization of resource personnel in evaluating, planning programs, and carrying out the subsequent applications. Toward this end, substantial amounts of money and time will be needed—at least for some years—until an adequate pool of well-trained teachers for the retarded are available who can utilize fully modern techniques of evaluation and teaching and who can utilize other personnel in cooperative efforts in the program.

ORIENTATION TO THE FUTURE

We have made great strides in gaining a better understanding of mental retardation and in methods of dealing with it. We are still far short of the goals which leaders in the field have defined and we still have to face enormous problems. We can do no more than repeat our summary of the current needs that we have presented in our previous edition of this work, for they are still urgent needs.

1. *Prevention.* Mental retardation is a multifaceted problem. Its causes are multiple rather than unitary; they are interactive rather than simplex. Greatly expanded research programs are needed (some of them interdisciplinary) to study far more intensively the genetic, biological, cultural, and experiential factors in mental retardation. Only on the basis of more definitive findings can we hope to establish adequate preventive measures and adequate counseling procedures.

2. *Pregnancy and Genetic Counseling.* Many types of mental retardation could be prevented or could be ameliorated if the knowledge we already possess were put to proper use. We have discussed some of these conditions in previous chapters. Adequate programs of genetic counseling are essential, and funds must be made available to support the continuing counseling process and to support the family. In addition to offering expert advice and counseling, the program must deal with the nutritional-economic-social-cultural needs of the family.

3. *Infancy and Preschool Programs.* The care, nurturance, and training of the child and the child's family are part of an ongoing process. With the knowledge already available, great improvement may be made by providing resources and facilities for programs at the infant and preschool levels. Most likely, the schools are the appropriate agencies to administer such programs, with the active support and cooperation of social and community agencies. Research is urgently needed to evaluate the effectiveness of experimental and control programs.

4. *School Programs.* We have dealt at great length with some of the school programs that have been developed. We believe that much more innovation, combined with adequately planned research programs, is needed to consider some of the alternate proposals and provisions that have been advocated. We have stressed the importance of individualizing instruction and the merits of flexibility in planning and programming. One proposal that has received much attention in school programs is *accountability.* This term has been variously defined by different groups, but in general focuses on the desirability of holding educators and others accountable, or responsible, for the educational and behavioral outcomes of the programs. Gallagher (1972) has proposed that educators and parents formulate and sign a contract specifying the amount of progress that should be expected. Some schools have even contracted outside organizations specializing in personnel and training procedures to accomplish outcomes over a defined period of time. The whole idea of accountability is very complex. Although schools should be held accountable in a general sense, and although their programs should be carefully evaluated and improved when necessary, the idea of a specific contract for specific amounts of improvement is hazardous, in our opinion. For one thing, it assumes that we know far more than we actually do about the course of improvement in specific areas; hence, educators may attempt to meet contractual obligations, if forced to do so, by any means available—and at considerable expense to the child and the teacher. More important than this, the mechanical focus on contractual goals may greatly limit the creative, human, and intangible values that are an essential part of the educational process. These and other considerations should cause us to be highly cautious about the excessive or unthinking use of accountability programs.

5. *Vocational Training and Job Placement.* Much progress has been made in this area, but much more can be done. The aim of vocational training and on-the-job training should be employability. Much more remains to be done in integrating school programs with the needs of the individual and the community. Most retarded children can learn the kinds of personal and job skills that will enable them to support themselves or to contribute to their own support. To accomplish this, more attention needs to be given to the whole area of job training. Beyond this, there must be adequate provision for job placement, replacement when necessary, and counseling during the process of placement and adjustment.

6. *Personal and Family Counseling.* We devoted an entire chapter to parental reactions and family problems (chapter 10) because of the special problems in this area that often tend to be neglected. If we are to attain the full

social development of the retarded that we desire, programs of counseling for the retarded individual and for the individual's family must be greatly expanded. Available resources for counseling and psychotherapy are limited for the nonretarded population; they are even more limited for the adult retarded person and family. The total process of constructive adaptation of the mentally retarded to the community, as well as to a job, can be greatly facilitated by wise, effective counseling. Too often, the process terminates abruptly after the retarded individual leaves school.

7. *Education of the Community.* The problems of the retarded individual also are problems of the community—in some cases, they have been created by the community. Through education, much can be done to improve the community's understanding of these problems. The mass media can be used effectively in such programs, but they will need stimulation, financial support, and guidance. In the end, all of the programs for the retarded will stand or fall on whether the community understands and accepts that retardation is their problem, too.

REFERENCES

Abel, T. M. Resistances and difficulties in the psychotherapy of mental retardates. *Journal of Clinical Psychology,* 1953, *9,* 107–109.

Abelson, R. B., and Johnson, R. C. Heterosexual and aggressive behaviors among institutionalized retardates. *Mental Retardation,* 1969, *7,* 28–30.

Abt Associates. *Assessment of Selected Sources for Severely Handicapped Children and Youth, 5 Vols. Cambridge, Massachusetts: Abt Associates, 1974.*

Accreditation Council of Facilities for the Mentally Retarded (AC/FMR). Questionnaire for Superintendents of Public Residential Facilities that Have Not Applied for Survey. Chicago: Joint Commission on Accreditation of Hospitals, Evaluation Project, 1975.

Ackerson, L. Inferiority attitudes and their correlations among children examined in a behavior clinic. *Journal of Genetic Psychology,* 1943, *62,* 85–96.

Adams, J. Adaptive behavior and measured intelligence in the classification of mental retardation. *American Journal of Mental Deficiency,* 1973, *78,* 77–81.

Adams, J., McIntosh, E. I., and Weade, B. L. Ethnic background, measured intelligence, and adaptive behavior scores in mentally retarded children. *American Journal of Mental Deficiency,* 1973, *78,* 1–6.

Affleck, G. G. Role-taking ability and the interpersonal tactics of retarded children. *American Journal of Mental Deficiency,* 1976, *80,* 667–670.

Ainsworth, M. D. S. *Infancy in Uganda: Infant Care and Growth of Love.* Baltimore: Johns Hopkins Press, 1967.

Allen, R. M., Haupt, T. D., and Jones, R. W. Visual perceptual abilities and intelligence in mental retardates. *Journal of Clinical Psychology,* 1965, *21,* 299–300.

Alley, G. R. Perceptual-motor performances of mentally retarded children after systematic visual-perceptual training. *American Journal of Mental Deficiency,* 1969, *73,* 247–250.

Allport, G. W. *Pattern and Growth in Personality.* New York: Holt, Rinehart, & Winston, 1961.

Allport, G. W., and Odbert, H. S. Trait names: A psychological study. *Psychological Monographs,* 1936, *47,* No. 211.

Alper, A. E. An analysis of the Wechsler intelligence scale for children with institutionalized retardates. *American Journal of Mental Deficiency,* 1967, *71,* 624–630.

Alper, A. E., and Horne, B. M. Changes in IQ of a group of institutionalized mental defectives over a period of two decades. *American Journal of Mental Deficiency,* 1959, *64,* 472–475.

Ames, L. B., Metraux, R. W., and Walker, R. N. *Adolescent Rorschach Responses,* rev. ed. New York: Bruner/Mazel, 1971.

Anastasi, A. *Psychological Testing,* 4th ed. New York: Macmillan, 1976.

Anastasi, A., and Foley, J. P. A proposed reorientation to the heredity-environment controversy. *Psychological Review,* 1948, *55,* 239–249.

Anderson, D. E., and Coleman, R. O. The use of a receptive/cognitive approach in language habilitation. In Margary, J. F. et al. (eds.). *Piagetian Theory and Its Implications for the Helping Professions.* Proceedings of the 6th Interdisciplinary Conference. Los Angeles: University of Southern California, 1977.

Anderson, J. R. *Language, Memory and Thought.* Hillsdale, New Jersey: Lawerence Erlbaum Associates, 1976.

Andrew, G., Hartwell, S. W., Hutt, M. L., and Walton, R. E. *The Michigan Picture Test.* Chicago: Science Research Associates, 1955.

APA Psychology Monitor, 1977a, 8, November, p. 4.

APA Psychology Monitor, 1977b, 8, December, p. 5.

Appley, M. H. (ed.). *Adaptation-level Theory.* New York: Academic Press, 1971.

Aring, C. D. Senility. *American Medical Archives of Internal Medicine,* 1957, *100,* 519–528.

Asher, E. J. The inadequacy of current intelligence tests for testing Kentucky Mountain children. *Journal of Genetic Psychology,* 1935, *46,* 480–486.

Astin, A. W., and Ross, S. Glutamic acid and human intelligence. *Psychological Bulletin,* 1960, *57,* 429–434.

Astrachan, M. Group psychotherapy with mentally retarded female adolescents and adults. *American Journal of Mental Deficiency,* 1955, *60,* 152–156.

Ausubel, D. P. Negativism as a phase of ego development. *American Journal of Orthopsychiatry,* 1950, *20,* 796–805.

Ausubel, D. P. *Ego Development and Personality Disorders.* New York: Grune and Stratton, 1952.

Averill, J. Grief: Its nature and significance. *Psychological Bulletin,* 1968, *70,* 721–728.

Azrin, N. H., and Wesolowski, M. D. Eliminating habitual vomiting in a retarded adult by positive practice and self-correction. *Journal of Behavior Therapy,* 1975, *6,* 145–148.

Babab, E. Y. Pygmalion in reverse. *Journal of Special Education,* 1977, *11,* 81–90.

Babab, E. Y., and Budoff, M. *A Preliminary Manual of the Series Learning Potential Test.* Unpublished manuscript, Research Institute for Educational Problems, Cambridge, Massachusetts, 1971.

Badt, M. I. Levels of abstraction in vocabulary definitions of mentally retarded school children. *American Journal of Mental Deficiency,* 1958, *63,* 241–246.

Baer, D. M., Peterson, R. F., and Sherman, J. A. The development of imitation by reinforcing behavioral similarity to a model. *Journal of Experimental Analysis of Behavior,* 1967, *10,* 405–416.

Baker, B. L. Support systems for the parent as therapist. In Mittler, P. (ed.). *Research to Practice in Mental Retardation,* Vol. I. *Care and Intervention.* Baltimore: University Park Press, 1977.

Baker, B. L., Heifetz, L. J., and Brightman, A. J. *Parents as Teachers.* Cambridge, Massachusetts: Behavioral Education Projects, 1973.

Bakwin, H. Loneliness in infants. *American Journal of Disturbances in Children,* 1942, *63,* 34.

Baldwin, A. L. The effect of home environment on nursery school behavior. *Child Development,* 1949, *20,* 49–61.

Baldwin, A. L. *Behavior and Development in Childhood.* New York: Holt, Rinehart & Winston, 1955.

Balla, D. A., Nutterfield, E. C., and Zigler, E. Effects of institutionalization on retarded children: A longitudinal, cross-institutional investigation. *American Journal of Mental Deficiency,* 1974, *78,* 530–549.

Balthazar, E. E. *Balthazar Scales of Adaptive Behavior.* II. Scales of Social Adaptation. Palo Alto, California, Consulting Psychologists Press, 1973.

Balthazar, E. E. *Balthazar Scales of Adaptive Behavior for the Profoundly and Severely Mentally Retarded.* I. *Scale of Functional Independence,* rev. ed. Palo Alto, California: Consulting Psychologists Press, 1976a.

Balthazar, E. E. *Training the Retarded at Home or in School. A Manual for Parents, Teachers and Home Trainers.* Palo Alto, California: Consulting Psychologists Press, 1976b.

Balthazar, E. E., and Stevens, H. A. Scaler techniques for program evaluation with the severely mentally retarded. *Mental Retardation,* 1969, *7,* 25–29.

Bandura, A. The influence of rewarding and punishing consequences to the model in the acquisition and performance of imitative responses. Unpublished manuscript, Stanford University, 1962.

Bandura, A. Vicarious processes: a case of no-trial learning. In Berkowitz, L. (ed.). *Advances in Social Psychology,* Vol. 2. New York: Academic Press, 1965.

Bandura, A., and Jeffrey, R. W. Role of symbolic coding and rehearsal processes in observational learning. *Journal of Personality and Social Psychology,* 1973, *26,* 122–130.

Bandura, A., and Walters, R. H. *Social Learning and Personality Development.* New York: Holt, Rinehart and Winston, 1963.

Barnett, C. D., and Cantor, G. N. Discrimination set in defectives. *American Journal of Mental Deficiency,* 1957, *62,* 334–337.

Baroff, G. S. Current theories on the etiology of mongolism. *Eugenics Quarterly,* 1958, *5,* 212–215.

Baron, J. Temperamental profile of children with Down's Syndrome. *Developmental Medicine and Child Neurology,* 1972, *14,* 640–643.

Barrett, B. H. Behavior analysis. In Wortis, J. (ed.). *Mental Retardation and Developmental Disabilities,* Vol. IX, New York: Bruner/Mazel, 1977.

Barsch, R. H. The concept of regression in the brain injured child. *Exceptional Children,* 1960, *27,* 84–89.

Baumeister, A. A. The use of the WISC with mental retardates: A review. *American Journal of Mental Deficiency,* 1964, *69,* 183–185.

Baumeister, A. A. Learning abilities of the mentally retarded. In Baumeister, A. A. (ed.). *Mental Retardation.* Chicago: Aldine, 1967.

Baumeister, A. A. The American residential institution: Its history and character. In Baumeister, A. A., and Butterfield, E. (eds.). *Residential Facilities for the Mentally Retarded in the United States.* Worcester, Massachusetts: Hefferman Press, 1970.

Baumeister, A. A., Bartlett, J. A., and Hawkins, W. F. Stimulus trace as a predictor of performance. *American Journal of Mental Deficiency,* 1963, *67,* 726–729.

Baumeister, A. A., and Ellis, N. R. Delayed response performance of retardates. *American Journal of Mental Deficiency,* 1963, *67,* 714–722.

Bayley, N. On the growth of intelligence. *American Psychologist,* 1955, *10,* 805–810.

Bayley, N., and Schaefer, E. S. Maternal behavior and personality development from the Berkeley Growth Study. Presented at Regional Research Council, Child Development and Child Psychiatry, Iowa City, April, 1960.

Beargie, R. A., James, V. L., and Greene, J. N. Growth and development of small-for-date newborns. *Pediatric Clinics of North America,* 1970, *17,* 159.

Beery, K. E. *Models for Mainstreaming.* San Francisco: University of California, 1972.

Begab, M. J. The major dilemma of mental retardation: Shall we prevent it? (Some implications of research in mental retardation.) *American Journal of Mental Deficiency,* 1974, *78,* 519–529.

Begab, M. J. The mentally retarded and society: Trends and issues. In Begab, M. J., & Richardson, S. A. (eds.). *The Mentally Retarded and Society: A Social Science Perspective.* Baltimore: University Park Press, 1975.

Begab, M. J. Some priorities in research in mental retardation. In Mittler, P. (ed.). *Research to Practice in Mental Retardation,* Vol. I. *Care and Intervention.* Baltimore: University Park Press, 1977.

Begab, M. J., and Richardson, S. A. (eds.). *The Mentally Retarded and Society: A Social Science Perspective.* Baltimore: University Park Press, 1975.

Beier, D. C. Behavior disturbances in the mentally retarded. In Stevens, H. A., and Heber, R. (eds.). *Mental Retardation: A Review of Research.* Chicago: University of Chicago Press, 1964.

Beier, E. G., Gorlow, L., and Stacey, C. L. The fantasy life of the mental defective. *American Journal of Mental Deficiency,* 1951, *55,* 582–589.

Belch, P. J. An investigation on the effect of different questioning strategies on the reading comprehension scores of secondary level educable mentally retarded students. Unpublished doctoral dissertation, West Virginia University, 1974.

Bell, J. E. *Projective Techniques.* New York: David McKay, 1948.

Bellak, L., and Bellak, S. S. *Children's Apperception Test.* Chicago: Stoelting, 1950.

Belmont, I., Belmont, L., and Birch, M. D. The perceptual organization of complex arrays by educable mentally subnormal children. *Journal of Nervous and Mental Diseases,* 1969, *149,* 241–253.

Benaron, H. B. W., et al. Effect of anoxia during labor and immediately after birth on the subsequent development of the child. *American Journal of Obstetrics and Gynecology,* 1960, *80,* 1129–1142.

Benda, C. E. *Developmental Disorders of Mentation and Cerebral Palsies.* New York: Grune and Stratton, 1952.

Bender, L. *A Visual Motor Gestalt Test and Its Clinical Use.* New York: American Orthopsychiatric Association Monograph, No. 3, 1938.

Bender, L., and Andermann, K. Brain damage in blind children with retrolental fibroplasia. *Archives of Neurology,* 1965, *12,* 644–649.

Bennett, G. K. *Hand-Tool Dexterity Tests: Manual.* New York: Psychological Corporation, 1947.

Bennett, G. K. *Test of Mechanical Comprehension, Form AA: Manual.* New York: Psychological Corporation, 1948.

Benoit, E. P. The play of problem children. *American Journal of Mental Deficiency,* 1955, *60,* 41–55.

Benoit, E. Towards a new definition of mental retardation. *American Journal of Mental Deficiency,* 1959, *63,* 559–565.

Bereiter, C., and Engelmann, S. *Teaching Disadvantaged Children in the Preschool.* Englewood Cliffs, New Jersey: Prentice-Hall, 1966.

Bergin, A. E., and Strupp, H. H. *Changing Frontiers in the Science of Psychotherapy.* Chicago: Aldine-Atherton, 1972.

Bergin, A. E., and Suinn, R. M. Individual psychotherapy and behavior therapy. In Rosenzweig, M. R., & Porter, L. W. (eds.). *Annual Review of Psychology.* Palo Alto, California: Annual Reviews, 1975.

Bergman, M., and Fisher, L. The value of the Thematic Apperception Test in mental deficiency. *Psychiatry Quarterly Supplement,* 1953, *27,* 22–42.

Berkson, G., Hermelin, B., and O'Connor, N. Physiological responses of normals and institutionalized mental defectives to repeated stimuli. *Journal of Mental Deficiency Research,* 1961, *5,* 30–39.

Berman, L. L. Learning. In Wortis, (ed.). *Mental Retardation and Developmental Disabilities: An Annual Review,* Vol. VII. New York: Bruner/Mazel, 1975.

Bernard, C. Leçons sur les Propriétés Physiologiques et les Altérations. Patologiques des Liquides de l'Organisme (2 Vols.) Paris: Bailliere, 1859.

Bettleheim, B. *Love is Not Enough.* New York: Free Press, 1950.

Bettleheim, B. *The Empty Fortress.* New York: Free Press, 1967.

Betts, E. A. *Ready to Read Tests: Manual.* Meadville, Pennsylvania: Keystone View Co., 1934.

Bialer, I. Conceptualization of success and failure in mentally retarded and normal children. *Journal of Personality,* 1961, *29,* 303–320.

Bijou, S. W. A functional analysis of retarded mental development. In Ellis, N. R. (ed.). *International Review of Research in Mental Retardation,* Vol. 1. New York: Academic Press, 1963.

Bijou, S. W., Birnbrauer, J. S., Kidder, J. S., and Tague, C. Programmed instruction as an approach to teaching of reading, writing, and arithmetic to retarded children. *Psychological Record,* 1966, *73,* 505–522.

Bijou, S. W., and Peterson, R. F. The psychological assessment of children: A functional analysis. In McReynolds, P. (ed.). *Advances in Psychological Assessment,* Vol. 2. Palo Alto, California: Science and Behavior, 1971.

Biller, H., and Borstelman, L. Intellectual level and sex role development in mentally retarded children. *American Journal of Mental Deficiency,* 1965, *70,* 443–447.

Binder, V., Binder, A., and Rimland, B. *Modern Therapies.* Englewood Cliffs, New Jersey: Prentice-Hall, 1976.

Binet, A., and Henri, V. La psychologie individuelle. *Anné Psychologie,* 1895, *2,* 411–463.

Birch, J. W. *Mainstreaming.* Reston, Virginia: Council for Exceptional Children, 1974.

Bjornson, J. Behavior in phenylketonuria. *Archives of General Psychiatry,* 1964, *10,* 65–69.

Blackman, L., and Smith, M. P. *The Development and Evaluation of a Curriculum for Educable Retardates Utilizing Self-Instructor Devices or Teaching Machines.* Bordentown, New Jersey: Johnstone Training Center, 1964.

Blanchard, I. Speech patterns and etiology in mental retardation. *American Journal of Mental Deficiency,* 1964, *68,* 612–617.

Blanton, L. P. The relationship of organizational abilities to the comprehension of connected discourse in educable mentally retarded and nonretarded children. Unpublished doctoral dissertation, Indiana University, 1974.

Blanton, L. P., Sitko, M. C., and Gillespie, P. H. Reading and the mildly retarded: Review of research. In Mann, L., and Sabatino, D. A. (eds.) *The Third Review of Special Education.* New York: Grune and Stratton, 1976.

Blatman, S. Narcotic poisoning of children (1) through incidental ingestion of methadone and (2) in utero. *Pediatrics,* 1974, *54,* 329–332.

Blatt, B. The physical, personality, and academic status of children who are mentally retarded attending special classes compared with children who are mentally retarded attending regular classes. *American Journal of Mental Deficiency,* 1958, *62,* 810–818.

Blatt, B., and Kaplan, F. *Christmas in Purgatory: A Photographic Essay.* Boston: Allyn and Bacon, 1966.

Blattner, R. *Phenylketonuria: Phenylpyruvic aciduria. Journal of Pediatrics,* 1961, *59,* 294–298.

Blau, T. H. *Torque and schizophrenic vulnerability: As the world turns. American Psychologist,* 1977, *32,* 997–1005.

Blodgett, H. C. The effect of the introduction of reward upon the maze performance of rats. University of California Publications in Psychology, 1929, 4, 113–134.

Bloom, B. S. Stability and Change in Human Characteristics. New York: Wiley, 1964.

Blum, A. The relationship between flexibility in children and their parents. Child Development, 1959, 30, 304.

Blum, G. S. The Blacky Pictures: A Technique for Exploration of Personality Dynamics. New York: Psychological Corporation, 1950.

Boles, G. Personality factors in mothers of cerebral palsied children. Genetic Psychology Monographs, 1959, 59, 159–161.

Bolles, R. C. Reinforcement, expectancy, and learning. Psychological Review, 1972, 79, 394–409.

Bonneau, C. A. Paradigm regained? Cognitive behaviorism revisited. American Psychologist, 1974, 29, 297–304.

Böök, J. A., Schut, J. W., and Reed, S. C. A clinical and genetic study of microcephaly. American Journal of Mental Deficiency, 1953, 57, 637.

Borberg, A. Clinical and Genetic Investigations into Tubero-Sclerosis. Copenhagen: Munksgaard, 1951.

Borg, W. R., and Hamilton, E. R. Comparison between a performance test and criteria of instructor effectiveness. Psychological Reports, 1956, 2, 111–116.

Borokowski, J. G., and Wanchura, P. B. Mediational processes in the retarded. In Ellis, N. R. (ed.). International Review of Research in Mental Retardation, Vol. 7. New York: Academic Press, 1974.

Bortner, M., and Birch, H. G. Patterns of intellectual ability in emotionally disturbed and brain damaged children. Journal of Special Education, 1969, 3, 351–369.

Bortner, M., and Birch, H. G. Cognitive capacity and cognitive competence. American Journal of Mental Deficiency, 1970, 74, 735–744.

Bosiclair, C., and Dubreuil, G. La pensée précausale chez un groupe d'enfants martiniquais. In Benoit, J. Montréal, Centre de Reserches Caraibes, Université de Montréal, 1974.

Bourne, L. E., Ekstrand, R. B., and Dominoski, R. L. The Psychology of Thinking. Englewood Cliffs, New Jersey: Prentice-Hall, 1971.

Bowlby, J. Child Care and the Growth of Love. Baltimore: Penguin Books, 1953.

Bowlby, J. Attachment and Loss, Vol. I. Attachment. New York: Basic Books, 1969.

Braddock, D. Opening Closed Doors. The Deinstitutionalization of Disabled Individuals. Reston, Virginia: Council for Exceptional Children, 1977.

Braga, J., and Braga, L. Growing with Children. New York: Pergamon Press, 1974.

Braginsky, D. D., and Braginsky, B. M. Hansels and Gretels: Studies of Children in Institutions for the Mentally Retarded. New York: Holt, Rinehart, and Winston, 1971.

Brandon, M. W. G., Kirman, B. H., and Williams, C. E. Microcephaly. Journal of Mental Science, 1959, 105, 721–747.

Breger, L. From Instinct to Identity: The Development of Personality. Englewood Cliffs, New Jersey: Prentice-Hall, 1974.

Brenner, C. An Elementary Textbook of Psychoanalysis, rev. ed. New York: International Universities Press, 1973.

Brody, S. Patterns of Mothering, 2nd ed. New York: International Universities Press, 1970.

Brody, S., and Axelrad, S. Anxiety and Ego Formation in Infancy. New York: International Universities Press, 1970.

Broman, S. Y., Nichols, P. L., and Kennedy, W. A. Preschool IQ: Prenatal and Early Developmental Correlates. New York: John Wiley, 1975.

Bromwich, R. M. Focus on maternal behavior in infant intervention. American Journal of Orthopsychiatry, 1976, 46, 439–446.

Bronfenbrenner, U. *Is Early Intervention Effective,* Vol. II. New York: Cornell University Children's Bureau, 1974.

Browder, J. A., Ellis, L., and Neal, J. Foster homes: Alternatives to institutions? *Mental Retardation,* 1974, *12,* 33–36.

Brown, D., and Jones, E. Using the Bell Adjustment Inventory with the mentally retarded. *Rehabilitation Counseling Bulletin,* 1970, *13,* 288–294.

Brown, L., Huppler, B. Pierce, L., Scheuerman, N., and Sontag, E. Teaching young trainable students to report behavioral events. *Education and Training of the Mentally Retarded,* 1974, *9,* 15–22.

Brown, L., and Perlmutter, L. Training functional reading to trainable level retarded students. *Education and Training of the Mentally Retarded,* 1971, *6,* 64–84.

Brown, M. M. What's being missed in parent-infant counseling? Paper presented at the 11th Annual Conference, Association for Care of Children in Hospitals, Denver, Colorado, March 24–27, 1976.

Browning, P. L. *Mental Retardation: Rehabilitation and Counseling.* Springfield, Illinois: Charles C. Thomas, 1974.

Bruhl, H., Arneson, J. F., and Bruhl, M. G. Effect of low-phenylalanine diet on older phenylketonuria patients. (Long-range controlled study.) *American Journal of Mental Deficiency,* 1964, *69,* 225–235.

Bruininks, R. H. Physical and motor development of retarded persons. In Ellis, N. R. (ed.). *International Review of Research in Mental Retardation,* Vol. 7. New York: International Universities Press, 1974.

Bruininks, R. H., Rynders, J. E., and Gross, J. C. Social acceptance of mildly retarded pupils in resource rooms and special classes. *American Journal of Mental Deficiency,* 1974, *78,* 377–388.

Bruner, J. S. The course of cognitive development. *American Psychologist, 1964, 19,* 1–16.

Buchwald, A. M. Effects of "right" and "wrong" on subsequent behavior: A new interpretation. *Psychological Review,* 1969, *76,* 132–143.

Budoff, M. The relative utility of animals and human figures in a picture story test for young children. *Journal of Projective Techniques,* 1960, *24,* 347–352.

Budoff, M. Animal versus human figures in a picture story test for young mentally backward children. *American Journal of Mental Deficiency,* 1963, *68,* 245–250.

Budoff, M., and Purseglove, E. M. Peabody Picture Vocabulary Test: Performance of institutionalized mentally retarded adolescents. *American Journal of Mental Deficiency,* 1963, *67,* 756–760.

Buffmire, J. A. The stratician model. In Deno, E. N. (ed.). *Instructional Alternatives for Exceptional Children,* 1973.

Burks, B. S. The relative influence of nature and nurture upon mental development: a comparative study of foster parent-child resemblance and true parent-child resemblance. In *27th Yearbook, National Society for the Study of Education,* Vol. 1. 1928, 219–316.

Burnett, A. Comparisons of the PPVT, Wechsler-Bellevue, and Stanford-Binet scales on educable retardates. *American Journal of Mental Deficiency,* 1965, *69,* 712–715.

Buros, O. K. *The Mental Measurements Yearbook,* Vol. 7. Highland Park, New Jersey: Gryphon Press, 1972.

Burt, C. Intelligence and mental ability. *Eugenics Review,* 1957, *49,* 137–139.

Burt, C. The genetic determination of differences in intelligence: A study of monozygotic twins reared together and apart. *British Journal of Psychology,* 1966, *57,* 137–153.

Burton, T. A., Burton, S: F., and Hirshhoren, A. For sale: The state of Albama. (A commentary on litigation and the institutionalized retardate.) *Journal of Special Education,* 1977, *11,* 59–64.

Butterfield, E. C. The role of environmental factors in the treatment of institutionalized mental retardates. In Baumeister, A. A. (ed.). *Mental Retardation*. Chicago: Aldine, 1967.

Cain, L. F., and Levine, S. *Effects of Community and Institutional School Programs on Trainable Mentally Retarded Children*. Council on Exceptional Children Research Monographs, 1963, No. B-1.

Caldwell, B. The rationale for early intervention. *Exceptional Children,* 1970, *36,* 712–723.

Caldwell, B., and Guze, S. A study of the adjustment of parents and siblings of institutionalized and non-institutionalized children. *American Journal of Mental Deficiency,* 1960, *64,* 845–861.

Calhoun, K. S., and Matherne, P. The effect of varying schedules of time-out on aggressive behavior of a retarded girl. *Journal of Behavior Therapy,* 1975, *6,* 139–143.

Cannon, W. B. *The Wisdom of the Body,* rev. ed. New York: W. W. Norton, 1963.

Capobianco, R. J., and Knox, S. IQ estimates and the index of family integration. *American Journal of Mental Deficiency,* 1964, *68,* 718–721.

Carroll, J. B. *Language and Thought*. Englewood Cliffs, New Jersey: Prentice-Hall, 1964.

Carson, P., and Morgan, S. B. Behavior modification of food aversion in a profoundly retarded female: A case study. *Psychological Reports,* 1974, *34,* 954.

Carter, J. W., and Bowles, J. W. A manual on qualitative aspects of psychological examining. *Journal of Clinical Psychology,* 1948, *4,* 109–150.

Cashdan, A., and Jeffree, D. M. The influence of home background on the development of severely abnormal children. *British Journal of Medical Psychology,* 1966, *39,* 313–318.

Casler, L. Maternal deprivation: A critical review of the literature. *Monographs of the Society for Research in Child Development,* 1961, *26,* No. 2.

Cattell, J. Mc. Mental tests and measurement. *Mind,* 1890, *15,* 373–380.

Cattell, P. *The Measurement of Intelligence in Infants and Young Children*. New York: Psychological Corporation, 1947.

Cattell, R. B. *Personality*. New York: McGraw-Hill, 1950.

Cattell, R. B. *Anxiety, Motivation and Measurement*. New York: Harcourt, Brace and World, 1957.

Cattell, R. B. *Personality and Social Psychology*. San Diego, California: Robert R. Knapp, 1964.

Cattell, R. B. *Abilities: Their Structure, Growth, and Action*. Boston: Houghton Mifflin, 1971.

Cawley, J. J., Goodstein, H. W., and Burrow, W. H. *Reading and Psychomotor Ability among Mentally Retarded and Average Children*. Storrs, Connecticut: University of Connecticut, 1968.

CBS–TV Reports. *Hunger in the U.S.A.* Summer, 1968.

Cegelka, P. T. Sex role stereotyping in special education. A look at secondary work-study programs. *Exceptional Children,* 1976, *42,* 323–331.

Centerwall, S. A., and Centerwall, W. R. A study of children with mongolism reared in the home compared with those reared away from home. *Pediatrics,* 1960, *25,* 278–285.

Centerwall, W. R. and Centerwall, S. A. Phenylketonuria, the story of its discovery. *Journal of History of Medicine,* 1961, *16,* 192–296.

Chaffin, J. D., Spellman, C. R., Regan, C. E., and Davison, R. Two follow-up studies of former educable retarded students from the Kansas work-study project. *Exceptional Children,* 1971, *37,* 339–347.

Chaney, C. M., and Kephart, N. C. *Motoric Aids to Perceptual Training*. Columbus, Ohio: Charles E. Merrill, 1968.

Chao, D. Congenital neurocutaneous syndromes in children: II. Tuberous sclerosis. *Journal of Pediatrics,* 1959, *55,* 447–459.

Charles, D. C. Ability and accomplishments of persons earlier judged mentally deficient. *Genetic Psychology Monographs,* 1953, *47,* 3–71.

Chase, H. P., Dabiere, C. S., Welch, N. N., and O'Brien, D. Intrauterine nutrition and brain development. *Pediatrics,* 1971, *47,* 491–500.

Chasey, W. C., Swartz, J. D., and Chasey, C. G. Effect of motor development on body image scores for institutionalized mentally retarded children. *American Journal of Mental Deficiency,* 1974, *78,* 440–445.

Chazan, M. The incidence and nature of maladjustment among children in schools for the educationally subnormal. *British Journal of Educational Psychology,* 1964, *34,* 292–304.

Chein, I. *The Science of Behavior and the Image of Man.* New York: Basic Books, 1972.

Chess, S., and Korn, S. Temperament and behavior disorders in mentally retarded children. *Archives of General Psychiatry,* 1970, *23,* 122–130.

Children's Bureau. *Infant Mortality: A Challenge to the Nation.* Washington, D.C.: U.S. Department of Health, Education and Welfare, 1966.

Cianci, V. Objectives of home training. *Training School Bulletin,* 1953, *50,* 23–29.

Cicerelli, V. G. *The Impact of Head Start. An Evaluation of the Effects of Head Start on Children's Cognitive and Affective Development,* Vol. 7. Springfield, Virginia: Clearing House, 1969.

Clark, A. D., and Richards, C. J. Auditory discrimination among economically disadvantaged and non-disadvantaged preschool children. *Exceptional Children,* 1966, *33,* 259–262.

Clarke, A. D. B., Clarke, A. M., and Reiman, S. Cognitive and social changes in the feeble-minded—three further studies. *British Journal of Psychology,* 1958, *49,* 144–157.

Clarke, A. D. B., and Cookson, M. Perceptual-motor transfer in imbeciles: A second series of experiments. *British Journal of Psychology,* 1962, *53,* 321–330.

Clarke, C. A. The prevention of Rh isoimmunization. In McKusick, V. A., and Clairborne, R. (eds.). *Medical Genetics.* New York: Hospital Practice Publishing Co., 1973.

Clarke-Stewart, K. A. Interactions between mothers and their young children: Characteristics and consequences. *Monographs of the Society for Research in Child Development,* 1973, *38,* Serial No. 153.

Clausen, B. Quo vadis AAMD? *Journal of Special Education,* 1971, *6,* 51–60.

Cleverdon, D., and Rosenzweig, L. E. A work-play program for the trainable mental deficient. *American Journal of Mental Deficiency,* 1955, *60,* 56–70.

Cobb, H. V. Self-concept and the mentally retarded. *Rehabilitation Research,* 1961, *2,* 21–25.

Cobb, H. V. The forecast of fulfillment: A review of research on predictive assessment of the adult retarded for social and vocational adjustment. New York: Teachers College Press, Teachers College, Columbia University, 1972.

Cochran, I. L., and Cleland, C. Manifest anxiety of retardates and normals matched as to academic achievement. *American Journal of Mental Deficiency,* 1963, *67,* 539–542.

Collmann, R. D., and Newlyn, D. Changes in Terman-Merrill IQs of mentally retarded children. *American Journal of Mental Deficiency,* 1958, *63,* 307–311.

Collmann, R. D., and Stoller, A. Epidemiology of congenital anomalies of the central nervous system with special reference to the patterns in the state of Victoria, Australia. *Journal of Mental Deficiency Research,* 1962, 22–37.

Condell, J. S. Parental attitudes toward mental retardation. *American Journal of Mental Deficiency,* 1966, *71,* 85–92.

Condon, W. S., and Sanders, L. W. Neonate movement is synchronized with adult speech: interactional participation and language acquisition. *Science,* 1974, *183,* 99–101.

Conley, R. W. *The Economics of Mental Retardation.* Baltimore: Johns Hopkins, 1973.

Conroy, J. W., and Derr, K. E. *Survey and Analysis of the Habilitation and Rehabilitation Status of the Mentally Retarded with Associated Handicaps*. Washington, D.C.: Department of Health, Education and Welfare, 1971.

Courville, C. B., and Edmondson, H. A. Mental deficiency from intrauterine exposure to radiation. *Bulletin of Los Angeles Neurology Society,* 1958, *23,* 11–20.

Cowen, E. L., Dorr, D., Trost, M. A., and Izzo, L. D. Follow-up study of maladapting children seen by nonprofessionals. *Journal of Clinical and Consulting Psychology,* 1972, *39,* 235–238.

Craighead, W. E., and Mercatoris, M. Mentally retarded residents as paraprofessionals. *American Journal of Mental Deficiency,* 1973, *78,* 339–347.

Crawford, J. E. and Crawford, D. M. *Small Parts Dexterity Test: Manual*. New York: Psychological Corporation, 1949.

Credido, S. G. A construct validity study of a measure of perceptual approach-avoidance. Unpublished doctoral dissertation, University of Detroit, 1975.

Cromwell, R. L. Selected aspects of personality development in mentally retarded children. *Exceptional Children,* 1961a, *28,* 44–51.

Cromwell, R. L. Personality evaluation. In Baumeister, A. A. (ed.). *Mental Retardation: Appraisal, Education, and Rehabilitation*. Chicago: Aldine, 1961b.

Cromwell, R. L. Personality evaluation. In Baumeister, A. A. (ed.). *Mental Retardation*. Chicago: Aldine, 1967.

Cronbach, L. J. *Essential of Psychological Testing,* 3rd ed. New York: Harper and Row, 1970.

Cronbach, L. J., and Meehl, P. E. Construct validity. *Psychological Bulletin,* 1955, *52,* 281–302.

Cruickshank, W. M., Bentzen, F. A., Ratzeber, F. H., and Tannhouser, M. T. *A Teaching Method for Brain-Injured and Hyperactive Children*. Syracuse, New York: Syracuse University Press, 1961.

D'Amelio, D. *Severely Retarded Children: Wider Horizons,* Columbus, Ohio: Charles E. Merrill, 1971.

Daniels, L. K., and Hansen, K. P. Effects of social reinforcement and visual feedback on work production among mentally retarded sheltered workshop clients. *Psychological Reports,* 1976, *39,* 664.

Das, J. P., and Pivato, E. Malnutrition and cognitive functioning. In Ellis, N. R. (ed.). *International Review of Research in Mental Retardation,* Vol. 8. New York: Academic Press, 1976.

Davids, A., Spencer, D., and Talmadge, M. Anxiety, pregnancy, and childbirth abnormalities. *Journal of Consulting Psychology,* 1961, *25,* 74–77.

Davis, D. R. A disorder of mental retardation. *Journal of Mental Subnormality,* 1961, *7* (1 Whole Part No. 12), 13–21.

Davis, K. Final note on a case of extreme isolation. *American Journal of Sociology,* 1947, *52,* 432–437.

Davis, L. J. The internal consistency of the WISC with the mentally retarded. *American Journal of Mental Deficiency,* 1966, *70,* 714–716.

Deci, E. L. *Intrinsic Motivation*. New York: Plenum Press, 1975.

Deich, R. Reproduction and recognition as indices of perceptual impairment. *American Journal of Mental Deficiency,* 1968, *73,* 9–12.

DeMeyer, M., and Ferster, C. Teaching new social behavior to schizophrenic children. *American Academy of Child Psychiatry,* 1962, *1,* 443–461.

Denhoff, E. The impact of parents on the growth of exceptional children. *Exceptional Children,* 1960, *26,* 271–274.

Dennis, W. The effect of cradling upon the onset of walking in Hopi children. *Journal of Genetic Psychology,* 1940, *25,* 74–77.

Dennis, W. Causes of retardation among institutional children. *Iranian Journal of Genetic Psychology,* 1960, *96,* 47–59.

Denny, M. R. Memory and transformations in concept learning. *Journal of Experimental Psychology,* 1969, *79,* 63–68.

Deno, E. N. Where do we go from here? In Deno, E. N. (ed.). *Instructional Alternatives for Exceptional Children.* Reston, Virginia: Council for Exceptional Children, 1973.

Dentler, R. A., and Mackler, B. The Porteus Maze Test as a predictor of functioning abilities of retarded children. *Journal of Consulting Psychology,* 1962, *26,* 50–55.

Dilea, C. L. The use of the token economy with mentally retarded persons in a music therapy setting. *Journal of Music Therapy,* 1975, *12,* 155–160.

Dingman, H. F., and Meyers, C. E. The structure of intellect in the mental retardate. In Ellis, N. R. (ed.). *International Review of Research in Mental Retardation,* Vol. 1. New York: Academic Press, 1966.

Dingman, H. F., and Tarjan, G. Mental retardation and the normal distribution curve. *American Journal of Mental Deficiency,* 1960, *64,* 991–994.

Doll, E. A. Definition of mental deficiency. *Training School Bulletin,* 1941a, *37,* 163–164.

Doll, E. A. The essentials of an inclusive concept of mental deficiency. *American Journal of Mental Deficiency,* 1941b, *46,* 214–219.

Donnell, G. N., Collado, M., and Koch, R. Growth and development of children with glactosemia. *Pediatrics,* 1961, *58,* 836–864.

Drash, P. H. Habilitation of the retarded child: A remedial program. *Journal of Special Education,* 1972, *6,* 149–159.

Duckworth, E. Piaget rediscovered. *Journal of Research in the Science of Teaching,* 1964, *2, 3.*

Dugdale, R. L. *The Jukes: A Study of Crime, Pauperism, Disease, and Heredity.* New York: Putnam, 1877.

Dunn, L. M. Special education for the mildly retarded. Is much of it justifiable? *Exceptional Children,* 1968, *35,* 5–22.

Dunn, L. M. (ed.). *Exceptional Children in the Schools: Special Education in Transition.* New York: Holt, Rinehart and Winston, 1973.

Dunn, L. M., and Kirk, S. A. Impressions of Soviet psychoeducational service and research in mental retardation. *Exceptional Children,* 1963, *29,* 299–311.

Dunn, L. M., Neville, D., Bailey, C. F., Pochanart, P., and Pfost, P. The effectiveness of three reading approaches and an oral language stimulation program with disadvantaged children in the primary grades: An interim report after one year of the cooperative reading project. IMRID Behavioral Science Monographs (No. 7). Nashville: George Peabody College for Teachers, 1967.

Dunn, P. *The Peabody Picture Vocabulary Test Manual.* Minneapolis: American Guidance Services, 1959.

Durrell, D. D. *Analysis of Reading Difficulty: Manual of Directions.* New York: Harcourt, Brace and World, 1937.

Edgar, C. L., Kohler, H. F., and Hardness, S. A. A new method for toilet training developmentally disabled children. *Perceptual and Motor Skills,* 1975, *41,* 63–69.

Educational Policies Commission. *Policies for Education in American Democracy.* Washington, D.C.: National Education Association, 1946.

Egan, R. Should the educable mentally retarded receive driver education? *Exceptional Children,* 1967, *33,* 323.

Ehrman, L. Omenn, G. S., and Caspar, E. (eds.). *Genetics, Environment and Behavior: Implications for Educational Policy*. New York: Academic Press, 1972.

Eisenberg, L. Emotional determinants of mental deficiency. *American Medical Association Archives of Neurology and Psychiatry*, 1958, *80*, 119–121.

Ellis, N. R. The stimulus trace and behavioral inadequacy. In Ellis, N. R. (ed.). *Handbook of Mental Deficiency: Psychological Theory and Research*. New York: McGraw-Hill, 1963.

Ellis, N. R. Memory processes in retardates and normals. In Ellis, N. R. (ed.). *International Review of Research in Mental Retardation*, Vol. 4. New York: Academic Press, 1970.

Elvidge, A. E., Branch, C. L., and Thompson, C. B. Observations in a case of hydrocephalus treated with diamox. *Journal of Neurosurgery*, 1957, *14*, 628–639.

Epstein, M. H., Hallahan, D. P., and Kauffman, J. M. Implications of the reflectivity-impulsivity dimension for special education. *Journal of Special Education*, 1975, *9*, 11–25.

Erelenmeyer-Kimling, L., and Jarvik, K. L. F. Genetics and Intelligence: A review. *Science*, 1963, *142*, 1477–1478.

Eriksen, C. W. Psychological defenses and 'ego strength' in the recall of completed and incomplete tasks. *Journal of Abnormal and Social Psychology*, 1954, *45*, 45–50.

Erikson, E. H. The problem of ego identity. *American Psychoanalytic Association*, 1956, *4*, 58–121.

Erikson, E. H. *Childhood and Society*, rev. ed. New York: W. W. Norton, 1964.

Escalona, S. K. Feeding disturbances in very young children. *American Journal of Orthopsychiatry*, 1945, *15*, 76–80.

Estes, W. K. Reward in human learning: Theoretical issues and strategic choice points. In Glaser, R. (ed.). *The Nature of Reinforcement*. New York: Academic Press, 1971.

Evans, J. L. *Principles of Programmed Learning*. New York: Grolier, 1962.

Ewert, J. C., and Green, M. W. Conditions associated with the mother's estimate of the ability of her retarded child. *American Journal of Mental Deficiency*, 1957, *62*, 521–533.

Fahmy, M. *Initial Exploring of the Skilluk Intelligence*. Cairo, Egypt: Dar Misr Printing House, 1954.

Falconer, D. S. The inheritance of liability to disease with variable ages of onset, with particular references to diabetes mellitus. *Annuals of Human Genetics*, 1967, *31*, 1–20.

Farber, B. The effect of the severely mentally retarded child on family integration. *Society for Research in Child Development, Monograph*, 1959, *24*, No. 71. Yellow Springs, Ohio: The Antioch Press.

Farber, B. Perceptions of crisis and related variables in the impact of a retarded child on the mother. *Journal of Health and Human Behavior*, 1961, *1*, 108–118.

Farber, B. Effects of a severely retarded child on the family. In Trapp, P. E., and Himelstein, P. (eds.). *Readings on the Exceptional Child*. New York: Appleton-Century-Crofts, 1962.

Farber, B. *Mental Retardation: Its Social Context and Social Consequences*. Boston: Houghton Mifflin, 1968.

Farber, B., and Jenné, W. C. Family organization and parent-child communication: Parents and siblings of a retarded child. *Monographs of the Society for Research in Child Development*, 1963, *28*, No. 7.

Farber, B., and Royce, E. The mentally retarded: Valuable individuals or superfluous population. In Mittler, P. (ed.). *Research to Practice in Mental Retardation*, Vol. I. Baltimore: University Park Press, 1977.

Farley, G. K., and Blom, G. E. Mental health consultation to schools. In Mann, L., and

Sabatino, D. A. (eds.). *The Third Review of Special Education.* New York: Grune and Stratton, 1976.

Favell, J. E., Larsen, L. A., Seller, V., Boyd, L., St. Clair, J., Fleeman, G., and Jackson, L. Belvedere House: A group home program for severely retarded boys. Paper presented at Annual Meeting, American Association on Mental Deficiency, Chicago, June 1976.

Fenichel, O. *The Psychoanalytic Theory of Neurosis.* New York: W. W. Norton, 1945.

Ferster, C. B., and Simmons, J. Behavior therapy with children. *Psychological Record,* 1966, *16,* 65–71.

Feuerstein, R. *The Dynamic Assessment of Retarded Performers.* Baltimore: University Park Press, 1978.

Feuerstein, R., and Krasilowsky, D. Intervention strategies for the significant modification of cognitive functioning in the disadvantaged adolescent. *Journal of American Academy of Child Psychiatry,* 1972, *11,* 572–582.

Field, D. Long-term effects of conservation training with educationally subnormal children. *Journal of Special Education,* 1974, *8,* 237–241.

Finch, S. M. *Fundamentals of Child Psychiatry.* New York: W. W. Norton, 1960.

Fine, R. H., and Dawson, J. C. A therapy program for the mildly retarded adolescent. *American Journal of Mental Deficiency,* 1964, *69,* 23–30.

Finley, J. C., and Thompson, J. An abbreviated Wechsler Intelligence Scale for Children, for use with educable mentally retarded. *American Journal of Mental Deficiency,* 1958, *63,* 473–480.

Fisher, K. Effects of perceptual-motor training on the educable mentally retarded. *Exceptional Children,* 1971, *38,* 264–266.

Fisher, L. A., and Wolfson, I. N. Group therapy of mental defectives. *American Journal of Mental Deficiency,* 1953, *57,* 463–476.

Fishler, K., Koch, R., Donnell, G. N., and Graliker, B. Psychological correlates in glactosemia. *American Journal of Mental Deficiency,* 1966, *71,* 116–125.

Fix, A. J., and Haffke, E. A. *Basic Psychological Therapies: Comparative Effectiveness.* New York: Human Science Press, 1976.

Flavell, J. H. *The Developmental Psychology of Jean Piaget.* Princeton, New Jersey: Van Nostrand, 1963.

Fleishman, E. A. *The Structure and Measurement of Physical Fitness.* Englewood Cliffs, New Jersey: Prentice-Hall, 1964.

Foale, M. The special difficulties of the high-grade mental defective adolescent. *American Journal of Mental Deficiency,* 1956, *60,* 867–877.

Fodor, N. *The Search for the Beloved,* reprinted 1972. New York: Hermitage Press, 1949.

Forbes, L. Some psychiatric problems related to mental retardation. *American Journal of Mental Deficiency,* 1958, *62,* 637–641.

Ford, M. The Application of the Rorschach Test to Young Children. *University of Minnesota Institute for Child Welfare Monographs,* No. 23, 1946.

Fowle, G. M. The effect of the severely mentally retarded child on his family. American Journal of Mental Deficiency, 1968, *73,* 466–473.

Francis, R. J., and Rarick, G. L. *Motor Characteristics of the Mentally Retarded.* Cooperative Research Bulletin No. 1, USOE 35005. Washington, D. C: Government Printing Office, 1960.

Frandsen, A. N., McCullough, B. R., and Stone, D. R. Serial versus consecutive order administration of the Stanford Binet Intelligence Scales. *Journal of Consulting Psychology,* 1950, *14,* 316–320.

Frankel, H. M. Portland Public Schools' prescriptive education program. In Mann, L., and Sabatino, D. A. (eds.). *The Third Review of Special Education.* New York: Grune and Stratton, 1974.

Freeberg, N. E., and Payne, D. T. Parental influence on cognitive development: A review. *Child Development,* 1967, *38,* 65–87.

Freud, A., and Burlingham, T. D. *War and Children.* 1943 Reprint Edition. Westport, Connecticut: Greenwood Press, 1973.

Freud, S. *The Problem of Anxiety.* New York: W. W. Norton, 1936.

Freud, S. *A General Introduction to Psychoanalysis.* Garden City, New York: Doubleday, 1943.

Fried, A. Report of four years' work at the Guidance Clinic for Retarded Children, Essex County, New Jersey. American Journal of Mental Deficiency, 1955, *60,* 83–89.

Fries, M. E. The child's ego development and the training of adults in his development. In *The Psychoanalytic Study of the Child,* Vol. 2. New York: International Universities Press, 1946.

Fromm, E., and Hartman, L. D. *Intelligence: A Dynamic Approach.* Garden City, New York: Doubleday, 1955.

Frostig, M., and Harris, D. *The Frostig Program for the Development of Visual Perception: Teacher's Guide.* Chicago: Follett, 1968.

Furth, M. G. Intellectual health in school. What can Piaget's theory contribute? In Magary, J. F., Poulsen, M. K., Levinson, P. J., and Taylor, P. A. (eds.). *Piagetian Theory and its Implications for the Helping Professions.* Proceedings of the Sixth Interdisciplinary Conference. University Park, Los Angeles: University of Southern California, 1977.

Gallagher, E. E. The special education contract for mildly handicapped children. *Exceptional Children,* 1972, *38,* 527–535.

Gallagher, J. J. Measurement of personality development in preadolescent mentally retarded children. *American Journal of Mental Deficiency,* 1959, *64,* 299–301.

Gallagher, J. J. *The Tutoring of the Brain-Injured Mentally Retarded Child.* Springfield, Illinois: Charles G. Thomas, 1960.

Gallagher, J. J. New directions in special education. *Exceptional Children,* 1967, *33,* 441–447.

Gallagher, J. J., and Moss, J. New concepts of intelligence and their effect on exceptional children. *Exceptional Children,* 1963, *30,* 1–4.

Gampel, D. H., Gottlieb, J., and Harrison, R. N. Comparison of classroom behavior of special class EMR, integrated EMR, low IQ, and nonretarded children. *American Journal of Mental Deficiency,* 1974, *79,* 16–21.

Garber, H., and Heber, F. R. *The Milwaukee Project: Early Intervention as a Technique to Prevent Mental Retardation.* Storrs, Connecticut: University of Connecticut Technical Papers, 1973.

Garber, H., and Heber, R. The Milwaukee Project: Indications of the effectiveness of early intervention in the prevention of mental retardation. In Mittler, P. (ed.). *Research to Practice in Mental Retardation.* Vol. I, *Care and Intervention.* Baltimore: University Park Press, 1977.

Gardner, W. I. Personality concomitants of mental retardation. In Wilcox, R. K. (ed.). *Strategies for Behavioral Research in Mental Retardation.* Madison, Wisconsin: University of Wisconsin, 1961.

Gardner, W. I. Social and emotional adjustment of mildly retarded children and adolescents. *Exceptional Children,* 1966, *33,* 97–106.

Garfield, S. L., Wilcott, J. B., and Milgram, N. A. Emotional disturbance and suspected mental deficiency. *American Journal of Mental Deficiency,* 1961, *66,* 23–29.

Garrison, K. C. *Psychology of Adolescence.* Englewood Cliffs, New Jersey: Prentice-Hall, 1956.

Garrison, M. Jr. Personality: Another view. In Wortis, J. (ed.). *Mental Retardation and Developmental Disabilities*, Vol. VII. New York: Bruner/Mazel, 1975.

Garton, M. D. *Teaching the Educable Mentally Retarded.* Springfield, Illinois: Charles C. Thomas, 1961.

Gates-MacGinitie Reading Tests and Gates-MacGinitie Readiness Skills Test. New York: Psychological Corporation, 1965.

Gates, A. I., and McKillop, A. S. *Gates-McKillop Reading Diagnosis Test.* New York: Psychological Corporation, 1973.

Gesell, A., and Amatruda, C. S. *Developmental Diagnosis,* 2nd ed. New York: Hoeber Medical Division, Harper and Row, 1949.

Gesell, A., et al. *Gesell Developmental Schedules.* New York: Psychological Corporation, 1949.

Gesell, A., and Ilg, F. L. *Infant and Child in the Culture of Today,* rev. ed. New York: Harper and Row, 1974.

Geshuri, Y. Observational learning: Effects of reward and response patterns. *Journal of Educational Psychology,* 1972, *63,* 374–380.

Gibby, R. G. *A Manual for the Intelligence Rating Scale.* Richmond, Virginia: Science Research Institute, 1969.

Gibson, J. J. The useful dimensions of sensitivity. *American Psychologist,* 1963, *18,* 1–15.

Giles, D. K., and Wolf, M. M. Toilet training institutionalized severe retardates. *American Journal of Mental Deficiency,* 1966, *70,* 766–780.

Gilmer, B., Miller, J. O., and Gray, S. W. *Intervention with Mothers and Young Children: A Study of Intra-Family Effects.* Nashville, Tennessee: Demonstration Center for Early Education, George Peabody College, 1970.

Ginsberg, E., and Bray, D. W. *The Uneducated.* New York: Columbia University Press, 1953.

Glass, G. V. Note on Jensen and Rohwer's mental retardation, mental age and learning rate. *Journal of Educational Psychology,* 1969, *60,* 415–416.

Goddard, H. H. *Feeblemindedness: Its Causes and Consequences.* New York: Macmillan, 1926.

Goertzen, S. M. Speech and the mentally retarded child. *American Journal of Mental Deficiency,* 1957, *62,* 244–253.

Gold, E. M. A broad view of maternity care. *Children,* 1962, *9,* 52–58.

Gold, M. Research on the habilitation of the retarded: The present, the future. In Ellis, N. R. (ed.). *International Review of Research in Mental Retardation,* Vol. 6. New York: Academic Press, 1973.

Golden, M., and Birns, R. Social class and cognitive development in infancy. *Merrill-Palmer Quarterly,* 1968, *14,* 139ff.

Golden, M., and Birns, R. Social class and intelligence. In Lewis, M. (ed.). *Origins of Intelligence—Infancy and Early Childhood.* New York: Plenum Press, 1976.

Goldfried, M. R., Stricker, G., and Weiner, J. B. *Rorschach Handbook of Clinical Research Applications.* Englewood Cliffs, New Jersey, 1971.

Goldstein, H. *The Development of the Illinois Index of Self-Derogation.* Project Report No. SAE 8204. Washington, D.C.: United States Office of Health, Education and Welfare, 1964.

Goldstein, H., Moss, J., and Jordan, L. The efficacy of special class training of the development of mentally retarded children. USOE Project No. 619, United States Office of Education, 1965.

Goldstein, K. *The Aftereffects of Brain Injuries in War.* New York: Grune and Stratton, 1942.

Goodenough, F. L. *Exceptional Children.* New York: Appleton-Century-Crofts, 1951.

Goodenough, F. L. Experiments of raising the IQ. In Dennis, W. (ed.). *Readings in Child Psychology.* Englewood Cliffs, New Jersey: Prentice-Hall, 1951.

Goodman, H., Gottlieb, J., and Harrison, R. H. Social acceptance of EMR's integrated into a nongraded elementary school. *American Journal of Mental Deficiency,* 1972, *76,* 412–417.

Goodnick, B. A case of pseudoretardation. *Psychological Newsletter,* 1959, *10,* 331–335.

Goodstein, H., Kahn, H., and Cawley, J. The achievement of educable mentally retarded children on the Key Math Diagnostic Achievement Test. *Journal of Special Education,* 1976, *10,* 61–70.

Gordon, D. A., and Baumeister, A. A. The use of verbal medication in the retarded as a function of developmental level and response availability. *Journal of Experimental Child Psychology,* 1971, *12,* 95–105.

Gordon, H. Mental and scholastic tests among retarded children. An enquiry into the effects of school on the various tests. London: *Bulletin of Education Pamphlet,* No. 44, 1924.

Gorelick, M. C. The assessment of vocational realism of educable mentally retarded adolescents. *American Journal of Mental Deficiency,* 1963, *68,* 154–157.

Gorlow, L., Butler, A. J., and Guthrie, G. M. Correlates of self-attitudes of retardates. *American Journal of Mental Deficiency,* 1963, *67,* 462–466.

Gorth, W. P., and Hambleton, R. K. Measurement considerations for criterion-referenced testing and special education. *Journal of Special Education,* 1973, *6,* 303–314.

Goshen, C. E. Mental retardation and maternal neurotic attitudes. *Archives of General Psychiatry,* 1963, *9,* 168–174.

Gottlieb, J. Attitudes of Norwegian and American children toward mildly retarded children in special class. *Journal of Special Education,* 1974, *8,* 313–319.

Gottlieb, J., and Budoff, M. Social acceptability of retarded children in nongraded schools differing in architecture. *American Journal of Mental Deficiency,* 1973, *78,* 412–417.

Gottlieb, J., and Davis, J. E. Social acceptance of EMR's during overt behavioral interaction. In *Studies in Learning Potential.* Cambridge, Massachusetts: Research Institute for Education, vol. 2, 1971.

Gottlieb, J., and Siperstein, G. M. Attitudes toward mentally retarded persons: Effects of attitude referent specificity. *American Journal of Mental Deficiency,* 1976, *80,* 376–381.

Graham, F. K., Ernhart, C. B., Craft, M., and Berman, P. W. Brain injury in the preschool child: Some developmental considerations. *Psychological Monographs,* 1963, *77,* 573–574.

Gray, S. W. Home-based programs for mothers of young children. In Mittler, P. (ed.). *Research to Practice in Mental Retardation: Vol. 1, Care and Intervention.* Baltimore: University Park Press, 1977.

Gray, S. W., and Klaus, R. A. The early training project: A seventh year report. Child Development, 1970, *41,* 909–924.

Gray, W. S. *Standardized Oral Reading Paragraphs: Manual.* Bloomington, Illinois: Public School Publishing Co., 1915.

Greenacre, P. The early predisposition to anxiety. In Tompkins, S. S. (ed.). *Contemporary Psychopathology.* Cambridge, Massachusetts: Harvard University Press, 1943.

Greenacre, P. The biological economy of birth. In *The Psychoanalytic Study of the Child,* Vol. 1. New York: International Universities Press, 1945.

Greenfield, D. B. Novelty and familiarity as redundant cues in retardate discrimination learning. *Journal of Experimental Child Pyschology,* 1976, *21,* 289–302.

Grigsby, C. E., and Harshman, H. W. Teaching strategy and learning rate. *Mental Retardation,* 1977, *15,* 27–29.

Grinker, R. R., and Spiegel, J. P. *Men under Stress.* New York: McGraw-Hill, 1945.

Grossman, H. J. (ed.). *Manual on Terminology and Classification in Mental Retardation.* Baltimore: Garamond/Pridemark Press, 1973.

Gruen, G. E., and Zigler, E. Expectancy of success and the probability of learning of middle-class, lower-class, and retarded children. *Journal of Abnormal Pyschology,* 1968, *73,* 343–352.

Gruenwald, P. Chronic fetal distress and placental insufficiency. *Biology of the Neonate,* 1963, *5,* 215–265.

Guilford, J. P. *Personality.* New York: McGraw-Hill, 1959.

Guilford, J. P., and Hoepfner, R. *The Analysis of Intelligence.* New York: McGraw-Hill, 1971.

Guskin, S. L., Bartel, N. R., and MacMillan, D. L. Perspective of the labeled child. In Hobbs, N. (ed.). *Issues in the Classification of Children,* Vol. 2. San Francisco: Jossey-Bass, 1975.

Guthrie, E. R. *The Psychology of Learning.* New York: Harper, 1935.

Guthrie, G. M., Butler, A. J., and Gorlow, L. Patterns of self-attitudes of retardates. *American Journal of Mental Deficiency,* 1961, *66,* 222–229.

Guthrie, G. M., Butler, A. J., and Gorlow, L. Non-verbal expression of self-attitudes. *American Journal of Mental Deficiency,* 1964, *69,* 462–466.

Guthrie, G. M., Butler, A., Gorlow, L., and White, G. N. Non-verbal expression of self-attitude of retardates. *American Journal of Mental Deficiency,* 1963, *67,* 42–49.

Guthrie, R., and Susi, A. A simple phenylalanine method for detecting phenylketonuria in large populations of newborn infants. *Pediatrics,* 1963, *31,* 338–342.

Guyette, A., Wapner, S., Werner, H., and Davidson, J. Some aspects of space perception in mental retardates. *American Journal of Mental Deficiency,* 1964, *69,* 90–100.

Haddad, H. M., and Wilkins, L. Congenital anomalies associated with gonadal aplasia: Review of 55 cases. *Pediatrics,* 1959, *23,* 885.

Hagedorn, H. J. et al. *A Working Manual of Simple Program Evaluation Techniques for Mental Health Centers.* Rockville, Maryland: National Institute of Mental Health, 1976.

Hagen, J. W. The effect of distraction on selective attention. *Child Development,* 1967, *38,* 685–694.

Hall, C. S., and Domhoff, B. A. A ubiquitous sex difference in dreams. *Journal of Abnormal and Social Psychology,* 1963, *66,* 278–280.

Hall, H. V., Price, A. B., Shinedling, M., Preizer, S., and Massey, R. M. Control of aggressive behavior in a group of retardates using positive and negative reinforcement procedures. *Training School Bulletin,* 1973, *70,* 179–186.

Hallahan, D. P., Stainbach, S., Ball, D. W., and Kauffman, J. M. Selective attention in cerebral palsied and normal children. *Journal of Abnormal Child Psychology,* 1973, *1,* 280–291.

Hallenbach, C. E. Evidence for a multiple process view of mental deterioration. Paper presented at Midwest Psychological Association, 1963.

Halpern, A. S., Browning, P. L., and Brummer, E. R. Vocational adjustment of the mentally retarded. In Begab, M. J., and Richardson, S. A. (eds.). *The Mentally Retarded and Society: A Social Science Perspective.* Baltimore: University Park Press, 1975.

Hammons, G. W. Educating the mildly retarded: A review. *Exceptional Children,* 1972, *38,* 565–570.

Haring, N. G., Hayden, A. H., and Nolen, P. A. Accelerating approximate behaviors of children in a Head Start program. *Exceptional Children,* 1969, *35,* 773–784.

Haring, N. G., and Stables, J. M. The effect of gross motor development on visual perception and eye-hand coordination. *Physical Therapy,* 1966, *46,* 129–135.

Harlow, H. F. *Learning to Love.* San Francisco: Albion Press, 1971.

Harris, L. M. Reactions of adolescent mentally deficient girls to a permissive atmosphere in an academic atmosphere. *American Journal of Mental Deficiency,* 1953, *57,* 434–446.

Harris, L. M. A method for studying and treating behavior problems in the classroom. *American Journal of Mental Deficiency,* 1955, *59,* 595–600.

Harter, S., and Zigler, E. The assessment of effectance motivation in normal and retarded children. *Developmental Psychology,* 1974, *10,* 169–180.

Hartmann, H. Comments on the psychoanalytic formulation of the ego. In Freud, A. et al. (eds.). *The Psychoanalytic Study of the Child,* Vol. 5. New York: International Universities Press, 1950.

Hartmann, H., Kris, E., and Lowenstein, R. M. Comments on the formation of pyschic structure. In Freud, A. et al. (eds.). *The Psychoanalytic Study of the Child,* Vol. 2. New York: International Universities Press, 1947.

Haworth, M. R. *The Primary Visual Motor Test.* New York: Grune and Stratton, 1970.

Hayden, A. H., and Haring, N. G. The acceleration and maintenance of developmental gains in Down's syndrome school-age children. In Mittler, P. (ed.). *Research to Practice in Mental Retardation,* Vol. 1. *Care and Intervention.* Baltimore: University Park Press, 1977.

Haywood, R. C. Perceptual handicap: fact or artifact. *Child Study,* 1966–67, *28,* 2–13.

Hebb, D. O. *The Organization of Behavior,* New York: John Wiley and Sons, 1949.

Hebb, D. O. The motivating effects of exteroceptive stimulation. *American Psychologist,* 1958, *13,* 109–113.

Heber, R. F. A manual on terminology and classification in mental retardation. *American Journal of Mental Deficiency,* 1959, *64,* Monograph Supplement No. 2.

Heber, R. F. Progress report II: An experiment in the prevention of cultural-familial retardation. Proceedings of the 3rd Congress, IASSMD, The Hague, 1973.

Heber, R. F. The Milwaukee Project: A study of the use of family intervention to prevent cultural-familial mental retardation. In *Exceptional Infant,* Vol. 3. *Assessment and Intervention.* New York: Bruner/Mazel, 1975.

Heber, R. F., Dever, R., and Conry, J. The influence of environmental and genetic variables on intellectual development. *Behavior Research in Mental Retardation.* Eugene, Oregon: University of Oregon, 1968.

Heber, R. F., and Garber, H. An experiment in the prevention of cultural-familial familial retardation. Paper presented at the 2nd Congress of the International Association for the Scientific Study of Mental Deficiency, Warsaw, Poland, August 25–September 2, 1970.

Heber, R. F., and Garber, H. *An Experiment in the Prevention of Cultural-Familial Mental Retardation.* Madison, Wisconsin: Rehabilitation and Training Center, University of Wisconsin, 1971.

Heber, R. F., Harrington, S., Garber, H., and Thelan, M. An experiment in the prevention of socio-cultural retardation: The Milwaukee Project. Presented at the 96th Annual Meeting, American Association of Mental Deficiency, Minneapolis, May 18, 1972.

Heber, R. F., and Stevens, H. A. *Research in Mental Retardation.* Chicago: University of Chicago Press, 1963.

Heider, F. *The Psychology of Interpersonal Relations.* New York: John Wiley and Sons, 1958.

Heifetz, L. J. Professional preciousness and the evolution of parent strategies. In Mittler, P. (ed.). *Research to Practice in Mental Retardation,* Vol. I. *Care and Intervention.* Baltimore: University Park Press, 1977.

Heinstein, M. I. Behavioral correlates of breast-bottle regimes under varying parent-infant relationships. *Monographs of the Society for Research in Child Development.* 1963, *28,* No. 4.

Heiser, K. F. Psychotherapy in a residential school for mentally retarded children. *Training School Bulletin,* 1954, *50,* 211–218.

Heller, A. W. The resource room: Mere change or real opportunity for the handicapped? *Journal of Special Education,* 1972, *6,* 396–375.

Helsel, E. D. Residential services. In Wortis, J. (ed.). *Mental Retardation and Developmental Disabilities,* Vol. 3. New York: Bruner/Mazel, 1971.

Hermelin, B., and O'Connor, N. Short-term memory in normal and subnormal children. *American Journal of Mental Deficiency,* 1964, *69,* 121–125.

Hertzig, H., Birch, H., Thomas, A., and Mendez, O. Class and ethnic differences in the responsiveness of preschool children to cognitive demands. *Monographs of the Society for Research in Child Development,* 1968, 33, 1.

Hess, R. D., and Shipman, V. Early experiences and the socialization of cognitive modes in children. *Child Development,* 1965, *36,* 869–886.

Hewett, F. M., and Forness, S. R. *Education of Exceptional Learners.* Boston: Allyn and Bacon, 1974.

Hildreth, G., et al. *Metropolitan Achievement Tests: Manual for Interpreting.* New York: Harcourt, Brace and World, 1948.

Hildreth, G., and Griffiths, N. L. *Metropolitan Reading Readiness Test: Directions for Administering and Scoring.* New York: Harcourt, Brace and World, 1949.

Hilgard, E. R. *Divided Consciousness: Multiple Controls in Human Behavior.* New York: John Wiley and Sons, 1977.

Himmelstein, P. Use of the Stanford-Binet Form L–M with retardates: A review of recent research. *American Journal of Mental Deficiency,* 1968, *72,* 691–699.

Hirsch, E. A. The adaptive significance of commonly described behavior of the mentally retarded. *American Journal of Mental Deficiency,* 1959, *63,* 644–649.

Hobbs, N. (ed.). *Issues in the Classification of Children,* Vols. 1 and 2. San Francisco: Jossey-Bass, 1975.

Hoch, P. H., and Zubin, J. (eds.). *Anxiety.* New York: Hafner Press, 1964 (Reprint).

Hodges, H. F., and Felling, J. P. Types of stressful situations and their relation to trait anxiety and sex. *Journal of Consulting Psychology,* 1970, *34,* 333–337.

Hoefstaetter, P. R. The changing composition of intelligence: a study of the t-technique. *Journal of Genetic Psychology,* 1954, *85,* 159–164.

Holtzmann, W. H. The Holtzman Inkblot Technique. In Rabin, A. I. (ed.). *Projective Techniques in Personality Assessment.* New York: Springer Publishing Company, 1968.

Hovland, C. The generalization of conditioned responses. *Journal of Genetic Psychology,* 1937, *17,* 125–148.

Howarth, E., and Cattell, R. B. The multivariate experimental contribution to personality research. In Wolman, B. B. (ed.). *Handbook of General Psychology.* Englewood Cliffs, New Jersey: Prentice-Hall, 1973.

Hull, C. L. *A Behavior System.* New Haven, Connecticut: Yale University Press, 1952.

Hull, F. M. Speech impaired children. In Dunn, L. M. (ed.). *Exceptional Children in the Schools.* New York: Holt, Rinehart and Winston, 1963.

Hundziak, M., Maurer, R., and Watson, L. Operant conditioning in the toilet training of several mentally retarded boys. *American Journal of Mental Deficiency,* 1965, *60,* 120–124.

Hungerford, R. H. Editor's page. *American Journal of Mental Deficiency,* 1955, *60,* ii–iii.

Hungerford, R. H., DeProspo, C. J., and Rosenzweig, L. E. Education of the mildly handicapped child in childhood and adolescence. *American Journal of Mental Deficiency,* 1952, *57,* 214–228.

Hunt, E., Frost, N., and Lunneberg, C. Individual differences in cognition: A new approach to intelligence. In Bower, G. H. (ed.). *The Psychology of Learning and Motivation,* Vol. 7. New York: Academic Press, 1973.

Hunt, J. McV. *Intelligence and Experience.* New York: Ronald Press, 1961.

Hunt, J. McV. Environment, development, and scholastic achievement. In Deutsch, M., Katz, I., and Jensen, A. R. (eds.). *Social Class, Race, and Psychological Development.* New York: Holt, Rinehart and Winston, 1968.

Hunt, J. McV. *The Challenge of Incompetence and Poverty.* Urbana, Illinois: University of Illinois Press, 1969.

Hunt, N. *The World of Nigel Hunt: The Diary of Mongoloid Youth.* New York: Garrett, 1967.

Hurley, J. R. Parental malevolence and children's intelligence. *Journal of Consulting Psychology,* 1967, *31,* 199–204.

Hurley, O. L. The categorical/noncategorical issue: Implications for teacher trainers. Conference Proceeding, University of Missouri-Columbia, 1971. Also in Kirk, S. A., and Lord, F. E. *Exceptional Children.* Boston: Houghton Mifflin, 1974.

Hutt, M. L. The use of projective methods of personality measurement in Army medical installations. *Journal of Clinical Psychology,* 1945a, *1,* 134–140.

Hutt, M. L. A tentative guide for the administration and interpretation of the Bender-Gestalt Test. U. S. Army, Adjutant General's School, 1945b.

Hutt, M. L. A clinical study of "consecutive" and "adaptive" testing with the revised Stanford-Binet. *Journal of Consulting Psychology,* 1947, *11,* 93–103.

Hutt, M. L. *The Hutt Adaptation of the Bender-Gestalt Test,* 2nd. ed. New York: Grune and Stratton, 1969.

Hutt, M. L. The significance of perceptual adience-abience in child development. In Siva Sankar, D. V. (ed.). *Mental Health in Children,* Vol. II. Westbury, New York: 1976.

Hutt, M. L. *The Hutt Adaptation of the Bender-Gestalt Test,* 3rd ed. New York: Grune and Stratton, 1977a.

Hutt, M. L. *Psychosynthesis: Vital Therapy.* Oceanside, New York: Dabor Science Publications, 1977b.

Hutt, M. L. Adience-abience. In Woody, R. H. (ed.), *Encyclopedia of Clinical Assessment.* San Francisco: Jossey Bass, In press.

Hutt, M. L., and Briskin, G. J. *The Hutt Adaptation of the Bender-Gestalt Test.* New York: Grune and Stratton, 1960.

Hutt, M. L., and Dates, B. G. Reliabilities and interrelationships of two HABGT scales in a male delinquent population. *Journal of Personality Assessment,* 1977, *41,* 353–357.

Hutt, M. L., Dates, B. G., and Reid, D. M. The predictive ability of HABGT scales for a male delinquent population. *Journal of Personality Assessment,* 1977, *41,* 492–496.

Hutt, M. L., and Feueretile, D. The clinical meanings and predictions of a measure of perceptual adience-abience. Paper presented at American Psychological Association, Philadelphia, 1963.

Hutt, M. L., and Gibby, R. G., *Patterns of Abnormal Behavior.* Boston: Allyn and Bacon, 1957.

Hutt, M. L., and Gibby, R. G. *The Child: Development and Adjustment.* Boston: Allyn and Bacon, 1959.

Hutt, M. L., and Gibby, R. G. *An Atlas for the Hutt Adaptation of the Bender-Gestalt Test.* New York: Grune and Stratton, 1970.

Hutt, M. L., and Miller, D. Social values and personality development. *Journal of Social Issues,* 1949, *5,* 2–49.

Hutt, M. L., and Miller, L. J. Further studies of a measure of adience-abience. *Journal of Personality Assessment,* 1975, *39,* 123–128.

Hutt, M. L., and Miller, L. J. Interrelationships of psychopathology and adience-abience. *Journal of Personality Assessment,* 1976, *40,* 135–139.

Inhelder, B., and Piaget, J. *The Growth of Logical Thinking from Childhood to Adolescence.* New York: Basic Books, 1958.

Institute of Medicine, National Academy of Sciences. Infant death: An analysis by maternal risk and health care. ISBN No. 0–309–02119–7, 1973.

Institute for the Study of Mental Retardation and Related Disabilities, and the University Council for Educational Administration. *Special Education and Litigation for Professional and Educational Practice.* Ann Arbor, Michigan, unpublished, 1972.

Isaacson, R. L. *The Retarded Child: A Guide for Parents and Friends.* Niles, Indiana: Argus Communications, 1974.

Isaacson, R. L., and Hutt, M. L. *Psychology: The Science of Behavior,* 2nd ed. New York: Harper and Row, 1971.

Jackson, L., and Todd, K. M. *Child Treatment and the Theory of Play.* New York: Ronald Press, 1950.

Jacobs, J., and Pierce, M. The social position of retardates with brain damage-associated characteristics. *Exceptional Children,* 1968, *34,* 677–681.

James, W. *Principles of Psychology.* New York: Henry Holt, 1890.

Jeffrey, D. M., McConkey, R., and Hewson, S. A. Parental involvement project. In Mittler, P. (ed.). *Research to Practice in Mental Retardation,* Vol. I. *Care and Intervention.* Baltimore: University Park Press, 1977.

Jensen, A. R. How much can we boost the IQ and scholastic achievement? *Harvard Educational Review,* 1969, *39,* 1–123.

Jensen, A. R. The role of mediation in mental development. *Journal of Genetic Psychology,* 1971, *118,* 39–70.

Jensen, A. R., and Rohwer, W. D. Jr. The effect of verbal mediation on the learning and retention of paired-associates by retarded adults. *American Journal of Mental Deficiency,* 1963, *68,* 80–84.

Jensen, A. R., and Rohwer, W. D. Jr. Mental retardation, mental age, and learning rate. *Journal of Educational Psychology,* 1968, *59,* 402–403.

Jervis, G. A. The mental deficiencies. In Arieti, S. (ed.). *American Handbook of Psychiatry,* Vol. 2. New York: Basic Books, 1959.

Johnson, G. O. A study of the social position of mentally handicapped children in the regular grades. *American Journal of Mental Deficiency,* 1950, *65,* 60–89.

Johnson, G. O. *A Comparative Study of the Personal and Social Adjustment of Mentally Handicapped Children Placed in Special Classes with Mentally Handicapped Children who Remain in Regular Classes.* Syracuse, New York: Syracuse Research Institute, 1961.

Johnson, G. O., and Blake, K. A. *Learning Performance of Retarded and Normal Children.* Syracuse, New York: Syracuse University Press, 1960.

Johnson, W. Darley, F., and Spriesterbach, D. C. *Diagnostic Methods in Speech Pathology.* New York: Harper, 1963.

Jones, R. L. Labels and stigmas in special education. *Exceptional Children,* 1972, *38,* 533–564.

Jordan, T. E. *The Mentally Retarded,* 3rd ed. Columbus, Ohio: Charles E. Merrill, 1972.

Jordan, T. E., and DeCharms, R. The achievement motive in normals and retarded children. *American Journal of Mental Deficiency*, 1960, *65,* 42–45.

Junkala, J. Task analysis and instructional alternatives. *Academic Therapy*, 1972, *8,* 33–40.

Kagan, J. The first critical period. In Janis, I., Mahl, G. F., Kagan, J., and Holt, R. R. *Personality: Dynamics, Development, and Assessment.* New York: Harcourt, Brace and World, 1969.

Kagan, J. On class differences and early development. In Dennenberg, V. (ed.). *Education of the Infant and Young Child.* New York: Academic Press, 1970.

Kagan, J., and Havemann, E. *Psychology: An Introduction,* 2nd ed. New York: Harcourt Brace Jovanovich, 1972.

Kagan, J., and Moss, H. A. Maternal influences on early IQ scores. *Psychological Reports,* 1958, *4,* 655–661.

Kalckar, H. M., Kinoshita, J. H., and Donnell, G. N. Glactosemia: Biochemistry, genetics, pathophysiology and developmental aspects. *Biology of Brain Dysfunction,* 1973, *1,* 31–88.

Kanfer, F. H., and Phillips, J. S. *Learning Foundations for Behavior Therapy.* New York: John Wiley and Sons, 1970.

Kanner, L. *A Miniature Text Book of Feeblemindedness.* New York: Child Care Publications, 1949.

Kanner, L. Parents' feelings about retarded children. *American Journal of Mental Deficiency,* 1953, *57,* 375–383.

Kanner, L. Parent counseling. In Rothstein, H. (ed.). *Mental Retardation.* New York: Holt, Rinehart and Winston, 1961.

Kanner, L. *Child Psychiatry,* 4th ed. Springfield, Illinois: Charles C. Thomas, 1972.

Kansas City, Public Schools. A curriculum guide for teachers of pupils, educable but mentally retarded, Grades 7–12. Kansas City, Missouri: Public Schools, July 1959 (Secondary Curriculum Guide, 109).

Karnes, M. B. *Helping Young Children Develop Language Skills: A Book of Activities.* Arlington, Virginia: Council for Exceptional Children, 1968.

Karnes, M. B., Hodgins, A., and Teska, J. An evaluation of two preschool programs for disadvantaged children. A traditional and a highly structured experimental school. *Exceptional Children,* 1968, *34,* 667–676.

Karnes, M. B., Teska, J. A., and Hodgins, A. S. *A Longitudinal Study of Disadvantaged Children Who Participated in Three Different School Programs.* Champaign, Illinois: University of Illinois, Research for Exception Children, 1969.

Kass, N., and Stevenson, H. W. The effects of pretraining reinforcement conditions on learning by normal and retarded children. *American Journal of Mental Deficiency,* 1961, *66,* 76–80.

Kawi, A. A., and Pasamanick, B. Prenatal and parental factors in the development of childhood reading disorders. *Monographs of the Society for Research in Child Development,* 1959, No. *4,* Serial 73.

Keller, S. The social world of the urban slum child: Some early findings. *American Journal of Orthopsychiatry,* 1963, *33,* 823–831.

Kelley, T. L., Madden, R., Gardner, E. F., Terman, L. M., and Ruch, G. M. *Stanford Achievement Test: Manuals for Primary, Elementary, Intermediate, and Advanced Batteries.* New York: Harcourt, Brace and World, 1953.

Kendler, T. S. An ontogeny of mediational deficiency. *Child Development,* 1972, *43,* 1–17.

Kennedy, R. J. R. A Connecticut community revisited: A study of social adjustment of a group of mentally deficient adults in 1948 and 1960. In Jordan, T. E. (ed.). *Perspectives in Mental Retardation.* Carbondale, Illinois: Southern University Press, 1965.

Kenney, E. Mother-retarded child relationships. *American Journal of Mental Deficiency,* 1967, *71,* 631–636.

Kent, G. H., and Shakow, D. Grade series of form boards. *Personnel Journal,* 1928, *7,* 115–120.

Kephart, N. C. Perceptual-motor aspects of learning disabilities. *Exceptional Children,* 1967, *72,* 422–427.

Kephart, N. C. *The Slow Learner in the Classroom,* 2nd ed. Columbus, Ohio: Charles E. Merrill, 1971.

Kern, W. H., and Pfaeffle, H. A comparison of social adjustment of mentally retarded children in various educational settings. *American Journal of Mental Deficiency,* 1965, *67,* 407–413.

Kiesler, C. A. *The Psychology of Commitment: Experiences Linking Behavior to Belief.* New York: Academic Press, 1971.

Kilman, B. and Fisher, G. An evaluation of the Finley-Thompson abbreviated form of the WISC for undifferentiated brain damaged and familial retardates. *American Journal of Mental Deficiency,* 1960, *64,* 742–746.

Kinsey, A. C., Pomeroy, W. B., and Martin, C. E. *Sexual Behavior in the Human Male.* Philadelphia: W. B. Saunders, 1948.

Kirk, S. A. *Educating Exceptional Children.* Boston: Houghton Mifflin, 1962.

Kirk, S. A., and Johnson, G. O. *Educating the Retarded Child.* Boston: Houghton Mifflin, 1951.

Kirk, S. A., Karnes, M. B., and Kirk, W. B. *You and Your Retarded Child: A Manual for Parents of Retarded Children.* Palo Alto California: Pacific Books, 1968.

Kirk, S. A., and Kirk, W. D. *Psycholinguistic Learning Disabilities: Diagnosis and Remediation.* Urbana, Illinois: University of Illinois, 1971.

Kirk, S. A., and McCarthy, J. J. The Illinois Test of Psycholinguistic Abilities: An approach to differential diagnosis. *American Journal of Mental Deficiency,* 1961, *66,* 399–412.

Kirk, S. A., McCarthy, J. J., and Kirk, W. D. *Illinois Test of Psycholinguistic Abilities,* rev. ed. Urbana, Illinois: University of Illinois Press, 1968.

Kirkendall, D. R., and Ismail, A. H. The ability of personality variables in discriminating among three intellectual groups of preadolescent boys and girls. *Child Development,* 1970, *41,* 1173–1181.

Kirman, B. Drug-therapy in mental handicap. *British Journal of Psychiatry,* 1975, *127,* 545–549.

Klaus, M. H., and Kennell, J. H. *Maternal-Infant Bonding.* St. Louis: C. V. Mosby Co., 1976.

Klausmeier, H., and Check, J. Relationships among physical, mental, achievement, and personality measures in children of low, average, and high intelligence at 113 months of age. *American Journal of Mental Deficiency,* 1959, *63,* 1059–1068.

Klein, M. The development of conscience in the child. In Lorand, S. (ed.). *Psychoanalysis Today.* New York: International Universities Press, 1944.

Klein, M. H., Dittman, A. T., Parloff, M. B., and Gill, M. Behavior therapy: Observations and reflections. *Journal of Clinical and Counseling Psychology,* 1969, *33,* 259–266.

Klein, R. E., Irwin, M., Engle, P. L., Townsend, J. Lehtig, A., Martell, R., and Delgado, H. Data from an international study. In Mittler, P. (ed.). *Research to Practice in Mental Retardation. Vol. I. Care and Intervention.* Baltimore: University Park Press, 1977.

Klineberg, O. *Negro Intelligence and Selective Migration.* New York: Columbia University Press, 1935.

Knight, D., Ludwig, A. J., Strazzulla, M., and Pope, L. The role of varied therapists in the rehabilitation of the retarded child. *American Journal of Mental Deficiency,* 1957, *61,* 508–515.

Knobloch, H., and Pasamanick, B. Syndromes of minimal cerebral damage in infancy. *Journal of the American Medical Association,* 1959, *170,* 1384–1387.

Koch, R., and Dobson, J. *The Mentally Retarded Child and His Family: A Multidisciplinary Approach.* New York: Bruner/Mazel, 1971.

Kolstoe, O. P. Programs for the mildly retarded: A reply to critics. In Drew, C. D., Hardmann, M. L., and Bluhm, H. P. (eds.). *Mental Retardation: Social and Educational Perspectives.* St. Louis: C. V. Mosby Co., 1977.

Koppitz, E. M. *The Bender-Gestalt Test for Young Children.* New York: Grune and Stratton, 1963.

Koppitz, E. M. *The Bender-Gestalt Test for Young Children,* Vol. II. New York: Grune and Stratton, 1975.

Kornetsky, C., Humphries, O., and Evarts, E. V. A comparison of the psychological effects of certain centrally acting drugs in man. *Archives of Neurology and Psychiatry,* 1957, *77,* 318–324.

Kramm, E. R. *Families of Mongoloid Children.* Washington, D.C.: U.S. Government Printing Office, 1963.

Krause, F. J. The President's Committee on Mental Retardation looks ahead twenty-five years. In Mittler, P. (ed.). *Research to Practice in Mental Retardation.* Vol. I. *Care and Intervention.* Baltimore: University Park Press, 1977.

Krop, D., and Smith, C. R. Effect of special education on the Bender-Gestalt performance of the mentally retarded. *American Journal of Mental Deficiency,* 1969, *73,* 693–699.

Kugel, R., Lundgren, R. Jr., and Fedge. A. A comparison of two laboratory techniques for early detection of phenylketonuria. *American Journal of Mental Deficiency,* 1966, *71,* 244–248.

LaCrosse, R. E., Lee, P. C., Litman, F., Ogilvie, D. M., Stoolsky, S. S., and White, B. L. The first six years of life: A report on current research and educational practice. *Genetic Psychology Monograph,* 1970, *82,* 161–266.

LaDu, B., Howell, R., Michael, P., and Sober, E. A quantative method for the determination of phenylalanine and tyrosine blood and its application in the diagnosis of phenylketonuria in infants. *Pediatrics,* 1963, *31,* 338–342.

Lambie, D. Z., and Weikart, D. P. Ypsilanti Carnegie infant education project. In Helmuth, J. (ed.). *Disadvantaged Child,* Vol. 3. New York: Bruner/Mazel, 1970.

Lang, D. Segregation of poor and minority children into classes for the mentally retarded by the use of IQ tests. *Michigan Law Review,* 1973, *71,* 1212–1250.

Larsen, L. A. Community services necessary to program effectively for the severely/profoundly handicapped. In Sontag, E. (ed.). *Educational Programming for the Severely/Profoundly Handicapped.* Reston, Virginia: Division on Mental Retardation, Council for Exceptional Children, 1977.

Lassers, L. R., and Low, G. Symposium on assessing and developing communicative effectiveness in mentally retarded children. *Asha,* 1960, *2,* 377.

Laufer, M., and Denhoff, E. Hyperkinetic behavior in children. *Journal of Pediatrics,* 1957, *50,* 403–474.

Laurendeau, M., and Pinard, A. *Causal Thinking in the Child.* New York: International Universities Press, 1962.

Lawrence, D. H., and Festinger, L. *Deterrents and Reinforcement: The Psychology of the*

Insufficient Reward. Chevy Chase, Maryland: National Institute of Mental Health, 1970 (first published in 1962).

Lawrence, E. A., and Winschel, J. F. Self-concept and the retarded: Research and issues. *Exceptional Children*, 1973, *39*, 310–319.

Lazarus, R. S., et al. The effects of pyschological stress upon performance. *Psychological Bulletin*, 1952, *49*, 293–317.

Lazerson, M. Educational institutions and mental subnormality: Notes on writing a history. In Begab, M. J., and Richardson, S. A. *The Mentally Retarded and Society: A Social Science Perspective.* Baltimore: University Park Press, 1975.

Lejeune, J. Gautier, M., and Turpin, R. Study of the somatic chromosomes of nine mongoloid idiot children. In Boyer, S. H. (ed.). *Papers on Human Genetics.* Englewood Cliffs, New Jersey: Prentice-Hall, 1959.

Leland, H. Mental retardation and adaptive behavior. *Journal of Special Education,* 1972, *6*, 71–80.

Lepper, M. R., and Greene, D. Turning play into work: Effect of adult surveillance and extrinsic rewards on children's intrinsic motivation. *Journal of Personality and Social Psychology*, 1975, *31*, 479–586.

Lerch, H. A. et al. *Perceptual-Motor Learning: Theory and Practice.* Palo Alto, California: Peek Publications, 1974.

Lerner, J. W. *Children with Learning Disabilities.* Boston: Houghton Mifflin, 1971.

Lesser, G. S., Fifer, G., and Clark, D. H. Mental abilities of children from different social class and cultural groups. *Monographs of the Society for Research in Child Development*, 1965, *30*, 4.

Levine, B. A. Resistance to extinction as a function of the IQ and reinforcement ratios among retarded children. *Journal of Mental Deficiency Research*, 1976, *20*, 25–30.

Levitt, E. Higher order and lower order responses of mentally retarded and nonretarded children at the first-grade level. *American Journal of Mental Deficiency*, 1972, *77*, 13–20.

Levy, E., and McLeod, W. The effects of environmental design on adolescents in an institution. *Mental Retardation*, 1977, *15*, 28–32.

Lewin, K. *Dynamic Theory of Personality.* New York: McGraw–Hill, 1935.

Lewis, E. D. Types of mental deficiency and their social significance. *Journal of Mental Science*, 1933, *79*, 298–304.

Lewis, H. B. *Shame and Guilt in Neurosis.* New York: International Universities Press, 1971.

Lewis, J. F. The community and the retardate: A study in social ambivalence. In Eyman, R. K., Meyers, C. E., and Tarjan, G. (eds.). *Sociobehavioral Studies: Mental Retardation.* Los Angeles: American Association on Mental Deficiency, Monograph No. 1, 1973.

Lewis, M. A. A comparison of self-concept, academic achievement and attitude toward school and adaptive behavior of elementary school children identified as educable mentally retarded in four different school environments. Unpublished doctoral dissertation, University of Michigan, 1973.

Lichtenberg. P. and Norton, D. C. *Cognitive and Mental Development in the First Five Years of Life.* Chevy Chase, Maryland: National Institute of Mental Health, 1970.

Lieberman, M. A., Yalom, I. D., and Miles, M. B. Impact on participants. In Solomon, L. N., and Berzon, B. (eds.). *New Perspective on Encounter Groups.* San Francisco: Jossey-Bass, 1972.

Liebowitz, H. Waskow, I., Loeffler, N., and Glaser, F. Intelligence level as a variable in the perception of shape. *Quarterly Journal of Experimental Psychology*, 1959, *11*, 108–112.

Lilly, M. S. Improving social acceptance of low sociometric status, low achieving students. *Exceptional Children,* 1971, *37,* 341–347.

Lindsey, D. B. Emotions. In Stevens, S. S. (ed.). *Handbook of Experimental Psychology.* New York: John Wiley and Sons, 1951.

Lippman, L., and Goldberg, I. I. *Anatomy of the Pennsylvania Case and Its Implications for Exceptional Children.* New York: Teachers College, Columbia University, 1973.

Lippman, R., Perry, T., and Wright, S. The biochemical basis of mental dysfunction. II. Mental Deficiency (Amentia). *Metabolism-Clinical Experimental,* 1958, *7,* 274–330.

Lloyd-Still, J. D., Hurwitz, I., Wolff, P. H., and Schwachman, H. Intellectual development after severe malnutrition in infancy. *Pediatrics,* 1974, *54,* 306–311.

Loew, C. A., Grayson, H., and Loew, G. H. *Three Psychotherapies: A Clinical Comparison.* New York: Bruner/Mazel, 1975.

Louttit, R. T. Chemical facilitation of intelligence among the mentally retarded. *American Journal of Mental Deficiency,* 1965, *69,* 495–499.

Lovaas, O. I., Freitas, L., Nelson, K., and Whalen, C. The establishment of imitation and its use for the development of complex behavior in schizophrenic children. *Behavior Research and Therapy,* 1967, *5,* 171–181.

Lowenfeld, V. *Creative and Mental Growth.* New York: Macmillan, 1952.

Lowrey, G. H., et al. Early diagnostic criteria of congenital hypothyroidism. *American Journal of Diseases of Children,* 1958, *96,* 131–143.

Lubin, N. M. The effect of color in the Thematic Apperception Test productions of mentally retarded subjects. *American Journal of Mental Deficiency,* 1955, *60,* 366–370.

Lyle, J. G. The effect of an institutional environment upon the verbal development of imbecile children: Verbal intelligence. *Journal of Mental Deficiency Research,* 1959, *3,* 122–128.

MacGillivray, R. C. The larval psychoses of idiocy. *American Journal of Mental Deficiency,* 1956, *60,* 57–74.

Mackie, R. P. Spotlighting advances in special education. *Exceptional Children,* 1965, *32,* 77–81.

Mackie, R. P. Special Education in the United States: Statistics, 1948–1966. New York: Teachers College Press, Columbia University, 1969.

MacMillan, D. L., and Forness, S. P. Behavior modification: Limitations and liabilities. *Exceptional Children,* 1970, *37,* 291–297.

MacMillan, D. L., Jones, R. L., and Aloia, G. F. The mentally retarded label: A theoretical analysis and review of research. *American Journal of Mental Deficiency,* 1974, *79,* 241–261.

MacMillan, D. L., and Keogh, B. K. Normal and retarded children's expectancy for failure. *Developmental Psychology,* 1971, *4,* 343–348.

MacQuarrie, T. W. *MacQuarrie Tests of Mechanical Aptitude:* Manual. Los Angeles: California Test Bureau, 1943.

Mahoney, M. J. *Cognition and Behavior Modification.* Cambridge, Massachusetts: Ballinger, 1974.

Mahoney, M. J. The sensitive scientists in empirical humanism. *American Psychologist,* 1975, *30,* 864–867.

Mahoney, M. J., and Mahoney, K. Self-control techniques with the mentally retarded. *Exceptional Children,* 1976, *42,* 338–339.

Malamud, N. Recent trends in classification of neuropathological findings in mental deficiency. *American Journal of Mental Deficiency,* 1954, *58,* 438–447.

Maloney, M. P., Ball, T. S., and Edgar, C. L. Analysis of the generalizability of sensory-motor training. *American Journal of Mental Deficiency*, 1970, *74,* 458–469.

Malpass, L. F. Programmed instruction for retarded children. In Baumeister, A. A. (ed.). *Mental Retardation.* Chicago: Aldine, 1967.

Malpass, L. F., Brown, R., and Hoke, D. The utility of progressive matrices with normal and retarded children. *Journal of Clinical Psychology*, 1960, *16,* 350.

Malpass, L. F., Mark, S., and Palerma, D. Responses of retarded children to the Children's Manifest Anxiety Scale. *Journal of Educational Psychology*, 1960, *51,* 305–308.

Mann, L. Are we fractioning too much? *Academic Therapy*, 1970, *5,* 85–91.

Mann, L. Psychometric phrenology. *Journal of Special Education*, 1971, *5,* 3–14.

Manocha, S. L. *Malnutrition and Human Development.* Springfield, Illinois: Charles C. Thomas, 1972.

Marchand, J. G. Changes of psychometric test results in mental defective employment care patients. *American Journal of Mental Deficiency*, 1956, *60,* 133–139.

Martin, G. L., and Lowther, G. H. Kim Kare: A community residence program for severe and profound retardates in a large institution. Paper presented at International Symposium on Behavior Modification, Minneapolis, 1972.

Martin, G., and Powers, R. Attention span: An operant conditioning analysis. *Exceptional Children*, 1967, *33,* 555–570.

Martin, H. P. Microcephaly and mental retardation. *American Journal of Diseases of children*, 1970, *119,* 128–131.

Martin, W. E. *Programs of the Bureau of Education for the Handicapped.* Washington, D. C.: Unites States Office of Education, 1970.

Martin, W. E. *Estimated Number of Handicapped Children in the United States.* Washington, D. C.: United States Office of Education, 1971.

Masland, R. L. The prevention of mental retardation: A survey research. *American Journal of Mental Deficiency*, 1958, *62,* 994–1012.

Maslow, A. H. *Motivation and Personality.* New York: Harper & Row, 1954.

Maslow, A. H. (ed.). *Motivation and Personality,* 2nd ed. New York: Harper & Row, 1970.

Matheny, A. Improving diagnostic forecasts made on a developmental scale. *American Journal of Mental Deficiency*, 1967, *71,* 371–375.

Matthews, C., and Levy, L. Response sets and manifest anxiety scores in a retarded population. *Child Development*, 1961, *32,* 577–584.

May R. *The Meaning of Anxiety.* New York: Ronald Press, 1950.

Mayer, C. L. The relationship of early special class placement and self-concepts of mentally handicapped children. *Exceptional Children*, 1966, *33,* 77–81.

Maze, S. R. On some corruptions of the doctrine of homeostasis. *Psychological Bulletin*, 1953, *60,* 405–412.

McAshan, H. H. *Writing Behavioral Objectives.* New York: Harper and Row, 1970.

McCarthy, J. J. Notes on the validity of the ITPA. *Mental Retardation*, 1965, *3,* 25–26.

McCarver, R. B. Placement of the retarded in the community: Prognosis and outcome. In Ellis, N. R. (ed.). *International Review of Research in Mental Retardation,* Vol. 7. New York: Academic Press, 1974.

McCarver, R. B., and Craig, E. M. Placement of the retarded in the community: Prognosis and outcome. In Ellis, N. R. (ed.). *International Review of Research in Mental Retardation,* Vol. 7. New York: Academic Press, 1974.

McCulloch, T. L., Reswick, J., and Irving, R. Studies of word learning in mental defectives. *American Journal of Mental Deficiency*, 1955, *60,* 133–139.

McLachlan, D. G. Emotional aspects of the backward child. *American Journal of Mental Deficiency*, 1955, *60,* 323–330.

Meacham, J. Patterns of memory abilities in two cultures. *Developmental Psychology,* 1975, *11,* 50–53.

Mead, M. *Male and Female.* New York: William Morrow, 1949.

Meichenbaum, D. H., and Turk, L. Implications of research on disadvantaged children and cognitive training programs for educational television: Ways of improving "Sesame Street." *Journal of Special Education,* 1972, 6, 27–42.

Mein, R. Use of the PPTV with severely subnormal patients. *American Journal of Mental Deficiency,* 1962, *67,* 269–273.

Meisgeiger, C. A review of critical issues underlying mainstreaming. In Mann, L., and Sabatino, D. A. (eds.). *The Third Review of Special Education.* New York: Grune and Stratton, 1976.

Menninger, K., Mayman, M., and Pruyser, P. *The Vital Balance.* New York: Viking Press, 1963.

Menolascino, F. J. Psychiatric aspects of mongolism. *American Journal of Mental Deficiency,* 1965, *69,* 653–666.

Menolascino, F. J. *Challenges in Mental Retardation: Progress, Ideology and Services.* New York: Human Sciences Press, 1977.

Menolascino, F. J., and Egger, M. L. *Medical Dimensions in Mental Retardation.* Lincoln, Nebraska: University of Nebraska Press, 1978.

Mental Health Law Project. *Basic Rights of the Mentally Handicapped.* Washington, D.C.: United States Government Printing Office, 1973.

Mercer, J. R. Patterns of family crisis related to reacceptance of the retardate. *American Journal of Mental Deficiency,* 1966, *71,* 19–31.

Mercer, J. R. *Labeling the Mentally Retarded.* Berkeley, California: University of California Press, 1973a.

Mercer, J. R. The myth of 3 percent prevalence. In Tarjan, G., Eyman, R. K., and Meyers, C. E. (eds.). *Sociobehavioral Studies in Mental Retardation.* Monograph of the American Association of Mental Deficiency, No. 1, 1973b.

Mercer, J. R. Psychological assessment and the rights of children. In Hobbs, N. (ed.). *Issues in the Classification of Children,* Vol. 1. San Francisco: Jossey-Bass, 1975.

Mesibov, G. B. Alternatives to the principle of normalization. *Mental Retardation,* 1976, *14,* 30–32.

Metz, J. R. Conditioning generalized imitation in autistic children. *Journal of Experimental Child Psychology,* 1965, *2,* 389–399.

Meyerowitz, J. H. Parental awareness of retardation. *American Journal of Mental Deficiency,* 1967, *71,* 637–643.

Meyers, E. L. *Proceedings of the Missouri Conference on the Categorical/Noncategorical Issue in Special Education.* Columbia, Missouri: Univeristy of Missouri Press, 1971.

Milkovich, L., and van den Berg, B. J. Effects of prenatal meprobamate and chlordiasepoxide hydrochloride on human embryonic and fetal development. *New England Journal of Medicine,* 1974, *291,* 1268–1271.

Miller, M. B., and Gottlieb, J. Projection of affect after task performance by retarded and non-retarded children. *American Journal of Mental Deficiency,* 1972, *77,* 149–156.

Mittler, P. (ed.). *Research to Practice in Mental Retardation,* Vol. I. *Care and Intervention.* Baltimore: University Park Press, 1977.

Mohr, G. J., Richmond, J. B., Garner, A. M., and Eddy, E. J. A program for the study of children with psychosomatic disorders. In Caplan, G. (ed.). *Emotional Problems of Early Childhood.* New York: Basic Books, 1955.

Monroe, J. D., and Howe, C. E. The effects of integration and small class on the acceptance of retarded adolescents. *Education and Training of the Mentally Retarded,* 1971, *5,* 23–26.

Monroe, M. *Reading Aptitude Tests: Manual.* Boston: Houghton Mifflin, 1935.

Montagu, M. F. A. Constitutional and prenatal factors in infant and child health. In Senn, J. E. (ed.). *Symposium on the Healthy Personality.* New York: Josiah Macy, Jr. Foundation, 1950.

Montenegro, H., Lira, M. I., and Rodriguez, S. Early psychological stimulation program for infants (from birth to 24 months of age) of low socioeconomic class. In Mittler, P. (ed.). *Research to Practice in Mental Retardation,* Vol. I. *Care and Intervention.* Baltimore: University Park Press, 1977.

Morgan, C. D., and Murray, H. A. A method for investigating phantasies: The Thematic Apperception Test. *Archives of Neurology and Psychiatry,* 1935, *34,* 289–306.

Morris, E. F. Casework training needs for counseling parents of the retarded. *American Journal of Mental Deficiency,* 1955, *59,* 513.

Morrison, E., and Pothier, P. Two different remedial motor training programs and the development of mentally retarded preschoolers. *American Journal of Mental Deficiency,* 1972, *77,* 251–278.

Morse, W. C. If schools are to meet their responsibility to all children. *Childhood Education,* 1970, *46,* 299–303.

Mosier, H. D., and Dingman, H. F. Sexually deviant behavior in Klinefelter's syndrome. *Journal of Pediatrics,* 1960, *3,* 479–483.

Murphy, D. P., et al. Microcephaly following maternal pelvic irradiation for the interruption of pregnancy. *American Journal of Roentological Therapy,* 1942, *48,* 356–359.

Murphy, L. B., et al. *The Widening World of Childhood.* New York: Basic Books, 1962.

Murray, M. A. Needs of parents of retarded children. *American Journal of Mental Deficiency,* 1959, *63,* 1078–1088.

Nadler, H. L., Inouye, T., and Hsia, D. Y. Y. Classical glactosemia. In Hsia, D. Y. Y. (ed.). *Glactosemia.* Springfield, Illinois: Charles C. Thomas, 1969.

Naor, E., Rocca, A., and Balthazar, E. E. BSAB-II training reliability. Unpublished study, 1972.

National Association for Retarded Children. Classification and placement in special education classes: An NARC position statement. Unpublished paper, September 1, 1970.

National Association of Health. Advancement of knowledge for the nation's health. A report prepared for the President of the United States. Bethesda, Maryland: 1967.

Neuer, M. The relationship between behavior disorders in children and the syndrome of mental deficiency. *American Journal of Mental Deficiency,* 1947, *52,* 143–147.

Neuhaus, M. Modifications in the administration of the WISC performance subtests for children with profound hearing loss. *Exceptional Children,* 1967, *33,* 573–574.

Newman, H. H., Freeman, F. N., and Holzinger, K. J. *Twins: A Study of Heredity and Environment.* Chicago: University of Chicago Press, 1937.

Nihira, K. Factorial dimensions of adaptive behavior in the adult retardate. *American Journal of Mental Deficiency,* 1969, *73,* 868–878.

Nihira, K., Foster, R., Shellhaus, M., and Leland, H. *AAMD Adaptive Behavior Scale, 1974 Revision.* Washington, D.C.: American Association of Mental Deficiency, 1974.

Nihira, K., Foster, R., Shellhaus, M., and Leland, H. *AAMD Adaptive Behavior Scale: Public School Version.* Washington, D.C. American Association on Mental Deficiency, 1976.

Nihira, K., and Shellhaus, M. Study of adaptive behavior: Its rationale, method, and implications in rehabilitation programs. *Mental Retardation,* 1970, *8,* 11–16.

Norman, R. P. Extreme response tendency as a function of emotional adjustment and stimulus ambiguity. *Journal of Consulting and Clinical Psychology*, 1969, 33, 406–410.

Northcutt, M. P. *Comparative Effectiveness of Classroom and Programmed Instruction in the Teaching of Decimals to Fifth-Grade Children.* Ann Arbor, University of Microfilms, 1963.

O'Brien, M., and Schofield, L. J. The effects of positive and negative reinforcement in manual dexterity testing. *Journal of Clinical Psychology*, 1975, *31*, 74–77.

O'Connor, J. *Administration and Norms for the Finger Dexterity Test, Work Sample No. 16, and Tweezer Dexterity Test, Work Sample No. 17.* Technical Reports of Human Engineering Laboratory, No. 16, 1938.

Ogdon, D. P. WISC IQ's for the mentally retarded. *Journal of Consulting Psychology*, 1960, *24*, 177–188.

Olshansky, S., Schonfeld, J., and Sternfeld, L. Mentally retarded or culturally different? *Training School Bulletin*, 1962, *59*, 18–21.

Orme, J. E. The colored progressive matrices as a measure of intellectual subnormality. *British Journal of Medical Psychology*, 1961, *34*, 291.

Ornitz, E. and Ritvo, E. R. Perceptual inconstancy in early infantile autism. *Archives of General Psychiatry*, 1968, *18*, 76–98.

Osler, S. F., and Fivel, M. W. Concept attainment: The role of age and intelligence in concept attainment by induction. *Journal of Experimental Psychology*, 1961, *62*, 1–8.

Oxford Universal Dictionary, 3rd ed. London: Oxford University Press, 1955.

Pacella, M. The performance of brain-damaged mental retardates on successive trials of the Bender-Gestalt. *American Journal of Mental Deficiency*, 1965, *69*, 723–728.

Parmelee, A. H. Planning intervention for infants at high risk by developmental evaluation. In Mittler, P. (ed.). *Research to Practice in Mental Retardation*, Vol. I. *Care and Intervention.* Baltimore: University Park Press, 1977.

Parmelee, A. H., and Haber, A. Who is the "risk" infant? In Osofsky, H. J. (ed.). *Clinical Obstetrics and Gynecology*, Vol. 16. Hagerstown: Harper and Row, 1973.

Parnicky, J. Kahn, H., and Burdett, A. Preliminary efforts at determining the significance of retardates' vocational interests. *American Journal of Mental Deficiency*, 1965, *70*, 383–389.

Pasamanick, B., Knobloch, H., and Lilenfeld, A. M. Socioeconomic status and some precursors of neuropsychiatric disorder. *American Journal of Orthopsychiatry*, 1956, *26*, 594–601.

Paterson, D. G., et al. *Minnesota Spatial Relations Test: Manual.* Minneapolis: Educational Testing Bureau, 1930a.

Paterson, D. G., et al. *Minnesota Mechanical Assembly Test: Manual.* Chicago: Stoelting, 1930b.

Paul, J. L., Turnbull, A. P., and Cruickshank, W. M. *Mainstreaming: A Practical Guide.* Syracuse: Syracuse Unversity Press, 1977.

Pavlov, I. P. *Conditioned Reflexes.* London: Oxford University Press, 1927.

Payne, J. E. The deinstitutional backlash. *Mental Retardation*, 1976, *14*, 43–45.

Payne, J. S., and Mercer, C. D. Head Start. In Goodwin, S. E. (ed.). *Handbook on Contemporary Education.* New Jersey: Bowker, 1974.

Peck, J. R. A comparative investigation of the learning and social adjustment of trainable children in public school facilities, segregated community centers, and state residential centers. USOE Project No. 6430, United States Office of Education, 1960.

Peck, R. F. Family patterns correlated with adolescent personality structure. *Journal of Abnormal and Social Psychology,* 1958, *57,* 347–350.

Perline, I., and Levinsky, D. Controlling the maladaptive classroom behavior in the severely retarded. *American Journal of Mental Deficiency,* 1968, *73,* 74–78.

Peters, E. N., Pumphrey, M. W., and Flax, N. Comparison of retarded and nonretarded children in the dimensions of behavior based on recreation groups. *American Journal of Mental Deficiency,* 1974, *79,* 87–94.

Peterson, C. P. Retention of mentally retarded children in a community school program: Behaviors and teacher ratings as predictors. *Mental Retardation,* 1977, *15,* 46–49.

Peterson, D. *Functional Mathematics for the Mentally Retarded.* Columbus, Ohio: Charles E. Merrill, 1973.

Peterson, G. Factors related to the attitudes of non-retarded children toward their EMR peers. *American Journal of Mental Deficiency,* 1974, *79,* 412–416.

Piaget, J. *The Origins of Intelligence in Children.* New York: International Universities Press, 1952.

Piaget, J. *Main Trends in Psychology.* New York: Harper and Row, 1970.

Piaget, J. *Equilibration des Structures.* Paris: Universitaire de France, 1975.

Piaget, J., and Inhelder, B. *The Psychology of the Child.* New York: Basic Books, 1969.

Pinard, A., and Lavoie, G. Perception and conservation of length: Comparative study of Rwandese and French-Canadian children. *Perceptual and Motor Skills,* 1974, *39,* 363–368.

Porteus, S. D. Mental tests for the feebleminded: A new series. *Journal of Psycho-Asthenics,* 1915, *19,* 200–213.

Porteus, S. D. *The Maze Test and Clinical Psychology.* Palo Alto, California: Pacific Books, 1959.

Poulsen, H. Maturation and learning in the improvement of some instinctive activities. *Medd. Dansk Naturh. Foren,* 1951, *113,* 155–170.

Powell, L. F. The effect of extra stimulation and maternal involvement on the development of low-birth infants and on maternal behavior. *Child Development,* 1974, *45,* 106–113.

President's Committee on Mental Retardation. *Report to the President: Mental Retardation: Century of Decision.* Washington, D.C.: March 1976a.

President's Committee on Mental Retardation. *The Known and the Unknown.* Washington, D.C., 1976b.

President's Panel on Mental Retardation. *A Program for National Action to Combat Mental Retardation.* Washington, D.C.: United States Government Printing Office, 1962.

Pringle, M. L. K., and Bossio, V. A study of deprived children, Part I. Intellectual, emotional and social development. *Vita Humana,* 1968, *1,* 65–92.

Prouty, R. W., and McGarry, F. M. The diagnostic/prescriptive teacher. In Deno, E. N. (ed.). *Instructional Alternatives for Exceptional Children.* Arlington, Virginia: Council for Exceptional Children, 1972.

Rabin, A. I. (ed.). *Projective Techniques in Personality Assessment.* New York: Springer Publishing Co., 1968.

Rabkin, L., and Rabkin, K. Kibbutz children. *Psychology Today,* 1969, *3,* No. 440.

Ramey, C. T., and Campbell, F. A. Prevention of developmental retardation in high-risk children. In Mittler, P. (ed.). *Research to Practice in Mental Retardation,* Vol. I. *Care and Intervention.* Baltimore: University Park Press, 1977.

Rank, B. Aggression. In Freud, A., et al. (eds.). *The Psychoanalytic Study of the Child,* Vols. 3–4. New York: International Universities Press, 1949.

Rank, O. *The Trauma of Birth.* New York: Harcourt, Brace and World, 1929.

Ransohoff, J., Shulman, K., and Fishman, R. A. Hydrocephalus: A review of etiology and treatment. *Journal of Pediatrics,* 1960, *56,* 399–411.

Rapaport, D. *Diagnostic Psychological Testing,* Vol. 2. Chicago: Yearbook Medical Publishers, 1946.

Rarick, G. L. (ed.). *Physical Activity: Human Growth and Development.* New York: Academic Press, 1973.

Rarick, G. L., and Dobbins, D. A. *Basic Components in Motor Performance of Educable Mentally Retarded Children: Implications for Curriculum Development.* Washington, D.C.: United States Office of Education, 1972.

Raven, J. C. *Guide to the Standard Progressive Matrices.* London: H. K. Lewis, 1960.

Ray, A. B., and Shottick, A. L. Short-term and long-term recall of familiar objects by trainable and educable mentally retarded and normal individuals of comparable mental age. *American Journal of Mental Deficiency,* 1976, *81,* 183–189.

Razik, T. A. (ed.). *Bibliography of Programmed Instruction and Computer Assisted Instruction,* Vol. 1. Englewood Cliffs, New Jersey: Educational Technology Publishers, 1971.

Redd, W. H. Attention span and generalization of task-related stimulus control: Effects of reinforcement contingencies. *Journal of Experimental Child Psychology,* 1972, *13,* 527–539.

Reger, R., and Koppmann, M. The child-oriented resource room program. *Exceptional Children,* 1971, *37,* 460–462.

Reitan, R. M., and Boll, T. L. Neuropsychological correlates of minimal brain dysfunction. *Annals of the New York Academy of Sciences,* 1973, *205,* 65–88.

Retjo, A. Music as an aid in the remediation of learning disabilities. *Journal of Learning Disabilities,* 1973, *6,* 286–295.

Rettig, J. H. Chlorpromazine for the control of psychomotor excitement in the mentally deficient. *Journal of Nervous Disorders,* 1955, *122,* 190–194.

Ribble, M. *The Rights of Infants.* New York: Columbia University Press, 1943.

Riccuitto, H. N. Malnutrition and psychological development. In Nurmberger, J. I. (ed.). *Biological and Environmental Determinants of Early Development.* Baltimore: Williams and Wilkins, 1973.

Richards, T. W., and Sands, R. *Mongoloid Children Living at Home.* Santa Monica, California: Kennedy Child Study Center, 1963.

Richardson, R. E. Effects of motor training on intellectual functioning, social competency, body image, and motor proficiency of trainable mentally retarded children. Doctoral dissertation, George Peabody College, Nashville, Tennessee, 1970.

Richter, D. C. Biology of drives. *Psychosomatic Annual Review of Physiology,* 1942, *4,* 451.

Richter, D. C. Total self-regulatory functions in animals and human beings. *Harvey Lectures,* 1943, *38,* 63.

Rigrodsky, S., and Steer, M. D. Mowrer's theory applied to speech habilitation of the mentally retarded. *Journal of Speech Disorders,* 1961, *26,* 237–243.

Rimland, B. *Infantile Autism: the Syndrome and Its Implications for a Neural Theory of Behavior.* New York: Appleton-Century-Crofts, 1964.

Ringness, T. A. Self-concept of children of low, average, and high intelligence. *American Journal of Mental Deficiency,* 1961, *65,* 453–461.

Rioch, M. J., et al. National Institute of Mental Health pilot study in training mental health counselors. *American Journal of Orthopsychiatry,* 1963, *33,* 678–689.

Ritvo, E. R., Ornitz, E. M., and Tanguay, P. E. Clinical neurophysiologic and neurobiochemical studies in autism. In Sankasr, D. V. Siva (ed.). *Mental Health in Children,* Vol. II. Westbury, New York: PJD Publications, 1976.

Robinson, N. M., and Robinson, H. B. *The Mentally Retarded Child,* 2nd ed. New York: McGraw-Hill, 1976.

Rogers, C. R. *Counseling and Psychotherapy.* Boston: Houghton Mifflin, 1942.

Rohrs, F. W., and Haworth, M. R. The 1960 Stanford-Binet, WISC and Goodenough tests with mentally retarded children. *American Journal of Mental Deficiency,* 1962, *66,* 853–859.

Roos, P. The U. S. constitution: Is it for sale? *Journal of Special Education,* 1977, *11,* 65–68.

Rorschach, H. *Psychodiagnostik: Methodik und Ergebnisse enines Wahrnehmungs-diagnostichen Experiments. Deutenlassen von Zufallsformen,* 1st ed. Bern: Bircher, 1921.

Rorschach, H. *Psychodiagnostics: A Diagnostic Test Based on Apperception.* New York: Grune and Stratton, 1942.

Rose, J. Factors in the development of handicapped children. Proceedings of the 1958 Woods School Conference, May 2–3, 1958.

Rosen, L. Selected aspects in the development of the mother's understanding of her men-tally retarded child. *American Journal of Mental Deficiency,* 1955, *59,* 522–528.

Ross, D. M. Retention and transfer of mediation set in paired-associate learning of educable retarded children. *Journal of Educational Psychology,* 1971, *62,* 322–327.

Ross, D. M., and Ross, S. A. Facilitative effect of mnemonic strategies on multiple-associ-ate learning in EMR children. *American Journal of Mental Deficiency,* 1978, *82,* 460–468.

Ross, D. M., Ross, S. A., and Downing, M. L. Intentional training vs. observational learning of mediational strategies in EMR children. *American Journal of Mental Deficiency,* 1973, *78,* 292–299.

Royfe, E. H. A systems analysis of an historic mental retardation institution: A case study of Elwyn Institute, 1852–1970. Ed. D. dissertation, Temple University, 1972.

Rucker, C. N., and Vincenso, F. M. Maintaining social acceptance gains made by mentally retarded children. *Exceptional Children,* 1970, *36,* 679–680.

Sabatino, D. A., Ysseldyke, J. E., and Woolston, J. Diagnostic-prescriptive training with mentally retarded children. *American Journal of Mental Deficiency,* 1973, *78,* 7–14.

Sackett, G. P. Unlearned responses, differential rearing experience, and the development of social attachment by rhesus monkeys. In *Primate Behavior Developments in Field and Laboratory Research,* Vol. 1. New York: Academic Press, 1970.

Saenger, G. *Factors Influencing the Institutionalization of Mentally Retarded Individuals in New York City.* Albany, New York: Interdepartmental Health Resources Board, 1960.

Sameroff, A. J. Infant risk factors in developing deviancy. Paper presented at International Association for Child Psychiatry and Allied Professions, Philadelphia, July, 1974.

Sameroff, A. J., and Chandler, M. J. Reproductive risk and the continuum of caretaking casualty. In Horowitz, F. D. (ed.). *Review of Child Development Research,* Vol. 4. Chicago: University of Chicago Press, 1975.

Sanders, R., Smith, R. S., and Weinman, R. S. *Chronic Psychoses and Recovery.* San Fran-cisco: Jossey-Bass, 1967.

Santosefano, S., and Stayton, S. Training the preschool retarded child in focusing attention: A program for parents. *American Journal of Orthopsychiatry,* 1967, *37,* 732–743.

Sarason, I. G. Intellectual and personality correlates of test anxiety. *Journal of Abnormal and Social Pathology,* 1959, *59,* 272–275.

Sarason, I. G. Empirical findings and theoretical problems in the use of anxiety scales. *Psychological Bulletin,* 1960, *57,* 403–415.

Sarason, I. G. Experimental approaches to test anxiety. In Spielberger, C. D. (ed.). *Anxiety: Current Trends in Theory and Research.* New York: Academic Press, 1972.

Sarason, S. B. *Psychological Problems in Mental Deficiency.* New York: Harper and Row, 1949.

Sarason, S. B. *The Psychological Sense of Community: Prospects for a Community Psychology.* San Francisco: Jossey-Bass, 1974.

Sarason, S. B., Davidson, K. S., Lighthall, F. F., Waite, R. R., and Ruebush, B. K. *Anxiety in Elementary School Children.* New York: Wiley, 1960.

Sarason, S. B., and Gladwin, T. Psychological and cultural problems in mental subnormality: A review of research. *American Journal of Mental Deficiency,* 1958, *62,* 1115–1307.

Sarason, S. B., and Mandler, G. A study of anxiety and learning. *Journal of Abnormal and Social Psychology,* 1952a, *47,* 166–173.

Sarason, S. B., and Mandler, G. Some correlates of test anxiety. *Journal of Abnormal and Social Psychology,* 1952b, *47,* 810–817.

Sargent, H. Projective methods: Their origins, theories, and their applications in personality research. *Psychological Bulletin,* 1945, *42,* 257–293.

Schacter, S. *Emotion, Obesity, and Crime.* New York: Academic Press, 1971.

Scheerenberger, R. C. A model for deinstitutionalization. *Mental Retardation,* 1974, *12,* 3–7.

Scheerenberger, R. C. A study of public residential facilities. *Mental Retardation,* 1976, *14,* 32–35.

Schiefelbusch, R. L. The development of communication skills. In Schiefelbusch, R. L., and Smith, J. (eds.). *Research in Speech and Hearing for Mentally Retarded Children.* Conference Report, United States Office of Education, No. F010, 1963.

Schild, S. The family of the retarded child. In Koch, R., and Dobson, J. (eds.). *The Mentally Retarded Child and His Family.* New York: Bruner/Mazel, 1971.

Schippes, W., and Kenowitz, L. Special education futures: A forecast of events affecting the education of exceptional children, 1975–2000. Washington, D.C.: National Association of State Directors of Special Education, February 1975.

Schlanger, B. B. Speech measurements of institutionalized mentally handicapped children. *American Journal of Mental Deficiency,* 1953, *58,* 114–122.

Schlottmann, R. S., and Anderson, V. N. Social and play behavior of institutionalized mongoloid and nonmongoloid retarded children. *Journal of Psychology,* 1975, *91,* 201–206.

Schopler, E. Treatment of autistic children. In Mittler, P. (ed.). *Research to Practice in Mental Retardation,* Vol. I. *Care and Intervention.* Baltimore: University Park Press, 1977.

Schroeder, G. M. and Baer, D. M. Effects of concurrent and serial training of generalized vocal imitation in retarded children. *Developmental Psychology,* 1972, *6,* 193–201.

Schulman, J. L., and Stern, S. Parents' estimate of the intelligence of retarded children. *American Journal of Mental Deficiency.* 1959, *63,* 969–698.

Schurr, K. T., Joiner, L. M., and Towne, R. C. Self-concept research on the mentally retarded. *Mental Retardation,* 1970, *5,* 679–680.

Schweinhart, L. S., and Weikart, D. P. Research Report—Can preschool education make a lasting difference? Results of follow-up through eighth grade for the Ypsilanti Perry Preschool Project. *Bulletin of the High/Scope Foundation,* 1977, No. 4. High/Scope Foundation, Ypsilanti, Michigan.

Sears, R. R., Macoby, E. F., and Levin, H. *Patterns of Child Rearing.* New York: Harper and Row, 1957.

Sechzer, J. A., Faro, M. D., and Windle, W. F. Studies of monkeys asphyxiated at birth: Implications for minimal cerebral dysfunction. *Seminars in Psychiatry,* 1973, *5,* 19–34.

Séguin, E. *Idiocy and its Treatment by the Physiological Method.* New York: Columbia University Press, 1907.

Shaffer, L. F., and Shoben, E. J. *The Psychology of Adjustment,* 2nd ed. Boston: Houghton Mifflin, 1956.

Shepard, T. H. Teratogenicity from drugs: an increasing problem. *Disease-a-Month.* Chicago: Yearbook Medical Publishers, 1974.

Shepps, R., and Zigler, E. Social deprivation and rigidity in the performance of organic and familial retardates. *American Journal of Mental Deficiency,*1962, *67,* 262–268.

Shuman, R. M., Leech, R. W., and Alvord, E. C. Jr. Neurotoxicity of hexachlorophene in the human: I. A clinicopathologic study of 248 children. *Pediatrics,* 1974, *54,* 680–695.

Sidman, M., and Stoddard, L. T. The effectiveness of fading in programming a simultaneous form discrimination for retarded children. *Journal of Exceptional Analysis of Behavior,* 1967, *10,* 3–5.

Siegel, L. J. Cerebral trauma—concept and evaluation of psychopathological aftermaths. *Diseases of the Nervous System,* 1953, *14,* 163–171.

Silverstein, A. B. WPPSI IQs for the mentally retarded. *American Journal of Mental Deficiency,* 1969, *73,* 446.

Silverstein, A. B. The measurement of intelligence. In Ellis, N. R. (ed.). *International Review of Research in Mental Retardation,* Vol. 4. New York: Academic Press, 1970.

Silverstein, A. B., and Mohan, P. J. Conceptual area analysis of test performance of mentally retarded adults. *Journal of Abnormal and Social Psychology,* 1963, *66,* 255–260.

Sitko, M. C., and Semmel, M. I. The effects of phrasal cueing on free recall of the mentally retarded. In Mann, L., and Sabatino, D. A. (eds.). *First Review of Special Education,* 1972.

Skeels, H. M. Mental development of children in foster homes. *Journal of Genetic Psychology,* 1938, *2,* 33–43.

Skeels, H. M. Adult stature of children with contrasting early life experience: A follow-up study. *Child Development Monographs,* 1966, *31.*

Skeels, H. M., and Dye, H. B. A study of the effects of differential stimulation on mentally retarded children. *Proceedings of the American Association on Mental Deficiency,* 1939, *44,* 114–136.

Skinner, B. F. *The Behavior of Organisms.* New York: Appleton, 1938.

Skinner, B. F. *Science and Human Behavior.* New York: Macmillan, 1953.

Skinner, B. F. *The Technology of Teaching.* New York: Appleton-Century-Crofts, 1968.

Skinner, B. F. *Beyond Freedom and Human Dignity.* New York: Alfred A. Knopf, 1971.

Skinner, C. W. Jr. The rubella problem. *American Journal of Diseases of the Child,* 1961, *101,* 104–112.

Skodak, M. Mental growth of adopted children. *Journal of Genetic Psychology,* 1950, *77,* 3–9.

Skodak, M., and Skeels, H. M. A final follow-up study of 100 adopted children. *Journal of Genetic Psychology,* 1949, *75,* 85–125.

Slivkin, S., and Bernstein, N. R. Goal-directed group therapy for retarded adolescents. *American Journal of Psychotherapy,* 1968, *22,* 35–45.

Sloan, W. Some statistics in institutional provision for the mentally handicapped. *American Journal of Mental Deficiency,* 1955, *59,* 380–387.

Smirnov, A. A., and Zinchenko, P. I. Problems in the psychology of memory. In Cole, M., and Maltzman, I. (eds.). *A Handbook of Contemporary Soviet Psychology.* New York: Basic Books, 1969.

Smith, J. Group language development for educable mental retardates. *Exceptional Children,* 1962, *58,* 59–62.

Smith, J. O., and Arkans, J. R. More than ever: A case for the special class. In Schmid, R. E., Moneypenny, J., and Johnson, R. (eds.). *Contemporary Issues in Special Education.* New York: McGraw-Hill, 1977.

Smith, R. M. *An Introduction to Mental Retardation.* New York: McGraw-Hill, 1971.

Smith, R. M. *Clinical Teaching: Methods of Instruction for the Retarded,* 2nd ed. New York: McGraw-Hill, 1974.

Smith, R. M., and Neisworth, J. T. *Modifying Retarded Behavior.* Boston: Houghton-Mifflin, 1973.

Smokoski, F. The mentally retarded are different. *Mental Retardation,* 1971, 9, 52–53.

Snyder, L. K., Lovitt, T. C., and Smith, J. O. Language training for the severely retarded: Five years of behavioral analysis research. *Exceptional Children,* 1975, *42,* 7–15.

Soeffing, M. Y. New assessment techniques for mentally retarded and culturally differ-ent—a conversation with Jane R. Mercer. In Drew, C. J., Hardman, M. L., and Bluhm, H. P. (eds.). *Mental Retardation: Social and Educational Perspectives.* St. Louis: C. V. Mosby Co., 1977.

Sontag, E. (ed.). *Educational Programming for the Severely and Profoundly Handicapped.* Reston, Virginia: Division on Mental Retardation, Council for Exceptional Children, 1977.

Sontag, E., Smith, J., and Sailor, W. The severely/profoundly handicapped: Who are they? Where are we? *Journal of Special Education,* 1977, *11,* 5–11.

Spearman, C. *The Abilities of Man.* New York: Macmillan, 1927.

Spence, K. W. A theory of emotionally based drive (D) and its relationship to performance in simple learning situations. *American Journal of Psychology,* 1958, *13,* 131–141.

Spence, K. W. *Behavior Theory and Conditioning.* New Haven, Connecticut: Yale University Press, 1971.

Spicker, H. H. Intellectual development through early childhood education. *Exceptional Children,* 1971, *37,* 629–640.

Spielberger, C. D. (ed.). *Anxiety and Behavior.* New York: Academic Press, 1966.

Spielberger, C. D., Lushene, R. E., and McAdoo, W. G. Theory and measurement of anxiety. In Cattell, R. B. (ed.). *Handbook of Modern Personality Theory.* Chicago: Aldine, 1970.

Spitz, H. H. Consolidating facts into the schematized learning and meaning system of educable retardates. In Ellis, N. R. (ed.). *International Review of Research in Mental Retardation,* Vol. 6. New York: Academic Press, 1973.

Spitz, H. S., and Blackman, L. S. A comparison of mental retardates and normals on figural after-effects and reversible figures. *Journal of Abnormal and Social Psychology,* 1959, *58,* 105–110.

Spitz, R. A. The smiling response: A contribution to the ontogenesis of social relations. *Genetic Psychology Monographs,* 1946, *34,* 57–125.

Spitz, R. A. The importance of the mother-child relationship during the first years of life: A symposium in five sketches. *Mental Health Today,* 1948, *7,* 1–14.

Spitz, R. A. The role of ecological factors in emotional development in infancy. *Child Development,* 1949, *20,* 145–156.

Spitz, R. A. Psychiatric therapy in infancy. *American Journal of Orthopyschiatry,* 1950, *20,* 622–633.

Spivak, G., and Spotts, J. The Devereaux child behavior scale: Symptom behavior in la-tency-age children. *American Journal of Mental Deficiency,* 1965, *69,* 839–853.

Spivak, G., and Spotts, J. Adolescent symptomatology. *American Journal of Mental Deficiency,* 1967, *72,* 74–95.

Spradlin, J. E. Assessment of speech and language of retarded children: The Parsons language sample. *Journal of Speech and Hearing Disorders Monograph Supplement,* 1963, *10,* 831.

Stacey, C. L., and Gill, M. R. The relationship between Raven's colored matrices and two tests of general intelligence for 172 subnormal adult subjects. *Journal of Clinical Psychology,* 1955, *11,* 86–87.

Steisel, I. M., Friedman, G., and Wood, C. Jr. Interaction patterns in children with phenylketonuria. *Journal of Consulting Psychology,* 1967, *31,* 162–168.

Stenquist, J. L. Measurement of mechanical ability. *Teachers College, College, Columbia University Contributions to Education,* No. *130,* 1923.

Stephens, B. Piagetian theory: Applications for the mentally retarded and the visually handicapped. In Magary, J. F., Poulsen, M. K., and Taylor, P. J. (eds.). *Piagetian Theory and Its Implications for the Helping Professions.* (Proceedings of the Sixth Interdisciplinary Conference.) Los Angeles: University of Southern California, 1977.

Stephens, E. Defensive reactions of mentally retarded adults. *Social Casework,* 1953,.*34,* 119–124.

Sterba, R. *Introduction to the Psychoanalytic Theory of the Libido. Nervous and Mental Diseases* Monograph, No. *68,* 1942.

Stern, C. *Principles of Human Genetics,* 3rd. ed. San Francisco: Freeman, 1973.

Sternlicht, M. Establishing an initial relationship in group psychotherapy with delinquent retarded male adolescents. *American Journal of Mental Deficiency,* 1964, *69,* 39–41.

Sternlicht, M. Personality: One view. In Wortis, J. (ed.). *Mental Retardation and Developmental Disabilities,* Vol. VII. New York: Bruner/Mazel, 1975.

Sternlicht, M., and Siegel, L. Institutional residence and intellectual functioning. *Journal of Mental Deficiency Research,* 1968, *12,* 119–127.

Sternlicht, M., Silverg, E. F. The relationship between fantasy aggression and overt hostility in mental retardates. *American Journal of Mental Deficiency,* 1965, *70,* 486–488.

Sternlicht, M., and Wexler, H. L. Cathartic tension reduction in the retarded: An experimental demonstration. *American Journal of Mental Deficiency,* 1966, *70,* 609–617.

Stewart, L. H. Change in personality test scores during college. *Journal of Consulting Psychology,* 1964, *11,* 211–220.

Stott, D. H. *Studies of Troublesome Children.* New York: Humanities Press, 1966.

Strauss, A. A., and Kephart, N. C. *Psychopathology and Education of the Brain-Injured Child: Progress in Theory and Clinic,* Vol. 2. New York: Grune and Stratton, 1955.

Strauss, A. A., and Lehtinen, L. E. *Psychopathology and Education of the Brain-Injured Child.* New York: Grune and Stratton, 1947.

Stubblefield, H. W. Religion, parents and mental retardation. *Mental Retardation,* 1965, *3,* 8–11.

Sullivan, H. S. *Conceptions of Modern Psychiatry.* Washington, D.C : William Alanson White Psychiatric Foundation, 1947.

Symonds, P. M. *The Psychology of Parent-Child Relationships.* New York: Appleton-Century-Crofts, 1938.

Symonds, P. M. *Symonds Picture Story Test: Manual.* New York: Bureau of Publications, Teachers College, Columbia University, 1948.

Symposium. Counseling the mentally retarded and their parents. *Journal of Clinical Psychology,* 1953, *9,* 99–124.

Tarjan, G. Research in mental deficiency with emphasis on etiology. *Bulletin of the Menninger Clinic,* 1960, *24,* 57–69.

Tarjan, G. Classification and mental retardation: Issues arising in the fifth WHO seminar on psychiatric diagnosis, classification, and statistics. *American Journal of Psychiatry,* 1972, *128,* 34–45.

Tarjan, G., et al. Natural history of mental deficiency in a state hospital: III. Selected characteristics of first admissions and their environments. *American Journal of Diseases of Children,* 1961, *101,* 195–205.

Tarjan, G., Wright, S. W., Eyman, R. K., and Keeran, C. V. Natural history of mental retardation: Some aspects of epidemiology. *American Journal of Mental Retardation.* 1973, *77,* 369–379,

Terman, L. M., and Merrill, M. A. *Measuring Intelligence.* Boston: Houghton Mifflin, 1937.

Terman, L. M., and Merrill, M. A. *The Stanford-Binet Intelligence Scale.* Boston: Houghton Mifflin, 1960.

Terman, L. M., and Merrill, M. A. *Stanford-Binet Scales. Manual for Third Revision, Form L-M.* Iowa City, Iowa: Houghton Mifflin, 1973.

Thewatt, R. C. Predictions of school learning disabilities through the use of the Bender-Gestalt Test: A validation of Koppitz' scoring technique. *Journal of Clinical Psychology,* 1963, *19,* 216–217.

Thiel, E. *Design for Daily Living: A Framework for Curriculum Development for Children and Youth with Intelligent Handicaps.* Tallahassee, Florida: Florida State University, 1960.

Thomas, A., and Chess, S. *Temperament and Development.* New York: Bruner/Mazel, 1977.

Thompson, C. E., and Bachrach, A. J. The use of color in the Thematic Apperception Test. *Journal of Projective Techniques,* 1951, *15,* 173–184.

Thompson, W. R. Influence of prenatal maternal anxiety on emotionality in young rats. *Science,* 1957, *125,* 698–699.

Thorn, M., Schulman, J. and Kasper, J. Reliability and stability of the WISC for a group of mentally retarded boys. *American Journal of Mental Deficiency,* 1962, *67,* 455–457.

Thorndike, E. L. *Animal Intelligence.* New York: Macmillan, 1911.

Thorndike, E. L., et al. *The Measurement of Intelligence.* New York: Bureau of Publications, Teachers College, Columbia University, 1926.

Thorne, F. C. Counseling and psychotherapy with mental defectives. *American Journal of Mental Deficiency,* 1948, *52,* 263–271.

Thorpe, J. S., and Swartz, J. D. Level of perceptual development as reflected in responses to the Holtzman Inkblot Techniques. *Journal of Personality Assessment,* 1965, *29,* 380–386.

Thurston, S. R. Counseling the parents of the severely handicapped. *Exceptional Children,* 1960, *26,* 351–354.

Thurstone, L. L. *Primary Mental Abilities.* Chicago: University of Chicago Press, 1938.

Thurstone, L. L. *Thurstone Interest Schedule: Manual.* New York: Psychological Corporation, 1947.

Thurstone, L. L. The criterion problem in personality research. *Psychometric Laboratory Reports,* No. 78. Chicago: University of Chicago Press, 1952.

Thurstone, L. L., and Ackerman, L. The mental growth curve for the Binet tests. *Journal of Educational Psychology,* 1929, *20,* 569–583.

Thurstone, T. G. An evaluation of educating the handicapped children in special classes and in regular classes. USOE Project No. 6452, United States Office of Education, 1959a.

Thurstone, T. G. An evaluation of educating mentally handicapped children in special classes and regular classes. Unites States Office of Education, Cooperative Research Project No. OE–SAE 6452. Chapel Hill: University of North Carolina, 1959b.

Tiegs, E. W., and Clark. W. W. *California Achievement Tests: Manuals of Directions for*

Primary, Elementary, Intermediate, and Advanced Batteries. Los Angeles: California Test Bureau, 1951.

Tiffin, J. *Examiner Manual for the Purdue Pegboard.* Chicago: Science Research Associates, 1948.

Tiffin, J., and Asher, E. J. The Purdue Pegboard: Norms and studies of reliability and validity. *Journal of Applied Psychology,* 1948, *32,* 234–247.

Tillman, M. H. Differential performance of normals and retardates on the WISC as predicted by stimulus trace theory. Unpublished Master's thesis, University of Chicago, 1965.

Tizard, J. The prevalence of mental subnormality. *Bulletin of World Health Organization,* 1953.

Tizard, J. *Community Services for the Mentally Retarded.* London: Oxford University Press, 1964.

Tolman, E. C. Cognitive maps in rats and men. *Psychological Review,* 1948, *55,* 189–208.

Tolman, E. C. *Purposive Behavior in Animals and Men.* New York: Appleton, 1967. Originally published in 1932.

Tolor, A., and Schulberg, H. C. *An Evaluation of the Bender-Gestalt Test.* New York: Grune and Stratton, 1960.

Townsend, P. W., and Flanagan, J. J. Experimental preadmission program to encourage retarded children. *American Journal of Mental Deficiency,* 1976, *80,* 562–569.

Travis, L. *Speech Pathology.* New York: Appleton-Century-Crofts, 1931.

Tredgold, A. F., and Soddy, K. *A Textbook of Mental Deficiency,* 11th ed. Baltimore: Williams and Wilkins, 1970.

Trippe, M. J. The social psychology of exceptional children: Part II, In terms of factors in society. *Exceptional Children,* 1959, *26,* 171–175.

Tulchin, S. H. The pre-Rorschach use of ink blots. *Rorschach Research Exchange,* 1940, *4,* 1–7.

Turnure, J. E. Types of verbal elaboration in paired-associate performance of educable mentally retarded children. *American Journal of Mental Deficiency,* 1971, *76,* 306–312.

Turnure, J. E., and Walsh, M. K. Extended verbal mediation in the learning and reversal of paired-associates by EMR children. *American Journal of Mental Deficiency,* 1971, *76,* 60–67.

Tymchuk, A. J. Personality and sociocultural retardation. *Exceptional Children,* 1973, *38,* 721–728.

Tyor, P. L. Segregation or surgery: The mentally retarded in America. Unpublished doctoral dissertation, Northwestern University, 1972.

Ullman, D. G. Breadth of attention and retention in mentally retarded and intellectually average children. *American Journal of Mental Deficiency,* 1974, *76,* 640–648.

U. S. Office of Education. Bureau of Education for the Handicapped, Aid to States Branch, 1976.

Vail, D. J. An unsuccessful experiment in group therapy. *American Journal of Mental Deficiency,* 1955, *60,* 144–151.

Valeutti, P. Integration vs. segregation: A useless dialectic. *Journal of Special Education,* 1969, *3,* 405–408.

Vandenberg, S. G., Stafford, R. E., and Brown, A. M. (eds.). *Genetics, Environment and Behavior: Implications for Educational Policy.* New York: Academic Press, 1968.

Van Riper, C. G. *Speech Correction: Principles and Methods,* 5th ed. Englewood Cliffs, New Jersey: Prentice-Hall, 1972.

Vernon, P. E. *The Structure of Abilities.* New York: John Wiley and Sons, 1950.

Vitello, S. J. The institutionalization and deinstitutionalization of the mentally retarded in the United States. In Mann, L., and Sabatino, D. A. (eds.). *The Third Review of Special Education.* New York: Grune and Stratton, 1976.

Wabash Center for the Mentally Retarded. *Guide to Early Developmental Training.* Boston: Allyn and Bacon, 1977.

Walker, G. H. Social and emotional problems of the retarded child. *American Journal of Mental Deficiency,* 1950, *55,* 132–138.

Wallace, G., and Kauffman, J. M. *Teaching Children with Learning Problems.* Columbus, Ohio: Charles E. Merrill, 1973.

Wallin, J. E. Prevalence of mental retardation. *School and Society,* 1958, *86,* 55–56.

Ware, J. R., Baker, R. A., and Sipowics, R. R. Performance of mental deficients on a simple vigilance task. *American Journal of Mental Deficiency,* 1962, *66,* 647–650.

Warren, K. An investigation of the effectiveness of the educational placement of mentally retarded children in a special class. *Dissertation Abstracts,* 1962, *23,* 2211.

Waterhouse, I. K., and Child, I. L. Frustration and the quality of performance. III: An experimental study. *Journal of Personality,* 1953, *21,* 298–311.

Watson, G. Some personality differences in children related to strict or permissive parental discipline. *Journal of Psychology,* 1957, *44,* 227–249.

Watson, R. I. *The Clinical Method in Psychology.* New York: Harper Brothers, 1951.

Waugh, N. C., and Norman, D. A. Primary memory. *Psychological Review,* 1965, *72,* 89–104.

Weber, R. W. An approach to the use of musical instruments in the education of the "trainable" mentally retarded. Doctoral Dissertation, Teachers College, Columbia University, 1966.

Webster, D. R., and Azrin, N. H. Required relaxation: A method of inhibiting adaptive-disruptive behavior of retardates. *Behavior Research and Therapy,* 1973, *11,* 67–78.

Webster, T. G. Unique aspects of emotional development in mentally retarded children. In Menolascino, F. J. (ed.). *Psychiatric Approaches to Mental Retardation.* New York: Basic Books, 1970.

Wechsler, D. *The Measurement of Adult Intelligence,* 3rd ed. Baltimore: Williams and Wilkins, 1944.

Wechsler, D. *Manual for the Wechsler Intelligence Scale for Children.* New York: Psychological Corporation, 1949.

Wechsler, D. Cognitive, conative, and nonintellectual intelligence. *American Psychologist,* 1950, *5,* 78–83.

Wechsler, D. *The Measurement and Appraisal of Adult Intelligence.* Baltimore: Williams and Wilkins, 1958.

Wechsler, D. *Manual for the Wechsler Preschool and Primary Scale of Intelligence.* New York: Psychological Corporation, 1967.

Wechsler, D. *Wechsler Intelligence Scale for Children — Revised.* New York: Psychological Corporation, 1974.

Weikhart, D. P., Rogers, L., Adcock, C., and McClelland, D. *The Cognitively Oriented Curriculum: A Framework for Preschool Teachers.* Urbana, Illinois: University of Illinois–NAEYC, 1971.

Weiner, B. Assessment: Beyond psychometry. *Exceptional Children,* 1967, *33,* 367–370.

Weingold, J. T., and Hormuth, R. P. Group guidance of parents of mentally retarded children. *Journal of Clinical Pyschology,* 1953, *9,* 118–124.

Weintraub, F. J. Recent influences of law regarding the identification and educational placement of children. *Focus on Exceptional Children,* 1972, *4,* 1–11.

Weir, M. W. Mental retardation, technical comment. *Science,* 1967, *157,* 576.

Weller, T. H., and Hanshaw, J. B. Virologic and clinical observations on cytomegalic inclusion disease. *New England Journal of Medicine,* 1962, *266,* 1233.

Wellman, B. L. Iowa studies on the effects of schooling. In *39th Yearbook, National Society for the Study of Education,* Vol. 2, 1940, 377–399.

Wertheimer, M. Studies in the theory of Gestalt psychology. *Psychologische Forschung, 1923, 4,* 301–350.

West, R., Ansberry, M., and Carr, A. *The Rehabilitation of Speech,* 3rd ed. New York: Harper, 1957.

Whitney, E. A. Mental deficiency, 1955. *American Journal of Mental Deficiency,* 1955, *60,* 676–683.

Wiener, G., Crawford, E. E., and Snyder, R. T. Some correlates of overt anxiety in mildly retarded patients. *American Journal of Mental Deficiency,* 1960, *64,* 735–739.

Wiest, G. Psychotherapy with the mentally retarded. *American Journal of Mental Deficiency,* 1955, *59,* 64–65.

Wigglesworth, J. S. Malnutrition and brain development. *Developmental Medical Child Neurology,* 1969, 11, 792–803.

Wile, I. S., and Davis, R. The relation of birth to behavior. *American Journal of Orthopsychiatry,* 1951, *11,* 320–324.

Wilkins, L. The thyroid gland. *Scientific American,* 1960, *202,* 119–129.

Willey, N. R. , and McCandless, B. R. Social stereotypes for normal, educable mentally retarded, and orthopedically handicapped children. *Journal of Special Education,* 1973, *7,* 283–285.

Williamson, M., Koch, R., and Henderson, R. Phenlyketonuria in school-age retarded children. *American Journal of Mental Deficiency,* 1968, *72,* 740–747.

Windle, C. Prognosis of mental subnormals. *American Journal of Mental Deficiency,* 1962, *66,* 23–25.

Wine, J. Test anxiety and direction of attention. *Psychological Bulletin,* 1971, *76,* 92–105.

Winick, M., and Rosso, P. Effects of malnutrition on brain development. *Biology of Brain Dysfunction,* 1967, *1,* 301–317.

Wolfensberger, W. Schizophrenia in mental retardates: Three hypotheses. *American Journal of Mental Deficiency,* 1960, *64,* 704–706.

Wolfensberger, W. The correlation between Peabody Picture Vocabulary Test and achievement scores among retardates. *American Journal of Mental Deficiency,* 1962, *67,* 450–451.

Wolfensberger, W. Counseling parents of the retarded. In Baumeister, A. A. (ed.). *Mental Retardation.* Chicago: Aldine, 1967.

Wolfensberger, W. The origin and nature of our institutional models. In Kugel, R. B., and Wolfensberger, W. (eds.). *Changing Patterns in Residential Services for the Mentally Retarded.* President's Committee on Mental Retardation, Washington, D.C., 1969.

Wolfensberger, W. *The Principle of Normalization in Human Services.* Toronto: National Institute on Mental Retardation, 1972.

Wolfensberger, W., and Menolascino, F. Basic considerations in evaluating drugs to stimulate cognitive development in retardates. *American Journal of Mental Deficiency,* 1969, *73,* 414–423.

Wolff, P. H. Observations on the early development of smiling. In Foss, B. M. (ed.). *Determinants of Infant Behavior,* Vol. 2. New York: John Wiley, 1963.

Wood, J., Johnson, K., and Omori, V. In utero exposure to the Hiroshima atomic bomb. *Pediatrics,* 1967, *39,* 385–392.

Wood, N. E. *Communication Problems and their Effects on the Learning Potential of the Mentally Retarded Child.* U.S. Office of Education, CRP # 184, 1960.

Woodcock, R. W., and Dunn, L. M. *Efficacy of Several Approaches for Teaching Reading to the Educable Retarded.* U.S. Office of Education Project No. 5-0392. Nashville, Tennessee: George Peabody College for Teachers, 1967.

Woodward, M. Concepts of number in the mildly subnormal child studied by Piaget's method. *Journal of Child Psychology and Psychiatry,* 1961, *2,* 249-259.

Worchel, T., & Worchel, P. The parental concept of the mentally retarded child. *American Journal of Mental Deficiency,* 1961, *65,* 782-788.

Wortis, J. Introduction: The role of psychiatry in mental retardation services. In Wortis, J. (ed.). *Mental Retardation and Developmental Disabilities,* Vol. IX. New York: Bruner/Mazel, 1977.

Wunsch, W. L. Some characteristics of mongoloids evaluated at a clinic for children with retarded development. *American Journal of Mental Deficiency,* 1957, *62,* 122-130.

Yando, R., and Zigler, E. Outerdirectedness in the problem-solving of institutionalized and noninstitutionalized normal and retarded children. *Developmental Psychology,* 1971, *4,* 277-288.

Yarrow, L. J. The relationship between nutritive sucking experiences in infancy and non-nutritive sucking in childhood. *Journal of Genetic Psychology,* 1954, *84,* 149-162.

Yarrow, L. J. Research in dimensions of early maternal care. *Merrill-Palmer Quarterly,* 1963, *9,* 101-114.

Yarrow, L. J. Separation from parents during early childhood. In Hoffman, M. L., and Hoffman, L. W. (eds.). *Review of Child Development,* Vol. 1. New York: Russell Sage Foundation, 1964.

Yarrow, L. J., Rubenstein, J. L., and Pederson, F. A. *Infant and Environment: Early Cognitive and Motivational Development.* Washington, D.C.: Hemisphere Publishing Corporation, 1975.

Yoder, P., and Forehand, R. Effect of modeling and verbal cues upon concept acquisition of nonretarded and retarded children. *American Journal of Mental Deficiency,* 1974, *78,* 566-570.

Ysseldyke, J. E. Diagnostic-prescriptive teaching: The search for aptitude-treatment interactions. In Mann, L., and Sabatino, D. A. (eds.). *The First Review of Special Education.* Philadelphia: JSE Press, 1973.

Zeaman, D. One programmatic approach to retardation. In Routh, D. K. (ed.). *The Experimental Psychology of Mental Retardation.* Chicago: Aldine, 1973.

Zeaman, D., and House, B. J. An attention theory of retardate discrimination learning. Progress Report No. 3, Research Grant M-1099, National Institute of Mental Health, Bethesda, Maryland, November 1962a.

Zeaman D., and House, J. B. Approach and avoidance in the discrimination learning of retardates. *Child Development,* 1962b, *33,* 355-372.

Zeaman, D., and House, B. J. The role of attention in retardate discrimination learning. In Ellis, N. R. (ed.). *Handbook of Mental Deficiency.* New York: McGraw-Hill, 1963.

Ziegler, S., and Hambleton, D. Integration of young TMR children into a regular elementary school. *Exceptional Children,* 1976, *48,* 459-461.

Zigler, E. Research on personality structure in the retardate. In Ellis, N. R. (ed.). *International Review of Research in Mental Retardation,* Vol. 1. New York: Academic Press, 1965.

Zigler, E. Motivational determinants in the performance of retarded children. *American Journal of Orthopsychiatry,* 1966, *36,* 848-856.

Zigler, E. Familial retardation: A continuing dilemma. *Science,* 1967, *155,* 292.

Zigler, E. Developmental versus difference theories of mental retardation and the problem of motivation. *American Journal of Mental Deficiency,* 1968, *72,* 536–556.

Zigler, E., and Unell, E. Concept-switching in normal and feebleminded children as a function of reinforcement. *American Journal of Mental Deficiency,* 1962, *66,* 651–657.

Zimmerman, F. T., and Ross, S. Effects of glutamic acid and other amino acids on maze learning in the white rat. *Archives of Neurology and Psychiatry,* 1944, *51,* 446–451.

Zimmerman, I. L., and Woo-Sam, J. Research with the Wechsler Intelligence Scale for Children. *Journal of Clinical Psychology,* 1972, April Monograph Supplement, *33.*

Zisfein, L., and Rosen, M. Self-concept and mental retardation. *Mental Retardation,* 1974, *12,* 15–19.

Zuk, G. H. Autistic distortions in parents of retarded children. *Journal of Consulting Psychology,* 1959a, *23,* 171–176.

Zuk, G. H. The religious factors and the role of guilt in parental acceptance of the retarded child. *American Journal of Mental Deficiency,* 1959b, *64,* 139–147.

Zwerling, I. Initial counseling of parents with mentally retarded children. *Journal of Pediatrics,* 1954, *44,* 469–479.

Index of Names

Index of Subjects